INTERNET SYSTEM HANDBOOK

INTERNET SYSTEM HANDBOOK ▫ ▫ ▫ ▫

EDITORS

Daniel C. Lynch

Marshall T. Rose

ADDISON-WESLEY PUBLISHING COMPANY, INC.

Reading, Massachusetts • Menlo Park, California • New York
Don Mills, Ontario • Wokingham, England • Amsterdam • Bonn
Sydney • Singapore • Tokyo • Madrid • San Juan • Milan • Paris

This book was acquired, developed, and produced by
Manning Publications Co., 3 Lewis Street, Greenwich, CT 06830
Managing Editor: Lee E. Fitzpatrick

Library of Congress Cataloging–in–Publication Data
Internet system handbook/edited by Daniel C. Lynch and Marshall T. Rose.
    p. cm.
Includes bibliographical references and index.
ISBN 0–201-56741-5
1. Internet (Computer network)   I. Lynch, Daniel C.   II. Rose, Marshall T.
TK5105.875.I57I58   1993
004.6'7--dc20   92-20245
                                                        CIP

1 2 3 4 5 6 7 8 9 10-HA-95949392

Brief Contents

Contents

Preface

The Internet community spans every continent across the globe. The Internet is so large that its size can only be estimated, and it is evolving so quickly that its rate of growth can only be guessed. It is so diverse that it uses hundreds of different technologies, and is so decentralized that its administrators don't even know each other. The Internet is an electronic infrastructure that enables intense communications between colleagues, competitors, and disciplines. Despite these extremes, the Internet community is bound together by a framework of computer communications networking protocols and infrastructure.

This book, which describes and explains this framework, is written by the very people who made it all happen! We, the Editors, are deeply indebted to all of these authors who took the time to carefully explain their segment of the Internet System. The goal has been to provide practitioners with the knowledge and insight needed to use and extend this framework.

The word system has its roots in the ancient Greek and it stands for order and interrelatedness between the parts of a whole. It means the parts hang together as a collective entity. The word *System* in our title emphasizes that the book's contents have been written with a view of the Internet and its underlying technologies, its operation, its past and its future, all as interrelated parts of a whole. We hope that many newcomers, and some old hands, will find this comprehensive point of view of practical use as they read the *Handbook*.

We have divided the *Internet System Handbook* in four parts. The first part describes the historical evolution of the Internet community, examining the early motivations and how technologies are developed for a constantly changing and ever more demanding community. The second part considers the technologies themselves, and how they have evolved over time. The third part explains how the technologies are managed to provide a cohesive infrastructure for the community. The final part examines new trends in the community and postulates how the technology and infrastructure must adapt. Following these four parts, there is an annotated bibliography and some information on how to find out more about special topics.

This book was written for the competent engineer, manager, and administrator. Although the chapters form an organized progression from start to finish, they are sufficiently self-contained that the book can also be used as a reference guide when the reader needs information on a particular subject. One of the Editors believes that this book will find a prominent place on your bookshelf, the other believes that you will lock this book in your desk every night. Either way, we are confident you will find the *Internet System Handbook* to be your favorite reference on Internet technology and infrastructure.

Many people besides the Editors and authors have lent their talents and energy to the creation of this handbook. Our gratitude goes out especially to Marjan Bace, Lee Fitzpatrick, Steve Goldstein, Ole Jacobsen and Carole Steding.

DANIEL C. LYNCH
President and Founder, Interop Company

MARSHALL T. ROSE
Theorist, Implementor, and Agent Provocateur

Acronyms

AARNET	Australian Academic and Research Network
AD	Autonomous Domain
AFS	Andrew File System
ANS	Advanced Network & Services
AO	Abort Output
AP-CCIRN	Asian Pacific Coordinating Committee for International Research Networks
ARP	Address Resolution Protocol
ARPA	Advanced Research Projects Agency (former name for DARPA)
ARPANET	ARPA experimental packet-switched network
AS	Applicability Statements or Autonomous System
ASN.1	Abstract Syntax Notation One
ASTA	Advanced Software Technology and Algorithms
ATM	Asynchronous Transfer Mode
AYT	Are You There
B-ISDN	Broadband Integrated Services Digital Network
BARRNet	Bay Area Regional Research Network
BBN	Bolt Beranek and Newman
BER	Basic Encoding Rules

BF	Bellman-Ford
BGP	Border Gateway Protocol
BITNET	Because It's Time Network
BOF	Birds of a Feather
BOOTP	Bootstrap Protocol
BRHR	Basic Research and Human Resources
BRK	Break
CA*NET	Canadian Academic and Research Network
CAB	Communication Accelerator Board
CAT	Common Authentication Technology
CCIRN	Coordinating Committee for Intercontinental Research Networks
CCITT	International Telephone and Telegraph Consultative Committee
CEC	Commission of the European Communities
CERN	Organization Europene pour la Recherche Nucléaire
CERT	Computer Emergency Response Team
CIDR	Classless Interdomain Routing
CLNP	Connectionless Network Layer Protocol
CLNS	Connectionless Networks Service
CMIP	Common Management Information Protocol
CMIS	Common Management Information Service
CMOT	CMIP over TCP
CMU	Carnegie Mellon University
CNRI	Corporation for National Research Initiatives
CONS	Connection-Oriented Network Service
COPS	Computerized Oracle and Password System
COSINE	Cooperation for OSI Networking in Europe
CREN	Corporation for Research and Education Networks
CSNET	Computer Science Network
CUG	Closed User Group
DARPA	Defense Advanced Research Projects Agency
DASS	Distributed Authentication Service
DCA	Defense Communications Agency
DDN	Defense Data Network
DEC	Digital Equipment Corporation

DES	Data Encryption Standard
DET	Data Entry Terminals
DF	Don't Fragment
DFL	Deterministic Fragment Loss
DIB	Directory Information Base
DIT	Directory Information Tree
DM	Data Mark
DNS	Domain Name System
DOD	Department of Defense
DQS	Distributed Queuing System
DR	Designated Router
DSA	Directory System Agent
DSAP	Destination Service Access Point
DT	Data Transfer
DUA	Directory User Agent
EARN	European Academic and Research Network
EC	Erase Character
EEC	European Economic Community
EEPG	European Engineering Planning Group
EGP	Exterior Gateway Protocol
EL	Erase Line
EOF	End-of-file
EOR	End-of-record
EOS	Earth Observation System
ESNET	Energy Sciences Network
ESOC	European Space Operations Centre
EUNET	European UNIX Network
EUREKA	European advanced research program covering EEC and EFTA countries
Euro-CCIRN	European Coordinating Committee for Intercontinental Research Networks
EXPN	Expand
FARNET	Federation of Academic Research Networks
FC	Frame Control

FDDI	Fiber Distributed Data Interface
FEPG	Federal Engineering Planning Group
FF	Ford-Fulkerson
FIX	Federal Interconnection Exchange
FNC	Federal Networking Council
FOX	DARPA Field Operational X.500
FQDN	Fully Qualified Domain Names
FRICC	Federal Research Internet Coordinating Committee
FTAM	File, Transfer Access, and Management
FTP	File Transfer Protocol
GA	Go Ahead
GCM	General Circulation Model
GGP	Gateway-to-Gateway Protocol
GMT	Greenwich Mean Time (see UT)
GOSIP	Government OSI Profile
GSFC	Goddard Space Flight Center
GSTN	General Switched Telephone Network
HDTV	High-Definition Television
HEMS	High-Level Entity Management System
HEPNET	High-Energy Physics Network
HIPPI	High-Performance Parallel Interface
HPCC	High-Performance Computing and Communications
I-D	Internet Drafts
IAB	Internet Architecture Board (formerly Internet Activities Board)
IAC	Interpret As Control
IANA	Internet Assigned Numbers Authority
IANW	International Academic Networkshop
ICB	International Cooperation Board
ICCB	Internet Configuration Control Board
ICCC	International Conference on Computers and Communication
ICMP	Internet Control Message Protocol
IDPR	Inter-Domain Policy Routing Protocol
IDRP	Inter-Domain Routing Protocol
IEN	Internet Experiment Note

IEPG	Intercontinental Engineering Planning Group
IESG	Internet Engineering Steering Group
IETF	Internet Engineering Task Force
IFIP	International Federation of Information Processing
IGMP	Internet Group Management Protocol
IGP	Interior Gateway Protocol
IHL	Internet Header Length
IMP	Interface Message Processor
INENG	Internet Engineering
INRIA	Institut National de la Recherche en Informatique et Automatique
INWG	International Network Working Group
IP	Internet Protocol or Interrupt Process
IPTO	Information Processing Techniques Office
IRG	Internet Research Group
IRTF	Internet Research Task Force
IS-IS	Intermediate System to Intermediate System
ISI	Information Sciences Institute
ISN	Initial Sequence Number
ISO	International Organization for Standardization
ISOC	Internet Society
ISODE	ISO Developmental Environment
IXI	International X.25 Infrastructure
KDC	Key Distribution Host
LAN	Local Area Network
LAT	Local Area Terminal Protocol
LBL	Lawrence Berkeley Laboratory
LCP	Link Configuration Protocol
LFN	Long Fat Networks
LITA	Library and Information Technology Association
LLC	Logical Link Control
LLNL	Lawrence Livermore National Laboratory
LME	Layer Management Entity
LSP	Link State Packet
LSRR	Loose Source and Record Route

MAC	Media Access Control
MCNC	Microelectronics Center of North Carolina
MF	Move Fragment
MIB	Management Information Base
MIDS	Matrix Information and Directory Services
MIME	Multipurpose Internet Mail Extensions
MMDF	Multi-Memo Distribution Facility
MRTT	Most recent RTT measurement
MSFC	Marshall Space Flight Center
MSL	Maximum Segment Lifetime
MSP	Mid-level Service Provider
MSS	Maximum Segment Size
MTBF	Mean Time Between Failures
MTTR	Mean Time To Repair
MTU	Maximum Transmission Unit
MX	Mail-Exchange
NA-CCIRN	North American Coordinating Committee for International Research Networks
NACC	Necessary Ad-Hoc Coordinating Committee, CCIRN
NADF	North American Directory Forum
NASA	National Aeronautics and Space Administration
NAT	Network Address Translation
NATO	North Atlantic Treaty Organization
NCC	Network Control Center
NCP	Network Control Protocol
NDRE	Norwegian Defence Research Establishment
NEARnet	New England Academic and Research Network
NFS	Network File System
NIC	Network Information Center
NIH	National Institute of Health
NIST	National Institute of Standards and Technology
NLM	National Library of Medicine
NLST	Name List
NMR	Nuclear Magnetic Resonance

NNTP	Network News Transfer Protocol
NOC	Network Operations Center
NOP	No Operation
NPL	National Physical Laboratory
NPLDN	NPL Data Network
NREN	National Research and Education Network
NSAP	Network Service Access Point
NSF	National Science Foundation
NSFNET	National Science Foundation Network
NSI	NASA Science Internet
NSS	Nodal Switching System
NTP	Network Time Protocol
NTS	Network Time System
NUSIRG	Northwestnet User Services Internet Resource Guide
NVP	Network Voice Protocol
NVRAM	Nonvolatile Random Access Memory
NVT	Network Virtual Terminal
NWG	ARPA Network Working Group
OARnet	Ohio Academic Resources Network
OSI	Open Systems Interconnection
OSPF	Open Shortest Path First
PACCOM	Pacific rim networking organization
PAWS	Protection Against Wrapped Sequence
PCB	Protocol Control Block
PDU	Protocol Data Unit
PEM	Privacy Enhanced Mail
PI	Protocol Interpreter
PMTUD	Path MTU Discovery
POP	Point of Presence or Post Office Protocol
PPP	Point-to-Point Protocol
PSI	Performance Systems International
PSRG	Privacy and Security Research Group
PTM	Packet Transfer Mode
PTT	Public Telephone and Telegraph

PVP	Packet Video Protocol
RARE	Réseaux Associés pour la Recherche Européenne (Association of European Research Networks)
RARP	Reverse ARP
RCPT	Recipient
RFC	Request For Comments
RIP	Routing Information Protocol
RIPE	Réseaux IP Européens
RLP	Resource Location Protocol
ROAD	Routing and Addressing Group
RPC	Remote Procedure Call
RR	Resource Records
RST	Reset
RTMP	Routing Table Maintenance Protocol
RTO	Retransmit Timeout
RTT	Round-Trip Time
RTTM	Retransmission Time Measurement
SAA	Statistics Acquisition Agent
SACK	Selective Acknowledgment
SAML	Send And Mail
SAP	Servive Access Point
SATNET	DARPA experimental packet-switched satellite network
SB	Subnegotiation
SCH	Statistics Collection Host
SDE	Security Data Exchange
SDH	Synchronous Digital Hierarchy
SE	End Subnegotiation
SEX	Sigma Executive
SGA	Suppress Go Ahead
SGMP	Simple Gateway Management Protocol
SLIP	Serial Line Internet Protocol
SMDS	Switched Multimegabit Data Service
SMI	Structure of Management Information
SMTP	Simple Mail Transfer Protocol

SNA	System Network Architecture, IBM's networking protocol suite
SNAP	Subnetwork Access Protocol
SNMP	Simple Network Management Protocol
SOML	Send Or Mail
SONET	Synchronous Optical Network
SPAN	Space Physics Analysis Network
SPIRES	Stanford Public Information and Retrieval System
SRI	Stanford Research Institute
SRT	Source Routing Transparent
SRTT	Smoothed RTT estimate
SSAP	Source SAP
SSRR	Strict Source and Record Route
ST	Stream Protocol
SUNet	Stanford University Network
SUSP	Suspend
SWITCH	Swiss National Network for Research and Education
SWS	Silly-Window Syndrome
TAC	Terminal Access Controller
TCP	Transmission Control Protocol
TCSEC	Trusted Computer System Evaluation Criteria
TFTP	Trivial File Transfer Protocol
TID	Transfer Identifier
TIP	Terminal Interface Processors
TNI	Trusted Network Interpretation
TOS	Type-Of-Service
TS	Technical Specifications
TSIG	Trusted Systems Interoperability Group
TTL	Time-To-Live
UCL	University College London
UDP	User Datagram Protocol
UT	Universal Time (formerly Greenwich Mean Time)
UUCP	UNIX-to-UNIX Copy Protocol
UUNET	UNIX-to-UNIX Network
VRFY	Verify

WAIS	Wide Area Information Services
WAN	Wide Area Network
WKS	Well-Known Service
WPP	White Pages Pilot
XDR	eXternal Data Representation
XNS	Xerox Network System

Contributors

David A. Borman is a Senior Programmer/Analyst at Cray Research, Inc., and is the Project Leader for the TCP/IP code in the UNICOS kernel. He has been active in the Internet Engineering Task Force since 1988, and was a member of the Internet Host Requirements Working Group. Currently he is a member of the Internet Engineering Steering Group, and is the Area Director for the Transport and Services Area. He is probably best known for his involvement with the promotion of high-speed TCP, and for demonstrating the protocol running at near-gigabit speeds. He received his BA in Mathematics, with a concentration in Computer Science, from St. Olaf College in 1983.

David A. Borman wrote the chapter *A Practical Perspective on Host Networking*.

Scott O. Bradner has been involved in the design, operation, and use of data networks at Harvard University since the early days of the ARPANET. He was involved in the design of the Harvard High-Speed Data Network (HSDN), the Longwood Medical Area network (LMAnet) and the New England Academic and Research network (NEARnet). He is currently chair of the technical committees of both LMAnet and NEARnet.

Mr. Bradner is a consultant at the Harvard Office of Information Technology, Network Service Division, where he works on the design and development of network-based applications and is the director of the Harvard Network Device Test Lab. He is a frequent speaker at technical conferences and is an instructor for Interop Company.

Scott O. Bradner wrote the chapter *A Practical Perspective on Routers*.

Hans-Werner Braun joined the San Diego Supercomputer Center as a Principal Scientist in January 1991, where he has focused on NSF-funded efforts for NREN engineering and network performance related research. Between 1983 and 1991 he worked at the University of

Michigan, on network infrastructure. He became very involved in the early stages of the NSFNET networking efforts. He has been Principal Investigator on the NSFNET backbone project since the 1987 NSFNET award to Merit; he also managed Merit's Internet Engineering group. Between 1978 and 1983 he worked at the Regional Computing Center of the University of Cologne in West Germany on network engineering.

AT SDSC, Braun is Co-Principal Investigator and Executive Committee member of the CASA gigabit network research project. He was a member of the National Science Foundation's Network Program Advisory Group (NPAG), and in particular, its Technical Committee (NPAG-TC), between November 1986 and late 1987; he served as chair of the NPAG-TC starting in February 1987. Braun has been a member of the Engineering Planning Group of the Federal Networking Council since its beginnings in early 1989; he is also a member of the Intercontinental Engineering Planning Group and of the Internet Architecture Board. Braun received a diploma in Engineering in 1978 from the University of Cologne.

Hans-Werner Braun co-authored the chapter *Tools for an Internet Backbone.*

Jeffrey D. Case is a coauthor of the Simple Network Management Protocol. He currently is the President of SNMP Research, Inc., where he has produced one of the leading vendor-independent reference implementations of the SNMP for agents and manager stations, including the first commercial implementation of the SNMP security proposals. He also is a Professor of Computer Science at the University of Tennessee, where he teaches, conducts research in networking and network management, and directs the Computer Science Laboratories. Case was named as one of the top 25 networking Visionaries for 1991 by *Communications Week* for his work "as one of the SMNP architecture's developers and chief implementors." Dr. Case received his PhD from the University of Illinois in 1983.

Jeffrey D. Case wrote the chapter *Network Management.*

Charles E. Catlett is the Associate Director for Computing and Communications at the National Center for Supercomputing Applications, the NSF-sponsored supercomputing center located at the University of Illinois at Urbana-Champaign. His responsibilities include all computing and communications operation and management, as well new technologies development and integration. He is Principal Investigator for NCSA's work on the BLANCA gigabit/sec testbed, one of five government- and industry-funded testbeds. He was previously the Manager of the Networking Development group at NCSA, where he established programs in high-performance distributed applications, high-performance mass storage archives, wide-area network needs analyses, and local-area gigabit LANs. Catlett received a BS in Computer Engineering from the University of Illinois at Urbana-Champaign in 1983.

Charles E. Catlett wrote the chapter *Internet Evolution and Future Directions.*

Vinton G. Cerf is currently Vice President of the Corporation for National Research Initiatives, where he has managed the Digital Library, Electronic Mail, and Internet research programs since 1986. From 1982 to 1986, Dr. Cerf worked at MCI Communications, where he developed MCI Mail. He worked at the Defense Advanced Research Projects Agency from 1976 to 1982, where he led the packet communications, internetting and security efforts and served as principal scientist in the Information Processing Techniques Office. At Stanford University, from 1972 to 1976, he taught electrical engineering and computer science, and coinvented the TCP/IP protocol suite. At UCLA, from 1967 to 1972, he managed the Network Measurement Center and helped develop the host protocols for the ARPANET. At IBM he performed systems engineering on the QUIKTRAN time-sharing system.

Dr. Cerf is a member of the Association for Computing Machinery (ACM), and has served as chairman of LA-SIGART (1968), chairman of SIGCOMM (1987–1991), and a member of the ACM Council (1991–1992). He was elected a Fellow of the IEEE in 1988, and received the Koji Kobayashi Award in 1992. Dr. Cerf served as a member of the Internet Architecture Board from 1986 to 1989, and as its chairman from 1989 to 1992. He is a coorganizer of the Internet Society, and was elected its president in 1992. Dr. Cerf has served on numerous national and international committees and commissions, technical advisory boards and boards of charitable organizations. With his wife, Sigrid, he works on a Shakespeare video-captioning project, and in his copious spare time enjoys science fiction, gourmet cooking, and the collection and consumption of fine wines. Dr. Cerf received a BS in Mathematics in 1965 from Stanford University, and his MS (1970) and PhD (1972) in Computer Science from UCLA.

Vinton G. Cerf wrote the chapter *Core Protocols*.

A. Lyman Chapin wrote COBOL applications for Systems and Programs (NZ) Ltd. in Lower Hutt, New Zealand during 1974–1975. After a year traveling in Australia and Asia, he joined the newly formed Networking group at Data General Corporation (DG) in 1977. At DG, he was responsible for the development of software for distributed resource management (operating system-embedded RPC), distributed database management, X.25-based local- and wide-area networks, and OSI-based transport, internetwork, and routing functions for DG's open-system products. In 1987, he formed the Distributed Systems Architecture group, and was responsible for the development of DG's Distributed Application Architecture (DAA) and for the specification of the directory and management services of DAA. He moved to Bolt Beranek and Newman (BBN) in 1990 as the Chief Network Architect in BBN's Communications Division, where he serves as a consultant to the Systems Architecture group and the coordinator for BBN's open system standards activities. He has been the chairman of ANSI-accredited task group X3S3.3, which is responsible for Network and Transport layer standards, since 1982; and has been chairman of the ACM Special Interest Group on Data Communication (SIGCOMM) since July 1991. Chapin is chairman of the Internet Architecture Board, of which he has been a member since 1989. He lives with his wife and two young daughters in Hopkinton, Massachusetts. He received his BS in Mathematics in 1973 from Cornell University.

A. Lyman Chapin wrote the chapter *The Billion-Node Internet*.

David H. Crocker is a principal at The Branch Office, a consultancy specializing in strategic market planning and technical system architectures for communications products and services. Mr. Crocker has participated in the development of internetworking capabilities since 1972, first as part of the ARPANET research community and more recently in the commercial sector. He wrote the current Internet standard for electronic mail header formats and was a director and principal architect for MCI Mail. Mr. Crocker currently serves as the IETF Area Director for Standards Management, attempting to facilitate the community's development of technical specifications. Mr. Crocker received his BA degree in Psychology from UCLA in 1975, an MA degree from the Annenberg School of Communication at USC in 1977, and interrupted his doctoral studies in Computer Science at the University of Delaware to join Vint Cerf in developing MCI Mail.

David H. Crocker wrote the chapter *Evolving the System*.

Stephen D. Crocker is Vice President of Trusted Information Systems, Inc. in Glenwood, Maryland. His responsibilities include overseeing research and development projects in network security and program verification, including development of a reference version of Privacy Enhanced Mail for the Internet, code level verification of portions of the operational code in the Defense Data Network routers, and with UCLA, development of a trusted version of the Ficus distributed file system. He was previously Director of the Computer Science Laboratory at the Aerospace Corporation in El Segundo, California. Dr. Crocker also serves as the Area Director for Security in the Internet Engineering Task Force and as Treasurer of the IEEE Technical Committee on Security and Privacy. Dr. Crocker received a PhD in Computer Science from the UCLA in 1977.

Stephen D. Crocker wrote the chapter *Operational Security*.

Elise Gerich joined Merit Network, Inc., in January 1988 as the Systems Project Coordinator of the Merit team that engineered, managed, and operated the NSFNET backbone. Ms. Gerich's responsibilities have focused on technical interfaces and policy interactions between mid-level networks, sister Federal agencies, and international network research organizations. She represents the National Science Foundation at Federal Engineering Planning Group meetings and serves as the North American co-chair of the International Engineering Planning Group. Elsevier Science Publishers published two papers by Ms. Gerich in *Computer Networks and ISDN Systems 23* (1991). The papers are titled, "Management and operation of the NSFNET backbone" and "Expanding the Internet to a global environment but...how to get connected?" Ms. Gerich is a graduate of the University of Michigan.

Elise Gerich co-authored the chapter *Tools for an Internet Backbone*.

Stephen Kent is the Chief Scientist of BBN Communications, a division of Bolt Beranek and Newman Inc., where he has been engaged in network security research and development activities for over a decade. His work has included performance analysis of security mechanisms, the design and development of user authentication and access control systems, network layer encryption and access control systems for packet networks, secure transport layer and electronic message protocols, and the design of a multilevel secure directory system.

Dr. Kent has served as the chair of the Privacy and Security Research Group of the Internet Research Task Force and as a member of the Internet Architecture Board since 1985. He served on the Secure Systems Study Committee of the National Research Council of the Sciences, and is a member of the NRC technical assessment panel for the NIST Computer Systems Laboratory. He was a charter member of the board of directors of the International Association for Cryptologic Research.

Dr. Kent is the author of two book chapters and numerous technical papers on packet network security, and has served as a referee, panelist, and session chair for a number of security-related conferences. He has lectured on the topic of network security on behalf of government agencies, universities, and private companies throughout the United States, Western Europe, and Australia. Dr. Kent received his BS in Mathematics from Loyola University of New Orleans, and his SM, EE, and PhD in Computer Science from MIT. He is a member of the Internet Society, ACM, and Sigma Xi, and appears in *Who's Who in the Northeast* and *Who's Who of Emerging Leaders*.

Stephen Kent wrote the chapter *Architectural Security*.

Raman Khanna is the Director of Networking Systems at Stanford University. His responsibilities include management and operation of SUNet, the campuswide data and video network, and institutional academic computing resources. He is also responsible for the development and integration of new technologies into Stanford's distributed computing environment. Raman has been working, consulting, and lecturing in the field of computer networks and distributed computing since 1984. He has a special interest in the development of distributed services and tools for network and systems management. Raman holds a BS in Electrical Engineering, an MS in Computer Science, and an MBA in High Technology Management.

Raman Khanna co-authored the chapter *Tools for an Internet Component*.

Barry M. Leiner is a Senior Staff Scientist at the Universities Space Research Association. Dr. Leiner rejoined Universities Space Research Association (USRA) in June 1992, where he provides technical support to the Federal High Performance Computing and Communications Program. In particular, he focuses on the National Research and Education Network (NREN) and the Distributed Software Information System. From September 1990 to June 1992, Dr. Leiner was Director of Research at Advanced Decision Systems (ADS), a division of Booz-Allen, Hamilton, Inc., where he was responsible for formulating and executing corporate research directions. Prior to ADS, Dr. Leiner was Assistant Director of the Research Institute for Advanced Computer Science (RIACS), located at NASA Ames Research Center and operated by USRA. In that position, he formulated and carried out research programs ranging from the development of advanced computer and communications technologies, to the application of such technologies to scientific research. Prior to coming to RIACS, he was Assistant Director for C3 Technology in the Information Processing Techniques Office of DARPA. In that position, he was responsible for a broad range of research programs aimed at developing the technology base for large-scale surviv-able distributed command, control, and communication systems. Prior to that, he was Senior Engineering Specialist with Probe Systems, Assistant Professor of Electrical Engineering at Georgia Tech, and Research Engineer with GTE Sylvania.

Dr. Leiner received the best paper of the year award in the *IEEE Aerospace and Electronic Systems Transactions* in 1979 and in the *IEEE Communications* Magazine in 1984. He is a Senior Member of the IEEE and a member of ACM, Tau Beta Pi and Eta Kappa Nu.He received his BEEE from Rensselaer Polytechnic Institute in 1967 and his MS and PhD from Stanford University in 1969 and 1973, respectively.

Barry M. Leiner wrote the chapter *Globalization of the Internet.*

Brian Lloyd is a Network Architect and operates a consulting firm, Lloyd & Associates, that specializes in the design and implementation of internetworks. In addition he has been active with the Internet Engineering Task Force as the chairman of the Point-to-Point Protocol working group. Mr. Lloyd has performed extensive research and development in the area of dial-up internetworking and was the original architect for the Telebit NetBlazer product. Mr. Lloyd was educated in Mathematics and Computer science at the United States Air Force Academy and at the University of California at San Diego.

Brian Lloyd co-authored the chapter *Tools for an Internet Component.*

Daniel C. Lynch, President and Founder of Interop Company, is a member of the ACM, IEEE, and the Internet Architecture Board, and was recently named by *Communications Week* as one of the top 25 Visionaries of 1991. Lynch, has been active in computer networking, with primary focus in probating the understanding of network operational behavior, for over 20 years. Since 1985, the semiannual INTEROP Conference and Exhibition has been the major vehicle for his efforts.

He received undergraduate training in Mathematics and Philosophy from Loyola University in Los Angeles, and obtained a Master's Degree in Mathematics from UCLA in 1965.

Daniel C. Lynch wrote the chapter *Historical Evolution.*

Paul V. Mockapetris is Program Manager for Networking in the Computing Systems Technology Office of the Defense Advanced Research Projects Agency (DARPA). He is on loan from the Information Sciences Institute of the University of Southern California. His responsibilities at DARPA included the oversight of both defense- and HPCC-sponsored research in internet technology, gigabit R&D, optical networks, and other areas. He previously was the architect of the Domain Name System at ISI, implemented hardware and software components of the Distributed Computer System while at UC Irvine, and has interests in distributed computing and computer networks. Dr. Mockapetris holds a PhD in Information and Computer Science from UC Irvine, and BS degrees in Physics and Electrical Engineering from MIT.

Paul V. Mockapetris wrote the chapter *Directory Services.*

Jeffrey C. Mogul has been an active participant in the Internet community, and is the author or coauthor of several Internet Standards. Since 1986, he has been a researcher at the Digital Equipment Corporation Western Research Laboratory, working on network and operating systems issues for high-performance computer systems. His primary research interests include network monitoring, network performance improvements, and file system design issues. He is a member of ACM, the Internet Society, Sigma Xi, the IEEE Computer Society, and Computer Professionals for Social Responsibility. He received an SB from the MIT in 1979, his MS from Stanford University in 1980, and his PhD from the Stanford University Computer Science Department in 1986.

Jeffrey C. Mogul wrote the chapter *IP Network Performance*.

Radia Perlman's work has had a profound impact on networking. For the past 12 years she has been designing protocols for Digital Equipment Corporation (DEC). Her work on DECnet routing has been adopted by ISO as the ES-IS and IS-IS protocols, and her work on robust and efficient distribution of link state packets has been adopted for the OSPF protocol. She also designed the spanning tree algorithm used by bridges. She holds numerous patents in the field, and is the author of the book *Interconnections: Bridges and Routers*. Her PhD thesis at MIT presented a practical design for a network resistant to sabotage. She is the author of the book *Interconnections: Bridges and Routers*.

Radia Perlman wrote the chapter *Routing Protocols*.

Jon Postel is the Associate Director for Networking of the HPCC Division of the Information Sciences Institute of the University of Southern California. Dr. Postel has been involved in the development of computer communication protocols and applications from the early days of the ARPANET. He currently is a member of the Internet Architecture Board, and servers as the *RFC* Editor. His current interests include multimachine internetwork applications, multimedia conferencing and electronic mail, very large networks, and very high speed communications. Dr. Postel received a BS and MS in Engineering and a PhD in Computer Science from UCLA.

Jon Postel wrote the chapter *Main Applications*.

John S. Quarterman is Senior Technical Partner in Texas Internet Consulting, and consults in networks and open systems, with particular emphasis on TCP/IP networks, UNIX systems and standards. He wrote the CACM article *Notable Computer Networks*, in October 1986, and the book, *The Matrix: Computer Networks and Conferencing Systems Worldwide*, Digital Press, in 1990. He is editor of *Matrix News*, a monthly newsletter about contextual issues crossing network, geographic, and political boundaries, and is Secretary of Matrix Information and Directory Services, Inc., of Austin.

John S. Quarterman wrote the chapter *Annotated Bibliography*.

Marshall T. Rose is Principal at Dover Beach Consulting, Inc., a California-based computer-communications consultancy. He spends half of his time working with clients, and the other half involved in self-supported, openly-available projects. Rose lives with internetworking technologies, such as TCP/IP, OSI, network management, and directory services, as a theorist, implementor, and agent provocateur. He is the author of four professional texts—on Open Systems Interconnection (*The Open Book*), Internet Management (*The Simple Book*), OSI Directory Services (*The Little Black Book*) and Electronic Mail (*The Internet Message*)—all published by Prentice-Hall. Rose received his PhD degree in Information and Computer Science from the University of California, Irvine, in 1984. His subscriptions to *The Atlantic* and *Rolling Stone Magazine* are in good standing.

Barry Shein is founder and president of Software Tool & Die, which manages The World, the oldest public access Internet system. He currently serves on the Boards of Directors of USENIX and The Sun User Group, and is a Technical Editor, and frequent contributor for two technical magazines (*Sun Expert* and *RS/Magazine*). Among his current projects are The On-line Book Initiative (creating a large, freely redistributable on-line textbase), and InterSuite, a software project conducted jointly with The Electronic Frontier Foundation to create a new user interface to the Internet. He taught Computer Science at Boston University for a decade, and as a staff member, led the design and implementation of the university's campuswide academic network and computing environment. Previously, he was on the medical research staff at Harvard where he worked with some of the earliest UNIX systems. Mr. Shein has a Master's (ABD) in Computer Science from Boston University and a Bachelor's degree from Cornell.

Barry Shein wrote the chapter *Creating New Applications*.

William Yundt is Executive Director of the Bay Area Regional Research Network, a mid-level regional network founded with support from the National Science Foundation in 1987, and is also Director of Networking and Communication Systems at Stanford University. In the former role, he has been responsible for the creation and development of a wide-area network organization that currently serves over 150 educational, research and industrial sites in California. At Stanford, he has management responsibility for campuswide communication systems and services; voice, data, and video. He was instrumental in the creation and development of SUNet, the campus-wide computer and video network, which serves the needs of over 100 departments, 200 buildings, and 20,000 people; currently connecting over 10,000 networked computers and terminals. He has worked in the field of computer networking since 1980, having earlier worked in management of university computer centers, large-scale computer performance monitoring and measurement, computer resource allocation systems, and computer applications in a defense research laboratory. Mr. Yundt serves on the board of directors of the Federation of American Research Networks (FARNET), the Networld Advisory Board, has served as a director of the Corporation for Research and Education Networking (CREN), Network Users Association, Seminars for Academic Computing and other professional and trade organizations. He received his BS in Chemistry in 1962 and an MBA in 1965 from UCLA.

William Yundt co-authored the chapter *Tools for an Internet Component*.

PART I   □ □ □ □ □

INTRODUCTION

CHAPTER 1   ❏ ❏ ❏ ❏

Historical Evolution

DANIEL C. LYNCH

CONTENTS

We begin the *Internet System Handbook* with a brief explanation of how the Internet came into being. No one could foresee the global community that would be enabled by the initial, pioneering research into packet-switching. Indeed, the payoffs of the technology had little to do with the original goals of the research! On the other hand, who can argue with success?

1.1 "THE GRANDDADDY OF COMPUTER NETWORKS"

The Internet—today used by over four million people in more than 100 countries to access and exchange information—is widely considered the granddaddy of computer networks. Users range from educators, researchers, government officials, and business personnel, to private citizens exchanging e-mail messages with friends. How did all this begin?

1.2 PURPOSE

First, let's look at the original purpose of the Advanced Research Projects Agency Network, more commonly known as the ARPANET. The ARPANET was intended to provide communication between computers in a way that permitted a very broad range of interactions: remote login access to distant computers; sharing of files and other resources; and, while not in the original plan, the use of intersite electronic mail. In addition, an important goal was to improve and expand computer research productivity through the sharing of resources.

The ARPANET had some pretty lofty goals, but they all focused on one end result: that any user or program on any of the networked computers be able to utilize any program or subsystem on any other computer without having to modify the remote program. To accomplish this goal, two main computing problems prevalent in 1969 had to be solved. First, most computer centers—in both public and private sectors—operated autonomously. To exchange files, reformatting was required. To utilize another center's software, it had to be modified. Second, training was a real problem. Users had to be trained for each different computer they used. A final objective of the ARPANET was to permit access from general-purpose computer centers to specialized computers, i.e., those designed for specialized tasks, such as information retrieval, compiling, and list processing. This dramatically expanded the capabilities of each computer center. The result was the ARPANET, the first packet-switched, store-and-forward, host-to-host digital network of computers.

1.3 THE HISTORY

Many people believe that the Internet has its roots in Paul Baran's early concepts. Then at RAND Corporation, Baran—who many consider to be the father of networking—presented his ideas in a series of reports published by RAND in the early 1960s. These ideas later came to fruition through the ARPANET.

During the same period, Leonard Kleinrock was writing his dissertation, *Communication Nets: Stochastic Message Flow and Delay,* at MIT. This created a role model of sorts for the design and performance evaluation of networks.

Well before the ARPANET became a reality, J.C.R. Licklider believed computers could be linked to a network. He later became the first director of the Advanced Research Projects Agency of the Department of Defense (DOD) Information Processing Techniques Office (ARPA/IPTO).

In 1965, MIT's Lincoln Laboratory commissioned Thomas Marill and his colleagues at Computer Corporation of America, in Cambridge, Massachusetts, to study computer networking—on a subcontract under the Laboratory's DARPA contract. Leading the effort at MIT's Lincoln Laboratory was Lawrence Roberts, who later went on to become head of DARPA/IPTO.

This study, which took place in late 1965, resulted in the report *A Cooperative Network of Time-Sharing Computers.* The report suggested that a three-computer network be constructed, so experiments could be carried out. About one year later, Computer Corporation of America was awarded a contract to conduct the linking of two computers, a Systems Development Corporation AN/FSQ-32 and Lincoln Laboratory's TX-2. The experiment, which linked host computers directly, was successful. In fact, a small Digital Equipment Corporation computer at ARPA was later added to this group, which is now referred to as "The Experimental Network."

Another technical development that had an impact on the ARPANET was a broad system design of the National Physical Laboratory (NPL) Data Network, undertaken at NPL in Middlesex, UK under D.W. Davies. This design was similar to the network proposed by Paul Baran. And similar to the ARPANET, the NPL design proposed that local networks be constructed with interface computers that would multiplex among a number of user systems and communicate with a high-level network.

However, the real basis for the Internet was an experiment launched in 1968 by IPTO to connect computers over a shared network. The original purpose of ARPANET was to carry command and control information during a nuclear "event," but the undertaking soon became a straight research project without a specific application. (I have to add my opinion here that the real secret to the success of the Internet is that it built up wonderful momentum in the early years because the hearts of the researchers were pure; there were no computer system vendors involved.)

As the basic research arm of the Department of Defense, DARPA (ARPA became DARPA in 1972 to better reflect its defense posture) funds basic research in numerous technologies and basic sciences. DARPA does not perform research functions, and doesn't even have laboratories on its premises. Instead, it defines research problems, funds groups and individuals (often from universities, private industry, and nonprofit organizations) to conduct the research. Then it manages the programs.

The 1968 experiment focused on tying together a few geographically dispersed, dissimilar computers—called *hosts* because they housed the data and computational resources used by attached terminals (think of these as the *guests*)—so the resources on the computers could be accessed by many more users. This was especially important in the late 1960s, when computing power didn't come cheaply. Many of the technical pieces that made up the ARPANET had been attempted in some form by 1968, but no attempt had ever been made to compile them into a large resource-sharing computer network.

In the two years preceding the actual experiment, DARPA promoted interest in the ARPANET project within the government and with IPTO contractors. Later, the fundamental structure of the network was decided, a request for quotation was written, and a contractor was selected. In 1967, work was started on how to exchange messages between different pairs of computers in the proposed network, as well as on selecting the types of communications lines and data sets. At this time, Frank Westervelt, then of the University of Michigan, developed a position paper on the interhost communication protocol, which would include character and block transmission, error checking and retransmission, and computer and user identification.

Based on Westervelt's paper, an ad hoc Communication Group was appointed to consider the problem of connecting all the computers by dialup telephone lines and data sets, so that a computer on the network could communicate with any other computer through the phone lines.

A notable development occurred at a meeting of this group when Wes Clark, then of Washington University, proposed that a small computer be inserted between each participant's computer (the host) and the phone line. This idea was developed further by DARPA, and became the basis for the Interface Message Processor (IMP). IMPs are small, special-purpose computers connected to each other by phone lines. They provide the sub-network through which hosts communicate.

By October 1967, a number of topics were being discussed by the Communication Group, including IMP-to-host communication, message formatting, protocols, dynamic routing, queuing, error control, and measurements. During this time, ARPA decided to lease 50-Kb communications lines instead of the previously proposed 2.4-Kb lines. To speed the handling of messages, each IMP would be connected to at least two other IMPs via the leased lines, and would use store-and-forward techniques. Each IMP would accept messages of up to 8,000 bits from a host computer, break them into packets of 1,000 bits, and route (i.e., direct) the individual packets to the location of the receiving system.

The Communication Group met several more times over the next several months, exchanging ideas—both far fetched and real world. Keep in mind that this group was meeting before the procurement had been awarded to anyone (by the way, it was unusual for an IPTO procurement to be competitive, as was this one). This meant that the people involved had no official guidelines, and no idea what form the host–IMP interface would take, or even what functions the IMP would provide. Given this much free rein, the group began to focus on extreme circumstances, including application-specific protocols, with code downloaded to user sites.

In July 1968, a *Request For Proposal* for the network was sent to prospective bidders. Twelve proposals were received, and four were chosen as possible candidates to receive the IMP contract. Additional technical briefings were requested from these four, final negotiations were conducted with two finalists, and finally, in December 1968, one company—Bolt Beranek and Newman (BBN)—was awarded the contract.

According to Bolt Beranek and Newman's *A History of the ARPANET: The First Decade*, there were two primary problems in building the ARPANET:

1 To construct a "subnetwork" consisting of telephone circuits and switching nodes whose reliability, delay characteristics, capacity, and cost would facilitate resource sharing among the computers on the network.

2 To understand, design, implement the protocols and procedures within the operating systems of each connected computer, in order to allow the use of the new subnetwork by those computers in sharing resources.

On January 2, 1969, teams of researchers began their work on the experiment, under contract from IPTO. In February 1969 the group met for the first time with BBN. BBN's team was led by Frank Heart, Bob Kahn, Severo Ornstein, and Will Crowther. You could think of it as a clash of great minds: The university-based researchers and graduate students working with IPTO quickly realized that BBN, the private sector contractor, was most concerned with getting bits to flow quickly and reliably, but hadn't thought much beyond that.

About this time the collective group (graduate students and BBN) decided to start recording the minutes of each meeting. Not wanting to offend anyone, the group established two basic ground rules:

1 Anyone could say anything.

2 Nothing was official.

Steve Crocker then labeled the first notes *Request for Comments*, and a new way of recording technical information—the *RFC*—was born. This group met at what is now (in networking circles) a famous retreat. In the summer of 1969 Larry Roberts, then of IPTO, invited a small group of representatives (mostly graduate students) from the selected sites—the University of California at Los Angeles (UCLA), SRI International (then Stanford Research Institute), the University of California at Santa Barbara (UCSB), and the University of Utah—to Snowbird, Utah to work on the definition and design of the network. This group was to become known as the Network Working Group.

The first Working Group meeting was chaired by Elmer Shapiro of SRI. Steve Crocker (then at UCLA) recalls in the *RFC Reference Guide* that in addition to himself, Jeff Rulifson attended from SRI, Ron Stoughton from UCSB, and Steve Carr from Utah. (In his chapter of the *RFC Reference Guide*, Crocker apologizes to anyone he may have left out. I'd like to do the same; reconstructing events from nearly 25 years ago isn't always easy or 100% accurate!)

At this early stage, the attendees knew that a network was in the works, but nothing more. In fact, a funny aside is that when the graduate students came to this meeting, they thought the big "network geniuses" would tell them the design of the network and would assign them work. Instead, they found out that there were no geniuses in the back room and that there was no grand design—the students would have to use their talents to invent this thing! The results were some pretty far-reaching thoughts; namely, to address this problem of diverse machine interoperability, that they'd actually have to invent stuff that worked on any operating system, any file format, and any terminal type.

It would be misleading to make it sound like everything the network designers touched turned to gold. They had to face many uphill battles, not the least of which was dealing with operating systems that viewed themselves as the only machine; cooperation among computers simply did not exist in 1969. The schedule was an aggressive one: the first IMP was to be delivered to UCLA on September 1, 1969, with the other three due at monthly intervals. Based on the Honeywell 316 minicomputer, these IMPs required custom hardware and software to fulfill their role as providers of the subnetwork.

Steve Crocker's group at UCLA was hustling to build a host–IMP hardware interface. Mike Wingfield, another UCLA graduate student, was recruited to build the interface, and he completed it in just five and a half weeks.

On September 1, the network's first of four IMPs arrived at UCLA, having been shipped from BBN. The computer was plugged in and the software was restarted from where it had been halted prior to shipping; it worked beautifully. Shortly thereafter, this IMP began the packet-switching experiment between itself and the three other IMPs, which were located at SRI, UCSB, and the University of Utah.

The four sites, respectively, were running an SDS Sigma 7 with the SEX (Sigma EXecutive) operating system, an SDS 940 with the Genie operating system, an IBM 360/75 with OS/MVT (some believe it may have been OS/MFT), and a DEC PDP-10 with the Tenex operating system. Why were these four sites chosen? They had many ARPA computer science research contractors.

SRI received the second IMP at the beginning of October. By now, ARPA was intensely interested. On November 21, Larry Roberts and Barry Wessler visited UCLA, and a Telnet-like connection to SRI was demonstrated.

However, a snag occurred late in 1969. The graduate students had been frantically working on the network, and had come to the decision that the first set of protocols would include only Telnet and FTP functions, with only asymmetric, *client–server* relationships supported. In December 1969, a meeting with Larry Roberts in Utah surfaced a difference of opinion on that point. Roberts felt that more was needed, and over the following months, a symmetric *host–host* protocol was designed, and an abstract implementation of the protocol, known as Network Control Protocol, was defined. At this point the group envisioned an architectural layering of protocols, with Telnet, FTP, and other protocols as first examples.

From the outset, the IMPs were designed to automatically and periodically examine themselves and their environments to locate problems and failures. These results were then reported back to a Network Control Center (NCC) at BBN, which kept the IMPs functioning properly by detecting and analyzing unusual occurrences, and fixing them before they became major problems. By also providing field maintenance for the IMPs and Terminal Interface Processors (TIPs), the NCC became the first netwide service on the ARPANET.

In addition to the NCC at BBN, arrangements were made with UCLA to develop and run a Network Measurement Center, which was to determine the performance of the network. SRI was given the task of operating a Network Information Center (NIC) to collect information about the network and host resources, while also generating computer-based tools for storing and accessing that information.

The ARPANET evolved from being a lab experiment exploring the possibility of creating a network consisting of a few geographically dispersed computers, to a system in which many different networks interconnect.

To accomplish that sort of internetwork linkage, researchers needed to come up with something that could span the panoply of different manufacturers' networking protocols, data lines, hardware, etc. Their answer was TCP/IP (Transmission Control Protocol/Internet Protocol), which they designed during 1973–74. The purpose was to connect different networks to each other and still have the hosts talk to each other.

These original network architects had wonderful foresight: They predicted there would be an endless variety of transmission types that were going to solve particular problems. For example, if you need mobility, you can't have wires, or if you need super-high speed, copper won't work—you need lasers or microwave. So, that was the reasoning behind TCP/IP: to provide support for solving these problems and specifically to provide:

- Interoperability between heterogeneous systems

- End-to-end communication across a multitude of diverse networks

- Robust and automatic operation in the face of failures of data links.

At the same time, the applications running on the network were very simple: Telnet (remote login), FTP (file transfer), and e-mail. Electronic mail wasn't even in the original plan—it was an afterthought! Around 1971, two programmers at BBN decided to send each other messages, not just data. Before that, the true purpose of the network was strictly resource sharing—passing data files back and forth, and logging in to remote systems. At the time, no one realized the significance of e-mail; truly, a new era of communication was being ushered in.

No recounting of history is complete without an anecdote or two. Bob Kahn, who was directly involved in the ARPANET while at BBN, then DARPA, reminisces in the October 1989 issue of *ConneXions—The Interoperability Report*:

> Probably one of the most striking {anecdotes}, in its way, was when we were in the first stages of building and debugging the network, which had about 10 nodes at the time. We could tell—from our remote facilities—where problems were occurring in various parts of the net, such as errors in phone lines. This was before the phone companies had similar facilities in their own central offices.
>
> I remember calling from Cambridge to a telephone company central office in California to inquire about high error rates on a certain line. First of all, the telephone company didn't understand why someone from Boston was calling about a line in California. And when we explained why, they said "How could you possibly know what is happening on lines across the country?" And three minutes after I called, the line actually broke.

The network had been declared an immediate success, thanks to the initial experiment. Interest in the Network Working Group started to grow rapidly, with 50 to 100 people attending the meetings in the early 1970s, compared to the original five or six attendees in late 1960s.

A significant experiment on the network took place at MIT in October 1971. Representatives from each of the four sites were in attendance, and each person tried to log in to the other sites. It was successful, with the exception of one site that was completely down. The experiment holds a place in the interoperability history books.

Then, in October 1972, the first public demonstration of the network was held at the International Conference on Computers and Communications (ICCC) in Washington, DC. It was an interoperability demonstration consisting of terminals talking to different hosts on the ARPANET, running different applications. More than 1,000 attendees got to witness the unveiling of the net, which then involved about 40 terminals accessing many large computers from different vendors on the net. I saw the actual 16-mm film of this event, complete with the audio interviews. As you can imagine, there was more than one person exclaiming, "Wow! What is this thing?" It certainly made a big impact.

In early 1973, the first satellite link in the network was introduced—from California to Hawaii. By the end of that year, the first very distant hosts were connected to the network over telephone lines.

I became involved with the ARPANET in April 1973 at SRI. As I mentioned, the people responsible for the research program decided that the basic architecture they'd invented for the network was not general enough for what was going to be happening in the "real world." Thus, TCP was developed during the mid, 1970s. Meanwhile, the ARPANET ran with its own set of growing pains. In 1978, TCP/IP was declared (in the usual government dictate method) the preferred way to send information from one computer to another. Until then, all of the network was built by the researchers—with no vendor involvement of any kind until the late 1970s; it was pure research and development.

By the way, TCP/IP wasn't always known by its current name. In its early stages, it was known as the Kahn–Cerf protocol, after its major architects: Bob Kahn, then from DARPA, and Vinton Cerf, then at Stanford University.

By the mid, 1970s, the network had developed into a fully operational DOD computer network. On July 1, 1975, the administration of the ARPANET was transferred to the DOD Defense Communications Agency (DCA), with a six-month phase-over period from July 1 to December 31. This transition took place because the network had become operational and less of an experiment, and because DCA was better suited to the administration of a working facility. In addition, DCA was charged with managing the Network Control Center and the Network Information Center.

In the late 1970s international standards were created for computer-to-computer communications. The International Organization for Standardization (ISO) has been working for more than a decade to make the ARPANET capabilities a central component of all computing. ISO is finally achieving consensus. Why didn't ISO take the TCP/IP protocol suite "as is?" There are two main reasons:

- The "rest of the world" did not want US manufacturers to have an unfair advantage selling into world markets by virtue of their existing TCP/IP products.

- A number of enhancements to applications built on top of TCP/IP were incorporated that would make ISO-based products more useful than TCP/IP-based products.

In the early 1980s, DARPA funded Berkeley UNIX and decided to put TCP/IP into it. The government wanted to buy UNIX, but AT&T's version didn't have enough features for its purposes, so it funded Berkeley to add the desired features. One primary component missing from AT&T's UNIX was, of course, TCP/IP.

Berkeley UNIX was adopted by the vendor community in the early 1980s, and soon became widespread. At this time the use of the Internet protocols boomed.

In 1981, I took charge of the effort of converting the ARPANET to run only TCP/IP, rather than any of the original protocols, such as the defunct Network Control Protocol (NCP), which had been developed at UCLA under Steve Crocker's guidance. This meant I had to get hundreds of programmers and sites to change hundreds of programs so the whole thing would begin working on a single flag day—January 1, 1983. It took two years of scheduling, pleading, begging, and cajoling. I can guarantee you that there will never be another flag day in networking history, because there will never again be a single overseer of the Internet. During the time of my flag day, "orders" came only from the single overseer, which at that time happened to be the government.

In the early 1980s, the ARPANET was split in to two parts: the military went on MIL-NET, while research and development and other sectors stayed on the ARPANET. This was to provide operational separation, and perhaps security separation—in case that ever became a problem. The DOD ran and paid for everything.

Then, in 1985 and 1986, the National Science Foundation in Washington, DC became very interested in the Internet and decided that it wanted to proliferate the technology to lots of universities, not just the cream-of-the-crop institutions that had been involved to date (MIT, Stanford, Berkeley, UCLA, etc.). NSF began to put money into the effort.

In the late 1980s, NSF began constructing the NSFNET, a supercomputer network conceived by Dennis Jennings. It's interesting that Jennings was a Computer Center Director from University College, Dublin on exchange with NSF. The father of the NSFNET was Irish, not American!

NSF planners envisioned a system based on a "backbone" connecting supercomputer centers that in turn would interconnect with autonomously administered wide-area networks serving different communities of researchers, and with campus networks.

In the late 1980s, the Internet started creeping all over the globe, to Europe, Australia, Canada, South America, and beyond. (University College, London had been involved since the very early days of the Internet.)

The Internet even had its day in the spotlight of the general public, albeit with negative notoriety. On November 1, 1988, an e-mail message was sent from the NASA Ames Research Center to the Internet's TCP-IP mailing list: "We are currently under attack from an Internet Virus." A self-replicating worm ran amok across the Internet for several days, infecting thousands of host computers, disrupting the connectivity of the Internet itself. This event raised the awareness of the vulnerability of the Internet.

The original ARPANET became a bit of a victim of its own success. Demands on the ARPANET exceeded its capability and original purview. As a result of newer technologies and organizational restructuring, the DOD decided to disband the ARPANET in 1990. In its place, the NSFNET backbone, together with other agency networks (such as NASA and Department of Energy networks), became the principal backbone networks for the Internet. NSFNET contracts for the operation of the backbone of the Internet—the largest portion of the network. But, because the Internet follows a mesh design, a backbone is not an absolute necessity.

As for TCP/IP, it's easy to judge its success; just look at the number and caliber of vendors offering TCP/IP today, including IBM, DEC, AT&T, Amdahl, Hewlett-Packard, Bull, Siemens, Unisys, Tandem, Sun Microsystems, Apple, Cray, CDC, Data General, and Prime. There are also myriad networking companies that have sprung up to serve the needs of customers: 3Com, ACC, Cisco Systems, Proteon, FTP Software, Network General, Spider Systems, Ungermann-Bass, Hughes LAN Systems, Novell, SynOptics, Cabletron, Network Systems Corporation, Wellfleet, Xyplex, Wollongong, and many more.

In some countries, you can even get TCP/IP connectivity services from the telephone company. The US is seeing an emerging public offering of TCP/IP services via SMDS from the telephone companies. Private companies also have been created to provide these services: Performance Systems International (PSI), Advanced Network & Services (ANS), and UUNET are among the early entrants in this field. In total, well over 400 vendors offer TCP/IP products worldwide.

1.4 WHO MANAGES THE INTERNET?

The Internet is a cooperative effort among all the diverse networks that make up the larger network. Founded in the early 1980s, the Internet Architecture Board (IAB) oversees the architecture and receives reports from the Internet Engineering Task Force (IETF), which has rapidly become a major international standards-making body, and the Internet Research Task Force (IRTF), which develops and maintains networking and internetworking information science experiments.

The IAB is a collection of concerned, knowledgeable people. It is truly an architecture group, and not an operations group. Over the years it has evolved into a board of about a dozen people who act as overseers of some 50 subcommittees that do the lion's share of the work in the IETF. The IRTF consists of researchers looking to the future of the Internet. In June 1992, the IAB, the IETF, and the IRTF were moved into the Internet Society, a new nonprofit international organization. The Internet Society will raise money through voluntary membership dues, with the funds collected providing for a few full-time people to spread the knowledge of the Internet's growth.

1.5 GROWTH RATE

The Internet provides electronic mail, file transfer capabilities, and remote login. Special electronic mail procedures are also used to support news distribution applications and bulletin boards. The Internet's major backbones currently support transfer rates from T1 (1.5 Mbits/sec) to DS-3 (45 Mbits/sec). In September 1991, domestic traffic through just one major US Internet backbone exceeded a terabyte—that's equal to a trillion bytes per month.

The IAB has estimated that the Internet has a monthly growth rate in computer hosts of 10–15%, making it by far the most rapidly growing electronic network in the world. At this writing, traffic growth on the major backbones of the Internet exceeds 25% per month—unprecedented growth that is resulting in major engineering efforts to accommodate the anticipated size, complexity, and traffic.

1.6 THE INTERNET'S SUCCESS

It's almost impossible to recognize every group and every individual who helped the Internet grow to be what it is today. It would take countless volumes to describe fully all that has taken place around this wonderful invention. What I've tried to do instead is give the reader a snapshot of the Internet's roots—the "Reader's Digest Condensed Version" of sorts.

It's true that the Internet has experienced unbelievable growth and notoriety; it was used extensively during the Russian coup attempt and during Operation Desert Storm. The secret of its success is that it is a living and evolving system. Used by millions daily, it is important enough to be constantly improved. The purpose of this handbook is to help those who depend on the Internet to understand it better so that they can become part of the process of evolving the Internet.

CHAPTER 2 ❏ ❏ ❏ ❏

Globalization of the Internet

BARRY M. LEINER

CONTENTS

It is a common misconception that internetworking technology is a product that was "built in the US for use in the US." Indeed, the Internet community has had substantial European participation from its very beginning. Further, the level of global participation is so large that it is beyond the scope of the *Internet System Handbook* to detail developments in each region; at best we can focus on several, but not all of these.

2.1   INTRODUCTION

At the initial meeting of what was to become the Coordinating Committee for Intercontinental Research Networks (CCIRN), David Nelson of the US Department of Energy welcomed us with an inspirational speech. He spoke of the emerging global research village, and laid down a challenge to us to bring into place the highways of that global research village. This vision of unity has caused a set of disconnected research activities to evolve into networking, and has caused ad hoc network activities supporting specific science communities to evolve into the global set of interconnected networks we find today.

Our goal in this chapter is to give the reader a feeling for the evolution of the Internet from the set of research, scientific, and commercial networks into the interconnected set of networks we have today. Our perspective (because of the history of Internet development, as well as the background of the author) will tend to be from the point of view of the interactions of the US with the various entities around the globe, and will tend to emphasize the role of the Transmission Control Protocol/Internet Protocol (TCP/IP) environment. Furthermore, we shall not attempt to give comprehensive descriptions of the various networks that comprise the worldwide Internet. Readers interested in the details of the various networks are advised to consult LaQuey[1] or Quarterman[2] for overviews of the individual networks and pointers on the details of each.

First, we will discuss the background of internetworking from the international perspective. Then we will describe the current state of the global Internet. We will discuss organizational activities unique to the international environment, focusing on the three aspects of coordination: policy, research and development, and engineering and operations. Finally, we will cover the technical implications of the continued global growth of the Internet.

2.2   THE BACKGROUND OF INTERNATIONAL
  INTERNETWORKING

Packet-switching technology has been an international activity from its very inception. The underlying concepts, which were presented initially by Baran,[3] led to seminal experimental work by Larry Roberts[4] at the Defense Advanced Research Projects Agency (DARPA) and Donald Davies[5] at the UK National Physical Laboratory. The Advanced Research Projects

Agency Network (ARPANET) had a satellite-based extension into Europe, with nodes in London and Norway.[6]

2.2.1   DARPA-Related International Activities

A major motivation for the development of the TCP/IP protocol suite was the need to tie together wide-area networks based on long-haul telephone lines (e.g., ARPANET) and satellite links (e.g., SATNET),[7] with local area networks (e.g., the Ethernet)[8] and packet radio networks providing mobile access.[9] Packet radio networking was actively being explored both in the United States[10] and in the UK.[11] In the initial research on TCP/IP,[12] as it was being specified, researchers at Stanford collaborated on test implementations with colleagues at Bolt Beranek and Newman, and University College London (UCL). The first tests, of TCP, in1975 were conducted using a wide-area satellite link on the ARPANET, which connected UCL to the US. Later, this group was joined by researchers at the Norwegian Defence Research Establishment (NDRE). In fact, the initial connectivity went by satellite from the US to Norway, and then by "land" to the UK.

Thus, from the early days of the Internet, there was international cooperation and motivation. Once the development of internet technology was begun in earnest (spearheaded by DARPA), many of the parties involved in the development of packet-switching technologies internationally began to cooperate with DARPA in experimenting with this new capability.[13, 14] A primary vehicle for cooperating in this exploration was not needed the ARPANET, and later the Internet, working groups. In the 1970s and early 1980s, there was considerable international participation in these working groups, with regular meetings being held in Europe.

In addition, in 1981, the International Cooperation Board (ICB) was formed to facilitate cooperation among several NATO countries in the research and development of computer networking and its applications. An initial focus of the precursor activities of the ICB was experimentation with satellite packet-switching technology,[7] with the vehicle being the SATNET, the experimental network being developed by DARPA. The SATNET had nodes in Germany, the United Kingdom, Italy, and Norway, as well as the US. Once this network was established, though, interest expanded to experimentation with integrating the SATNET into the experimental Internet, and the ability of the Internet to support interesting military command and control applications.

2.2.2   US-Based International Research Networks

Once the feasibility of packet-switching technology was established, a number of "grass roots" networking activities began in the research communities. These took place not only in the computer science research communities, but also in other science communities (e.g., physics and space science) where scientists had a clear need for remote access to computing resources and information, as well as to major physics and space research facilities.

By the early 1980s, only about 20 universities were connected to the ARPANET. There were many more that could not be served because DARPA funding was constrained by its charter (to support militarily relevant research and development), and therefore was restricted in its ability to provide general networking support for the computer science community. As a result, two networks were established to provide more general support. The first, the Computer Science Network (CSNET), was aimed at providing interconnection to the computer science academic and industrial community. The second, the Because It's Time Network (BITNET), provided a general computer network capability to the academic campus computing community.

One early networking activity evolved around the space science community. NASA initially established the Space Physics Analysis Network (SPAN) to support the space physics community. It soon proved to be so popular that its role was expanded to general research network support for the space science community. Similarly, the high energy physics community identified the need for networking and established the High Energy Physics Network (HEPNET). Because of the early prevalence of computers manufactured by Digital Equipment Corporation (DEC) in the science communities, both the SPAN and HEPNET communities chose to base their networks on DECnet protocols.

Another community-based network was growing at the same time, and was based on the UNIX™ operating system. This network, known as USENET, links machines using the UNIX-to-UNIX Copy Protocol (UUCP) to provide file transfer and, consequently, news and electronic mail functions.

Each of these community network activities soon became international. BITNET expanded into the European academic community in the form of the European Academic and Research Network (EARN). HEPNET very early recognized the international nature of high energy physics, and expanded its network into Europe as the European HEPNET. Similarly, SPAN and USENET expanded into Europe, the latter as EUNET. CSNET expanded into Europe and the Pacific Rim via its Phonenet mail relay component.

2.2.3   European Networking Activities

In addition to the networking activities starting in the US and expanding around the globe, a number of networking activities were originating in other countries. Several European nations developed internal networks with various goals and methods. In many of these cases, networking services for specific communities (e.g., the research and academic communities) were developed and implemented by using underlying public X.25 networks as the carrier service. A prime example of such networking is JANET (Joint Academic Network) in the United Kingdom, which provides an interconnecting wide-area network service to the academic community, and is based on X.25 networking, achieving speeds up to 2 Mbits/sec.

As a direct consequence of the growing speed of international standardization, Europe turned its attention to providing compatible networking across its constituents—through the International Organization for Standardization (ISO), which focused on the model for OSI (see Chapter 1) coupled with related standardization activities in the Comité Consultatif International de Télégraphique et Téléphonique (CCITT). Because of the strong influence of the public carriers on networking service, the focus in Europe has been on the interconnection of X.25 networks. The Cooperation for OSI Networking in Europe project (COSINE) was initiated (under the EUREKA framework) to develop and implement the techniques needed to interconnect the various national networks into a European computer communications infrastructure.[15] A COSINE Policy Group was formed to oversee the project, consisting of 19 countries plus the CEC was formed to oversee the project. The CEC, acting on behalf of the Policy Group, contracted with Réseaux Associés pour la Recherche Européenne (RARE) for a specification phase, followed by an implementation phase. One of the project's major components is to provide an International X.25 Infrastructure (IXI); i.e., a backbone X.25 network linking the various X.25 national and regional networks.[16]

While OSI- and X.25-based networking constituted the major formal thrusts throughout Europe in providing networking for the research community, there also was considerable interest in TCP/IP-based networking. The availability of local area networks and workstations that supported TCP/IP resulted in a growing TCP/IP-based infrastructure in Europe. This infrastructure tended to coexist with the OSI-based infrastructure, with OSI dominating in some parts of Europe and TCP/IP dominating in others. Efforts in the US agencies to provide a well-supported infrastructure to their researchers via coordinated networking programs (e.g., NASA Science Internet, NSI; NSFNET; and Energy Science Network, ESNET), and their focus on the TCP/IP protocol suite as the interim basis for such networking, provided additional support for using and coordinating TCP/IP in Europe and elsewhere, as the agency-based networks reached out around the globe providing connections to support their programs. Recently, an initiative called EBONE92 was launched to provide a multiprotocol 2-Mbits/sec backbone network to interconnect various national networks, as well as provide connectivity to the global internet.[17] This backbone is intended to provide IP services, as well as a pilot Connectionless Network Service (CLNS).

Toward the end of the 1980s and the beginning of the 1990s, a new series of events began to change the shape of European networking. As global political realities began to change the landscape of the political and economic world in Europe through the opening up of eastern Europe, these same changes began to have repercussions in the networking environment. The lowering of the barriers between the west and the east brought with it increasing pressures for networking connections. The result has been a substantially increased pace of such network connections, beginning with the extension of EARN into a number of countries in eastern Europe, and more recently, connections for X.25 and TCP/IP networking. Along with these connections have come a number of policy issues, and the situation is changing almost daily.

2.2.4 Other International Research Network Activities

While the research and other networking activities in Europe and the US were substantial, they were by no means the only networking activities taking place throughout the globe.

Networks like CA*NET in Canada, AARNET in Australia, and national network initiatives in Brazil and Japan are but a few examples. As we shall see, the Internet has a large and growing global constituency. This growth has come about primarily from two driving forces. The first is the ubiquity of the underlying technology. The easy availability of TCP/IP networking in many workstations and computers, coupled with widespread activity in international standardization and its accompanying infrastructure, has made it much more straightforward to put into place effective networks. Second and no less significant, the growing globalization of research communities and economies has made it critical to have an effective underlying communications infrastructure, which increasingly has meant a computer communications infrastructure.

As an example, the various research interests in Brazil are coordinating the development of a Brazilian research network.[18] Since the establishment of its first BITNET connection in September 1988, the Brazilian national academic and research network has grown to cover most of the important centers in the country by mostly BITNET technology, with some islands of UUCP, DECnet (HEPNET), and TCP/IP. The principal links use dedicated circuits having speeds between 1200 bits/sec and 9600 bits/sec, but a number of sites use dialup telephone circuits or X.25 switched data circuits of the public data network operated by the state telecommunications monopoly. Currently, around 50 sites are connected to the network, including most state capitals, and many institutions in the Rio de Janeiro–São Paulo region. This network is currently connected to the US through three dedicated circuits. Pushing forward even further, a workshop was held in Rio de Janeiro in October 1991 to explore academic networking cooperation in the Latin American and Caribbean regions. Similar activities are taking place around the globe.

2.3   CURRENT GLOBAL INTERNET

The pace of international network connectivity has grown by leaps and bounds in the past several years. In fact, we can be totally confident that this section will be significantly out of date by the time it is in print. Nevertheless, we will attempt to paint a picture of the current state of global network connectivity and services.

Figure 2.1 shows the growth of TCP/IP networks based on the policy-routing tables of the NSFNET routers.* It is clear that, while the total number of networks grows, so does the number of non-US networks. In the year from December 1990 to December 1991, the total number of nets increased by 96% (from 2190 to 4305).† During this same period, the number of international nets increased by 135% (from 615 to 1450). In other words,

---

*   We use the NSF router tables because of the role that national and regional backbone networks play in the overall routing structure. These backbone networks, when interconnected, form the global backbone of the Internet, and typically have the best information regarding network numbers, etc.

†   The most recent figures show the number of networks to be in excess of 5000.

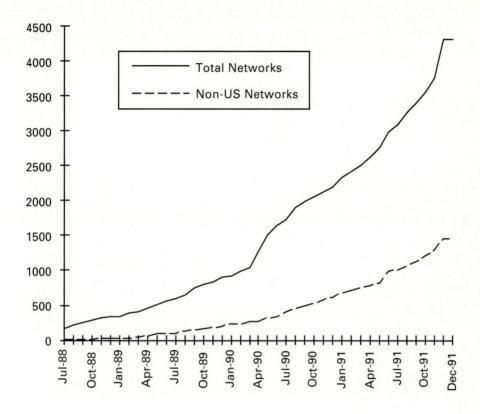

Figure 2.1   Networks seen from NSFNET (Data Courtesy of Hans-Werner Braun and Merit, Inc.)

the growth in the number of non-US nets was half again the total growth. This is just one indication of the significant globalization of the Internet.

As noted above, network connectivity has consisted of growth in multiple protocol domains—TCP/IP, OSI, and DECNET. Increasingly, and especially in the research and academic networks, the various domains have coordinated their connections to the point where their connectivity can be described in terms of three levels:

1   Basic Level.   At the first level, basic link connectivity is provided. This is commonly provided either through the use of leased lines or by using the available public packet data network infrastructure, which is commonly X.25-based.

2   Network Level.   The next level of connectivity provides network connection, for example, so that end-to-end TCP connectivity may be established. This level of connection is typically provided through the use of a single protocol suite, but often by sharing link or physical connectivity between networks using multiple protocol suites.

3 Application Level.   In the final level, user network services are provided, such as electronic mail, by providing the connection of similar networking services between different protocol suites. This often takes the form, for example, of application gateways between OSI and TCP/IP services.

In this section, we will describe the current state of international networking from the perspectives of these levels.

2.3.1   International Link Connectivity

The thrust toward international user and network connectivity has given rise to a large number of intercontinental and international links. These links carry a number of protocols (sometimes shared and sometimes dedicated), and likewise serve both infrastructural (general) and specific requirements.

As an example, we consider the link interconnectivity between the US and Europe. Figure 2.2 shows a portion of the link connectivity between the US and Europe in April 1991. As can easily be seen, there are a large number of links, serving a variety of purposes. Most of the lines operate at approximately 64 Kbits/sec or below, and tend to serve a specific need, either infrastructural (such as the line between Oslo and College Park, which connects NORDUNET and the US research network infrastructure) or specific (such as the link between MSFC and ESOC, which supports the DECNET portion of NSI). In addition to specific links, a concept is emerging, colloquially known as "fat pipes," in which larger bandwidths (typically fractions of T1) are purchased and shared among several networks. An example is the fat pipe between GSFC and London that is shared by NSI, ESNET, and DARPA.

The proliferation of international link connectivity can easily be observed by looking at the network maps of some of the major networks. Figure 2.3 shows a recent map of the NSI. These networks are connected to a wide variety of regional, national, and local networks around the globe.

The mere existence of so many links causes some operational coordination and topology difficulties. We will discuss later some efforts to coordinate the engineering and planning of links.

It is of interest to compare networks like NSI to the infrastructural network of NSFNET. The NSI mission is to support the networking needs of NASA science and research projects. Hence, international connectivity for NSI is established because of specific requirements from NASA organizations. The connectivity reflects this mission, and tends to be organized to connect to specific non-US organizations.

NSFNET, on the other hand, is chartered to serve the broad scientific, research, and education community of the US. As a result, it is organized to interconnect regional and local networks that serve that community. The connectivity, then, tends to be organized around national and regional networks.

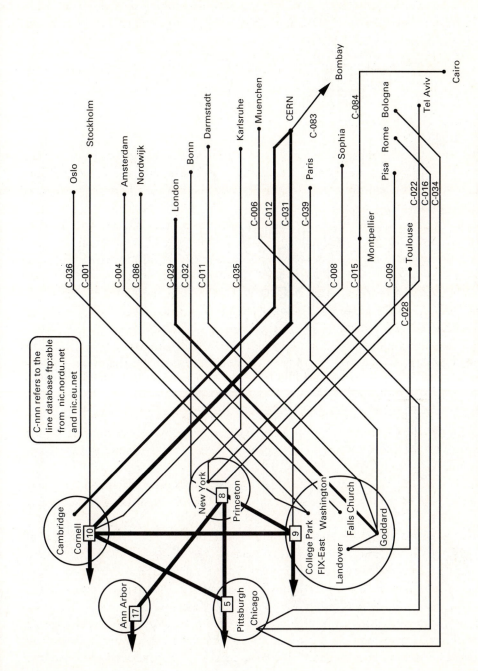

Figure 2.2 US–Europe link connectivity (Courtesy of Bernhard Stockman, NORDUNET)

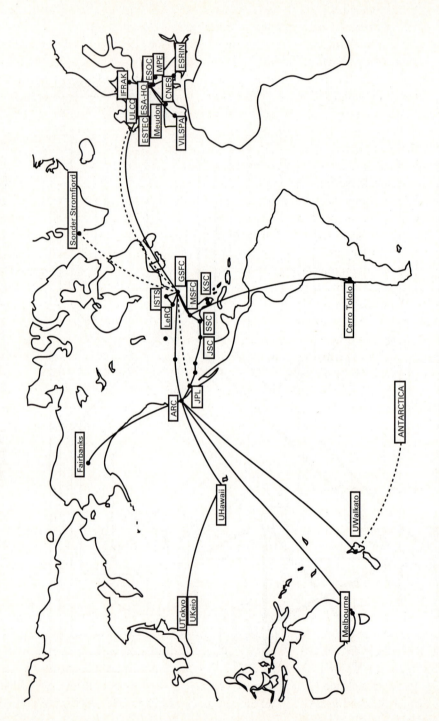

Figure 2.3   NSI international connectivity (Courtesy of NASA Science Internet Project Office)

As with all generalizations, this example ignores an important aspect of cooperation between the agencies. As active members of the Federal Networking Council, NASA and NSF cooperate in the provision of networking service to the research and education communities. In particular, this allows NASA (NSI) to obtain networking service for its user community through use of the more infrastructural NSFNET connections. This results in considerable cost savings, and has been an effective means for accomplishing a portion of the NSI mission. Similar observations hold for other agencies, such as DOE and the ESNET.

Of course, connectivity is far broader than just the interconnections to US networks. International connectivity covers all the continents and is growing. In particular, the connectivity is based on a combination of leased (sometimes shared) lines and utilization of the international public packet-switching infrastructure based on X.25 protocols. We find all forms of "mix and match," including running TCP/IP over X.25, TP4 over TCP/IP, etc.

Another important trend, alluded to above, is toward aggregating requirements and using the result to share larger bandwidth links. This allows for a larger bandwidth to be obtained for the same cost, as a result of economies of scale. Furthermore, because of the nature of packet switching, this also allows for better performance, since combining requirements and sharing a larger bandwidth results in shorter delays for a given total loading and throughput. We see this trend occurring across the Internet. The first case was the fat pipe between GSFC and London noted above. Additional fat pipes are in the planning stages for Europe and the US, and to support Pacific rim connectivity.

A final trend in international connectivity is the expansion of connectivity into what was formerly known as Eastern Europe. Changes in the political situation have been accompanied by an increase in such connectivity, starting with the expansion of EARN. Connectivity is being established between the various networks of the RARE members and the former Eastern Europe networks. The impact of these changes is discussed below.

2.3.2 Network Level Connectivity

International network connectivity is being driven by two complementary forces. The first is the existence of a number of networks in each region of the world, driving toward network connection. The second is the existence of scientific and other collaborations, driving a requirement for user connectivity, and therefore driving toward an expansion of the discipline-based research networks (e.g., NSI).

The interconnection of networks is visible throughout the Internet. The various DEC-NET networks, such as HEPNET and SPAN, are connected internationally and are used to support the science community. Similarly, and on a larger scale, we see the interconnection and coordination of TCP/IP networks around the globe, in such diverse locations as Europe, Japan, Australia, Brazil, and Canada. Similar comments may be made regarding the BITNET network family (including EARN) and the various networks based on OSI/X.25 protocols.

Table 2.1   Country networks observed on NSFNET backbone:* Total Networks, 2869; Total Countries, 37

Argentina	1	Hong Kong	1	Norway	9
Australia	102	Hungary	1	Poland	2
Austria	18	Iceland	1	Portugal	6
Belgium	2	India	1	Puerto Rico	3
Brazil	10	Ireland	3	Singapore	1
Canada	163	Israel	17	Spain	10
Chile	1	Italy	37	Sweden	30
Czechoslovakia	1	Japan	69	Switzerland	38
Denmark	3	Korea	9	Tunisia	1
Finland	15	Mexico	6	United Kingdom	53
France	113	The Netherlands	56	United States	190
Germany	156	New Zealand	16	Yugoslavia	1
Greece	6				

* Courtesy of Merit, Inc. and NSFNET.

As an indication of the growth of international network-level interconnectivity, we again turn to the traffic statistics on the NSFNET backbone. Table 2.1 shows the networks as observed on the backbone in November 1991 (not counting networks that were not recognized as being from a country). It seems that not a day goes by without a few more networks being added to the routing tables. Although the number of US networks still dominates, there is great diversity in the nations that are interconnected.

The Internet, of course, includes more than just those networks using the TCP/IP protocols. Table 2.2 shows the connectivity of countries (by ISO two-letter code) with respect to several network connection technologies (BITNET, TCP/IP, UUCP, and FIDONET) as of December 1991. We see from this table that at the time 89 countries had some connectivity, and 11 more countries were planning connections.

While most of this discussion has been in terms of the various networks supporting the research and education communities, we have recently seen a significant and increasingly important rise in the provision of networking service by for-profit carriers and service providers. Examples include networks in Sweden and Finland that have heavy involvement of the respective Public Telephone and Telegraph (PTT) companies (as well as a number of commercial service providers in the US). Because of the tradition of cooperation among common carriers in providing global telephone service, this may lead to even more coordinated global service in the Internet.

Thus, we are seeing a globalization of the various networks, with technical divisions between protocol suites being more of an impediment to communications than the national and regional differences.

Table 2.2 National connectivity.* Connection codes: B, ≥ 5 BITNET links; I, Operational IP connectivity; U, ≥ 5 domestic UUCP sites; F, ≥ 5 domestic FIDONET sites; x, Uncertain; b, < 5 BITNET links; i, IP operational connectivity soon; u, < 5 domestic UUCP sites; f, < 5 domestic FIDONET sites; N, new connections expected.

AR	---N	CU	--u-	HU	biUF	MY	b-uF	SC	--u-
AR	BIUF	CY	b-U-	ID	--u-	MZ	---N	SE	BIUF
AT	BIUF	DE	BIUF	IE	BIUF	NA	--u-	SG	bIuF
AU	-IUF	DK	BIUF	IL	BIuF	NC	--u-	SL	-- -
BE	BIUF	DO	--u-	IN	bIU-	NE	--u-	SN	--u-
BF	--u-	EC	b-u-	IS	-IUf	NI	--u-	SU	b-UF
BG	--UF	EG	b-u-	IT	BIUF	NL	BIUF	TG	--u-
BO	--u-	ES	BIUF	JP	BIUF	NO	BIUF	TH	--uF
BR	BIUF	ET	---f	KE	---N	NZ	-IuF	TN	bI--
BW	---f	EW	--UF	KR	BIUf	PE	x-u-	TR	B---
BY	--uf	FI	BIUF	KW	b---	PF	---N	TW	B-uF
CA	BIUF	FJ	--u-	LK	--u-	PG	--u-	UA	--UF
CG	---N	FR	BIUF	LS	---N	PH	--uF	US	BIUF
CH	BIUF	GB	bIUF	LT	--uF	PL	biUF	UY	x-uf
CL	BIUf	GF	--u-	LU	b-uF	PR	BIUF	VE	--u-
CM	---N	GL	---f	LV	--UF	PT	bIUF	VU	---N
CN	--u-	GP	--u-	ML	--u-	PY	--u-	YU	B-U-
CO	b-u-	GR	BIUF	MO	---F	RE	---N	ZA	-IUF
CR	b-u-	GT	--u-	MQ	--u-	RO	---N	ZM	---N
CS	BiUF	HK	B--F	MX	BIuf	SA	B---	ZW	---f

2.3.3 Application Connectivity

The existence of networks supporting different protocol suites, combined with the need for users to communicate, results in a need for application-level connectivity between the different protocol suites. While this is true within a single nation or region, the problem is exacerbated on an international level. Because of the inevitable tendency to have greater uniformity within a nation or region than internationally or intercontinentally, the international differences tend to be larger, and the solutions tend to be less uniform.

Nevertheless, as a result of the high degree of international cooperation (see below), we are seeing the installation of well-supported application gateways and the development of appropriate interoperability mechanisms. These tend to be installed to serve regional needs, but by the same token are used to support international connectivity.

A prime example is the installation of electronic mail gateways. These proliferate throughout the US, Europe, and elsewhere, and result in an effective global electronic mail network. This is not to imply that there are no technical and performance issues that need to be addressed.

The issues of effective electronic mail gateways tend to be ones of detail, of making sure that the right mappings are present between the various protocol suites. Dealing with other applications can be more difficult, and we have seen much less progress in those areas. For example, although effective file transfer has been desirable across protocol suites, the most common method is to require the user to log onto an intermediate host having a connection to both networks or protocols. Similar mechanisms are used for remote login. Achieving more effective connection between the various protocol suites is a subject of on going research and development activity across the global Internet.

At the application level, there is also considerable cooperation in the provision of network and user services. Ranging from the assignment of network numbers and domain names through to white pages services, we are seeing the establishment of a powerful international infrastructure. At this level, perhaps more than in any other area, we are seeing a selection of the best of the various protocol suites, and their use to provide needed services to the broad community. For example, white pages services based on X.500 are being used to provide electronic mail addresses and related information, regardless of the underlying protocol suite of either the interrogator or the subject of the search. This, in the author's opinion, is an important trend, and one that is likely to continue.

2.4   ORGANIZATIONAL ACTIVITIES

The Internet began as a multiorganizational activity, and as such has always required a substantial coordinating activity. Even in the early days of its development under DARPA leadership, there was a set of working groups, beginning with the ARPA Network Working Group (NWG) and continuing to the Internet Research Group (IRG) and its associated committees. With the expansion of the activity beyond DARPA and beyond the research community, the importance of these coordinating activities has grown. The evolution of the Internet Architecture Board (IAB), the expansion of the Internet Engineering Task Force (IETF), and the recent initiation of the Internet Society bear witness to this growth.

As an example of the extent of international internetworking activity, Table 2.3 shows the anticipated attendance at the INET'91 conference held in Copenhagen. The actual attendance was 378 people from 58 countries, which demonstrates the widespread interest in networking across the globe.

Internet coordination activities have always had an international component, but the global explosion of the Internet in the last few years has given rise to increased need for and level of international coordination. In this section, we will discuss the evolution and current state of these coordination activities.

Table 2.3   Estimated INET'91 attendance[*]

Total: 354 from 54 countries					
Algeria	1	Finland	10	Nigeria	1
Argentina	2	France	26	Norway	4
Australia	4	Germany	22	Peru	1
Austria	2	Greece	5	Poland	9
Belgium	7	Guinea	1	Portugal	1
Bolivia	2	Hungary	3	Saudi Arabia	1
Brazil	1	Iran	4	Spain	5
Cameroun	1	Ireland	3	Sweden	14
Canada	3	Israel	7	Switzerland	9
Chile	1	Italy	20	Tanzania	1
China	1	Japan	17	Tunisia	1
Costa Rica	1	Kenya	1	Turkey	7
CSFR	3	Korea	7	United Kingdom	8
Cyprus	1	Luxembourg	1	United States	78
Denmark	19	Malaysia	1	USSR (including the	
Dominican Republic	1	Mexico	1	Baltic States)	5
Ecuador	2	The Netherlands	13	Yugoslavia	2
Egypt	8	New Zealand	1	Zambia	1
Fiji	1	Nicaragua	1	Zimbabwe	1

[*] Courtesy of Larry Landweber and Frode Greisen.

2.4.1   Early Worldwide Coordination Activities

As mentioned above, there was international cooperation even in the very early days of ARPANET and Internet development. One vehicle used by DARPA to facilitate this cooperation was the International Cooperation Board (ICB). The ICB had representatives from NATO countries and organizations interested in collaborative research in networking and in networking applications to support military command and control. Started in 1981, the ICB, continues to perform this function, and currently consists of representatives from the countries listed in Table 2.4. Initially, its focus was on the coordination of the DARPA experimental satellite network (SATNET). More recently, the satellite components of the

Table 2.4   ICB member organizations

Germany	SHAPE Technical Center
Italy	United Kingdom
The Netherlands	United States

interconnection have been replaced by terrestrial networks, and the coordination activity focus has moved to interesting command and control applications.

Another independent international coordination activity was based on the annual informal International Academic Networkshop meetings (IANW), which were organized initially by Peter Kirstein, and later by Larry Landweber. These meetings, held from 1982 to 1989, were attended at first by network implementors from Europe and the US, and later were expanded to include representatives from Latin America and the Pacific Rim. They laid the foundation for much of the early cooperation between academic computer science groups developing networks around the world. Both the CCIRN (described below) and the INET conferences are outgrowths of the IANWs.

As networking became more pervasive in the scientific community, appropriate coordination activities grew around the scientific networks. Each of the early scientific networks—SPAN, HEPNET, and BITNET—coordinated their networking activities via formal and informal working groups. For example, HEPNET maintained coordinating working groups in the US and in Europe. HEPNET and SPAN coordinated with each other and with other DECNETs.

In 1983, CSNET negotiated an agreement with DARPA that allowed it to gateway electronic mail from CSNET-affiliated institutions and networks outside the US to the ARPANET. This was the first formal agreement allowing such relaying.

Beginning in the mid-1980s, we began to see a higher level of coordination as networking became more pervasive. In particular, 1986 saw the formal formation of Réseaux Associés pour la Recherche Européene (RARE),[19] which has been highly influential in the evolution of global networking coordination, and hence is worth understanding.

2.4.2 RARE

RARE is an association of networking organizations and users in Europe whose goal is to foster cooperation and "develop a harmonized communications infrastructure." RARE actively supports the "principles of Open Systems Interconnection (OSI), as defined by the International Standards Organization (ISO) [Sic]" and actively supports profiling activities. In addition, as a direct result of the influence of IETF activities and discussions in the CCIRN, RARE has incorporated the Réseaux IP Européens (RIPE). RIPE is a body coordinating TCP/IP activities in Europe.

RARE membership is of four types. The formal membership is national, as is shown in Table 2.5. In addition, RARE has associate national members (e.g., Czechoslovakia), international members (e.g., CERN), and liaison members (e.g., the Corporation for Research and Education Networking, CREN). Examples of the activities undertaken by RARE include COSINE, which is aimed at establishing an interconnected set of networks and network services based on OSI protocols; the European Engineering and Planning Group (discussed below); and an annual networking workshop. In addition, RARE has formed seven working groups to aid in achieving its objectives.

Table 2.5   RARE national members

Austria	Iceland	Portugal
Belgium	Ireland	Spain
Denmark	Italy	Sweden
Finland	Luxembourg	Switzerland
France	The Netherlands	The United Kingdom
Germany	Norway	Yugoslavia
Greece		

2.4.3   Evolution of the CCIRN

In 1987, the pace of global research networking was rapidly increasing. NSFNET was well on its way to becoming the major networking backbone in the US, and was establishing a sizable number of connections to other countries. The European program of international networking, primarily being carried forward through the auspices of RARE, was becoming a reality. Other countries and regions were carrying their network activities forward and were coordinating on an ad hoc basis.

In November of that year, following an IANW held in Princeton, several key people from networking in the US and Europe met in Washington, DC, to discuss the needs and methods of coordinating the ever larger international networking activities. A vision was articulated at that meeting of the global research networks serving as an infrastructure for the global research community. To accomplish that vision, an informal coordinating body was formed, originally titled the Necessary Ad Hoc Coordinating Committee (NACC). Cochaired by Bill Bostwick, chairman of the Federal Research Internet Coordinating Committee (FRICC),[*] and by James Hutton, secretary-general of RARE, the NACC represented an initial attempt to provide coordination among the various research networks. Within months its name was changed to the Coordinating Committee for Intercontinental Research Networks and a formal charter was adopted (shown in Table 2.6).

It was decided that, while the goal of the NACC/CCIRN was global networking, it would be pragmatic to begin with the US and Europe. Thus, the initial membership of the CCIRN included US government personnel and members of European networking organizations. In addition, representatives of the IAB and the ICB were specifically included. The two cochairpersons of the CCIRN were responsible for arranging the specific membership from the US and Europe.

Over the years, there has been an expansion of the membership as the CCIRN moves toward achieving its global objectives. The US membership was broadened to include non-

---

[*]   As a somewhat interesting aside, while one might think that the FRICC was formed prior to the NACC, in fact it was the other way around. The formation of the NACC highlighted the need for an informal coordinating group for US Government research in networking. The FRICC was formed shortly after the initial 1987 meeting.

Table 2.6   CCIRN Terms of Reference

COORDINATING COMMITTEE FOR INTERNATIONAL RESEARCH NETWORKING (CCIRN)

---

1. Terms of Reference

The purpose of the CCIRN is to agree and progress a set of activities to achieve inter-operable networking services between participating entities (currently North America and Europe) to support open research and scholarly pursuit. Policy, management, and technical issues will be examined, based on agreed requirements. More precisely, the committee aims to:

  a. stimulate cooperative intercontinental research by promoting enhanced interoperable networking services, specifically
- promoting the evolution of an open, international research network in line with official policies on the use of international standards,
- coordinating and facilitating effective use of the international networks to enhance the quality of research and scholarship.

  b. optimize use of resources and to coordinate international connections of the networks represented on the CCIRN

  c. coordinate development of international network management techniques

  d. exchange results of networking research and development

2. Membership

CCIRN members should represent an organization with an active interest in developing a continental network with the aims described above in section 1 (Terms of Reference).

In North America these organizations are Federal Agencies which form the Federal Internet, initially: DARPA, NASA, DHHS, DOE, NSF and the IAB and a representative from the Canadian Research Ministry. The North American CCIRN takes responsibility for assembling the appropriate members. In Europe these organizations are those which promote cooperative international networking. Initially, RARE, COSINE, EARN, EUNET, HEP and CERN, SPAN and ESA, the CEC and the ICB. The RARE Executive Committee takes responsibility for assembling the appropriate members.

Observers may be invited at the joint discretion of the co-chairs.

---

government membership, such as FARNET[*] and CREN. The various Canadian networking organizations were included, and the representation was viewed to be regional (North America, Europe, etc.). Membership from the Pacific Rim networking community was included via PACCOM.[†] This expansion continues as regions like Eastern Europe and South America become involved.

Current membership in the CCIRN is shown in Table 2.7. The chairpersons of the CCIRN in July 1991 were William Bostwick (who also serves as the executive director of the US FNC) and Kees Neggers (who also serves as vice president of RARE.)

The CCIRN activities have encouraged the formation of regional coordination bodies. While the US Government, for example, had been coordinating its activities through the

---

[*] Federation of Academic and Research Networks. An association of US regional networks serving academic and research communities.

[†] Pacific Communications. At that time, the coordinating activity for intercontinental research networking in the Pacific Rim region.

Table 2.7 CCIRN membership (August 1991)

Asia/Pacific Rim	Internet Activities Board
Europe	North America
International Cooperation Board	

FCCSET, the CCIRN resulted in the broader coordination of the North American Coordinating Committee for International Research Networks (NA-CCIRN), which includes US and Canadian government and nongovernment research network organizations. Similarly, in Europe, the European Coordinating Committee for Intercontinental Research Networks (Euro-CCIRN) was formed as a somewhat broader set of organizations than RARE itself (although RARE continues to act as the lead organization). Recently, the Asia Pacific Coordinating Committee for International Research Networks (AP-CCIRN) has been formed, broadening the group and charter of PACCOM. The First Inter-American Networking Workshop was held in October 1991 in Brazil, to foster cooperative efforts in academic networking, and focused on an intended Latin American and Caribbean network. While these are not solely due to the CCIRN, the existence of the CCIRN as a model for international cooperation in research networking has certainly been a positive force in that direction.

2.4.4 Coordination of Engineering Planning

As the CCIRN has proceeded to take on the coordination of the research networking infrastructure internationally and intercontinentally, the major challenge of coordinating the engineering of the intercontinental network has surfaced. Much as in the US, where there was a need for engineering coordination between the various Federal networks (satisfied by the Federal Engineering Planning Group, FEPG), as well as the broader research and commercial networks (currently not very well satisfied), and similarly in Europe, where RARE coordinated a good deal of the engineering work, there is a need for coordination of the intercontinental links and operations.

In 1990, the CCIRN began to organize the Intercontinental Engineering Planning Group (IEPG), originally under the leadership of Phill Gross (chair of the IETF). The IEPG works to support the CCIRN by providing the engineering planning and coordination required to "make the Internet work." It comprises engineers from the various constituent networks represented in the CCIRN and is focused on intercontinental and interregional engineering (as opposed to network engineering within a single network, country, or region.) Table 2.8 shows the charter of the IEPG. The IEPG is currently cochaired by Geoff Huston (Australia), Bernhard Stockman (Sweden), and Elise Gerich (USA).

Much as the CCIRN has helped foster regional coordination, so has the IEPG. As a direct result of CCIRN and IEPG activities, a European Engineering Planning Group (EEPG) has been formed to foster the development of a European backbone infrastruc-

Table 2.8   IEPG Terms of Reference

INTERCONTINENTAL ENGINEERING PLANNING GROUP (IEPG)

---

1.   Statement of Goal and Purpose

The Intercontinental Engineering Planning Group (IEPG) is a technical engineering group working under the auspices of the Coordinating Committee for Intercontinental Research Networking (CCIRN). The goal of the IEPG is to work toward a more technically coordinated environment of global networking infrastructural services in keeping with the spirit of the CCIRN, including the goal of integrating international standards.

The CCIRN serves as a coordinating body among organizations which are planning or operating intercontinental computer networks. The IEPG, as an adjunct to the CCIRN, will provide the technical and engineering coordination to supplement CCIRN policy-level guidelines.

2.   The Role of the IEPG

The IEPG will support the CCIRN in working towards coordination of the operations and planning of global networking infrastructural services. The IEPG will work with the CCIRN to develop and maintain a workplan, and to prioritize specific technical topics in this workplan on which to focus attention.

In pursuing its goals, the IEPG will strive to:

a.   coordinate topology planning among CCIRN members to optimize networking capabilities. This could include the recommendation of new intercontinental connections to supplement or replace existing interconnections. It could include commenting on the impact on global operations of links planned by member or other organizations.

b.   coordinate the operations and management of existing networking infrastructure to promote smooth global operations and interoperable global services. This could include coordination of registration, routing, monitoring, and other networking services as required to smoothly operate a global infrastructure.

c.   promote the introduction of new networking services through the proposal and coordination of pilot projects.

The IEPG is not a technical development group. It will accomplish its goals by focusing on the use of existing technology and by coordination between its members. Where existing methods or technology are deficient, the IEPG will provide this information to other already existing developmental organizations. The IEPG will also strive to liaise with other existing operations coordination groups.

3.   Membership

The IEPG membership is made up of network engineers selected by the CCIRN member bodies. IEPG membership is intended to be based on a stable membership of technical experts. The IEPG chair may invite non-member experts on a particular issue on a temporary basis.

---

ture.[20] Similarly, AP-CCIRN and North America have or are forming engineering planning groups.

2.4.5   Globalization of the IAB and the IETF

The engineering groups discussed above are concerned with the coordination of operational engineering and planning. These must be based on a set of technologies, which in the network world is primarily instantiated through a set of standards and protocols. Of course, in the Internet world, this is the province of the IAB and the IETF.

As noted above, the scope of the IAB and the IETF has always transcended national boundaries. The focus of the IAB and its predecessors has always been on technology, independent of nationality, and has always had some participation from around the world, particularly from Europe.

In the last few years, though, the increasing use of the TCP/IP protocol suite (as well as integration of other protocol suites, particularly OSI) to support both research and commercial networks throughout the world has caused a great increase in the international interest in this technology. This in turn has caused the IAB and the IETF to pay much more attention to the international ramifications of the technology. In the next section, we will discuss some of the technical implications of internationalization. In addition, though, there are implications with respect to coordination activities. In particular, the IAB and the IETF have always functioned through fostering close interaction between the participants (individual researchers and engineers). This has meant a relatively high degree of communications, including face-to-face meetings. The logistical difficulties of maintaining this high level of interaction in an international environment is an obstacle to the continued unified approach taken in the Internet community, and must be overcome.

To give the reader a feeling for the current state of IETF globalization, the meeting of the IETF held in Santa Fe in November 1991 had 25 non-US attendees out of a total of 337 attendees. From another viewpoint, 9% (5 out of 56) chairpersons of IETF working groups are from countries other than the US. These figures illustrate the move toward increased globalization of the IETF, and at the same time, the problems of obtaining high levels of participation given the logistical difficulties of international meetings and committees.

Possibilities being explored to mitigate these difficulties include regional subcommittees of the IAB, the IETF, and working groups, and more intensive use of voice and video teleconferencing facilities. The hope is that the very progress being made in the technical community (such as high-speed networking and unified protocols) may be the solution to these problems.

2.5   TECHNICAL IMPLICATIONS OF GLOBALIZATION

The continued global growth of the Internet has some significant technical implications that must be addressed by the Internet community. These are not new implications, and are seen even within each nation. However, the international context for these issues exacerbates the technical difficulties, as well as the political difficulties of addressing them.

One such issue is that of dealing with multiple protocol suites. Currently, the dominant protocols encountered in the research and education community are TCP/IP, DECnet, and OSI. When one deals with a single network, or a tightly coordinated set of networks, the tendency is to select one of these protocol suites and make it the standard. Using a single protocol suite has decided technical advantages in terms of both performance and function, and hence this is a good strategy when possible.

However, when one moves into the larger community, and particularly into the international context, the difficulty of getting global consensus on the selection of a single protocol suite becomes overwhelming. This is due to several factors—some political, some economic, and some technical. For example, in some regions of the world, the dominant network services are tightly coupled to the provision of common carrier services (telecommunications links). In this case, the tendency is to focus on connection-oriented services provided by the common carriers. On the other hand, some regions have focused on building networks based on leased lines, and have seen the network as driven by the end nodes (computers and local-area networks). In such networks, the connectionless mode has dominated, due to the focus on interconnecting connectionless-based LANs. This division not only leads to a selection of different protocol suites, but also may lead to the selection of different network provisions within a protocol suite (e.g., CLNS versus CONS in the OSI protocol suite).

International network coordination bodies like the CCIRN are loath to attempt to select and enforce a single protocol internationally, and probably would be unable to do so. Hence, the focus of international internetworking in addressing the multiple protocol suite is to find a method for coexistence and interoperability. We therefore find the three levels of connectivity discussed above. A challenge for the Internet research and development community then is to develop mechanisms for the integration of multiple protocol suites within the Internet that maximize the functionality and performance of the end-to-end system.

In particular, since it appears that several of the proprietary protocol suites will migrate to OSI or TCP/IP, mechanisms are needed to allow for the maximal interoperability and coexistence of OSI and TCP/IP protocols, and of OSI CONS and CLNS. In addition, recognizing that the Internet continues to change, these mechanisms need to allow for evolution and incorporation of new technologies and techniques.

The IAB and the IETF Steering Group (IESG) held an architectural retreat in San Diego in June 1991. One of the topics covered at that meeting was approaches to the multiprotocol Internet. A description was formulated of a natural tendency of the protocol evolution process to accommodate multiple protocols, and at the same time drive toward integrating the best of the protocol suites into a single basis. This process is outlined in Figure 2.4.

In this process, the assumption is that there is a core protocol suite that acts as the focus of attention. Note that this core suite depends on the community discussing this issue, and there need not be a single core suite. Other protocol suites are then accommodated in the system through two mechanisms. The first is the sharing of resources, allowing multiple protocol suites to share such items as circuits, gateways or routers, and host computers. The second mechanism is the development of interoperability techniques (e.g., protocol translation), allowing end-to-end functions (e.g., electronic mail, file transfer)

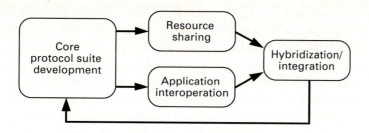

Figure 2.4 Process of multiprotocol Internet

etc.) to be accomplished across multiple networks using different protocol suites. These two mechanisms accommodate the existence of multiple protocol suites but do not drive back toward the high functionality and performance obtained from a single protocol suite.

That benefit results from the integration part of the process. The core protocol suite is evolved by incorporating the best of the other protocols. Incorporation of X.500 directory services mechanisms into the TCP/IP protocol suite is an example of this process at work. The result is to create a counter-pressure to the tendency toward divergence, not necessarily to achieve a single protocol suite.

Internationalization exacerbates another technical difficulty of the Internet—the accommodation of a large dynamic range of bandwidth and error rates in the underlying communications infrastructure. Within a single region or country, while there is a significant range of bandwidths and error rates, the major networks tend to be able to operate from a more limited range. For example, in the US, the major backbone networks operate over communications links ranging from T1 to T3, and need to accommodate lower speeds (56 Kbits/sec and below) and higher speeds (10–100 Mbits/sec) in local areas. However, in many countries, particularly some of the less developed regions, obtaining 56-Kbits/sec long-haul links at low error rates can be difficult. Thus, the international Internet must be designed to be more flexible and accommodating of different levels of technology than is typical in a single region.

This is not a problem unique to the international setting. For example, consider that, in the US, the results of the new initiative in High Performance Computing and Communications (HPCC) are intended to be a technology capable of supporting networking in the range of multiple gigabits per second. Providing effective networking services across both the gigabit network and the lower-speed T3, T1, and DS0 networks will be a major challenge.

One challenge that appears to be on its way to being mitigated through other changes is the international aspect of privacy and security. Just a few short years ago, it appeared that the difficulties of dealing with the presence of sensitive (not military) US and other NATO resources on the Internet, coupled with the expanding connectivity into areas of the world that were perceived at that time as being unfriendly to NATO interests, would pose challenges to the Internet technology and management that were beyond our abilities to cope with them. The subsequent easing of international tensions appears to be resulting in a relaxing of the requirements to the point where solutions now appear feasible (although by no means has this problem been solved).

Perhaps the most important challenge to the technical community lies in the provision of effective international networking application services. Even a service as "simple" as electronic mail requires dealing with the multiplicity of languages and alphabets. While it may be somewhat acceptable to specify the protocols in a single language, user-oriented services cannot be dealt with so simply. An example of an early attempt to deal with this issue is the current effort to expand the specification of the Internet electronic mail protocol to deal with national character sets.

This challenge can be extended to the more general one of dealing with cultural differences across the international Internet. These differences show up in unanticipated ways, and the community will need to maintain flexibility, both technically and procedurally, to deal with them.

2.6 SUMMARY

There is an ever-increasing number of international activities using the Internet as the supporting infrastructure. A good example is a pair of simulated space missions being run cooperatively by 21 schools from 5 nations. One mission is an imaginary Russian space station (MIR-1) being operated by a Finnish–Russian Language School in Helsinki, and getting ground support from Moscow School #117. The other mission is a US space shuttle "manned" by a school in Cleveland, with ground support coming from schools in the US, Czechoslovakia, Finland, and New Zealand. It was planned (as of November 1991) to have the shuttle dock at the MIR-1. International cooperation has included weather reports from around the world, articles written by student journalists, and solar observatory reports.[21]

2.7 ACKNOWLEDGMENTS

The author would like to express his appreciation to the following for providing insightful and most helpful comments as well as much needed information: Vinton Cerf, Hans-Werner Braun, Frode Greisen, Larry Landweber, Kees Neggers, Michael Stanton, and Bernhard Stockman.

REFERENCES

1   T.L. LaQuey, Ed., *The User's Directory of Computer Networks*, Digital Press, Bedford, 1990.

2   J.S. Quarterman, *The Matrix: Computer Networks and Conferencing Systems Worldwide*, Digital Press, Bedford, 1990.

3   P. Baran et al., *On Distributed Communications*, Vols. 1–11, RAND Corporation Research Documents,1964.

4   L.G. Roberts, The evolution of packet switching, *Proc. IEEE*, Vol. 66, No. 11, 1978.

5   D.W. Davies et al., A digital communications network for computers giving rapid response at remote terminals, *ACM Symp. Operating Systems Problems*, 1967.

6   V.G. Cerf and R E. Kahn, ARPANET Maps 1969–1990, *Computer Communication Review*, Vol. 20, No. 5, 1990.

7   I.M. Jacobs, R. Binder, and E.V. Hoversten, General purpose packet satellite networks, *Proc. IEEE*, Vol. 66, No. 11, 1978.

8   D.D. Clark K.T. Pogran and D.P. Reed, An introduction to local area networks, *Proc. IEEE*, Vol. 66, No. 11, 1978.

9   R.E. Kahn et al., Advances in packet radio technology, *Proc. IEEE*, Vol. 66, No. 11, 1978.

10 B.M. Leiner D.L. Nielson and F.A. Tobagi, Eds., Special Issue on Packet Radio Networks, *Proc. IEEE*, Vol. 75, No. 1, 1987.

11 B. Davies and B.M. Leiner, Packet radio and internetworking, STC Workshop on Interoperability, 1985.

12 V.G. Cerf and P.T. Kirstein, Issues in packet-network interconnection, *Proc. IEEE*, Vol. 66, No. 11, November 1978.

13 V.G. Cerf and R.F. Kahn, A protocol for packet network interconnection, *IEEE Transactions on Communications*, Vol. COM-22, No. 5, 1974.

14 B.M. Leiner et al., The DARPA Internet protocol suite, *IEEE Communications Magazine*, Vol. 25, No. 3, 1985.

15 P. Tindemans, COSINE: Ready to move into implementation phase, *Computer Networks and ISDN Systems*, Vol. 17, Nos. 4 and 5, 1989.

16 C. Michau, The IXI pilot project, *Computer Networks and ISDN Systems*, Vol. 17, Nos. 4 and 5, 1989.

17   *Towards a Single European Infrastructure: Report of the RARE Task Force on the Establishment of the Operational Unit for the Supply of Network and Information Services to the R&D Community,* RARE Report RSTF, Vol. 91, No. 5, 1991.

18   M.A. Stanton, private communications.

19   *RARE Annual Report 1990,* RARE secretariat, 1991.

20   K. Neggers, European Engineering Planning Group (EEPG)—Summary Report, *Computer Networks and ISDN Systems,* Vol. 23, Nos. 1–3, 1991.

21   T. Grundner, Ammunition for K–12 Networkers, posting to Consortium for School Networking Discussion Forum List, 1991.

CHAPTER 3 ❏ ❏ ❏ ❏

Evolving the System

DAVID H. CROCKER

CONTENTS

The Internet is a dynamic place. New communities are constantly joining to take advantage of its extensive facilities. During this process, the Internet must evolve to meet the requirements of each new community. This process is rarely painless but it is surprisingly successful.

3.1 THE STANDARDS PROCESS THAT WASN'T

Although the Internet technical community can trace its origins back to a research program begun in 1968, it is only within the last few years that its role in establishing effective and popular communications standards has received broad commercial and international support. The tensions between research experimentation with interesting-but-untested ideas and the enhancement and protection of an installed operating base have been a part of the community since its earliest days. It is the bane of the research community that its work usually is immediately, directly, and clearly useful, but experiments sometimes fail— much to the consternation of the users of the network. This is particularly true with testing that takes place on the operational network.

The predecessor to the Internet, the ARPANET, provided a platform for experimentation with the new packet-switching technology that the ARPA (now DARPA) community developed. The work was distributed among research organizations around the US, and included Western Europe. Researchers used the new technology to facilitate their own interactions, as well as for conducting experiments. This network mediated collaboration, based upon the open exchange of ideas via electronic mail and on-line distribution of documents, led to the Internet culture of today and was fully in place by 1973. The Internet technical community is organic, fluid, and diverse, encouraging participation from the widest possible population of individual contributors, with its membership changing informally and flexibly. The community comprises strong research, academic, and engineering personalities, with open debate and open sharing of results and software. Efforts are more often the result of individual champions than of organizational planning or directives.

The engineering orientation toward immediate use of the technology creates a pressure for simple, clean, and practical architecture that can be developed in a timely manner, as opposed to permitting extended deliberation in search of an ultimate "complete" solution that would require a profile for specifying a useful subset. The philosophy is to build something now, use it, and then modify it as needed. This tends to produce components that are architecturally lean. The public nature of the community's review process also tends to favor architectures that are extensible, since members of the community can see avenues for incorporating their own features. Using incremental improvement to existing technology is sometimes criticized as "lacking foresight," but there is the very concrete rebuttal that the Internet's 10-year history of production use, now with an installed base of many thousands of networks and millions of users, suggests that the process works. The process has repeatedly developed solutions that satisfy near-term requirements and the necessary long-term extensibility.

From its inception, the Internet community has been dynamic, aggressive, and outspoken in its pursuit of focused technical problems, and has insisted upon the minimum of bureaucracy. However, the Internet's technology forms the basis of an industry generating expenditures of billions of dollars per year and producing intense competitive pressures. This requires the standards process to ensure that a level playing field exists for all participants, and that requires a bureaucracy.

At its simplest, the Internet standards process combines the components of a pragmatic engineering style with a social insistence upon wide-ranging input and review. The community's current tensions come from the technical dilemma of continuing to explore and expand the technology while protecting the installed base of users, and of continuing to incorporate ideas from the broadest base of contributors while still producing specifications that are clear, tight, and timely.

This chapter discusses the activities that created the Internet technology, in the context of solutions that are known as "open systems." The Internet standards process is then presented in terms of its current organizational structure, its mechanisms for conducting discussions and disseminating information, and its processes for producing its "products." The chapter ends with some commentary on challenges facing the community.

3.1.1   A Small Community of Interest

ARPA commissioned the core ARPANET packet-switching technology to be developed by Bolt Beranek and Newman. However, the development of services on the attached host computers was left primarily to the loosely organized initiative of bright, highly motivated graduate students.[1] Not knowing any better, they chose various services to be developed and met in collaborative sessions according to whatever topics interested the individuals, after which some industrious participant would document design decisions. Eventually, protocol specifications emerged.

The informality of the process had the detriment of relying entirely upon the energies of one or a few "champions" rather than the more deliberate outcome resulting from an organizational commitment. Documentation tended to be somewhat incomplete at the start, and was not revised in a timely fashion. On the other hand, the documentation had the great advantage of being produced quickly, while being only part of the shared knowledge needed to produce interoperable systems. Other information came from attending the working group meetings. Another feature of the informality was that a scribe could make "enhancements" to the specification and have them implicitly accepted—if no one objected too loudly. For example, before 1982 the ARPANET had no independent electronic mail transport protocol: prior to that time, electronic mail was sent by using two special commands in the File Transfer Protocol (FTP). These were added after working group discussions were completed, and were based upon a private, casual suggestion made to the working group's scribe.

Since the community was geographically distributed, but specifications and ideas needed quick dissemination, an on-line publication series called *Request for Comments* (*RFC*) was initiated in 1969. The name very accurately reflected the desires of authors. *RFC* documents were explicitly viewed as working documents to be used within a relatively small community. They ranged from casual ideas to detailed specifications, and from expressions of operations concerns to whimsical fantasy. If an idea seemed attractive, an individual might spontaneously specify a protocol, or a group might meet to discuss it further. If a protocol seemed useful, someone implemented it, and if the implementation was useful, it was copied to similar systems on the net.

To be sure, the working groups provided a strong focus on technical problems, such as the development of basic connectivity, which now is called transport or "lower layers." Since the total population of this community was only about 100, and initially there was only one network, it was possible to maintain considerable consistency across the "architecture" without full documentation or formal enforcement of conformance rules.

3.1.1.1   An Early Coordination Body

Whereas the ARPANET research developed a single packet-switching technology, it was clear by 1974 that networking needed to span multiple communications media and multiple administrative domains. Early work on the TCP/IP suite was part of a funded research program by DARPA; it was begun as a separate effort from the on going ARPANET work, and with the goal of developing the ability to interconnect packet networks. Its project communications were informal until 1977, when the participants began their own publication series, called *Internet Experiment Notes* (*IEN*). By 1983, participants were publishing their notes as part of the *RFC* series, since the TCP/IP suite was coming into use within the larger community, and a separate series only added administrative complexity. A stronger indication of the acceptance of TCP/IP was the decision by the US DOD to adopt the suite as a military standard. Simultaneously, the DOD converted the ARPANET to use the suite, and separated the ARPANET research and academic com-munity from a produc-tion-only military community.

Two years before this, the effort had matured and grown to the point that the DARPA program manager decided to form an advisory group, called the *Internet Configuration Control Board* (ICCB), that would give DARPA technical advice on the management of the Internet research program. Initially consisting of eight members, this was the genesis of the management structure that is in place today.

Because the bulk of the funding for TCP/IP research and development initially came from the US military establishment, there is a natural tendency to assume that the work was fundamentally biased toward the needs of the US. One of the three original research groups to work on TCP/IP was University College, London, in England. The ICCB and the *International Collaboration Board* (ICB) were formed at the same time and usually met in parallel, the latter often in Europe or Canada. The ICB had a European focus, with the goal of coordinating requirements of transatlantic and NATO use of TCP/IP, particularly in the context of the multisite Atlantic Packet Satellite Network (SATNET), which included Norway, the UK, Italy, and Germany.

By the middle of 1984, the ICCB efforts had evolved to the point that DARPA reorganized it into the *Internet Activities Board* (*IAB*), with each member of the ICCB becoming chair of a task force. The initial task forces were:

- Applications
- Autonomous Systems
- Gateway Algorithms
- Interoperability
- Privacy
- New End-to-End Services
- Robustness and Survivability
- Security
- Tactical Internetting
- Testing.

It is curious and reassuring that the range of skills and interests of the existing members of the ICCB provided a one-to-one match with the range of required activities in the reorganized IAB. In 1986, a new task force was added, called *Internet Engineering* (INENG), which was the forerunner to the current Internet group whose responsibility is the development of standards.

3.1.1.2   *The Present Structure Emerges*

In 1987, 40–50 people attended each technical meeting. By 1989, attendance was up to 150 and the basic tension between long-term research goals and near-term engineering requirements caused yet another reformation, this time creating the split into the *Internet Engineering Task Force* (re-acronymed to IETF) and the *Internet Research Task Force* (IRTF), both of which reported to the IAB. A more detailed description of the current organizational structure is contained in Section 3.2.

During the late 1980s, an Internet industry was emerging, causing the IAB technical activities to be viewed as establishing commercially viable standards. The commercial sector needed far more detailed and current documentation than was initially available. Also, the research community's tendency to modify specifications when convenient began to be mediated by the need to give vendors enough specification stability for reasonable development and deployment cycles. As the community grew, reliance upon the informal communication of essential information became unacceptable, so a more bureaucratic process developed.

Meetings were held four times per year, for about three days, in various locations around North America. This required a substantial investment in time and travel costs; yet there was always pressure to add more to each agenda. Currently, there are three week-long meetings per year. Meeting sites are chosen according to the availability of sites wishing to host the event and handle its logistics. Although the meetings originally were held at the host site—often a university—the logistics became unwieldy, and meetings now are held entirely within a conference hotel. The details of arranging IETF meetings have become sufficiently complex that the assistance of professional staff is required, although the efforts of the host organization remain essential.

Each year has seen a considerable increase in attendance at the IETF meetings and in the number of working groups. Although the IETF was separated into a distinct activity, there were too many groups for the IETF Chair to administer single handedly, so the *Internet Engineering Steering Group* (IESG) was formed, with a set of *Area Directors* who have expertise in various technical topics and who oversee the activities of the working groups. At the July 1992 IETF meeting, 675 people attended. The workload from a community this size is stressing the expanded management structure, and it's not clear that simply adding more management layers, or increasing the number of Area Directors, will suffice. This issue is discussed more below, but it's worth first considering the field in which the Internet technology process has come to play.

3.1.2   On the Meaning of "Open"

Internet technology comes under the rubric of *open systems*. Unfortunately, the term is used with several very different meanings, resulting in serious confusion among consumers. During the 1970s and 1980s vendors provided highly functional networking systems, each one proprietary and often having unpublished interface specifications. Other vendors could compete only by the difficult and time-consuming process of reverse engineering the proprietary products. This increased the profit margins of the proprietary vendors, but decreased customers' choices. Once customers chose a vendor's architecture, they were virtually locked into that company's products; at a minimum, the vendor dictated all changes in the architecture. The commercial pressure for open systems has been specifically intended to let customers obtain products from a variety of vendors, potentially buying each component with a competitive bid. But there are different ways to create multiple sources of a product, so the remainder of this section considers the options, and particularly the types of organizations that produce open systems. A detailed and literate discussion of several standards processes will be found in Quarterman.[2]

3.1.2.1   *Open Publication*

It is possible for a vendor to publish the specifications of its proprietary technology. This allows a third-party *aftermarket* to exist, usually selling products at a lower price than the vendor who owns the specification. At any time, however, the vendor may choose to change the specification and delay publication of the changes until after it has released its own new products. While it's certainly not true that all vendors assert this leverage, it is important that they *can*, and that changes to the specification will be responsive only to the original vendor's assessment of what is needed.

Another concern is that specifications are not universally available. For example, requiring consortium membership with high membership fees effectively restricts the free flow of information from the community at large. Certainly consortia have a special advantage by controlling the content of a specification, while preventing community-wide review of their choices. While this still allows products to come from multiple vendors, they can exercise undue influence over the usual free-market processes. On the other hand, consortium members can argue different points of view, and can move more quickly than most standards processes.

3.1.2.2   Open Ownership

Traditional, "accredited" standards bodies have relatively liberal rules of membership, and conduct open meetings. They publish their specifications, though usually for a significant price, making them available to any customer or vendor. No single company or market-driven consortium controls the specifications. This allows vendors to work from a reasonably level playing field. Work is done only at meetings, which are held at venues around the world. This requires major investment by anyone wishing to attend, constituting an implicit barrier to broad-based participation.

Usually the development of a specification is done in small working groups that have varied membership, but formal voting rights are restricted. This means that one part of the community may dominate the decision process. More often, formal voting serves to delay work rather than to bias technical choices. Further, the charges for copies of a specification often are high enough to limit real access, since many people cannot afford charges of $100 and more per copy, or $1000 and more for a set of specifications.

3.1.2.3   Open Development

In the extreme, a group that develops specifications could be open to everyone interested in participating, possibly even allowing work to be conducted without travel by using a wide-access data network, and then making the resulting specifications available at little or no charge and in a highly convenient on-line format to anyone interested in reading them. On the surface, such an environment would seem not to be viable. The diversity would make it unlikely that it could be managed to a productive end, and it's unclear that it could derive an adequate operating budget. However, this is the gist of the Internet standards process!

At its core, the process relies precisely upon the enthusiasm of its participants rather than upon formal assignment of tasks to members. If a topic lacks an adequate constituency, it's not pursued. If a topic has diverse constituencies, they are free to go their own ways and the market chooses among them. Anyone may participate in the on-line discussions, with no incremental charge for contributing to the development of a specification.

Continuing on-line discussion, away from the face-to-face meetings, allows progress to be made quickly. There is no incremental charge for learning about a document's progress: Anyone may obtain an on-line copy of draft specifications. In general, however, future funding for this process is somewhat problematic. Direct government expenditure funded the development of the technology and its core operational infrastructure. Increasingly, funding for network operations is coming from the commercial sector. The community relies on technical contributions from volunteers, with each participant being self-supporting. However, the core of the standards process uses various logistics, administration, and operations personnel with government funding.

3.2 ORGANIZATION OF THE INTERNET TECHNICAL COMMUNITY

The structure of the current Internet technology and standards processes has been in place since 1989. As described earlier, it comprises a technical oversight and coordination body now called the *Internet Architecture Board* (IAB), which oversees a long-term exploratory body called the *Internet Research Task Force* (IRTF), and a near-term and standards-oriented body, called the *Internet Engineering Task Force* (IETF). Two small secretariats, largely funded by the US government, provide administrative and logistics support to the community. Registration and publication services round out the essential components in the structure of the standards organization.

3.2.1 The Internet Architecture Board (IAB)

The IAB has responsibility for developing Internet technology. It comprises about 15 international volunteers from industry, research, and government, including participation from Europe. As the Internet community has grown and diversified, so has the IAB membership. The group has been self-sustaining, holding sway by virtue of the credibility of its members. The IAB is not formally accountable to a traditional standards organization or any government agency, but the Federal Networking Council consortium of US agencies has provided funding for some of the support, administration, and operations tasks described below. Teleconference meetings occur regularly, with several face-to-face meetings per year. Minutes of meetings are published "on the Internet," as discussed below.

The success of the Internet and its technology, in particular with its expanding commercial market and international scope, has created pressure for a more formal affiliation. There was some exploration of an association with an existing standards body, but without productive outcome. The result was the formation in January 1992 of a professional organization called the *Internet Society* (ISOC). In June 1992, the IAB was placed under ISOC, and given responsibility for the "oversight of the architecture of the worldwide multiprotocol Internet," including continued standards and publication efforts as described here.[3] As part of the move, the IAB changed its name to the *Internet Architecture Board* (from Internet Activities Board), since the IAB does not, in fact, participate directly in the operational activities of any Internet component.

It's no small point that the emphasis within the IAB's ISOC charter specifies "multiprotocol." The Internet is moving from pure TCP/IP advocacy and use to a broader scope. Certainly, ISO's and CCITT's protocols are part of this larger set, but so are popular proprietary protocols. Whenever there's a technical problem to be solved and an adequate Internet constituency to work on the solution and then use it, it's fair game. While the term *Internet* used to be equivalent to the technology of the TCP/IP suite, it now encompasses a larger range of interoperable services in the globally connected data networking world.

Most oversight groups serve primarily to set basic policy and then review the decisions of subordinate groups, making sure that *i*'s and *t*'s are dotted and crossed. While the IAB certainly performs these functions, it also works to embody a consistent but evolving vision of the Internet architecture, serving as a final editorial and technical review board for the quality of Internet standards. On the technical side, the IAB endeavors to ensure that new developments are consistent with the overall protocol architecture, and that they reflect the experience that has accumulated over the 20-year history of the community. The IAB is also concerned about policy issues pertaining to the overall IAB/IETF operation as a technical standards body, for example, ensuring cooperative relationships with other standards bodies.

As with other aspects of the standards process, policies and procedures continue to undergo evaluation and change. Recently, the IAB has instituted the practice of conducting a formal review for each specification submitted to it, and providing written feedback in a style typical of refereed journals. This seems to be adding greatly improved crispness to the evaluation process. In general, it is proving to be a procedural challenge to ensure that the IAB's expertise is tapped early enough in the standardization process to avoid having specification efforts pursue unproductive paths.

3.2.2   The Internet Research Task Force (IRTF)

At the level of direct technical development, the IRTF pursues long-term projects that carry some risk of failure, hence the term *research* in its name. Activities within the IRTF, therefore, are given time and space to consider broad architectural issues and to conduct the deeper analyses that may be required for major changes or additions to the Internet technology. For example, the Privacy and Security Research Group has developed a proposed enhancement to the Internet electronic mail service, called Privacy Enhanced Mail, which has been submitted to the IETF for standardization. The IETF has formed a working group for this, and it is making the changes that are deemed necessary by working group members. Other IRTF topics include the End-to-End Research Group and the Autonomous Networks Research Group. The former considers basic issues in achieving reliable and efficient transfer of data between processes, and the latter attends to the challenge of interconnecting services among mutually suspicious participants.

3.2.3   The Internet Engineering Task Force (IETF)

The IETF develops the specifications that become Internet Standards, and it provides a forum for ongoing discussion about Internet technology and operations. Emphasis is placed upon engineering near-term solutions to problems and upon enhancing features. Projects must have a clear market of users and an adequate source of workers willing to spend the needed development time. As discussed earlier, development is primarily done in *working groups*. These are formally chartered with a chair, a scope of work, a schedule, and a stated set of deliverables. Approximately 80 working groups are active at the time of this writing, and 675 people attended the Summer 1992 IETF meeting. Meetings are held three times a year, for one week each. However, most working groups conduct the bulk of their business over the Internet, through on-line discussion groups, and may meet separately.

   With such a large set of activities and so many participants, the chair of the IETF needs help in managing the process. In 1989 the *Internet Engineering Steering Group* (IESG) was formed, with members who have expertise in various aspects of Internet technology and operations. Called *Area Directors*, they oversee portions of the IETF working group activities (i.e., Areas), but with considerable discussion and decision-making being made by the Steering Group as a whole. The specific sets of areas and working groups vary, with the essential feature being the functioning of the IESG as a general coordination and quality control body, facilitating the creation and operation of working groups. Working group activities often touch more than one Area, so that assignment of an effort may be according to the preferences of the Area Directors, rather than any strict partitioning. Currently, the IETF Areas are divided into

- Applications

- User Services

- OSI Integration

- Internet Services

- Routing & Addressing

- Security

- Network Management

- Operational Requirements

- Standards Management.

Applications

The Applications Area attends to existing and new protocols for providing end-user capabilities, such as interactive access, remote data access, electronic mail, and standard application support infrastructures. Application services developed for the Internet are fundamentally distinguished from many other distributed processing efforts by the need to ensure that the services will operate throughout the global Internet, rather than in a more limited context, such as a single local-area network.

User Services

The User Services Area provides a forum for service providers and others who are interested in improving the quality of the information available to users of the Internet. In general, this Area does not pursue the establishment of formal standards, although it does participate in the development of guidelines, such as the *Site Security Handbook* discussed in Chapter 16. Coordination of support services, such as end-user network information centers that include the Internet Repository described in Section 3.3, also fall into the User Services Area.

OSI Integration

The Internet does not have a history as a hotbed of OSI technical activity, so the OSI Integration Area has provided a base of expertise, and a platform for pursuing incorporation of the OSI suite into the Internet. There is an increasing indication that use of OSI protocols will be by component, rather than by wholesale adoption of the entire OSI stack. This includes the possibility of hybrid solutions, such as running OSI applications over a TCP/IP transport infrastructure,[4] and may extend into such unexpected avenues as the use of OSI internetworking protocol, CLNP, within an otherwise normal TCP suite. That is, it may result in the operation of TCP over CLNP!

Internet Services

The Internet Services Area attends to the basic issue of moving raw data from one end-system host, through intermediate system routers, to destination end systems. Thus, this Area covers such topics as the operation of IP on a very wide range of local- and wide-area media, functions of routers, and low-level internetwork control mechanisms, such as ICMP.

Routing and Addressing

The scaling requirements imposed by the dramatic growth of the Internet means that it is remarkably difficult for a router to know where next to send a datagram. Worse, the 32-bit IP address field is inadequate for the long term. The Routing and Addressing Area was created to provide adequate focus on these issues. It pursues the development of routing protocols for the Internet, and the extension of routing protocols that have been developed elsewhere but are candidates for use within the Internet. Routing and addressing are sufficiently complex topics to warrant the allocation of a separate Area, rather than being included as part of Internet Services, although the two Areas frequently share oversight of working group activities. The topic is considered more extensively in Chapter 17.

Security

Broadly, the Security Area seeks development of capabilities that support protection of the network infrastructure against unauthorized tampering, protection of network users against compromise of data confidentiality and integrity, and protection of network services against unauthorized use. Since detailed consideration of security issues is unfamiliar territory outside of specialized technical and government communities, the Security Area also pursues the development of security-related policies appropriate to the operation of the Internet, and assessment of the capabilities and risks present in technical options. Security technology and techniques also makes this an appropriate Area for considering the application of formal analytic techniques to evaluate protocols for correctness and robustness.

Network Management

As the Internet grew to have multiple backbone service providers and thousands of attached networks, the technical community began to pursue the development of tools for controlling operation, and detecting and resolving problems, within the Network Management Area. Now that a core system for conducting management exchanges has been accepted, most development is focused on the definition of topic-specific management information, for example, characterizing the operation of IP over different transmission media. However, a recent proposal seeks to enhance the exchange mechanism. Generally, the purview of the Area is the development of common mechanisms for management of all the devices that may be present in the Internet.

Operational Requirements

The Operational Requirements Area seeks to provide coordination among Internet service operations groups, to develop operations techniques, and to ensure that technical development allows proper system-wide operation. Working-group efforts include the development of a common trouble-ticket system, to facilitate Internet-wide tracking of operational problems, as well as the pursuit of operational guidelines to establish a common basis for end-user expectations.

Standards Management

The Standards Management Area is a staff function that attends to the IETF's conformance to its own standards procedures, and the enhancement of those procedures as needed. In effect, this provides the IESG with a parliamentarian.

The diversity, style, and size of the IETF's work load tends to lead an Area Director into the role of shepherd rather than active instigator. Activities for each Area tend to overlap with others, and assignment of a working group to a specific Area is often a matter of convenience. Work in Applications, Internet Services, and Routing and Addressing is predominantly the direct development of specific pieces of technology. Network Management, Security, User Services, OSI Integration, and Operational Requirements also have specific projects, but very often provide expert assistance to working groups in other Areas. The high degree of overlap and cross assistance correctly suggests that IETF technical work is conducted with a general, systems-oriented perspective, rather than keeping areas of technical expertise separate from each other. Area Directors are selected by the chair of the IETF, and some Areas are broad enough to need more than one Director. The review and guidance of an Area's technical work often is assisted by selected groups of expert advisers. The IESG meets regularly by teleconference and has an open session during the IETF meetings. Minutes are published on the Internet.

Working groups provide the core platform for IETF productivity. They have a formal chair and charter, and are created and terminated with IESG approval and announcement to the IETF. Each operates in a manner dictated by its membership, and membership is entirely open. Since anyone may participate in the on-line discussion or may attend meetings, one could claim that IETF membership is a state of mind.

The chair's job is to find a productive path, in a manner that is largely acceptable to the membership. The process is labeled "consensus-based" in that no formal votes are recorded, and there is a general desire to resolve differences by navigation and negotiation, rather than by fiat. Consensus-based decision-making is generally viewed as consuming a particularly great deal of time and energy. Worse, it is impossible to resolve all differences. So, efficient working groups benefit from a strong, diplomatic chair who can help the group surface and present issues clearly. Such a chair also helps the group to choose options, without endless debate and—what is worse—constant rehashing of issues. Rehashing decisions is a particular danger, since participation in working groups is so fluid. People new to a working group may not be aware of the group's discussion history and usually are directed to the working group's on-line archive of messages. This is of mixed benefit, since archives often are many, many megabytes and can take a very long time to read, no matter how fast one's network connection.

3.2.4 Internet Assigned Numbers Authority (IANA)

A great many aspects of the Internet protocols are subject to extension, usually by assignment of new values for existing attributes. Services like Telnet and FTP depend on the assignment of "well-known" TCP and UDP ports for initiation of the service; and numerous options are defined with IP, TCP, and the other protocols. To coordinate the assignment of ports, values for options, and the like, the Internet has established the *Internet Assigned Number Authority* (IANA), which is operated by the University of Southern California's Information Sciences Institute (USC-ISI). Anytime a specification permits extensions, the task of registering those extensions and assigning an appropriate extension name or number is performed by IANA.

Registration with IANA does not make an extension a "standard" but rather standardizes the mechanism of referring to it. This distinction is fundamental. IANA's task is to standardize the way systems refer to resources and mechanisms. The IAB/IETF's task of standardization creates consensus about the nature and details of those mechanisms. IANA requires a specification for any extension. Authors are encouraged to publish their specifications, particularly through the *Request for Comments* series, and also are encouraged to seek standardization, when appropriate, but these are not required. IANA will register an extension that is not published, as long as a formal specification exists. New extensions are registered frequently, and the published summary list may not be current. At the time of this writing, *RFC 1060* is the most recent version.[5] Requests for specific details about extensions, such as the current list of network management information base values, should be sent to

        iana@isi.edu

3.2.5   *Request for Comments*

Formal and archival publication of individual ideas, organizational notices, IAB standards specifications, and other items of interest are made available through the *RFC* publication series, which is also operated by USC-ISI. The series retains its original name from the time it served as the primary means of communicating ideas among the distributed community of ARPANET researchers. Over time, it has become best known as the means of publishing Internet Standards, but formal status as a standard is separately assigned, by the IAB. Hence many *RFC* documents are not IAB standards. The continuing need for an informal mechanism for disseminating ideas and specifications has resulted in the creation of the Internet Drafts directory, which is described below.

In fact, the status of *RFC* documents was quite ambiguous for many years. *RFC 733*, the first formal specification of a convention for formatting ARPANET mail, was also the first *RFC* presumptuous enough to call itself a standard, engendering some heated comments within the community. Only within recent years has the assignment of standards status become formal and distinct, while the *RFC* series continues to serve a wide range of Internet interests. Some *RFC* documents also engage in the whimsical, primarily with a publication date of April first.

The *RFC* Editor is a member of the IAB, and coordinates release of relevant documents with the IESG, to assist the working group process. Basic style and format rules are enforced, with considerable attention paid to timely publication. A copy of the *RFC* style guide was published as *RFC 1111*.[6]

For information about submitting a document to be published as an *RFC*, send a message to

        rfc-editor@isi.edu

The current list of *RFC* documents can be obtained by retrieving the file

```
rfc/rfc-index.txt
```

from an Internet Repository, as discussed below and detailed in the Appendix. To receive announcements of the publication of new *RFC* documents, send a message to:

```
rfc-announce@isi.edu
```

As the formal import of *RFC* publication has increased along with the total number of documents, some special categories of *RFC* documents have been defined. One covers documents that provide useful tutorial material about the Internet and Internet technology for end users. These are called *FYI (For Your Information)*, and have their own numbering system, in addition to the *RFC* number.[7] An *RFC* number is assigned to a specific version of a document, and changes when a new version is issued. An *FYI* number is assigned to the generic document and stays constant across new versions.

The current list of *FYI* documents can be obtained by retrieving the file

```
fyi/fyi-index.txt
```

from an Internet Repository.

To facilitate maintaining a clear distinction between publication as an *RFC* and assignment of standards status, a subseries of *RFC* documents called *STD* has been developed and is structured in the same way as the *FYI* series.[8] That is, when a document is revised, a new *RFC* number is assigned, but the associated *STD* number is not. Also, a single *STD* number may apply to multiple documents when they compose a single, integrated specification, such as for the Domain Name Service.

The current list of *STD* documents can be obtained by retrieving the *RFC* directory, with the filename

```
rfc/std-index.txt
```

from an Internet Repository.

As the Internet standardization process has become increasingly formal, so has the need to publish an official list of the standards. Previously, a summary was produced by the *RFC* Editor as a general service. More recently, quarterly publication of a summary was made a formal action by the IAB. It's issued with the title *IAB Official Protocol Standards;*[9] check the *RFC* index for its current number.

3.2.6   The IAB and IETF Secretariats

The size and operation of the IAB and its components requires logistical and administrative assistance. When the community was quite small, this overhead was part of the original research funding. As such funding declined and the community grew, support was largely a volunteer effort. In recent years, agencies that have been members of the *Federal Networking Council* (FNC) have provided funding for some of the support, administration, and operations needs of the IAB and IETF. The originators of TCP/IP, Robert Kahn and Vinton Cerf, both at the Corporation for National Research Initiatives, have received support from the FNC members allowing them to operate an IETF Secretariat. The Secretariat currently includes an Executive Director for the IETF and a Secretary for the IESG, both of whom participate in the IESG. A three-person administrative staff handles all of the logistical details for the IETF meetings each year, as well as a number of smaller events within the IAB. Jon Postel and Robert Braden, both of the Information Sciences Institute of the University of Southern California, participated in the original ARPANET and Internet technical efforts, and currently act, respectively, as the Executive Director of the IAB and the Chair of the IRTF. They also operate the IANA and *RFC* publication services, with partial funding from an FNC member organization. Recently, attendees at IETF meetings have been charged a fee on a cost recovery basis. One goal of affiliation with ISOC is to allow more formal treatment of the IAB's financial requirements and to diversify its funding.

3.2.7   International Coordination and Collaboration

In recent years, the IAB technical community has had limited participation outside of the US, although Internet technology is becoming quite popular in Europe and the Pacific Rim. Europe has two organizations, RARE and RIPE, which employ, coordinate, and develop Internet technology, and there now is cross-membership with the IAB and the IESG, although such membership is on an individual, rather than organizational, level. The European body that is roughly equivalent to the IAB is *Réseaux Associés pour la Recherche Européenne* (RARE). Separately, *Réseaux IP Européens* (RIPE) is an organization of the academic community, and its coordination with the IETF is informal. On a selected basis, RARE technical groups are cross-authorized for IETF-related work, and this may be an indication of the IAB's ability to collaborate on the development of Internet standards by organizations that are not wholly part of the IETF.

Along a technical vein, the work of the IETF is attempting to include internationalization as a factor when making design decisions. In fact, the recent enhancement to Internet electronic mail, MIME, was instigated with the specific goal of permitting Internet messages to be in character sets other than ASCII, to support other languages.

3.3   INFORMATION EXCHANGE

One aspect of the Internet technical community's style of operation that has been a long-standing benefit and that is gaining increasingly general appreciation is its extremely easy and open access to technical and operational information. Work in the IAB, the IRTF, and the IETF relies upon this. Since anyone can obtain the source material or observe (and participate in) development discussions, "mysticism" about the technology is reduced. The standards process is significantly aided by the larger population of potential contributors that results from greatly reducing the effort required to join and become a productive participant. Electronic mail and bulletin board services provide the means for discussion, and on-line repositories provide the archives and reference materials for those discussions. Broadly, Internet technical communication, therefore, is by face-to-face meetings, on-line discussion, and on-line document repositories.

3.3.1 Mailing Lists

Each IETF working group has an on-line mailing list, with an address specified in the group's charter. Many such lists are interconnected to the Usenet bulletin board service, often under the `net.tcp` newsgroup.[10] Each mailing list has a central address from which messages are fanned out (or "exploded") to recipients and other, subordinate mailing lists. Large lists are operated in a hierarchical, distributed manner, with most recipients receiving copies of messages in a few hours. A general-purpose mailing list for the IETF is:

```
ietf@nri.reston.va.us
```

The Internet convention is to send administrative messages to the list name with `-request` appended. Therefore subscription or removal requests must be sent to:

```
ietf-request@nri.reston.va.us
```

Under *no* circumstances should such requests be sent to the actual mailing list, since many thousands of people will receive it. Checking with local network or systems operations staff is advisable, since a subscriber's local organization may have its own list exploder.

It is a curious phenomenon of computer-based group communications that participants often indulge in language that they would not be likely to use in a face-to-face confrontation. Known as "flaming," such behavior often includes intense personal attacks predictably sidetracking the group discussion. Flaming is remarkably common in public e-mail discussions, though quite rare in other forums; it would be helpful for behavioral or social researchers to study the reasons this occurs. To reduce a novice's learning time, an extremely useful primer is *Toward an Ethics and Etiquette for Electronic Mail*.[11] An extensive discussion about available networking collaboration services can be found in *The Matrix*,[10] and a highly literate consideration of the technology's impact can be found in *Connections: New Ways of Working in the Networked Organization*.[10]

3.3.2 Meetings

Often viewed as definitive events in the Internet standards process, week-long IETF meetings bring together much of its technical community. The bulk of the week is spent in parallel working group sessions and *Birds of a Feather* (BOF) exploratory meetings. However, time is reserved for meetings of the IETF plenary, to hear operations and technical reports pertinent to the community, and to permit presentation and discussion of recent and pending IESG actions. As attendance at the meetings has grown, a major challenge has been to balance scheduling. Simply extending the length of meetings is no longer possible, since even the most dedicated IETF members value their weekends.

Face-to-face meetings of working groups permit detailed and intense discussion of open issues, and they form the meat of an IETF week. There is a tendency to treat these meetings as definitive in the decision-making process. Consequently, failure to attend can leave a participant at a disadvantage. Unfortunately, going to IETF meetings may not ensure one's ability to participate in relevant working group meetings because the sessions are held in parallel, which forces members to choose among groups with competing schedules. It can be argued that this hones attendance to a committed core, permitting more efficient decision-making, but it also can be argued that potentially valuable input is lost. In reality, the decision-making process in the IETF is rather fluid, and valid concerns may be raised at any reasonable time. Regardless of its timing, a sufficiently perceptive argument can, and does, cause review of a decision.

As the IETF has grown, the creation of working groups has become more formal and, therefore, more difficult. Recently, BOF sessions have been permitted to meet to test the waters for new topics and potential working groups. In effect, BOF sessions are a market research and planning tool, to test whether the IETF has a sufficient constituency for a working group and to formulate the basic approach for group efforts. In general, a BOF should convene at only one IETF meeting, since a series of such BOF sessions might be construed as conducting a working group without formal approval. This would mean that the participants would be operating under the cover of the IETF, without formal reporting or accountability.

To receive IETF meeting announcements, send a request to:

```
ietf-rsvp@nri.reston.va.us
```

3.3.3   Internet Repositories

The amount of on-line information that is publicly available around the Internet is astonishing. The highly distributed nature of Internet administration allows any organization to make its own decision to provide information. Most documents are available in a simple ASCII-based format. While quite constraining, this format has the very major advantage of being universally convenient for simple processing, such as searching, viewing, and printing. This is another example of the Internet choosing a simple alternative for immediate utility and finding that it provides a basic benefit to the operational infrastructure. There is considerable desire to use an enhanced presentation format, but none is universally acceptable. Experiments in the use of PostScript™ have demonstrated enough difficulty to place it as secondary to the use of simple ASCII.

For the purposes of this chapter, the most significant source of files is a redundantly stored collection that is formally operated as the *Internet Repository*. It contains files pertinent to the IAB, the IESG, the IETF, and the Internet at large. Copies of the Repository are maintained at sites that are geographically distributed around the Internet, to facilitate access. In addition to providing interactive retrieval, many repository sites provide retrieval via electronic mail. SRI International, in Menlo Park, California, offers printed and CD-ROM versions of *RFC* and other Internet documents. Announcements of new documents are sent to the IETF mailing list. Also, some organizations may maintain their own copy of all or part of the official Repository. The reader is encouraged to explore the directories in the Repository as described in the Appendix. Directories are provided for the IAB, the IESG, and the IETF. Two other directories that are basic to the standards process are discussed in the following sections.

Repository sites and other Internet-based public archives are accessible interactively, using a convention with the Internet's FTP service. FTP transfers entire files between machines; it has a simple user–password identification scheme. For public access, some files are made accessible through *Anonymous Login*. The convention is that the user gives the word anonymous as a username and the user's own name as a password. (Some sites require that the password be the user's full e-mail address.) Electronic mail retrieval is accomplished by sending a message to a special e-mail address, with the structured request for information in the subject line or, more commonly, the body of the message.

The Repository contains copies of the *RFC* publications and the IAB, IESG, and IESG working documents, such as meeting minutes. However, the most active portion of the Repository contains documents in progress and support documents, primarily for IETF working groups, called *Internet Drafts* (I-D). The I-D directory is explicitly for short-term use, and no archival copies are kept. Any document may be placed there for community access and reference. A document that has not been changed within six months is removed, as it is when formally published as a *Request for Comments*. Internet Drafts are not intended to be cited in publications or Requests for Proposal, since there's no guarantee that any document will be available for an adequate period of time. In effect, I-Ds now serve the role that *Request for Comments* documents originally served in the early days of the ARPANET.

I-Ds may come from a working group or an individual contributor. For information about submitting a document for storage in the I-D directory, send a query to

```
internet-drafts@nri.reston.va.us
```

The format rules for I-Ds may be obtained from the Internet Repository, in the file

```
internet-drafts/1id-guidelines.txt
```

The perceptive reader will have noticed that the file name begins with an Arabic 1. This is a trick designed to make the filename appear early in the list of files in the Internet-Drafts directory.

3.4 OFFICIAL LABELS

Over time, the process has become increasingly formal and detailed. Specifications are separated into those that seek to be standards and those that do not. Moreover, there's a distinction between specification of *how* a procedure works, and *when* it's to be employed. This section discusses these categories and the IAB processes that produce the specifications.

Whether a standards body operates as a *de facto* or *de jure* agency, it can never dictate market purchases or government requirements, although the nature of its position may permit it to constrain or influence such activity. Ultimately, only customers can dictate the success of a standard. The job of the standards body, therefore, is simply to produce documents that serve as common descriptions, and attempt to sway customer usage by force of credibility. That is, a standard represents a consensus of some group as to one way to accomplish a task. Whether that group has correctly anticipated or understood the needs of the market is not clear until the market votes with its money. Since producing specifications is expensive, some effort is needed to determine the existence of an audience prior to beginning development, and as work progresses, to ensure that it is responsive to the audience's need.

3.4.1 Standards Track Products

A document intended to be an Internet Standard goes through four stages of development, with three formal maturity levels. The first is basic development, during which time the specification has no formal status and might not result in a submission to the standards process. When the specification is stable, has a sufficient constituency, and has no known omissions or problems, it may formally enter the standards track as a *Proposed Standard*. In general, testing before standardization is an important principle of the Internet process. Although implementation and testing are not required in all cases before entering the standards track, they generally are encouraged. Specifications represent many subtle choices in the range of possible solutions, and their complexity and impact upon the Internet often is not well understood. Implementation and testing yield this information in a way that static analysis cannot. Final judgment about the need for such experience, prior to entering the standards track, is left to the IAB.

A specification may be submitted for elevation to the status of *Draft Standard* when there exist at least two independent implementations that have interoperated to test all functions, and when the specification has been a Proposed Standard for at least 6 months. The nature of testing is such that it may well uncover problems. If these are sufficiently minor, then the specification may be fixed without affecting progress along the standards track. Major changes, however, introduce instability and decrease the base of understanding that has developed for a specification, usually necessitating its being required to reenter the process as a Proposed Standard. Determination of the degree of impact often is subjective, but upward compatibility is a good discriminator. This concern about impact relates to the technical content of the specification. Major changes to the writing style of the document—as long as it does not change the bits that are sent over the wire—generally will not affect progress along the standards track, although a small amount of additional time may be indicated to give the community an opportunity to review the new version and convince itself of its semantic stability.

It should be noted that another cornerstone of the Internet culture is to produce at least one "reference" implementation of a specification, and to make it generally available to the Internet, possibly even placing it in the public domain. However, this is not a requirement for standardization, though it's a remarkably effective method of assisting the adoption of a specification in the operating Internet. Equally strong is the development of implementations prior to submission for Proposed Standard status, even when not formally required by the IAB.

When a Draft Standard has gained significant field experience, providing a clear demonstration of community interest in using the specification, and has held its status for at least 4 additional months, it may be elevated to the status of full *Internet Standard*. If a specification does not reach Internet Standard within 24 months after becoming a Proposed Standard, the IESG is required to review the work for viability, and may terminate any further effort.

When an existing Internet Standard specification is revised, there's a clear need to attend to issues of transition for the installed base of users. The handling of the old and new specifications will vary, according to the needs of the user community and the alternatives that are feasible for the specific service. As appropriate, elevation of a new version to full Internet Standard status may cause the previous version to be labeled obsolete immediately, or an explicit transition plan may be specified. The choice largely will depend upon the extent to which the older specification has a satisfied installed base or the new specification provides substantial improvement. In any event, new versions go through the entire standards process.

3.4.2   Non-Standards Track Products

The Internet relies upon many documents that are not categorized as official Standards. Such documents may explain or document technical or operational problems or their solutions. They may invite comment or simply provide status about work in progress. The Internet encourages freely sharing such reports and discussions.

Documents that are produced by other standards bodies, other organizations, or individuals simply wishing to make their work available to the Internet may publish a version as an *RFC*, with the status *Informational*. These are not Internet Standards, and are not intended to be the subject of formal Internet effort.

Specifications that are not on the standards track but for which the author seeks to gain Internet experience, may be published as *Experimental*. The specifications may change, may be incomplete in some respects, or may contain significant errors. However, the specification's author wishes to encourage technical review and experience, possibly for later consideration in the standards process.

Since the term *Experimental* conjures uncomfortable images in the commercial sector, it often is difficult to obtain vendor participation in gaining experience with Internet specifications that are labeled Experimental. In recognition of this, the IAB may create the *Prototype* status. The basic requirements for Prototype would be the same as for Experimental, but there would be an implicit expectation that such specifications already had received considerable group development effort and review, and would be quite likely to enter the standards track, although they would not yet be viewed as being sufficiently well understood.

Finally, specifications that are ready for retirement, due to lack of interest, obsolescence, or the like, are moved to the status of *Historic*. Linguists have noted that the correct term is *historical,* but the existing term has too much history behind it to make a change now.

3.4.3 Categories of Specifications

The bulk of the IAB standards are technical descriptions of network-based exchange procedures, called protocols. Any document that specifies conventions for the interchange of information is called a *Technical Specification* (TS). While these have historically been for computer–computer exchanges, the IAB is considering other interchange specifications, such as common textual formats for exchanges among human users or *application programming interfaces* (API) to support multiple network-related end-user services. However, the appropriateness of such standardization will depend upon its improving the utility of networked systems.

Separate from indicating *how* a task is to be accomplished is specifying *when* it should be accomplished, that is, indicating the context that is appropriate for its use. Technical Specifications serve the former function, and *Applicability Statements* (AS) accomplish the latter. A TS should contain a basic AS section, indicating the general use to which the specification should be put, or it may contain all of the AS detail. In some cases, a major category of device or service can be described by an AS that covers more than one TS. These are known as *Requirements* documents. The major examples of these are the suite of documents for *Host Requirements*[13] and *Requirements for gateways,*[14] which detail and clarify the TS documents for end systems and intermediate systems, respectively. The latter document is under revision, with the tentative new name of *Requirements for IP Routers,* but it has not been released at the time of this writing. The Internet develops independent Applicability Statements whenever there is a need to clarify proper usage of a specification or service. Generally, this is a factor only for specifications that are Standards.

The use of Applicability Statements derives from the need to assign an appropriate requirement label for individual specifications. The process of standardization produces an assessment about the stability and completeness of the specification but gives no guidance about the importance in using it. To this end, Internet specifications are given a basic assignment of *Required, Recommended, Elective, Limited*, or *Not Recommended*. The first three are used for standards, the fourth is most appropriate to Experimental or Prototype specifications, and the last applies to Historic documents. The only specifications that received the label Required were specifications for the Internet Protocol and its companion, the Internet Control Message Protocol (ICMP), since they formed the common glue to the entire Internet. Given the move to a multiprotocol environment, it's not clear that even these two documents warrant a blanket label of Required.

3.5   THE CURRENT STANDARDS PROCESS

This chapter has discussed the organization of the Internet's standards development community, the categories of Internet standards, and the mechanisms available for conducting standards business. All that's left is to describe the process that combines these pieces into a factory for the creation of communication technology products.

More than anything else, Internet standards are produced by the combination of individual effort and community need. In its way, it's a remarkably market-driven process, with the formal procedures designed primarily to keep things public and to give contributors an equal opportunity. The process succeeds due to the enthusiasm of contributors and those charged with oversight of the process. Until recently, the process was not documented, and the current specification of the procedures is acknowledged to be incomplete. It was a first attempt to document *current* procedures. As with the Internet technology itself, the procedures and the document are undergoing review and refinement as experience is gained in their use and as the conditions of their use change. *RFC 1310: The Internet Standards Process*[15] may have been reissued by the time this chapter is published.

A basic view is that the formal processes *embody* the philosophy of the Internet, rather than replace it; detailed rules often take on their own life. On the other hand, managing the process entirely at the discretion of the personalities responsible for it could lead to charges of bias. Hence, the development of formal Internet standards procedures is proceeding in a fashion very similar to the way the Internet develops technology. Practice largely precedes documentation, with the written specification then being reviewed and modified as experience is gained.

3.5.1   Criteria

The evaluation and acceptance of specifications desiring standards status entails a set of criteria that are simple in concept but subjective in assessment. Whenever debate about a candidate specification becomes heated, it is particularly useful to review the degree to which it satisfies the following list. A specification must demonstrate:

• *Competence.*   The specification must be technically sound and consistent with the overall Internet architecture.

- *Constituency.*   There must be a significant set of potential providers and of potential users and an indication that they will, in fact, use the services provided by the specification.

- *Coherence.*   The specification must be written clearly and cleanly.

- *Consensus.*   The specification must reflect an adequate consensus of the technical community.

3.5.2 Procedures

Broadly, a simple three-stage sequence takes place. A specification is developed. Then it's reviewed, and if reviewed favorably, it's approved. The process is made somewhat more complicated by the demands for fairness in the development process and thoroughness in the review process. The sequence occurs at each of the three formal levels of the standards track. That is, the procedures are applied iteratively. A specification goes through the entire procedural cycle to become a Proposed Standard, then again to become a Draft Standard, and one last time to become an Internet Standard.

Development of a specification usually takes place in the context of a group operating under charter from the IESG. Formal chartering of a working group is a major event, since it permits public review of the working group's goals, and public indication of support for the working group's existence. Specifications also may come from other standards groups, other organizations, or individual contributors. If a specification is not placed in a working group, the IESG may solicit reviews from experts, prior to recommending it for standardization. While not strictly required, processing specifications through a working group greatly facilitates establishing the technical adequacy and community constituency of a specification, and the acceptance of specifications that are entirely outside of a working group context has become quite rare.

In general, the IAB seeks to avoid pursuing developments that are redundant with the efforts of other standards bodies or that otherwise might conflict with their work. To this end, there are efforts to coordinate working group efforts with relevant organizations, often by virtue of cross-attendance by members. At its best, the coordination can result in having the IETF explore ideas and preliminary specifications on behalf of other standards bodies, in recognition of the quicker metabolism allowed in the IETF context. It also is possible that the needs of the Internet will dictate pursuing a course that is not compatible with specific efforts of an outside group.

In any event, work from other standards bodies is not directly standardized by the IAB. Rather, such work may be incorporated by reference, either in a TS or an AS. This also applies to other outside work, as long as a copy of the cited specification is generally available. Publication as an Informational *RFC* is one of the means of establishing this availability. The work of individuals and other organizations carries an automatic concern about ownership. Any outside work may be incorporated by reference into an AS or a TS.

In this circumstance, the original work is not made an IAB standard. Rather, its use in a larger context is specified by an IAB document and made standard. On the other hand, it may be that the original authors of a specification wish to have it directly made an Internet Standard. The IAB encourages such actions, but it will only make an Internet Standard of work for which the IETF has control over all changes. That is, the outside creators of a specification must be willing to give over their ownership, although their participation in the IETF's standardization of the work is highly desirable. Of course, the final test of the authors' willingness is their acceptance of working group decisions, which may run contrary to their preferences.

Review and approval of a specification involves the IESG, the IAB, and the entire IETF. Only the IAB may formally approve elevation in the standards process, but all three components of the technical community are called upon to review it and make comments. When the working group has completed its own review and has reached a consensus, it submits the final specification to the I-D directory and recommends formal action by the IESG. The IESG then polls the community, by issuing a *Last Call* to the IETF mailing list; this may be accompanied by an announcement or presentation at an IETF plenary. Such announcements are intended only as a final safety check, rather than for obtaining an extensive review, and last minute interventions are discouraged in favor of early participation in the technical work.

The relevant Area Director submits the specification to the IESG, which in turn makes a recommendation to the IAB. In general, specifications that have enough effort and support to get this far are reasonably certain to be approved. The caveat is that the IAB performs its own thorough technical and procedural review, and often develops significant questions that need to be resolved. When these are satisfied, the IAB decision is communicated to the IETF mailing list.

The procedures for this sequence have become increasingly detailed, and the Secretariat is developing a formal state diagram to describe it and indicate timing, conditions, and alternatives. It also has developed an automated tracking system. One is given pause upon realizing that the small, obscure efforts of a specialized research community have grown to the point of requiring such bureaucratic assistance. And it does require that. The first time the tracking tool was run, a very large number of specifications were discovered to be overdue for elevation or dismissal.

3.5.3 Conflict Resolution

Organization, procedures, and participation are well and good, but the development of acceptable Internet standards requires achieving accord, often in the midst of considerable disagreement. Working groups, the IETF plenary, the IESG, and the IAB each have opportunities to review and comment on a specification, and the working group does the original design and specification. Each, therefore, needs to resolve internal disagreements. There also may be disagreements between the working group and the IESG or the IAB.

In an organization with formalized membership and voting, disagreements ultimately can be resolved procedurally. The IAB/IETF community rarely has that option. Most disagreements are resolved by debate and negotiation, predicated upon agreement about basic goals. The biggest challenge to this takes place in the working groups. Here, membership can be large and diverse, and participation quite intermittent. As is always true, basic engineering views may differ dramatically.

In general, it's worth distinguishing basic differences in taste and philosophy from questions of technical sufficiency. A difference in philosophy is unlikely to be resolved by discussion. When issues are minor, participants may bargain on various points. (One participant may prefer dashes, and another may prefer parentheses, but they are likely to agree that the difference is minor.) When issues are major, common ground is rarely found. If one point of view clearly dominates the working group, the minority view eventually must give ground. If the two views each have sufficient support, it may be necessary to form independent working groups. The groups then proceed at their own pace and develop their own following. To the extent that it is important for the Internet community to state a preference or choose a single alternative, this is best accomplished through the development of experimental and operational experience, allowing strengths and weaknesses to be assessed concretely. Unfortunately, major disagreements have occasionally been resolved rather less smoothly than this description implies.

In the IETF's history, these differences have occurred regularly, with the debate sometimes being strident and public. In 1987, the IETF decided to develop a network management protocol. A three-way battle developed among proponents of the High-Level Entity Management System (HEMS), the Simple Gateway Monitoring Protocol (SGMP), developed by Internet service providers and some router vendors, and proponents of OSI's Common Management Information Protocol, to be used over TCP (CMOT). During an initial high-level technical summit,[16] there was an attempt to resolve the differences among the groups; the authors of HEMS graciously removed their specification from consideration; the proponents of SGMP (to be refined and renamed SNMP) and CMOT agreed to maintain data compatibility. However, even this level of cooperation was not feasible. Notable was the amount of warfare conducted in the trade press. Ultimately, another summit was called, by which time SNMP already dominated the market.[17]

Often, these differences are handled with far less theatre. The IETF recently began to pursue enhancements to its electronic mail service, based upon the Simple Mail Transfer Protocol (SMTP, *RFC 821*) and the formats specified in *RFC 822*, with a particular interest in allowing support for international character sets. Initial working group meetings produced a debate between those who wished to modify the mail transport protocol, SMTP, to allow full 8-bit traffic, and those who wished instead to modify the mail format specification, *RFC 822*, to allow encoding of 8-bit data inside the message for transport over the current 7-bit paths. Eventually, two different working groups were formed, with some members participating in both groups. It seems likely that both groups will have their efforts become standardized and used in the Internet, all without bloodshed.

But what happens when IETF members claim that a specification is technically flawed or, worse, that their points of view were not given an adequate hearing?

Differences in philosophy and taste are expected to be stated and resolved early. The IESG and IAB generally are not sympathetic to those criticizing the basic efforts of a group when a specification is being submitted for standardization after the working group has completed its job. Those that do the specification work have a *prima facie* case in favor of their choices. On the other hand, the claim that a specification simply "won't work" is always serious, and is attended to. Such claims may turn out to be criticisms about philosophy, recast in more acceptable terms, but they *always* are taken seriously by the IESG and IAB, and are investigated. So, too, are criticisms of unfairness.

In spite of the development of formal group procedures, the Internet standards process works by virtue of individual efforts, and the community knows this. Those managing the process are particularly careful to respond to criticisms of the process. There's an intense desire to make sure that the process is equitable. A claim of unfairness or technical inadequacy may be pursued through an appeals hierarchy formed by the working group chair, the relevant Area Director, the Area Director for Standards Management, the IETF Chair, and the members of the IAB. In each case, a claimant who is not satisfied with a response may attempt to sway the next person in order. In reality, the process tends to be abbreviated. The working group chair usually is not approached formally, since the concern usually pertains to the conduct of the group. Once an Area Director or the IETF Chair is approached, there usually is a round of private discussions. If the issue cannot then be resolved, it is brought before the full IESG. If the claimant is not satisfied with the outcome, an appeal to an IAB member usually brings the matter before the full board.

In all cases, the person approached will investigate the claim, seeking comments from other participants or review of the working group's on-line archive and meeting minutes. If necessary, an independent assessment will be obtained. A criticism that is formally submitted to the IESG or the IAB will receive a formal response. If the criticisms are found to have substance, then discussions are held with the relevant participants to determine an adequate resolution.

3.6 EVALUATION

On the way to creating a communication technology designed to connect different media and networks, a small research community invented a new way to develop standards. Whatever technical or procedural criticisms might be lodged against this new way, its success is undeniable. Other standards bodies have moved towards shorter development cycles, and new groups have copied the Internet's open and pragmatic style of doing business. While participants in the Internet have long enjoyed its free-ranging style, comparisons with other standards processes have been taken seriously only recently, as the Internet's technology has developed into an industry, and as the Internet has continued to succeed in producing essential enhancements.

Open specification, open participation, convenient access to information, extremely direct and concrete technical goals, and a requirement for early implementation and testing all combine to ensure that a specification works and is useful in a timely manner. The challenge to the Internet, now, is to sustain these key strengths in the face of massive growth, an installed base that requires basic stability of operation, and increasing concern for accountability in the standards process. In this section we will consider these challenges and possible responses to them. These are topics under significant debate within the Internet, and there are no dominant lines of argument, so the material presented here is intended more to stimulate thought and discussion than to describe a plan for success in the future.

3.6.1   Scaling the Installed Base

Designing protocols for a networked system is made particularly difficult by the potential number of its components and by their asynchronous operation and interaction. Within the duration of a single Internet session, throughput, delay, and reliability behaviors can range over many orders of magnitude. Candidate Internet protocol standards must take these factors into account, rather than focus on more limited application, yet most participants in the IETF are new to this level of technical scope. Too, modifications to existing services must be made in a fashion that preserves the safe operation of the installed base. Either a change must be demonstrated to have no effect on the base, or a clear transition plan must be characterized. Most upgrades to Internet protocols seek to support upward compatibility or parallel operation. For more complicated changes, formal transition planning may be necessary. Such transition specifications have not typically been a part of working group efforts to enhance or revise existing services, although this may become necessary. In reality, major transitions of networked systems often are so difficult that the process of moving an installed base safely may dictate many characteristics of the final system. Although the Internet service is a collection of connected but independent systems, their dynamics very much interact. So, it is essential that additions to the service be manageable on a global scale.

3.6.2   Economies of the Scales

There is a tendency for Internet enthusiasts to refer to various aspects of its operation as "free," thereby creating an opportunity for detractors to dismiss the community as unrealistic. However, the Internet does have a very real philosophy of standards-making economics that is unique and viable. As with most such groups, technical contributors are volunteers from many organizations, and they obtain their own funding. Most are "volunteers" only to the extent that they persuade their employers to contribute the funding and allocate the employee's time to standards efforts.

But any process of standards-making needs a support infrastructure of people and services. The Internet distributes these among numerous organizations. Hence, the cost of any single organization's efforts may be quite small. There are fewer than 10 full-time workers devoted to the Internet standards organization infrastructure, and all of the on-line storage and access that is essential to the smooth conduct of business is provided as incremental capabilities by organizations already attached to the Internet. Hence, high degrees of openness and interaction can be accommodated with extremely small increments of effort or expense, and it can be argued that this is the major strength of the process. By making the infrastructure cost small, the community can develop, distribute, and revise specifications quickly and cheaply, obtaining significant feedback about their appropriateness. Hence, it is not difficult or expensive to try out new ideas and let the community provide the market feedback needed to decide which specifications are most needed. The overall benefit of funding the infrastructure that makes this style of operation feasible is massive.

3.6.3 Improving Anticipation

The Internet technical community has the basic philosophy that it is better to gain operational experience early and refine a technology than to plan for every contingency prior to implementation. For one thing, it is impossible to predict long-term needs; for another, "fully planned" architectures have a tendency to be ponderous and, in the rapidly changing world of network technology, to find themselves overtaken by obsolescence before they can be realized. The philosophy of incremental enhancement has worked well, but the current market-driven funding for technical contributions is causing the standards process to seek additions and refinements to some problems later than may be safe. By the time the network management standards were being developed, interoperation of Internet service providers was quite difficult, due to a lack of diagnostic tools. In general, this was overcome only by extraordinary degrees of personal cooperation and trust, unlike typical interactions among competitors. By the time a new external system routing protocol was developed, it was nearly impossible to add networks to the Internet, since configuration was almost entirely by hand. By the time the IP address space limitations are fixed, we may well have run out of IP addresses.

None of these situations developed suddenly. In every case, there were signals several years in advance of the problems reaching critical need. The difficulty is in finding ways to initiate the required, concerted efforts within a system that lies predicated upon the happenstance of contributions made by individual champions with independent funding.

3.6.4 Scaling the Process

If there is any one phenomenon with which networking technologists have experience, it is congestion control. Networking is predicated on the statistics of resource sharing. One of the earliest lessons of the ARPANET was that packet-switching controls work well under conditions of transient congestion, and poorly under conditions of sustained congestion. When the traffic level is too high for too long, the only choices are to reduce the traffic or to increase the capacity of the network.

There is a strong argument for claiming that current levels of IETF activity are at saturation. Logistics and administrative overhead are quite difficult, and the IESG and IAB management are working at capacity. It is not clear that the usual method of adding more people or more layers to the management structure will help, since it will at least increase the impact of administration. Some members of the IETF community already view the overhead of the process as excessive. In fact, some standards-like groups have formed independently, hoping to avoid the bureaucracy. Within the IETF, the large number of working groups also makes it extremely difficult for the scarce resource of senior technical contributors to assist all adequately.

What to do?

There are only two choices: reduce the traffic or increase the capacity of the system. At the moment, there is no obvious way to increase the capacity of the standards process that will help. But the working groups exist due to community interest and need, so it is unclear that the traffic can be reduced. In any event, this issue is very much a matter of current discussion and debate. By way of contributing to the philosophical aspects of the discussion, some insight can be obtained by reading "On Being the Right Size."[18]

3.6.5   Individual Effort and the Working Group Process

The mythology of the Internet standards process is that a working group develops specifications according to the consensus of its members. As working groups are increasingly attended by those new to the community and lacking a deep background in the technology, the effort to bring them "up to speed" increases, potentially slowing down the group's progress. Too, the larger a working group is, the more difficult it is to reach a consensus. Even so, the mythology often is true. However, this chapter has emphasized that an Internet technical specification is the work of one or a few individuals. In reality, working groups rarely participate in the step-by-step specification effort. Rather, the detailed work is performed by the core individuals, and the working group provides a technical backstop to catch errors, and a sanity check for overall acceptability to the group—and therefore to the community. Internet specifications carry the personal stamp of their authors far more than is true of other standards bodies. Internet developers are free to gambol in the technical fields, listening only to their intellectual consciences, and then offer the results to the community for direct adoption. With traditional, accredited standards bodies, the work of incorporating such offerings involves very large adjustment to the needs of various members and their organizations. With the Internet, some adjustments usually are made, too, but they typically are few and are agreed to quickly.

All of this suggests that one approach to the handling of IETF growth is to find a means of reemphasizing the work of individuals while still permitting working groups their proper role of review and refinement. It is essential that this balance allow contributors—those who do the real work—to pursue specifications fully, according to their own vision, and allow the rest of the community whatever controls are essential to guarantee openness for a level playing field and adequacy for technical competence.

REFERENCES

1   J.K. Reynolds and J.B. Postel, *The Request for Comments Reference Guide*, *RFC 1000*, August, 1987.

2   J.S. Quarterman and S. Wilhelm, *UNIX, POSIX, and Open Systems: The Open Standards Puzzle*, Addison-Wesley, Reading, 1993.

3   L. Chapin, *Draft IAB charter as part of ISOC communication to the IETF mailing list*, 15 April 1992.

4   M.T. Rose and D.E. Cass, *ISO transport services on top of the TCP: Version 3, RFC 1006*, May 1987; and M.T. Rose, *The Open Book: A Practical Perspective on OSI*, Prentice Hall, 1990.

5   J.K. Reynolds and J.B. Postel, *Assigned Numbers, RFC 1060*, March 1990.

6   J.B. Postel, *Request for comments on Request for Comments: Instructions to RFC authors, RFC 1111*, August 1989.

7   G. Malkin and J.K. Reynolds, *FYI on FYI—Introduction to the FYI Notes, RFC 1150, FYI 1*, Marsh 1990.

8   J.B. Postel, Ed., *Introduction to the STD notes, RFC 1311*, March 1992.

9   J.B. Postel, Ed., *IAB official protocol standards, RFC 1280*, March 1992.

10 J.S. Quarterman, *The Matrix: Computer Network and Conferencing Systems Worldwide*, Digital Press, Bedford, 1990.

11 N.Z. Shapiro and R.H. Anderson, *Toward an Ethics and Etiquette for Electronic Mail*, R-3283-NSF/RC, Rand Corporation, Santa Monica, 1985.

12 L. Sproull and S. Kiesler, *Connections: New Ways of Working in the Networked Organization*, MIT Press, Cambridge, 1991.

13 R.T. Braden, *Perspective on the host requirements RFC documents RFC documents, RFC 1127*, 1989; *Requirements for Internet hosts—communication*

layers, RFC 1122, (R.T. Braden, Ed.) 1989; and *Requirements for Internet hosts—application and support, RFC 1123* (R.T. Braden, Ed.), 1989.

14 R.T. Braden and J.B. Postel *Requirements for Internet gateways, RFC 1009,* 1987.

15 L. Chapin, *The Internet Standards Process, RFC 1310,* 1992.

16 V.G. Cerf, *IAB recommendations for the development of Internet network management standards, RFC 1052,* 1988.

17 V.G. Cerf, *Report of the second Ad Hoc Network Management Review Group, RFC 1109,* August 1989.

18 J.B.S. Haldane, On Being the Right Size, in *Possible Worlds.* Harper Brothers, 1928. Reprinted in *The World of Mathematics* (Names R. Newman, Ed.) Simon and Schuster, New York, 1956 (To be issued as an Informational *RFC*).

APPENDIX

Internet Repository Locations

Chapter 19 discusses a wide range of information and sources. This Appendix provides detail about access to the Internet Repository, which is replicated in many locations around the Internet. Private copies also are maintained.

RFC and Internet-Draft documents may be obtained via e-mail or FTP from many repositories. The primary repositories will have a *RFC* or I-D available when it is first announced, as will many secondary repositories. Some secondary repositories may take a few days to make available the most recent documents.

Primary Repositories

Documents can be obtained via FTP from `NIC.DDN.MIL`, `FTP.NISC.SRI.COM`, `NIS.NSF.NET`, `NISC.JVNC.NET`, `VENERA.ISI.EDU`, `WUARCHIVE.WUSTL.EDU`, `SRC.DOC.IC.AC.UK`, or `FTP.CONCERT.NET`.

1 `NIC.DDN.MIL` (aka `DIIS.DDN.MIL`)—*RFC* documents can be obtained via FTP from `NIC.DDN.MIL`, with the pathname `rfc/rfcnnnn.txt` (nnnn refers to the number of the *RFC*). Log in with FTP username `anonymous` and password `guest`.

Contact:

`ScottW@NIC.DDN.MIL`

2 `FTP.NISC.SRI.COM`—*RFC* documents can be obtained via FTP from `FTP.NISC.SRI.COM`, with the pathname `rfc/rfcnnnn.txt` or `rfc/rfcnnnn.ps` (`nnnn` refers to the number of the *RFC*). Log in with FTP username `anonymous` and password `guest`. To obtain the *RFC* Index, use the pathname `rfc/rfc-index.txt`.

SRI also provides an automatic mail service for sites that use FTP. Address the request to `MAIL-SERVER@NISC.SRI.COM`, and indicate in the body of the message the *RFC* to be sent as in send `rfcnnnn` or send `rfcnnnn.ps`, where `nnnn` is the *RFC* number. Multiple requests may be included in the same message by listing the send commands on separate lines. To request the *RFC* Index, the command should read: `send rfc-index`.

Contact:

`rfc-update@nisc.sri.com`

3 `NIS.NSF.NET`—To obtain *RFC* documents from `NIS.NSF.NET` via FTP, log in with username `anonymous` and password `guest`; then connect to the *RFC* directory (`cd RFC`). The file name is of the form `RFCnnnn.TXT-1` (`nnnn` refers to the number of the *RFC*).

The NIS also provides an automatic mail service for sites that cannot use FTP. Address the request to `NIS-INFO@NIS.NSF.NET`, and leave the subject field of the message blank. The first line of the text of the message must be `SEND RFCnnnn.TXT-1`, where `nnnn` is replaced by the *RFC* number.

Contact:

`Jo_Ann_Ward@UM.CC.UMICH.EDU`

4 `NISC.JVNC.NET`—*RFC* documents can also be obtained via FTP from `NISC.JVNC.NET`, with the pathname `rfc/RFCnnnn.TXT.v` (`nnnn` refers to the number of the *RFC*, and `v` refers to the version number of the *RFC*).

JvNCnet also provides a mail service for sites that cannot use FTP. Address the request to `SENDRFC@JVNC.NET` and in the subject field of the message indicate the *RFC* number, as in `Subject: RFCnnnn` where `nnnn` is the *RFC* number. Please note that a *RFC* whose number is less than 1000 does not need a leading 0; for example, `RFC932` is fine. No text is needed in the body of the message.

Contact:

`Becker@NISC.JVNC.NET`

5 `VENERA.ISI.EDU`—*RFC* documents can be obtained via FTP from `VENERA.ISI.EDU`, with the pathname `in-notes/rfcnnnn.txt` (`nnnn` refers to the

number of the *RFC*). Log in with FTP username anonymous and password guest.
RFC documents can also be obtained via electronic mail from VENERA.ISI.EDU by
using the *RFC*-INFO service. Address the request to rfc-info@isi.edu with a message body of:

```
Retrieve: RFC
Doc-ID: RFCnnnn
```

Note that nnnn refers to the number of the *RFC* (always use 4 digits—the DOC-
ID of *RFC 822* is RFC0822). The RFC-INFO@ISI.EDU server provides other ways of
selecting *RFC* documents based on keywords and such; for more information send a
message to rfc-info@isi.edu with the message body help:help.

Contact:

RFC-Manager@ISI.EDU

6 WUARCHIVE.WUSTL.EDU—*RFC* documents can also be obtained via FTP from
WUARCHIVE.WUSTL.EDU, with the pathname info/rfc/rfcnnnn.txt.Z. (nnnn refers
to the number of the *RFC*, and Z indicates that the document is in compressed form).

At WUARCHIVE.WUSTL.EDU the *RFC* documents are in an "archive" file system,
and various archives can be mounted as part of an NFS file system. Please contact
Chris Myers (see contact address) if you want to mount this file system in your NFS.

Contact:

chris@wugate.wustl.edu

7 SRC.DOC.IC.AC.UK—*RFC*   documents   can   be   obtained   via   FTP   from
SRC.DOC.IC.AC.UK with the pathname rfc/rfcnnnn.txt.Z or rfc/rfcnnnn.ps.Z.
(nnnn refers to the number of the *RFC*). Log in with FTP username anonymous and
your e-mail address as password. To obtain the *RFC* Index, use the pathname
rfc/rfc index.txt.Z. (The trailing Z indicates that the document is in compressed
form.)

SRC.DOC.IC.AC.UK also provides an automatic mail service for those sites in the
UK which cannot use FTP. Address the request to info-server@doc.ic.ac.uk with
a Subject: line of "wanted," and a message body of:

```
    request sources
    topic path rfc/rfcnnnn.txt.Z
    request end
```

Here nnnn refers to the number of the *RFC*. Multiple requests may be included in
the same message by giving multiple "topic path" commands on separate lines. To

request the *RFC* Index, the command should read: topic path `rfc/rfc-index.txt.Z`
The archive is also available using NIFTP and the ISO FTAM system.

Contact:

`ukuug-soft@doc.ic.ac.uk`

8   `FTP.CONCERT.NET`—To obtain *RFC* documents from `FTP.CONCERT.NET` via FTP, log
in with username `anonymous` and your internet e-mail address as password. The *RFC*
documents can be found in the directory `/rfc`, with file names of the form:
`rfcnnnn.txt` or `rfcnnnn.ps`, where `nnnn` refers to the *RFC* number. This repository
is also accessible via WAIS and the Internet Gopher.

Contact:

`rfc-mgr@concert.net`

Secondary Repositories

In the following list, `nnnn` is the *RFC* number.

Sweden
Host:	`sunic.sunet.se`
Directory:	`rfc`
Host:	`chalmers.se`
Directory:	`rfc`

Germany
Site:	University of Dortmund
Host:	`walhalla.informatik.uni-dortmund.de`
Directory:	`pub/documentation/rfc`
Notes:	*RFC* documents in compressed format

France
Site:	Institut National de la Recherche en Informatique et Automatique (INRIA)
Address:	`info-server@inria.fr`
Notes:	*RFC* documents are available via e-mail to the above address. Info Server manager is Mireille Yamajako (`yamajako@inria.fr`).

Netherlands
Site:	EUnet
Host:	`mcsun.eu.net`
Directory:	`rfc`
Notes:	*RFC* documents in compressed format

Finland
Site:	FUNET
Host:	`funet.fi`
Directory:	`rfc`
Notes:	*RFC* documents in compressed format. Also provides e-mail access by sending mail to `archive-server@funet.fi`.

Norway
Host:	`ugle.unit.no`
Directory:	`pub/rfc`

Denmark
>Site: University of Copenhagen
>Host: `ftp.diku.dk (freja.diku.dk)`
>Directory: `rfc`

Australia and Pacific Rim
>Site: munnari
>Contact: `Robert Elz <kre@cs.mu.OZ.AU>`
>Host: `munnari.oz.au`
>Directory: `rfc`
>Notes: *RFC* documents in compressed format `rfcnnnn.Z` postscript *RFC* documents `rfcnnnn.ps.Z`

United States
>Site: cerfnet
>Contact: `help@cerf.net`
>Host: `nic.cerf.net`
>Directory: `netinfo/rfc`
>Site: uunet
>Contact: `James Revell <revell@uunet.uu.net>`
>Host: `fto.uu.net`
>Directory: `inet/rfc`

United States / Mexico
>Site: SESQUINET
>Contact: `rfc-mgr@sesqui.net`
>Host: `nic.sesqui.net`
>Directory: `pub/rfc`

- Requests for special distribution of *RFC* documents should be addressed to either the author of the *RFC* in question, to NIC@NIC.DDN.MIL, or to NISC@NISC.SRI.COM. Submissions for Requests for Comments should be sent to POSTEL@ISI.EDU. Please consult *RFC 1111, Instructions to RFC Authors,* for further information.

- Requests to be added to or deleted from this distribution list should be sent to RFC-REQUEST@NIC.DDN.MIL

- Changes to this file `rfc-retrieval.txt` should be sent to Joyce K. Reynolds (JKRey@ISI.EDU).

- Details on obtaining *RFCs* via FTP or e-mail may be obtained by sending an e-mail message to `rfc-info@ISI.EDU` with the message body `help: ways_to_get_rfcs`. For example:

  ```
  To: rfc-info@ISI.EDU
  Subject: getting rfcs

  help: ways_to_get_rfcs
  ```

PART II □ □ □ □ □

TECHNOLOGIES

CHAPTER 4   ❑ ❑ ❑ ❑

Core Protocols

VINTON G. CERF

CONTENTS

CONTENTS   (Continued)

At the heart of the Internet are two protocols, IP and TCP, which provide two very different functions. The IP, or Internet Protocol, smoothes over the differences between different kinds of network technologies, so that they offer a common set of delivery services, regardless of their physical characteristics. The TCP, or Transmission Control Protocol, provides reliability over the IP-mesh.

4.1   INTRODUCTION

This chapter provides some perspective on the evolution of the technical concepts behind the TCP/IP protocol suite, and the protocols that are used to support the functions of the Internet and transport layers of the architecture. Although this chapter focuses only on elements of the TCP/IP protocol suite, readers should be aware that the Internet system is evolving into a multiprotocol environment.

The original motivation for the development of the TCP/IP protocol suite came from the US Defense Advanced Research Projects Agency (DARPA) in 1973. The ARPANET had been successfully deployed, and in October 1972, had been publicly demonstrated at the International Computer Communications Conference in Washington, DC. This first wide area packet network was soon joined by two other DARPA-developed applications of packet-switching technology: packet radio and packet satellite.[1-3] R.E. Kahn, who was responsible for these two programs at DARPA, also was one of the principal architects of the ARPANET,[4] and recognized both the potential for further applications of packet switching in different media and the problem of integrating these different manifestations of packet switching into a coherent whole for military applications.[27] Kahn began an "internetting" research effort at DARPA in 1973, concurrent with the development of the packet radio and packet satellite technologies.

Nearly concurrent with the DARPA internetting efforts, local area network concepts were emerging in parallel, most notably at the Xerox Palo Alto Research Center, where Robert Metcalfe and David Boggs were experimenting with a 3-Mbits/sec local network they called the Ethernet.[9] A similar effort, using a ring concept, was being explored by David J. Farber at University of California, Irvine.[10]

An important characteristic of the Ethernet, packet radio nets, and packet satellite nets was that they used shared communication channels. The sources of traffic contended for access to the shared channels in such a way that packet loss was a distinct possibility. The so-called best-efforts systems introduced a degree of uncertainty in end-to-end delivery that had been hidden in the ARPANET by internal retransmission mechanisms (i.e., within the network). These new packet systems offered far greater flexibility in the utilization of shared transmission capacity, at the price of needing increased machinery at the periphery to recover from loss. The problem of providing reliable, end-to-end communication between computers using multiple packet networks was the central focus of the internetting research effort. Kahn brought this problem to my attention in early 1973, and he and I developed the conceptual approach to solving the internetting problem.[6] The detailed specification and implementation of the protocol became the primary design problem occupying my attention, and that of my graduate students and several colleagues. Several assumptions were key to the architecture that evolved. It was assumed that the networks themselves could not be altered to accommodate concatenated use. Moreover, since each medium was quite different in its communications and error characteristics, it was assumed that the end-to-end protocol would have to deal with passage through networks supporting different maximum length packets.

These basic assumptions led to the idea of a gateway between the networks that would know about the end-to-end protocol used by the hosts that were communicating across the multiple networks. The hosts would encapsulate the end-to-end packets in the network protocol of the net to which the host was directly attached, but would address the packet to the next gateway. The gateway would decapsulate the packet, examine an end-to-end global address to determine where to send the packet in the next network, encapsulate the packet in the network level protocol of the next network, and address this encapsulated packet to the next gateway or the target (destination) host. Over the course of the evolution of the TCP/IP protocol suite, the term *gateway* was replaced by the term *router*, and *gateway* came to refer to a relay that operated at a higher level of protocol than IP (*gateway* is used now to refer to protocol translating relays, such as might be used to link two different electronic mail networks). Figure 4.1 illustrates the general concept of hosts, routers, networks, and encapsulation and decapsulation.

End-to-end sequencing and reliability would be accomplished by end-to-end checksumming, and retransmission between the source and destination hosts and flow control would also be achieved by end-to-end cooperation. Minimal assumptions were made about the communications capability of each participating network. It was assumed that each net could support the transmission of datagrams that were not guaranteed to be delivered. This was a best-effort assumption that placed most of the responsibility for reliability on the end points in the concatenated set of networks. Even the gateways would not perform retransmission, so as to avoid accumulating any state information in them about end-to-end communication.

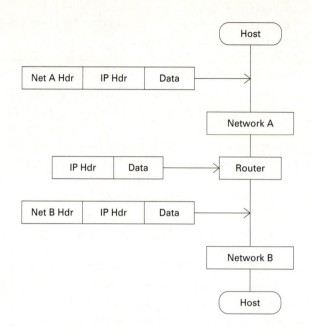

Figure 4.1   Encapsulation and decapsulation of IP packets across routers in an internet

The concept of layering had emerged clearly in the development of the ARPANET protocols,[5] and played a central role in the evolution of the TCP/IP architecture. In the earliest stages of development, only a single protocol, the Transmission Control Protocol (TCP), was proposed.[6] Since the packets produced by this end-to-end protocol were encapsulated by hosts and gateways into the network level packets of each network, TCP was thought of as a layer 4 protocol, in the language of the OSI reference model.[7] Two versions of the TCP protocol had been developed and tested at Stanford, University College, London (UCL), and Bolt Beranek and Newman (BBN), when a new requirement was introduced by the development of packet voice capability in the ARPANET. One of the primary researchers in this area, Danny Cohen at USC Information Sciences Institute, argued that TCP functionality should be split between what was required end-to-end for reliability, flow control, and so on, and what was required hop-by-hop to get from one network to another via gateways, without consideration for reliability, retransmission, and the like. Cohen pointed out that some communication applications require timeliness more than they require fully sequenced and reliable delivery, and that packet voice was one such application.[8]

This line of reasoning led to the separation of the original TCP protocol into two components: the Internet Protocol (IP) and the new Transmission Control Protocol (TCP). To accommodate the nonsequenced, transaction-like applications, including packet voice, a simple User Datagram Protocol (UDP) was devised to operate in parallel with the

Layer	Example
Application	FTP, Telnet, SMTP, X-Windows
Transport	UDP, TCP, TP4, Routing
Internet	ICMP, IP, CLNP
Subnetwork	Ethernet, X.25, FDDI, Token Ring
Link	HDLC, PPP, SLIP
Physical	RS232, V.35, 10BaseT, fiber, etc.

Figure 4.2   Internet layering

sequenced, reliable data stream TCP above the common end-to-end, best-effort, datagram protocol IP.

This separation placed IP at layer 4 above the network layer, and TCP and UDP at layer 5. For years, this caused confusion in discussions with OSI researchers, until it became common to consider the internetworking function to be a network level service. Layer 3 was split into two sublayers in the OSI reference model: one layer for internet service and a lower one for the particular network, leaving the end-to-end protocols to operate as transport layer services at layer 4. Figure 4.2 illustrates the layering. Various characterizations of the resulting TCP/IP architecture may be found.[6, 25, 26, 28]

Readers may find it interesting that an attempt was made to merge the still-developing TCP protocol with efforts in Europe that became the basis for the OSI protocol suite. A paper was offered by V. Cerf, A. McKenzie, R. Scantlebury, and H. Zimmermann[11] as a result of efforts in Working Group 6.1 of the Telecommunications Committee of the International Federation of Information Processing (IFIP 6.1). IFIP 6.1 started out as the International Network Working Group (INWG) formed at the ICCC72 meeting mentioned above, at which the ARPANET was publicly demonstrated. An international collaborative research effort ensued, affiliating with IFIP in 1974. As things turned out, the momentum behind the TCP effort had reached such a high level that it was not possible to divert it in the fashion proposed by Cerf et al. In another universe, perhaps....

The internetting experiment started by DARPA in 1973 led to the evolution of a system of networks, called the Internet, which is global in scope. As of this writing, over 7500 networks are interlinked, supporting over 1,000,000 computers, and millions of users in over three dozen countries. In this chapter, the term *Internet* is used in reference either to this global system or to the standards used in its operation. The term *internet* is used when referring to any collection of networks that may or may not make use of the Internet standards.

The next sections in this chapter will examine IP and its associated Internet Control Message Protocol (ICMP), Internet Group Management Protocol (IGMP), UDP, and TCP in more detail. Readers are cautioned, however, that this chapter is not a substitute for examination of the official IAB standard documents.[12–19]

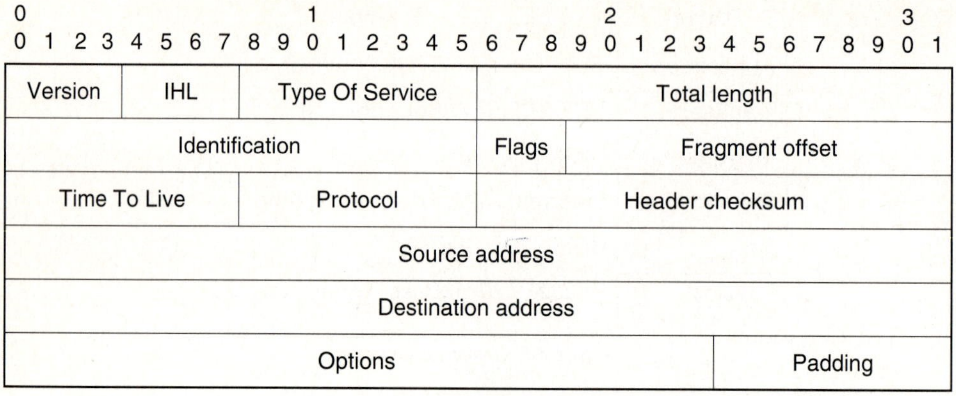

```
 0                      1                      2                      3
 0 1 2 3 4 5 6 7 8 9 0 1 2 3 4 5 6 7 8 9 0 1 2 3 4 5 6 7 8 9 0 1
```

Version	IHL	Type Of Service	Total length		
Identification			Flags	Fragment offset	
Time To Live		Protocol	Header checksum		
Source address					
Destination address					
Options				Padding	

Figure 4.3   Internet datagram header. Note that each "tick" represents 1 bit

4.2   INTERNET PROTOCOL

IP provides for the carriage of datagrams from a source host to destination hosts, possibly passing through one or more gateways (routers) and networks in the process. A datagram is a finite-length packet of bits containing a header and a payload. The header information identifies the source, destination, length, handling advice, and other characteristics of the payload contents. The payload is the actual data transported. Figure 4.3 illustrates the format of a standard Internet packet.

Both hosts and routers in an internet are involved in the processing of the IP headers. The hosts must create them on sending, and process them on receipt,[16, 17] and the routers must examine them for the purpose of making routing decisions, and modify them as the IP packets make their way from the source to the destination.[19, 37]

4.2.1   Version Number

This 4-bit field specifies which version of the Internet packet format is in use. The purpose of this field is to allow more than one version of IP packet format to be in use at one time, to aid in transitions from one form to another. The current standard uses IP version 4. An experimental Stream Protocol uses[36] IP version 5, and a follow-on Stream Protocol II uses[39] IP version 6.

4.2.2   Internet Header Length (IHL)

This 4-bit field specifies the length of the header of the Internet packet in 32-bit words. Padding is used, if necessary, to extend the header to a multiple of 32 bits.

4.2.3   Type Of Service (TOS)

The purpose of this header field is to identify the nature of the service to be provided to a datagram marked with any particular value for Type Of Service. As this chapter is being written, the interpretation of this field and, indeed, its format and values, are being reconsidered by the Internet Engineering Task Force. There is a high likelihood that the current standard interpretations outlined[12] in *RFC 791* will be changed by the IAB to reflect the IETF working group recommendations.[20] For completeness, the current standard is outlined here, and the likely revision is offered. Readers should refer to the *RFC* documents and Official Protocols documents for up-to-date information.

The material that follows discusses the standard interpretation of the Type-Of-Service field (as of this writing). As is shown in Figure 4.4, this field is broken into a precedence field and an additional 5 bits, three of which are associated with delay, reliability, and throughput. The remaining 2 bits are not defined,[12] and must be set to 0. The theory behind the original design was that different networks would offer varying classes of service. Since the Internet Protocol rides above the network layer, and since internet packets may pass through many networks without the explicit knowledge of the sender, only an abstract sense of service class seemed definable. Each host and router would map these abstract requirements into the appropriate lower level network service class, if available, when encapsulating the packet for further propagation.

At the time that IP was being specified, considerable attention was paid to the requirements of the US military, since the research effort was funded by DARPA. It is no surprise, then, that the precedence field contained specifications reflecting typical military traffic precedence classes, as shown in Figure 4.4. At present, few commercial routers implement precedence handling in a way that affects the forwarding of packets. An obvious application would be to allow router and host configuration to limit traffic entering the internet to be above some specified precedence. Such a mechanism can be used to reduce traffic on an internet as is often needed under crisis conditions.

With regard to Type Of Service, the major choice is a three way trade-off between low delay, high reliability, and high throughput. As shown in Figure 4.4, these three parameters are treated as independent values, which, in theory, can be asserted alone or in combination to achieve a particular desired effect for the service provided to a given internet packet. Of course, any assertion of Type Of Service can only be realized if the network into which the internet packet is injected has a class of service that matches the particular combination of Type-Of-Service markings selected.

The potential new interpretation of the Type-Of-Service octet is illustrated in the lower half of Figure 4.4. In this new view, the precedence values are as defined above,[12] but the Type Of Service is expressed as a 4-bit field, which can take on up to 16 different values. Not all values are defined, and the values that have been defined are chosen to be compatible with the previous interpretation of bits 3–5, so as to make introduction of a new interpretation minimally harmful to deployed routers.

Current interpretation:

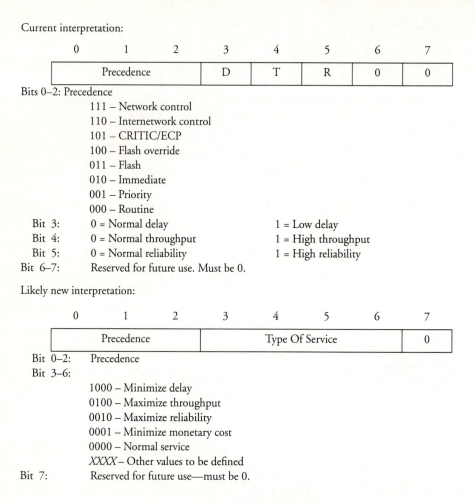

Bits 0–2: Precedence

        111 – Network control
        110 – Internetwork control
        101 – CRITIC/ECP
        100 – Flash override
        011 – Flash
        010 – Immediate
        001 – Priority
        000 – Routine

Bit 3:	0 = Normal delay	1 = Low delay
Bit 4:	0 = Normal throughput	1 = High throughput
Bit 5:	0 = Normal reliability	1 = High reliability
Bit 6–7:	Reserved for future use. Must be 0.	

Likely new interpretation:

Bit 0–2:   Precedence
Bit 3–6:

        1000 – Minimize delay
        0100 – Maximize throughput
        0010 – Maximize reliability
        0001 – Minimize monetary cost
        0000 – Normal service
        XXXX – Other values to be defined

Bit 7:   Reserved for future use—must be 0.

Figure 4.4   Type Of Service

Considerable attention is given in Almquist[20] to the way in which routers should interpret the 4-bit Type-Of-Service field in selecting the next hop for the packet, and in determining whether to generate any advisory or error indications if the packet's service requirements cannot be met. In particular, the prevailing view is that if there does not exist a path producing the desired Type Of Service, but there does exist a path to the destination using a different Type Of Service, or perhaps no special service at all, the path should be taken on the premise that asserting a TOS should not penalize the sender if a preferred path doesn't exist.

The Type Of Service capability of the Internet Protocol will become increasingly important as networks emerge that have the ability to deliver specific classes of services, and offer certain service guarantees.

D = Don't-fragment bit

      D = 0; May fragment if required
      D = 1; Do not fragment

M = More-fragments bit

      M = 0; Last fragment
      M = 1; More fragments exist

Figure 4.5   Fragmentation and reassembly

4.2.4   Total Length

This 16-bit field specifies the total length of the internet datagram in octets. This allows for packets up to 65,536 octets long. It is required that all hosts and routers service packets up to 576 octets in length without any need for fragmentation (see the next section). The 576-octet value allows for 512 octets of data, 20 octets of header (typical) and 44 octets for options or lower layer protocol headers.

4.2.5   Fragmentation

A key element of the design of IP is the capability to allow internet packets to be broken into smaller, but still syntactically valid, internet packets for routing through networks with a Maximum Transmission Unit (MTU) less than the size of the packet originally sent. The principal motivation for this feature was that the sending host might have little or no idea which networks the traffic would be routed through, and therefore, might have no way to adjust packet sizes to fit. With dynamic, adaptive routing in the routers, packet paths might vary in real time, outside the control of the source host.

    Three fields in the Internet packet header are used to support the fragmentation of packets: a 16-bit identification field, a 13-bit fragment offset field, and a 3-bit flag field, which indicates whether fragmentation is allowed, and if so, whether the particular packet is the last one. See Figure 4.5. The identification field is used to allow a reassembling host to collect together all the fragments of a given packet for reassembly. Note that fragmentation may take place at a variety of routers, not just one, and that paths may vary, so that the receiving host is the only place at which all reassembly can be reasonably attempted. The fragment offset field simply indicates where in the original packet the data of the fragment fits. The first fragment has offset value zero (0).

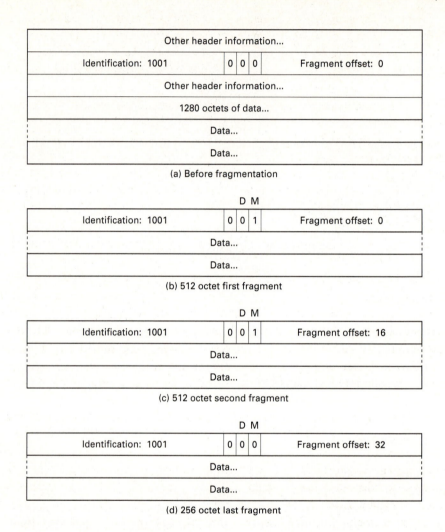

Figure 4.6   Fragmenting an Internet datagram. Note that the Internet packet header is abridged for simplicity

There are two flags defined in the 3-bit flag field. The high-order bit is always 0. The Don't-Fragment bit is used to mark whether packets are permitted to be fragmented or not. The More-Fragment bit is used to indicate when it is set, that the packet is *not* the last in the series of fragment. An example of a fragmented packet is shown in Figure 4.6.

There has always been debate about the utility of fragmentation. In many circumstances, especially where long packets on highly reliable local area nets are sent across wide area networks, being able to fall back upon fragmentation has been helpful. By the same token, however, if a fragment fails to arrive at the destination host for reassembly, the entire original internet datagram has to be resent (unless the source can reconstruct and resend exactly the same datagram with the same identifier). In the original design, there was only one end-to-end protocol, TCP, and the fragmentation and reassembly process were intimately related to the TCP retransmission and reassembly process. When IP was split off from TCP, the fragmentation process was made applicable to all higher level protocols.

In the example of Figure 4.6, a 1280-octet Internet Packet has been split into two 512-octet fragments and one 256-octet fragment. The more-fragments bit is set in the first two fragments, and reset in the last. The offset field is set to reflect where the data in each fragment starts, relative to the beginning of the data in the original packet. Generally, the identifier field must be selected at the source to be unique relative to the combination of source address, destination address, and protocol identifier fields. Obviously, the identifier value should not be reused by the source until all fragments have drained from the internet. Reassembly techniques are discussed in detail in *RFC 791* and *RFC 815*.[12, 44]

As networks increase in speed, a natural tension will develop between the identifier uniqueness necessary for fragment reassembly to work, and the maximum rate at which data can be sent through the network. For example, suppose a pair of hosts were sending data using a particular protocol (e.g., TCP) in maximum-size Internet packets containing 65,536 octets of data each. A total of 2^{16} packets of length 2^{16} octets could be sent before an identifier had to be reused. The total number of bits sent (not counting lower level protocol overhead) is $2^3 \times 2^{16} \times 2^{16} = 2^{35}$, or about 32 gigabits ($32 \times 10^9$ bits). At a gigabit per second, this would take about 32 seconds. Depending on the worst case packet or fragment lifetime in the internet, there might not be adequate margin to ensure fragment identifier uniqueness.

The problem would be dramatically exacerbated if the original packets had to be much smaller to account for the MTU allowed at the originating host's network. For example, if the source were to send 8192-octet packets that had to be fragmented to pass through some intermediate network, then the maximum amount of data that could be sent before exhausting the identifier space would be approximately $2^3 \times 2^{13} \times 2^{16} = 2^{32}$ or about 4 gigabits. At gigabit speeds, it would take only 4 seconds to consume the identifier space.

It seems probable that as internets move toward higher end-to-end speeds, these concerns will motivate architectural reconsideration of these basic facilities. Some evidence of this can be found in *RFC* documents[49, 50] in which consideration is given to methods for modifying TCP to accommodate transmission over paths with high bandwidth$\times$ delay product (e.g., cross-country gigabit speed networks, and satellite links).

4.2.6   Time To Live (TTL)

This 8-bit field was originally intended to be used to specify how long, in seconds, an internet packet could persist in the internet before being discarded by a router or a host. The maximum value of 255 seconds seemed more than enough for all practical purposes. However, few, if any, routers actually used timers to decrement the TTL field. Moreover, the quantization into seconds meant that even if a packet made it through a router in a few tens of milliseconds or less, it would have to be charged one second because of the coarseness of the TTL field. Effectively, this field has become a kind of maximum hop count. The current default value[45] is 32. Even with this interpretation, it seems reasonable to hope that no packet would experience a hop count as large as the maximum value without actually being in some kind of loop. The current complexity of the Internet, however, may dictate an increase in the default value.

4.2.7   Protocol Identifier

This 8-bit field is used to identify which upper level protocol is embedded in the internet packet. A list of assigned protocol identifiers is maintained by the Internet Assigned Numbers Authority and is documented periodically.[45] Table 4.1 lists some of the assignments for the better-known protocols, but readers are advised to refer to the latest edition of *Assigned Numbers* for up-to-date information.

4.2.8   Checksum

Although the Internet Protocol provides only a best-efforts service, it is important to ensure that the header information has not been damaged in its store-and-forward transit across the Internet. A header checksum is part of the IP design.[12,33] This is an extremely simple 16-bit 1's complement of the 16-bit sum of the header contents. The use of 1's complement arithmetic, although slightly awkward for today's 2's complement machines, has the merit that a result can be readily computed 8 bits, 16 bits, or 32 bits at a time, and can be computed incrementally.[34]

The checksum has to be recalculated at each "hop" from one router to the next because some values in the IP header may change. Obvious examples include the TTL field, which is decremented on each hop; various option fields (e.g., source/record route, and timestamps); and length and fragment markings if fragmentation is required. After adjusting the IP header, careful implementations will regenerate the checksum using the incremental approach: this will help the next hop detect if a header has been inadvertently corrupted during processing (e.g., due to memory or coding errors). Thus, the ability to incrementally compute the checksum is an important feature.

4.2.9   Addressing

One of the most critical functions of the Internet Protocol is to establish a global address space that allows every network in the Internet to be uniquely identified. For the global Internet, a central network identifier allocation service (an Internet Registry), ensures that uniqueness is preserved,[21] while allowing the actual assignment of network identifiers to be distributed for efficiency. The Internet Assigned Numbers Authority (IANA) is responsible

Table 4.1 Assigned Internet protocol numbers

Decimal	Keyword	Protocol
0		Reserved
1	ICMP	Internet Control Message Protocol
2	IGMP	Internet Group Management Protocol
3	GGP	Gateway-to-Gateway Protocol
4		Unassigned
5	ST	Stream Protocol
6	TCP	Transmission Control Protocol
7		Assigned
8	EGP	Exterior Gateway Protocol
9	IGP	any private interior gateway
10		Assigned
11	NVP-II	Network Voice Protocol
12-16		Assigned
17	UDP	User Datagram Protocol
18-28		Assigned
29	ISO-TP4	ISO Transport Protocol Class 4
30-34		Assigned
35-60		Unassigned
61		Any host internal protocol
62-71		Assigned
72-75		Unassigned
76-79		Assigned
80	CLNP	ISO Connectionless Protocol (CLNP)
81	VMTP	VMTP
82	SECURE-VMTP	SECURE-VMTP
83	VINES	VINES
84		Assigned
85	NSFNET-IGP	NSFNET-Internal Gateway Protocol
86-87		Assigned
88	IGRP	IGRP
89	OSPF	Open Shortest Path First Protocol
90-91		Assigned
92-254		Unassigned
255		Reserved

for the allocation and assignment of network numbers (among many other identifiers[45]), but has traditionally delegated this responsibility to organizations equipped to carry out the process.

Historically, the Internet address space has been flat in the sense that little structure was applied to the network addresses. In the initial implementation of IP, a network address was a 32-bit field consisting of 8 bits of network number and 24 bits of host identifier. At that time, 24 bits was actually enough to embed the lower level network addresses in the host identifier field with the 8-bit network number prefixed to indicate to which network the IP datagram was to be routed. This state of affairs was quickly rendered simple-minded by the rapid spread of local area networks (LANs), for example, Ethernets, which had a 48-bit host identifier that could not be embedded in 24 bits, and which numbered far more than the 256 networks that could be identified in the original 8-bit network number field.

The network addressing structure was revised to accommodate three classes of address: A, B, and C. Class A retained the 24-bit host identifier field, but only 7 bits for network number. Class B used 16 bits for host identifiers and 14 bits for network number. Class C allocated 21 bits for network number and 8 bits for host identifier. The restructured address space allowed for a small number of class A networks (128), a larger number of class B networks (14,284), and many more class C networks (2,097,152). In each category, network numbers 0 and "all 1s" are reserved. Figure 4.7 illustrates the various classes and their structure.

A convention for expressing IP addresses was developed in which the 32-bit value is represented as four 8-bit values: $X.X.X.X$. Each field had a range of 0–255, so the "minimum" address is 0.0.0.0, and the "maximum" is 255.255.255.255.

Certain special case addresses were defined to help deal with initialization and with debugging:

<127><any>	"Internal host loopback address"
<0><0>	"This host on this network"
<0><host-number>	"Specified host on this network"

These special addresses are not intended for general use on the Internet, but are used either for debugging (first case) or in an initialization procedure in which a host learns its own IP address.

The explosion of local area networks led to the realization that the flat addressing conventions in the Internet exacted a price: the passing of large quantities of information among routers identifying which networks could be reached by each router. In facilities where large numbers of LANs were interconnected, it was observed that much of the internal network structure could be hidden from outside view by means of subnetting. Subnetting allows a network complex to be seen, from the outside, as a single network.[22] Typically, a 32-bit mask is associated with a subnetted address so that the network-related portion (<net>+<subnet>) of the Internet address can be extracted and used for routing purposes within the subnetted complex. Outside of that complex, only the <net> portion needs to be "known." The technique reduces the amount of routing information that has to be exchanged in the global Internet, and represents one of the natural benefits of using even a primitive hierarchical address structure.

A common practice is to assign a class B network address to a collection of local area networks. To the outside world, and in particular, to the routers, this complex appears to be a single, class B network. However, the first N bits of the host address might actually be the subnet identifier. Instead of assigning 15 class C network numbers to the complex, for instance, a single class B address might be assigned in which the first 4 bits of the host field are treated as the subnet identifier.

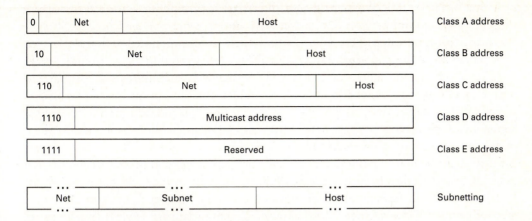

Figure 4.7   IP addressing structure

Local area network technology brought more than population explosion to the Internet system. It also brought the concept of convenient broadcasting to all terminations on the LAN. This versatile capability was reflected in the Internet addressing structure by associating addresses of the forms

255.255.255.255	"Broadcast on THIS net only"
<net>.255.255.255	"Broadcast on class A <net>"
<net>.255.255	"Broadcast on class B <net>"
<net>.255	"Broadcast on class C <net>"
<net><subnet><all 1s>	"Broadcast on subnet <subnet>"

with datagram broadcast service.[23, 35] For the last four cases above, the broadcast packet is routed through the Internet in the usual fashion, and is broadcast *only* at the target net or subnet. This is a powerful feature, which allows a host remote from a given network to make use of broadcast probing of the host resources on the remote target LAN or LAN complex. Such facilities can be instrumental in resource discovery, distributed file and database searching, and so on.

LANs also introduced the concept of multicasting, in which only a subset of the terminations on the LAN were targeted to receive a particular transmission. This subset of broadcasting is attractive in a variety of distributed applications, including computer-assisted conferencing and distributed database maintenance. This concept is captured in the Internet architecture through special Internet class D addresses (see Figure 4.7 and Table 4.2), in which multicast-addressed packets are routed (and duplicated at routers when necessary) to all targets that are part of the multicast group.[24]

The realization of multicasting in a wide area network (WAN) environment is a nontrivial undertaking. The routing system must be made aware of which networks have hosts participating in each multicast group, so that the arrival of a multicast-addressed packet can trigger proper forwarding to the destination networks. To avoid an avalanche of duplicative replication of multicast packets by multiple routers, a spanning-tree of routers is constructed as part of the multicast routing algorithm, to route and duplicate multicast packets. This capability, the subject of considerable debate and experimentation,[38] is only just beginning to make its way into actual deployed implementations in the Internet system.

Finally, for completeness, class E addresses have been reserved for future extensions. See Figure 4.7. As this text is being prepared, there is a major effort underway within the IETF to develop a new addressing and routing architecture for the Internet. The present system is reaching its design limitations, and the Internet is growing at 10–20% per month. For example, from October 1990 to January 1992, the number of networks routed across the NSFNET backbone leapt from 2,000 to over 4,400! The number of hosts in the system exploded from 1000 in October 1984 to over 720,000 in January 1992.[40] Two limits are being stressed simultaneously:

1 The ability to transfer voluminous routing information in a timely way to all routers that need it

2 The availability of network numbers, especially of the Class B variety (the most popular for LAN complexes using subnetting).

This topic is taken up again below.

A discussion of addressing would be incomplete without reference to the mechanisms that permit binding of IP addresses to lower level network addresses. In the case of Ethernet LANs, for example, routers need to encapsulate IP packets in a properly addressed Ethernet packet. Ethernets use 48-bit addresses on the LAN. What is needed is a way for

Table 4.2   Internet multicast addresses. When used on an Ethernet or IEEE 802 network, the 23 low-order bits of the IP Multicast address are placed in the low-order 23 bits of the Ethernet or IEEE 802 net multicast address 1.0.94.0.0.0

Source: *Assigned Numbers,*[45] *RFC 1060*	
224.0.0.0	Reserved
224.0.0.1	All hosts on this subnet
224.0.0.2	All gateways on this subnet (proposed)
224.0.0.3	Unassigned
224.0.0.4	DVMRP routers
224.0.0.5	OSPF all routers
224.0.0.6	OSPF designated routers
244.0.0.7–244.0.0.255	Unassigned
224.0.1.0	VMTP managers group
224.0.1.1	NTP network time protocol
224.0.1.2–224.0.1.4	Assigned
244.0.1.5–244.0.1.255	Unassigned
224.0.2.1	Assigned
232.x.x.x	VMTP transient groups

the router to learn the binding of IP to 48-bit LAN address. An Address Resolution Protocol (ARP)[29] has been devised that allows a router (or any host) to broadcast a query containing an IP address, and receive back the associated LAN address. A related protocol, Reverse ARP (RARP),[30] can be used to ask which IP address is bound to a given LAN address. Routers typically use these protocols and cache the results, so that they can minimize the need for broadcasting when forwarding packets into the LAN from the outside world. ARP is easiest to implement in network environments where broadcasting is readily supported. In some circumstances, it has proven effective to let one device act to respond to ARP queries on behalf of one or more others, functioning as a kind of proxy. In fact, this is sometimes referred to as *proxy ARP.*

Although routing is discussed later, it is useful to mention that the concept of the Autonomous System (AS) or Administrative Domain (AD) has emerged in a way that might, ultimately, influence the way in which addressing is organized in the Internet architecture. Autonomous Systems are collections of routers falling under a common administrative authority. The routers commonly use the same routing protocol within the AS (although this is not, strictly speaking, an absolute requirement). The concept of the AS is sufficiently well embedded in the architecture that unique identifiers are assigned to Autonomous Systems although these identifiers are not used, at present, for addressing purposes.[46] They are, however, used in certain kinds of routing designs, and might, therefore, be considered a part of a hierarchical addressing structure that starts with the high-level aggregation of Autonomous Systems of routers, and reaches down to networks, sub-networks, and finally, hosts. AS numbers are 16-bit values, and if they were used as part of an address structure, would extend the current 32-bit address space to 48 bits. The discussions surrounding the rapid growth of the Internet suggest that even this extension may be inadequate for the next 20 years.

In this context, it is worth mentioning one other small detail related to routing. In the earliest conceptions of the Internet architecture, it was thought that routers would be interconnected largely by way of lower level networks. Thus, each router would have an address in the lower level network address structure, and because the network would have an Internet network number, the ports on the router connecting to the network would have Internet addresses. In fact, however, routers produced by vendors were often used to form store-and-forward networks built up by linking routers to each other by means of dedicated circuits. Rather than use up an entire network number (even a class C one) on each such interrouter links, the lines were unnumbered and the router ports associated with the Internet network number of at least one of the numbered networks was associated with the router. Typically, each router is connected to at least *one* network that has been assigned an Internet identifier, so this works out in practice, and conserves the use of network identifiers.[19, 37]

To finish this section on Internet addressing, it seems appropriate to mention another important binding function: binding of Internet host addresses to host domain names. At higher levels in the Internet protocol architecture, especially in dealing with users, it is convenient to assign readable, nonnumeric identifiers to hosts in the Internet. For example, one of the hosts I use is called `nri.reston.va.us`. Other well-known hosts include `nic.ddn.mil`, `isi.edu`, `note.nsf.gov`, `cs.ucl.ac.uk`, and `sophia.inria.fr`, just to mention a few. The rightmost strings (*us, mil, edu, gov, uk,* and *fr*) are called top-level domains in the Internet Domain Name System (DNS).[31, 32] Chapter 11 discusses the DNS in detail.

4.2.10   Options

Internet packets may contain zero or more option fields. The entire option field and each option is variable in length, and options may appear in one of two formats:

1   A single octet option (option-type)

2   A three-field option containing: an option-type octet, an option-length octet, and the actual option-data octets. The option-length octet counts the option-type octet and the option-length octet, as well as the option-data octets.

The option-type octet is viewed as having three subfields:

• 1-bit copy flag (0, copy on fragmentation; 1, don't)

• 2-bit option class

• 5-bit option number.

The option classes are:

• 0   Control

• 1   Reserved for future use

• 2   Debugging and measurement

• 3   Reserved for future use.

The defined Internet options are illustrated in Table 4.3.

4.2.10.1   End-of-Option List

Type=0

This option indicates the end of the option list. This might not coincide with the end of the Internet header according to the Internet header length. It is used at the end of all the options, not at the end of each option, and only needs to be used if the end of the options would not otherwise coincide with the end of the Internet header. The list may be copied, introduced, or deleted, on fragmentation or for any other reason.

Table 4.3 Internet options summary

| Type | | Octet | Description |
Decimal	Binary	length	
0	00000000	-	End-of-Option List. This option occupies only 1 octet; it has no length octet. Used to mark the end of all options in the datagram.
1	00000001	-	No Operation. This option occupies only 1 octet; it has no length octet. It is used for alignment.
130	10000010	var.	Basic Security Option.[48] Security level and authority indicators (US Government only).
131	10000011	var.	Loose Source Routing. Used to route the Internet datagram based on information supplied by the source; route is automatically recorded.
68	01000100	var.	Internet Timestamps.
133	10000101	var.	Extended Security Option[48] (US Government only).
7	00000111	var.	Record Route. Used to trace the route an internet datagram takes.
136	10001000	4	Stream ID. Used to carry the stream identifier.
137	10001001	var.	Strict Source Routing. Used to route the internet datagram based on information supplied by the source; route is automatically recorded.

4.2.10.2 No Operation

Type=1

This option may be used between options, for example, to align the beginning of a subsequent option on a 32-bit boundary. It may be copied, introduced, or deleted, on fragmentation or for any other reason.

4.2.10.3 Basic Security Option

This option provides a way for hosts to mark Internet packets with the security level and classification authority associated with the contents of the packet. This option has had a very checkered history, and has been essentially associated with US Government requirements. A more general security marking option is under consideration by the IETF. Readers should be aware that *RFC 791* and predecessors[48] to *RFC 1108* are essentially out of date, although it is known that there are implementations of pre-*RFC 1108* security specifications in the field.

This option is used by end systems and intermediate systems of an internet to:

Table 4.4 US classification levels

Value	Name
00000001	(Reserved 4)
00111101	Top Secret
01011010	Secret
10010110	Confidential
01100110	(Reserved 3)
11001100	(Reserved 2)
10101011	Unclassified
11110001	(Reserved 1)

1   Transmit from source to destination in a network standard representation the common security labels required by computer security models

2   Validate the datagram as appropriate for transmission from the source and delivery to the destination

3   Ensure that the route taken by the datagram is protected to the level required by all protection authorities indicated on the datagram. To provide this facility in a general internet environment, interior and exterior gateway protocols must be augmented to include security label information in support of routing protocols.

The basic security option must be copied on fragmentation, and appears at most once in an unfragmented datagram. Some security systems require that this be the first option if more than one is carried in the IP header, but this is not a generic requirement. The format for this option is as follows:

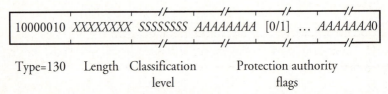

Type=130   Length Classification   Protection authority
                      level   flags

The length is variable, depending on the number of protection authority indications required. The minimum length is 3 octets, since protection authority indicators are optional. If only 1 octet of flags is needed, this octet is terminated by a zero-bit in the low-order bit position; otherwise, this bit is a 1 and another octet is appended.

The classification level (*SSSSSSS*) is encoded as shown in Table 4.4: These values represent the US classification levels at which the datagram must be protected. The value encodings are chosen to achieve a minimum Hamming distance of 4. *Reserved* values are invalid until assigned.

The protection authority flag field identifies the National Access or Special Access Programs that specify protection rules for transmission and processing of information con-

**Table 4.5 Assigned bits of the first octet of the
protection authority flag field**

Bit number	Authority
0	GENSER
1	SIOP-ESI
2	SCI
3	NSA
4	DOE
5,6	Unassigned
7	(Field termination indicator)

tained in the datagram. The authority flags do not represent accreditation authorities. Additional protection authority flag field assignments will be made by the Internet Assigned Numbers Authority only on the recommendation of DISA DISDB, Washington DC, 20305-2000.

The currently assigned bits of the first octet of the protection authority flag field are shown in Table 4.5. Bits are numbered, with bit 0 at the high-order end and bit 7 at the low-order end.

The field termination indicator in the low-order bit is set to 0 if this is the only octet present in the protection authority field. If another is appended, then the termination indicator is set to 1.

A set of system configuration parameters is also defined in association with the use of this option. Please refer to *RFC 1108* for details. See also Section 4.2.10.6 for a brief description of the extended security option.

4.2.10.4 Loose Source and Record Route

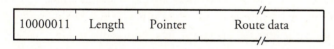

Type=131

The loose source and record route (LSRR) option provides a means for the source of an Internet datagram to supply routing information to be used by the gateways in forwarding the datagram to the destination, and to record the route taken.

The option begins with the option type code. The second octet is the option length, which includes the option type code, and is followed by the length octet, the pointer octet, and length-3 octets of route data. The third octet is the pointer into the route data, and indicates the octet at which the next source address to be processed begins. The pointer is relative to the beginning of this option, and the smallest legal value for the pointer is 4.

A source route is composed of a series of Internet addresses. Each Internet address is 32 bits or 4 octets. If the pointer is greater than the length, the source route is empty (and the recorded route full), and the routing is to be based on the destination address field.

If the address in the destination address field has been reached, and the pointer is not greater than the length, the next address in the source route replaces the address in the destination address field, the recorded route address replaces the source address just used, and the pointer is increased by 4.

The recorded route address is the Internet module's own Internet address as it is known in the environment into which this datagram is being forwarded.

This procedure of replacing the source route with the recorded route (though its order is the reverse of that recorded by a source route) means that the option (and the IP header as a whole) remains a constant length as the datagram progresses through the Internet.

This option is called a *loose source route* because the gateway or host IP is allowed to use any route of any number of other intermediate routers to reach the next address in the route.

The option must be copied on fragmentation, and appears at most once in a datagram. See Section 4.2.10.7 for record route error handling.

4.2.10.5   Internet Timestamps

01000100	Length	Pointer	oflw	flg
Internet address				
Timestamp				
⋮				

Type = 68

The option length of a timestamp is the number of octets in the option, counting the type, length, pointer, and overflow or flag octets (the maximum length is 40). The pointer is the number of octets from the beginning of this option to the end of timestamp plus 1 (i.e., it points to the octet beginning the space for next timestamp). The smallest legal value is 5. The timestamp area is full when the pointer is greater than the length. The overflow (4 bits) is the number of IP routers that were unable to register timestamps due to lack of space.

The flag values (4 bits) are

- 0   Timestamps only, stored in consecutive 32-bit words

- 1   Each timestamp preceded with Internet address of the registering entity

- 3   Internet address fields prespecified. An IP module only registers its timestamp if it matches its own address with the next specified Internet address.

The timestamp is a right-justified, 32-bit time, in milliseconds, since midnight Universal Time (UT). If the time is not available in milliseconds, or cannot be provided with respect to midnight UT, then any time may be inserted as a timestamp, provided the high-order bit of the timestamp field is set to 1 to indicate the use of a nonstandard value.

The originating host must compose this option with a large enough timestamp data area to hold all the timestamp information expected. The size of the option does not change due to adding timestamps. The initial contents of the timestamp data area must be zero or Internet address/zero pairs.

If the timestamp data area is already full (i.e., if the pointer exceeds the length) the datagram is forwarded without inserting the timestamp, but the overflow count is incremented by 1.

If there is some room, but not enough for a full timestamp to be inserted, or if the overflow count itself overflows, the original datagram is considered to be in error and is discarded. In either case, an ICMP parameter problem message may be sent to the source host.[3]

The Timestamps option is not copied upon fragmentation. It is carried in the first fragment, and appears at most once in a datagram.

4.2.10.6 Extended Security Option

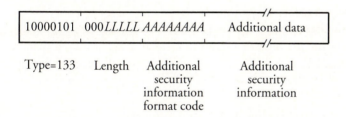

This option must be copied on fragmentation, and may appear more than once in a single, unfragmented datagram. This option is not yet fully specified, and development work is still in progress. An *RFC* will be published for each Additional Security Information Format Code, describing syntax and algorithmic processing rules to determine whether a datagram bearing such an extended security option should or should not be accepted. Any datagram containing the extended security option must contain a basic security option. The minimum length of this option is 3 octets (the additional security information field may be absent).

Format codes are assigned by the Internet Assigned Numbers Authority only upon recommendation by DISA DISDB, Washington, DC 20305-2000.

4.2.10.7 Record Route

The record route option provides a means to record the route of an Internet datagram. The option begins with the option type code. The second octet is the option length, which includes the option type code, the length octet, the pointer octet, and length-3 octets of route data. The third octet is the pointer into the route data, indicating the octet that

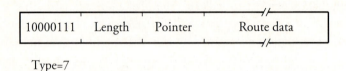

Type=7

begins the next area in which to store a route address. The pointer is relative to this option, and the smallest legal value for the pointer is 3.

A recorded route is composed of a series of Internet addresses. Each Internet address is 32 bits, or 4 octets. If the pointer is greater than the length, the recorded route data area is full. The originating host must compose this option with a large enough route data area to hold all the addresses expected. The size of the option does not change due to adding addresses. The initial contents of the route data area must be 0.

When a router routes a datagram, it checks to see if the record route option is present. If it is, the router inserts its own Internet address into the recorded route as known in the environment into which this datagram is being forwarded, beginning at the octet indicated by the pointer, and increments the pointer by 4.

If the route data area is already full (i.e., if the pointer exceeds the length), the datagram is forwarded without inserting the router's address into the recorded route. If there is some room but not enough for a full address to be inserted, the original datagram is considered to be in error and is discarded. In either case, an ICMP parameter problem message may be sent to the source host.[13]

This option is not copied on fragmentation and goes in the first fragment only. It appears at most once in a datagram.

4.2.10.8   Stream Identifier

10001000	00000010	Stream ID
Type = 136	Length = 4	

This option was defined to allow hosts to bind a datagram to transmission via a preallo-cated stream in the subnet into which the datagram was injected. The Atlantic Satellite net-work providing this feature is no longer in service.[3] Readers should refer[39] to *RFC 1190* for the most recent specification of the use of this option. Note that this option is allowed only in version 5 Internet Headers.

4.2.10.9   Strict Source and Record Route

This option is essentially identical to the loose source and record route option, except that the router or host must send the datagram directly to the next address in the source route, through only the directly connected network indicated in the next address, to reach the

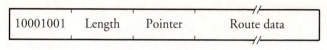

Type=137

next router or destination host specified in the route. See Section 4.2.10.7 for record route error handling.

The option must be copied on fragmentation, and appears at most once in a datagram.

4.2.11 Padding

The internet header padding is used to ensure that the internet header ends on a 32-bit boundary. The padding consists of 0s.

4.2.12 Routing

Routing is a major subject in its own right, and readers should refer to Chapters 5 and 7 in this book on that topic. Since routing of Internet Protocol packets is fundamental to the architecture, a brief summary of concepts and protocols in use is given here to provide context. As was illustrated in Figure 4.1, the basic model of the Internet consists of networks connected by routers. A brief tutorial on events involved in routing Internet packets through a system of networks and routers is given in *RFC 1180*.[65] Protocols for delivering information to all routers about how to decide where to send Internet packets next are called routing protocols.

The first Internet routing protocol developed, called Gateway-to-Gateway Protocol (GGP), was documented in an Internet Experiment Note,[51] and updated in a later *RFC*.[74] The protocol was similar to the one initially developed for the ARPANET IMPs, and involved a simple, distributed distance vector computation. A similar algorithm was introduced into the Xerox Network System (XNS) under the name Routing Information Protocol (RIP), and was adapted for use in some parts of the Internet.[52] It soon became clear that these simple algorithms had difficulty adapting to dynamic changes in connectivity, leading to routing loops and "black holes" of one kind or another. To create an opportunity for further experimental exploration of different routing protocols, the concept of Autonomous Systems was developed, as mentioned in Section 4.9.

In theory, all routers associated with a given AS make use of a common Interior Gateway Protocol (IGP) for the purposes of routing datagrams throughout the AS. In practice, a number of interior routing protocols are in use in the Internet, and within a given AS, multiple routing protocols are sometimes used. In the latter case, procedures are invoked that support the transfer of routing information from one protocol to another within the AS.

Autonomous Systems of gateways (routers) exchange reachability information by means of an Exterior Gateway Protocol (EGP). Thus within an AS, one or more IGPs are in use, and between AS's, an EGP is used. The first such EGP was developed at Bolt Beranek and Newman.[53, 54] Much of the knowledge and folklore about implementing gateways (routers) was summarized, first in Strazisar,[51] and later, by Braden.[37] Requirements for router implementation are complex, and a massive new document is in process,[56] and likely to be published as an *RFC* in the spring of 1992. With regard to concepts and terminology, a new term, *administrative domain* (or *routing domain*) has been introduced to support the management of multiple routing systems in the Internet.[67, 73]

As the Internet grew larger and more complex, it became clear that the available IGPs (GGP and RIP) were not sufficient, and that EGP was similarly unsatisfactory to cope with increasing scale. A major initiative within the IETF was launched to develop new routing protocols to cope with this growth. Based on concepts developed for improving ARPANET routing,[57] and those used in the Open Systems Interconnection (OSI) Intermediate System to Intermediate System (IS-IS) intradomain routing protocol,[66, 69] an Open Shortest Path First (OSPF) linkstate routing algorithm was developed.[58, 64] Concurrently, exploration of the adaptation of the OSI IS-IS to routing OSI connectionless packets (CLNP) and IP packets was also initiated.[59] OSFP has been adopted as the common IGP for the Internet. Both OSPF and IS-IS are in use in various parts of the Internet.

On the EGP front, a new exterior gateway protocol has been developed, called the Border Gateway Protocol (BGP).[60–63] BGP offers considerably more topological flexibility than its predecessor, EGP, and is in increasing use in the Internet. A protocol similar to BGP, but for routing of OSI CLNP packets, is now being standardized in the OSI community under the name Inter-Domain Routing Protocol (IDRP).

Research efforts are under way to discover more flexible routing architectures, which might permit the expression of policy in the routing algorithms.[68] For example, if identifiable kinds of traffic should be routed in certain ways, a policy routing algorithm might be able to take this into account. Research in this area is being carried out under the rubric of *interdomain policy routing*, and a protocol, Inter-Domain Policy Routing protocol (IDPR), is the subject of an experimental program supported by DARPA.

4.3   INTERNET CONTROL MESSAGE PROTOCOL (ICMP)

IP is used as the basic communication mechanism for carrying traffic in an internet between hosts, between hosts and gateways (routers), and between routers. Because the Internet Protocol is a best-efforts datagram protocol, failure to deliver a packet is not an occasion for an error message from the node that lost the packet. However, there are occasions when something is detectably wrong with the packet format, with the selection of a router, or with the condition of some intermediate node in the internet, and it is helpful if such abnormal conditions can be reported to the source of the datagram for possible remedial action. To support the reporting of errors and responses to queries about remote conditions, an Internet Control Message Protocol (ICMP) has been defined. ICMP is logically layered above the Internet Protocol, with a protocol identifier value of 1 in the protocol

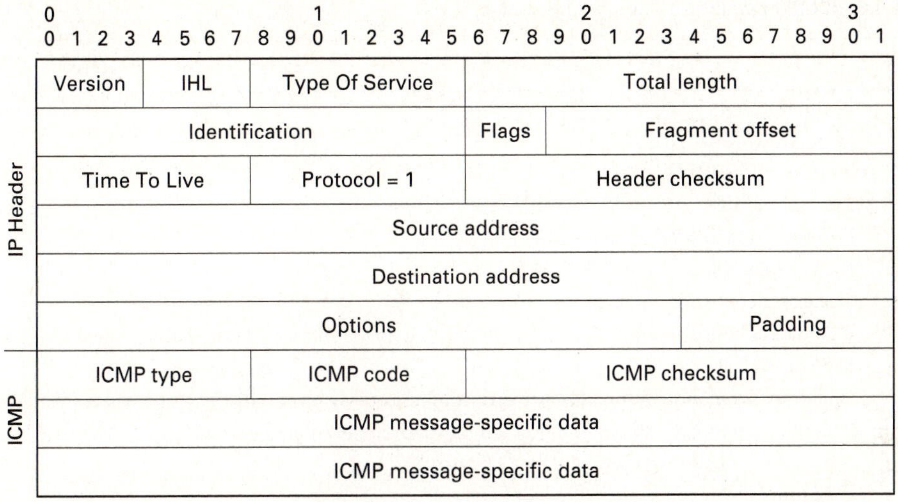

0		1		2		3	

0 1 2 3 4 5 6 7 8 9 0 1 2 3 4 5 6 7 8 9 0 1 2 3 4 5 6 7 8 9 0 1

IP Header

Version	IHL	Type Of Service	Total length	
Identification			Flags	Fragment offset
Time To Live		Protocol = 1	Header checksum	
Source address				
Destination address				
Options			Padding	

ICMP

ICMP type	ICMP code	ICMP checksum	
ICMP message-specific data			
ICMP message-specific data			

Figure 4.8   Internet control message protocol format. Note that each "tick" represents 1 bit

field of a standard IP packet. The format is illustrated in Figure 4.8. In effect, an ICMP packet looks just like an IP packet with some additional information attached. However, ICMP is considered an integral part of IP, and any implementation of the Internet Protocol must also include ICMP.

ICMP is of interest both to hosts (endpoints in the Internet) and to routers (intermediate points). Some ICMP messages are considered appropriate only for routers to generate; others may be generated by hosts or routers. It is never permitted for an ICMP message to be generated as the result of receiving an ICMP message. This rule is applied to prevent infinite recursion of ICMP message generation. Indeed, the restrictions are spelled out in *RFC 1122*:[16]

An ICMP error message *must not* be sent as the result of receiving:

• An ICMP error message

• A datagram destined to an IP broadcast or IP multicast address

• A datagram sent as a link-layer broadcast

• A noninitial fragment

• A datagram whose source address does not define a single host, e.g., a 0 address, a loopback address, a broadcast address, a multicast address, or a Class E address.

Many of these restrictions are designed to prevent "broadcast storms" that have resulted from hosts returning ICMP error messages in response to broadcast datagrams.

Table 4.6   ICMP destination unreachable codes

Code	Meaning
0	Net unreachable
1	Host unreachable
2	Protocol unreachable
3	Port unreachable
4	Fragmentation needed; don't-fragment flag set
5	Source route failed
6	Destination network unknown
7	Destination host unknown
8	Source host isolated
9	Communication with destination network administratively prohibited
10	Communication with destination host administratively prohibited
11	Network unreachable for selected Type Of Service
12	Host unreachable for selected Type Of Service
13	Communication administratively prohibited due to filtering
14	Host precedence violation. Requested precedence for this packet is not permitted.
15	Precedence cutoff in effect. The network operators have imposed a minimum level of precedence required for acceptance of any packets.

There are two classes of ICMP messages: ICMP error messages and ICMP query messages. Every ICMP error message includes the Internet header, and at least the first 8 data octets of the datagram that triggered the error; more than 8 octets may be sent. The defined messages, and whether they are sent by hosts or routers, are outlined below. As always, reference to the relevant *RFC* documents[13, 16, 56, 70] is recommended for implementation and further technical detail.

4.3.1   Destination Unreachable

ICMP type = 3	ICMP code	ICMP checksum
Unused (must be 0)		
Internet header + 64 bits of original IP packet data		

The destination address of the IP packet carrying this ICMP message is taken from the source address of the original IP packet. The defined ICMP codes for this type of message are shown in Table 4.6.

Codes 0, 1, 4–12 may be received from a router. Codes 2 and 3 may be received from a host. Code 8 is considered obsolete, and codes 0 or 1 are preferred. Codes 9 and 10 are intended for use with end-to-end encryption devices, and additional codes (13–15) are proposed for nonencryption-related administrative restrictions, and for citing precedence processing problems. It is proposed that some configurations of routers be permitted that will suppress codes 13–15 (amounting to silent discarding of unserviceable packets).

4.3.2 Redirect

ICMP type = 5	ICMP code	ICMP checksum
Gateway/router internet address		
Internet header + 64 bits of original IP datagram data		

Redirect messages are sent by routers to advise the sources of IP packets that a different router should be selected to forward this traffic. Note that routers use Interior or Exterior Gateway Protocols to apprise each other of preferred routing choices. The redirect ICMP is principally for router-to-host communication.

The destination address of the ICMP message is taken from the source address of the IP packet that generated the ICMP error message. The data following the type/code/check-sum section contains the address of the preferred router to which this packet should have been sent. Receiving hosts should update their local routing tables. If the new router address is not on the same connected (sub-)net through which the redirect message arrived, the ICMP message should be silently discarded.

The various defined types of ICMP redirect messages are listed in Table 4.7. References to *Network*, *Host*, and *Type Of Service* refer to those values in the destination address or TOS fields of the IP packet that triggered the ICMP message. The addition of subnetting into the architecture has led to ambiguity in the interpretation of codes 0 and 2, and it is now contemplated to prohibit the generation of these two codes.

IP packets containing source route instructions do not generate redirect ICMP messages.

Table 4.7   ICMP redirect messages

Code	Meaning
0	Redirect datagrams for the Network
1	Redirect datagrams for the Host
2	Redirect datagrams for the Type Of Service and Network
3	Redirect datagrams for the Type Of Service and Host

4.3.3 Source Quench

ICMP type = 4	ICMP code = 0	ICMP checksum
Unused (must be 0)		
Internet header + 64 bits of original IP packet data		

A router may discard Internet packets if it does not have sufficient buffer space to queue them for output to the next network. If a router discards a packet, it may send a source quench ICMP message to the source of the discarded Internet packet. Destination hosts may also send source quench messages. There is only one code (0) for this type of ICMP. Handling of source quench messages has been the subject of considerable debate in the Internet research and engineering communities. Experimental proposals for the use of this mechanism have been published,[71, 72] and it is required that protocols above the IP layer be prepared to receive source quench advice. General handling of congestion and flow control, outside of specific end-to-end protocol mechanisms, such as those found in the Transmission Control Protocol, is still the subject of experiment and research. Debate still continues on the use of source quench versus other methods of congestion control.[80, 81]

4.3.4 Time Exceeded

ICMP type= 11	ICMP code	ICMP checksum
Unused		
Internet header + 64 bits of original IP packet data		

The destination address of this ICMP message is taken from the original source address in the IP packet triggering the ICMP error message. This message is generated for one of two reasons:

- Code = 0   Time To Live exceeded in transit

- Code = 1   Fragment reassembly time exceeded

If the TTL field of the original IP packet has been decremented to 0, the datagram is discarded, and the router may return the time-exceeded ICMP. Hosts may time out in attempting to reassemble a fragmented Internet packet. When this occurs, the partially reassembled packet is discarded, and the host may (but is not required to) send a time-exceeded ICMP.

Routing loops are the most likely cause of TTL exhaustion although, with a rapidly growing Internet, the initial choice of TTL may have been too small to accommodate the necessary transit time (or hop count) required to reach the selected destination.

4.3.5 Parameter Problems

ICMP type= 12	ICMP code	ICMP checksum
Pointer (opt.)	Unused	
Internet header + 64 bits of original IP packet data		

The destination address of the ICMP packet is taken from the source address of the Internet packet triggering the error. Hosts and routers may both generate this ICMP error message. There are two type codes defined:

- Type = 0   Pointer value references the octet in the original IP packet that caused the problem. For example, 1 indicates a Type-Of-Service field value error. If there are options present, 20 indicates that the type code of the first option is not valid.

- Type = 1   There is no pointer present (the field is unused and set to 0) or a required option is missing (e.g., basic security option is missing).

This message is only sent if the error caused the IP packet to be discarded at the source of the ICMP error message.

4.3.6 Echo Request and Echo Reply

ICMP type=0/8	ICMP code = 0	ICMP checksum
Identifier	Sequence number	
Data....		

An echo request ICMP packet is type 0, and a reply is type 8. The source and destination addresses of the echo reply ICMP are taken from the echo request packet and reversed (the echo reply is sent *to* the source of the echo request). The data sent in the echo request should be returned in the echo reply. Record route, source route, and timestamp IP options, if present in the echo request IP packet, must also be processed and included in the return IP packet containing the ICMP echo reply. The identifier and sequence number fields are available to assist a receiving host to match an echo reply to an echo request sent earlier. These fields may be 0.

4.3.7 Information Request and Reply

ICMP type=15/16	ICMP code = 0	ICMP checksum
Identifier	Sequence number	
⋮		

This ICMP packet was originally intended to allow self-configuring systems, such as diskless workstations, to discover their IP network numbers at boot time. The Reverse ARP and BOOTP protocols proved better mechanisms, and these ICMP message types (15 and 16) are not in use in normal practice.

4.3.8   Timestamp and Timestamp Reply

ICMP type=13/14	ICMP code = 0	ICMP checksum
Identifier		Sequence number
Originator timestamp		
Receive timestamp		
Transmit timestamp		

The destination address of the timestamp reply messages is taken from source address of the timestamp request message. The source address of the reply is the responder's IP address (which should be the same as the destination address of the timestamp request message). Type 13 identifies a timestamp request and type 14, a timestamp reply.

An ICMP timestamp server returns a timestamp reply for every timestamp request message it receives. A timestamp message to a broadcast or multicast address may be silently discarded and ignored. If the source route option is present in the IP packet carrying the timestamp request, then the proper return route must be used. Record route and timestamp IP options must be processed appropriately, independently of processing the timestamp request.

The originator timestamp marks the time that the sender last touched the message before sending it. The receive timestamp marks the time that the timestamp server first touched the ICMP message on receipt. The transmit timestamp marks the time that the server last touched the message on sending the timestamp reply. The identifier and sequence fields may be used by the receiver of the timestamp reply to match it with the corresponding timestamp request.

The preferred form for a timestamp value (the "standard value") is in units of milliseconds since midnight UT. Since millisecond accuracies are not uniformly available, servers must at least update their clocks 15 times or more per second. Moreover, the accuracy of the value should be comparable to operator-set CPU clocks (which is to say, within a few minutes of the actual Universal Time).

Servers may make use of the Network Time Protocol[77] and various external sources (e.g., WWVB radio clocks, Stratum 1, 2, or 3 services, etc.) to maintain clock accuracy within acceptable tolerances.

4.3.9 Address Mask Request and Reply

ICMP type 17/18	ICMP code = 0	ICMP checksum
Identifier		Sequence number
Address mask		

This ICMP message pair may be used at boot time, for example, to help a host, such as a diskless workstation, determine the subnet address mask in use on the networks to which it is attached. The address mask request may be broadcast, and the response, if there is no specific host source address, may also be broadcast. Typically, this mode of operation is discouraged, and if broadcast replies are needed, the narrowest possible responding broadcast should be used. Normally, the destination address used in the address mask reply ICMP packet is the source address of the address mask request packet.

The responder, which may be a host, a gateway or a special server, should return the 32-bit network + subnetwork mask in the address mask field. The response should match the subnet over which the request was received. Multihomed hosts may need to make queries on all nets to which they are attached.

The need for this feature is outlined in documentation on the use of subnets in the Internet architecture.[78, 79]

4.3.10 Router Advertisement and Solicitation Messages

ICMP type=9/10	ICMP code = 0	ICMP checksum
Num addr	Addr entry size	Lifetime
Router address 1		
Preference level 1		
Router address 2		
Preference level 2		
⋮		

The purpose of this pair of ICMP messages is to support router discovery in multicast environments.[70] The basic notion is that hosts (and routers) can listen for periodic router advertisement messages that are multicast to the "all-hosts" group in a local multicast environment. Hosts just joining the system can also solicit information about available routers using the multicast router solicitation message.

Router advertisements (ICMP type = 9) are unsolicited or elicited in response to a router solicitation (ICMP type = 10) message. In either case, the advertisement contains zero or more router entries. The *Num addr* field indicates the number of router entries the advertisement contains and the *Addr entry size* field indicates the length of each router entry in 32-bit words. In the present standard, this is equal to 2. The *Lifetime* field indicates for what period of time, in seconds, the router entry should be considered valid. The default for this value is 1800 seconds (30 minutes). Every pair of 32-bit fields in each router entry contains the 32-bit IP address of the router and a "preference" value indicating which router the respondent considers it preferable for the inquirer to use. These values are signed, 32-bit quantities. Higher values indicate higher preference.

Routers are not supposed to advertise too often; the default value is once every 7–10 minutes. Hosts or others soliciting router information should not do so too often and, if they fail to obtain a response after three attempts, should cease soliciting for a period of time.

Router solicitations and advertisements are typically sent to well-known multicast addresses: 224.0.0.2 (all routers in the local net multicast group) or 224.0.0.1 (all systems in the local net multicast group).

4.4 INTERNET GROUP MANAGEMENT PROTOCOL (IGMP)

Although the protocol for managing Internet multicast groups is still under development, for completeness, a brief discussion of it is included in this chapter. Interested readers are referred to *RFC 1122* and *RFC 1045* for more details of the mechanisms proposed for managing multicast groups and for applying the technology to higher level applications.[24,55] IGMP should be thought of in terms similar to ICMP insofar as IGMP is really considered to be a part of the IP service.

RFC 1122 characterizes the facilities needed to permit hosts to engage in IP multicasting. Still in development are the details of router support for this capability in wide area implementations. The basic service permits a source to send datagrams to all members of a multicast group. There are no guarantees of delivery to any or all targets in the group. Permanent multicast group identifiers have been defined in the Class D address space (see Section 4.2.9) for:

- All hosts (in the local network) 224.0.0.1

- All routers (in the local network) 224.0.0.2

All other class D addresses are dynamically bound to groups of hosts using the IGMP protocol procedures. The range of Class D addresses includes 224.0.0.0–239.255.255.255. The first of these is not assigned to any group.

If the TTL field of the carrying IP packet has the value 1, then the multicast is confined to the immediately attached local network. If TTL exceeds 1, then the multicast message is forwarded by multicast routers to the target networks where it is injected as a multicast message.

Three levels of support for IGMP are contemplated:

- Level 0   No support for multicast

- Level 1   Send, but do not receive multicast

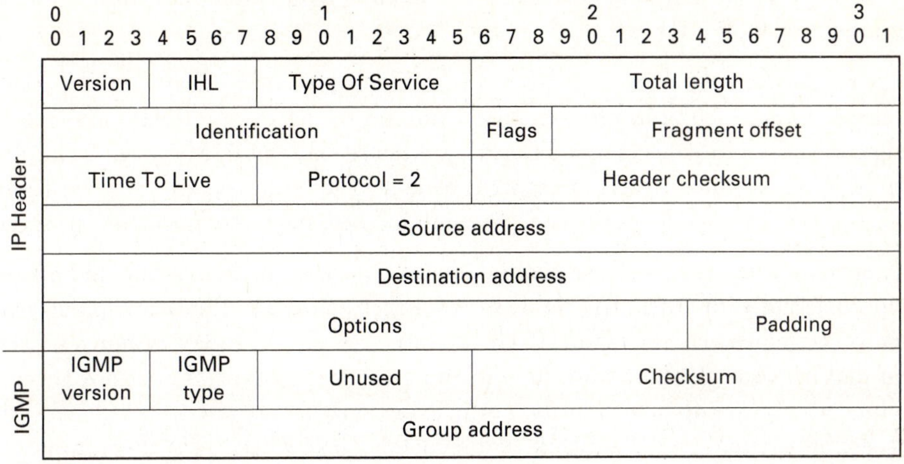

```
 0                    1                    2                    3
 0 1 2 3 4 5 6 7 8 9 0 1 2 3 4 5 6 7 8 9 0 1 2 3 4 5 6 7 8 9 0 1
```

Version	IHL	Type Of Service	Total length
Identification		Flags	Fragment offset
Time To Live		Protocol = 2	Header checksum
Source address			
Destination address			
Options			Padding
IGMP version	IGMP type	Unused	Checksum
Group address			

(IP Header: rows 1–6; IGMP: rows 7–8)

Figure 4.9   Internet group multicast protocol format. Note that each "tick" represents 1 bit

- Level 2   Full Support (send and receive) for multicast.

The basic IGMP services include two functions:

- JoinHostGroup (group IP address, network interface)

- LeaveHostGroup (group IP address, network interface).

The network interface identifier may be omitted if the host has only one network interface. If there are multiple network interfaces, the host may join different multicast groups on different interfaces. No ICMP error messages are to be generated by hosts on receipt of multicast messages (to avoid various kinds of broadcast storms and meltdowns).

IGMP is specified[24] in *RFC 1112* and uses IP packets with the format shown in Figure 4.9. It is required to be implemented by all hosts conforming to level 2 of the IP multicasting specification. IGMP messages are encapsulated in IP datagrams, with an IP protocol number of 2. Referencing Figure 4.9, the IGMP fields have the values and meanings listed in Table 4.8.

4.4.1 Informal Protocol Description

Multicast routers send Host Membership Query messages (queries) to discover which host groups have members on their attached local networks. Queries are addressed to the all-hosts group (address 224.0.0.1), and carry an IP TTL of 1.

Hosts respond to a query by generating Host Membership Reports (reports), reporting each host group to which they belong on the network interface from which the query was received.

To avoid an "implosion" of concurrent reports and to reduce the total number of reports transmitted, two techniques are used:

1   When a host receives a query, rather than sending reports immediately, it starts a report delay timer for each of its group memberships on the network interface of the incoming query. Each timer is set to a different, randomly-chosen value between 0 and D seconds. When a timer expires, a report is generated for the corresponding host group. Thus, reports are spread out over a D-second interval, instead of occurring all at once.

2   A report is sent with an IP destination address equal to the host group address being reported, and with an IP TTL of 1, so that other members of the same group on the network can overhear the report. If a host hears a report for a group to which it belongs on that network, the host stops its own timer for that group and does not generate a report for that group. Thus, in the normal case, only one report will be generated for each group present on the network, by the member host whose delay timer expires first.

Note that the multicast routers receive all IP multicast datagrams, and therefore need not be addressed explicitly. Further note that the routers need not know which hosts belong to a group, only that at least one host belongs to a group on a particular network.

There are two exceptions to the behavior described above. First, if a report delay timer is already running for a group membership when a query is received, that timer is not reset to a new random value, but rather is allowed to continue running with its current value. Second, a report delay timer is never set for a host's membership in the all-hosts group (224.0.0.1), and that membership is never reported.

If a host uses a pseudorandom number generator to compute the reporting delays, one of the host's own individual IP address should be used as part of the seed for the generator, to reduce the chance of multiple hosts generating the same sequence of delays. A host

Table 4.8   IGMP fields

IGMP Version	1	*RFC 1112*
	0	*RFC 988*—obsolete
Type	1	Host Membership Query
	2	Host Membership Report
Unused		Zeroed when sent, ignored when received.
Checksum		The checksum is the 16-bit 1's complement of the 1's complement sum of the 8-octet IGMP message. For computing the checksum, the checksum field is zeroed.
Group Address		In a Host Membership Query message, the group address field is zeroed when sent, ignored when received.
		In a Host Membership Report message, the group address field holds the IP host group address of the group being reported.

should confirm that a received report has the same IP host group address in its IP destination field and its IGMP group address field, to ensure that the host's own report is not cancelled by an erroneous received report. A host should quietly discard any IGMP message of type other than host membership query or host membership report.

Multicast routers send queries periodically to refresh their knowledge of memberships present on a particular network. If no reports are received for a particular group after some number of queries, the routers assume that group has no local members, and that they need not forward remotely originated multicasts for that group onto the local network. Queries are normally sent infrequently (no more than once a minute), so as to keep the IGMP overhead on hosts and networks very low. However, when a multicast router starts up, it may issue several closely spaced queries to build up its knowledge of local memberships quickly.

When a host joins a new group, it should immediately transmit a report for that group, rather than waiting for a query, in case it is the first member of that group on the network. To cover the possibility of the initial report being lost or damaged, it is recommended that it be repeated once or twice after short delays. (A simple way to accomplish this is to act as if a query had been received for that group only, setting the group's random report delay timer.)

Note that, on a network with no multicast routers present, the only IGMP traffic is the one or more reports being sent whenever a host joins a new group.

4.4.2 Implementation on an Ethernet

As an example, on an Ethernet, the low-order 23 bits of the IP multicast address are inserted into the low-order 23 bits of the Ethernet multicast address (01-00-5E-00-00-00 hex) to effect a multicast transmission. Since there are actually 28 bits of IP multicast address, up to 2^5 (32) IP group addresses will map to the same Ethernet multicast address. Receiving hosts must check to verify that the received packet is for an IP multicast address to which the receiving host belongs.

4.5 USER DATAGRAM PROTOCOL (UDP)

UDP[14] is a simple extension to IP that supports multiplexing of datagrams exchanged between pairs of Internet hosts. The format of a UDP packet is shown in Figure 4.10. UDP is protocol number 17 when carried in an Internet Protocol packet. Sixteen-bit source and destination port numbers are associated with a UDP packet. If no particular source or destination port indication is required, these fields may be set to 0. Typically, a receiving process must obtain or be assigned a port number, and must be "listening" on that port for an arriving User Datagram to be delivered on that port. Arrival of a UDP packet destined for a port on which no "listen" is pending should give rise to an ICMP "port unreachable" message.

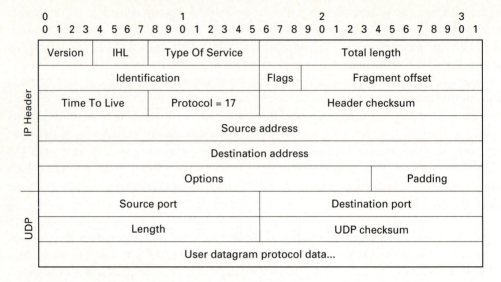

Figure 4.10   Internet protocol and user datagram protocol headers. Note that each "tick" represents 1 bit

The length field in the UDP packet is the number of octets in the UDP packet, including the UDP header and data. This length does not include the IP header and any options it may carry. The checksum is computed using a pseudo-header which is logically prefixed to the UDP packet, as illustrated in Figure 4.11. The UDP length appears twice in this figure, once in the pseudo-header and once in the UDP packet itself. The checksum is computed over the pseudo-header and the UDP header and data.

The checksum is simply the 1's complement of the 16-bit 1's complement sum of all the octets in the pseudo-header, the UDP header, and UDP data. Note that if the computed value of the checksum is 0, it is transmitted as all 1's. In 1's complement arithmetic, there are two values of zero, 0 and all 1's. By this convention, if no checksum is computed, the checksum field is sent with the value 0.

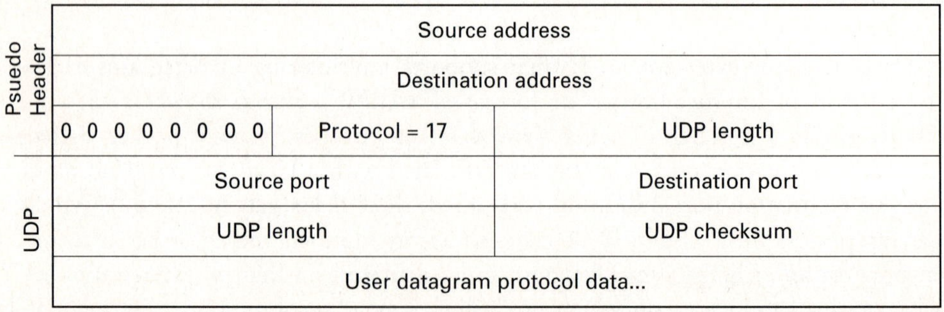

Figure 4.11   Pseudo-header prefix on UDP packet for checksum computation

UDP is almost a null protocol. It offers only multiplexing and checksumming, nothing else. Higher level protocols using UDP must provide their own retransmission, packetization, reassembly, flow control, congestion avoidance, and so on, if any are required. By itself, UDP is no more reliable than the underlying IP. UDP should pass up to the next layer any IP option that it receives, and should accept option specifications and other important IP parameters from higher level protocols that it should pass downward to IP. Similarly, all ICMP error messages received should be passed upward to the application lying above UDP.

UDP uses the same well-known ports (0–255) as the Transmission Control Protocol (TCP). Ports outside that range can be freely assigned on a dynamic basis. Interested readers are referred to *Assigned Numbers*[45] and Appendix A for a list of all port assignments currently made for use by UDP clients (i.e., higher level protocols).

4.6 TRANSMISSION CONTROL PROTOCOL (TCP)

TCP is a protocol designed to operate above the Internet Protocol layer and to provide to its clients at higher layers of protocol a reliable, sequenced, flow-controlled end-to-end octet stream. An analysis of the performance and characteristics of the predecessor to TCP, Network Control Protocol (NCP),[85] operating on the ARPANET, strongly influenced the direction of the TCP design. As was noted in Section 4.1, the original internetworking concepts developed in 1973–74 did not separate end-to-end from intermediate functions required to communicate reliably across multiple networks.

The original concepts behind TCP were expressed in a 1974 paper[6] that posited the idea of associations between pairs of communicating processes in hosts on a network of networks. These associations bound together the combination of a source host address or port, and a destination host address or port which defined a globally unique instance of interprocess communication. It had been hoped that there would be no necessity for any kind of "connection set-up," but analysis by several researchers[82–84] led to the inescapable conclusion that some kind of exchange was needed to ensure that arriving packets were current and not old, wandering duplicates that suddenly emerged from the Internet at an unpropitious moment.

The rationale for many of the TCP mechanisms can be understood through the following observations:

1 TCP operates above IP, and IP provides only a best-efforts datagram transmission service.

2 End-to-end recovery from unreliability by retransmission leads to the need for sequence numbering, both for reordering and for duplicate detection.

3 Flow control requires that both ends uniquely agree on which information may now be sent at any time, and which information has been received and acknowledged.

4 In a concatenation of many packet networks, it is possible for a packet to circulate in one or more networks for an indeterminate amount of time, only to emerge at a moment when it may cause the maximum confusion for the receiving party.

5 Termination of a full-duplex exchange of information should be graceful in the sense that both sides should be aware when one side has completed all its transmissions and has received all that it has been sent.

6 Every process should be able to engage in multiple "conversations" with the same or other processes without confusion.

7 Because different networks have different maximum packet sizes they can carry, the arrival of information in a particular segment should not have any semantic significance. Rather, the stream should be reassembled, and any semantic or syntactic markings should be embedded in the data stream and interpreted by the application receiving it.

4.6.1   TCP Service Model

Drawing on *RFC 793* and *RFC 1122*,[15, 16] this section characterizes the basic features of the Transmission Control Protocol, as viewed by processes using it to communicate with other processes in an internet.

TCP provides a reliable, serial communication path, or virtual circuit, between processes exchanging a full-duplex stream of octets. Each process is assumed to reside in an internet host that is identified by an Internet Protocol address. Each process has a number of logical, full-duplex ports through which it can set up and use TCP connections. A host is identified by its IP address (see Section 4.2.9), and a port is identified by a 16-bit value. A port–IP address combination is called a *socket*. The TCP service provides port identifiers to processes on request (or a process is imbued with a set of them at system initialization in the case of well-known ports, which are associated with common processes and services). A pair of sockets forms a connection that links the processes by a reliable, serial, two-way data stream.

It is important to realize that a socket may be involved in more than one connection. In Figure 4.12, for example, socket [132.151.1.1] is associated with two connections.[23] It is the connection that TCP uses to distinguish among pairs of communicating processes, not just the local socket identifiers.

A set of low-numbered ports have been set aside as well-known ports. All systems on an internet, if they provide the associated well-known services, do so using the well-known ports. The Appendix lists the current well-known ports used by applications running over TCP and UDP.[45] In addition, there are a set of reserved ports which, while not considered well-known, are nevertheless in common use. These are also listed in the Appendix.

Processes making use of the TCP service expect to be able to OPEN a connection actively or passively (sometimes called LISTEN), SEND and RECEIVE information, determine the STATUS of a connection, CLOSE the connection, and if need be, ABORT

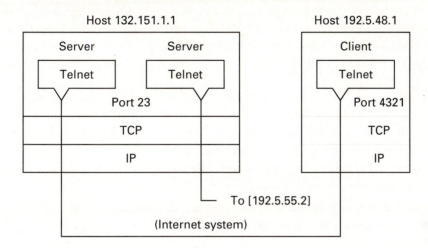

Well-known server Telnet socket: [132.151.1.1] (23)

Client Telnet socket: [192.5.48.1] (4321)

Connection: [132.151.1.1] (23) and [192.5.48.1] (4321)

Connection: [132.151.1.1] (23) and [192.5.55.2] (5464)

Figure 4.12   Internet ports, sockets, and connections

it. Each of these basic services may involve the specification of various parametric values, including the local port or foreign socket associated with the connection, timeouts and precedence associated with the connection, security features, and various options that may be required for the connection. If information destined for the other end of the connection is being buffered at the source, a push capability is available that allows an application to force the information to be transmitted, assuming flow control requirements from the other side have been met.

It is also possible to convey to the other side that information of an urgent character has been introduced into the data stream. The receiver is given a signal that there exists urgent information in the serial stream and sufficient additional data to know when all urgent information has been received. This feature permits applications individually to determine how they will deal with high-priority information without binding the TCP implementation to any built-in semantics. The CLOSE operation is graceful in the sense that the connection is not terminated until both sides have verified that each has finished sending and that all information in transit has been received. The ABORT feature permits a more abrupt closure of the connection, when needed, without these parting handshakes.

Neither the push nor the urgent mechanisms should be considered record markers. Multiple "pushes" may be aggregated into a single emission from the source TCP, and multiple calls to send "urgent" data may be collapsed into a single signal reporting that there is urgent information in the serial stream up to a particular point. The urgent information may be interspersed with less urgent information in the same serial stream, so any markings associated with urgency must be embedded in the serial stream for examination by the application using the TCP connection.

Some systems have implemented a FLUSH capability, which causes data that have been provided to TCP by the application but have not yet been transmitted to be flushed from the "to be sent" queue. This feature allows an application to respond to changing conditions by clearing out unsent data. Since this may result in a partial delivery of information to the receiving application, the application level protocol needs to have a way to resynchronize the state of both ends above the TCP level.

4.6.2 Basic Parameters of TCP Connections

The basic assumption is that TCP must achieve reliable, sequenced delivery of a stream of octets by means of an underlying, unreliable datagram service (IP). To achieve this, TCP makes use of retransmission on timeouts and positive acknowledgments on receipt of information. Because retransmission can cause both out-of-order arrival and duplication of data, sequence numbering of all information sent is critical. In the TCP design, every octet of information sent has an implicit 32-bit sequence number. Information to be sent on a TCP connection is broken into segments, which are encapsulated in IP datagrams for transmission. These, in turn, may be encapsulated in lower level frames at lower levels in the protocol hierarchy (e.g., in Ethernet packets, or HDLC frames).

Flow control in TCP makes use of a window technique in which the receiving side of the connection reports to the sending side the sequence numbers it may transmit at any time and those it has received contiguously thus far. The latter process is sometimes referred to as *cumulative* acknowledgment, and allows both sides to minimize the amount of information kept about the state of each connection and which data have been successfully sent. This does not preclude more complex implementations in which out-of-order arrivals of data are carefully tracked for efficiency. There have been various proposals over time to add a selective acknowledgment capability that would allow received information to be acknowledged before missing information has arrived. Thus far, such a facility has not been generally agreed, in part because its implementation requires the cooperation of the sender to remember these out-of-order acknowledgments to avoid unnecessary retransmissions. The notion is gaining some currency, however, as very high speed networks in the gigabit range are considered, because the latency of these networks leads to the potential for large amounts of data to be in flight before an acknowledgment can be received.

The basic format of a TCP segment is illustrated in Figure 4.13. TCP segments are embedded in IP datagrams for transmission. Source and destination port identifiers, together with the source and destination IP addresses taken from the IP header, form the socket pair that make up a TCP connection identifier. The sequence and acknowledgment

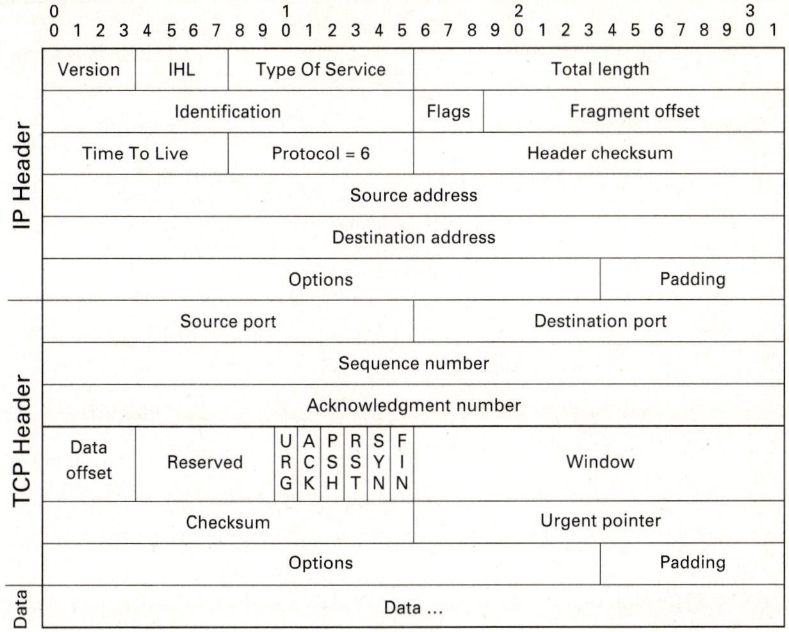

0		1		2		3	

```
 0 1 2 3 4 5 6 7 8 9 0 1 2 3 4 5 6 7 8 9 0 1 2 3 4 5 6 7 8 9 0 1
```

IP Header

Version	IHL	Type Of Service	Total length

Identification	Flags	Fragment offset

Time To Live	Protocol = 6	Header checksum

Source address

Destination address

Options	Padding

TCP Header

Source port	Destination port

Sequence number

Acknowledgment number

Data offset	Reserved	U R G	A C K	P S H	R S T	S Y N	F I N	Window

Checksum	Urgent pointer

Options	Padding

Data

Data ...

Figure 4.13 TCP header with IP wrapper. Note that each "tick" represents 1 bit

numbers are used to identify which data are being sent and which data have been received by the party sending the TCP segment. The Data Offset field is used to indicate the number of 32-bit words in the TCP header. Padding is used, when necessary, to ensure that TCP headers are always a multiple of 32 bits long. The reserved field must be set to 0.

A variety of flags are available for signalling special conditions (e.g., URG, for "urgent data present"; ACK, for "acknowledgment field is valid"; PSH, for "push the arriving data up to the application level"; RST, for "reset the connection"; SYN, for "begin connection by synchronizing sequence numbers"; and FIN, for "signal the finishing of transmission).

The window field indicates the number of octets, beginning with the one whose sequence number value is in the acknowledgment field, that the sender of the segment is prepared to accept.

The checksum field is the 16-bit 1's complement of the 1's complement sum of all 16-bit words in the header and text. If a segment contains an odd number of header and text octets to be checksummed, the last octet is padded on the right with 0s to form a 16-bit word for checksum purposes. While computing the checksum, the checksum field is replaced with 0s. The checksum covers a 96-bit pseudo-header prefixed, conceptually, to the TCP header. This pseudo-header contains the source address, the destination address, the protocol ID field, and the TCP length field. TCP length is the length of the TCP header plus the data length in octets (a computed, not a transmitted, value). These field

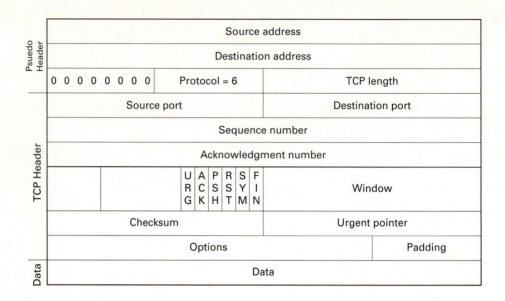

Figure 4.14   TCP checksum with pseudo-header. Note that each "tick" represents 1 bit

values are taken or computed from the IP and TCP headers. The fields over which the TCP checksum is computed are illustrated in Figure 4.14.

The Urgent Pointer is a 16-bit value representing an offset from the sequence number of the packet carrying the Urgent Pointer. The sum of the sequence number and Urgent Pointer is the sequence number of the *last octet of urgent data.* As is pointed out in *RFC 1122,*[16] the TCP specification, *RFC 793,*[15] incorrectly says that the Urgent Pointer points to the octet after the last octet of urgent data. TCP implementations should report the existence of urgent data to the upper applications and provide a way for these applications to know when all outstanding urgent data have been read.

There are a variety of options that can be carried in TCP headers, and these are summarized in the subsections below. As is shown in Figure 4.13, options occupy the last part of the TCP header and are padded to a multiple of 32 bits, if necessary, so that the data can start on a 32-bit boundary. Multiple options may be present in a TCP header. There are two formats for each option:

1   A single octet

2   A three-part option, containing an octet identifying what type of option is present, another indicating the length in octets of the option (up to 255 octets), and finally the octets making up the value or content of the option itself. Recall that the Data Offset field indicates where the TCP data begin, and that the options may not fill the entire space in the TCP header between the end of the Urgent Pointer and the start of data. Implementers must not mistake padding for options!

4.6.2.1   End of Option List

00000000

Option kind = 0
Option length = 1
Option data = N/A

This option code indicates the end of all options in the TCP header. It may not necessarily coincide with the end of the TCP header according to the Data Offset field. It is used at the end of all options, not the end of each option, and is only necessary if the last octet of the last option does not coincide with the last octet of the TCP header.

4.6.2.2   No-operation

00000001

Option kind = 1
Option length = 1
Option data = N/A

This option code may be used between options, for example, to align a subsequent option on a 32 bit boundary (or other octet boundary), if desired. There is no guarantee that this option will be exercised, so receivers must be prepared to process options which start on arbitrary octet boundaries.

4.6.2.3   Maximum Receive Segment Size Option

00000010	00000100	Max segment size

Option kind = 2
Option length = 4
Option data = Maximum Receive Segment Size

If this option is present, it communicates the maximum segment size, in octets, that the sender of the option is willing to receive on the associated TCP connection. This option is only to be sent in the initial segment of a TCP connection (one in which the SYN flag is set). If this option is not used, any segment size may be sent to the receiver. Note that the maximum possible value of the maximum receive segment size option coincides with the maximum possible size of the window allowed for flow control purposes.

This option can be used together with the MTU available[47] to adapt TCP connections to network parameters present at the time the connection is being set up. Note that the maximum receive segment size does not include the TCP header. The default IP datagram size, including the IP header, is 576 octets. Without options, the IP and TCP headers are 20 octets each. The default maximum receive segment size is thus: 576 – 40 = 536 octets.

It is helpful to note that once either the default or explicitly maximum receive segment size has been communicated to each party, each implicitly has a maximum send segment size that is determined by the other party's maximum receive segment size.

4.6.2.4   Window Scale Option

00000011	00000011	Shift

Option kind = 3
Option length = 3
Option data = Amount by which to scale received window

The shift amount is the number of bits by which the receiver right-shifts the true receive-window size, to scale it into a 16-bit value to be sent in the TCP header. The value may be 0 (offering to scale while applying a factor of 1 to the window size). Both sending and receiving TCPs must exchange window scale options for the scaling to take place in either direction.

In effect, all window calculations are expanded from 16 to 32 bits. Since TCP determines whether an incoming data segment is old or new by testing whether its sequence number is within 2^{31} octets of the left edge of the window (expected next sequence number), the left edge of the window has to be at least 2^{31} away from the right edge (a window length away from the left edge). Moreover, the sender and receiver windows are at most out of phase by the window size, so $2 \times$ the maximum window must be less than 2^{31}, or the maximum-window must be less than 2^{30}. This limits the safe scaling factor to 14, yielding an effective window of 2^{30} or about 10^9 octets.

This option must be sent with the connection-initiating SYN segment. See also Section 4.6.5.5.

4.6.2.5   SACK-Permitted Option

00000100	00000010

Option kind = 4
Option length = 2

This option confirms that the sender is willing to accept selective acknowledgments from the receiver. It must be sent with the connection-initiating SYN segment.

4.6.2.6   SACK Option

00000101	Variable relative origin	Block size	

Option kind = 5
Option length = variable
Option data = list of blocks of received data

The Selective Acknowledgment (SACK) option is used to convey acknowledgment information over an established connection. It is used by the data receiver to inform the sender of noncontiguous blocks of data that have been received and queued for delivery. The receiver is still awaiting receipt of data to fill in gaps between the received blocks. The operation of the SACK option is advisory in nature, and if ignored, the regular acknowledgments found in TCP headers will continue to work correctly.

Each block of received and queued data is characterized by two 16-bit values. The relative origin specifies the first sequence number of the block, relative to the acknowledgment value in the packet containing this option. The block size is the size in octets of the block of contiguous data.

There are some complexities when using selective acknowledgment in the presence of the scaling option.[50]

4.6.2.7 TCP Echo Option

00000110	00000110	4 bytes of information to be echoed

Option kind = 6
Option length = 6
Option data = 4 bytes of data to be echoed back

To initiate use of the TCP option, the first one must be sent with the connection-initiating SYN packet (to accommodate TCP implementations which break when they receive options other than in the SYN packet). A TCP Echo request should *only* be sent if one was received with the connection-initiating SYN packet.

When used to assist in round-trip time measurement, the four bytes sent will define the time at which the data segment was transmitted.

4.6.2.8 TCP Echo Reply Option

00000111	00000110	4 bytes of echoed data

Option kind = 7
Option length = 6
Option data = four bytes of data echoed back

A TCP which receives an ECHO option responds with an ECHO reply option in the next segment (e.g., the ACK segment). If multiple echo requests are outstanding, the TCP must choose the newest segment with the oldest sequence number to which to respond. To use this option, the TCP must send a TCP echo option in its SYN segment and receive one in the SYN segment of the other TCP. See also Section 4.6.5.5.

TCP *A* STATE		TCP *B* STATE
1. CLOSED		LISTEN
2. SYN-SENT	→ <SEQ=100><CTL=SYN>	→ SYN-RECEIVED
3. ESTABLISHED	← <SEQ=300><ACK=101><CTL=SYN,ACK>	← SYN-RECEIVED
4. ESTABLISHED	→ <SEQ=101><ACK=301><CTL=ACK>	→ ESTABLISHED

Figure 4.15   Basic three-way handshaking for connection synchronization

4.6.3   TCP Connection Set-Up

Sequential numbering of the TCP octet data stream is fundamental to the way in which TCP works. To ensure that both sides of a TCP connection unambiguously know what the initial sequence number is for each side's data stream, the initiation of a TCP connection involves the verified exchange of initial or synchronizing sequence numbers. The SYN flag bit mentioned in Section 4.6.2 is used to mark the first packet of a TCP three-way hand-shake.[83, 84] The purpose of this exchange is, primarily, to make it possible to reject old, duplicate packets (possibly from earlier connections) that might arrive and be improperly accepted as valid. It also has the virtue that it unambiguously identifies the start of the sequence of octets so it is clear how to order them at the receiving site, since arrivals are not constrained to be in proper sequence (due to TCP retransmissions and possible alternate routings at the IP level).

4.6.3.1   *Normal Connection Establishment*

Figure 4.15 illustrates a typical example of a three-way handshake. In this instance the receiving TCP is in a passive (listening) state awaiting an incoming connection request from the initiating side. The initiating side, (TCP *A*), sends a TCP segment containing no data, but an initial sequence number (100) and an indication that this is the initial segment of the TCP connection (CTL references the control flags in the TCP header; SYN means the synchronization flag is set). In effect, TCP *A* says it will number all its data on this con-nection, starting with 100. The SYN flag consumes the first octet of the sequence number space and is associated with this first octet sequence number. TCP *A* remembers it has sent this initial SYN packet by entering the SYN-SENT state, as is shown in Figure 4.15. TCP *B* receives the TCP segment, enters the SYN-RECEIVED state, and responds with a TCP segment of its own, acknowledging receipt of the initial SYN packet by setting its acknowl-edgment number field to 101 (saying that it is expecting an octet numbered 101 next; it has received all other octets sent so far). It also sets the SYN flag and says that it (TCP *B*) will start with sequence number 300. At Line 4, TCP *A* acknowledges receipt of the SYN from TCP *B* and, when TCP *B* receives this, it enters the ESTABLISHED state. At this

TCP *A* STATE		TCP *B* STATE
1. CLOSED		CLOSED
2. SYN-SENT	→ <SEQ=100><CTL=SYN>	...
3. SYN-RECEIVED	← <SEQ=300><CTL=SYN>	← SYN-SENT
4.	... <SEQ=100><CTL=SYN>	→ SYN-RECEIVED
5. SYN-RECEIVED	→ <SEQ=100><ACK=301><CTL=SYN,ACK>	...
6. ESTABLISHED	← <SEQ=300><ACK=101><CTL=SYN,ACK>	← SYN-RECEIVED
7.	... <SEQ=100><ACK=301><CTL=SYN,ACK>	→ ESTABLISHED

Figure 4.16 Simultaneous connection synchronization

point, both sides know which sequence numbers the other will use, both have acknowledged this fact, and the exchange of data may begin.

A similar scenario is illustrated in Figure 4.16, except in this case both sides initiate a connection simultaneously. Considerable effort was put into the TCP design to allow for this case. When it occurs, a single TCP connection is set up, and both sides know this. This ability to treat a simultaneous initiation as a request for one connection is one thing which distinguishes TCP from other connection-oriented protocols, which usually wind up creating two independent connections under these circumstances. In a distributed environment in which many autonomous processes are initiating connections with one another as equal partners (rather than client–server pairs), this is a fundamentally important feature. Astute readers of *RFC 793* will notice that Figure 8 of that document is incorrect, and that Figure 4.16 is the correct revision.

4.6.3.2 Detecting Old Duplicate Connection Initiations

One of the principal motivating factors behind the three-way handshake in TCP is to detect that an old, duplicate SYN packet has arrived. Figure 4.17 illustrates one example of this case. A legitimate SYN packet is sent (Line 2), but is delayed while an old one from an earlier session arrives (Line 3). When the ACK for the old duplicate returns at Line 4, TCP *A* responds with a reset (RST) packet (Line 5). When the RST packet arrives at TCP *B*, while TCP *B* is in an unsynchronized state (SYN-SENT or SYN-RECEIVED), that TCP returns to the active or passive connection initiation state it started in (note that it is important to remember whether the connection started passively or actively), and either waits (in LISTEN state) or reinitiates the active connection initiation attempt after a suitable timeout period. In the example given, the real SYN packet was delayed and arrives, as intended, at TCP *B*, and the rest of the three-way handshake is completed.

Another anomalous condition can occur when one side of a TCP connection has "crashed," but this is not yet known to the other. The resulting connection is considered to

TCP *A* STATE		TCP *B* STATE
1. CLOSED		LISTEN
2. SYN-SENT	→ <SEQ=100><CTL=SYN>	...
3. (duplicate)	... <SEQ=90><CTL=SYN>	→ SYN-RECEIVED
4. SYN-SENT	← <SEQ=300><ACK=91><CTL=SYN>	← SYN-RECEIVED
5. SYN-SENT	→ <SEQ=91><CTL=RST>	→ LISTEN
6.	... <SEQ=100><CTL=SYN>	→ SYN-RECEIVED
7. SYN-SENT	← <SEQ=400><ACK=101><CTL=SYN,ACK>	← SYN-RECEIVED
8. ESTABLISHED	→ <SEQ=100><ACK=401><CTL=SYN,ACK>	→ ESTABLISHED

Figure 4.17   Detecting an old duplicate SYN

be half-open and the TCP protocol needs to have a way to detect this case. If the side which has crashed receives an ordinary data-bearing TCP packet from the still-open side, the crashed side will respond with a fabricated reset (RST) packet inducing the other side to abort the connection. Figure 4.18 illustrates another case where the side that crashes makes an attempt to open a new instance of the previous connection. The side that was still open (half-open) needs to be induced to abort the connection.

At Line 1, TCP *A* crashes, and on recovering, the previously open connection is considered closed. The application using this connection attempts to reinitiate a connection with its correspondent served by TCP *B*. When the initial SYN packet arrives at Line 3, TCP *B* is not sure what to do, but in its ESTABLISHED state, it assumes that the attempt to synchronize the connection is not appropriate and simply responds with an acknowledgment of what it thinks the state of the connection is. TCP *A*, on the other hand, recognizes the

TCP *A* STATE		TCP *B* STATE
1. (Crash)		(send 300, receive 100)
2. CLOSED		ESTABLISHED (half-open)
3. SYN-SENT	→ <SEQ=400><CTL=SYN>	→ (??)
4. (!!)	← <SEQ=300><ACK=100><CTL=ACK>	← ESTABLISHED (half-open)
5. SYN-SENT	→ <SEQ=100><CTL=RST>	→ (Abort!!)
6. SYN-SENT		→ CLOSED
7. SYN-SENT	← <SEQ=400><CTL=SYN>	→
8. ESTABLISHED	→ <SEQ=100><ACK=401><CTL=SYN,ACK>	→ ESTABLISHED

Figure 4.18   Half-open connection discovery

TCP *A* STATE		TCP *B* STATE
1. (Crash)		(send 300, receive 100)
2. (??)	← <SEQ=300><ACK=100><DATA=10><CTL=ACK>	← ESTABLISHED (half-open)
3. (!!)	→ <SEQ=100><CTL=RST>	→ (Abort!!)

Figure 4.19   Active side causes half-open connection discovery

ACK as inappropriate (acknowledging something that TCP A did not send recently) and sends a reset packet at Line 4 to TCP *B*. Believing this RST packet, TCP *B* aborts and closes the connection on its end. When TCP *A* resends the SYN packet, things then proceed normally (assuming that TCP *B* is either now passively LISTENing on the connection or actively trying to initiate it again).

Connection resets can be induced when data arrives on a connection that is no longer recognized at the receiving side, as is illustrated in Figure 4.19. Unsolicited SYN packets can also induce connection resets as is shown in Figure 4.20.

As a general rule, resets are sent when a segment (packet) arrives that apparently is not for the current connection. A reset must not be sent if it is not clear that this is the case. The following rules apply to reset generation and processing:

1   If the connection does not exist (i.e., is CLOSED), then a reset is sent in response to any incoming segment except another reset. SYNs addressed to nonexistent connections are rejected by this means.

   If the incoming segment has an ACK field, the reset is constructed by taking its SEQUENCE number value from the ACK field of the offending, incoming segment. Otherwise, the reset packet has a sequence number of 0 and the ACK field is set to the sum of the sequence number and segment length of the incoming packet that caused a problem in the first place. The connection remains CLOSED.

2   If the connection is in any nonsynchronized state (LISTEN, SYN-SENT, or SYN-RECEIVED), and the incoming segment acknowledges something not yet sent, or if

TCP *A* STATE		TCP *B* STATE
1. LISTEN		LISTEN
2. LISTEN	... <SEQ=500><CTL=SYN>	→ SYN-RECEIVED
3. (??)	← <SEQ=700><ACK=501><CTL=SYN,ACK>	← SYN-RECEIVED
4. LISTEN	← <SEQ=501><CTL=RST>	→ (Return to LISTEN)
5. LISTEN		LISTEN

Figure 4.20   Passive sockets reset on receipt of old SYN packet

the incoming segment lacks other proper attributes (e.g., appropriate security or precedence indicators), then a reset should be sent. The SEQUENCE and ACK fields of the reset packet are generated as for Case (1).

3 If the connection is in a synchronized state (ESTABLISHED, or any other state in which the connection is known), then any unacceptable segment (e.g., improper sequence or acknowledgment values) must elicit only an empty (i.e., non-data-bearing) acknowledgment segment containing the current send-sequence number and an acknowledgment indicating the next sequence number expected to be received. The connection does not change its state.

There are more details to be found about reset processing in *RFC 793* and *RFC 1122* for readers interested in additional precision.

4.6.3.3 Selecting Initial Sequence Numbers

There is no restriction in the protocol design on the reuse of a pair of sockets (which define a connection). New instances (incarnations) of old connections may encounter problems if the new incarnation uses a sequence number recently used by an earlier incarnation. It is desired that connections be reusable, especially after a crash of the host, without introducing problems with reuse of sequence numbers and subsequent confusion over which packets contain the data associated with the most recent incarnation. We also do not want to impose any more restrictions than necessary on the reuse of a given connection.

In the present design, it is assumed that a (possibly fictitious) initial sequence number generator is ticking at the rate of one tick per 4 microseconds. The initial sequence number space cycles approximately every 4.55 hours. It is assumed that segments do not stay in the network for this long so that, by the time the ISN has recycled, any previous use of the segment sequence number will have long since left the network. This assumption is affected by the advent of very high speed networks which can consume sequence number space at extremely high speeds. This aspect of sequence number selection is dealt with in Section 4.6.5.6.

Despite careful design of the protocol, a crash of a host may cause it to lose all knowledge of any previous connections and possibly also any knowledge of how long it has been down. For such cases, the TCP design requires that a recovering host not initiate or respond to any new connection requests for the maximum segment lifetime which, in the TCP specification, is two minutes. This quiet time observance can be avoided if there is knowledge of the last sequence numbers used on all recent connections, but it is easy to see that a host could recover with incorrect data (e.g., boot up from old tapes) and operate on erroneous assumptions about the previously used sequence numbers.

The alternative, discussed in Section 4.6.5.6, is to make use of timestamps in TCP packets for the purpose of determining their freshness.

TCP *A* STATE		TCP *B* STATE
1. ESTABLISHED		ESTABLISHED
2. Close FINWAIT-1	→ <SEQ=100><ACK=300><CTL=FIN,ACK>	→ CLOSED-WAIT
3. FINWAIT-2	← <SEQ=300><ACK=101><CTL=ACK>	← CLOSED-WAIT
4. TIMEWAIT	← <SEQ=300><ACK=101><CTL=FIN,ACK>	(Close) ← LAST ACK
5. TIMEWAIT	→ <SEQ=101><ACK=301><CTL=ACK>	CLOSED
6. CLOSED (after 2 × maximum segment lifetimes)		

Figure 4.21   Normal close sequence

4.6.4 Connection Closing

TCP connections are full-duplex in concept, and therefore, the closing of a connection by one side does not necessarily imply that the other side has finished sending on its own behalf. The TCP CLOSE operation means more "I have no more data to send" than "I will take no more data." This means that applications using TCP should continue to read incoming data until told there is no more, even if, on the send side, the application has ceased to transmit data and has informed the operating system that it is done.

There are three cases to consider in analyzing the graceful close of a TCP connection:

1 The local TCP initiates the close in response to the using application's request.

2 The remote TCP initiates the close (by sending a segment containing a FIN control flag).

3 Both sides close simultaneously.

The point of graceful closing is that both sides decide when they have no more data to send and both confirm they have received all data sent. Only after all this is the connection terminated. The mechanisms for achieving this involve additional states in the life of a TCP connection.

In the first case, the local TCP initiates the closing. This is illustrated in Figure 4.21. At Line 2, TCP *A* sends a segment with a FIN control, indicating it will send no more data. The connection enters a state awaiting the acknowledgment of its FIN and also the receipt of a FIN from the other side. At Line 3, TCP *A* gets the acknowledgment of its FIN and enters a new state awaiting the FIN from the other TCP. At Line 4, TCP *A* receives the FIN from the other side, acknowledges it, and then waits for twice the maximum segment lifetime before discarding knowledge of this TCP connection. TCP *B*, on receipt of the FIN in Line 2, enters a state awaiting word from its application (user) that it is finished

TCP *A* STATE		TCP *B* STATE
1. ESTABLISHED		ESTABLISHED
2. (Close)		(Close)
FINWAIT-1	→ <SEQ=100><ACK=300><CTL=FIN,ACK>	... FINWAIT-1
	← <SEQ=300><ACK=100><CTL=FIN,ACK>	←
	... <SEQ=100><ACK=300><CTL=FIN,ACK>	→
3. CLOSING	→ <SEQ=101><ACK=301><CTL=ACK>	... CLOSING
	← <SEQ=301><ACK=300><CTL=ACK>	←
	... <SEQ=101><ACK=301><CTL=ACK>	→
4. TIMEWAIT	← <SEQ=300><ACK=101><CTL=FIN,ACK>	(Close)
(2MSL)		TIMEWAIT
(CLOSED)		(2MSL)
		(CLOSED)

Figure 4.22   Simultaneous close sequence

sending, too, and responds with an ACK on Line 3. At Line 4, the application using TCP *B* closes its side of the connection, and sends its FIN indicator. TCP *A* acknowledges this in Line 5, and awaits the expiration of a timer set for two maximum segment lifetimes before dropping its knowledge of the connection. The second case looks like the first, except TCP *A* and TCP *B* reverse roles. The third case is illustrated in Figure 4.22.

4.6.5   Data Communications with TCP

As was pointed out in Section 4.6.2, every octet of data sent on a TCP connection has an associated 32-bit sequence number, including the SYN and FIN flags that begin and end the connection. These are treated as occupying sequence space so that they can be retransmitted, if necessary, and duplicate detection will work. The initial sequence number is selected in such a way as to minimize the reappearance in the internet of packets from an earlier incarnation of the same connection. This may be done by choosing the initial sequence number based on a time-of-day clock, by randomizing the initial choice, or by delaying the start of a new connection to increase the likelihood that any datagrams from an earlier TCP connection have drained from the system.

4.6.5.1   *Window Management*

As a means of controlling the flow of segments, TCP uses the notion of a window to determine how many and which octets a source TCP is permitted, by the receiving TCP, to send on a given TCP connection. Window size values are communicated in each TCP header: the receiver of a packet indicates in the header of an acknowledgment packet how many

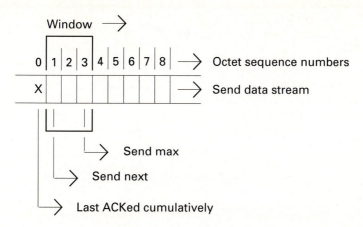

Figure 2.23   The initial SEND window

octets may be sent and also, based on the acknowledgment field value in the packet header, which octet sequence numbers are candidates to be sent. The receiving TCP may adjust the window size to reduce or increase the amount of data it is willing to accept as it sends acknowledgments of previously received data. Typically, a window size is established by each receiving end of a TCP connection at the beginning of a TCP connection, and is adjusted in size as needed. It is considered an error to shrink the window in such a way that it takes back permission granted earlier to send data.

To see how this works in some simple cases, Figure 4.23 illustrates the case of a source TCP that has been given permission to send up to three octets of data to a destination TCP. Initially, the window is 3 octets long, and from the point of view of the sender, no data have yet been sent into the window (which starts at 1 for pedagogical purposes). Figure 4.24 shows the state of affairs after two octets have been sent. None of the data have been

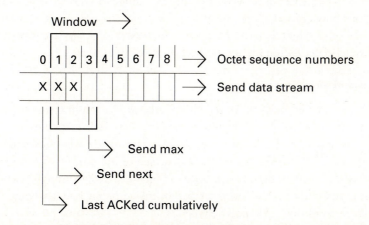

Figure 2.24   The SEND window after two octets

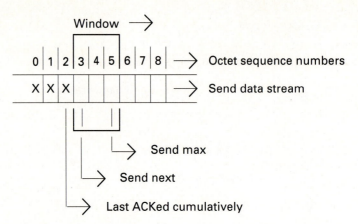

Figure 2.25   The SEND window after first two octets ACKed

acknowledged yet, so the left edge of the window remains over octets 1–3 and the next sequence number to use, 3, is also the maximum which is permitted.

Figure 4.25 illustrates the state of affairs after the first two octets are acknowledged. The left edge of the window has advanced, as has its right edge. The last cumulatively acknowledged packet sequence number has similarly advanced.

The basic scheme, which is worked bidirectionally (one for each side of the TCP connection), has a natural self-pacing. In the absence of any interfering traffic, an acknowledgment is typically sent shortly after the receipt of a data packet. Since it takes a finite time to send each data packet at the source TCP, the interval between arrival of acknowledgments tends to reflect the interval between data packet arrivals at the destination. The self-pacing effect advances the window at the sender in step with its advance at the receiver.

Windows may be set to 0 to stop transmissions from the sender. To detect the possibility that the receiver has crashed, it is permitted for the sender to send small amounts of data into a closed window (probing the closed window) at infrequent intervals. It is recommended that the probe interval be exponentially increased each time a probe transmission fails to be acknowledged before the retransmission timeout expires.

4.6.5.2   Retransmission Timeouts

If a segment is lost in the network, timeouts are used at the sending side to recover from the loss. The setting of timeouts is a delicate and critical matter. If the sender is too impatient and retransmits early, the network resources are unnecessarily consumed with extra traffic. If the timeout is too long, the effective data rate of the transmission will be reduced because recovery from a lost datum is too slow. Since the delay through a store-and-forward network is variable, determination of an optimal timeout and adjusting it to reflect changing network conditions is a major challenge.

Two important refinements of TCP implementation were developed by Van Jacobson,[90] and Philip Karn and Craig Partridge.[91] The original round-trip time estimators only worked in circumstances that gave rise to small variance in round-trip times. On low-speed lines, for instance, the apparent round-trip times can vary dramatically with packet size, giving rise, under the original algorithms, to unstable timeout values and poor throughput. Moreover, retransmissions, unless properly accounted for, could pollute round-trip time estimates (e.g., an acknowledgment from the original packet is attributed to being sent in response to a retransmission, leading to incorrectly short round-trip times).

The proper measurement of round-trip time helps to minimize unnecessary retransmissions and can contribute to proper setting of window sizes. A suitably set window can allow a kind of pipelining to take place, permitting the sender to make full use of the effective capacity of the network, despite the existence of a possibly long delay for acknowledgments to be returned.

Karn[91] specifies which measured round-trip times should be incorporated into the round-trip time estimation. Van Jacobson[90] recommends a way of smoothing the estimated round-trip times, taking into account the measured variance. These values are factored into the retransmission timeout used by the sender to recover from lost segments. It should be noted that the retransmission timeout in TCP is backed-off exponentially on the possibility that failure to receive an acknowledgment is caused, not by packet loss, but by congestion (see also Section 4.6.5.4).

The recommended initial starting values for round-trip time and for retransmission timeout are 0 seconds and 3 seconds, respectively. To accommodate operation of TCP in high-speed LANs and across large internets, the lower and upper bounds on the retransmission timeout need to be in fractions of seconds and at double the maximum segment lifetime (or 240 seconds), respectively.

Note that error recovery is aided by the fact that every octet in a segment has an implicit sequence number. Duplicate packets caused by retransmissions are easily detected and supernumerary data discarded, even if segments are reformed (regrouped) at the sender when retransmitted.

4.6.5.3 Silly Window Syndrome

D. Clark identified an anomaly in the behavior of window-based flow control schemes,[86] and named it *silly window syndrome*. In this syndrome, a stable pattern of small window size updates develops so that the sender has little opportunity to send large chunks of data, despite the fact that, if the sender just waited a little while, a larger window would be available and a more efficient transmission scheme would result. Essentially, the syndrome manifests itself when the receiver advances the right edge of the window as soon as it has some buffer space to receive and when the sender sends data, no matter how small the increment in the right edge of the window. The resulting sequence of tiny packets reduces throughput dramatically. The syndrome can be initiated by sending a small packet of data which, when acknowledged by the receiver, advances the window by a small amount. If the sender then immediately sends a small amount of data again (bound by available space in the send window) rather than waiting for more space to be made available as other previously-sent data are acknowledged, the cycle is perpetuated.

The problem only happens when there is a large and rather continuous amount of data to send—once the system goes quiescent, the problem clears itself up. The solution to silly window syndrome essentially consists of three simple algorithms first specified by David Clark:[86]

1   The sender refrains from sending if the usable window is smaller than 25% of the window size advertised by the receiver. Usable window means the sequence numbers associated with octets not yet sent, which the receiver would accept because they lie within the scope of the window size carried in the acknowledgment packet.

2   The receiver reduces the actual advertised receive window if the reduction doesn't represent more than 50% of the actual space available.

3   The receiver refrains from sending an acknowledgment at all if the push flag was not set in the incoming segment header and there is no revised window information to send back. A timer is used to make sure that acknowledgments eventually are sent back to avoid unnecessary retransmission.

Nagle noticed that this syndrome was exacerbated by sending a number of small segments when they could have been coalesced into a larger one.[92] The present recommendations for TCP implementation take Nagle's notion of coalescing segments into account, to minimize the instigation of silly window syndrome.

4.6.5.4   *Congestion Control*

Use of the TCP protocol in actual internets containing gateways of varying and sometimes limited capacity led to the observation that improperly tuned TCP implementations could readily congest one or more gateways by sending too quickly and building up large, persistent queues of packets. Van Jacobson took up this problem and produced rather interesting and very useful results, which have been replicated and extended by others.

Van Jacobson's scheme to reduce congestion at gateways by suitable TCP tuning[90] is summarized in Wang and Crowcroft:[87]

> Jacobson's algorithm consists of two separate window adjustment algorithms: slow-start and congestion avoidance. Before slow-start is implemented, TCP always sends a full window's worth of back-to-back packets to the network when it starts initially or restarts after a timeout. To avoid overwhelming a slow bottleneck with bursts of packets, the slow-start algorithm sets the congestion window to 1 and then opens the window exponentially to the slow-start threshold ssthresh. The congestion avoidance algorithm is a timeout-based multiplicative decrease/adding increase algorithm. When a timeout (for receiving an anticipated acknowledgment) is encountered, the threshold, ssthresh, is reduced to half the current window size and then

the congestion window is reduced to 1. During the slow-start phase, each acknowledgment increases the congestion window by 1. After the congestion window reaches ssthresh, the congestion window is increased by 1/(congestion window) for each acknowledgment seen.

Obviously, the actual sending size window should not exceed the receiver-provided receive window, and the algorithm takes this into account.

4.6.5.5 Long-Delay Networks

Combinations of network bandwidth and round-trip times can combine to prevent effective utilization of the network resources. The product of network speed and round-trip time is sometimes referred to as the *delay-bandwidth product*. When this is larger than the offered window size, throughput suffers while the sender delays sending until acknowledgment is received for the amount of data previously transmitted. If the delay-bandwidth product exceeds the maximum possible window size, no amount of procedural adjustment can overcome the problem.

A second problem in high-delay network environments is exaggerated by the cumulative acknowledgment scheme used in TCP. In effect, if a single segment is lost, many of those which follow it and arrive safely cannot be acknowledged until the missing one has been retransmitted. They may well be unnecessarily retransmitted if the round-trip time is long, since the retransmission timers will expire on them before the cumulative acknowledgment can be received after recovering the lost segment. The third problem is that round-trip times must be continuously measured to properly adjust the retransmission timeouts to current network conditions. Failure to do so can lead to serious congestion or very poor capacity utilization. Because round-trip time computations can be time-consuming, some implementations of TCP time only one segment per window. For small windows, this may be an adequate measurement, but for the very large windows required in high-delay networks, such estimates are inadequate.

Jacobson and Braden propose[50] to adjust the interpretation of offered window sizes, use selective acknowledgment, and use a TCP *echo* option for round-trip timing independent of retransmission to overcome these problems.

The Window Scale Option increases the effective window size by 2^S where S is the window scaling factor. Under the present definitions, S is less than or equal to 14, yielding an effective window size of up to 2^{30}, or 1 gigabyte.

To allow the receiver to advise the sender of data arriving out of order (to avoid unnecessary retransmissions by the sender), a selective acknowledgment scheme has been proposed (see options 4.6.2.5 and 4.6.2.6). The selective acknowledgments are advisory in nature and TCPs not implementing them will continue to function, but possibly not as effectively in high delay or high bandwidth-delay environments.

Table 4.9   Network speeds

Network	bits/sec	bytes/sec	Wrap time
ARPANET	56 Kbits/sec	7 Kbytes/sec	3×10^5 sec (~3.6 days)
DS1	1.5 Mbits/sec	190 Kbytes/sec	10^4 sec (~3 hours)
Ethernet	10 Mbits/sec	1.25 Mbytes/sec	1700 sec (~30 min)
DS3	45 Mbits/sec	5.6 Mbytes/sec	380 sec
FDDI	100 Mbits/sec	12.5 Mbytes/sec	170 sec
Gigabit	1000 Mbits/sec	125 Mbytes/sec	17 sec

Finally, the echo and echo reply options are used to implement a more reliable round-trip time measurement scheme through the use of timestamps in the options, rather than inferring these times from packet acknowledgments.

4.6.5.6   High-Speed Networks

Gigabit networks are now starting to emerge in the research community and TCP, because of its limited window size (65,536 octets maximum), does not effectively utilize the potential transmitting capacity of such high-speed networks, if the delay for acknowledgments exceeds the time it takes to transmit a full, maximum-sized window. Van Jacobson, and Braden and Zhang[49, 50] describe methods for overcoming these limitations.

High-speed networks pose an additional challenge because they may consume sequence space faster than the networks contemplated in the original TCP design. If this happens, it is possible that old duplicate packets will be mistaken for current ones and accepted, violating the primary function of TCP, which is to deliver data in sequence and with 100% integrity. Duplicate use of sequence numbers may occur either because they are reused during the same connection before all previously sent packets using that sequence number have been delivered, or because a previous instance of the connection has left packets in the network and a new instance is started before the old packets have disappeared.

The rapid use of sequence space is, in part, a function of the capacity of networks to accept traffic and the permission by the receiver to accept the data. Assuming no limitations of the latter variety, Table 4.9 illustrates the time it takes for the available sequence space to wrap-around at varying network speeds.[49] Clearly, at speeds beyond 45 Mbits/sec, the wrap time approaches the assumed maximum segment lifetime (120 seconds), and is too small to be enforced by the Internet TTL mechanism.

Van Jacobson, Braden and Zhang propose to use TCP timestamps in the TCP Echo and TCP Echo Reply options. Basically, the idea is that any arriving segment whose timestamp is earlier than the timestamp of the most recently accepted segment should be discarded as an old duplicate. See *RFC 1185* for details.

The other possible way in which a sequence number may be inappropriately reused is after a system crash in which the system state is lost (in particular, all knowledge of previ-

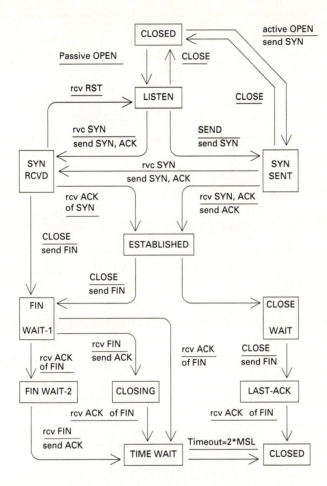

Figure 4.26   TCP Connection state diagram

ous connections is gone). The standard TCP specification requires that a quiet-time be enforced after system recovery.[15] This is specified as twice the maximum segment lifetime. A similar pause is recommended after a connection is closed to ensure that both sides can be assured that the close has been successful. If all TCPs made use of Timestamped packets, and if system clocks could be guaranteed to be monotonic over system crashes, some of the quiet-time delays could be eliminated.

4.6.6   TCP Connection States

It may be helpful to see the entire state diagram for the lifetime of a TCP connection. This is illustrated in Figure 4.26, and corrects omissions identified in *RFC 1122*. The meanings of the states are roughly as follows:

LISTEN   Represents waiting for a connection request from any remote TCP
                    and port.

SYN-SENT   Represents waiting for a matching connection request after having
                    sent one.

SYN-RECEIVED   Represents waiting for a confirming connection request acknowledg-
                    ment after having both received and sent a connection request.

ESTABLISHED   Represents an open connection; data received can now be delivered
                    to the upper layer protocol. This is the normal state for the data
                    transfer phase of the connection.

FIN-WAIT-1   Represents waiting for a connection termination request from the
                    remote TCP, or an acknowledgment of the connection termination
                    previously sent.

FIN-WAIT-2   Represents waiting for a connection termination request from the
                    remote TCP.

CLOSE-WAIT   Represents waiting for a connection termination request (CLOSE)
                    from the upper layer protocol.

CLOSING   Represents waiting for a connection termination request acknowledg-
                    ment from the remote TCP.

LAST-ACK   Represents waiting for an acknowledgment of the connection termi-
                    nation request previously sent to the remote TCP (which includes an
                    acknowledgment of its connection termination request).

Readers are cautioned that all nuances of the TCP protocol cannot be expressed in one
terse diagram. Implementers should consult the full specifications and other referenced
publications that deal with advisable implementation practices.

4.7   FUTURE EVOLUTION OF THE TCP/IP PROTOCOLS

As this chapter is being written, the Internet system, which uses the TCP/IP protocols, is
undergoing exponential growth in size, traffic, and variety of uses. Apart from the predictable arrival of gigabit LANs and WANs, which will certainly have an impact on the performance and requirements to be met by the TCP/IP protocols, this scaling has other effects.
Security has become far more critical, especially in the presence of commercial use of the
technology. With wider application, a much broader swath of users is incorporated into the
ambit of the Internet, for example, and this increases some of the risks associated with connecting to it. These requirements drive continuing evolution of the security architecture of
the Internet, as well as the serious need for revision of the addressing and routing structure
of the system. The present target is to revise the addressing and routing capability to

accommodate up to one billion networks each with up to one billion terminations. To achieve this goal while maintaining reasonable backward compatibility with the very large and growing installed base is a major challenge.

New commercial services, such as Switched Multimegabit Data Service, Frame Relay, SONET fiber links, and gigabit LANs and WANs, together with new workstation capabilities including sound and video, are producing yet another demanding requirement: multiple types of service. Video conferencing and voice teleconferencing have been demonstrated on the Internet with datagram-based protocol, but large quantities of such traffic probably cannot be supported without paying additional attention to handling different types of service at gateways and routers, and in the end-to-end protocols. The 1990s will likely prove to be highly consequential for the TCP/IP protocol suite. The protocol will either adapt to the new requirements emerging from the Internet or it will be replaced by something that does meet these needs.

REFERENCES

1   V.G. Cerf, Packet Communication Technology, in *Protocols and Techniques for Data Communication Networks* (F.F. Kuo, Ed.), Prentice Hall, New York, 1980.

2   R.E. Kahn, S.A. Gronemeyer, J. Burchfiel, and R.C. Kunzelman, Advances in Packet Radio Technology, *Proc. IEEE*, Vol. 66, No. 11, pp. 1468–1496, November 1978.

3   I.M. Jacobs, R. Binder, and E.V. Hoversten, General Purpose Packet Satellite Networks, *Proc. IEEE*, Vol. 66, No. 11, pp. 1448–1467, November 1978.

4   F.E. Heart, R.E. Kahn, S.M. Ornstein, W.R. Crowther, and D.C. Walden, The interface message processor for the ARPA computer network, in *Proceedings of the Spring Joint Computer Conference*, AFIPS Press, Vol. 36, pp. 551–567, 1970.

5   C.S. Carr, S. Crocker, and V.G. Cerf, HOST-HOST Communication Protocol in the ARPA Network, in *Proceedings of the Spring Joint Computer Conference*, AFIPS Press, Vol. 36, pp. 589–597. Reprinted in *Computer Networking*, Blanc and Cotton, Eds., IEEE Press, 1976, p. 7.

6   V.G. Cerf and R.E. Kahn, A Protocol for Packet Network Intercommunications, *IEEE Transactions on Communication*, Vol. COM-22, No. 5, pp. 637–648, May 1974, Reprinted in *Computer Networking*, Blanc and Cotton, Eds., IEEE Press, 1976, pp. 95–106.

7   M.T. Rose, *The Open Book: A Practical Perspective on Open Systems Inter-connection*, Prentice Hall Series in Innovative Computing, Prentice Hall, Englewood Cliffs, 1989.

8   D. Cohen, Issues in transnet packetized voice communication, *Proceedings of the Fifth Data Communications Symposium*, 10–13 September 1977, Snowbird, Utah, p. 6. IEEE Catalog Number 77CH1260-9C.

9   D.R. Boggs and R.M. Metcalfe, Ethernet: Distributed packet switching for local computer networks, *Communications of the Association for Computer Machinery*, Vol. 19, No. 7, pp. 395–404, July 1976.

10 D.J. Farber and K.C. Larson, *The system architecture of the distributed computer system—The communications system*, presented at the Symposium on Computer Networks, Polytechnic Institute of Brooklyn, New York, April 1972.

11 V. Cerf, A. McKenzie, R. Scantlebury, and H. Zimmermann, Proposal for an International End to End Protocol, *ACM SIGCOMM Computer Communications Review*, Vol. 6, No. 1, pp. 63–89, January 1976.

12 J. Postel, *Internet Protocol, RFC 791*, September 1981.

13 J. Postel, *Internet Control Message Protocol, RFC 792*, September 1981.

14 J. Postel, *User Datagram Protocol, RFC 768*, August 1980.

15 J. Postel, *Transmission Control Protocol, RFC 793*, September 1981.

16 R. Braden, Ed., *Requirements for Internet Hosts—Communication Layers, RFC 1122*, October 1989.

17 R. Braden, Ed., *Requirements for Internet Hosts—Applications and Support, RFC 1123*, October 1989.

18 J. Postel, Ed., *IAB Official Protocol Standards, RFC 1250*, August 1991.

19 P. Almquist, Ed., *Router Requirements, RFC* in progress, check current issue of *IAB Official Protocol Standards* for reference; probable date of issue is second quarter, 1992.

20 P. Almquist, *Type Of Service in the Internet Protocol Suite, RFC* in progress, check current issue of *IAB Official Protocol Standards* for reference; probable date of issue is second quarter, 1992.

21 V. Cerf, *IAB Recommended Policy on Distributed Internet Identifier Assignment and IAB Recommended Policy Change to Internet "Connected Status," RFC 1174*, August 1990.

22 J. Mogul and J. Postel, *Internet Standard Subnetting Procedure, RFC 950*, August 1985.

23 J. Mogul, *Broadcasting Internet Datagrams in the Presence of Subnets, RFC 922*, October 1984.

24 S. Deering, *Host Extensions for IP Multicasting, RFC 1112*, August 1989.

25 J. Postel, C. Sunshine, and D. Cohen, *The ARPA Internet Protocol, Computer Networks*, Vol. 5, No. 4, July 1981.

26 B. Leiner, J. Postel, R. Cole, and D. Mills, *The DARPA Internet Protocol Suite, Proceedings INFOCOM 85*, IEEE, Washington, DC, March 1985.Also in *IEEE Communications Magazine*, March 1985.

27 V.G. Cerf and R.E. Lyons, Military Requirements for Packet Switched Networks and Their Implications for Protocol Standardization, *EASCON 1982 Proceedings*. Also, *Proceedings of the SHAPE Technology Center Symposium of the Interoperability of Automated Data Systems*, November 1982.

28 V.G. Cerf and E. Cain, The DOD Internet Architecture Model, *Proceedings of the SHAPE Technology Center Symposium on the Interoperability of Automated Data Systems*, November 1982. Also *Computer Networks*, Vol. 7, No. 5, October 1983.

29 W. Plummer, *An Ethernet Address Resolution Protocol, RFC 826*, September 1982.

30 R. Finlayson, T. Mann, J. Mogul, and M. Theimer, *A Reverse Address Resolution Protocol, RFC 903*, June 1984.

31 P. Mockapetris, *Domain Names—Concepts and Facilities, RFC 1034*, November 1987.

32 P. Mockapetris, *Domain Names—Implementations and Specifications, RFC 1035*, November 1987.

33 R. Braden, D. Borman, and C. Partridge, *Computing the Internet Checksum, RFC 1071*, September 1988.

34 T. Mallory and A. Kullberg, *Incremental Updating of the Internet Checksum, RFC 1141*, January 1980.

35 J. Mogul, *Broadcasting Internet Datagrams, RFC 919*, October 1984.

36 J. Forgie, *ST-A Proposed Internet Stream Protocol*, Internet Experiment Note 119, September 1979.

37 R. Braden, *Requirements for Internet Gateways, RFC 1009*, June 1987.

38 D. Waitzman, C. Partridge, and S. Deering, *Distance Vector Multicast Routing Protocol, RFC 1075*, November 1988.

39 C. Topolcic, *Experimental Internet Stream Protocol Version 2 (ST-II), RFC 1190*, October 1990.

40 M. Lottor, *Internet Growth (1981–1991), RFC 1296*, January 1992

41 M. Stahl, *Domain Administrators Guide, RFC 1032*, November 1987.

42 M. Lottor, *Domain Administrators Operations Guide, RFC 1033*, November 1987.

43 W. Prue and J. Postel, *A Queueing Algorithm to Provide Type Of Service for IP Links, RFC 1046*, February 1988.

44 D.D. Clark, *IP Datagram Reassembly Algorithms, RFC 815*, July 1982.

45 J.K. Reynolds and J.B. Postel, *Assigned Numbers, RFC 1060*, March 1990.

46 S. Kirkpatrick, M. Recker, and M. Stahl, *Internet Numbers, RFC 1166*, July 1990.

47 J. Mogul, *Path MTU Discovery, RFC 1191*, November 1990.

48 S. Kent, *Basic Security Option, RFC 1108*, November 1991.

49 V. Jacobson, R. Braden, and L. Zhang, *TCP Extension for High-Speed Paths, RFC 1185*, October 1990.

50 V. Jacobson and R. Braden, *TCP Extensions for Long-Delay Paths, RFC 1072*, October 1988.

51 V. Strazisar, *How to Build a Gateway*, IEN 109, Bolt Beranek and Newman, August 1979.

52 C.L. Hedrick, *Routing Information Protocol, RFC 1058*, June 1988.

53 E. Rosen, *Exterior Gateway Protocol (EGP), RFC 827*, October 1982.

54 D. Mills, *Exterior Gateway Protocol Formal Specification, RFC 904*, April 1984.

55 D. Cheriton, *Versatile Message Transaction Protocol: Protocol Specification (VMTP), RFC 1045*, February 1988.

56 P. Almquist, *Router Requirements, RFC* in progress, February 1992.

57 J.M. McQuillan, I. Richer, and E. Rosen, The New Routing Algorithm for the ARPANET, *IEEE Transactions on Communications*, Vol. COM-28, No. 5, pp. 711–719, May 1980.

58 J. Moy, *OSPF Version 2, RFC 1247*, July 1991.

59 R. Callon, *Use of OSI IS-IS for Routing in TCP/IP and Dual Environments,* *RFC 1195,* December 1990.

60 K. Lougheed and Y. Rekhter, A *Border Gateway Protocol 3 (BGP-3),* *RFC 1267,* October 1991.

61 Y. Rekhter and P. Gross , Eds., *Application of the Border Gateway Protocol in the Internet, RFC 1268,* October 1991.

62 Y. Rekhter, Ed., *Experience with the BGP Protocol, RFC 1266,* October 1991.

63 Y. Rekhter, Ed., *BGP Protocol Analysis, RFC 1265,* October 1991.

64 J. Moy, Ed., *Experience with the OSPF Protocol, RFC 1246,* July 1991.

65 T. Socolofsky and C. Kale, *A TCP/IP Tutorial, RFC 1180,* January 1991.

66 D. Oran, *OSI IS-IS Intra-Domain Routing Protocol, RFC 1142,* February 1990 (ISO DP 10589)

67 S. Hares, *Administrative Domains and Routing Domains—A Model for Routing in the Internet, RFC 1136,* December 1989.

68 D.E. Estrin, *Policy Requirements for Inter-Administrative Domain Routing, RFC 1125,* November 1989.

69 Y. Rehkter, *The NSFNET Backbone SPF-based Interior Gateway Protocol, RFC 1074,* October 1988.

70 S.E. Deering, Ed., *ICMP Router Discovery Messages, RFC 1256,* September 1991.

71 W. Prue and J. Postel, *Something a Host Could Do with Source Quench: The Source Quench Introduced Delay (SQUID), RFC 1016,* July 1987.

72 A. McKenzie, *Some Comments on SQUID, RFC 1018,* August 1987.

73 M. Little, *Goals and Functional Requirements for Inter-Autonomous System Routing, RFC 1126,* October 1989.

74 R. Hinden, *The DARPA Internet Gateway, RFC 823,* September 1982.

75 B. Croft and J. Gilmore, *BOOTP—UDP Bootstrap Protocol, RFC 951,* September 1985

76 J.K. Reynolds, *BOOTP Vendor Information Extensions, RFC 1084,* December 1988.

77 D. Mills, *Network Time Protocol (Version 2) Specification and Implementation, RFC 1119,* September 1989.

78 J. Mogul and J. Postel, *Internet Standard Subnetting Procedure, RFC 950*, August 1985.

79 J. Mogul, *Internet Subnets, RFC 917*, October 1984.

80 A. Mankin, G. Hollingsworth, G. Reichlen, K. Thompson, and R. Wilder, *Evaluation of Internet Performance—FY89*, Technical report MTR-89W00216, MITRE Corporation, February 1990.

81 G. Finn, A Connectionless Congestion Control Algorithm, *Computer Communications Review*, Vol. 19, No. 5, Special Interest Group on Communication, Association for Computing Machinery, October 1989.

82 Y. Dalal, C. Sunshine, Connection Management in Transport Protocols, *Computer Networks*, Vol. 2, No. 6, pp. 454–473, December 1978.

83 R. Tomlinson, Selecting Sequence Numbers, *Proceedings ACM SIGOPS/SIGCOMM Interprocess Communication Workshop*, March 1975, pp. 11–23. These proceedings also appeared in *ACM Operating Systems Review*, Vol. 9, No. 3, July 1975.

84 Y. Dalal, More on Selecting Sequence Numbers, *Proceedings ACM SIGOPS/SIGCOMM Interprocess Communication Workshop*, March 1975, pp. 25–36. These proceedings also appeared in *ACM Operating Systems Review*, Vol. 9, No. 3, July 1975.

85 V. Cerf, An Assessment of ARPANET Protocols, in *Proceedings of the Jerusalem Conference on Information Technology*, 1974. Also in J. McQuillan and V. Cerf, *A Practical View of Computer Communication Protocols*, IEEE Computer Society, 1978, pp. 92–110.

86 D.D. Clark, *Window and Acknowledgment Strategy in TCP, RFC 813*, July 1982.

87 Z. Wang and J. Crowcroft, Eliminating Periodic Packet Losses in the 4.3-Tahoe BSD TCP Congestion Control Algorithm, *Computer Communication Review*, ACM SIGCOMM, Vol. 22, No. 2, pp. 9–16, April 1992.

88 L. Zhang, S. Shenker, and D. Clark, Observations on the Dynamics of a Congestion Control Algorithm: the Effects of Two-Way Traffic, *Proceedings ACM SIGCOMM'91*, September 1991.

89 Z. Wang and J. Crowcroft, A New Congestion Control Scheme: Slow Start and Search (Tri-S), *Computer Communication Review*, ACM SIGCOMM, Vol. 21, No. 1, January 1991.

90 Van Jacobson, Congestion Avoidance and Control, in *Proceedings ACM SIGCOMM'88*, August 1988, pp. 314–329.

91   P. Karn and C. Partridge, Round-Trip Time Estimation, in *Proceedings ACM SIGCOMM'87*, August 1987.

92   J. Nagle, *Congestion Control in IP/TCP, RFC 896*, January 1984.

APPENDIX

Port Numbers

This list is taken from *RFC 1060* (J.K. Reynolds and J.B. Postel, *Assigned Numbers, RFC 1060*, March 1990). Readers are urged to seek the most recent issue of *Assigned Numbers* for a more accurate survey.

Ports are used in the TCP to name the ends of logical connections which carry long-term conversations. For the purpose of providing services to unknown callers, a service contact port is defined. This list specifies the port used by the server process as its contact port. The contact port is sometimes called the "well-known port." To the extent possible, these same port assignments are used with the UDP. The assigned ports use a small portion of the possible port numbers. The assigned ports have all except the low order eight bits cleared to zero. The low order eight bits are specified here.

Decimal	Keyword	Description
0		Reserved
1	TCPMUX	TCP Port Service Multiplexer
2-4		Unassigned
5	RJE	Remote Job Entry
7	ECHO	Echo
9	DISCARD	Discard
11	USERS	Active Users
13	DAYTIME	Daytime
15		Unassigned
17	QUOTE	Quote of the Day
19	CHARGEN	Character Generator
20	FTP-DATA	File Transfer [Default Data]
21	FTP	File Transfer [Control]
23	TELNET	Telnet
25	SMTP	Simple Mail Transfer
27	NSW-FE	NSW User System FE
29	MSG-ICP	MSG ICP
31	MSG-AUTH	MSG Authentication
33	DSP	Display Support Protocol
35		any private printer server
37	TIME	Time
39	RLP	Resource Location Protocol
41	GRAPHICS	Graphics
42	NAMESERVER	Host Name Server

Decimal	Keyword	Description
43	NICNAME	Who Is
44	MPM-FLAGS	MPM FLAGS Protocol
45	MPM	Message Processing Module [recv]
46	MPM-SND	MPM [default send]
47	NI-FTP	NI FTP
49	LOGIN	Login Host Protocol
51	LA-MAINT	IMP Logical Address Maintenance
53	DOMAIN	Domain Name Server
55	ISI-GL	ISI Graphics Language
57		any private terminal access
59		any private file service
61	NI-MAIL	NI MAIL
63	VIA-FTP	VIA Systems - FTP
65	TACACS-DS	TACACS-Database Service
67	BOOTPS	Bootstrap Protocol Server
68	BOOTPC	Bootstrap Protocol Client
69	TFTP	Trivial File Transfer
71	NETRJS-1	Remote Job Service
72	NETRJS-2	Remote Job Service
73	NETRJS-3	Remote Job Service
74	NETRJS-4	Remote Job Service
75		any private dial out service
77		any private RJE service
79	FINGER	Finger
81	HOSTS2-NS	HOSTS2 Name Server
83	MIT-ML-DEV	MIT ML Device
85	MIT-ML-DEV 0	MIT ML Device
87		any private terminal link
89	SU-MIT-TG	SU/MIT Telnet Gateway
91	MIT-DOV	MIT Dover Spooler
93	DCP	Device Control Protocol
95	SUPDUP	SUPDUP
97	SWIFT-RVF	Swift Remote Vitural File Protocol
98	TACNEWS	TAC News
99	METAGRAM	Metagram Relay
101	HOSTNAME	NIC Host Name Server
102	ISO-TSAP	ISO-TSAP
103	X400	X400
104	X400-SND	X400-SND
105	CSNET-NS	Mailbox Name Nameserver
107	RTELNET	Remote Telnet Service
109	POP2	Post Office Protocol - Version 2
110	POP3	Post Office Protocol - Version 3
111	SUNRPC	SUN Remote Procedure Call
113	AUTH	Authentication Service
115	SFTP	Simple File Transfer Protocol
117	UUCP-PATH	UUCP Path Service

Decimal	Keyword	Description
119	NNTP	Network News Transfer Protocol
121	ERPC	Encore Expedited Remote Proc. Call
123	NTP	Network Time Protocol
125	LOCUS-MAP	Locus PC-Interface Net Map Server
127	LOCUS-CON	Locus PC-Interface Conn Server
129	PWDGEN	Password Generator Protocol
130	CISCO-FNA	CISCO FNATIVE
131	CISCO-TNA	CISCO TNATIVE
132	CISCO-SYS	CISCO SYSMAINT
133	STATSRV	Statistics Service
134	INGRES-NET	INGRES-NET Service
135	LOC-SRV	Location Service
136	PROFILE	PROFILE Naming System
137	NETBIOS-NS	NETBIOS Name Service
138	NETBIOS-DGM	NETBIOS Datagram Service
139	NETBIOS-SSN	NETBIOS Session Service
140	EMFIS-DATA	EMFIS Data Service
141	EMFIS-CNTL	EMFIS Control Service
142	BL-IDM	Britton-Lee IDM
143	IMAP2	Interim Mail Access Protocol v2
144	NEWS	NewS
145	UAAC	UAAC Protocol
146	ISO-TP0	ISO-IP0
147	ISO-IP	ISO-IP
148	CRONUS	CRONUS-SUPPORT
149	AED-512	AED 512 Emulation Service
150	SQL-NET	SQL-NET
151	HEMS	HEMS
152	BFTP	Background File Transfer Program
153	SGMP	SGMP
154	NETSC-PROD	NETSC
155	NETSC-DEV	NETSC
156	SQLSRV	SQL Service
157	KNET-CMP	KNET/VM Command/Message Protocol
158	PCMail-SRV	PCMail Server
159	NSS-Routing	NSS-Routing
160	SGMP-TRAPS	SGMP-TRAPS
161	SNMP	SNMP
162	SNMPTRAP	SNMPTRAP
163	CMIP-Manage	CMIP/TCP Manager
164	CMIP-Agent	CMIP/TCP Agent
165	XNS-Courier	Xerox
166	S-Net	Sirius Systems
167	NAMP	NAMP
168	RSVD	RSVD
169	SEND	SEND
170	Print-SRV	Network PostScript

Decimal	Keyword	Description
171	Multiplex	Network Innovations Multiplex
172	CL/1	Network Innovations CL/1
173	Xyplex-MUX	Xyplex
174	MAILQ	MAILQ
175	VMNET	VMNET
176	GENRAD-MUX	GENRAD-MUX
177	XDMCP	X Display Manager Control Protocol
178	NextStep	NextStep Window Server
179	BGP	Border Gateway Protocol
180	RIS	Intergraph
181	Unify	Unify
182	Unisys-Cam	Unisys-Cam
183	OCBinder	OCBinder
184	OCServer	OCServer
185	Remote-KIS	Remote-KIS
186	KIS	KIS Protocol
187	ACI	Application Communication Interface
188	MUMPS	MUMPS
189	QFT	Queued File Transport
190	GACP	Gateway Access Control Protocol
191	Prospero	Prospero
192	OSU-NMS	OSU Network Monitoring System
193	SRMP	Spider Remote Monitoring Protocol
194	IRC	Internet Relay Chat Protocol
195	DN6-NLM-AUD	DNSIX Network Level Module Audit
196	DN6-SMM-RED	DNSIX Session Mgt Module Audit Redirect
197	DLS	Directory Location Service
198	DLS-Mon	Directory Location Service Monitor
198-200	Unassigned	
201	AT-RMTP	AppleTalk Routing Maintenance
202	AT-NBP	AppleTalk Name Binding
203	AT-3	AppleTalk Unused
204	AT-ECHO	AppleTalk Echo
205	AT-5	AppleTalk Unused
206	AT-ZIS	AppleTalk Zone Information
207	AT-7	AppleTalk Unused
208	AT-8	AppleTalk Unused
209-223		Unassigned
224-241		Reserved
243	SUR-MEAS	Survey Measurement
245	LINK	LINK
246	DSP3270	Display Systems Protocol
247-255		Reserved

UNIX Ports

By convention, ports in the range 256 to 1024 are used for "Unix Standard" services.

Listed here are some of the normal uses of these port numbers.

Service name	Port/ Protocol	Description
echo	7/tcp	
discard	9/tcp	sink null
systat	11/tcp	users
daytime	13/tcp	
netstat	15/tcp	
qotd	17/tcp	quote
chargen	19/tcp	ttytst source
ftp-data	20/tcp	
ftp	21/tcp	
telnet	23/tcp	
smtp	25/tcp	mail
time	37/tcp	timserver
name	42/tcp	nameserver
whois	43/tcp	nicname
nameserver	53/tcp	domain
apts	57/tcp	any private terminal service
apfs	59/tcp	any private file service
rje	77/tcp	netrjs
finger	79/tcp	
link	87/tcp	ttylink
supdup	95/tcp	
newacct	100/tcp	[unauthorized use]
hostnames	101/tcp	hostname
iso-tsap	102/tcp	tsap
x400	103/tcp	
x400-snd	104/tcp	
csnet-ns	105/tcp	CSNET Name Service
pop-2	109/tcp	pop postoffice
sunrpc	111/tcp	
auth	113/tcp	authentication
sftp	115/tcp	
uucp-path	117/tcp	
nntp	119/tcp	usenet readnews untp
ntp	123/tcp	network time protocol
statsrv	133/tcp	
profile	136/tcp	
NeWS	144/tcp	news
print-srv	170/tcp	
exec	512/tcp	remote process execution;authentication performed using passwords and UNIX login names
login	513/tcp	remote login á la Telnet; automatic authentication performed based on privileged port numbers and distributed databases that identify "authentication domains"
cmd	514/tcp	like exec, but automatic authentication is performed as for login server
printer	515/tcp	spooler

Service name	Port/Protocol	Description
efs	520/tcp	extended filename server
tempo	526/tcp	newdate
courier	530/tcp	rpc
conference	531/tcp	chat
netnews	532/tcp	readnews
uucp	540/tcp	uucpd
klogin	543/tcp	
kshell	544/tcp	krcmd
dsf	555/tcp	
remotefs	556/tcp	rfs server
chshell	562/tcp	chcmd
meter	570/tcp	demon
pcserver	600/tcp	Sun IPC server
nqs	607/tcp	nqs
mdqs	666/tcp	
rfile	750/tcp	
pump	751/tcp	
qrh	752/tcp	
rrh	753/tcp	
tell	754/tcp	send
nlogin	758/tcp	
con	759/tcp	
ns	760/tcp	
rxe	761/tcp	
quotad	762/tcp	
cycleserv	763/tcp	
omserv	764/tcp	
webster	765/tcp	
phonebook	767/tcp	phone
vid	769/tcp	
rtip	771/tcp	
cycleserv2	772/tcp	
submit	773/tcp	
rpasswd	774/tcp	
entomb	775/tcp	
wpages	776/tcp	
wpgs	780/tcp	
mdbs_daemon	800/tcp	
device	801/tcp	
maitrd	997/tcp	
busboy	998/tcp	
garcon	999/tcp	
blackjack	1025/tcp	network blackjack
bbn-mmc	1347/tcp	multi media conferencing
bbn-mmx	1348/tcp	multi media conferencing
orasrv	1525/tcp	oracle
ingreslock	1524/tcp	

Service name	Port/ Protocol	Description
issd	1600/tcp	
nkd	1650/tcp	
dc	2001/tcp	
mailbox	2004/tcp	
berknet	2005/tcp	
invokator	2006/tcp	
dectalk	2007/tcp	
conf	2008/tcp	
news	2009/tcp	
search	2010/tcp	
raid-cc	2011/tcp	raid
ttyinfo	2012/tcp	
raid-am	2013/tcp	
troff	2014/tcp	
cypress	2015/tcp	
cypress-stat	2017/tcp	
terminaldb	2018/tcp	
whosockami	2019/tcp	
servexec	2021/tcp	
down	2022/tcp	
ellpack	2025/tcp	
shadowserver	2027/tcp	
submitserver	2028/tcp	
device2	2030/tcp	
blackboard	2032/tcp	
glogger	2033/tcp	
scoremgr	2034/tcp	
imsldoc	2035/tcp	
objectmanager	2038/tcp	
lam	2040/tcp	
interbase	2041/tcp	
isis	2042/tcp	
rimsl	2044/tcp	
dls	2047/tcp	
dls-monitor	2048/tcp	
shilp	2049/tcp	
NSWS	3049/tcp	
rfa	4672/tcp	remote file access server
commplex-main	5000/tcp	
commplex-link	5001/tcp	
padl2sim	5236/tcp	
man	9535/tcp	
UDP PORT ASSIGNMENTS		
echo	7/udp	
discard	9/udp	sink null
systat	11/udp	users
daytime	13/udp	

Service name	Port/Protocol	Description
netstat	15/udp	
qotd	17/udp	quote
chargen	19/udp	ttytst source
time	37/udp	timserver
rlp	39/udp	resource
name	42/udp	nameserver
whois	43/udp	nicname
nameserver	53/udp	domain
bootps	67/udp	bootp
bootpc	68/udp	
tftp	69/udp	
sunrpc	111/udp	
erpc	121/udp	
ntp	123/udp	
statsrv	133/udp	
profile	136/udp	
snmp	161/udp	
snmp-trap	162/udp	
at-rtmp	201/udp	
at-nbp	202/udp	
at-3	203/udp	
at-echo	204/udp	
at-5	205/udp	
at-zis	206/udp	
at-7	207/udp	
at-8	208/udp	
biff	512/udp	used by mail system to notify users of new mail received; currentlyreceives messages only from processes on the same machine
who	513/udp	maintains data bases showing who's logged in to machines on a local net and the load average of the machine
syslog	514/udp	
talk	517/udp	like tenex link, but across machine - unfortunately, doesn't use link protocol (this is actually just a rendezvous port from which a tcp connection is established)
ntalk	518/udp	
utime	519/udp	unixtime
router	520/udp	local routing process (on site); uses variant of Xerox NS routing information protocol
timed	525/udp	timeserver
netwall	533/udp	for emergency broadcasts
new-rwho	550/udp	new-who
rmonitor	560/udp	rmonitord
monitor	561/udp	
meter	571/udp	udemon
elcsd	704/udp	errlog copy/server daemon
loadav	750/udp	
vid	769/udp	

Service name	Port/Protocol	Description
cadlock	770/udp	
notify	773/udp	
acmaint_dbd	774/udp	
acmaint_transd	775/udp	
wpages	776/udp	
puparp	998/udp	
applix	999/udp	Applix ac
puprouter	999/udp	
cadlock	1000/udp	
hermes	1248/udp	
wizard	2001/udp	curry
globe	2002/udp	
emce	2004/udp	CCWS mm conf
oracle	2005/udp	
raid-cc	2006/udp	raid
raid-am	2007/udp	
terminaldb	2008/udp	
whosockami	2009/udp	
pipe_server	2010/udp	
servserv	2011/udp	
raid-ac	2012/udp	
raid-cd	2013/udp	
raid-sf	2014/udp	
raid-cs	2015/udp	
bootserver	2016/udp	
bootclient	2017/udp	
rellpack	2018/udp	
about	2019/udp	
xinupageserver	2020/udp	
xinuexpansion1	2021/udp	
xinuexpansion2	2022/udp	
xinuexpansion3	2023/udp	
xinuexpansion4	2024/udp	
xribs	2025/udp	
scrabble	2026/udp	
isis	2042/udp	
isis-bcast	2043/udp	
rimsl	2044/udp	
cdfunc	2045/udp	
sdfunc	2046/udp	
dls	2047/udp	
shilp	2049/udp	
rmonitor_secure	5145/udp	
xdsxdm	6558/udp	
isode-dua	17007/udp	

CHAPTER 5 ❑ ❑ ❑ ❑

Routing Protocols

RADIA PERLMAN

CONTENTS

157

A routing protocol keeps track of how to forward data through the network from a source to a destination. As the Internet has enjoyed explosive growth, we have seen extensive research into and deployment of new routing technologies. The tasks a modern routing protocol faces are daunting: not only must it determine the optimal path through the network, but it must do so in the face of administrative policies and intermittent outages.

5.1   INTRODUCTION

This chapter explains what routing protocols do and how there got to be so many of them. People talk about various types of routing protocols, which will be explained. There are intradomain and interdomain protocols, distance vector, link state, and path vector protocols. There are devices known as *bridges* that have their own forms of routing protocols. There are also many protocols in the Network Layer, for instance CLNP, IP, ES-IS, ARP, and X.25, that are not routing protocols. This chapter attempts to explain how all these protocols fit together. The main focus of this chapter is on routing protocols,[1] so although the other pieces of the Network Layer are mentioned, they are not described in detail. The concepts behind the routing protocols are discussed in detail, but the exact details of individual routing protocols are not stressed. For the latest packet formats and other protocol details, the reader is referred to the current specifications.

In the OSI Reference Model,[2] the function of the Network Layer is to allow communication between a source and a destination that are not directly connected. Instead, they are connected by a sequence of packet switches that are, in turn, connected by various types of technologies. The packet switches must cooperate to calculate paths through the network. The ISO terminology for packet switches in the Network Layer is *Network Layer Relays*. Most people refer to them as *routers*. The ISO terminology for packet switches in the Data Link Layer is *Data Link Layer relays*. Most people refer to these as *bridges*. *Physical layer relays* are known as *repeaters*. It is not exactly clear what it means for a packet switch to operate in one layer rather than another. In reality, the definition of the layer in which a protocol operates depends only upon which type of committee (network or Data Link Layer) adopted the standard. Bridges, like routers, do routing; however, the routing protocols used by bridges tend to be simpler than those used by routers.

This chapter discusses the main types of routing protocols prevalent in networks today. The remainder of the introduction describes where routing protocols fit into the Network Layer. It discusses the service provided by the Network Layer, components of the Network Layer, and types of routing protocols. The remainder of the chapter discusses various aspects of routing protocols, including distance vector, link state, bridge spanning tree, bridge source routing, multiprotocol routing, and interdomain routing.

5.1.1 Connection-Oriented Versus Connectionless Service

There are two basic models for the type of service the network might provide. One is known as *connection-oriented*, and the other is known as *connectionless*. The connection-oriented service is similar to the telephone network. When node *A* wishes to communicate with node *B*, it goes through a conversation set-up procedure. Once the network informs *A* that the conversation has been successfully established, *A* can start transmitting data to *B*. Proponents of the connection-oriented service tend to believe the network should also provide reliable service, meaning that the network takes the responsibility of delivering all packets transmitted by *A* to *B* in order, without loss, corruption, or duplication. Connectionless service is similar to the postal service. No set-up procedure occurs. Instead, each piece of data is individually addressed and launched into the network, which makes its best effort to deliver it to the destination. Although proponents of both philosophies tend to fervently believe in their approaches, there are technical advantages that can be claimed for either, so both types of networks exist.

A connection-oriented service is used as follows:

1   Send a *call request* packet, which contains the complete addresses of the source and destination.

2   Receive, from the network, notification that the call has been successfully set up, together with a short call identifier.

3   Send data packets, identified by the call identifier (the source and destination addresses do not appear).

4   Send a *clear request* packet, to notify the network to terminate the call.

A connectionless service is used simply by transmitting data packets that have the complete source and destination addresses.

5.1.2 Components of the Network Layer Protocol

The type of protocol that claims to be a Network Layer Protocol tends to view the network as a black box, and describes the interface only to the network. Three examples are X.25, IP,[3] and CLNP.[4] IP is the Internet community's protocol. X.25 was developed by CCITT, and has been adopted by ISO. CLNP has also been adopted by ISO. The adoption of two protocols by ISO was the result of the wars between the connectionless and the connection-oriented camps. X.25 is the connection-oriented protocol, and CLNP is the connectionless protocol. IP is also a connectionless protocol. CLNP is derived from IP, and the main difference is the size of the addresses. IP's addresses are 4 octets, whereas CLNP's addresses are variable length, with a maximum of 20 octets.

IP and CLNP basically consist of a data packet that includes the source and destination addresses, fragmentation and reassembly information, and various options, such as allowing the source to include a route in the packet. X.25 basically consists of data packets and a call set-up packet, which sets up a call and assigns the conversation a 12-bit number. There are other control packets in X.25 for informing about the status of calls and hanging up calls. Unlike IP and CLNP, X.25 data packets do not require a source or destination address. Instead they are identified by the 12-bit number assigned to the conversation. Also, since X.25 attempts to provide reliable service, each data packet contains a message number, and must be acknowledged.

Another piece of the Network Layer consists of neighbor discovery. The purpose of this is to allow nodes to attach to the network and automatically be assimilated. X.25 has no such function. It is assumed that assimilating a new subscriber requires a procedure in which information about the new subscriber is manually configured into the network. ISO's neighbor discovery protocol that goes along with CLNP is known as ES-IS[5] (for End System to Intermediate System). IP's neighbor discovery protocol consists of ARP[6] and ICMP.[7] Neighbor discovery allows end nodes to announce themselves to routers and vice versa, and for nodes on a common link (such as a LAN) to discover the Data Link Layer address of their Network Layer neighbors. The major difference between ES-IS and ARP is that ARP requires a portion of the address to be reserved for distinguishing nodes on one link from nodes on other links. The implications of this are discussed below.

The third piece of the Network Layer consists of the routing protocol. A packet switch needs a "forwarding table," which consists of a mapping from a destination address to a forwarding direction. For instance, a packet switch with 5 ports might have an entry mapping destination D to port 3. If port 3 is a multiaccess link, for instance a LAN, the forwarding table must not only specify the port, but also must specify an address on that port to which the packet should be forwarded. Early networks had human beings maintaining the forwarding table. The purpose of a routing protocol is for the routers to cooperate to maintain their forwarding tables without human intervention. They must calculate good paths, taking advantage of new routers and links as they are added to the network, and route around failed links or routers.

The remainder of this chapter discusses the different types of routing protocols available, and also discusses the impact of addressing on routing.

5.1.3   Types of Routing Protocols

The most popular types of routing protocols are *distance vector* and *link state*. There are many routing protocols based on distance vector routing. Examples are the original ARPANET routing algorithm, RIP, IGRP (Cisco's proprietary routing protocol), DECnet Phases III and IV, RTMP (AppleTalk's routing protocol), and variants of RIP used for routing IPX and XNS.[8, 9] (Indeed, the RIP for XNS was the first, and the other RIPs are descendents.) Examples of link state routing protocols are the replacement routing protocol for the ARPANET, DECnet Phase V (which has been adopted by ISO and is known as IS-IS), and OSPF. In addition to distance vector and link state protocols, there are other types of routing protocols. Bridges use spanning tree routing and bridge source routing. These types of protocols are discussed in detail in later sections.

Networks are often partitioned into *domains*, also known as *autonomous systems*. Some people believe* that a different type of routing should occur between domains. The type of protocol that routes between domains is known in the ISO community as an *interdomain routing protocol*. In the IP community it is known as an *exterior gateway protocol* (EGP). Within domains the routing protocol is known as an *intradomain routing protocol* (the ISO name), or *interior gateway protocol* (IGP, the IP name).

Interdomain routing can be done with manual configuration (after all, one of the arguments behind using a different type of routing protocol for interdomain routing is that one does not trust routers in a different domain, and all routing protocols, including those being proposed for interdomain routing, require the cooperation of all interdomain routers). Theoretically the interdomain routers could use the same sort of distance vector or link state routing protocol designed for intradomain routing, but the proponents of the new interdomain routing protocol standards believe a much more flexible form of routing is required to accommodate various sorts of *policy routing*.[10]

Interdomain routing protocols for IP include EGP (the original IP interdomain routing protocol, which is being replaced by BGP), BGP (the replacement of EGP which will greatly surprise anyone who habitually skips the first phrase in a sentence), and IDPR, a fancier and higher-functionality interdomain routing protocol that is unlikely to replace BGP, but is considered important for its work on policy routing. The only proposed interdomain routing protocol for CLNP is IDRP, which is similar to BGP but has had more features added. Some people (including me) advocate adding IP support to IDRP, so that both IP and CLNP can be routed with one interdomain routing protocol.

5.2 DISTANCE VECTOR ROUTING

Distance vector protocols are sometimes called Bellman–Ford, or Ford–Fulkerson algorithms after early work in the field.[11] In a distance vector protocol, each router is responsible for keeping track and informing its neighbors of its distance to each destination. The router computes its distance to a destination based on its neighbors' distance to the destination. The only information a router must know *a priori* is its own ID and the cost of its links to each neighbor. Suppose a router R with 5 ports has been configured with costs $c1$, $c2$, $c3$, $c4$, and $c5$ for each of the ports, respectively. Suppose the neighbor on port 1 informs R that it is $d1$ from some destination D. The neighbor on port 2 informs R that it is $d2$ from D, and so forth, with the neighbor on port 5 informing R that it is $d5$ from D. R

---

* Indeed, I had originally written "people believe" and not "some people believe" in the apparently mistaken belief that I was the only person who was not convinced that interdomain routing required a totally new type of routing protocol. However, to my delight, one of the reviewers suggested I change it to "some people" because that reviewer is also not convinced.

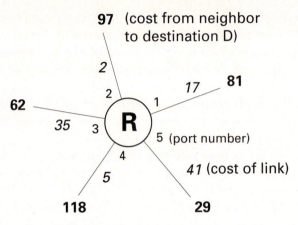

Figure 5.1   Example of distance vector routing

then can figure out its own distance to *D*. If *R* is at *D*, then *R*'s distance to *D* is 0. Otherwise, *R*'s distance to *D* is the minimum of $(c_i + d_i)$, for $i = 1, ..., 5$. If *R* receives a packet addressed to destination *D*, *R* should forward it through port *i*. Consider an example, shown in Figure 5.1.

The path from *R* to *D* through port 1 has cost 17+81, or 98. The path from *R* to *D* through port 2 has cost 2+97, or 99. The path from *R* to *D* through port 3 is 35+62, or 97. The path from *R* to *D* through port 4 is 5+118, or 123. The path from *R* to *D* through port 5 is 41+29, or 70. Therefore, the best choice for *R* to send data toward *D* is to forward the packet through port 5. *R* will list 70 in its distance vector as its distance to *D*, and will list port 5 in its forwarding table as its direction of forwarding to destination *D*.

Distance vector protocols have generally lower performance than link state protocols because of their speed of convergence. Distance vector protocols adapt to changes in topology less quickly than do link state protocols, and until the protocol adapts to a change in topology, routing can be disrupted.

The most serious reason for the slow convergence of distance vector routing is known as the *count-to-infinity* problem, illustrated in the very simple network shown in Figure 5.1.

Let us consider *A*, *B*, and *C*'s opinions of their distance to *C*, and let us assume that the cost of each link is 1 (which is the same as routing based on minimizing the number of hops). *C* will consider itself 0 from the destination (itself). *B*, based on hearing its right-hand neighbor's report of a path of length 0 to the destination, will assume itself to be 1 from *C*. *A*, based on *B*'s report of being 1 from *C*, will assume itself to be 2 from *C*.

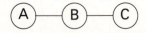

So far everything is wonderful. If *A* receives a packet with destination address *C*, it will forward it to *B*, which will forward the packet to *C*, which, one hopes, will be delighted to receive it. Now assume that *C* fails, or that the link to *C* fails. *B* no longer has a neighbor reporting a path to *C* of cost 0, but it still has a neighbor (*A*) reporting a path to *C* of cost 2. Therefore *B* will decide that it is now 3 from *C*, and that if it were to receive a packet for *C*, it should forward the packet toward *A*. When *B* reports its new distance vector to *A*, *A* will conclude itself to now be 4 from *C*, and will still forward packets for *C* toward *B*. This process repeats until *A* and *B* count to a large enough value that they conclude *C* is indeed not reachable. Until they reach the agreed-upon maximum value, packets for *C* will loop between *A* and *B*, further slowing down the convergence of the routing protocol, since the looping data packets will consume some CPU time and bandwidth.

An enhancement to distance vector routing that most protocols use is known as *split horizon*. The rule in split horizon routing is that the distance to a destination *D* is not reported on the link that is being used to forward packets destined for *D*. In the example above, *A* would not have informed *B* that *A* could reach *C*. When *B*'s link to *C* broke, *B* would have had to conclude *C* was unreachable. When *B* informed *A* that *C* was unreachable, *A* would then also have concluded that *C* was unreachable, and the protocol would converge without risking counting to infinity.

Sadly, split horizon works only on loops of two routers. Consider the topology shown below.

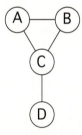

Consider everyone's distance to *D*. *D* will be 0 from *D*, *C* will be 1 from *D*, and *A* and *B* will each be 2 from *D*. The split horizon rule will result in neither *A* nor *B* telling *C* about its distance to *D*. If *D* were to crash, *C* would immediately conclude *D* to be unreachable, and would report that to *A* and *B*. However, this would not make *A* and *B* conclude *D* was unreachable. Depending on the timing of events, a variant of the following scenario would occur: *B* will conclude itself to be 3 from *D* (having heard from *A* that *A* was 2 from *D*). *B*, through split horizon, will inform *A* that *B* thinks *D* is unreachable, and *B* will inform *C* that *B* is 3 from *D*. *C* will now assume itself to be 4 from *D*, and that *D* is in the direction of *B*. *C* will inform *A* that *C* is 4 from *D*, and *A* will now conclude itself to be 5 from *D*. The count-to-infinity behavior will still exist, but it will involve a loop of three routers.

The count-to-infinity behavior is much worse if a cost function other than hops is used. If the cost of a link has a wider dynamic range than 1—for instance, if the cost of a link can range between 1 and 100—then the cost of a path might plausibly be as large as several thousand, and a loop of links with low costs would take considerable time to converge. Some distance vector protocols pass around hops, as well as a cost function. The best route is selected based on cost, which allows more intelligent route selection, but the destination is detected to be unreachable when the hops increase beyond a configured maximum value.

Another attempt to ameliorate the convergence problem is the use of a *holddown timer*, which is supposed to give the network time to propagate "bad news" about a route before routers switch to better routes.

All of these methods help the convergence problem somewhat, but link state routing protocols always converge more quickly than distance vector protocols. Even if the count-to-infinity problem were to be solved, a link state protocol still would converge more quickly because a routing protocol message can be instantly forwarded, so information can spread as quickly as a message can physically propagate through the network. In contrast, a router cannot pass information about a topological change downstream from the event until it has run its routing algorithm. There is other functionality that one gains with a link state protocol, like the ability to easily know the entire topology of the network.

Distance vector routing does have the advantage of simplicity, and it uses less memory in the routers than link state routing. But since the investment in routers is a very small fraction of the cost of a network, saving implementation investment or memory in the routers is no longer felt to be an adequate offset of the loss in functionality or of the increase in convergence time.

5.3   LINK STATE ROUTING

In a link state protocol, each router is responsible for determining the identities of its neighbors, and constructing a *link state packet* (LSP), which lists its neighbors and the cost of the link to each. The LSP is transmitted to all of the other routers, which are responsible for storing the most recently generated LSP from each other router. Given this information (the LSP database) it is possible to calculate routes.

The first deployed link state routing protocol was developed by BBN for the ARPANET.[12] Current link state routing protocols use the basic idea, which is for routers to generate LSPs, reliably flood them to all the other routers, and then compute routes, but improvements have been added. Many of the improvements were designed for IS-IS (DECnet Phase V). Another modern link state protocol is OSPF, which used many of the IS-IS ideas, given that it was designed after IS-IS, but which diverged somewhat from the IS-IS design. The improvements that have been made to link state routing protocols since the ARPANET routing protocol are:

1   The ARPANET method for distributing LSPs had excessive overhead and was not stable. A self-stabilizing protocol for LSP distribution that also required much less bandwidth was designed for IS-IS, and adopted by OSPF.

2   If a network is very large, it is necessary to partition it into pieces (which are often called *level 1 subnetworks* or *areas*). This is known as making the network *hierarchical*. It not only allows larger networks, but also a certain amount of protection. Routing can be designed so that routing within an area will not be disrupted by routing proto-col faults in other areas.

     A problem, which is called the area partition problem (discussed below), arises when a routing protocol is hierarchical. A method for automatically detecting and repairing partitioned areas was designed for IS-IS.

3   A second problem, called the level 2 net partition problem, arises when a routing pro-tocol is hierarchical. OSPF is designed to allow the repair of a partitioned level 2 net-work, but in contrast to the IS-IS area partition mechanism, the OSPF mechanism requires manual configuration of repair paths, and manual deletion of such paths when they are no longer required. IS-IS requires the level 2 network to be connected.

4   The ARPANET protocol assumed all connections were point-to-point links. Many nodes can be connected with a LAN. Modeling a LAN as a fully connected set of nodes attached with point-to-point links would be extremely inefficient. IS-IS introduced mechanisms for electing one router on a LAN, known as the *designated router* (DR), to report the membership of the LAN, and to ensure reliable and efficient LSP distribu-tion on the LAN. OSPF also uses a DR, but has a somewhat different design for LSP distribution on the LAN. OSPF has a more complex mechanism for choosing a DR, and elects not only a DR, but a backup DR as well.

5   Given that a router has limited memory, it is possible for the network to grow beyond the maximum size supportable by some router. If the router simply crashed as a result of its LSP database overflowing the available space, it would not be possible to use net-work management to reconfigure the router. If the router simply ignored the fact that it was routing based on an incomplete database, routing loops might form and cause problems for any routes that traversed it. IS-IS has mechanisms for dealing with over-loaded routers that cause them to remain reachable via network management.

   The following sections discuss the details of link state routing protocols.

5.3.1   Computation of Routes

Assume that a router has an LSP database that consists of the most recently generated LSP from each other router. The goal of a route computation is to generate a forwarding database that will tell the router the neighbor to which it should forward packets for any destination.

   The Dijkstra algorithm involves two temporary databases that are used to construct a tree of shortest paths from a router to each destination. One database is known as PATH, which contains the best known path for each possible destination. Entries in PATH consist of (destination, path cost, forwarding direction). The other database is known as TENT (for "tentative"), which consists of the best path found so far during the computation. Entries in TENT have the same form as those in PATH.

The Dijkstra algorithm can be stated as follows:

1   Start by placing (self, 0, 0) in PATH.

2   For an entry (D, cost, direction) just placed in PATH, examine D's LSP. For each neighbor N of D, that is listed in D's LSP with a link cost from D to N of c, see if (N, cost x,...) is already in TENT or PATH. If (N, x, direction) is not already listed, or is listed with a cost x > (cost+c), then place (N, cost+c, direction) in TENT.

3   If TENT is empty, terminate the algorithm. Otherwise, find the triple (X, c,...) having the minimal c, move that entry to PATH, and go to Step 2.

Let us work through an example (see Figure 5.2).

5.3.2   Distribution of LSPs

Routers run a neighbor-to-neighbor protocol to determine the identities of their neighbors. Each then constructs an LSP consisting of

1   The identity of the router generating the LSP

2   A sequence number

3   The time left until LSP should be discarded

4   A list of neighbors, and the cost of the link to each.

The LSP is to be broadcast to all other routers, and each router must keep a copy of the most recently generated LSP from each other router. The sequence number is supposed to enable routers that are remote from the source of an LSP to determine, given two LSPs, which one was most recently generated.

The ARPANET used the following LSP distribution mechanism:

1   Sequence numbers wrap around, which means that after reaching the maximum value, the sequence numbers restart from the smallest value. If the maximum value is n, then a is defined to be less than b if:

$a < b$ and $b - a < n/2$
$a > b$ and $a - b > n/2$

2   If an LSP from source S is received from neighbor N, and its sequence number is greater (according to the definition above) than the sequence number of the LSP stored from S (if any), then the stored LSP is replaced by the received LSP, and the received LSP is marked as needing to be transmitted to all neighbors other than N.

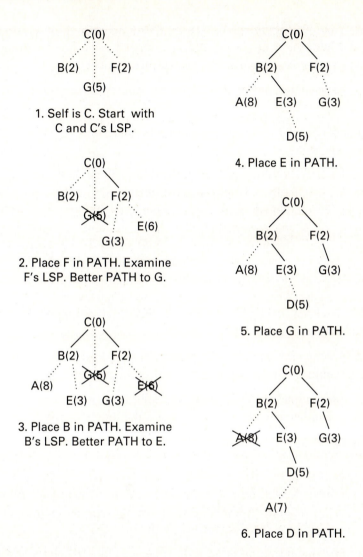

1. Self is C. Start with
   C and C's LSP.

2. Place F in PATH. Examine
   F's LSP. Better PATH to G.

3. Place B in PATH. Examine
   B's LSP. Better PATH to E.

4. Place E in PATH.

5. Place G in PATH.

6. Place D in PATH.

Figure 5.2   Dijkstra computation as done by **C**. The number following the node name represents the
cost of the best path known from **C** to that node

Otherwise, if the sequence number indicates that the LSP is a duplicate or older, the
received LSP is discarded.

3   The Time-To-Live field is set by the source to the maximum value by the source (8, in
    units of 8 seconds, for a total of 64 seconds).

4   A router that has stored an LSP decrements its Time-To-Live field after 8 seconds.

5　If an LSP's Time-To-Live field is 0, then the LSP is no longer propagated, and another LSP received from the same source, with nonzero Time-To-Live, is accepted as newer than the one in memory, regardless of its sequence number.

6　A router must generate a new LSP at least every minute (before its old LSP's Time-To-Live expires).

7　A router that has just been booted must wait 90 seconds for its old LSP to expire before it generates a new one.

This protocol is not self-stabilizing,[13] and indeed brought down the ARPANET in 1981 when a router, due to a hardware fault, generated several LSPs for itself in rapid succession, with random sequence numbers. With sequence numbers that wrap, it is possible to have sequence numbers a, b, and c, such that $a < b < c < a$. The result was that the sick router's LSPs became a virus. Each router that processed one of these LSPs overwrote the one in memory and generated more copies of the bad LSP, since it thought that this LSP was newer and needed to be flooded to all neighbors. The Time-To-Live field never changed because the routers never held an LSP long enough to decrement the field.

The problem has been analyzed,[14] and has since been further simplified.[15] The currently accepted method of efficient and fault tolerant LSP distribution is as follows:

1　LSPs contain a sequence number field, but it is large (at least 32 bits), never expected to reach the maximum value in normal operation, and it does not wrap.

2　LSPs are compared solely by their sequence numbers. In other words, if an LSP from S is stored and another is received from S, then the one with the numerically higher sequence number is considered "more recent," regardless of the value in the Time-To-Live field.

3　LSPs get purged from the database when they are very old (on the order of an hour). The age is estimated based on the Time-To-Live field (which is recommended to be considerably larger than the ARPANET's 3-bit field). Every router must decrement the Time-To-Live field by at least 1 before forwarding the LSP.

4　To synchronize the expiration of an LSP, when an LSP's Time-To-Live reaches 0, a router refloods the LSP. In terms of the flooding procedure, an LSP with 0 Time-To-Live is considered "newer" than one with the same sequence number and nonzero Time-To-Live. After some time has elapsed since the LSP's Time-To-Live became 0, the LSP is deleted from memory.

5　Because the purging time is on the order of an hour, new LSPs do not need to be generated frequently (as was the case in the ARPANET). Instead, new LSPs need to be generated on the order of once an hour.

6　A router always starts with the lowest sequence number. It is not necessary to wait for the old LSP to be purged (as was the case in the ARPANET). If the network retains memory of a previous LSP with higher sequence number, the previous LSP will be reflooded back to the source, which can then issue a newer LSP with a higher sequence number.

This protocol was proven correct by Professor Nancy Lynch (of MIT). Besides being self-stabilizing, it is much more efficient than the ARPANET scheme, since it does not require very frequent periodic generation of LSPs, and it does not require a newly rebooted router to wait before participating in the network.

5.3.3 Hierarchy

If a network becomes too large, several factors overload the routing protocol. The LSP database might become too large to fit into memory, too much CPU might be required to compute routes, too much bandwidth might be consumed in keeping the LSP databases up to date, or the network might be unstable because link changes might be too frequent. To deal with these issues, routing protocols allow the network to be partitioned into areas. Within an area, the level 1 routers keep track of all the nodes and links. Level 2 routers keep track of where the areas are, but they are not concerned with the detail inside the areas. In general, a level 2 router will also act as a level 1 router in one area.

To use a routing protocol in a hierarchical way, it is convenient for the Network Layer addresses to be geographically hierarchical, as in:

Area	ID

All the nodes in a particular area will have the same value for the area portion of their address. A level 1 router looks at the area portion of the address. If the area portion of the destination address in a packet matches the router's area address, it routes the packet based on the ID portion of the address. If the area portion does not match the router's area, it routes the packet toward a level 2 router, which routes the packet based solely on the area portion of the address.

If the address is not hierarchical, it is still possible to use a routing protocol in a hierarchical manner. A level 1 router first checks to see if the destination is reachable within the area. If it does not know how to reach the destination, it forwards the packet to a level 2 router. The addressing defined in CLNP and IP allows the summarization of level 2 addresses. In CLNP, level 2 routers use the address prefixes. A packet is routed toward the most specific address prefix match. In IP, level 2 routing is to a masked address. The most specific match is the one with the mask that has the most 1 bits.

Note that when people talk about "IP routing" they are really talking about level 2 routing, though that is not the terminology used. The IP address consists of two parts, one which specifies the link, and one which specifies the host on the link. Therefore, according to the terminology above, the part of the IP address that specifies the link (the part in which the "subnet mask" has 1s) really is the "area" part of the address. The part of the IP address that specifies the host (the part in which the subnet mask has 0s) is the "ID" part of the address. Level 1 routing in IP is trivial, since the first level of addressing hierarchy in IP is restricted to a single link. When OSPF discusses "areas," it is really discussing a third level of routing. I have heard people complain about ISO routing because "it requires routers to know about individual hosts." ISO routing would be equivalent to IP routing if an area were restricted to be a single link. IP routers have to keep track of hosts on the links to which they are directly attached (in their "ARP caches"). ISO routers similarly have to keep track of hosts on the links to which they are directly attached. If people really believe it is infeasible for routers to keep track of hosts on links other than the ones to which they are attached, it can be done with ISO routing simply by making each link a separate area. The difference between ISO and IP routing is that ISO routing does not *require* this restriction. If routers are capable of keeping track of hosts on more links, ISO allows many links to be combined into a single area, which benefits level 2 because level 2 routing then has fewer destinations of which to keep track (level 2 routing has to keep track of all the areas).

IPX and AppleTalk Network Layer addresses do not have summarization capability for level 2 addresses, at least not at this time. (Note that AppleTalk destinations consist of "network number ranges," which look like summarization, but actually are not.) A network number range defines a single LAN in AppleTalk. The only way a network number range can be considered to be a summary is if it allows a grouping of LANs to be reported as if it were a single destination.) If there is no way of summarizing addresses within a particular network protocol suite, then the level 2 routers have a very difficult task, because they must keep track of all the level 2 addresses in the network.

5.3.4   The Area Partition Problem

If links within an area break, it is possible for the area to be *partitioned*, which means there is no level 1 path from one part of the area to another part of the area (See Figure 5.3). If there are level 2 routers in each portion, and the level 2 network is connected, the partitions are physically connected, but conventional level 1 routing will not be able to allow nodes in different partitions to communicate. Another problem is that nodes from other areas will have difficulty communicating with nodes in the partitioned area, because packets might be routed to the wrong partition.

IS-IS solves this problem by having enough information in the level 2 LSP so that level 2 routers can determine that the area has been partitioned. Once level 2 routers in area X determine that X is partitioned, say into partitions $X1$ and $X2$, a level 2 router in $X1$, say $R1$, and a level 2 router in $X2$, say $R2$, repair X by using the level 2 path between $R1$ and $R2$ as a level 1 link. Data packets between the two partitions are encapsulated in an additional header, which means that if $R1$ receives a packet with source A and destination B, $R1$ will add a header indicating $R1$ as source and $R2$ as destination, and will forward the packet over the level 2 network toward $R2$. $R2$ removes the outer header and continues the original packet along its path.

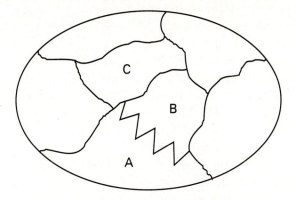

Figure 5.3   Partitioned area

5.3.5   Efficient Use of LANs

All nodes connected to a LAN are Data Link Layer neighbors. If the routing protocol were to simply consider all pairs of nodes on the LAN as neighbors, then each router on the LAN would issue an LSP listing all the nodes on the LAN. Also, the LSP distribution would be very inefficient if every router needed to transmit every LSP to every other router on the LAN, and receive acknowledgments from every other router on the LAN.

IS-IS and OSPF solve the LSP database size problem by considering the LAN as a pseudo-node. One router is elected designated router (DR). In IS-IS the DR is the router with the highest ID (with an optionally configured priority field). In OSPF, the DR is based on similar criteria, but once chosen, it remains the DR until it goes down. In IS-IS, given a particular set of routers, the same one will always be chosen DR. In OSPF, which router is designated depends on the history of which routers were up at which point. I don't believe that the differences between these two schemes are very significant. The IS-IS scheme is clearly much simpler (and I believe something more complicated had better be a *lot* better to be justified). Some people claim its *determinism*, i.e., the fact that, given a particular set of routers, the same one will always be elected DR, is a major advantage. (I don't think that's very important.) The OSPF designers felt that having the DR change unnecessarily causes disruptions on the network. Indeed, in OSPF the DR keeps a lot of state, since it needs to keep track of which routers on the LAN have acknowledged which LSPs (this is not necessary in IS-IS, as will be seen shortly). For that reason, OSPF not only elects a DR, but also a backup DR. The backup DR passively participates in the same work the DR does, so that it will have enough state to take over quickly in case the DR fails.

In IS-IS the DR gives a name to the LAN by appending an octet to its own ID. For example, assume a LAN has routers *R1, R2, R3, R4,* and *R5,* and perhaps 100 end nodes with IDs *S1, S2, ..., S100.* Suppose *R5* is elected DR. It might name the LAN *R5.22.* Each of *R1, R2, R3, R4,* and *R5* will claim a single link in their LSP, a link to *R5.22*. *R5*, in addition to its own LSP (claiming a link to *R5.22*), issues another LSP claiming to be *R5.22*, listing as neighbors *R1, R2, R3, R4, R5, S1, ..., S100*.

OSPF has a similar mechanism. The DR issues an LSP on behalf of the LAN that lists all the routers on the LAN. Because OSPF is used for routing IP (instead of CLNP), the OSPF DR does not individually list the end nodes on the LAN, but instead gives the IP the address and mask for the LAN. This is not a difference between the two protocols as routing protocols—if IS-IS were used for routing IP, or if OSPF were used for routing CLNP, they'd each list the same information.

The second LAN efficiency problem deals with the reliable distribution of LSPs on the LAN. The naive extension to the flooding procedure designed for distribution of LSPs on point-to-point links would have each router on a LAN transmit each LSP to each other router on the LAN, and collect acknowledgments from each other router on the LAN. This is obviously inefficient. IS-IS solves this problem by having no explicit acknowledgments to LSPs on the LAN. Instead, a router that has an LSP to forward to the LAN simply multicasts the LAN to the other routers. A router that receives an LSP on the LAN will not multicast the same LSP on the LAN. Theoretically, if no packets get lost, only a single router would issue an LSP on the LAN. However, packets do get lost, so it is important that lost LSPs get detected.

IS-IS detects lost LSPs by having the DR periodically broadcast a summary of the LSP database in a packet known as a CSNP (Complete Sequence Numbers Packet). It lists the source IDs of all LSPs, together with their sequence numbers. Based on the CSNP, a receiving router can determine whether it has missed an LSP (in which case it will explicitly request the LSP from the DR), or whether it has a more recent LSP than the DR, in which case the receiving router will multicast the LSP on the LAN to the other routers.

OSPF has a different mechanism for efficiently and reliably distributing LSPs on a LAN. In OSPF a router on a LAN that has an LSP to forward on the LAN transmits the LSP to the DR. The DR then multicasts the LSP to all the routers, and collects acknowledgments. If the DR does not receive an acknowledgment from some subset of the routers, it transmits individual copies of the LSP to those routers until it does receive acknowledgments.

5.3.6 Database Overload

An implementation of a router typically has only finite storage for the LSP database. There are two reasons why the space may not be adequate, and the router might receive an LSP for which it has no storage. The first reason is a *static overload*, which means that the network really has become so large that the router will not be able to store the LSP database. The second reason is a *temporary overload*. It can happen, just because of the ordering of events, that the LSP database is temporarily larger than necessary. An example of such an event is when the DR on a large LAN goes down. The DR's previous pseudo-node LSP is still in the other routers' databases. The new DR on the LAN will give the LAN a new ID, and until the old LSP times out (a half-hour), other routers will have to temporarily store twice as much information about that LAN.

If nobody thought about this problem, basically there would be two strategies that an implementation might follow. It might crash, or it might ignore the fact that it can't hold all the LSPs, and route the best it can. Crashing is inconvenient because if the problem is truly temporary, it is unfortunate that the router will not recover without human intervention. Crashing is also inconvenient because then the router is not available via network management. However, the other strategy (routing based on an incomplete LSP database) can be very dangerous, and can cause widespread misrouting.

IS-IS solves the problem by having a router that cannot store its LSP database set a flag in its LSP indicating that it is overloaded. Other routers then treat it as an end node. They will route to it but not through it. The overloaded router then is available via network management. If some time goes by in which the router has not needed to refuse an LSP from a neighbor, the router will clear the flag in its LSP, so that in the case of a temporary problem the network will recover without human intervention.

5.4   BRIDGE ROUTING PROTOCOLS

Bridges came about because of the need to interconnect LANs when the end nodes on the LANs had no Network Layer protocol. Routers require that a compatible Network Layer protocol be running in the end nodes.

There were two forms of bridge proposed to the IEEE 802.1 committee. One was known as the *transparent bridge*, or *spanning tree bridge*. The other was known as the *source routing bridge*. The transparent bridge was just that—a method of interconnecting LANs without changing the end nodes. Source routing bridges required a compatible protocol running in the end nodes. As such, the only reason source routing bridges are called *bridges* rather than *routers* is because the standard was adopted by a Data Link Layer committee. As is often the case with committees, although they initially chose the transparent approach, source routing did not go away, and is now considered officially as an optional "enhancement" on a transparent bridge.

5.4.1   Transparent Bridging

The basic idea behind a transparent bridge is that it acts as a station on two or more LANs, listens promiscuously to each data packet, stores the packet for forwarding, and forwards it onto every other LAN to which it is connected when the LAN arbitration protocol for the destination LAN indicates the medium is available. A transparent bridge is more clever than always forwarding every data packet. When a bridge receives a packet, it has a source address and a destination address. The bridge remembers the location from which it received the packet, and assumes that the source address resides on that link. Then, when the bridge is ready to forward a data packet, it checks whether it has remembered the location of the destination address. If the destination address resides on the same link from which the packet arrived, then the packet is not forwarded. If the destination address resides on a different link, the packet is forwarded, but only to the link from which the destination address was learned.

This idea works as long as there are no loops in the topology. Loops make it impossible to determine the location of the source, since there might be multiple routes to the source. But worse than that, loops cause proliferating packets. With a Network Layer protocol, loops are not as serious, since there is a Time-To-Live field in the header that will eventually kill the packet, and since routers never make extra copies of the packet when they forward it—they always forward it only in a single direction, and always identify the recipient. When a bridge forwards a packet, it may forward it in multiple directions (if the destination is unknown), and when it does forward it, it simply transmits it onto a LAN and then multiple bridges may receive the packet and forward it, multiplying the number of copies of the packet.

To enable people to plug transparent bridges into arbitrary topologies, bridges run a *spanning tree protocol*. The protocol prunes the current topology into a *spanning tree*; that is, a loop-free subset of the topology that has maximal coverage. Data packets are routed along the spanning tree, but may be filtered if bridges have learned the location of the destination.

The basic idea behind the spanning tree is similar to a distance vector routing protocol with a single destination. All bridges compute their distance from the bridge with the lowest ID, which is known as the *root bridge*. The routing control message that bridges send consists of the ID of the bridge that the transmitter assumes is the root, the cost to the root, and the ID of the bridge transmitting the control message. These control messages are not forwarded by bridges.

Given that a bridge needs only to compute its distance from the bridge with the lowest ID, and given that information about a bridge that is further from the root than another bridge on the same LAN is irrelevant to the computations of the other bridges on that LAN, there is no need for more than one bridge on a LAN to issue a spanning tree control message. The bridge on a LAN that can issue the "best" control message is known as the *designated bridge* on that LAN, and it alone issues spanning tree control messages. The "best" control message is defined as, in decreasing order of importance:

1   One with a lower root ID

2   One with a lower cost to the root

3   One with a lower ID of the bridge transmitting the control message.

Once a bridge figures out the ID of the root, its own distance to the root, which port should be used for forwarding a packet to the root, and which ports the designated bridge is on, the links selected for the spanning tree are any of those for which the bridge is the designated bridge, plus the link which is in the direction of the root bridge. Data packets received on links other than those selected for the spanning tree are dropped, but spanning tree control messages continue to be processed on those links.

Bridges have timers to recover from failures, and there are lots of other details to the transparent bridge routing protocol. Interestingly, even though the spanning tree algorithm is similar to a distance vector protocol, the bridge protocol does not suffer from the count-to-infinity problem of distance vector protocols.

5.4.2   Source Routing Bridging

The idea behind source routing bridging is that the source end node puts a route into each data packet's header. The way that the source end node discovers a route is by issuing an "explorer" packet that makes copies of itself for every possible path, with each copy keeping a diary of where it's been. Then the destination can choose a route, based on the received explorer packets, or send them all back to the source, and let the source choose a route.

Source routing certainly requires cooperation of the end nodes (they have to maintain route caches for destinations with which they are communicating). As such, it really is similar to a Network Layer protocol. The proponents of source routing bridges claim source routing bridging is better than transparent bridging because the optimal route between a source and a destination, and load splitting between conversation streams, can occur. However, in a reasonably richly connected network, the number of paths can be so great that the overhead involved in the route exploration process can quickly overwhelm any gains that might be had by more optimal routing of data packets.

The original source routing proposal was intended as an alternative to transparent bridging. However, it was difficult to make the schemes interwork. Therefore, the SRT (Source Routing Transparent) approach was standardized. In the SRT approach, there are two kinds of conformant bridges:

1   Transparent bridges

2   Transparent bridges that also recognize source routing information.

With the SRT approach, end nodes need not participate in source routing. It will always be possible to communicate with ordinary Data Link Layer packets without the source routing header (transparent packets). However, if end nodes have the capability to do route exploration and route caching, they can attempt to find a source routing path, which may or not be better than the path transparent packets would take between them.

5.5   MULTIPROTOCOL ROUTING

This section describes various methods of supporting multiple Network Layer protocols. All methods require a means of unambiguously identifying data packets from different protocols. Another problem is routing multiple Network Layer protocols, and there are several techniques that will be discussed in this section, including "ships in the night" (totally independent routing protocols), "integrated routing" (one routing protocol that carries information about all protocols), and "tunnels" (where a backbone WAN has one Network Layer protocol and other protocols are encapsulated within the backbone protocol).

5.5.1   Disambiguating Data Packets

A multiprotocol router is capable of receiving and processing multiple Network Layer protocols, for instance IP, CLNP, and AppleTalk. For that to be even theoretically possible, it must be possible to differentiate the various types of packets. Most Data Link Layer protocols provide a method of expressing the protocol type of the contents of what is to the Data Link Layer the "data" field. This is done by providing a "protocol type" field in the Data Link Layer header, which the Data Link Layer committee administers. That means there is one authority responsible for defining which protocols use which protocol type values. PPP[6] and IEEE 802 both have a protocol type field, though the 802 protocol type field is encoded in a rather strange way. The 802 committee originally thought it was better to have a separate demultiplexing field for the source address than for the destination address. This field was known as a service access point, or SAP. In the 802.2 header, there are defined two fields, SSAP (for *source service access point*) and DSAP (for *destination service access point*). However, the 802 committee assigned some protocols a fixed SAP value, in which case the SSAP and DSAP would be always the same value, and the SAP fields would really be the same as a protocol type field (the only difference is that the protocol type field would appear twice in the header). The SAP fields were too small to give every protocol a value. "Privileged protocols" were assigned a SAP value, and when a privileged protocol uses 802 encoding, it will set the DSAP and the SSAP to the same value, namely the value assigned to that protocol by the 802 committee. "Underprivileged protocols" will not be able to get a value. Instead, a single SAP value was assigned (AA hex), known as the SNAP SAP (for *subnetwork access protocol service access point*). If the DSAP and SSAP are equal to the SNAP SAP constant, then a protocol type field of sufficient length (5 octets) appears later in the header.

If some Data Link protocol such as HDLC is used, which does not contain a protocol type, then some convention must be defined for making the packets self-describing. A straightforward mechanism is to add a value to the beginning of what the data link header thinks is the "data" field, indicating the protocol type. Unfortunately, this approach has not been standardized, and there is no central place to register protocol type values, so currently, multivendor multiprotocol routing over HDLC and other Data Link protocols without protocol information, is not guaranteed.

5.5.2 Routing Multiple Routing Protocols

Other than being able to differentiate the data packets, a multiprotocol router must support all protocols visible to the end nodes. That means a router that supports IP must support ARP and ICMP. A router that supports CLNP must support ES-IS. However, there is no particular routing protocol that must be supported by a router to interwork with end nodes. It is only important for routers to be compatible with the other routers.

There are three methods of having a routing protocol support multiple Network Layer protocols. One is known as *ships in the night*, which means implementing completely separate routing protocols for each Network Layer protocol. A common combination is IS-IS for CLNP and OSPF for IP. Another method is known as *integrated routing*, in which a single routing protocol routes multiple Network Layer protocols. A third method is known as *tunnels*, in which a backbone WAN runs (at least one) common Network Layer protocol, and other Network Layer protocols are encapsulated as data packets in the common protocol when they are carried across the backbone.

Ships in the Night

This approach consists of simply running independent routing protocols for each Network Layer protocol. The assumption is that there are incompatible routing protocols running for different Network Layer protocols, and that different routers support different subsets of the Network Layer protocols. A ships-in-the-night approach will automatically calculate a path only through routers that support a particular Network Layer protocol, so encapsulation is never required. On the other hand, it also means that if no path to the destination exists through routers that support that Network Layer protocol, the destination will be unreachable.

Integrated Routing

Integrated routing means running a single routing protocol, and sharing information about the various Network Layer destination addresses. For instance, in a link state protocol, a router's LSP might list

1   The routers that are its neighbors

2   The CLNP end nodes

3   The (IP address, mask) for any LANs to which the router is connected

4   The network number range for any LANs with AppleTalk end nodes to which the router is connected.

This single routing protocol would be able to support CLNP, IP, and AppleTalk.

A protocol that is popularly used for integrated routing is IS-IS. *RFC 1195* details[17] how to support IP with IS-IS. Current work focuses on the support of IPX and AppleTalk as well.

It is not theoretically necessary for all IS-IS routers to support the same set of Network Layer protocols, but it is wise to have a restriction that there be at least one Network Layer protocol that they all support. For instance, assume all IS-IS routers support IP, but only some support AppleTalk. In that case, the routers that do not support AppleTalk will ignore the portion of LSPs that list AppleTalk destinations. They will store the field in their LSP database and forward it to their neighbors, but they will not attempt to interpret that portion of the LSP. A router that needs to forward an AppleTalk packet through a neighbor that does not support AppleTalk will encapsulate the AppleTalk packet in an IP header, with the IP destination address being the router adjacent to the AppleTalk destination.

Since forwarding a data packet is a time-critical step, it might be an advantage for routers in the backbone WAN not to need to parse multiple Network Layer protocols. Although *RFC 1195* assumes that data packets are carried in "native mode" (i.e., without encapsulation) if possible, it is a reasonable design decision to have all the data packets on the backbone WAN follow a single Network Layer protocol, and have the first router encapsulate the foreign protocol packet with a header directing the packet to the exit router that carries the packet from the backbone to the destination.

Integrated routing could also work perfectly well with a distance vector protocol. From the packet formats in RIP, it might appear that the designers expected RIP to support multiple Network Layer protocols simultaneously, since each RIP destination consists of an "address family" followed by 14 octets of address. The behavior of an integrated distance vector protocol is rather interesting. If a router that does not support a particular address family merely ignores that portion of the distance vector, and does not report unsupported address families in its own distance vector, then the routing protocol will compute a path, if it exists, that contains only routers supporting the address family of the destination. In this sense the integrated distance vector protocol performs like a ships-in-the-night implementation.

If, on the other hand, routers add to the accumulated cost and pass the entry on, even though they do not support that address family, then the best path to the destination will be computed, but the path might include routers that would not be able to process the particular Network Layer data packet format. Therefore, the packet must be encapsulated in a Network Layer header guaranteed to be supported by all routers. With integrated link state routing, the identity of the router closest to the destination is known, since that is the router that includes the destination in its LSP as a neighbor. In distance vector routing this information is not normally available. Therefore it would be necessary to include an encapsulation destination in each distance vector entry, in addition to the cost to the destination, the address family, and the destination address. Encapsulation would either occur at the first router (the first and last router must be able to support the advertised address family), or the packet could be carried in native mode as far as possible, until a router noticed it needed to be forwarded to a neighbor that did not support that protocol. (The "encapsulate only when necessary" strategy depends on a router neighbor handshaking protocol to determine the protocols ones' neighbors support, which may not be present in a distance vector protocol.)

In fact, work is progressing to make IDRP integrated. IDRP is officially known as a "path vector" protocol. A path vector protocol is similar to a distance vector protocol, but a list of the domains along the path is included as an attribute of the path to the destination.

Integrated routing makes configuration easier, since only a single routing protocol needs to be understood and managed. It has the benefits of minimizing memory, bandwidth, and CPU in the routers (since only a single routing protocol is running). It also minimizes implementation effort, since only a single routing protocol needs to be implemented.

Tunnels

Tunneling is the term used for encapsulating a protocol X packet in Network Layer protocol Y, where Y is the protocol running on the WAN backbone. The concept of a tunnel is not necessarily distinct from the concept of integrated routing.

In the simplest form of tunnel, protocol X routers are statically configured with the (protocol Y) Network Layer addresses of other protocol X routers. The protocol X routers then simply treat the backbone as if it were a multiaccess link. Usually they run a protocol X routing protocol, but the reachable protocol X addresses might be statically configured instead.

The routing protocol might allow a router, in its LSP, to inform other routers that it is a protocol X router. With this minimal amount of help from the routing protocol, the addresses of other protocol X routers need not be manually configured. (Note that if the network is hierarchical and there are protocol X routers in other areas, it is still possible for protocol Y to give the protocol X routers information about all the protocol X routers that are reachable on the backbone, but it is more work. It involves having the level 2 routers collect information about the protocol X routers in each area and distribute this information in their LSPs.)

Integrated routing implemented where encapsulation is done at the entrance to the backbone is another form of tunnel. It is interesting to compare the efficiency of this form of tunnel versus one in which the routing protocol allows protocol X routers to find each other, but protocol X routing information is passed as a separate protocol between the protocol X routers. Both forms of tunnel cause automatic discovery of protocol X neighbors and automatic computation of protocol X routes. The difference is that in the integrated approach, the protocol X information is piggybacked in the protocol Y LSP. It is not processed by the backbone routers, but it takes room in their LSP databases, and takes bandwidth when protocol Y LSPs are exchanged. When a protocol X routing protocol runs over the backbone, the protocol Y LSPs are smaller, but an exchange of information is required between all the protocol X routers. Which protocol is more efficient depends on the relative number of protocol X and backbone routers.

5.6   INTERDOMAIN ROUTING

Often it makes sense to partition the network into *domains*. The idea behind a domain is that it is administered by a single administrative plan, and an intradomain routing protocol routes within the domain.[*]

Routing between domains is done with an interdomain routing protocol. The claim is that routing between domains cannot be done with a standard intradomain routing protocol because interdomain routing is subject to complex tariff and legal constraints, and domains offer such different types of service, access control, and transit restrictions.

People would like to have the route to a destination depend on any combination of the following:

1   Source and destination routing domains

2   Source and destination nodes

3   Application

4   Contents of the message (e.g., personal, commercial, or government business)

5   The route the packet has traversed so far.

There is really no way for the routing protocol to accommodate all of these wishes. A reasonably efficient routing protocol that solves some problems, but certainly not the general case, is known as a path vector protocol, and is the basis of BGP[18] and IDRP.[19] BGP was developed for routing IP. IDRP is based on BGP, and has additional capabilities, such as the ability to merge routing domains into "confederations," that appear to be single domains from outside. Path vector protocols are similar to distance vector protocols, but they contain a complete description of the path to the destination, instead of merely a numerical cost. (In fact, BGP does not pass around a metric at all, and all routing decisions must be based on the enumerated path.) Listing the path prevents the count-to-infinity behavior, and allows more complex route preference algorithms, but it also requires significantly more memory and bandwidth, since the volume of routing control information is so much greater. IDRP and BGP may evolve in parallel, where each adopts features added by the other, or they may merge into a single integrated interdomain routing protocol.

Support of policies is done in BGP/IDRP by configuring each router with an algorithm for mapping the known characteristics of a route to a number, a configuration of rules for which routes to believe from which neighbors, and rules, for which routes are allowed to be told to which neighbors. It is interesting that BGP/IDRP allows each router to be configured with different rules, and the routing will still work. Optimal routes may not be achieved, but the scheme will not suffer from the kind of disruptions a link state protocol would suffer if

---

[*]   I admit that my definition of a domain is vague. That is because none of the definitions I've seen are particularly intelligible or accurate. It would be an interesting denial-of-service threat on the networking community to lock a bunch of us in a room until we came up with a definition we all agreed on.

routers were making decisions based on different criteria. This is because in BGP/IDRP, a router makes a choice as to how to get to a destination, and then reports that path to its neighbors. They may like the path or prefer a different one, but they know what the path is. Once a packet for that destination is passed to that router, it will take the path advertised.

A second routing protocol is known as IDPR, and is being developed for routing IP. It is a link state protocol in which complex routing constraints are accommodated by the use of source routing. The major complexity of IDPR is the specification of policies. Source routing is done by going through a route set-up procedure (as opposed to carrying a route in each data packet). A "unified approach" is being suggested as well, in which IDRP is used when possible, and a source route is chosen and set up (based on IDPR information or other information) when it is known that the IDRP chosen route is not desirable.

REFERENCES

1   R. Perlman, *Interconnections: Bridges and Routers,* Addison-Wesley, Reading, 1992.

2   H. Zimmerman, OSI Reference model—The ISO Model of Architecture for Open Systems Interconnection, *IEEE Transactions on Communications,* **Vol. COM**-28, No. 4, pp. 425–432, 1980.

3   J.B. Postel, *Internet Protocol, RFC 791,* 1981.

4   *Final Text of DIS 8473, Protocol for Providing the Connectionless-Mode Network-Service-RFC 994,* International Organization for Standardization, 1986.

5   *End System to Intermediate System Routing Exchange Protocol for use in Conjunction with ISO 8473, RFC 995,* International Organization for Standardization, 1986.

6   D.C. Plummer, *Ethernet Address Resolution Protocol: Or converting network protocol addresses to 48-bit Ethernet address for transmission on Ethernet hardware, RFC 826,* 1982.

7   J.B. Postel, *Internet Control Message Protocol, RFC 792,* 1981.

8   D.R. Boggs, J.F. Shoch, E.A. Taft, and R.M. Metcalfe, Pup: An Internetwork Architecture, *IEEE Transactions on Communications,* April 1980.

9   *Internet Transport Protocols,* Xerox System Integration Standard XSIS 028112, Xerox Corp., 1981.

10   D.D. Clark, *Policy Routing in Internet Protocols, RFC 1102,* 1989.

11 R.E. Bellman, *Dynamic Programming*, Princeton University Press, Princeton, 1957; and L.R. Ford, Jr. and D.R. Fulkerson, *Flows in Networks*, Princeton University Press, Princeton, 1962.

12 E. Rosen, J. Mayerson, P. Sevcik, G. Williams, and R. Attar, *ARPANET Routing Algorithm Improvements*, Vol. 1, BBN report 4473, 1980.

13 E. Rosen, Vulnerabilities of Network Control Protocols: An Example, *Computer Communications Review*, 1981.

14 R. Perlman, Fault-Tolerant Broadcast of Routing Information, *Computer Networks*, 1983.

15 R. Perlman, *Network Layer Protocols with Byzantine Robustness*, PhD thesis, MIT, 1988.

16 D. Perkins, *Point-to-Point Protocol for the Transmission of Multiprotocol Datagrams Over Point-to-Point Links*, RFC 1171, 1990.

17 R.W. Callon, *Use of OSI IS-IS for Routing in TCP/IP and Dual Environments*, RFC 1195, 1990.

18 R. Lougheed, *Border Gateway Protocol 3 (BGP-3)*, RFC 1267, 1991.

19 C. Kunzinger, *Protocol for the Exchange of Inter-Domain Routing Information Among Intermediate Systems to Support Forwarding of ISO 8473 PDUs*, CD 10747, 1991.

CHAPTER 6

Main Applications

JON POSTEL

CONTENTS

The Internet has long enjoyed applications which provide good functionality supported by excellent engineering. Indeed, many users view the applications as enabling communication, rather than the underlying connectivity protocols. It is also amusing to note that although the term "client-server" came into vogue only a few years ago, the Internet applications have used such a model for over a decade!

6.1   INTRODUCTION

The Internet system (called the *Internet* in this chapter) has a layered architecture, and within this architecture a suite of protocols (sometimes called the *TCP/IP protocol suite*) has been developed.[1–5] This chapter focuses on the applications in this suite of protocols. Nearly all of the applications are implemented on one or the other of two system protocols: the Transmission Control Protocol (TCP) [6, 7] or the User Datagram Protocol (UDP).[8] The TCP provides a reliable end-to-end data stream connection for process-to-process communication. The UDP provides process-level access to a simple datagram service with no reliability guarantees.

These system protocols (often called Transport Protocols or Layer 4 Protocols) are generally implemented in the operating system of the computer or network host. There can be (and are) other system protocols in the Internet Architecture and TCP/IP protocol suite.

This chapter discusses the applications that are widely implemented in the Internet, including computer mail, file transfer, remote terminal access, name lookup service, and time lookup service. In addition, some experimental applications are discussed, including Stream Protocol and Network Voice Protocol. It should be noted that the TCP/IP protocol suite is continuously evolving, and that new protocols are developed every year.

6.2   GENERAL FEATURES OF APPLICATIONS

The applications to be discussed take many forms, but two themes appear in several of them; one is the user-server model, and the other is the use of a particular form of requests and replies.

6.2.1   The User-Server Model

Many of the applications in the TCP/IP protocol suite are created according to the user-server model, sometimes called the client-server model. The user-server model concerns network communication passing between two programs or processes, one of which is the user process, and the other of which is the server process.

The user process is usually run on behalf of a human user who may be controlling it via a user interface, or the user process may be following prerecorded instructions. The user process usually is the active agent in the communication. It sends requests for information or requests for service to the server process and interprets the responses.

The server process usually is connected somehow to a set of system resources, such as the file system, or pseudo-terminals. The server process is usually passive, waiting for a service request from the user process, then performing the service action, and sending a response.

In implementation, the user process is normally straightforward, and can be implemented as an ordinary user program with no special operating system privileges (for example, it doesn't need to be "root"). The trick is that it usually has to pay attention to two independent and unpredictable input channels: (1) input from the user at the keyboard (or mouse), and (2) input from the network. This often takes two operating system processes.

The implementation of the server process is usually a bit more difficult, since the service often involves access to a resource provided by the operating system, such as the file system, or access to a log-in job.

When valuable or powerful resources are involved, access control becomes important. The communication between the user and the server processes must include some access control information. This usually takes the form of a login username and password.

Some simple services are provided without access controls when the information they provide is publicly available anyway, and when the act of providing the service does not change the state of the system.

As the Internet has grown from a small community of cooperating researchers to a large set of communities with various purposes, it has become increasingly important to include access controls on services, and to carefully examine any uncontrolled services for security flaws.

6.2.2 The Request and Reply Paradigm

Several applications make use of a communication pattern based on stylized requests (or commands) and replies. The requests and replies are ASCII strings terminated by (usually) a carriage return and a line feed. The requests always begin with a keyword, and may have other information. The replies always begin with a number, and usually have other text. The number in the reply is a code indicating the outcome of the request (success, hard failure, soft failure, or more information needed). There is also a code for informational messages.

There are five values for the first digit of the reply code:

1yz Positive preliminary reply
2yz Positive completion reply
3yz Positive intermediate reply
4yz Transient negative completion reply
5yz Permanent negative completion reply.

For each command or command sequence, there are three possible outcomes: success (S), failure (F), or error (E). Figure 6.1 is a state diagram that represents the general

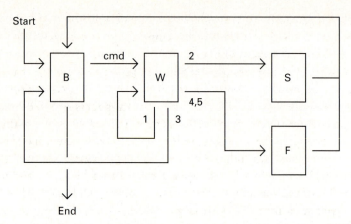

Figure 6.1   State diagram representing general sequencing and outcomes for commands and replies. The symbol **B** is for **begin**, and the symbol **W** is for **wait for reply**

sequencing and outcomes for commands and replies. Most actual commands have simpler state diagrams, since several of the possible paths are not allowed in particular cases.

There are also some applications that use the request and reply pattern, but replace the code numbers with a simple plus and minus. That is, if the request is successfully processed, the reply begins with a plus sign (+), or if the request is unsuccessful, the reply begins with a minus sign (–).

6.3   MAIL

6.3.1   Introduction

The most widely used application in the Internet community is computer mail (or electronic mail). This service allows users to compose memo-style messages and send them to other users or collections of users.

6.3.2   Simple Mail

The basic protocol for transmitting messages between the computers in the Internet is the Simple Mail Transfer Protocol (SMTP).[9] SMTP may be implemented above any reliable connection transport service; in the Internet, TCP is used. SMTP describes the allowed sequences of control messages passed between two computers to transfer a computer mail message. There are provisions for verifying that the two computers know that they are correctly connected, for identifying the message sender, for negotiating a set of recipients, and for delivering the message itself.

The format of the computer mail message (i.e., the memo-style header) is defined as well.[10] The content of the mail is limited to strings of ASCII text characters.

Users read and compose mail with a user interface application program. Most of these application programs provide extensive mail management functions to the users. These functions are not required, or even defined in the protocol specifications. Nonetheless, most users have available a mailbox that collects incoming messages, and functions that aid in reviewing the contents of the mailbox. Users may ask for a message list that shows (typically one line per message) the message number, the author, the date, and the subject of the message—some programs also indicate the length of the message. Other functions allow the user to read or print messages, to forward messages to other users, and to answer messages. For these functions the user may refer to the "current message" (usually the last message read), or refer to a message by message number—some systems also allow users to select a message (or set of messages) by author or subject keyword. Most application programs also provide extensive facilities for managing mailing lists, and for sending messages to groups of users by indicating only the name of a mailing list. One example of such application programs is MH developed by The RAND Corporation.[11]

6.3.3 Mail Transmission

Most of the material in this section is based on the specification of SMTP.[9, 12] However, this section is not to be used as a substitute for the actual specification, since some details have been left out.

Normally the user has a sophisticated program to prepare and examine mail. The interaction between this program and the SMTP modules is left up to the system designer for each operating system. Generally, the communication is through the file system. When the user has prepared a message to send, the user program leaves it in the file system, where it will be found by the sender-SMTP module (sometimes called the *mailer* program). When messages arrive, the receiver-SMTP program places them in the file system, where they will be found by the user program. The place in the file system where received messages are left is often called a *mailbox*. Usually, the mailbox is a file or directory private to the user, and the receiver-SMTP must execute as a privileged or *root* process to access it.

The SMTP design is based on the following model of communication: as the result of a user mail request, the sender-SMTP establishes a two-way transmission channel to a receiver-SMTP. The receiver-SMTP may be either the ultimate destination or an intermediate. SMTP commands are generated by the sender-SMTP, and sent to the receiver-SMTP. SMTP replies are sent from the receiver-SMTP to the sender-SMTP in response to the commands.

Once the transmission channel is established (for example, a TCP connection), the sender-SMTP sends a MAIL command, indicating the sender of the mail. If the receiver-SMTP can accept mail it responds with an OK reply. The sender-SMTP then sends a RCPT command identifying a recipient of the mail. If the receiver-SMTP can accept mail

Figure 6.2   Model for SMTP use

for that recipient, it responds with an OK reply; if not, it responds with a reply rejecting that recipient but not the whole mail transaction. The sender-SMTP and receiver-SMTP may negotiate several recipients. When the recipients have been negotiated the sender-SMTP sends the mail data, terminating with a special sequence. If the receiver-SMTP successfully processes the mail data it responds with an OK reply. The dialog is purposely in lock-step, one-step-at-a-time. See Figure 6.2.

Example of the SMTP Procedure

The SMTP example below shows mail sent by Smith at host Alpha.EDU, to Jones, Green, and Brown at host Beta.COM. Here, it is assumed that host Alpha contacts host Beta directly. S: indicates messages sent over the network by the sender-SMTP, and R: indicates messages sent over the network by the receiver-SMTP.

```
S: MAIL FROM:<Smith@Alpha.EDU>
R: 250 OK
S: RCPT TO:<Jones@Beta.COM>
R: 250 OK
S: RCPT TO:<Green@Beta.COM>
R: 550 No such user here
S: RCPT TO:<Brown@Beta.COM>
R: 250 OK

S: DATA R: 354 Start mail input; end with <CRLF>.<CRLF>
S: Blah blah blah...
S:...etc. etc. etc.
S: <CRLF>.<CRLF>
R: 250 OK
```

The mail has now been accepted for Jones and Brown. Green did not have a mailbox at host Beta. Since all this is normally done by the system in the background, i.e., while the user is doing something else or is not even logged on, the system mail programs (e.g., the sender-SMTP) will generate an error report, and send it as a message to the originator of the mail, in this case, Smith.

To provide the relay capability, the server-SMTP must be supplied with the name of the ultimate destination host, as well as the destination mailbox name.

The argument to the MAIL command is a <reverse-path>, which specifies whom the mail is from. The argument to the RCPT command is a <forward-path>, which specifies whom the mail is to. The <forward-path> is a source route, while the <reverse-path> is a return route (which may be used to return a message to the sender when an error occurs with a relayed message).

When the same message is sent to multiple recipients, SMTP encourages the transmission of only one copy of the data for all the recipients at the same destination host.

The mail commands and replies have a rigid syntax. Replies also have a numeric code. Commands and replies are not case sensitive. That is, a command or reply word may be uppercase, lowercase, or any mixture thereof. Note that this is not true of mailbox usernames. For some hosts the username is case-sensitive (though this is generally thought to be a bad practice), and SMTP implementations must take care to preserve the case of usernames as they appear in mailbox arguments. Host names are not case sensitive.

Commands and replies are composed of characters from the ASCII character set. When the transport service provides an 8-bit byte (octet) transmission channel, each 7-bit character is transmitted right justified in an octet, with the high-order bit cleared to zero.

When specifying the general form of a command or reply, an argument (or special symbol) will be denoted by a metalinguistic variable (or constant), for example, <string> or <reverse-path>, where the angle brackets indicate these are metalinguistic variables. However, some arguments use the angle brackets literally. For example, an actual <reverse-path> is enclosed in angle brackets, i.e., <John.Smith@ISI.EDU> is an instance of <reverse-path> (the angle brackets are actually transmitted in the command or reply).

There are three steps to SMTP mail transactions. The transaction is started with a MAIL command, which gives the sender identification. A series of one or more RCPT commands follows, giving the receiver information. Then a DATA command gives the mail data. Finally, the end of mail data indicator confirms the transaction.

The first step in the procedure is the MAIL command. The <reverse-path> contains the source mailbox:

    MAIL <SP> FROM:<reverse-path> <CRLF>

This command tells the receiver-SMTP that a new mail transaction is starting, and to reset all its state tables and buffers, including any recipients or mail data. It gives the <reverse-path> that can be used to report errors. If accepted, the receiver-SMTP returns a 250 OK reply.

The <reverse-path> can contain more than just a mailbox. The <reverse-path> is a reverse source routing list of hosts and source mailbox. The first host in the <reverse-path> should be the host sending this command.

The second step in the procedure is the RCPT command:

    RCPT <SP> TO: <forward-path> <CRLF>

This command gives a <forward-path> identifying one recipient. If accepted, the receiver-SMTP returns a 250 OK reply, and stores the <forward-path>. If the recipient is unknown, the receiver-SMTP returns a 550 Failure reply. This second step of the procedure can be repeated any number of times.

The <forward-path> can contain more than just a mailbox. It is a source routing list of hosts and the destination mailbox. The first host in the <forward-path> should be the host receiving this command.

The third step in the procedure is the DATA command:

    DATA <CRLF>

If accepted, the receiver-SMTP returns a 354 Intermediate reply, and considers all succeeding lines to be the message text. When the end of text is received and stored, the receiver-SMTP sends a 250 OK reply.

Since the mail data is sent on the transmission channel, the end-of-mail data must be indicated, so that the command and reply dialog can be resumed. SMTP indicates the end of the mail data by sending a line containing only a period. A transparency procedure is used to prevent this from interfering with the user's text.

Please note that the mail data includes the memo header items of the mail format, such as *Date*, *Subject*, *To*, *Cc*, and *From*.

The end of mail data indicator also confirms the mail transaction, and tells the receiver-SMTP to process the stored recipients and mail data. If accepted, the receiver-SMTP returns a 250 OK reply. The DATA command should fail only if the mail transaction was incomplete (for example, if it had no recipients), or if resources are not available.

This procedure is an example of a mail transaction; the commands must be used only in the order discussed above.

There are some cases where the destination information in the <forward-path> is incorrect, but the receiver-SMTP knows the correct destination. In such cases, one of the following replies should be used to allow the sender to contact the correct destination.

- 251 User not local; will forward to <forward-path>

  The 251 reply indicates that the receiver-SMTP knows the user's mailbox is on another host, and indicates the correct <forward-path> to use in the future. Note that the host, the user, or both may be different. The receiver takes responsibility for delivering the message.

- 551 User not local; please try <forward-path>

  The 551 reply indicates that the receiver-SMTP knows that the user's mailbox is on another host, and indicates the correct <forward-path> to use. Note that the host, the user, or both may be different. The receiver refuses to accept mail for this user, and the

sender must either redirect the mail according to the information provided, or return
an error response to the originating user.

SMTP provides as additional features, commands to verify a username or to expand a
mailing list. This is done with the commands VRFY and EXPN, which have character
string arguments. For the VRFY command, the string is a username; the response may
include the full name of the user and must include the mailbox of the user. For the EXPN
command, the string identifies a mailing list; the multiline response may include the full
name of the users, and must give the mailboxes on the mailing list.

Username is a fuzzy term and has been used purposely. If a host implements the VRFY
or EXPN commands, then at least local mailboxes must be recognized as "usernames." If a
host chooses to recognize other strings as usernames, it is allowed.

In some hosts the distinction between a mailing list and an alias for a single mailbox is a
bit fuzzy, since a common data structure may hold both types of entries, and it is possible
to have mailing lists of one mailbox. If a request is made to verify a mailing list, and a positive response can be given on receipt of a message so addressed, it will be delivered to
everyone on the list; otherwise, an error should be reported (e.g., "550 That is a mailing
list, not a user"). If a request is made to expand a username, a positive response can be
formed by returning a list containing one name, or an error can be reported (e.g., "550
That is a username, not a mailing list").

In the case of a multiline reply (which is normal for EXPN), exactly one mailbox is to be
specified on each line of the reply. In the case of an ambiguous request, for example,
"VRFY Smith," where there are two Smiths, the response must be "553 User ambiguous."

The case of verifying a username is straightforward as shown:
either

    S: VRFY Smith
    R: 250 Fred Smith <Smith@ZEPHYR.ISI.EDU>

or

    S: VRFY Smith
    R: 251 User not local; will forward to <Smith@TRADER.ISI.EDU>

or

    S: VRFY Jones
    R: 550 String does not match anything

or

    S: VRFY Jones
    R: 551 User not local; please try <Jones@TRADER.ISI.EDU>

or

    S: VRFY Gourzenkyinplatz
    R: 553 User ambiguous.

The case of expanding a mailbox list requires a multiline reply as shown:
Either

    S: EXPN Example-People
    R: 250-Jon Postel <Postel@ZEPHYR.ISI.EDU>
    R: 250-Fred Fonebone <Fonebone@TRADER.ISI.EDU>
    R: 250-Sam Q. Smith <SQSmith@TRADER.ISI.EDU>
    R: 250-Quincy Smith <@ZEPHYR.ISI.EDU:Q-Smith@VAXA.ISI.EDU>
    R: 250-<joe@foo-UNIX.XYZ.COM>
    R: 250 <xyz@bar-UNIX.XYZ.COM>

or

    S: EXPN Executive-Washroom-List
    R: 550 Access Denied to You

The character string arguments of the VRFY and EXPN commands cannot be further restricted, due to the variety of implementations of the username and mailbox list concepts. On some systems, it may be appropriate for the argument of the EXPN command to be a filename for a file containing a mailing list, but again, there is a variety of file-naming conventions in the Internet. The VRFY and EXPN commands are not included in the minimum implementation, and are not required to work across relays when they are implemented.

The main purpose of SMTP is to deliver messages to users' mailboxes.

At the time the transmission channel is opened there is an exchange to ensure that the hosts are communicating with the hosts they think they are. The following two commands are used in transmission channel opening and closing:

    HELO <SP> <domain> <CRLF>
    QUIT <CRLF>

In the HELO command, the host sending the command identifies itself; the command may be interpreted as saying "Hello, I am <domain>."

The SMTP commands define the mail transfer or the mail system function requested by the user. SMTP commands are character strings terminated by <CRLF>. The command codes themselves are alphabetic characters terminated by <SP>, if parameters follow and by <CRLF> otherwise. The syntax of mailboxes must conform to receiver site conventions.

A mail transaction involves several data objects that are communicated as arguments to different commands. The <reverse-path> is the argument of the MAIL command, the <forward-path> is the argument of the RCPT command, and the mail data is the argument of the DATA command. These arguments or data objects must be transmitted and held pending the confirmation communicated by the end of mail data indication, which finalizes the transaction. The model for this is that distinct buffers are provided to hold the types of data objects, that is, there is a <reverse-path> buffer, a <forward-path> buffer, and a mail data buffer. Specific commands cause information to be appended to a specific buffer, or cause one or more buffers to be cleared.

The HELLO (HELO) command is used to identify the sender-SMTP to the receiver-SMTP. The argument field contains the host name of the sender-SMTP. The receiver-SMTP identifies itself to the sender-SMTP in the connection greeting reply, and in the response to this command. This command, and an OK reply to it, confirm that both the sender-SMTP and the receiver-SMTP are in the initial state, that is, there is no transaction in progress and all state tables and buffers are cleared.

The MAIL (MAIL) command is used to initiate a mail transaction in which the mail data is delivered to one or more mailboxes. The argument field contains a <reverse-path>.

The <reverse-path> consists of an optional list of hosts, and the sender's mailbox. When the list of hosts is present, it is a "reverse" source route, and indicates that the mail was relayed through each host on the list (the first host in the list is the most recent relay). This list is used as a source route to return nondelivery notices to the sender. As each relay host adds itself to the beginning of the list, it must use its name as known in the environment to which it is relaying the mail, rather than the environment from which the mail came (if they are different). In some types of error-reporting messages (for example, undeliverable mail notifications) the <reverse-path> may be null.

The MAIL command also clears the <reverse-path> buffer, the <forward-path> buffer, and the mail data buffer, and inserts the <reverse-path> information from this command into the <reverse-path> buffer.

The RECIPIENT (RCPT) command is used to identify an individual recipient of the mail data; multiple recipients are specified by multiple uses of this command.

The <forward-path> consists of an optional list of hosts and a required destination mailbox. When the list of hosts is present, it is a source route, and indicates that the mail must be relayed to the next host on the list. If the receiver-SMTP does not implement the relay function, it may use the same reply it would for an unknown local user (550).

When mail is relayed, the relay host must remove itself from the beginning <forward-path> and put itself at the beginning of the <reverse-path>. When mail reaches its ultimate destination (the <forward-path> contains only a destination mailbox), the receiver-SMTP inserts it into the destination mailbox in accordance with its host mail conventions.

For example, mail received at relay host *A* with arguments

    FROM:<USERX@VENUS.ABC.EDU>
    TO:<@PLUTO.DEF.EDU,@MARS.GHI.EDU:USERC@EARTH.JKL.EDU>

will be relayed on to host *B* with arguments

    FROM:<@PLUTO.DEF.EDU:USERX@VENUS.ABC.EDU>
    TO:<@MARS.GHI.EDU:USERC@EARTH.JKL.EDU>.

This command causes its <forward-path> argument to be appended to the <forward-path> buffer.

The DATA command causes the receiver to treat the lines following the command as mail data from the sender. This command causes the mail data from this command to be appended to the mail data buffer. The mail data may contain any of the 128 ASCII character codes. As mentioned, mail data is terminated by a line containing only a period, that is the character sequence <CRLF>.<CRLF>, which is the end of mail data indication. The end of mail data indication requires that the receiver must process the stored mail transaction information. This processing consumes the information in the <reverse-path> buffer, the <forward-path> buffer, and the mail data buffer, and on the completion of this command these buffers are cleared. If the processing is successful, the receiver must send an OK reply. If the processing fails completely, the receiver must send a failure reply.

When the receiver-SMTP accepts a message either for relaying or for final delivery, it inserts at the beginning of the mail data a timestamp line. The timestamp line indicates the identity of the host that sent the message, the identity of the host that received the message (who is inserting the timestamp), and the date and time at which the message was received. Relayed messages will have multiple timestamp lines.

When the receiver-SMTP makes the "final delivery" of a message, it inserts at the beginning of the mail data a return path line. The return path line preserves the information in the <reverse-path> from the MAIL command. Here, *final delivery* means that the message leaves the SMTP world. Normally, this would mean it has been delivered to the destination user, but in some cases it may be further processed and transmitted by another mail system.

It is possible for the mailbox in the return path to be different from the actual sender's mailbox; for example, if error responses are to be delivered to a special error-handling mailbox.

The preceding two paragraphs imply that the final mail data will begin with a return path line, followed by one or more timestamp lines. These lines will be followed by the mail data header and body.

Special mention is needed of the response, and further action required when the processing following the end of mail data indication is partially successful. This could arise if, after accepting several recipients and the mail data, the receiver-SMTP finds that the mail data can be successfully delivered to only some of the recipients (for example, due to mailbox space allocation problems). In such a situation, the response to the DATA command must be an OK reply. But, the receiver-SMTP must compose and send an "undeliverable mail" notification message to the originator of the message. It must send either a single notification that lists all of the recipients that failed to get the message, or separate notification messages for each failed recipient. All undeliverable mail notification messages are sent using the MAIL command.

The TURN (TURN) command is used to reverse the roles of the sender-SMTP and the receiver-SMTP. A receiver-SMTP may refuse to change roles (there may be security and access issues involved in this decision).

The RESET (RSET) command specifies that the current mail transaction is to be aborted. Any stored sender, recipients, or mail data must be discarded, and all buffers and state tables must be cleared. The receiver must send an OK reply.

The VERIFY (VRFY) command asks the receiver to confirm that the argument identifies a user. If it is a username, the full name of the user (if known), and the fully specified mailbox are returned. This command has no effect on the <reverse-path> buffer, the <forward-path> buffer, or the mail data buffer.

The EXPAND (EXPN) command asks the receiver to confirm that the argument identifies a mailing list, and if so, to return the membership of that list. The full name of the users (if known), and the fully specified mailboxes are returned in a multiline reply. This command has no effect on the <reverse-path> buffer, the <forward-path> buffer, or the mail data buffer.

The HELP (HELP) command causes the receiver to send helpful information to the sender. The command may take an argument (e.g., any command name) and return more specific information as a response. This command has no effect on the <reverse-path> buffer, the <forward-path> buffer, or the mail data buffer.

The NOOP (NOOP) command does not affect any parameters or previously entered commands. It specifies no action other than that the receiver send an OK reply. This command has no effect on the <reverse-path> buffer, the <forward-path> buffer, or the mail data buffer.

The QUIT (QUIT) command specifies that the receiver must send an OK reply, and then close the transmission channel. The receiver should not close the transmission channel until it receives and replies to a QUIT command (even if there was an error). The sender should not close the transmission channel until it sends a QUIT command and receives the reply, even if there was an error response to a previous command). If the connection is closed prematurely, the receiver should act as if a RSET command has been received (canceling any pending transaction, but not undoing any previously completed transaction), and the sender should act as if the command or transaction in progress has received a temporary error (4xx).

The mail commands consist of a command code followed by an argument field. Command codes are four alphabetic characters. Upper and lowercase alphabetic characters are to be treated identically. Thus, any of the following may represent the mail command:

MAIL Mail mail MaIl mAIl

This also applies to any symbols representing parameter values, such as *TO* or *to* for the <forward-path>. Command codes and the argument fields are separated by one or more spaces. However, within the <reverse-path> and <forward-path> arguments case is important. In particular, in some hosts the user *smith* is different from the user *Smith*.

The detailed specification of the command and argument syntax is provided in *RFC 821*.[9]

Hosts are generally known by names that are translated to addresses in each host. Note that the name elements of domains are the official names—no use of nicknames or aliases is allowed.

Sometimes a host is not known to the translation function, and communication is blocked. To bypass this barrier two numeric forms are also allowed for host "names." One

FARNET has invited the IESG and and any IAB members attending the Santa Fe IETF to a dinner Monday, Nov 18th. This dinner is intended as a get to know each other affair. Details will be provided later by Susan Estrada.

Please RSVP to Susan (estradas@cerf.net) "real soon".

Greg Vaudreuil

The message headers are separated from the body of the message by an empty line. The message headers consist of a keyword, followed by a colon, and one or more values.

A header may be viewed as being composed of a field name followed by a colon and a field body, and terminated by a carriage return–line feed. The field name must be composed of printable ASCII characters, i.e., characters that have values between 33 and 126, decimal (except colon). The field body may be composed of any ASCII characters (except the carriage return or the line feed).

Certain field bodies of headers may be interpreted according to an internal syntax that some systems may wish to parse. These fields are called *structured fields*. Examples include fields containing dates and addresses. Other fields, such as *Subject* and *Comments*, are regarded simply as strings of text. Any field having a field body that is defined as other than simply text is to be treated as a structured field.

Due to an artifact of the notational conventions, the syntax indicates that, when present, some fields, must be in a particular order. Header fields are *not* required to occur in any particular order, except that the message body must occur *after* the header. It is recommended that, if present, headers be sent in the order Return-Path, Received, Date, From, Subject, Sender, To, Cc, etc. This specification permits multiple occurrences of most fields. Except as noted, their interpretation is not specified here, and their use is discouraged. The detailed specifications are found in *RFC 822*.[10]

Some systems permit mail recipients to forward a message, retaining the original headers, by adding some new fields. The mail standard supports such a service, through the Resent prefix to field names.

Whenever the string Resent begins a field name, the field is understood to have the same semantics as a field whose name does not have the prefix. However, the message is assumed to have been forwarded by an original recipient who attached the Resent field. This new field is treated as being more recent than the equivalent, original field. For example, the Resent-From indicates the person that forwarded the message, whereas the From field indicates the original author.

Use of such precedence information depends upon participants' communication needs. For example, this standard does not dictate when a Resent-From address should receive replies, in lieu of sending them to the From address.

In general, the Resent-fields should be treated as containing a set of information that is independent of the set of original fields. Information for one set should not automatically be taken from the other. The interpretation of multiple Resent fields of the same type is undefined.

In the remainder of the mail specification, occurrence of legal Resent fields are treated identically with the occurrence of fields whose names do not contain this prefix.

Tracing information is used to provide an audit trail for message handling. In addition, it indicates a route back to the sender of the message. The *Return-Path* field is added by the final transport system that delivers the message to its recipient. The field is intended to contain definitive information about the address and route back to the message's originator. The Reply-To field is added by the originator, and serves to direct replies. While the syntax indicates that a route specification is optional, every attempt should be made to provide that information in this field. A copy of the *Received* field is added by each transport service that relays the message. The information in the field can be quite useful for tracing transport problems.

The names of the sending and receiving hosts and time-of-receipt may be specified. The *via* parameter may be used, to indicate what physical mechanism the message was sent over, such as Internet or Phonenet, and the *with* parameter may be used to indicate the mail- or connection-level protocol that was used, such as the SMTP mail protocol, or X.25 transport protocol.

Some transport services queue mail; the internal message identifier that is assigned to the message may be noted, using the *id* parameter. When the sending host uses a destination address specification that the receiving host reinterprets, by expansion or transformation, the receiving host may wish to record the original specification, using the *for* parameter. For example, when a copy of mail is sent to the member of a distribution list, this parameter may be used to record the original address that was used to specify the list.

The standard allows only a subset of the combinations possible with the From, Sender, Reply-To, Resent-From, Resent-Sender, and Resent-Reply-To fields. The limitation is intentional.

The From field contains the identity of the persons who wished this message to be sent. The message-creation process should default this field to be a single, authenticated machine address, indicating the Agent (person, system, or process) entering the message. If this is not done, the Sender field must be present. If the From field *is* defaulted this way, the Sender field is optional, and is redundant with the From field. In all cases, addresses in the From field must be machine-usable (addr-specs) and may not contain named lists (groups).

The *Sender* field contains the authenticated identity of the *Agent* that is sending the message. It is intended for use when the sender is not the author of the message, or to indicate who among a group of authors actually sent the message. If the contents of the Sender field would be completely redundant with the From field, then the Sender field need not be present, and its use is discouraged (though still legal). In particular, the Sender field must be present if it is *not* the same as the From field.

The Sender mailbox specification includes a word sequence that must correspond to a specific agent (i.e., a human user or a computer program) rather than a standard address. This indicates the expectation that the field will identify the single *Agent* responsible for sending the mail, and will not simply include the name of a mailbox from which the mail was sent. For example, in the case of a shared login name, the name, by itself, would not be adequate. The local-part address unit, which refers to this agent, is expected to be a computer system term, and not (for example) a generalized personal reference that can be used outside the network text message context.

Since the critical function served by the Sender field is identification of the agent responsible for sending mail, and since computer programs cannot be held accountable for their behavior, it is strongly recommended that when a computer program generates a message, the *human* who is responsible for that program be referenced as part of the Sender field mailbox specification.

The *Reply-To* field provides a general mechanism for indicating any mailboxes to which responses are to be sent. Three typical uses for this feature can be distinguished. In the first case, the authors may not have regular machine-based mailboxes and therefore may wish to indicate an alternate machine address. In the second case, an author may wish additional persons to be made aware of, or responsible for, replies. A somewhat different use may be of some help to "text message teleconferencing" groups equipped with automatic distribution services: include the address of that service in the Reply-To field of all messages submitted to the teleconference; then participants can "reply" to conference submissions to guarantee the correct distribution of any submission of their own.

The Return-Path field is added by the mail transport service, at the time of final delivery. It is intended to identify a path back to the originator of the message. The Reply-To field is added by the message originator, and is intended to direct replies.

For systems which automatically generate address lists for replies to messages, the following recommendations are made:

- The Sender field mailbox should be sent notices of any problems in transport or delivery of the original messages. If there is no Sender field, then the From field mailbox should be used.

- The Sender field mailbox should *never* be used automatically, in a recipient's reply message.

- If the Reply-To field exists, then the reply should go to the addresses indicated in that field and not to the addresses indicated in the From field.

- If there is a From field, but no Reply-To field, the reply should be sent to the addresses indicated in the From field.

- Sometimes, a recipient may actually wish to communicate with the person that initiated the message transfer. In such cases, it is reasonable to use the Sender address.

This recommendation is intended only for automated use of originator-fields and is not intended to suggest that replies may not also be sent to other recipients of messages. It is up to the respective mail-handling programs to decide what additional facilities will be provided.

The *To* field contains the identity of the primary recipients of the message. The *Cc* field contains the identity of the secondary (informational) recipients of the message. The *Bcc* Field contains the identity of additional recipients of the message. The contents of this field are not included in copies of the message sent to the primary and secondary recipients. Some systems may choose to include the text of the Bcc field only in the author's copy, while others may also include it in the text sent to all those indicated in the Bcc list.

The *Message-ID* field contains a unique identifier (the local-part address unit) that refers to *This* version of *This* message. The uniqueness of the message identifier is guaranteed by the host that generates it. This identifier is intended to be machine readable and not necessarily meaningful to humans. A message identifier pertains to exactly one instantiation of a particular message; subsequent revisions to the message should each receive new message identifiers. The contents of the *In-Reply-To* field identify previous correspondence that a message answers. Note that if message identifiers are used in this field, they must use the msg-id specification format.

The contents of the *References* field identify other correspondence that this message references. Note that if message identifiers are used, they must use the msg-id specification format.

The *Keywords* field contains keywords or phrases, separated by commas. The *Subject* field is intended to provide a summary, or indicate the nature, of the message. The *Comments* field permits adding text comments onto the message without disturbing the contents of the message's body.

If included, the day-of-week field must specify the day implied by the date specification.

Time zone may be indicated in several ways. UT is Universal Time (formerly called Greenwich Mean Time), and GMT is permitted as a reference to Universal Time. The other forms are taken from ANSI standard X3.51-1975. One allows explicit indication of the amount of offset from UT; the other uses common 3-character strings for indicating time zones in North America.

A mailbox receives mail. It is a conceptual entity that does not necessarily pertain to file storage. For example, some sites may choose to print mail on a printer and deliver the output to the addressee's desk.

A mailbox specification comprises a person, system, or process name reference, a domain-dependent string, and a name domain reference. The name reference is optional, and is usually used to indicate the human name of a recipient. The name domain reference specifies a sequence of subdomains. The domain-dependent string is uninterpreted, except by the final subdomain; the rest of the mail service merely transmits it as a literal string.

An individual may have several mailboxes, and may wish to receive mail at whatever mailbox is convenient for the sender to access. The mail standard does not provide a means of specifying such an option.

A set of individuals may wish to receive mail as a single unit, i.e., on a distribution list. The <group> construct permits specification of such a list. Recipient mailboxes are specified within the bracketed part (i.e., group: mailboxes;). A copy of the transmitted message is to be sent to each mailbox listed. This standard does not permit recursive specification of groups within groups.

While a list must be named, it is not required that the contents of the list be included. In this case, the <address> serves only as an indication of group distribution and would appear in the form:

    name:;

Some mail services may provide a group-list distribution facility, accepting a single mailbox reference, expanding it to the full distribution list, and relaying the mail to the list's members. The mail standard provides no additional syntax for indicating such a service. Using the <group> address alternative, while listing one mailbox in it, can mean either that the mailbox reference will be expanded to a list, or that there is a group with one member.

It often is necessary to send mail to a site without knowing any of its valid addresses. For example, there may be mail system dysfunctions, or a user may wish to find out a person's correct address at that site.

The mail standard specifies a single, reserved mailbox address (local-part) that is to be valid at each site. Mail sent to that address is to be routed to a person responsible for the site's mail system or to a person with responsibility for general site operation. The name of the reserved local-part address is:

    Postmaster

so that Postmaster@domain is required to be valid. This reserved local-part must be matched without sensitivity to alphabetic case, so that *POSTMASTER*, *postmaster*, and even *poStmASteR* are to be accepted.

6.3.5   Domain Names in Mail

It is interesting to note that the concept of domain names and the supporting Domain Name System (DNS) (see Chapter 11) was just coming to fruition at the time the standards documents for mail were being written. So these documents were written with very little experience in using domain names. However, they have held up very well.

In the meantime, the use of domain names has exploded with the growth in the size of the Internet. Not only are hosts, that are in the Internet (those that communicate directly with TCP/IP) using domain names, but hosts in other networking systems using different underlying protocols may also use domain names.

A great deal of mail is relayed between different networking systems. Some of this is hidden from the users through the use of domain names and mail relay hosts. The DNS supports this by including a type of data record called a *mail exchanger*, or *MX* record.

The MX record allows a name to be registered and listed in the Internet DNS, and associated with a relay host that will forward mail to the named host in another networking system.

For example, the name Well.SF.CA.US is used to identify a particular computer that is not a TCP/IP Internet host and has no direct means of communicating with Internet hosts. An MX record has been established in the DNS as follows:

Well.SF.CA.US. 604800 MX 10 APPLE.COM.

which indicates that any mail intended for Well.SF.CA.US will be handled by APPLE.-COM. Another record in the DNS gives the Internet address for APPLE.COM:

apple.com IN A 130.43.2.2

showing that Internet computers can make a direct TCP connection to APPLE.COM to deliver mail.

Users of mail in the Internet need not be aware of this underlying mail relaying. As users, they see a domain name for the Well and use it just as they would the domain name for any computer on the Internet.

6.3.6 Mail Implementation Specifics

6.3.6.1 The Model

The SMTP specification is clear and contains numerous examples, so implementors should not find it difficult to understand. The following simply updates or annotates the specification consistent with current usage.

The mail format specification is a long and dense document, defining a rich syntax. Unfortunately, incomplete or defective implementations of it are common. In fact, nearly all of the many formats of the specification are actually used, so an implementation generally needs to recognize and correctly interpret all of the syntax.

Mail is sent by a series of request and response transactions between a client, the sender-SMTP, and a server, the receiver-SMTP. These transactions pass the message proper, which is composed of the header and the body, and SMTP source and destination addresses, which is referred to as the *envelope*.

The SMTP programs are analogous to the Message Transfer Agents (MTAs) of X.400. There will be another level of protocol software, closer to the end user, that is responsible for composing and analyzing message headers; this component is known as the *User Agent* in X.400, and we use that term in this document. There is a clear logical distinction between the User Agent and the SMTP implementation, since they operate on different levels of protocol. Note, however, that this distinction may not be exactly reflected in the structure of typical implementations of Internet mail. Often, there is a program known as the *mailer*

6.3.6.5   Receipt Command

A host that supports a receiver-SMTP must support the reserved mailbox Postmaster.

The receiver-SMTP may verify RCPT parameters as they arrive; however, RCPT responses must not be delayed beyond a reasonable time. Therefore, a 250 OK response to a RCPT does not necessarily imply that the delivery addresses are valid. Errors found after message acceptance will be reported by mailing a notification message to an appropriate address.

The set of conditions under which a RCPT parameter can be validated immediately is an engineering design choice. Reporting destination mailbox errors to the sender-SMTP before mail is transferred is generally desirable, to save time and network bandwidth, but this advantage is lost if RCPT verification is lengthy.

For example, the receiver can verify immediately any simple local reference, such as a single locally registered mailbox. On the other hand, the "reasonable time" limitation generally implies deferring verification of a mailing list until after the message has been transferred and accepted, since verifying a large mailing list can take a very long time. An implementation might choose not to defer validation of addresses that are nonlocal and therefore require a DNS lookup. If a DNS lookup is performed, but a soft domain system error (e.g., a timeout) occurs, validity must be assumed.

6.3.6.6   Data Command

Every receiver-SMTP (not just one that accepts a message for relaying or for final delivery) must insert a Received: line at the beginning of a message. In this line, called a timestamp line:

- The From field should contain both the name of the source host as presented in the HELO command, and a domain literal containing the IP address of the source, determined from the TCP connection.

- The (message queue) ID field may contain an @, but this is not required.

- The For field may contain a list of <path> entries when multiple RCPT commands have been given.

An Internet mail program must not change a Received: line that was previously added to the message header. Including both the source host and the IP source address in the Received: line may provide enough information for tracking illicit mail sources, and eliminate a need to explicitly verify the HELO parameter. Received: lines are primarily intended for humans tracing mail routes, primarily for diagnosis of faults.

When the receiver-SMTP makes final delivery of a message, it must pass the MAIL FROM: address from the SMTP envelope with the message, for use if an error notification message must be sent later. There is an analogous requirement when gatewaying from the Internet into a different mail environment.

Note that the final reply to the DATA command depends only upon the successful transfer and storage of the message. Any problem with the destination addresses must either have been reported in an SMTP error reply to the RCPT commands, or be reported in a later error message mailed to the originator.

The MAIL FROM: information may be passed as a parameter or in a Return-Path: line inserted at the beginning of the message.

6.3.6.7 SMTP Replies

A receiver-SMTP should send only the reply codes listed in the specification. A receiver-SMTP should use the text shown in examples whenever appropriate.

A sender-SMTP must determine its actions only by the reply code, not by the text (except for 251 and 551 replies); any text, including no text at all, must be acceptable. The space (blank) following the reply code is considered part of the text. Whenever possible, a sender-SMTP should test only the first digit of the reply code.

Interoperability problems have arisen with SMTP systems using reply codes that are not listed explicitly but are legal according to the theory of reply codes.

6.3.6.8 WKS Use in MX Processing

It had been recommended that the domain system be queried for well-known service (WKS) records, to verify that each proposed mail target supports SMTP. Later experience has shown that WKS is not widely supported, so the WKS step in MX processing should not be used.

6.3.6.9 Content Type

The set of optional header fields is expanded to include the Content-Type field. This field "allows mail reading systems to automatically identify the type of a structured message body and to process it for display accordingly." A User Agent may support this field.

6.3.6.10 Date and Time Specification

There is a strong trend towards the use of numeric time zone indicators, and implementations should use numeric time zones instead of time zone names. However, all implementations must accept either notation. If time zone names are used, they must be exactly as defined.

6.3.6.11 Local-part

The basic mailbox address specification has the form: local-part@domain. Here the *local-part*, sometimes called the lefthand side of the address, is domain dependent.

A host that is forwarding the message but is not the destination host implied by the right-hand-side domain must not interpret or modify the local-part of the address.

When mail is to be gatewayed from the Internet mail environment into a foreign mail environment, routing information for that foreign environment may be embedded within the local-part of the address. The gateway will then interpret this local-part appropriately for the foreign mail environment.

Although source routes are discouraged within the Internet there are non-Internet mail environments whose delivery mechanisms depend upon source routes. Source routes for extra-Internet environments can generally be buried in the local-part of the address while mail traverses the Internet. When the mail reaches the appropriate Internet mail gateway, the gateway will interpret the local-part and build the necessary address or route for the target mail environment.

For example, an Internet host might send mail to: a!b!c!user@gateway-domain. The complex local-part a!b!c!user would be uninterpreted within the Internet domain, but could be parsed and understood by the specified mail gateway.

An embedded source route is sometimes encoded in the local-part using % as a right-binding routing operator. For example, in:

    user%domain%relay3%relay2@relay1

the % convention implies that the mail is to be routed from *relay1* through *relay2*, and *relay3*, and finally to *user* at *domain*. This is commonly known as the *%-hack*. It is suggested that % have lower precedence than any other routing operator (e.g., !) hidden in the local-part; for example, a!b%c would be interpreted as (a!b)%c.

Only the target host (in this case, *relay1*) is permitted to analyze the local-part user%domain%relay3%relay2.

6.3.6.12   Domain Literals

A mailer must be able to accept and parse an Internet domain literal whose content (*dtext*) is a dotted-decimal host address.

An SMTP must accept and recognize a domain literal for any of its own IP addresses.

6.3.6.13   Common Address Formatting Errors

Errors in formatting or parsing mail addresses are, unfortunately, common. This section mentions only the most common errors. A User Agent must accept all valid mail address formats, and must not generate illegal address syntax.

- A common error is to leave out the semicolon after a group identifier.

- Some systems fail to fully-qualify domain names in messages they generate. The right-hand side of an @ sign in a header address field must be a fully qualified domain name.

For example, some systems fail to fully qualify the From: address; this prevents a "reply" command in the user interface from automatically constructing a return address.

Although the specification allows the local use of abbreviated domain names within a domain, the intent is that an Internet host must not send an SMTP message header containing an abbreviated domain name in an address field. This allows the address fields of the header to be passed without alteration across the Internet.

- Some systems mis-parse multiple-hop explicit source routes, such as:

  @relay1,@relay2,@relay3:user@domain

- Some systems overqualify domain names by adding a trailing dot to some or all domain names in addresses or message ids.

6.3.6.14 *Explicit Source Routes*

Internet host software should not create a header containing an address with an explicit source route, but must accept such headers for compatibility with earlier systems.

In an understatement, the specification says "The use of explicit source routing is discouraged." Many hosts have implemented source routes incorrectly, so the syntax cannot be used unambiguously in practice. Many users feel the syntax is ugly. Explicit source routes are not needed in the mail envelope for delivery. For all these reasons, explicit source route notations are not to be used in Internet mail headers.

It is necessary to allow an explicit source route to be buried in the local-part of an address, e.g., using the %-hack, to allow mail to be gatewayed into another environment in which explicit source routing is necessary. The vigilant will observe that there is no way for a User Agent to detect and prevent the use of such implicit source routing when the destination is within the Internet. We can only discourage source routing of any kind within the Internet as unnecessary and undesirable.

6.3.6.15 *SMTP Queueing Strategies*

The common structure of a host SMTP implementation includes user mailboxes, one or more areas for queueing messages in transit, and one or more daemon processes for sending and receiving mail. The exact structure will vary depending on the needs of the users on the host, and the number and size of mailing lists supported by it. We will describe several optimizations that have proved helpful, particularly for mailers supporting high traffic levels. Any queueing strategy must include:

- Timeouts on all activities

- Never sending error messages in response to error messages.

6.3.6.16 *Sending Strategy*

The general model of a sender-SMTP is one or more processes that periodically attempt to transmit outgoing mail. In a typical system, the program that composes a message has some method for requesting immediate attention for a new piece of outgoing mail, while mail that cannot be transmitted immediately must be queued, and periodically retried by the sender. A mail queue entry will include not only the message, but also the envelope information.

The sender must delay retrying a particular destination after one attempt has failed. In general, the retry interval should be at least 30 minutes; however, more sophisticated and variable strategies will be beneficial when the sender-SMTP can determine the reason for nondelivery.

Retries continue until the message is transmitted or the sender gives up; the give-up time generally needs to be at least 4–5 days. The parameters to the retry algorithm must be configurable. A sender should keep a list of hosts it cannot reach and corresponding time-outs, rather than just retrying queued mail items.

Experience suggests that failures are typically transient (the target system has crashed), favoring a policy of two connection attempts in the first hour the message is in the queue, and then backing off to retrying once every two or three hours.

The sender-SMTP can shorten the queueing delay by cooperation with the receiver-SMTP. In particular, if mail is received from a particular address, this is good evidence that any mail queued for that host can now be sent.

The strategy may be further modified as a result of multiple addresses per host, to optimize delivery time versus resource usage.

A sender-SMTP may have a large queue of messages for each unavailable destination host. If it retried all these messages in every retry cycle, there would be excessive Internet overhead, and the daemon would be blocked for a long period. Note that an SMTP can generally determine that a delivery attempt has failed only after a timeout of a minute or more; a 1-minute timeout per connection will result in a very large delay if it is repeated for dozens or even hundreds of queued messages.

When the same message is to be delivered to several users on the same host, only one copy of the message should be transmitted. That is, the sender-SMTP should use the command sequence: RCPT, RCPT,..., RCPT, DATA instead of the sequence: RCPT, DATA, RCPT, DATA, ..., RCPT, DATA. Implementation of this efficiency feature is strongly urged.

Similarly, the sender-SMTP may support multiple concurrent outgoing mail transactions to achieve timely delivery. However, some limit should be imposed to protect the host from devoting all its resources to mail.

The use of the different addresses of a multihomed host is discussed below.

6.3.6.17   Receiving Strategy

The receiver-SMTP should attempt to keep a pending listen on the SMTP port at all times. This will require the support of multiple incoming TCP connections for SMTP. Some limit may be imposed.

When the receiver-SMTP receives mail from a particular host address, it could notify the local sender-SMTP to retry any mail pending for that host address.

6.3.6.18 *Timeouts in SMTP*

There are two approaches to timeouts in the sender-SMTP: limit the time for each SMTP command separately, or limit the time for the entire SMTP dialogue for a single mail message. A sender-SMTP should use the former option, per-command timeouts. Timeouts should be easily reconfigurable, preferably without recompiling the SMTP code.

Timeouts are an essential feature of an SMTP implementation. If the timeouts are too long (or worse, if there are no timeouts), Internet communication failures or software bugs in receiver-SMTP programs can tie up SMTP processes indefinitely. If the timeouts are too short, resources will be wasted with attempts that timeout part way through message delivery.

If the second option is used, the timeout has to be very large, e.g., an hour, to allow time to expand very large mailing lists. The timeout may also need to increase linearly with the size of the message, to account for the time to transmit a very large message. A large fixed timeout leads to two problems: a failure can still tie up the sender for a very long time, and very large messages may still spuriously timeout (which is a wasteful failure).

Using the recommended first option, a timer is set for each SMTP command and for each buffer of the data transfer. The latter means that the overall timeout is inherently proportional to the size of the message.

Based on extensive experience with busy mail-relay hosts, the minimum per-command timeout values should be as follows:

- Initial 220 Message: 5 minutes. A Sender-SMTP process needs to distinguish between a failed TCP connection and a delay in receiving the initial 220 greeting message. Many receiver-SMTPs will accept a TCP connection but delay delivery of the 220 message until their system load will permit more mail to be processed.

- MAIL command: 5 minutes.

- RCPT command: 5 minutes. A longer timeout would be required if processing of mailing lists and aliases were not deferred until after the message was accepted.

- DATA initiation: 2 minutes. This is while awaiting the "354 Start Input" reply to a DATA command.

- Data Block: 3 minutes. This is while awaiting the completion of each TCP SEND call transmitting a chunk of data.

- DATA termination: 10 minutes. This is while awaiting the "250 OK" reply. When the receiver gets the final period terminating the message data, it typically performs processing to deliver the message to a user mailbox. A spurious timeout at this point would be very wasteful, since the message has been successfully sent.

A receiver-SMTP should have a timeout of at least 5 minutes while it is awaiting the next command from the sender.

6.3.6.19   *Reliable Mail Receipt*

When the receiver-SMTP accepts a piece of mail (by sending a 250 OK message in response to DATA), it is accepting responsibility for delivering or relaying the message. It must take this responsibility seriously; i.e., it must not lose the message for frivolous reasons, e.g., because the host later crashes or because of a predictable resource shortage.

If there is a delivery failure after acceptance of a message, the receiver-SMTP must formulate and mail a notification message. This notification must be sent using a null (<>) reverse-path in the envelope. The recipient of this notification should be the address from the envelope return-path (or the Return-Path: line). However, if this address is null (<>), the receiver-SMTP must not send a notification. If the address is an explicit source route, it should be stripped down to its final hop.

For example, suppose that an error notification must be sent for a message that arrived with MAIL FROM:<@a,@b:user@d>. The notification message should be sent to RCPT TO:<user@d>.

Some delivery failures after the message is accepted by SMTP will be unavoidable. For example, it may be impossible for the receiver-SMTP to validate all the delivery addresses in RCPT commands due to a "soft" domain system error or because the target is a mailing list (see the earlier discussion of RCPT).

To avoid receiving duplicate messages as the result of timeouts, a receiver-SMTP must seek to minimize the time required to respond to the final period that ends a message transfer.

6.3.6.20   *Reliable Mail Transmission*

To transmit a message, a sender-SMTP determines the IP address of the target host from the destination address in the envelope. Specifically, it maps the string to the right of the sign into an IP address. This mapping, or the transfer itself, may fail with a soft error, in which case the sender-SMTP will requeue the outgoing mail for a later retry.

When it succeeds, the mapping can result in a list of alternative delivery addresses rather than a single address, because of multiple MX records, multihoming, or both. To provide reliable mail transmission, the sender-SMTP must be able to try (and retry) each of the addresses in this list in order, until a delivery attempt succeeds. However, there may also be a configurable limit on the number of alternate addresses that can be tried. In any case, a host should try at least two addresses.

The following information is to be used to rank the host addresses:

1   Multiple MX Records—these contain a preference indication that should be used in sorting. If there are multiple destinations with the same preference and there is no clear reason to favor one (e.g., by address preference), then the sender-SMTP should pick one at random to spread the load across multiple mail exchanges for a specific organization.

2   Multihomed host—The destination host (perhaps taken from the preferred MX record) may be multihomed, in which case the domain name resolver will return a list of alternative IP addresses. It is the responsibility of the domain name resolver interface

to have ordered this list by decreasing preference, and SMTP must try them in the order presented.

Although the capability to try multiple alternative addresses is required, there may be circumstances where specific installations want to limit or disable the use of alternative addresses. The question of whether a sender should attempt retries using the different addresses of a multihomed host has been controversial. The main argument for using multiple addresses is that it maximizes the probability of timely delivery, and indeed, sometimes the probability of any delivery; the counter argument is that it may result in unnecessary resource use. Note that resource use is also strongly determined by the sending strategy.

Domain Name Support

Every Internet SMTP must include support for the Internet DNS. In particular, a sender-SMTP must support the MX record scheme.

Mailing Lists and Aliases

An SMTP-capable host should support both the alias and the list form of address expansion for multiple delivery. When a message is delivered or forwarded to each address of an expanded list form, the return address in the envelope (MAIL FROM:) must be changed to be the address of a person who administers the list, but the message header must be left unchanged; in particular, the From field of the message is unaffected.

An important mail facility is a mechanism for multidestination delivery of a single message, by transforming or expanding a pseudomailbox address into a list of destination mailbox addresses. When a message is sent to such a pseudomailbox (sometimes called an *exploder*), copies are forwarded or redistributed to each mailbox in the expanded list. We classify such a pseudomailbox as an *alias* or a *list*, depending upon the expansion rules:

1   Alias.   To expand an alias, the recipient mailer simply replaces the pseudo-mailbox address in the envelope with each of the expanded addresses in turn; the rest of the envelope and the message body are left unchanged. The message is then delivered or forwarded to each expanded address.

2   List.   A mailing list may be said to operate by redistribution rather than by forwarding. To expand a list, the recipient mailer replaces the pseudomailbox address in the envelope with each of the expanded addresses in turn. The return address in the envelope is changed so that all error messages generated by the final deliveries will be returned to a list administrator, not to the message originator, who generally has no control over the contents of the list, and will typically find error messages annoying.

6.3.6.21   Mail Gatewaying

Gatewaying mail between different mail environments, i.e., different mail formats and protocols, is complex, and does not easily yield to standardization. However, some general requirements may be given for a gateway between the Internet and another mail environment.

6.4 FILE TRANSFER

6.4.1 Introduction

The ability to copy files from one computer to another is provided by the File Transfer Protocol (FTP),[12, 17] and by the Trivial File Transfer Protocol (TFTP).[12, 18] FTP is implemented above TCP, and TFTP is implemented above UDP. Note that FTP is the often-used work-horse protocol for file transfers, while TFTP is, well, trivial, and used only in special circumstances.

6.4.2 File Transfer Protocol

Most of the material in this section is based on the specification of FTP.[12, 17] However, this chapter is not to be used as a substitute for the actual specification, since some details have been left out.

FTP provides mechanisms for authenticating users for file access control, setting file transmission parameters, identifying the files to be transferred, and a few file and directory maintenance functions. FTP has been in use for many years over the Internet.

6.4.2.1 Aspects of FTP

There are three relatively independent aspects to the FTP: Access Control, Filenames, and File Translation.

Access Control

FTP uses the same access control procedures that the hosts normally use for access control on files. In time-sharing systems, this generally means that users must log in by giving a name and a password (and in some systems an account number). FTP provides a means for communicating this identification information.

Filenames

There are two reasonable approaches to the question of what filenames to use in a file transfer protocol: the native filenames, or a new set of universal filenames. Establishing a universal naming convention requires providing a mapping between it and all the possible native naming conventions. The FTP uses the native filenames.

File Translation

Again, there are two reasonable choices for file format: use the local types, or create a new universal file type. Using a universal type requires all files to be translated from the local type to the universal type on transmission and from the universal type to a local type for

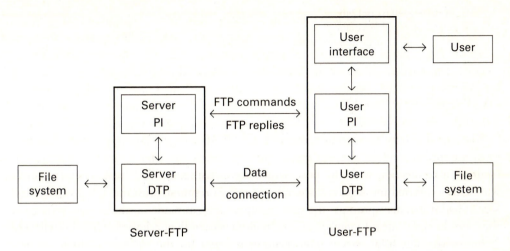

Figure 6.5 The FTP model

storage. The FTP uses the local types, with the provision of describing properties of the type such that a host can translate the transmitted file into an appropriate local type.

6.4.2.2 The FTP Model

FTP follows the user-server model of operation, with the additional feature that there are two functional units in each host and two connections between the hosts. At each host there is a protocol interpreter module (PI) and a data transfer module (DT). The two modules are linked internally to the host by some communication mechanism and shared state information. The user protocol interpreter sends commands to the server protocol interpreter over a control connection. The server protocol interpreter sends back replies over the same connection. The result of the command and reply exchange may be for the two data transfer modules to open a data connection between themselves and to actually transmit a data file. See Figure 6.5.

The FTP PIs, the user-PI, and the server-PI, exchange information via the request and reply paradigm. In fact, this technique was first developed for use in FTP.

6.4.2.3 An FTP Example

The following is a scenario as it normally appears to a UNIX user:

```
26% ftp
ftp> open ftp.nisc.sri.com
Connected to phoebus.NISC.SRI.COM.
220 phoebus FTP server (V.1.98 Fri Apr 19 11:57 1991) ready.
Name (ftp.nisc.sri.com:postel): anonymous
331 Guest login ok, send ident as password.
Password:
230 Guest login ok, access restrictions apply.
```

EBCDIC Type

This type is intended for efficient transfer between hosts that use EBCDIC for their internal character representation.

For transmission, the data are represented as 8-bit EBCDIC characters. The character code is the only difference between the functional specifications of EBCDIC and ASCII types.

End-of-line (as opposed to end-of-record—see the discussion of structure) will probably be rarely used with EBCDIC type for purposes of denoting structure, but where it is necessary the <NL> character should be used.

Image Type

The data are sent as contiguous bits that, for transfer, are packed into the 8-bit transfer bytes. The receiving site must store the data as contiguous bits. The structure of the storage system might necessitate the padding of the file (or of each record, for a record-structured file) to some convenient boundary (byte, word, or block). This padding, which must be all zeros, may occur only at the end of the file (or at the end of each record), and there must be a way of identifying the padding bits so that they may be stripped off if the file is retrieved. The padding transformation should be well publicized to enable a user to process a file at the storage site.

Image type is intended for the efficient storage and retrieval of files and for the transfer of binary data. It is recommended that this type be accepted by all FTP implementations.

Local Type

The data is transferred in logical bytes of the size specified by the obligatory second parameter, the byte size. The value of the byte size must be a decimal integer; there is no default value. The logical byte size is not necessarily the same as the transfer byte size. If there is a difference in byte sizes, then the logical bytes should be packed contiguously, disregarding transfer byte boundaries and with any necessary padding at the end.

When the data reaches the receiving host, it will be transformed in a manner that depends on the logical byte size and the particular host. This transformation must be invertible (i.e., an identical file can be retrieved if the same parameters are used), and should be well-publicized by the FTP implementors.

For example, a user sending 36-bit floating-point numbers to a host with a 32-bit word could send that data as local byte with a logical byte size of 36. The receiving host would then be expected to store the logical bytes so that they could be easily manipulated; in this example putting the 36-bit logical bytes into 64-bit double words should suffice.

In another example, a pair of hosts with a 36-bit word size may send data to one another in words by using TYPE L 36. The data would be sent in the 8-bit transmission bytes packed so that 9 transmission bytes carried two host words.

Format Control

The types ASCII and EBCDIC also take a second (optional) parameter; this is to indicate what kind of vertical format control, if any, is associated with a file. The following data representation types are defined in FTP:

A character file may be transferred to a host for one of three purposes: for printing, for storage and later retrieval, or for processing. If a file is sent for printing, the receiving host must know how the vertical format control is represented. In the second case, it must be possible to store a file at a host and then retrieve it later in exactly the same form. Finally, it should be possible to move a file from one host to another and process the file at the second host without undue trouble. A single ASCII or EBCDIC format does not satisfy all these conditions. Therefore, these types have a second parameter specifying one of the following three formats:

- Non Print.   This is the default format to be used if the second (format) parameter is omitted. Non Print format must be accepted by all FTP implementations. The file need contain no vertical format information. If it is passed to a printer process, this process may assume standard values for spacing and margins. Normally, this format will be used with files destined for processing or just storage.

- Telnet Format Controls.   The file contains ASCII/EBCDIC vertical format controls, i.e., <CR>, <LF>, <NL>, <VT>, <FF>, which the printer process will interpret appropriately. <CRLF>, in exactly this sequence, also denotes end-of-line.

- Carriage Control (ASA).   The file contains ASA (FORTRAN) vertical format control characters. In a line or a record formatted according to the ASA Standard, the first character is not to be printed. Instead, it should be used to determine the vertical movement of the paper that should take place before the rest of the record is printed.

The ASA Standard specifies the following control characters:

Character	Vertical Spacing
blank	Move paper up one line
0	Move paper up two lines
1	Move paper to top of next page
+	No movement, i.e., overprint

Clearly, there must be some way for a printer process to distinguish the end of the structural entity. If a file has record-structure (see below) this is no problem; records will be explicitly marked during transfer and storage. If the file has no record-structure, the <CRLF> end-of-line sequence is used to separate printing lines, but these format effectors are overridden by the ASA controls.

Data Structures

In addition to different representation types, FTP allows the structure of a file to be specified. Three file-structures are defined in FTP:

- File-structure, where there is no internal structure, and the file is considered to be a continuous sequence of data bytes

- Record-structure, where the file is made up of sequential records

- Page-structure, where the file is made up of independent indexed pages.

File-structure is the default to be assumed if the STRU command has not been used, but both file and record-structures must be accepted for *text* files (i.e., files with TYPE ASCII or EBCDIC) by all FTP implementations. The structure of a file will affect both the transfer mode of a file and the interpretation and storage of the file.

The "natural" structure of a file will depend on which host stores the file. A source-code file will usually be stored on an IBM Mainframe in fixed length records, but on a DEC TOPS-20 as a stream of characters partitioned into lines, for example by <CRLF>. If the transfer of files between such disparate sites is to be useful, there must be some way for one site to recognize the other's assumptions about the file.

With some sites being naturally file-oriented and others naturally record-oriented there may be problems if a file with one structure is sent to a host oriented to the other. If a text file is sent with record-structure to a host that is file-oriented, then that host should apply an internal transformation to the file based on the record-structure. Obviously, this transformation should be useful, but it must also be invertible, so that an identical file may be retrieved using record-structure. In the case of a file being sent with file-structure to a record-oriented host, there exists the question of what criteria the host should use to divide the file into records that can be processed locally. If this division is necessary, the FTP implementation should use the end-of-line sequence, <CRLF> for ASCII, or <NL> for EBCDIC text files, as the delimiter. If an FTP implementation adopts this technique, it must be prepared to reverse the transformation if the file is retrieved with file-structure.

File-Structure

File-structure is the default to be assumed if the STRU command has not been used. In file-structure there is no internal structure and the file is considered to be a continuous sequence of data bytes.

Record-Structure

Record-structures must be accepted for text files by all FTP implementations. In record-structure the file is made up of sequential records.

Page-Structure

To transmit files that are discontinuous, FTP defines a page-structure. Files of this type are sometimes known as random access files or even as *holey files*. In these files there is sometimes other information associated with the file as a whole (e.g., a file descriptor), or with a section of the file (e.g., page access controls), or both. In FTP, the sections of the file are called pages. See the FTP specification[12, 17] for the details of page-structure.

Establishing Data Connections

The mechanics of transferring data consists of setting up the data connection to the appropriate ports and choosing the parameters for transfer. Both the user- and the server-DTPs have a default data port. The user-process default data port is the same as the control connection port (i.e., U). The server-process default data port is the port adjacent to the control connection port (i.e., L-1).

The transfer byte size is 8-bit bytes. This byte size is relevant only for the actual transfer of the data; it has no bearing on representation of the data within a host's file system.

The passive data transfer process (this may be a user-DTP or a second server-DTP) will "listen" on the data port prior to sending a transfer request command. The FTP request command determines the direction of the data transfer. The server, upon receiving the transfer request, will initiate the data connection to the port. When the connection is established, the data transfer begins between DTPs, and the server-PI sends a confirming reply to the user-PI.

Every FTP implementation must support the use of the default data ports, and only the USER-PI can initiate a change to nondefault ports.

It is possible for the user to specify an alternate data port by use of the PORT command. The user may want a file dumped on a terminal server printer or retrieved from a third party host. In the latter case, the user-PI sets up control connections with both server-PIs. One server is then told (by an FTP command) to listen for a connection that the other will initiate. The user-PI sends one server-PI a PORT command indicating the data port of the other. Finally, both are sent the appropriate transfer commands.

In general, it is the server's responsibility to maintain the data connection—to initiate it and to close it. The exception to this is when the user-DTP is sending the data in a transfer mode that requires the connection to be closed to indicate EOF. The server must close the data connection under the following conditions:

1   The server has completed sending data in a transfer mode that requires a close to indicate EOF.

2   The server receives an ABORT command from the user.

3   The port specification is changed by a command from the user.

4   The control connection is closed legally or otherwise.

5   An irrecoverable error condition occurs.

Otherwise the close is a server option, the exercise of which the server must indicate to the user-process by either a 250 or 226 reply only.

Data Connection Management

- Default Data Connection Ports. All FTP implementations must support use of the default data connection ports, and only the user-PI may initiate the use of nondefault ports.

- Negotiating Nondefault Data Ports.   The user-PI may specify a nondefault user side data port with the PORT command. The user-PI may request the server-side to identify a nondefault server side data port with the PASV command. Since a connection is defined by the pair of addresses, either of these actions is enough to get a different data connection; still, it is permitted to use both commands to set new ports on both ends of the data connection.

- Reuse of the Data Connection.   When using the stream mode of data transfer the end of the file must be indicated by closing the connection. This causes a problem if multiple files are to be transferred in the session, due to the need for TCP to hold the connection record for a timeout period to guarantee reliable communication. Thus the connection cannot be reopened at once. There are two solutions to this problem. The first is to negotiate a nondefault port. The second is to use another transfer mode.

A comment should be made on transfer modes. The stream transfer mode is inherently unreliable, since one can not determine if the connection closed prematurely or not. The other transfer modes (Block and Compressed) do not close the connection to indicate the end-of-file. They have enough FTP encoding that the data connection can be parsed to determine the end of the file. Thus, using these modes one can leave the data connection open for multiple file transfers.

Transmission Modes

The next consideration in transferring data is choosing the appropriate transmission mode. There are three modes: one that formats the data and allows for restart procedures; one that also compresses the data for efficient transfer; and one that passes the data with little or no processing. In this last case the mode interacts with the structure attribute to determine the type of processing. In the compressed mode, the representation type determines the filler byte.

All data transfers must be completed with an end-of-file (EOF), which may be explicitly stated or implied by the closing of the data connection. For files with record-structure, all the end-of-record markers (EOR) are explicit, including the final one. For files transmitted in page-structure a *last-page* page type is used. In the rest of this discussion, byte means *transfer byte* except where explicitly stated otherwise.

For the purpose of standardized transfer, the sending host will translate its internal end-of-line or end-of-record denotation into the representation prescribed by the transfer mode and file-structure, and the receiving host will perform the inverse translation to its internal denotation. An IBM Mainframe record count field may not be recognized at another host, so the end-of-record information may be transferred as a 2-byte control code in Stream mode or as a flagged bit in a Block or a Compressed mode descriptor. End-of-line in an ASCII or EBCDIC file with no record-structure should be indicated by <CRLF> or <NL>, respectively. Since these transformations imply extra work for some systems, identical systems transferring nonrecord-structured text files might wish to use a binary representation and stream mode for the transfer.

The following transmission modes are defined in FTP: Stream, Block, and Compressed.

Stream Mode

The data is transmitted as a stream of bytes. There is no restriction on the representation type used; record-structures are allowed.

In a record-structured file, EOR and EOF will each be indicated by a 2-byte control code. The first byte of the control code will be all ones, the escape character. The second byte will have the low-order bit on, and zeros elsewhere for EOR, and the second low-order bit on for EOF; that is, the byte will have value 1 for EOR and value 2 for EOF. EOR and EOF may be indicated together on the last byte transmitted by turning both low-order bits on (i.e., the value 3). If a byte of all 1s was intended to be sent as data, it should be repeated in the second byte of the control code.

If the structure is a file-structure, the EOF is indicated by the sending host closing the data connection and all bytes are data bytes.

Block Mode

The file is transmitted as a series of data blocks preceded by one or more header bytes. The header bytes contain a count field and descriptor code. The count field indicates the total length of the data block in bytes, thus marking the beginning of the next data block (there are no filler bits). The descriptor code defines: last block in the file (EOF) last block in the record (EOR), restart marker or suspect data (i.e., the data being transferred is suspected of errors and is not reliable). This last code is *not* intended for error control within FTP. It is motivated by the desire of sites exchanging certain types of data (e.g., seismic or weather data) to send and receive all the data, despite local errors (such as magnetic tape read errors), and to indicate in the transmission that certain portions are suspect. Record-structures are allowed in this mode, and any representation type may be used.

The header consists of the 3 bytes. Of the 24 bits of header information, the 16 low-order bits shall represent byte count, and the 8 high-order bits represent descriptor codes as shown below.

Block Header

Descriptor 8 bits	Byte count 16 bits

The descriptor codes are indicated by bit flags in the descriptor byte. Four codes have been assigned, where each code number is the decimal value of the corresponding bit in the byte:

128	End of data block is EOR
64	End of data block is EOF
32	Suspected errors in data block
16	Data block is a restart marker

With this encoding, more than one descriptor coded condition may exist for a particular block. As many bits as necessary may be flagged.

The restart marker is embedded in the data stream as an integral number of 8-bit bytes representing printable characters in the language being used over the control connection (e.g., default—NVT-ASCII). <SP> (space, in the appropriate language) must not be used *within* a restart marker.

For example, to transmit a six-character marker, the following would be sent:

Descriptor code = 16	Byte count = 6	
Marker 8 bits	Marker 8 bits	Marker 8 bits
Marker 8 bits	Marker 8 bits	Marker 8 bits

Compressed Mode

There are three kinds of information to be sent: regular data, sent in a byte string; compressed data, consisting of replications or filler; and control information, sent in a 2-byte escape sequence. If $n > 0$ bytes (up to 127) of regular data are sent, these n bytes are preceded by a byte with the leftmost bit set to 0 and the rightmost 7 bits containing the number n. The Byte string is:

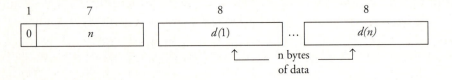

In a string of n data bytes $d(1),..., d(n)$ the count, n, must be positive.

To compress a string of n replications of the data byte d, the following 2 bytes are sent:.

2	6	8
1 0	n	d

A string of n filler bytes can be compressed into a single byte, where the filler byte varies with the representation type. If the type is ASCII or EBCDIC the filler byte is <SP> Space (ASCII code 32, EBCDIC, code 64). If the type is image or local byte, the filler is a zero byte.

A Filler string is:

2	6
1 1	n

The escape sequence is a double byte, the first of which is the escape byte (all 0s) and the second of which contains descriptor codes as defined in block mode. The descriptor codes have the same meaning as in Block mode, and apply to the succeeding string of bytes.

Compressed mode is useful for obtaining increased bandwidth on very large network transmissions at a little extra CPU cost. It can be most effectively used to reduce the size of output files, such as those generated by RJE hosts.

Error Recovery and Restart

There is no provision for detecting bits lost or scrambled in data transfer; this level of error control is handled by the TCP. However, a restart procedure is provided to protect users from gross system failures (including failures of a host, an FTP-process, or the underlying network).

The restart procedure is defined only for the Block and Compressed modes of data transfer. It requires the sender of data to insert a special marker code in the data stream with some marker information. The marker information has meaning only to the sender, but must consist of printable characters in the default or negotiated language of the control connection (ASCII or EBCDIC). The marker could represent a bit-count, a record-count, or any other information by which a system may identify a data checkpoint. The receiver of data, if it implements the restart procedure, would then mark the corresponding position of this marker in the receiving system, and return this information to the user.

In the event of a system failure, the user can restart the data transfer by identifying the marker point with the FTP restart procedure. The following example illustrates the use of the restart procedure.

The sender of the data inserts an appropriate marker block in the data stream at a convenient point. The receiving host marks the corresponding data point in its file system and conveys the last known sender and receiver marker information to the user, either directly or over the control connection in a 110 reply. In the event of a system failure, the user or controller process restarts the server at the last server marker by sending a restart command with the server's marker code as its argument. The restart command is transmitted over the control connection and is immediately followed by the command (such as RETR, STOR, or LIST) that was being executed when the system failure occurred.

FTP Restart Mechanism

The encoding of the restart information, which is specific to a particular file system and network implementation, is always generated and interpreted by the same system, either sender or receiver.

When an FTP that implements restart receives a Restart Marker in the data stream, it should force the data to that point to be written to stable storage before encoding the corresponding reply. An FTP sending Restart Markers must not assume that 110 replies will be returned synchronously with the data, i.e., it must not await a 110 reply before sending more data.

Two reply codes are defined for errors encountered in restarting a transfer:

- 554 Requested action not taken: invalid REST parameter. A 554 reply may result from a FTP service command that follows a REST command. The reply indicates that the existing file at the server-FTP cannot be repositioned as specified in the REST.

- 555 Requested action not taken: type or structure mismatch. A 555 reply may result from an APPE command or from any FTP service command following a REST command. The reply indicates that there is some mismatch between the current transfer parameters (type and structure), and the attributes of the existing file.

Note that the FTP Restart mechanism requires that Block or Compressed mode be used for data transfer, to allow the Restart Markers to be included within the data stream. The frequency of Restart Markers can be low.

Restart Markers mark a place in the data stream, but the receiver may be performing some transformation on the data as it is stored into stable storage. In general, the receiver's encoding must include any state information necessary to restart this transformation at any point of the FTP data stream. For example, in TYPE A transfers, some receiver hosts transform CR LF sequences into a single LF character on disk. If a Restart Marker happens to fall between CR and LF, the receiver must encode in the marker that the transfer must be restarted in a "CR has been seen and discarded" state.

Note that the Restart Marker is required to be encoded as a string of printable ASCII characters, regardless of the type of the data.

The specification says that restart information is to be returned to the user. This should not be taken literally. In general, the user-FTP should save the restart information in stable storage, e.g., by appending it to a restart control file. An empty restart control file should be created when the transfer first starts, and deleted automatically when the transfer completes successfully. It is suggested that this file have a name derived in an easily identifiable manner from the name of the file being transferred and the remote host name; this is analogous to the means used by many text editors for naming "backup" files.

There are three cases for FTP restart.

1   User-to-Server Transfer. The user-FTP puts Restart Markers <ssss> at convenient places in the data stream. When the server-FTP receives a Marker, it writes all prior

data to disk, encodes its file system position and transformation state as *rrrr*, and returns a "110 MARK *ssss* = *rrrr*" reply over the control connection. The user-FTP appends the pair *(ssss, rrrr)* to its restart control file

To restart the transfer, the user-FTP fetches the last *(ssss, rrrr)* pair from the restart control file, repositions its local file system and transformation state using ssss, and sends the command "REST *rrrr*" to the server-FTP.

2 Server-to-User Transfer.   The server-FTP puts Restart Markers *<ssss>* at convenient places in the data stream. When the user-FTP receives a Marker, it writes all prior data to disk, encodes its file system position and transformation state as *rrrr*, and appends the pair *(rrrr, ssss)* to its restart control file.

To restart the transfer, the user-FTP fetches the last *(rrrr, ssss)* pair from the restart control file, repositions its local file system and transformation state using *rrrr*, and sends the command "REST *ssss*" to the server-FTP.

3 Server-to-Server (third-party) Transfer.   The sending server-FTP puts Restart Markers *<ssss>* at convenient places in the data stream. When it receives a Marker, the receiving server-FTP writes all prior data to disk, encodes its file system position and transformation state as *rrrr*, and sends a "110 MARK *ssss* = *rrrr*" reply over the control connection to the User. The user-FTP appends the pair *(ssss, rrrr)* to its restart control file.

To restart the transfer, the user-FTP fetches the last (ssss, *rrrr*) pair from the restart control file, sends "REST *ssss*" to the sending server-FTP, and sends "REST *rrrr*" to the receiving server-FTP.

File Transfer Functions

The communication channel from the user-PI to the server-PI is established as a TCP connection from the user to the standard server port. The user protocol interpreter is responsible for sending FTP commands and interpreting the replies received; the server-PI interprets commands, sends replies and directs its DTP to set up the data connection and transfer the data. If the second party to the data transfer (the passive transfer process) is the user-DTP, then it is governed through the internal protocol of the user-FTP host; if it is a second server-DTP, then it is governed by its PI on command from the user-PI. In the description of a few of the commands it is helpful to be explicit about the possible replies.

FTP Commands: Access Control Commands

The following commands specify access control identifiers (command codes are shown in parentheses).

• User Name (USER).   The argument field is a string identifying the user. The user identification is that which is required by the server for access to its file system. This command will normally be the first command transmitted by the user after the control connections are made (some servers may require this). Additional identification information in the form of a password or an account command may also be required by some servers. Servers may allow a new USER command to be entered at any point in order to change the access control or accounting information. This has the effect of flushing any user, password, and account information already supplied and beginning the login sequence again. All transfer parameters are unchanged and any file transfer in progress is completed under the old access control parameters.

- Password (PASS).   The argument field is a string specifying the user's password. This command must be immediately preceded by the user name command, and, for some sites, completes the user's identification for access control. Since password information is quite sensitive, it is desirable in general to *mask* it or suppress typeout. It appears that the server has no foolproof way to achieve this. It is therefore the responsibility of the user-FTP process to hide the sensitive password information.

- Account (ACCT).   The argument field is a string identifying the user's account. The command is not necessarily related to the USER command, as some sites may require an account for login and others only for specific access, such as storing files. In the latter case the command may arrive at any time.

  There are reply codes to differentiate these cases for the automation: when account information is required for login, the response to a successful PASS command is reply code 332. On the other hand, if account information is *not* required for login, the reply to a successful PASS command is 230; and if the account information is needed for a command issued later in the dialogue, the server should return a 332 or 532 reply depending on whether it stores pending receipt of the ACCT command) or discards the command, respectively.

- Change Working Directory (CWD).   This command allows the user to work with a different directory or data set for file storage or retrieval without altering his login or accounting information. Transfer parameters are similarly unchanged. The argument is a pathname specifying a directory or other system-dependent file group designator.

- Change to Parent Directory (CDUP). This command is a special case of CWD, and is included to simplify the implementation of programs for transferring directory trees between operating systems having different syntaxes for naming the parent directory. The reply codes shall be identical to the reply codes of CWD.

- Structure Mount (SMNT).   This command allows the user to mount a different file system data structure without altering his login or accounting information. Transfer parameters are similarly unchanged. The argument is a pathname specifying a directory or other system-dependent file group designator.

- Reinitialize (REIN). This command terminates a USER, flushing all I/O and account information, except to allow any transfer in progress to be completed. All parameters are reset to the default settings and the control connection is left open. This is identical to the state in which a user finds himself immediately after the control connection is opened. A USER command may be expected to follow.

- Logout (QUIT).   This command terminates a USER and, if file transfer is not in progress, the server closes the control connection. If file transfer is in progress, the connection will remain open for result response and the server will then close it. If the user-process is transferring files for several users but does not wish to close and then reopen connections for each, then the REIN command should be used instead of QUIT.

    An unexpected close on the control connection will cause the server to take the effective action of an abort (ABOR) and a logout (QUIT).

Transfer Parameter Commands

All data transfer parameters have default values, and the commands specifying data transfer parameters are required only if the default parameter values are to be changed. The default value is the last specified value, or if no value has been specified, the standard default value is as stated here. This implies that the server must "remember" the applicable default values. The commands may be in any order except that they must precede the FTP service request. The following commands specify data transfer parameters:

- Data Port (PORT).   The argument is a host-port specification for the data port to be used in data connection. There are defaults for both the user and server data ports, and under normal circumstances this command and its reply are not needed. If this command is used, the argument is the concatenation of a 32-bit Internet host address and a 16-bit TCP port address. This address information is broken into 8-bit fields and the value of each field is transmitted as a decimal number (in character string representation). The fields are separated by commas. A port command would be:

  PORT h1,h2,h3,h4,p1,p2

    where *h1* is the high order 8 bits of the Internet host address.

- Passive (PASV).   This command requests the server-DTP to "listen" on a data port (which is not its default data port) and to wait for a connection, rather than initiate one upon receipt of a transfer command. The response to this command includes the host and port address this server is listening on.

- Representation Type (TYPE).   The argument specifies the representation type. Several types take a second parameter. The first parameter is denoted by a single character, as is the second Format parameter for ASCII and EBCDIC; the second parameter for local byte is a decimal integer to indicate byte size. The parameters are separated by a <SP> (Space, ASCII code 32).

The following codes are assigned for type:

```
A-ASCII                    N-Non-print

       →←              T-Telnet format effectors

E-EBCDIC                   C-Carriage Control (ASA)


I-Image


L <byte size>-Local byte Byte size
```

   The default representation type is ASCII Non Print. If the Format parameter is changed, and later just the first argument is changed, Format then returns to the Non Print default.

- File-structure (STRU). The argument is a single character code specifying file-structure. The following codes are assigned for structure:

  F   File (no record-structure)
  R   Record-structure
  P   Page-structure

The default structure is File.

- Transfer Mode (MODE).   The argument is a single character code specifying the data transfer modes. The following codes are assigned for transfer modes:

  S   Stream
  B   Block
  C   Compressed

The default transfer mode is Stream.

FTP Service Commands

The FTP service commands define the file transfer or the file system function requested by the user. The argument of an FTP service command will normally be a pathname. The syntax of pathnames must conform to server site conventions (with standard defaults applicable), and the language conventions of the control connection. The suggested default handling is to use the last specified device, directory or filename, or the standard default defined for local users. The commands may be in any order, except that a "rename from" command must be followed by a "rename to" command, and the restart command must be followed by the interrupted service command (e.g., STOR or RETR). The data, when transferred in response to FTP service commands, should always be sent over the data connection, except for certain informative replies. The following commands specify FTP service requests:

- Retrieve (RETR).   This command causes the server-DTP to transfer a copy of the file, specified in the pathname, to the server- or user-DTP at the other end of the data connection. The status and contents of the file at the server site shall be unaffected.

- Store (STOR).   This command causes the server-DTP to accept the data transferred via the data connection and to store the data as a file at the server site. If the file specified in the pathname exists at the server site, then its contents shall be replaced by the data being transferred. A new file is created at the server site if the file specified in the pathname does not already exist.

- Store Unique (STOU).   This command behaves like STOR, except that the resultant file is to be created in the current directory under a name unique to that directory. The 250 Transfer Started response must include the name generated.

- Append (with create) (APPE).   This command causes the server-DTP to accept the data transferred via the data connection and to store the data in a file at the server site. If the file specified in the pathname exists at the server site, then the data shall be appended to that file; otherwise the file specified in the pathname shall be created at the server site.

- Allocate (ALLO).   This command may be required by some servers to reserve sufficient storage to accommodate the new file to be transferred. The argument shall be a decimal integer representing the number of bytes (using the logical byte size) of storage to be reserved for the file. For files sent with record- or page-structure, a maximum record or page size (in logical bytes) might also be necessary; this is indicated by a decimal integer in a second argument field of the command. This second argument is optional, but when present should be separated from the first by the three characters <SP> R <SP>. This command shall be followed by a STOR or APPE command. The ALLO command should be treated as a NOOP (no operation) by those servers which do not require that the maximum size of the file be declared beforehand, and those servers interested in only the maximum record or page size should accept a dummy value in the first argument and ignore it.

- Restart (REST).   The argument field represents the server marker at which file transfer is to be restarted. This command does not cause file transfer but skips over the file to the specified data checkpoint. This command shall be immediately followed by the appropriate FTP service command which shall cause file transfer to resume.

- Rename From (RNFR).   This command specifies the old pathname of the file which is to be renamed. This command must be immediately followed by a "rename to" command specifying the new file pathname.

- Rename To (RNTO).   This command specifies the new pathname of the file specified in the immediately preceding "rename from" command. Together the two commands cause a file to be renamed.

- Abort (ABOR).   This command tells the server to abort the previous FTP service
  command and any associated transfer of data. The abort command may require "special action," to force recognition by the server. No action is to be taken if the previous
  command has been completed (including data transfer). The control connection is not
  to be closed by the server, but the data connection must be closed.

    There are two cases for the server upon receipt of this command: the FTP service
  command was already completed, or the FTP service command is still in progress. In
  the first case, the server closes the data connection (if it is open) and responds with a
  226 reply, indicating that the abort command was successfully processed. In the second case, the server aborts the FTP service in progress and closes the data connection,
  returning a 426 reply to indicate that the service request terminated abnormally. The
  server then sends a 226 reply, indicating that the abort command was successfully processed.

- Delete (DELE).   This command causes the file specified in the pathname to be
  deleted at the server site. If an extra level of protection is desired (such as the query,
  "Do you really wish to delete?"), it should be provided by the user-FTP process.

- Remove Directory (RMD).   This command causes the directory specified in the pathname to be removed as a directory (if the pathname is absolute) or as a subdirectory of
  the current working directory (if the pathname is relative).

- Make Directory (MKD).   This command causes the directory specified in the pathname to be created as a directory (if the pathname is absolute) or as a subdirectory of
  the current working directory (if the pathname is relative).

- Print Working Directory (PWD).   This command causes the name of the current
  working directory to be returned in the reply.

- List (LIST).   This command causes a list to be sent from the server to the passive
  DTP. If the pathname specifies a directory or other group of files, the server should
  transfer a list of files in the specified directory. If the pathname specifies a file then the
  server should send current information on the file. A null argument implies the user's
  current working or default directory. The data transfer is over the data connection in
  type ASCII or type EBCDIC. (The user must ensure that the TYPE is appropriately
  ASCII or EBCDIC). Since the information on a file may vary widely from system to
  system, this information may be hard to use automatically in a program, but may be
  quite useful to a human user.

- Name List (NLST).   This command causes a directory listing to be sent from server to
  user site. The pathname should specify a directory or other system-specific file group

descriptor; a null argument implies the current directory. The server will return a stream of names of files and no other information. The data will be transferred in ASCII or EBCDIC type over the data connection as valid pathname strings separated by <CRLF> or <NL>. (Again the user must ensure that the TYPE is correct.) This command is intended to return information that can be used by a program to further process the files automatically (e.g., in the implementation of a "multiple get" function).

- Site Parameters (SITE).   This command is used by the server to provide services specific to his system that are essential to file transfer but not sufficiently universal to be included as commands in the protocol. The nature of these services and the specification of their syntax can be stated in a reply to the HELP SITE command.

- System (SYST).   This command is used to find out the type of operating system at the server. The reply should have as its first word one of the system names listed in the current version of the Assigned Numbers document.

- Status (STAT).   This command shall cause a status response to be sent over the control connection in the form of a reply. The command may be sent during a file transfer (along with the Telnet IP and Synch signals) in which case the server will respond with the status of the operation in progress, or it may be sent between file transfers. In the latter case, the command may have an argument field. If the argument is a pathname, the command is analogous to the LIST command, except that data shall be transferred over the control connection. If a partial pathname is given, the server may respond with a list of filenames or attributes associated with that specification. If no argument is given, the server should return general status information about the server FTP process. This should include current values of all transfer parameters and the status of connections.

- Help (HELP).   This command will cause the server to send helpful information regarding its implementation status over the control connection to the user. The command may take an argument (e.g., any command name) and return more specific information as a response. The reply is type 211 or 214. It is suggested that HELP be allowed before entering a USER command. The server may use this reply to specify site-dependent parameters, e.g., in response to HELP SITE.

- Noop (NOOP).   This command does not affect any parameters or previously entered commands. It specifies no action other than that the server send an OK reply.

FTP follows the specifications of the Telnet protocol for all communications over the control connection. Since the language used for Telnet communication may be a negotiated option, all references in the following will be to the *Telnet language* and the corresponding *Telnet end-of-line code* (EOL). Currently, one may take these to mean, respectively, NVT-ASCII and <CRLF>.

FTP commands are *Telnet strings* terminated by the Telnet end-of-line code. The command codes themselves are alphabetic characters terminated by the character <SP> (space) if parameters follow, and by Telnet-EOL otherwise.

FTP commands may be partitioned as those specifying access-control identifiers, data transfer parameters, or FTP service requests. Certain commands (such as ABOR, STAT, QUIT) may be sent over the control connection while a data transfer is in progress. Some servers may not be able to monitor the control and data connections simultaneously, in which case some special action will be necessary to get the server's attention. The following ordered format is tentatively recommended:

1   User system inserts the Telnet Interrupt Process (IP) signal in the Telnet stream.

2   User system sends the Telnet Synch signal.

3   User system inserts the command (e.g., ABOR) in the Telnet stream.

4   Server-PI, after receiving Interrupt Process, scans the Telnet stream for *exactly one* FTP command.

For other servers this may not be necessary, but the actions listed above should have no unusual effect.

FTP Replies

Replies to FTP commands are devised to ensure the synchronization of requests and actions in the process of file transfer, and to guarantee that the user process always knows the state of the server. Every command must generate at least one reply, although there may be more than one; in the latter case, the multiple replies must be easily distinguished. In addition, some commands occur in sequential groups, such as USER, PASS and ACCT, or RNFR and RNTO. The replies show the existence of an intermediate state if all preceding commands have been successful. A failure at any point in the sequence necessitates the repetition of the entire sequence from the beginning. The details of the command-reply sequence are made explicit in a set of state diagrams below.

An FTP reply consists of a 3-digit number (transmitted as 3 alphanumeric characters) followed by some text. The number is intended for use by automata to determine what state to enter next; the text is intended for the human user. It is intended that the 3 digits contain enough encoded information that the user-process (the user-PI) will not need to examine the text and may either discard it or pass it on to the user, as appropriate. In particular, the text may be server-dependent, so there are likely to be varying texts for each reply code.

A reply is defined to contain the 3-digit code, followed by a space, <SP>, followed by one line of text (where some maximum line length has been specified), and terminated by the Telnet end-of-line code. The detailed list of reply codes can be found in *RFC 959.*[17]

Connections

The server protocol interpreter should listen on port L. The user or user protocol interpreter should initiate the full-duplex control connection. Server- and user-processes
should follow the conventions of the Telnet protocol. Servers are under no obligation to
provide for editing of command lines, and may require that it be done in the user host.
The control connection shall be closed by the server at the user's request after all transfers
and replies are completed.

The user-DTP must listen on the specified data port; this may be the default user port
(U) or a port specified in the PORT command. The server shall initiate the data connection from his own default data port (L-1) using the specified user data port. The direction
of the transfer used will be determined by the FTP service command.

Note that all FTP implementations must support data transfer using the default port,
and that only the user-PI may initiate the use of nondefault ports.

When data is to be transferred between two servers, A and B, the user-PI, C, sets up control connections with both server-PIs. One of the servers, say A, is then sent a PASV command telling him to listen on his data port rather than initiate a connection when he
receives a transfer service command. When the user-PI receives an acknowledgment to the
PASV command, which includes the identity of the host and port being listened on, the
user-PI then sends A's port, a, to B in a PORT command; a reply is returned. The user-PI
may then send the corresponding service commands to A and B. Server B initiates the connection and the transfer proceeds. The command-reply sequence is listed below where the
messages are vertically synchronous but horizontally asynchronous.

User-PI-Server *A*	User-PI-Server *B*
C→A: Connect	*C→B*: Connect
C→A: PASV	
A→C: 227 Entering Passive Mode	*A*1,*A*2,*A*3,*A*4,a1,a2
	C→B: PORT A1,A2,A3,A4,a1,a2
	B→C: 200 Okay
C→A: STOR	*C→B*: RETR
B→A: Connect to host-*A*, port-a	

If the data connection is to be closed following a data transfer where closing the connection
is not required to indicate the end-of-file, the server must do so immediately. Waiting until
after a new transfer command is not permitted because the user-process will have already
tested the data connection to see if it needs to do a listen; (remember that the user must listen on a closed data port *before* sending the transfer request). To prevent a race condition
here, the server sends a reply (226) after closing the data connection (or if the connection is
left open, a "file transfer completed" reply (250) and the user-PI should wait for one of
these replies before issuing a new transfer command).

Any time either the user or server see that the connection is being closed by the other side, it should promptly read any remaining data queued on the connection and issue the close on its own side.

Command Syntax

The commands begin with a command code followed by an argument field. The command codes are four or fewer alphabetic characters. Upper and lower case alphabetic characters are to be treated identically. Thus, any of the following may represent the retrieve command:

RETR Retr retr ReTr rETr

This also applies to any symbols representing parameter values, such as *A* or *a* for ASCII TYPE. The command codes and the argument fields are separated by one or more spaces.

The argument field consists of a variable length character string ending with the character sequence <CRLF> (carriage return, line feed) for NVT-ASCII representation; for other negotiated languages a different end-of-line character might be used. It should be noted that the server is to take no action until the end-of-line code is received.

The detailed specification of the command and argument syntax is found in *RFC 959*.[17]

Sequencing of Commands and Replies

The communication between the user and server is intended to be an alternating dialogue. As such, the user issues an FTP command and the server responds with a prompt primary reply. The user should wait for this initial primary success or failure response before sending further commands.

Certain commands require a second reply for which the user should also wait. These replies may, for example, report on the progress or completion of file transfer or the closing of the data connection. They are secondary replies to file transfer commands.

One important group of informational replies is the connection greetings. Under normal circumstances, a server will send a 220 reply, "awaiting input," when the connection is completed. The user should wait for this greeting message before sending any commands. If the server is unable to accept input right away, a "120 expected delay" reply should be sent immediately and a 220 reply when ready. The user will then know not to hang up if there is a delay.

Spontaneous Replies

Sometimes, *the system* spontaneously has a message to be sent to a user (usually all users). For example, "System going down in 15 minutes." There is no provision in FTP for such spontaneous information to be sent from the server to the user. It is recommended that such information be queued in the server-PI and delivered to the user-PI in the next reply (possibly making it a multiline reply).

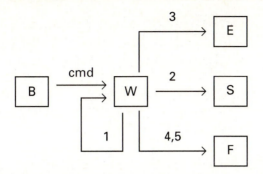

Figure 6.7   Model of FTP commands: APPE, LIST, NLST, REIN, RETR, STOR, and STOU

State Diagrams

Here, state diagrams are presented for a very simple-minded FTP implementation. Only the first digit of the reply codes is used. There is one state diagram for each group of FTP commands or command sequences.

The command groupings were determined by constructing a model for each command then collecting together the commands with structurally identical models.

For each command or command sequence there are three possible outcomes: success (S), failure (F), and error (E). In the state diagrams below the symbol B is used for *begin*, and the symbol W is for *wait for reply.*

Figure 6.6 represents the largest group of FTP commands: ABOR, ALLO, DELE, CWD, CDUP, SMNT, HELP, MODE, NOOP, PASV, QUIT, SITE, PORT, SYST, STAT, RMD, MKD, PWD, STRU, and TYPE.

The other large group of commands is represented by Figure 6.7: This diagram models the commands: APPE, LIST, NLST, REIN, RETR, STOR, and STOU.

Note that the second model could also be used to represent the first group of commands, the only difference being that in the first group the 100 series replies are unex-

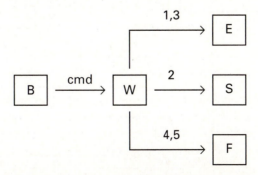

Figure 6.6   Model of FTP commands: ABOR, ALLO, DELE, CWD, CDUP, SMNT, HELP, MODE, NOOP, PASV, QUIT, SITE, PORT, SYST, STAT, RMD, MKD, PWD, STRU, and TYPE

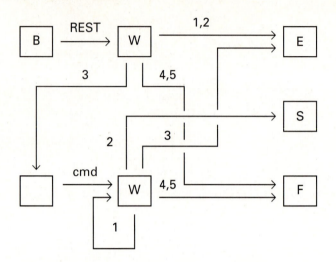

Figure 6.9   Model of the restart command

pected, and therefore treated as errors, while the second group expects (some may require) 100 series replies. Remember that at most, one 100 series reply is allowed per command.

The remaining diagrams model command sequences; perhaps the simplest of these is the rename sequence shown in Figure 6.8.

Figure 6.9 is a simple model of the restart command: where *cmd* is APPE, STOR, or RETR.

These three models are similar. The restart differs from the rename in Figure 6.8 only in the treatment of 100 series replies at the second stage. Remember that at most one 100 series reply is allowed per command.

The most complicated diagram is for the login sequence, which is shown in Figure 6.10.

Finally, Figure 6.11 is a generalized diagram that could be used to model the command and reply interchange.

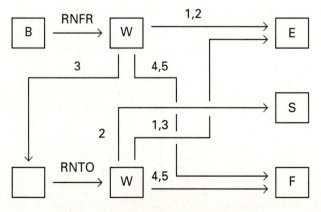

Figure 6.8   Model of the rename sequence

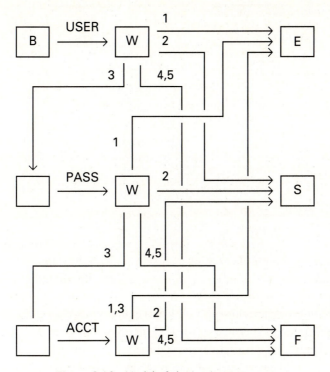

Figure 6.10   Model of the Login sequence

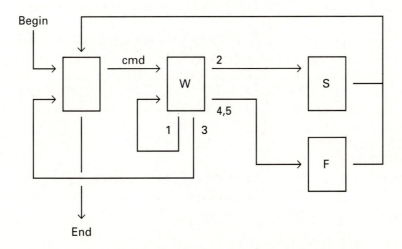

Figure 6.11   A general model of a command and reply interchange

6.4.2.5 FTP Implementation Specifics

FTP uses separate simultaneous TCP connections for control and for data transfer. The FTP protocol includes many features, some of which are not commonly implemented. However, for every feature in FTP, there exists at least one implementation.

Internet users have been unnecessarily burdened for years by deficient FTP implementations. Protocol implementors have suffered from the erroneous opinion that implementing FTP ought to be a small and trivial task. This is wrong, because FTP has a user interface, because it has to deal (correctly) with the whole variety of communication and operating system errors that may occur, and because it has to handle the great diversity of real file systems in the world.

LOCAL Type

An FTP program must support TYPE I (IMAGE, or binary type) as well as TYPE L 8 (LOCAL type with logical byte size 8). A machine whose memory is organized into m-bit words, where m is not a multiple of 8, may also support TYPE L m.

The command *TYPE L 8* is often required to transfer binary data between a machine whose memory is organized into, e.g., 36-bit words and a machine with an 8-bit byte organization. For an 8-bit byte machine, TYPE L 8 is equivalent to IMAGE.

TYPE L m is sometimes specified to the FTP programs on two m-bit word machines to ensure the correct transfer of a native-mode binary file from one machine to the other. However, this command should have the same effect on these machines as TYPE I.

Telnet Format Control

A host that makes no distinction between TYPE N and TYPE T should implement TYPE T to be identical to TYPE N. This provision should ease interoperation with hosts that do make this distinction.

Many hosts represent text files internally as strings of ASCII characters, using the embedded ASCII format effector characters (LF, BS, FF, ...) to control the format when a file is printed. For such hosts, there is no distinction between print files and other files. However, systems that use record-structured files typically need a special format for printable files (e.g., ASA carriage control). For the latter hosts, FTP allows a choice of TYPE N or TYPE T.

Page-Structure

Implementation of page-structure is *not recommended* in general. However, if a host system does need to implement FTP for random access or holey files, it must use the defined page-structure format rather than define a new private FTP format.

Data-Structure Transformations

An FTP transformation between record-structure and file-structure should be invertible, to the extent possible while making the result useful on the target host.

The specification required strict invertibility between record-structure and file-structure, but in practice, efficiency and convenience often preclude it. Therefore, the requirement is being relaxed. There are two different objectives for transferring a file: processing it on the target host, or just storage. For storage, strict invertibility is important. For processing, the file created on the target host needs to be in the format expected by application programs on that host. As an example of the conflict, imagine a record-oriented operating system that requires some data files to have exactly 80 bytes in each record. While STORing a file on such a host, an FTP server must be able to pad each line or record to 80 bytes; a later retrieval of such a file cannot be strictly invertible.

Data Connection Management

A user-FTP that uses STREAM mode should send a PORT command to assign a nondefault data port before each transfer command is issued.

This is required because of the long delay after a TCP connection is closed until its socket pair can be reused, to allow multiple transfers during a single FTP session. Sending a port command can be avoided if a transfer mode other than stream is used, by leaving the data transfer connection open between transfers.

PASV Command

A server-FTP must implement the PASV command. If multiple third-party transfers are to be executed during the same session, a new PASV command must be issued before each transfer command, to obtain a unique port pair. Note that the host number *h1,h2,h3,h4* is the IP address of the server host that is sending the reply, and that *p1,p2* is a nondefault data transfer port that PASV has assigned.

LIST and NLST Commands

The data returned by an NLST command must contain only a simple list of legal pathnames, such that the server can use them directly as the arguments of subsequent data transfer commands for the individual files.

The data returned by a LIST or NLST command should use an implied TYPE AN, unless the current type is EBCDIC, in which case an implied TYPE EN should be used.

Many FTP clients support macrocommands that will get or put files matching a wildcard specification, using NLST to obtain a list of pathnames. The expansion of multiple-put is local to the client, but multiple-get requires cooperation by the server.

The implied type for LIST and NLST is designed to provide compatibility with existing user-FTPs, and in particular, with multiple-get commands.

SITE Command

A server-FTP should use the SITE command for nonstandard features, rather than invent new private commands or unstandardized extensions to existing commands.

STOU Command

The STOU command stores into a uniquely named file. When it receives a STOU command, a server-FTP must return the actual filename in the "125 Transfer Starting" or the "150 Opening Data Connection" message that precedes the transfer. The exact format of these messages is hereby defined to be as follows:

```
125 FILE: pppp
150 FILE: pppp
```

where *pppp* represents the unique pathname of the file that will be written.

Telnet End-of-line Code

Implementors must not assume any correspondence between READ boundaries on the control connection and the Telnet EOL sequences (CR LF).

Thus, a server-FTP (or user-FTP) must continue reading characters from the control connection until a complete Telnet EOL sequence is encountered, before processing the command (or response, respectively). Conversely, a single READ from the control connection may include more than one FTP command.

FTP Replies

A server-FTP must send only correctly formatted replies on the control connection. A server-FTP should use the reply codes defined whenever they apply. However, a server-FTP may use a different reply code when needed, as long as the general rules are followed. When the implementor has a choice between a 4xx and 5xx reply code, a server-FTP should send a 4xx (temporary failure) code when there is any reasonable possibility that a failed FTP will succeed a few hours later.

A user-FTP should generally use only the highest-order digit of a 3-digit reply code for making a procedural decision, to prevent difficulties when a server-FTP uses nonstandard reply codes.

A user-FTP must be able to handle multiline replies. If the implementation imposes a limit on the number of lines and if this limit is exceeded, the user-FTP must recover, e.g., by ignoring the excess lines until the end of the multiline reply is reached.

A user-FTP should not interpret a 421 reply code ("Service not available, closing control connection") specially, but should detect closing of the control connection by the server.

Server implementations that fail to strictly follow the reply rules often cause FTP user programs to hang. It is important to choose FTP reply codes that properly distinguish between temporary and permanent failures, to allow the successful use of file transfer client daemons. These programs depend on the reply codes to decide whether or not to retry a failed transfer; using a permanent failure code (5xx) for a temporary error will cause these programs to give up unnecessarily.

When the meaning of a reply matches exactly the text shown in the specification, uniformity will be enhanced by using it verbatim. However, a server-FTP implementor is encouraged to choose reply text that conveys specific system-dependent information, when appropriate.

Connections

On a multihomed server host, the default data transfer port (L-1) must be associated with the same local IP address as the corresponding control connection to port L.

A user-FTP must not send any Telnet controls other than SYNCH and IP on an FTP control connection. In particular, it must not attempt to negotiate Telnet options on the control connection. However, a server-FTP must be capable of accepting and refusing Telnet negotiations (i.e., sending DONT or WONT).

Although the specification says: "Server- and user-processes should follow the conventions for the Telnet protocol ... [on the control connection]," it is not intended that Telnet option negotiation is to be employed.

Nonstandard Command Verbs

FTP allows experimental commands, whose names begin with X. If these commands are subsequently adopted as standards, there may still be existing implementations using the X form. At present, this is true for the directory commands:

Normal	Experimental
MKD	XMKD
RMD	XRMD
PWD	XPWD
CDUP	XCUP
CWD	XCWD

All FTP implementations should recognize both forms of these commands, by simply equating them with extra entries in the command lookup table.

A user-FTP can access a server that supports only the X forms by implementing a mode switch, or automatically using the following procedure: if the normal form of one of the above commands is rejected with a 500 or 502 response code, then try the experimental form; any other response would be passed to the user.

Idle Timeout

A server-FTP process should have an idle timeout, which will terminate the process and close the control connection if the server is inactive (i.e., no command or data transfer in progress) for a long period of time. The idle timeout time should be configurable, and the default should be at least 5 minutes.

A client-FTP process (the user-PI) will need timeouts on responses only if it is invoked from a program.

Without a timeout, a server-FTP process may be left pending indefinitely if the corresponding client crashes without closing the control connection.

Concurrency of Data and Control

The intent of the designers of FTP was that a user should be able to send a STAT command at any time while data transfer was in progress and that the server-FTP would reply immediately with status—e.g., the number of bytes transferred so far. Similarly, an ABOR command should be possible at any time during a data transfer.

Unfortunately, some small-machine operating systems make such concurrent programming difficult, and some other implementors seek minimal solutions, so some FTP implementations do not allow concurrent use of the data and control connections. Even such a minimal server must be prepared to accept and defer a STAT or ABOR command that arrives during data transfer.

Pathname Specification

Since FTP is intended for use in a heterogeneous environment, user-FTP implementations must support remote pathnames as arbitrary character strings, so that their form and content are not limited by the conventions of the local operating system.

In particular, remote pathnames can be of arbitrary length, and all the printing ASCII characters as well as space must be allowed. The specification allows a pathname to contain any 7-bit ASCII character except <CR> or <LF>.

Quote Command

A user-FTP program must implement a QUOTE command that will pass an arbitrary character string to the server and display all resulting response messages to the user.

To make this command useful, a user-FTP should send transfer control commands to the server as the user enters them, rather than saving all the commands and sending them to the server only when a data transfer is started.

The QUOTE command is essential to allow the user to access servers that require system-specific commands (e.g., SITE or ALLO), or to invoke new or optional features that are not implemented by the user-FTP. For example, QUOTE may be used to specify *TYPE A T* to send a print file to hosts that require the distinction, even if the user-FTP does not recognize that TYPE.

Displaying Replies to User

A user-FTP should display to the user the full text of all error reply messages it receives. It should have a verbose mode in which all commands it sends and the full text and reply codes it receives are displayed, for diagnosis of problems.

Maintaining Synchronization

The state machine in a user-FTP should be forgiving of missing and unexpected reply messages, to maintain command synchronization with the server.

6.4.3 Trivial File Transfer Protocol

In contrast to FTP, TFTP is a very simple protocol. There are no provisions for access control or user identification, so only public access files are generally available for transfer via TFTP. There is a provision for identifying the file to be transferred by name.

Since TFTP is implemented over UDP, which offers no reliability mechanism, TFTP must ensure the reliability of the file transfer itself. TFTP does this by a simple acknowledgment, timeout, and retransmission strategy. The file is sent in blocks, one at a time. After a block is sent the sending TFTP module waits for an acknowledgment. If the acknowledgment is not received within a timeout period, the block is retransmitted. Even though TFTP must implement some reliability mechanisms, the combination of IP plus UDP plus TFTP is much simpler than the combination of IP plus TCP plus FTP. TFTP works well in moving files between personal computers or workstations and file servers in high-speed local networks, and is occasionally used over long-haul networks.

Most of the material in this section is based on the specification of TFTP.[12, 18] However, this chapter is not to be used as a substitute for the actual specification since some details have been left out.

6.4.3.1 *Purpose*

TFTP is a simple protocol to transfer files, and therefore was named the Trivial File Transfer Protocol or TFTP. It has been implemented on top of the Internet User Datagram protocol (UDP or Datagram)[2] so it may be used to move files between machines on different networks implementing UDP. (This should not exclude the possibility of implementing TFTP on top of other datagram protocols.) It is designed to be small and easy to implement. Therefore, it lacks most of the features of a regular FTP. The only thing it can do is read and write files from or to a remote server. It cannot list directories, and currently has no provisions for user authentication. In common with other Internet protocols, it passes 8-bit bytes of data.

Two modes of transfer are currently supported: netascii; and octet, raw 8-bit bytes. Additional modes can be defined by pairs of cooperating hosts.

6.4.3.2 *Overview of the Protocol*

Any transfer begins with a request to read or write a file, which also serves to request a connection. If the server grants the request, the connection is opened and the file is sent in fixed length blocks of 512 bytes. Each data packet contains one block of data, and must be acknowledged by an acknowledgment packet before the next packet can be sent. A data packet of fewer than 512 bytes signals termination of a transfer. If a packet gets lost in the network, the intended recipient will timeout and may retransmit his last packet (which may be data or an acknowledgment), thus causing the sender of the lost packet to retransmit that lost packet. The sender has to keep just one packet on hand for retransmission, since the lock-step acknowledgment guarantees that all older packets have been received. Notice that both machines involved in a transfer are considered senders and receivers. One sends data and receives acknowledgments, the other sends acknowledgments and receives data.

Most errors cause termination of the connection. An error is signalled by sending an error packet. This packet is not acknowledged, and not retransmitted (i.e., a TFTP server or user may terminate after sending an error message), so the other end of the connection may not get it. Therefore, timeouts are used to detect such a termination when the error packet has been lost. Errors are caused by three types of events: not being able to satisfy the request (e.g., file not found, access violation, or no such user), receiving a packet which cannot be explained by a delay or duplication in the network (e.g., an incorrectly formed packet), and losing access to a necessary resource (e.g., disk full, or access denied during a transfer).

TFTP recognizes only one error condition that does not cause termination: the source port of a received packet being incorrect. In this case, an error packet is sent to the originating host.

This protocol is very restrictive in order to simplify implementation. For example, the fixed length blocks make allocation straightforward, and the lock-step acknowledgment provides flow control and eliminates the need to reorder incoming data packets.

6.4.3.3   *Relation to Other Protocols*

As mentioned, TFTP is designed to be implemented on top of the Datagram protocol. Since Datagram is implemented on the Internet protocol, packets will have an Internet header, a Datagram header, and a TFTP header. Additionally, the packets may have a header (Ethernet header, etc.) to allow them through the local transport medium. As shown below, the order of the contents of a packet will be: local medium header, if used, Internet header, Datagram header, TFTP header, followed by the remainder of the TFTP packet. (This may or may not be data, depending on the type of packet as specified in the TFTP header.) TFTP does not specify any of the values in the Internet header. On the other hand, the source and destination port fields of the Datagram header are used by TFTP and the length field reflects the size of the TFTP packet. The transfer identifiers (TIDs) used by TFTP are passed to the Datagram layer to be used as ports; therefore, they must be between 0 and 65,535.

The TFTP header consists of a 2-byte opcode field which indicates the packet's type (e.g., DATA, ERROR, etc.):

Local medium	Internet	Datagram	TFTP

6.4.3.4   *Initial Connection Protocol*

A transfer is established by sending a request (WRQ to write onto a foreign file system, or RRQ to read from it), and receiving a positive reply, an acknowledgment packet for write, or the first data packet for read. In general, an acknowledgment packet will contain the block number of the data packet being acknowledged. Each data packet has associated with it a block number; block numbers are consecutive and begin with 1. Since the positive response to a write request is an acknowledgment packet, in this special case the block number will be 0. (Normally, since an acknowledgment packet is acknowledging a data packet, the acknowledgment packet will contain the block number of the data packet being acknowledged.) If the reply is an error packet, then the request has been denied.

To create a connection, each end of the connection chooses a TID for itself, to be used for the duration of that connection. The TIDs for a connection should be randomly chosen, so that the probability that the same number is chosen twice in immediate succession is very low. Every packet has associated with it the two TIDs of the ends of the connection, the source TID and the destination TID. These TIDs are handed to the supporting UDP (or other datagram protocol) as the source and destination ports. A requesting host chooses its source TID as described above, and sends its initial request to the known TID 69 decimal (105 octal) on the serving host. The response to the request, under normal operation, uses a TID chosen by the server as its source TID, and the TID chosen for the previous message by the requester as its destination TID. The two chosen TIDs are then used for the remainder of the transfer.

As an example, the following shows the steps used to establish a connection to write a file. Note that WRQ, ACK, and DATA are the names of the write request, acknowledgment, and data types of the packets, respectively.

1   Host *A* sends a WRQ to host *B* with source = *A*'s TID, destination = 69.

2   Host *B* sends an ACK (with block number = 0) to host *A* with source = *B*'s TID, destination = *A*'s TID.

At this point the connection has been established and the first data packet can be sent by Host *A* with a sequence number of 1. In the next step, and in all succeeding steps, the hosts should make sure that the source TID matches the value that was agreed on in steps 1 and 2. If a source TID does not match, the packet should be discarded as erroneously sent from somewhere else. An error packet should be sent to the source of the incorrect packet, while not disturbing the transfer. This can be done only if the TFTP in fact receives a packet with an incorrect TID. If the supporting protocols do not allow it, this particular error condition will not arise.

The following example demonstrates a correct operation of the protocol in which the above situation can occur: Host *A* sends a request to host *B*. Somewhere in the network, the request packet is duplicated, and as a result two acknowledgments are returned to host *A*, with different TIDs chosen on host *B* in response to the two requests. When the first response arrives, host *A* continues the connection. When the second response to the request arrives, it should be rejected, but there is no reason to terminate the first connection. Therefore, if different TIDs are chosen for the two connections on host *B* and host *A* checks the source TIDs of the messages it receives, the first connection can be maintained while the second is rejected by returning an error packet.

that the ACK has been lost if it receives the final DATA packet again. The host sending the last DATA must retransmit it until the packet is acknowledged or the sending host times out. If the response is an ACK, the transmission was completed successfully. If the sender of the data times out and is not prepared to retransmit any more, the transfer may still have been completed successfully, after which the acknowledger or network may have experienced a problem. It is also possible in this case that the transfer was unsuccessful. In any case, the connection has been closed.

6.4.3.7 Premature Termination

If a request cannot be granted, or some error occurs during the transfer, then an ERROR packet (opcode 5) is sent. This is only a courtesy since it will not be retransmitted or acknowledged, so it may never be received. Timeouts must also be used to detect errors.

6.4.3.8 TFTP Implementation Specifics

TFTP provides its own reliable delivery with UDP as its transport protocol, using a simple stop-and-wait acknowledgment system. Since TFTP has an effective window of only one 512-octet segment, it can provide good performance only over paths that have a small delay-bandwidth product. The TFTP file interface is very simple, providing no access control or security. TFTP's most important application is bootstrapping a host over a local network, since it is simple and small enough to be easily implemented in EPROM. Vendors are urged to support TFTP for booting. The TFTP specification is written in an open style, and does not fully specify many parts of the protocol.

6.4.3.9 Sorcerer's Apprentice Syndrome

There is a serious problem, known as the Sorcerer's Apprentice Syndrome, in the protocol specification. While it does not cause incorrect operation of transfers (the file will always be transferred correctly if the transfer completes), this bug may cause excessive retransmission, which may cause the transfer to timeout.

Implementations must contain the fix for this problem: the sender (i.e., the side originating the DATA packets) must never resend the current DATA packet on receipt of a duplicate ACK.

The bug is caused by the protocol rule that either side, on receiving an old duplicate datagram, may resend the current datagram. If a packet is delayed in the network but later successfully delivered after either side has timed out and retransmitted a packet, a duplicate copy of the response may be generated. If the other side responds to this duplicate with a duplicate of its own, then every datagram will be sent in duplicate for the remainder of the transfer (unless a datagram is lost, breaking the repetition). Worse yet, since the delay is often caused by congestion, this duplicate transmission will usually cause more congestion, leading to more delayed packets, etc. Figure 6.12 is an example to help clarify this problem. Notice that once the delayed ACK arrives, the protocol settles down to duplicate all further

TFTP *A*	TFTP *B*
1 Receive ACK *X*-1 Send DATA *X*	
2	Receive DATA *X* Send ACK *X*
(ACK *X* is delayed in network, and A times out):	
3 Retransmit DATA *X*	
4	Receive DATA *X* Send ACK *X* again
5 Receive (delayed) ACK *X* Send DATA *X*+1	
6	Receive DATA *X*+1 Send ACK *X*+1
7 Receive ACK *X* again Send DATA *X*+1 again	
8	Receive DATA *X*+1 Send ACK *X*+1 again
9 Receive ACK *X*+1 Send DATA *X*+2	
10	Receive DATA *X*+2 Send ACK *X*+3
11 Receive ACK *X*+1 again Send DATA *X*+2 again	
12	Receive DATA *X*+2 Send ACK *X*+3 again

Figure 6.12 An example of the Sorcerer's Apprentice Syndrome

packets in sequences 5–8 and 9–12). The problem is caused not by either side timing out, but by both sides retransmitting the current packet when they receive a duplicate.

The fix is to break the retransmission loop, as indicated above. This is analogous to the behavior of TCP. It is then possible to remove the retransmission timer on the receiver, since the resent ACK will never cause any action; this is a useful simplification where TFTP is used in a bootstrap program. It is OK to allow the timer to remain, and it may be helpful if the retransmitted ACK replaces one that was genuinely lost in the network. The sender still requires a retransmit timer, of course.

6.4.3.10 Timeout Algorithms

A TFTP implementation must use an adaptive timeout. TCP retransmission algorithms provide a useful base to work from. At least an exponential backoff of retransmission timeout is necessary.

6.4.3.11 *Extensions*

A variety of nonstandard extensions have been made to TFTP, including additional transfer modes and a secure operation mode (with passwords). None of these have been standardized.

6.4.3.12 *Access Control*

A server TFTP implementation should include some configurable access control over what pathnames are allowed in TFTP operations.

6.4.3.13 *Broadcast Request*

A TFTP request directed to a broadcast address should be silently ignored. Due to the weak access control capability of TFTP, directed broadcasts of TFTP requests to random networks could create a significant security hole.

6.5   REMOTE TERMINAL ACCESS

The provision of remote terminal access was the very first service implemented in the network system. In the earliest design, the goal was to allow a user with an interactive terminal attached to one time-sharing computer to somehow use another computer as if the terminal were connected there. In this view of the problem there is considerable computing power available at both ends of the connection. The Telnet protocol was developed to provide this service.[12, 19, 20]

6.5.1   The Network Virtual Terminal

Telnet defines a Network Virtual Terminal (NVT), that is, an imaginary standard reference terminal. One task of an implementation of Telnet is to translate the characteristics of a real terminal into the characteristics of the NVT (and vice versa).

Telnet operates as follows: The user sits at the real terminal entering information to the User Telnet module. The Telnet module on the user computer translates that information to NVT-style information and sends it over the Internet to the server computer. At the server computer, the server Telnet module translates the NVT-style information to the form programs at that computer expect from local terminals. The information is given to the program being run on the server computer and any responses are sent back to the user via the reverse path and using the inverse series of translations.

The NVT approach requires translations between each type of real terminal and the NVT to be implemented. Without this approach, direct translations would be required between all pairs of types of real terminals. If there are N types of real terminals, the NVT approach requires on the order of N translations and the direct approach would require on the order of N^2 translations.

The implementation of the User Telnet module usually is quite straightforward and can be done as an ordinary process in the operating system environment and requiring no special privileges. The flow of data is from the real terminal through the operating system terminal handler code to the process that instantiates a User Telnet module. This process then translates the real terminal data to NVT data and sends it over the network via the operating system network handler code. Data coming from the remote host follows the reverse path. One tricky bit is that it is sometimes necessary to have separate processes for the two directions of data flow.

The server Telnet module implementation is much the same with the added problem that after the data from the network is translated from NVT to the local *real* terminal data it must be fed into a process (probably initially a shell in pre-login state) as if it came from a real terminal. Few operating systems allow one process to act as the operating system terminal handler code for another process in a completely general way. The implementation of the server Telnet module usually requires new code in the operating system. Since this was the case for many years, several current systems continue to implement the server Telnet module in the operating system for efficiency reasons.

NVT Controls

The NVT is defined to have some standard control codes, and nonprinting character functions. The control codes are transmitted with a preceding special code IAC meaning *interpret as control* the next octet. The nonprinting character functions are transmitted as plain data octets. Table 6.1 lists the NVT control codes.

6.5.2   Option Negotiation

While the NVT approach works quite well, the definition of the NVT is somewhat of a lowest-common-denominator kind of terminal, and many users have available on their real terminals features that are not defined in the NVT. Telnet provides for the use of features not defined in the basic NVT via negotiated options. The negotiation strategy is interesting in that it allows a Telnet module to refuse to use an optional feature without understanding the option in question.

Options are negotiated via an exchange of commands between the Telnet modules. The commands are DO, DONT, WILL, and WONT. Since options may be applied to each direction of data flow separately, the use of the option for each direction may be negotiated separately. The commands have the following interpretations:

DO	You please begin performing the option.
DONT	You please stop performing or do not begin performing the option.
WILL	I will begin performing the option.
WONT	I will stop performing or will not begin performing the option.

Table 6.1   NVT control codes

Name	Code	Meaning
IAC	255	Interpret the following octet(s) as controls.
NOP	241	No operation code.
BRK	243	NVT control code Break.
IP	244	Control code Interrupt Process.
AO	245	Control code Abort Output.
AYT	246	Control code Are You There.
EC	247	Control code Erase Character.
EL	248	Control code Erase Line.
GA	249	NVT Go Ahead signal.
EOR	239	End of Record
ABORT	238	Abort Process
SUSP	237	Suspend Process
EOF	236	End of File
NUL	0	No Operation
LF	10	Moves to the next line, at this horizontal position.
CR	13	Moves to the left margin of the current line.
BEL	7	Produces an audible or visible signal.
BS	8	Moves one character towards the left margin.
HT	9	Moves to the next horizontal tab stop.
VT	11	Moves to the next vertical tab stop.
FF	12	Moves to the top of the next page

For example, to begin using the option ABC one Telnet module sends WILL ABC. If the other Telnet module agrees, it responds DO ABC; if it disagrees (refuses the option), it sends DONT ABC.

Some options require further data to be exchanged to set the parameters of the option behavior. For example, an option to set Tab Stops needs to include the positions of the tab stops. To support this the SB and SE codes are defined to bracket the subnegotiation data, see Table 6.2. The currently defined options are listed in Table 6.3.

Of these, only Binary Transmission, Echo, Suppress Go Ahead, Status, and Timing Mark, are widely used—although the Line Mode option is rapidly gaining popularity.

6.5.3   Telnet Synchronization

When a user sitting at the keyboard and watching the output from the program being run decides that that output is not useful, he usually wants to halt that output and do something else. There are Telnet signals for interrupting a process (IP) and aborting output (AO). When these commands are used there may also be some data buffered between the

Table 6.2 Option negotiations

Name	Code	Meaning
WILL	251	Indicates the desire to begin performing, or confirmation that you are now performing, the indicated option.
WONT	252	Indicates the refusal to perform, or continue performing, the indicated option.
DO	253	Indicates the request that the other party perform, or confirmation that you are expecting the other party to perform, the indicated option.
DONT	254	Indicates the demand that the other party stop performing, or confirmation that you are no longer expecting the other party to perform, the indicated option.
SB	250	Indicates that what follows is subnegotiation of the indicated option.
SE	240	End of subnegotiation parameters.

user and the server (unprocessed user typing) or between the server and the user (unprinted program results). Cleaning out this unwanted data is the job of the Telnet Synch procedure.

The Synch procedure consists of sending a Data Mark (DM) code marked as TCP urgent data. When a receiving Telnet module is notified by TCP that there is urgent data to be processed, the Telnet module reads that data, discarding all but the Telnet signals. The end of the urgent data corresponds with a DM signal.

The Synch procedure is usually combined with the interrupt process function, so that the sequence IAC IP IAC DM is sent together as TCP urgent data. The specifications are:

DM 242 The data stream portion of a synch. This should always be accompanied by a TCP urgent notification.

6.5.4 Symmetry

Another feature of the design of the Telnet protocol is that it is reasonably symmetric. That is, the protocol functions and mechanisms may be used in either direction between the Telnet modules. This allows the Telnet protocol to be used to support user-to-user or process-to-process communication as well as the user-to-process communication commonly implemented.

6.5.5 Telnet Option Example

As an example of a Telnet Option a description of the Telnet Echo Option is included here. The command name and code are:

ECHO 1

The sender of the command

IAC WILL ECHO

Table 6.3   NVT options

Option	Name
0	Binary Transmission
1	Echo
2	Reconnection
3	Suppress Go Ahead
4	Approximate Message Size Negotiation
5	Status
6	Timing Mark
7	Remote Controlled Transmission and Echo
8	Output Line Width
9	Output Page Size
10	Output Carriage-Return Disposition
11	Output Horizontal Tab Stops
12	Output Horizontal Tab Disposition
13	Output Formfeed Disposition
14	Output Vertical Tabstops
15	Output Vertical Tab Disposition
16	Output Linefeed Disposition
17	Extended ASCII
18	Logout
19	Byte Macro
20	Data Entry Terminal
22	SUPDUP
22	SUPDUP Output
23	Send Location
24	Terminal Type
25	End of Record
26	TACACS User Identification
27	Output Marking
28	Terminal Location Number
29	Telnet 3270 Regime
30	X.3 PAD
31	Negotiate About Window Size
32	Terminal Speed
33	Remote Flow Control
34	Linemode
35	X Display Location
255	Extended-Options-List

requests to begin, or confirms that it will now begin, echoing data characters it receives over the Telnet connection back to the sender of the data characters. The sender of the command

    IAC WONT ECHO

demands to stop, or refuses to start, echoing the data characters it receives over the Telnet connection back to the sender of the data characters. The sender of the command

    IAC DO ECHO

requests that the receiver of this command begin echoing, or confirms that the receiver of this command is expected to echo, data characters it receives over the Telnet connection back to the sender. The sender of the command

    IAC DONT ECHO

demands the receiver of this command stop, or not start, echoing data characters it receives over the Telnet connection.

Default

The defaults are:

    WONT ECHO
    DONT ECHO

No echoing is done over the Telnet connection.

Motivation for the Option

The NVT has a printer and a keyboard that are nominally interconnected so that *echoes* need never traverse the network; that is to say, the NVT nominally operates in a mode where characters typed on the keyboard are (by some means) locally turned around and printed on the printer. In highly interactive situations it is appropriate for the remote process (command language interpreter, etc.) to which the characters are being sent to control the way they are echoed on the printer. In order to support such interactive situations, it is necessary that there be a Telnet option to allow the parties at the two ends of the Telnet connection to agree that characters typed on an NVT keyboard are to be echoed by the party at the other end of the Telnet connection.

Description of the Option

When the echoing option is in effect, the party at the end performing the echoing is expected to transmit (echo) data characters it receives back to the sender of the data characters. The option does not require that the characters echoed be exactly the characters received (for example, a number of systems echo the ASCII ESC character with something other than the ESC character). When the echoing option is not in effect, the receiver of data characters should not echo them back to the sender; this, of course, does not prevent the receiver from responding to data characters received.

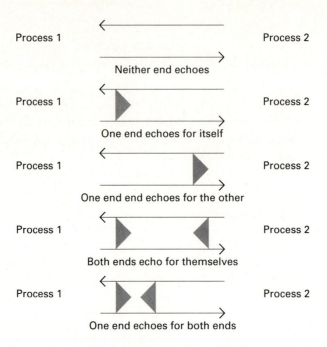

Figure 6.13　　Five modes of operation for echoing on a connection pair

The normal Telnet connection is two-way. That is, data flows in each direction on the connection independently; and neither, either, or both directions may be operating simultaneously in echo mode. Figure 6.13 shows the five reasonable modes of operation for echoing on a connection pair.

This option provides the capability to decide on whether or not either end will echo for the other. It does not, however, provide any control over whether or not an end echoes for itself; this decision must be left to the sole discretion of the systems at each end (although they may use information regarding the state of remote echoing negotiations in making this decision).

It should be noted that if *both* hosts enter the mode of echoing characters transmitted by the other host, then any character transmitted in either direction will be echoed back and forth indefinitely. Therefore, care should be taken in each implementation that if one site is echoing, echoing is not permitted to be turned on at the other end.

As discussed in the Telnet Protocol Specification, both parties to a full-duplex Telnet connection initially assume each direction of the connection is being operated in the default mode that is non-echo (non-echo means not using this option, and the same as DONT ECHO, WONT ECHO).

If either party desires to echo characters to the other party, or for the other party to echo characters to him, that party gives the appropriate command (WILL ECHO or DO ECHO) and waits (and hopes) for acceptance of the option. If the request to operate the connection in echo mode is refused, then the connection continues to operate in non-echo mode. If the request to operate the connection in echo mode is accepted, the connection is operated in echo mode.

After a connection has been changed to echo mode, either party may demand that it revert to non-echo mode by giving the appropriate DONT ECHO or WONT ECHO command (which the other party must confirm thereby allowing the connection to operate in non-echo mode). Just as each direction of the Telnet connection may be put in remote echoing mode independently, each direction of the Telnet connection must be removed from remote echoing mode separately.

Implementations of the echo option, as implementations of all other Telnet options, must follow the loop-preventing rules. Also, so that switches between echo and nonecho mode can be made with minimal confusion (momentary double-echoing, etc.), switches in mode of operation should be made at times precisely coordinated with the reception and transmission of echo requests and demands. For instance, if one party responds to a DO ECHO with a WILL ECHO, all data characters received after the DO ECHO should be echoed, and the WILL ECHO should immediately precede the first of the echoed characters.

The echoing option alone will normally not be sufficient to effect what is commonly understood to be remote computer echoing of characters typed on a terminal keyboard—the SUPPRESS-GO AHEAD option will normally have to be invoked in conjunction with the ECHO option to effect character-at-a-time remote echoing.

A Sample Implementation of the Option

The following is a description of a possible implementation for a simple user system called UHOST.

A possible implementation could be that, for each user terminal, the UHOST would keep 3 state bits: whether the terminal echoes for itself (UHOST ECHO always) or not (ECHO mode possible), whether the (human) user prefers to operate in ECHO mode or in non-ECHO mode, and whether the connection from this terminal to the server is in ECHO or non-ECHO mode. We will call these 3 bits P (physical), D (desired), and A (actual).

When a terminal dials up the UHOST the P-bit is set appropriately, the D-bit is set equal to it, and the A-bit is set to non-ECHO. The P-bit and D-bit may be manually reset by direct commands if the user so desires. For example, a user in Hawaii on a full-duplex terminal, would choose not to operate in ECHO mode, regardless of the preference of a mainland server. He should direct the UHOST to change his D-bit from ECHO to non-ECHO.

When a connection is opened from the UHOST terminal to a server, the UHOST would send the server a DO ECHO command if the MIN (with non-ECHO less than ECHO) of the P- and D-bits is different from the A-bit. If a WONT ECHO or WILL ECHO arrives from the server, the UHOST will set the A-bit to the MIN of the received request, the P-bit, and the D-bit. If this changes the state of the A-bit, the UHOST will send off the appropriate acknowledgment; if it does not, then the UHOST will send off the appropriate refusal if not changing meant that it had to deny the request (i.e., the MIN of the P-and D-bits was less than the received A-request).

If while a connection is open, the UHOST terminal user changes either the P-bit or D-bit, the UHOST will repeat the above tests and send off a DO ECHO or DONT ECHO, if necessary. When the connection is closed, the UHOST would reset the A-bit to indicate UHOST echoing.

While the UHOST's implementation would not involve DO ECHO or DON'T ECHO commands being sent to the server except when the connection is opened or the user explicitly changes his echoing mode, bigger hosts might invoke such mode switches quite frequently. For instance, while a line-at-a-time system was running, the server might attempt to put the user in local echo mode by sending the WONT ECHO command to the user; but while a character-at-a-time system was running, the server might attempt to invoke remote echoing for the user by sending the WILL ECHO command to the user. Furthermore, while the UHOST will never send a WILL ECHO command, and will only send a WONT ECHO to refuse a server-sent DO ECHO command, a server host might often send the WILL and WONT ECHO commands.

6.5.6 Implementation Specifics

Telnet is the standard Internet application protocol for remote login. It provides the encoding rules to link a user's keyboard and display on a client (user) system with a command interpreter on a remote server system. A subset of the Telnet protocol is also incorporated within other application protocols, e.g., FTP and SMTP.

Telnet uses a single TCP connection, and its normal data stream NVT mode is 7-bit ASCII with escape sequences to embed control functions. Telnet also allows the negotiation of many optional modes and functions.

Option Negotiation

Every Telnet implementation must include option negotiation and subnegotiation machinery. A host must carefully follow the rules to avoid option-negotiation loops. A host must refuse (i.e., reply WONT/DONT to a DO/WILL) an unsupported option. Option negotiation should continue to function (even if all requests are refused) throughout the lifetime of a Telnet connection. If all option negotiations fail, a Telnet implementation must default to, and support, an NVT.

Even though more sophisticated terminals and supporting option negotiations are becoming the norm, all implementations must be prepared to support an NVT for any user-server communication.

Telnet Go-Ahead Function

On a host that never sends the Telnet command Go-Ahead (GA), the Telnet server must attempt to negotiate the Suppress-Go-Ahead option (i.e., send WILL SGA). A User or Server Telnet must always accept negotiation of the Suppress-Go-Ahead option.

When it is driving a full-duplex terminal for which GA has no meaning, a User Telnet implementation may ignore GA commands.

Half-duplex (locked-keyboard) line-at-a-time terminals for which the Go-Ahead mechanism was designed have largely disappeared from the scene. It turned out to be difficult to implement sending the Go-Ahead signal in many operating systems, even on some systems that support native half-duplex terminals. The difficulty is typically that the Telnet server code does not have access to information about whether the user process is blocked awaiting input from the Telnet connection, i.e., it cannot reliably determine when to send a GA command. Therefore, most Telnet Server hosts do not send GA commands. The effect of these rules is to allow either end of a Telnet connection to veto the use of GA commands.

There is a class of half-duplex terminals that is still commercially important: data entry terminals, which interact in a full-screen manner. However, supporting data entry terminals using the Telnet protocol does not require the Go-Ahead signal.

Control Functions

The list of Telnet commands has been extended to include EOR (End-of-Record), with code 239. Both user and server Telnets may support the control functions EOR, EC, EL, and Break, and must support AO, AYT, DM, IP, NOP, SB, and SE. A host must be able to receive and ignore any Telnet control functions that it does not support.

Note that a server Telnet is required to support the Telnet IP (Interrupt Process) function, even if the server host has an equivalent in-stream function (e.g., Control-C, in many systems). The Telnet IP function may be stronger than an in-stream interrupt command, because of the out-of-band effect of TCP urgent data.

The EOR control function may be used to delimit the stream. An important application is data entry terminal support. There was concern that since EOR had not been defined in the basic specification, a host that was not prepared to correctly ignore unknown Telnet commands might crash if it received an EOR. To protect such hosts, the End-of-Record option was introduced; however, a properly implemented Telnet program will not require this protection.

Telnet Synch Signal

When it receives urgent TCP data, a user or server Telnet must discard all data except Telnet commands until the DM (and end of urgent) is reached.

When it sends Telnet interrupt process, a User Telnet should follow it by the Telnet Synch sequence, i.e., send as TCP urgent data the sequence "IAC IP IAC DM." The TCP urgent pointer points to the DM octet.

When it receives a Telnet IP command, a server Telnet may send a Telnet Synch sequence back to the user, to flush the output stream. The choice ought to be consistent with the way the server operating system behaves when a local user interrupts a process.

When it receives a Telnet AO command, a Server Telnet must send a Telnet synch sequence back to the user, to flush the output stream.

A User Telnet should have the capability of flushing output when it sends a Telnet IP. There are three possible ways for a User Telnet to flush the stream of server output data:

1   Send AO after the IP command. This will cause the server host to send a flush-buff-ered-output signal to its operating system. However, the AO may not take effect locally, i.e., stop terminal output at the user-Telnet end, until the server-Telnet has received and processed the AO and has sent back a Synch signal.

2   Send DO TIMING-MARK after the IP command, and discard all output locally until a WILL/WONT TIMING-MARK is received from the server-Telnet.

   Since the DO TIMING-MARK will be processed after the IP command at the server, the reply to it should be in the right place in the output data stream. However, the TIMING-MARK will not send a flush-buffered-output signal to the server operating system. Whether or not this is needed depends upon the server system.

3   Do both.

The best method is not entirely clear, since it must accommodate a number of existing server hosts that do not follow the Telnet standards in various ways. The safest approach is probably to provide a user-controllable option to select the method.

NVT Printer and Keyboard

In NVT mode, a Telnet should not send characters with the high-order bit set to 1, and must not send it as a parity bit. Implementations that pass the high-order bit to applications should negotiate binary mode.

Implementors should be aware that a strict reading of the specification allows a client or server expecting NVT ASCII to ignore characters with the high-order bit set. In general, binary mode is expected to be used for transmission of an extended (beyond 7-bit) character set with Telnet.

However, there exist applications that really need an 8-bit NVT mode, which is currently not defined, and these existing applications do set the high-order bit during part or all of the life of a Telnet connection. Note that binary mode is not the same as 8-bit NVT mode, since binary mode turns off end-of-line processing. For this reason, the requirements on the high-order bit are stated as *should*, not *must*.

The specification defines a minimal set of properties of an NVT; this is not meant to preclude additional features in a real terminal. A Telnet connection is fully transparent to all 7-bit ASCII characters, including arbitrary ASCII control characters.

For example, a terminal might support full-screen commands coded as ASCII escape sequences; a Telnet implementation would pass these sequences as uninterpreted data. Thus, an NVT should not be conceived as a terminal type of a highly restricted device.

Telnet Command Structure

Since options may appear at any point in the data stream, a Telnet escape character (known as IAC, with the value 255) to be sent as data must be doubled; i.e., sent twice.

Telnet Binary Option

When the Binary option has been successfully negotiated, arbitrary 8-bit characters are allowed. However, the data stream must still be scanned for IAC characters, any embedded Telnet commands must be obeyed, and data bytes equal to IAC must be doubled. Other character processing (e.g., replacing CR by CR NUL or by CR LF) must not be done. In particular, there is no end-of-line convention in binary mode.

The Binary option is normally negotiated in both directions, to change the Telnet connection from NVT mode to binary mode.

The sequence IAC EOR can be used to delimit blocks of data within a binary-mode Telnet stream.

Telnet Terminal-Type Option

The Terminal-Type option must use the terminal type names officially defined in *Assigned Numbers*,[36] when they are available for the particular terminal. However, the receiver of a Terminal-Type option must accept any name.

Telnet End-of-Line Convention

The Telnet protocol defines the sequence CR LF to mean *end-of-line*. For terminal input, this corresponds to a command-completion or end-of-line key being pressed on a user terminal; on an ASCII terminal, this is the CR key, but it may also be labeled *Return* or *Enter*.

When a server Telnet receives the Telnet end-of-line sequence CR LF as input from a remote terminal, the effect must be the same as if the user had pressed the end-of-line key on a local terminal. On server hosts that use ASCII, in particular, receipt of the Telnet sequence CR LF must cause the same effect as a local user pressing the CR key on a local terminal. Thus, CR LF and CR NUL must have the same effect on an ASCII server host when received as input over a Telnet connection.

A user Telnet must be able to send any of the forms: CR LF, CR NUL, and LF. A User Telnet on an ASCII host should have a user-controllable mode to send either CR LF or CR NUL when the user presses the end-of-line key, and CR LF should be the default.

The Telnet end-of-line sequence CR LF must be used to send Telnet data that is not terminal-to-computer (e.g., for Server Telnet sending output, or the Telnet protocol incorporated another application protocol).

To allow interoperability between arbitrary Telnet clients and servers, the Telnet protocol defined a standard representation for a line terminator. Since the ASCII character set includes no explicit end-of-line character, systems have chosen various representations, e.g.,

CR, LF, and the sequence CR LF. The Telnet protocol chose the CR LF sequence as the standard for network transmission.

Unfortunately, the Telnet protocol specification has turned out to be somewhat ambiguous on what characters should be sent from a client to a server for the end-of-line key. The result has been a massive and continuing interoperability headache, made worse by various faulty implementations of both user and server Telnets.

Although the Telnet protocol is based on a perfectly symmetric model, in a remote login session the role of the user at a terminal differs from the role of the server host. For example, the specification defines the meaning of CR, LF, and CR LF as output from the server, but does not specify what the user Telnet should send when the user presses the end-of-line key on the terminal; this turns out to be the point at issue.

When a user presses the end-of-line key, some user Telnet implementations send CR LF, while others send CR NUL (based on a different interpretation of the same sentence in the specification). These will be equivalent for a correctly-implemented ASCII server host, as discussed above. For other servers, a mode in the user Telnet is needed.

The existence of user Telnets that send only CR NUL when CR is pressed creates a dilemma for non-ASCII hosts: they can either treat CR NUL as equivalent to CR LF in input, thus precluding the possibility of entering a *bare* CR, or lose complete interworking.

Suppose a user on host *A* uses Telnet to log into a server host *B*, and then execute *B*'s user Telnet program to log into server host *C*. It is desirable for the server-user Telnet combination on *B* to be as transparent as possible, i.e., to make it appear as if *A* were connected directly to *C*. In particular, correct implementation will make *B* transparent to Telnet end-of-line sequences, except that CR LF may be translated to CR NUL or vice versa.

To understand Telnet end-of-line issues, one must have at least a general model of the relationship of Telnet to the local operating system. The server Telnet process is typically coupled into the terminal driver software of the operating system as a pseudo-terminal. A Telnet end-of-line sequence received by the server Telnet must have the same effect as pressing the end-of-line key on a real locally connected terminal.

Operating systems that support interactive character-at-a-time applications (e.g., editors) typically have two internal modes for their terminal I/O: a formatted mode, in which local conventions for end-of-line and other formatting rules are applied to the data stream, and a "raw" mode, in which the application has direct access to every character as it is entered. A server Telnet must be implemented in such a way that these modes have the same effect for remote as for local terminals. For example, suppose a CR LF or CR NUL is received by the server Telnet on an ASCII host. In raw mode, a CR character is passed to the application; in formatted mode, the local system's end-of-line convention is used.

Data Entry Terminals

In addition to the line-oriented and character-oriented ASCII terminals for which Telnet was designed, there are several families of video display terminals that are sometimes known as "data entry terminals" or DETs. The IBM 3270 family is a well-known example.

Two Internet protocols have been designed to support generic DETs: SUPDUP, and the DET option. The DET option drives a data entry terminal over a Telnet connection using (sub-) negotiation. SUPDUP is a completely separate terminal protocol, which can be entered from Telnet by negotiation. Although both SUPDUP and the DET option have been used successfully in particular environments, neither has gained general acceptance or wide implementation.

A different approach to DET interaction has been developed for supporting the IBM 3270 family through Telnet, although the same approach would be applicable to any DET. The idea is to enter a "native DET" mode, in which the native DET input/output stream is sent as binary data. The Telnet EOR command is used to delimit logical records (e.g., screens), within this binary stream.

The rules for entering and leaving native DET mode are as follows:

- The server uses the Terminal-Type option to learn that the client is a DET.
- It is conventional, but not required, that both ends negotiate the EOR option.
- Both ends negotiate the Binary option to enter native DET mode.

Option Initiation

When the Telnet protocol is used in a client/server situation, the server should initiate negotiation of the terminal interaction mode it expects.

The Telnet protocol was defined to be perfectly symmetrical, but its application is generally asymmetric. Remote login has been known to fail because *neither* side initiated negotiation of the required nondefault terminal modes. It is generally the server that determines the preferred mode, so the server needs to initiate the negotiation; since the negotiation is symmetric, the user can also initiate it.

A client (user Telnet) should provide a means for users to enable and disable the initiation of option negotiation.

A user sometimes needs to connect to an application service (e.g., FTP or SMTP) that uses Telnet for its control stream but does not support Telnet options. User Telnet may be used for this purpose if initiation of option negotiation is disabled.

Telnet Linemode Option

An important new Telnet option, linemode, has been proposed. The Linemode option provides a standard way for a user Telnet and a server Telnet to agree that the client, rather than the server, will perform terminal character processing. When the client has prepared a complete line of text, it will send it to the server in (usually) one TCP packet. This option will greatly decrease the packet cost of Telnet sessions and will also give much better user response over congested or long-delay networks.

The Linemode option allows dynamic switching between local and remote character processing. For example, the Telnet connection will automatically negotiate into single-character mode while a full screen editor is running, and then return to linemode when the editor is finished.

Hosts should implement the client side of this option, and may implement the server side of this option. To properly implement the server side, the server needs to be able to tell the local system not to do any input character processing, but to remember its current terminal state and notify the server Telnet process whenever the state changes. This will allow password echoing and full screen editors to be handled properly, for example.

Character Set Transparency

User Telnet implementations should be able to send or receive any 7-bit ASCII character. Where possible, any special character interpretations by the user host's operating system should be bypassed so that these characters can conveniently be sent and received on the connection.

Some character value must be reserved as meaning "escape to command mode;" conventionally, doubling this character (i.e., sending it twice) allows it to be entered as data. The specific character used should be user-selectable.

On Binary-mode connections, a user Telnet program may provide an escape mechanism for entering arbitrary 8-bit values, if the host operating system doesn't allow them to be entered directly from the keyboard.

The transparency issues are less pressing on servers, but implementors should take care in dealing with issues like masking off parity bits (sent by an older, nonconforming client) before they reach programs that expect only NVT ASCII, and properly handling programs that request 8-bit data streams.

Telnet Commands

A user Telnet program must provide a user the capability of entering any of the Telnet control functions IP, AO, or AYT, and should provide the capability of entering EC, EL, and BREAK.

TCP Connection Errors

A user Telnet program should report to the user any TCP errors that are reported by the transport layer.

Nondefault Telnet Contact Port

A user Telnet program should allow the user to optionally specify a nonstandard contact port number at the server Telnet host.

Flushing Output

A user-Telnet program should provide the user with the ability to specify whether or not output should be flushed when an IP is sent.

For any output flushing scheme that causes the user-Telnet to flush output locally until a Telnet signal is received from the server, there should be a way for the user to manually restore normal output, in case the server fails to send the expected signal.

6.5.7 Impact

The view expressed earlier that the goal of Telnet is to allow an interactive terminal attached to one computer to be used with the interactive programs on another computer had an impact on the Telnet protocol. Occasionally people speak of "connecting a terminal to the network." Technically, that is incorrect—only computers may be connected to the Internet. There are specially designed computers that are tailored to implement just those functions and protocols to support the connection of terminals so that users may access remote programs. Such computers are generally called *terminal servers*; one early example was called the Terminal Access Controller (TAC); it implements IP plus TCP and Telnet.[21, 22]

6.6 TRANSACTION APPLICATIONS

6.6.1 Introduction

Several Internet applications are transaction-oriented. These are particularly useful in environments composed of many smaller computers, such as professional workstations or personal computers, and local networks.

These applications are called transaction applications because they consist of simply one message from the user to the server, and one reply from the server to the user. Such applications may be implemented on either TCP or UDP, and several transaction applications are implemented on both.

Transaction applications are ideal candidates for implementation on a datagram base such as UDP. Two conditions must be met: the service operation is idempotent, and the data transfer will always fit in a datagram.

Several name lookup services have been implemented in the TCP/IP protocol suite. One is popularly called *Whois* (also known as *nicname*).[23] It returns information about a person given the last name or a unique ID (assigned by the Whois system). The information returned includes (if available) the organization, address, and phone number, the unique ID, and the computer mail mailbox of the person. If the name given is not unique, Whois returns a list of one-line descriptions of all the matches.

The time server simply returns the current time whenever it is contacted. The time is specified as the number of seconds since a reference date and time (UTC).[30]

More complex services are the Domain Name System and the Network Time System.

6.6.2 Domain Name System

The Domain Name System (DNS) is discussed in Chapter 11. It should be pointed out here, though, that the DNS is implemented as an application on top of UDP (and in a few cases on top of TCP). As an application it is a widely implemented distributed system providing a large database with distributed and replicated data storage.

6.6.3   Network Time System

The Network Time Protocol provides a means for maintaining accurate synchronized time among the participating hosts. In this system a distributed subnet of time servers operate in a self-organizing, hierarchical-master-slave configuration to synchronize local clocks within the subnet to national time standards.[24]

6.7   OTHER APPLICATIONS

6.7.1   Real-Time Video and Voice

DARPA has sponsored a major experiment in digital packet voice communication using the ARPANET, SATNET, and the WIDEBAND networks in particular, and the Internet in general. In the course of this work a system-level protocol, the Stream Protocol (ST),[31, 32] and two application level protocols, the Network Voice Protocol (NVP)[33, 34] and the Packet Video Protocol (PVP),[35] were developed.

The ST protocol provides a reserved capacity service (where possible given the underlying network technology). This is useful for real-time communication given the sensitivity to delay and variation in delay of this type of application. ST also provides a group addressing mechanism to support a "conference call" style application.

The NVP defines a format for digital packet voice using any of several coding techniques (including PCM, CVSD, and LPC). It also specifies a set of protocol messages for setting up and clearing calls, and establishing compatible coding and parameters.

The PVP defines the format for digital packet video use and of several coding techniques. In the current state of video coding technology each manufacturer has its own proprietary coding algorithm. The Packet Video Protocol provides a means to transmit several of these over packet networks.

6.7.2   Other

Many other applications and services are used in limited communities or on an experimental basis within the Internet community. In addition there are a number of limited use or experimental protocols at the service level; some of these may be considered specialized applications. Over 40 application-level protocols and over 20 service-level protocols identified as Internet Standards. Further information and references on these and other protocols may be found in the *Assigned Numbers*[36] and the *IAB Official Protocol Standards*.[37]

Following is a list of some of these protocols.

- Active Users Protocol
- Character Generator Protocol
- Cross Net Debugger Protocol
- Daytime Protocol
- Discard Protocol
- Echo Protocol
- Finger Protocol
- Graphics Protocol
- Host Monitoring Protocol
- Loader Debugger Protocol
- Logical Address Maintenance Protocol
- Login Host Protocol
- Mailbox Name Service
- Packet Radio Measurement Protocol
- Post Office Protocol
- Quote of the Day Protocol
- Reliable Data Protocol
- Remote Job Entry Protocol
- Remote Job Service
- Remote Telnet Service
- Remote Virtual Disk Protocol
- Resource Location Protocol

6.8 ACKNOWLEDGMENTS

The development of these protocols involved many people. It is not possible to acknowledge all of them, and I apologize to those who have contributed and are not mentioned here. Among the leading contributors are: Tom O'Sullivan, Abhay Bushan, Jim White, Ken Pogran, Eric Harslem, Wayne Hathaway, John Day, Buzz Owen, Alex McKenzie, Karen Sollins, Steve Crocker, Noel Chiappa, Bob Clements, Vint Cerf, Bob Bressler, Dave Mills, Nancy Neigus, Steve Carr, John Heafner, Bob Metcalfe, Dave Crocker, Will Crowther, Dave Clark, Ken Harrenstien, John Melvin, Bob Thomas, Paul Mockapetris, Danny Cohen, Ed Meyer, Dave Walden, Bill Duvall, Jeff Rulifson, Dick Watson, John Davidson, Bob Braden, and Michael Padlipsky.

The major sections of this chapter are substantially based on the documents specifying these protocols. My thanks to the many authors of those documents.

REFERENCES

1   B. Leiner, R. Cole, J. Postel and D. Mills, *The DARPA Internet Protocol Suite*, INFOCOM85, Washington, D.C., March, 1985.

2   V. Cerf and E. Cain, *The DoD Internet Architecture Model*, Computer Networks, V.7, N.5, October 1983.

3   R. Sproull and D. Cohen, *High-Level Protocols*, Proceedings of the IEEE, V.66, N.11, November 1978.

4   S. Crocker, J. Heafner, R. Metcalfe and J. Postel, Function-Oriented Protocols for the ARPA Computer Network, *Spring Joint Computer Conference*, AFIPS, May 1972.

5   M. Padlipsky, A *Perspective on the ARPANET Reference Model*, Proceedings of the IEEE INFOCOM83 Conference, San Diego, California, April 1983.

6   J. Postel, (Ed.), *Transmission Control Protocol-DARPA Internet Program Protocol Specification, RFC 793*, USC/Information Sciences Institute, September 1981.

7   MIL-STD-1778, *Transmission Control Protocol*, Defense Communications Agency, Department of Defense, August 1983. Available from: Naval Publications and Forms Center, Code 3015, 5801 Tabor Avenue, Philadelphia, Pennsylvania, 19120.

8   J. Postel, *User Datagram Protocol, RFC 768*, USC/Information Sciences Institute, August 1980.

9   J. Postel, *Simple Mail Transfer Protocol, RFC 821*, USC/Information Sciences Institute, August 1982.

10 D. Crocker, *Standard for the Format of ARPA Internet Text Messages, RFC 822*, Department of Electrical Engineering, University of Delaware, August 1982.

11 M.T. Rose and J. Romine, *MH.5: How to Process 200 Messages a Day and Still Get Some Real Work Done*, USENIX, Portland, Oregon, June 1985.

12 R. Braden, (Ed.), *Requirements for Internet Hosts—Applications and Support, RFC 1123*, Internet Engineering Task Force, October 1989.

13 J. Reynolds, J. Postel, A. Katz, G. Finn and A. DeSchon, *The DARPA Experimental Multimedia Mail System*, IEEE Computer, Vol. 18, No. 10, October 1985.

14   R. Thomas, H. Forsdick, T. Crowley, R. Schaaf, R. Tomlinson, V. Travers and G. Robertson, *Diamond: A Multimedia Message System Built on a Distributed Architecture*, IEEE Computer, V.18, N.12, December 1985.

15   J. Postel, *Internet Message Protocol, RFC 759*, USC/Information Sciences Institute, August 1980.

16   J. Postel, A *Structured Format for Transmission of Multi-Media Documents, RFC 767*, USC/Information Sciences Institute, August 1980.

17   J. Postel, *File Transfer Protocol, RFC 959*, USC/Information Sciences Institute, October 1985.

18   K. Sollins, *The TFTP Protocol (Revision 2), RFC 783*, MIT/LCS, June 1981.

19   J. Davidson, W. Hathaway, J. Postel, N. Mimno, R. Thomas, and D. Walden, *The ARPANET Telnet Protocol: Its Purpose, Principles, Implementation, and Impact on Host Operating System Design*, Proceedings of the Fifth Data Communications Symposium, ACM/IEEE, Snowbird, Utah, September 1977.

20   J. Postel and J. Reynolds, *Telnet Protocol Specification, RFC 854*, USC/Information Sciences Institute, May 1983.

21   S. Ornstein, F. Heart, W. Crowther, H. Rising, S. Russell, and A. Michel, The Terminal IMP for the ARPA Computer Network, *Spring Joint Computer Conference*, AFIPS, May 1972.

22   R. Clifford, *TAC User's Guide*, Report Number 4780, Bolt Beranek and Newman, September 1982.

23   K. Harrenstien, M. Stahl and E. Feinler, *Nicname/Whois, RFC 954*, SRI International, October 1988.

24   D. Mills, *Network Time Protocol (Version 2) Specification and Implementation, RFC 1119*, University of Delaware, September 1989.

25   J. Pickens, E. Feinler and J. Mathis, *The NIC Name Server-A Datagram-Based Information Utility*, Proceedings of the Fourth Berkeley Conference on Distributed Data Management and Computer Networks, August 1979.

26   P. Mockapetris, *The Domain Name System*, Proceedings of the IFIP 6.5 Working Conference on Computer Message Services, Nottingham, England, May 1984. Also available as RS-84-133, USC/Information Sciences Institute, June 1984.

27   P. Mockapetris, J. Postel and P. Kirton, *Name Server Design for Distributed Systems*, Proceedings of the Seventh International Conference on Com-

puter Communication, October 1984, Sidney, Australia. Also available as RS-84-132, USC/Information Sciences Institute, June 1984.

28   P. Mockapetris, *Domain Names-Concepts and Facilities*, *RFC 1034*, USC/Information Sciences Institute, November 1987.

29   P. Mockapetris, *Domain Names-Implementation and Specification*, *RFC 1035*, USC/Information Sciences Institute, November 1987.

30   J. Postel, and K. Harrenstien, *Time Protocol, RFC 868*, USC/Information Sciences Institute, May 1983.

31   C. Topolcic, (Ed.), *Experimental Internet Stream Protocol, Version 2 (ST-II)*, *RFC 1190*, IETF CIP Working Group, October 1990.

32   C. Weinstein and H. Heggestad, *Multiplexing of Packet Speech on an Experimental Wideband Satellite Network*, Proceedings of the Ninth AIAA Communications Satellite Systems Conference, San Diego, California, March 1982.

33   D. Cohen, *Specification for the Network Voice Protocol, RFC 741*, RR-75-39, USC/Information Sciences Institute, March 1976.

34   D. Cohen, *A Protocol for Packet Switching Voice Communication*, Proceedings of the IFIP TC6 Symposium on Computer Network Protocols, Liege, Belgium, February 1978.

35   S. Casner, K. Seo, W. Edmond and C. Topolcic, *N-Way Conferencing with Packet Video*, Proceedings of the Third International Workshop on Packet Video, March 22–23, 1990.

36   J. Reynolds and J. Postel, *Assigned Numbers, RFC 1060* USC/Information Sciences Institute, March 1990.

37   J. Postel, *IAB Official Protocol Standards*, *RFC 1250*, USC/Information Sciences Institute, August 1991.

38   N. Borenstein and N. Freed, *MIME (Multipurpose Internet Mail Extensions): Mechanisms for Specifying and Describing the Format of Internet Message Bodies, RFC 1341*, Bellcore, Innosoft, June 1992.

CHAPTER 7 ▫ ▫ ▫ ▫

A Practical Perspective on Routers

SCOTT O. BRADNER

CONTENTS

C O N T E N T S   (**Continued**)

There is a huge difference between "implementing the protocols" and "implementing a system." Without appreciation for system issues, an implementation can perform poorly or even fail to interoperate. We begin by looking at all the details that go into taking the specifications that deal with intermediate systems and realizing a production router.

7.1   INTRODUCTION

Many factors must be considered in the process of determining the specific network interconnection device that should be used in a particular situation. These factors range from the minutia of network design and applications to the larger issues of cost and politics. This chapter presents some background information on network interconnection devices and some suggestions about the choice criteria. The chapter does not attempt to evaluate the various design features available in the marketplace, but simply presents the information and leaves it to the reader to judge which vendor's products would best fit local requirements.

7.2   WHAT IS A ROUTER?

Routers represent one out of a spectrum of devices that may be used to connect parts of a data network or two or more local area networks (LANs). The interconnection devices are called local if they join two or more networks in a single location, and are called remote if one or more connections are made over a wide area circuit, like a telephone line.

7.2.1   Repeaters

The simplest interconnection device is a repeater. Repeaters operate at the ISO Physical Layer, and make two or more pieces of wire appear as one. Repeaters unconditionally copy bits of data from one port to another, sometimes gaining or losing bits at the beginning or end of packets when they do so. They do not check or regenerate checksums in the data

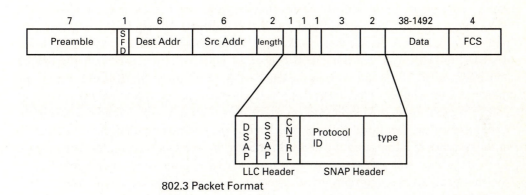

Ethernet Packet Format

802.3 Packet Format

Figure 7.1   Ethernet packet format: SFD—Start Frame Delimiter, Dest. Addr.—Destination address, Src Addr.—Source address, Type—protocol type, FCS—frame check sequence, DSAP—destination service access point, SSAP—source service access point, CNTRL—control

stream. They are transparent to protocols and are end-node transparent; that is, one computer transmitting data to another computer over a network does not (and cannot) know if there is a repeater between them.

7.2.2   Bridges

Bridges can be thought of as traffic-isolating repeaters. They operate at the ISO Data Link layer, and conditionally forward packets from one network port to another. Since bridges operate in store-and-forward mode with packets, they present a much longer processing delay than do repeaters. All packets are delayed by at least the length of time that it takes to transmit them on the slowest of the transit networks. There are three types of bridges used in data networks.

7.2.2.1   Transparent Bridges

Transparent bridges are used in networks like Ethernet and 802.3. As the name suggests, they are completely transparent to the end nodes on the network and are protocol independent. Transparent bridges maintain an internal database of the source addresses of all packets that have been seen on any of the connected networks. (See Figure 7.1 for a diagram of

an Ethernet packet format.) To ensure that all packets are seen, the bridge interfaces operate in promiscuous mode, capturing all packets on the attached LANs. Whenever a packet
is received, the bridge verifies the packet checksum (FCS) to be sure that valid data are
being used. Packets having bad checksums are discarded. The source address field in the
header is then checked against a database. A new database entry is created if this is a previously unknown address. The database entry consists of the hardware address, the port on
which it was seen, and a Timestamp to indicate when the entry was last updated. The
Timestamp and port number are updated if the address is already in the database. The
packet's destination address is then checked against the database. If the address is not in the
database, the packet is sent out on all connected network ports other than the one on
which it came in. If the address is in the database and the port in the database entry is not
the same as the one on which the packet was received, the packet is sent out from the listed
port. The packet is ignored if the port on which the packet was received and the port in the
database entry are identical. With this mechanism the end nodes do not have to be aware
of the presence of a bridge on the network, and yet the network traffic is segmented and a
particular packet will only travel where it needs to. In addition, most transparent bridges
run the spanning tree algorithm, which allows redundancy to be included in the physical
network design. The bridges interact to establish a unique path between all pairs of LANs.
Bridges having ports that are not part of the unique path block any ports that would cause
redundant paths. Keep-alive traffic between the bridges is used to discover a bridge or link
failure. The set of paths is recalculated whenever a failure is detected. This provides an
automatic fail-over to redundant pathways without requiring management interaction.

7.2.2.2 Source Route Bridges

The second type of bridge is the source route bridge. Source route bridges are used in token
ring networks. They also operate at the ISO Data Link Layer and are protocol independent, but they are not end node transparent. At the Data Link Level, the connected LANs
operate as separate networks, each with its own identity, but at the Network Layer and to
transport protocols these divisions are hidden, with the LANs appearing as one LAN. If the
high-order bit of the destination hardware address in a token ring packet is on, it indicates
that there is a path included in the packet header. (See Figure 7.2 for an example of a token
ring packet format.) The path consists of a series of up to seven route designators, each of
which consists of a 12-bit LAN identification number and a 4-bit bridge identification
number. The LAN ID value must be unique in the token ring Internet, but the bridge ID
must only be unique on its connected LANs. The source route bridge processes all packets
on the connected LANs whose high-order bits of the destination address are on. The
bridge examines the route designators to find the one that includes the LAN ID of the
LAN connected to the port on which it was received. If the next bridge ID in the path corresponds to the ID of the bridge doing the processing, then the following LAN ID is
checked to see if it corresponds to the ID of one of the LANs connected to the bridge. If
so, the packet is forwarded to the appropriate port. A direction bit in the packet header is

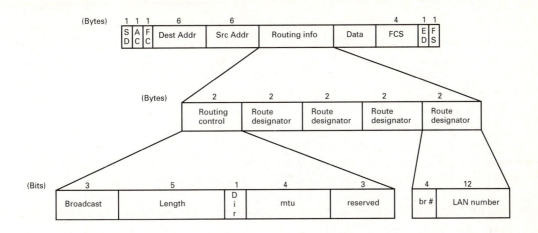

Figure 7.2 Token ring (802.5) packet format: SD—starting delimiter, AC—access control, FC—frame control, Dest Addr—destination address, Src Addr—source address, DIR—direction, MTU—maximum transmission unit, BR#—bridge number, FCS—frame checking sequence, ED—ending delimiter, FS,—frame status

used to indicate the direction in which to scan the route designators. This allows the end nodes in a conversation to copy, rather than reformat, the header of a response packet.

It is necessary for the initiator of a conversation through a network linked together with source route bridges to obtain the path to its intended destination and include it in the packet headers. The literature describes two methods that may be used to determine this path; both are used in IBM token ring networks. In the first method, a discovery packet is sent using an all-routes broadcast. All-routes addressing causes the packet to be forwarded by all bridges to all ports, except for the port on which it was received. This causes each LAN in the Internet to get a copy of the packet for each possible pathway between the packet source and the LAN. When forwarding an all-routes broadcast packet, each bridge appends its own route designator to the path in the packet header; thus when the packet arrives at the destination it includes a full path back to the source. The destination node replies to each of the discovery packets it receives using normal point-to-point addressing, by complementing the direction bit in the header. In the second method, the source sends the discovery packet by a single-route broadcast. A single-route broadcast uses a version of the spanning tree algorithm to ensure that all LANs in the Internet receive one (and only one) copy of the packet. The destination node then responds using an all-routes broadcast. In this method, the source will get a copy of the response for every route from the destination back to the source. In both cases, the original source will receive multiple responses and choose among them for the path it will use. Most implementations use the first response, assuming that it represents the fastest path. By complementing the direction bit,

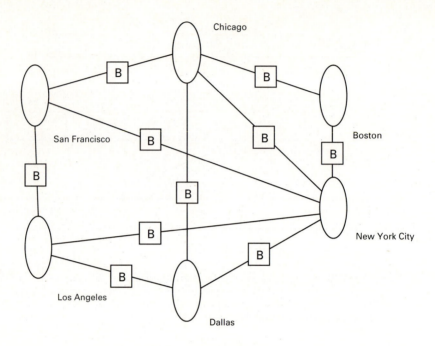

Figure 7.3   Sample source route: network home office in New York City and five
            branch offices; bridges indicated by **B**s

the same path is used for both directions of the conversation, thus ensuring symmetrical routing. The discovery process must be performed whenever a new connection is required or when an existing connection times out.

One area of concern in large networks using source route bridges (national SNA networks, for example) is the load that the route discovery process can place on a network. Most data networks are now designed with multiple pathways to increase the connection reliability. This produces an environment that can cause large numbers of discovery packets to reach some LANs for each one originally transmitted. An example of this is the network shown in Figure 7.3. A single all-routes discovery packet sent on the LAN in Los Angeles will generate 9 packets on the LAN in New York City (one for each path from Los Angeles to New York City). The addition of parallel redundancy (see Figure 7.4), as is often done, raises this to a number beyond my meager visualization ability. In a large source route network with a maximum of seven hops in each path and averaging only three pathways between LANs, a single transmitted discovery packet will cause over two thousand packets on the most remote LAN.

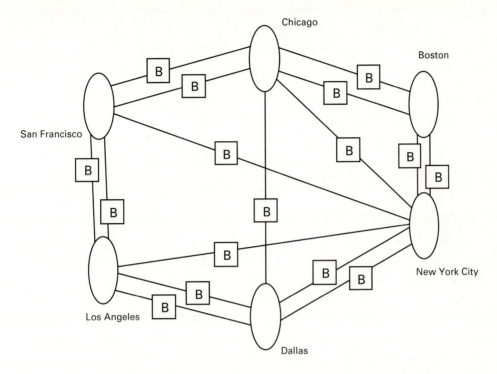

Figure 7.4   Sample route network with redundancy: home office in New York City and five branch offices; bridges indicated by **B**s

7.2.2.3 Combination Bridges

The third type of bridge is the combination bridge, also known as the mixed-media bridge. These devices are used to connect dissimilar types of networks, i.e., Ethernet to token ring, token ring to FDDI, etc. In the case of connecting the source route bridge world to the transparent bridge world (Ethernet to token ring, for example), these devices are seen as source route bridges to any connected token ring LAN, and as transparent bridges to the connected Ethernet LANs. Because the encapsulation formats for specific transport protocols differ between LAN types, these devices must be protocol specific. Two databases are maintained, one listing devices for the token ring ports, and one for the Ethernet ports. If a discovery packet is received from the token ring side, the requested MAC address is looked up in the non-token ring database. If a corresponding entry is found, the proper response is made using a LAN ID number that has been assigned to the Ethernet network. The token ring host is not able to differentiate between an Ethernet device and a token ring device found this way.

Combination bridges must also deal with the differing maximum packet length (a.k.a., Maximum Transmission Unit, or MTU) standards that apply to different types of LANs.

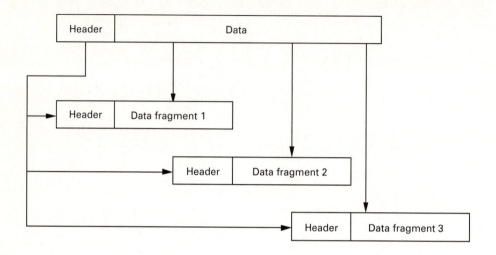

Figure 7.5   IP fragmentation

The MTU on Ethernet is 1518 octets (including the frame check sequence), 4K octets on a 4-Mb token ring, 17.6K octets on a 16-Mb token ring, and 8K octets on FDDI. A bridge forwarding packets between LANs may encounter cases where received packets exceed the MTU on the LAN on which they are to be transmitted. To deal with this sort of situation, many transport protocols support the breaking up of large packets into a series of smaller ones. This process is known as *segmentation* for some protocols, and as *fragmentation* for others. The procedures for this function differ between protocols. (See Figure 7.5.) This produces another protocol dependency in the bridge which, ostensibly, is a protocol-independent device.

Early combination bridges, particularly for Ethernet to FDDI, assumed that one LAN type would be used as a backbone connecting many LANs together, for example Ethernets in buildings' communication over a campuswide FDDI ring. In this case, there are no actual end nodes on the connecting network. A bridge could just encapsulate the packet from the Ethernet LAN and transmit it on the FDDI ring to another bridge, where the encapsulation process would be reversed and the packet would be retransmitted on that Ethernet LAN. There are advantages to this process. The bridge does not need to deal with any protocol-dependent functions, and can be made simpler and, often, faster. Also, at least in the case of Ethernet and FDDI, since the FDDI MTU is larger than the Ethernet MTU, the bridge does not require any fragmentation logic. Bridges that operate in this fashion are known as encapsulation bridges. (See Figure 7.6.)

In the cases where there are to be end node devices on both LAN types, encapsulation bridges cannot be used, since the encapsulated packet cannot be interpreted by the node. The bridges that convert packets from the format used on one type of LAN to the format

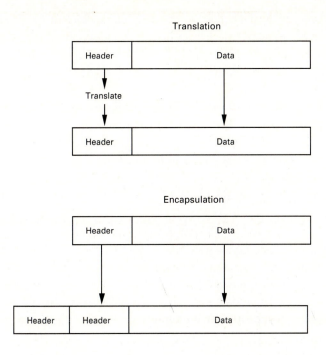

Figure 7.6   Encapsulation versus translation bridging

used on another are known as translation bridges. Most current combination bridges are protocol-dependent translation bridges.

7.2.3   Routers

By operating at the ISO Network Layer, routers make two or more pieces of wire look like two or more pieces of wire. The LANs are separated into distinct networks providing a much larger degree of management and traffic isolation. For example, packets addressed to the hardware broadcast address on one LAN are not forwarded to other LANs. Routers verify and, in many protocols, modify the packets that they forward, and recalculate new checksums. Routers are not end node transparent. If an end node needs to send a packet to a node on some other LAN through a router, the packet must be addressed to the router's hardware address. Therefore, the end nodes must have some procedure for obtaining that address. Routers are protocol specific: not all routers support all protocols, and not all protocols understand routers. One difference between a router and the various "routing bridges" that are advertised is that a router "runs" software that implements a routing protocol. This routing protocol is used to determine the next node along the path that a particular packet is to take, and performs whatever actions the protocol requires. An example of this is decrementing the TTL field in the TCP/IP packet header or incrementing the hop-count field in an AppleTalk packet header.

7.2.4 Gateways

Historically there has been an overlapping definition (or confusion) between the terms *router* and *gateway*. In the past few years, most of the networking community has come to agree that a *router* is as described above, and that a gateway involves application translation functions. Converting between ISO VT and IP Telnet would be done with a gateway.

7.3   ROUTERS VERSUS BRIDGES

The first step in selecting a router is to determine if a router is indeed the correct device to utilize for each network interconnection function. Since routers can be complex to configure and maintain, and, in general, are more expensive than bridges, they should be used where they are cost effective and the functionality required is beyond the capability of a bridge. There are many situations where the choice between the use of a bridge and a router is clear and, to most people, unambiguous.

7.3.1 Bridge Applications

The network traffic generated by a cluster of diskless or dataless workstations that access a specific server is mostly confined within the group of machines. Modern high-speed RISC-based servers and clients can generate a significant network load in normal operation. More than one such grouping on the same LAN can cause the LAN to become a bottleneck, at least for large packets. Isolating each grouping of computers from the building or campus backbone will eliminate many of these problems if the physical network topology will permit it. (See Figure 7.7 for examples of bridge applications.)

In a multistory building different departments are frequently on different floors. In some cases, these departments should be isolated for security reasons, for example, the development department from the sales department. Routers could be used for the analogous function networking, but in most cases bridges will provide the required isolation with no management effort required. The bridges will not forward packets off the "floor" if the packets are destined for other nodes on the same floor, nor will they forward traffic into a floor if it is destined for a known node elsewhere.

Data networks originated as local networks in which a packet sent by one node could be directly delivered to any other node in the network. This type of connectivity is used now to determine the extent of a single LAN. The LAN may consist of multiple physical sections joined together by repeaters or bridges. The collection of interconnected sections is referred to as a LAN as long as a packet addressed to the broadcast address will be received by all the nodes connected to any of the sections. Many protocols used in data networks

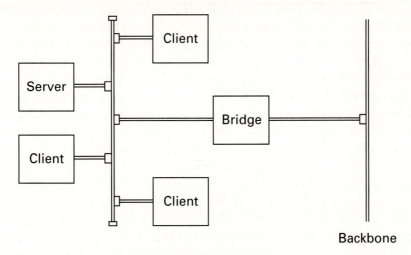

Workgroup cluster isolation

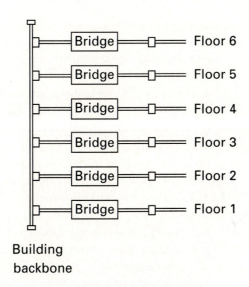

Isolate floors in a building

Figure 7.7   Bridge examples

were designed assuming this type of universal connectivity. DEC's Local Area Terminal
Protocol (LAT) is an example of such a nonroutable protocol. The actual LAT packets do
not have any fields to indicate which logical networks the packet is to travel between, since

the assumption of a single network was made when the protocol was designed. The connection of network segments so that this type of protocol can function must be done with bridges; if routers are used, they must be specifically enabled using the bridge mode available in many of them. An Internet can be created that appears as a collection of LANs to nodes communicating over TCP/IP, AppleTalk or IPX, but still seem to be a single LAN to nodes using LAT and other nonroutable protocols.

Connecting two small LANs together over a WAN link is another case where bridges may be preferable to routers, unless the traffic on the individual LANs is heavy or consists mostly of one or two routable protocols. There is less of a reason to invest in the management required by routers for this scale of installation.

Unless there is significant funding for resident expertise and management personnel, it is better to use bridges to interconnect LANs in a small internet that must support many transport protocols, particularly if the network has grown up from a single LAN. The conversion to a router-based environment will be difficult at best because it is difficult to know accurately the full range of protocols in use and where nonroutable protocols may predominate.

7.3.2   Router Applications

There are only a few clear cases where the use of routers to connect network segments is preferred. All of the regional and national multienterprise networks require a router as the connecting point between the enterprise network and the "outside world." Bridges are not available to connect network segments for some types of networks, such as Apple's LocalTalk and Novell's IPX. The devices that Apple and Novell once called *bridges* are actually routers and are now referred to as such. (See Figure 7.8.)

The price that is paid when routers are added to a network is mostly one of management. Under normal conditions it is very easy to manage a bridge-connected network. The network appears to be a single LAN, and all software that would work on a small LAN will work on the new extended LAN (barring problems introduced by the larger latency that might be present in a wide area LAN). New cable segments and new WAN connected sites may be added without any special configuration being required. The major problem with extensive bridge LANs springs from these same advantages—if something goes wrong on one segment it could easily affect the entire LAN. A misconfigured workstation in one building or city attempting to use the same IP address as an existing node will cause both nodes to become unusable over the network. A broadcast storm on the network segment in the basement of one building can cause VMS clusters all over the campus to crash and overload the campus mainframe. Bridge networks require a much higher level of management involvement during times of problems than does the alternative.

Replacing the bridges with routers provides the isolation required to ensure that local problems do not affect other areas. A misconfigured workstation could interfere with the operation of another workstation on the same LAN, but could not affect one across campus. The difficulty in simply making this replacement is the much greater level of expertise

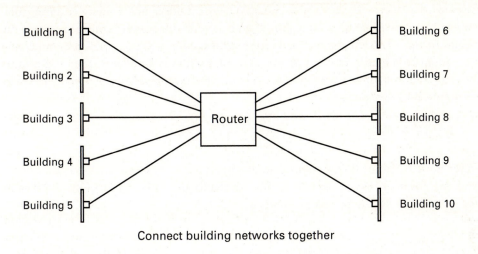

Connect building networks together

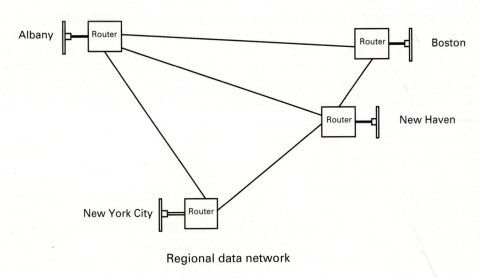

Regional data network

Figure 7.8 Router examples

required to configure and manage the routers. Unlike bridges, the level of management involvement is relatively constant, independent of whether there are problems on the network. Unfortunately, despite the efforts to simplify such systems by some router vendors, the expertise required can be quite expensive, and the tools required to complement the expertise are also expensive.

Despite what was said above, the choice between bridges and routers is more often determined by individual biases (religion, if you will) than by careful consideration of the situation. At times these biases are furthered by the actions of vendor sales personnel who espouse product line rather than function. A vendor who can only provide FDDI bridges can be expected to maintain that there is no requirement for routers functionally in whatever network is being discussed.

7.4   WHAT DOES A ROUTER HAVE TO DO?

A router must perform three functions simultaneously: it must forward packets between interfaces, it must receive and process packets containing routing information, and it must perform a number of management-related tasks.

7.4.1   Packet Handling

Routers receive packets that are addressed to them on their network interfaces, packets that are sent to the network's hardware broadcast address, and packets that are sent to multicast addresses (if the router subscribes to the multicast group). After a packet is received, its checksum is verified, the lower level network encapsulation (including the hardware addresses) is stripped off, and the remainder of the packet is forwarded to the software within the router that must deal with it. If the protocol address in the packet is the same or if the address of the router is the broadcast or a multicast address, the packet may contain management or routing information for the router. If not, the packet would be forwarded to another location, i.e., it will be "routed."

7.4.2   Packet Forwarding

When a packet to be forwarded is received by a router, the packet header is first checked to see if it contains an explicit path to the destination node. In some protocols—TCP/IP, for example—the sender of the packet is able to determine the full route that the packet must take: this is known as source routing. If the received packet contains such a path, the router forwards the packet to the next protocol address listed in the path. This forwarding process is analogous to the operation of source route bridges, although the paths are obtained using various routing procedures rather than by using the discovery mechanism. (See Figure 7.9.)

If source routing is not used, the router attempts to determine where the packet must go next. The packet might be destined for a device directly connected to a network to which the router is directly connected. If so, it is forwarded to the hardware address of that node. The packet might be destined for a node on a network to which the router knows a path. If so, it is sent to another router one step closer to the final destination. Another possibility is that the router might not know a pathway to the destination network but does have a "default path." A default path is used to point to a router that might have more complete

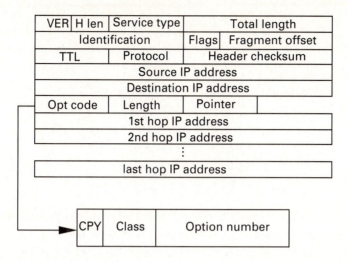

Figure 7.9   IP header with source route option: loose source routing: class = 0,
option number = 3, strict source routing: class = 0, option = 9

information of network reachability and might be able to deliver the packet. In this case, the first router forwards the packet using the default path. The final possibility is that the path to the destination network is not known and there is no default path. In this case the router discards the packet and, depending on the protocol of the packet and sometimes the options in the packet header, may return an error message back to the original sender of the packet.

Routers must often perform other operations on the packets that they forward. Many protocols have some mechanism to help eliminate routing loops in which a packet is endlessly bounced among a few routers and never gets to its correct destination. Routing loops can be a by-product of improper router configuration or instabilities in the network. A field in the packet header is used to keep track of how many routers the packet has traversed. In TCP/IP this is the Time-To-Live (TTL) field. This field is preset to a value by the device from which the packet is transmitted. The TTL field is decremented by each router that the packet traverses. If a router receives a packet that it should forward but which has already traversed as many routers as it is configured to cross (e.g., the TTL field is one), the packet will be discarded and, depending on the protocol, an error message might be returned to the original sender.

Routers, like combination bridges, must also segment a packet if the network on which it is to be sent cannot transport a packet of its size. Not all protocols can support this function. The resultant small packets are sent on to the destination, where they are reassembled into the original large packet. If a fragment is lost in transmission, the destination node must request a retransmission of the full (large) packet from the original source.

To allow traffic to and from the class B network 128.103 and disallow all other traffic

```
allow - IP from 128.103.0.0, mask=0.0.255.255 to 0.0.0.0, mask=255.255.255.255
allow - IP from 0.0.0.0, mask=255.255.255.255 to 128.103.0.0, mask=0.0.255.255
deny - IP from 0.0.0.0, mask=255.255.255.255 to 0.0.0.0, mask=255.255.255.255
```

To allow Telnet traffic out of 128.103 but deny Telnet in the other direction

```
allow - IP from 128.103.0.0, mask=0.0.255.255 to 0.0.0.0, port=23, mask=255.255.255.255
deny - IP from 0.0.0.0, mask=255.255.255.255 to 128.103.0.0, port=23, mask=0.0.255.255
```

Figure 7.10   Filter examples

Many routers can be configured to discard packets that they would normally forward if the packet fits specific criteria. This is known as filtering. (See Figure 7.10.) Filtering is often used for security reasons, such as keeping out external network traffic that could be a threat to the local network or keeping in network traffic that might contain information that should be kept confidential. When filtering is enabled, the router must check all incoming packets against a list of conditions and discard any that match, or discard all that do not match, depending on the filter design.

7.4.3   Routing Information Processing

Routers keep tables of networks about which they have information. These tables most often include the network address, some indication of the path or at least the next step in the path (known as the next-hop), some indication of the distance to the network, and a Timestamp indicating the last time the information was updated.

There are two different philosophies used in designing the routing protocols that maintain the network readability tables in the routers. The first type is distance vector, the second is link state. The TCP/IP Routing Information Protocol (RIP) and the AppleTalk Routing Table Maintenance Protocol (RTMP) are examples of distance vector routing protocols. The OSI Intermediate System-to-Intermediate System (IS-IS) protocol and the TCP/IP Open Shortest Path First (OSPF) are link state protocols. (See Chapter 5.)

In distance vector protocols, the routing information tables do not contain full pathways. They only contain the next-hop addresses, along with the "cost" of the path that is represented by this next-hop. The tables are maintained by having each router send out the contents of its own table from time to time. The outer routers in the network examine this information and compare their internal entries against the entry received. If the new entry concerns a network that is unknown, the information is added to the internal table. If the entry received is for a known network, and the cost of the path is less than that in the table, the table entry is updated with the new next-hop and cost. Otherwise the new information is disregarded. (See Figure 7.11.)

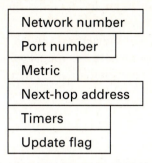

Figure 7.11   Sample routing table entry

In link state protocols the routers maintain an internal map of the network topology. This topology is maintained by each router in the network that is responsible for sending out information about any changes in the state of any of the communications links that are attached to it. Whenever a link state update is received, the router recalculates the network topology and then calculates a set of pathways through the network, one to each known network. This table of pathways may be used to insert a source route into a packet, or the first address in the path can be used as the "next-hop" in forwarding the packet.

For all types of routing, the router must send out information updates whenever the protocol requires them.

7.4.4   Management

All routers have one or more mechanisms to help manage the device and the networks attached to it. The router must respond to interactive commands over a serial line or via a network connection. The commands could include requests for changes in configuration or requests for status.

In addition, almost all routers, many bridges, and some other interconnect devices, such as Ethernet HUBs, include software to support the Simple Network Management Protocol (SNMP). SNMP permits detailed monitoring of the router functions and of the status of attached networks. Network management stations can use SNMP to control many aspects of router setup and behavior.

7.4.5   Miscellaneous Functions

There are a number of overhead functions that routers must also perform. For example, the status of each network interface must be checked periodically. Most routers do this with *keep-alive* packets. The network interface is "up" if the keep-alive packet is successfully transmitted. Some protocols, for example DECNET, also require keep-alive packets, so that other network devices can locate the router.

A router is also a host on each of the networks to which it is connected, and must execute all of the functions required of hosts for the network and protocol types being supported. Hosts must respond to address resolution requests, to echo requests, and the like.

7.5   NETWORK DESIGN

The topological design of the data network can have an effect on the router selection process. For example, router performance characteristics will play a far smaller role in networks that consist of LANs connected together with low-speed WAN links than in networks where the LANs are connected with an FDDI ring, but the latter might have a greater need for security filtering or out-of-band management. The following sections discuss some representative network topologies. (See Figure 7.12.)

7.5.1   Mesh Networks

The most reliable topology for data networks is a mesh design. The LANs are connected by point-to-point links, with each LAN having two or more links to other LANs. The dynamic routing protocols used by most protocols will ensure that individual link failures will not cause a LAN to become unreachable. Most mid-level networks and the NSFNET T1 backbone are examples of mesh networks.

7.5.2   Backbone Networks

One of the most common types of campus networks is a backbone network. Multiple LANs are connected to a common network designated as a backbone. Although there is no requirement that there be anything special about the backbone, the designation is one of topology more than mechanics, since a higher speed type of network is often used as the backbone. For example, Ethernet LANs in buildings can be connected to a common FDDI ring. This type of network is simpler to manage than a mesh design, but does not provide the potential reliability.

7.5.3   Star Networks

In star networks, individual LANs are connected through a single device. A similar design is used in cascading star designs, except that in this case clusters of LANs are first connected together and then to a common central device. Both of these designs have some management advantages over mesh and backbone networks. The centralization of equipment, often in the same location as the network operations center, minimizes the probability that repair will require travel to another location. It also minimizes the time it will take

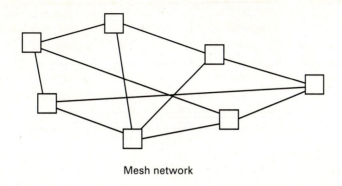

Mesh network

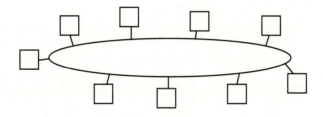

Backbone network

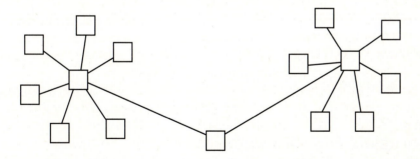

Cascaded star network

Figure 7.12   Network designs

to effect a repair, since often simply repatching a cable and reconfiguring a router will fix a problem. The effect of the obvious single point of failure exposure can be minimized by selecting routers whose modules can be "hot-swapped," or by actually duplicating the links in the design using another router with separate connections to each of the LANs.

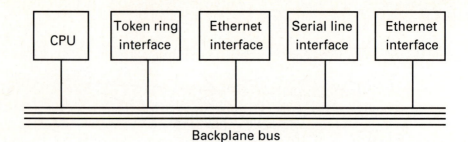

Central processing design

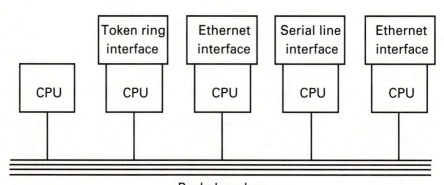

Multiprocessing design

Figure 7.13   Router designs

7.6   GENERAL ROUTER DESIGNS

There are only two basic designs for devices like multiport routers or bridges: the processing of the information can be done centrally, or it can be distributed. Given this restricted fundamental architecture, vendors have been able to develop a surprisingly wide range of differentiation in their products (at least in the eyes—and mouths—of their sales forces). (See Figure 7.13.)

7.6.1   Central Processing

The first advanced network interconnection devices were general-purpose computers that had two or more network interfaces. The UNIX system software, modified by the University of California at Berkeley, has included routines to support the routing of TCP/IP and Xerox's XNS protocols for many years. The same philosophy was used in early special-purpose computers at MIT, which were dedicated to the routing of data network traffic. Some of this work was used in the development of stand-alone routers by Proteon Inc. The majority of routers with four or fewer ports, and a few with more than four ports, use this single processor architecture. All of the required processing of the data, routing, and management packets are performed by the same CPU.

The use of innovative interface access designs, such as multiport memories and very high speed RISC processors, has produced single-processor routers with impressive aggregate packet-handling ability. The software design involved in this type of device is much simpler than that required for routers employing multiple processing elements.

7.6.2 Multiprocessing

A second trend in the design of routing devices divides the computing requirements among a number of separate processing elements. In most systems, these processing elements are general-purpose microprocessors, but a few routers, for example, the Cisco AGS+, employ specially designed logic subsystems instead of microprocessors. Usually there is a processing element associated with each network interface or set of network interfaces. Interface-specific functions, such as the queueing of received packets and handshaking with the LAN interface IC, are performed here.

A few of the more advanced systems take greater advantage of their multiprocessor architecture. In these routers, most of the tasks are distributed among the processors available. Packet forwarding and filtering decisions can be made by the processing element at the interface itself. A few even distribute the processing of some routing update information. At this writing, the one function that is still assigned to a specific processor in all routers is the interaction with SNMP.

7.7 CHOOSING A ROUTER

Many factors go into the decision to select a particular router from a particular vendor. Some of the factors listed below might seem unimportant, but all should have a place in the decision process.

7.7.1 Political and Economic

It is not at all unusual for the higher level management of an organization to decide on a vendor for political or economic reasons, and then leave only the choice between the different products of that vendor to the technical staff. If an organization will be remarketing a particular vendor's products, or has established a research relationship with a vendor, it is likely that the products from that vendor will be dictated for use in any networks within the organization. Many organizations have established internal regulations about the financial health required of their vendors. Products from small or new vendors, or from vendors with less than ideal credit ratings, may be excluded from consideration. The availability of a second source for products that would work in place of the ones selected is another requirement that can color the technical choice. This sort of requirement could also mean that only a specific complement of routing and transport protocols could be used in the network to ensure that there were multiple vendors able to supply routers.

7.7.2   Cost

All too frequently, the purchase and installation cost of network interconnection devices plays the determining role in the vendor and product selection. Unfortunately, the costs of device management, functionality, and operational expertise requirements often are not included in the equation. A router that boasts a low purchase cost could easily prove to have a much higher lifetime cost if other factors are realistically viewed. An inexpensive router that does not support some of the functions that may be required in the future might require expensive replacement or duplication as needs change.

7.7.3   Support

Routers have become complex devices, in their physical and electrical design and in the software required for the ever-changing repertoire of transport and routing protocols. Unless an organization expects to be entirely static and forego the benefits of the ongoing developments in the technology and understanding of routing and transport protocols, software support from the vendor is critical. In addition to evaluating the cost of the vendor's software support programs, the methods of communication that the vendor supports should be examined. Many router vendors now can provide software support via e-mail: questions can be asked of support personnel, and they can reply electronically. The presence of an active, open mailing list or USENET newsgroup can be of considerable assistance in the installation, configuration, and operation of any such device.

   In the past few years, router vendors have established connections to the Internet. Some provide access to on-line archives of documentation, software tools, or archives of mailing lists. In addition, the vendor's support people can use this connection to take a closer look at the devices in operation and to provide emergency software updates. This type of interactive support has become more important as the complexity of networks, routing protocols, and routers has grown. To many, it has become a vendor requirement.

7.7.4   Generational Migration

Router designs, like all electronics, evolve over time. A particular router from a vendor will generally be obsolete in some critical way within three to four years. The vendor's policies concerning the upgrading of old equipment could be quite important. As this is being written, a large regional network has just been told that its existing equipment will not be supported under future software releases. Some of the functionality being added in the new software is considered vital to the operation and growth of the network. The vendor is offering an upgrade program that appears to have a few problems. The upgrade must be completed within three months at a cost that is about equal to the full replacement of the equipment with another vendor's products. In addition, it is widely rumored that the vendor will switch to an entirely new router platform within a year or two. The prospect of spending the sums required, only to have to repeat the process in two years, is not pleasant.

The procedure required to migrate to a new version of software can become an issue. The update process is far easier if the new software can be distributed over the network and downloaded to some form of permanent storage on the individual routers than if an actual on-site swap of components is required.

The frequency and expense of generational migration could be an important consideration for any large network. A vendor that has a history of being more forthcoming in dealing with this sort of process may be a far better choice, even if there are other counter indications.

7.7.5 Purchasing Volume

To minimize the cost and turn-around time of maintenance, many organizations maintain a local supply of spare parts for their electronic equipment. This local stocking of spares is economically feasible only if the ratio between the number of in-service units of any part to the number of parts kept in local stock can be kept reasonable. It is not reasonable to stock a spare for a part of which there are few in use. A reasonable ratio would indicate that there should be five or ten parts of any one type in use before it is cost effective to stock one backup.

For an environment where local stocking of spares is required, there is less flexibility in the choice of particular products. Generally once a choice has been made, the organization is locked into that vendor unless a single network expansion or upgrade of equipment will result in the purchase of enough of some other vendor's product to be able to justify the purchase of the required spares.

7.7.6 Standards Tracking and Participation

None of the standards that describe transport or routing protocols are static. Rather, they are in a state of continual evolution. An examination of a vendor's track record in implementing new protocols and upgrading old implementations to reflect modified standards could be quite interesting. There are often subtle (and not so subtle) conflicts of interest during the evolution, adoption, and implementation of standards. A new routing protocol that performs the same function as one in which a vendor has already invested heavily in design and implementation may not show up as an option for quite a while.

Vendors who maintain an active participation in the committees and working groups that develop standards for the routers of the future are much more likely to have the resident expertise when it comes time to carry out the requirements. In addition, it is important to the future progress of Internet development that there be widespread vendor involvement in the standards process.

There are many standards that routers must meet. Each of the protocols that a router supports is defined in a set of standards. The operations that must be performed when exchanging routing information and forwarding data traffic are defined in another set of standards. Finally, because a router also acts as a host on a network, it must adhere to the standards that apply to the actions of hosts for the specific protocols.

Since most of the protocols that a router could support are closed rather than open, the relevant standards are defined by individual vendors. Generally, these vendors publish at least descriptions, if not fully detailed standards, for their protocols. Occasionally a vendor in some bid for exclusivity will attempt to keep the operational details of its protocol private. In many of these cases, if the protocol is seen to be an important one, router vendors will reverse engineer it. In these cases there will be no published standard, and if the vendor decides to change some features of the protocol in the future, incompatibilities could develop.

TCP/IP and the OSI are both open protocol suites, and their standards are readily available. The OSI standards have been developing over the years, and are well known for the deliberate pace of standards evolution. On the other hand, the *RFC* process that is used to establish standards in the TCP/IP arena can cause rapid changes and additions to the set of procedures and functions that a router supporting TCP/IP must implement. In addition to the numerous *RFC* documents defining transport, routing, and applications protocols, there are two sets of documents that should be of special concern during the selection of a router vendor. They are known as *Host Requirements* and *Router Requirements*.

7.7.7   Host Requirements

RFC 1122 and *RFC 1123*,[1] known collectively as the *Host Requirements RFC* documents, define the proper behavior of a host on a TCP/IP network. These documents are the result of a complete review of all relevant *RFC* documents, and contain clarifications and explanations of many of the issues in the implementation of TCP/IP. They also contain a list of specific *do's and don'ts,* with many functions characterized as *must, should, may, should not,* or *must not.* A careful comparison of routers offering TCP/IP support should include a check list from each vendor that details their support of the *Host Requirement's RFC* documents. Any variation from adherence to all *must* and *must not* requirements should be noted and explained.

A detailed review of the *Host Requirements RFC* documents is offered in Chapter 8, A Practical Perspective on Host Networking.

7.7.8 Router Requirements

The *Router Requirements* document[2] (in draft form as this is written), extends the *Host Requirements* review to cover the design and operation of TCP/IP routers. The draft is organized along the lines of the OSI seven-layer reference model, with sections on the Link Layer, Internet Layer, Transport Layer, and Application Layer, along with a special section discussing operations and maintenance. Like the *Host Requirements RFC* documents, the *Router Requirements* draft includes discussions of specific router functions at each of these layers, as well as a check list of *do's* and *don'ts*. Some of the more important requirements are reviewed below.

- Link Layer. A router must not establish ARP entries for broadcast or multicast IP addresses, and must not send a destination unreachable message solely because it does not have an ARP entry. The MTU of each logical interface must be configurable but must not accept a value that would violate the standards of the underlying Link Layer protocol. The draft also requires the ability to support the point-to-point protocol (PPP) on all serial lines.

- Internet Layer.   In addition to requiring support for IP, the draft also requires support of a number of IP options, including IP Source Routing, Record Route, and Timestamp, and specifies support of some Type-Of-Service functions. Routers are required to verify the header checksum, but must not provide a way to disable this check. They also must support IP fragmentation, but must not reassemble any fragments unless the router is the end node for the communication, and must properly decrement and check the TTL field. All frames received by a router that contain an invalid IP source address must be silently discarded. The Internet Control Message Protocol (ICMP) must be supported. The draft includes a number of specific ICMP-related requirements, including the ability to limit Source-quench messages if the router produces them, the ability to send host redirect messages and a prohibition of network redirect messages. Routers must respond to ICMP Echo Request, Address Mask Request, and Router Discovery messages. While forwarding data frames, routers must verify the correctness of the IP header and must silently discard all frames that fail the check. Routers must never forward frames received via a Link Level broadcast, and in most cases must not forward frames received via a Link Level multicast. They must also never forward a frame that is sent to the protocol broadcast address of 255.255.255.255, but must support the forwarding of net-directed broadcast frames. If a router ceases to forward frames, it must also cease advertising all non-third party routes.

- Transport Layer. Although routers are not required to implement any Transport Layer protocols, many do so to support remote management access. The *Router Requirements* draft dictates that if a router implements any Transport Layer protocol, it must be compliant with the appropriate sections of the *Host Requirements RFC* documents.

- Routing Protocols.   Routers supporting TCP/IP routing must support both the Routing Information protocol (RIP) and the Open Shortest Path First (OSPF) routing protocol for within-Autonomus System routing. Routers are not required to support between-AS routing, but if a router supports the Exterior Gateway Protocol (EGP), it must also support the Border Gateway Protocol (BGP).

- Network Management Protocols.   The *Router Requirements* draft requires that all TCP/IP routers be manageable by SNMP, including support for all SNMP functions. The specific wording permits management via an SNMP agent residing on a network device other than the router itself, as long as the management commands may be sent to any of the IP addresses assigned to the router's interfaces. The draft also lists some of the specific MIBs that the routers must support.

- Operations and Management.   Routers must have static configuration information, and must not forward frames after booting until some of the configuration process is complete. Routers must support both "in-band" (via the data network) and "out-of-band" (generally using a serial line) management access, and must be able to generate an ICMP Echo Request (ping).

7.7.9 Protocols Supported

There are all too many transport and routing protocols in use on data networks today. One router vendor currently supports about a dozen transport protocols, most with their associated routing protocols, as well as four IP-specific routing protocols, with one or two more announced, and bridge mode. Even this extensive offering does not include SNA, one of the most widely used transport protocols. Although few, if any, networks actually require all of these, it is tempting to select a vendor based on the length of the list rather than the depth of the support for the protocols that will be used. The selection process should examine the actual features of each offering, rather than simply relying on a check list of names, and should concentrate on the protocols that are, or will be, required on the network.

7.7.10 Interface Types Supported

It is obvious that any router that does not offer the types of interfaces that are needed in a particular network would not be a good choice for that network. Current, as well as future, interface requirements should be considered. If it is clear that 16-Mb token ring, FDDI or T3 serial connections are or will be required, then the vendor's plans for the support of these interface types must be explored.

There are large differences in the ability of different vendors to actually provide credible implementations of some interface types. For example, most vendors have relatively slow token ring interfaces on their routers. When selecting routers for a network where the primary requirement is the support of high-speed workstations and servers over a 16-Mb token ring, it might be best to concentrate on vendors who have demonstrated a history of offering token ring products.

7.7.11 Management

Management of routing devices includes two areas: centralized monitoring and control through the use of a management protocol like SNMP, and router features to assist in resolving network problems when they arise.

In the last few years, there has been widespread acceptance of SNMP as the management protocol of choice. There are still some vendors who, for reasons of philosophy or their own forecasting of the future, espouse the use of OSI-based protocols like CMOT, but this is not as much of an issue as it once was, since even those vendors also support SNMP. There is a bit of a problem with some vendors following the letter, but not the spirit of the SNMP standards, by implementing private MIBs rather than supporting MIBs defined by the various *RFC* documents and Internet Drafts. If a vendor does not follow the standards, it will be harder to integrate its devices into the operation of a common management system.

All too frequently in normal network operation it is necessary to determine why packets do not get from point *A* to point *B*. A number of router vendors have added functions to their devices to assist in this process. The TCP/IP ICMP Echo Request, also known as ping, is available in most routers supporting TCP/IP. At least one vendor includes a SNMP client, so that one can issue SNMP query commands to any SNMP-compliant device from routers at various places in the network. One function that would be quite helpful in this context is traceroute.

7.7.12 Security

There has been an evolution in the understanding of the proper role that the transport network and its interconnection devices should play in ensuring the security of the hosts and data accessible over the network. In the past, organizations like the Computer Emergency Response Team (CERT) have primarily emphasized host-based security. Passwords should be checked to ensure that they are not easy to guess or are not single words contained in the on-line dictionary. Security bugs should be repaired by the software vendors as soon as possible, and the fixed programs installed immediately upon receipt. The CERT and the *Site Security Handbook* (*RFC 1244*),[3] in addition to measures like this, are now recommending the installation of access control filters, at least in the routers that are used to connect an enterprise network to a regional or national backbone.

The current recommendation from the CERT is that the router be configured to permit the specific protocols that are known to be needed in communicating with the rest of the Internet, and to disallow the remainder. This does not have to be a blanket permission. Some protocols could be allowed only if the session was initiated from within the organiza-

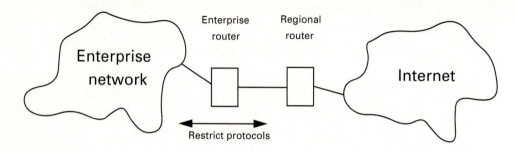

Figure 7.14   Guard router

tion, for example, outward-bound Telnet sessions, while disallowing inbound sessions. Other protocols should always be permitted, for example, Simple Mail Transfer Protocol and the name resolution protocol. Not all routers offer filtering capabilities (a.k.a., access lists) that are capable of implementing this type of control. The selection of a router to be placed at the border of an organization or at strategic locations within an enterprise network may depend on the availability of advanced filtering capabilities. (See Figure 7.14 for sample configuration for a guard router.)

The routers must be secure, in addition to helping to guard the systems on the network. Password-based access control should be a requirement, including on any out-of-band serial port connections. Multiple levels of access control can be a useful feature. Read-only access to the routers can be given to the busybodies, while retaining all actual controls under separate authorization. A desirable, though currently unavailable, feature would be access controlled by a system like Kerberos, which operates without transporting passwords over the network where they might be observed.

7.7.13   User Interface

The requirement to directly interact with a router is vastly reduced once it has been installed and configured, thus the ease of this interaction is of less importance than it might otherwise be. Even though there is little indication that most router vendors have in their employ someone with any formal training in human factors, the majority of interfaces are somewhat intuitive, and while not pleasant to use, at least are not painful. A few vendors seem to be making an attempt to impersonate the manufacturers of VCRs in the design of obscure interactions and procedures. Despite the apparent majority view, some router vendors have started to address this area, with somewhat encouraging results.

It is quite possible that in the near future most of the current requirements for interaction with a user interface on the individual router will be replaced by the ability to perform the same configuration and control operations using a network management protocol like SNMP.

7.7.14 Documentation

There is a remarkable range in the quality of documentation that accompanies router products. Some of it is extremely good, with clear, concise explanations of the features and design of protocols and device capabilities. Unfortunately, there is also some that is terse, rather than concise, and consisting more of lists than explanations. Since there is no consistency in setup procedures and commands across vendors, the quality of documentation can become quite important in the ongoing operation of a network. One factor to check in a vendor's documentation is the presence of a comprehensive index. It is quite beyond understanding how a vendor could expect users to operate this type of complex device without being able to use an index to locate the relevant sections of the often extensive manuals.

7.7.15 Physical

Whenever a network employs a star configuration with multiple links or LANs connected to one interconnection device, failure of the central device can have a catastrophic effect. Even if only one port or interface card were to fail, most systems require that the entire device be turned off to replace the failed component. A few vendors are beginning to take notice of the telecommunications products that have been available for years, and to offer the option of redundant power supplies, and the capability to replace modules without shutting off the power, a process known as hot-swap. In these systems only the connections to a particular card are affected when that card is replaced, unless the failed card provides some form of nonreplicated system control function. Except for redundant power supplies, this sort of ability is not relevant to smaller routers having only a few ports contained within a single module.

Routers are, on the whole, very reliable devices, and thus the features described above may seem to be of relatively little importance. This may be true in an environment that grew out of a research network and has always operated on a best-effort basis. It is not so true when the network in question is intended to replace some forms of existing corporate token ring networks. These bridge-based networks have, in the past, used point-to-point connections over telecommunications gear. Extremely high reliability is now expected in this type of network; many connections have never been down. The network managers have been able to provide almost perfect reliability guarantees, and are quite reluctant to switch to an environment in which a single board failure could cause dozens of sites to lose connectivity.

The mechanical design of the device should also be considered. If the case must be removed from a rack or disassembled to replace a module, or if most or all of the internal cables must be removed to get them out of the way, repair may take much longer than with a system where these conditions do not exist.

7.7.16 Operational Characteristics

There are a number of operational characteristics that might have an effect on the selection process. A router that will be used at the other end of a WAN link to an isolated location having no local general-purpose computers should be able to be rebooted without having to load its software and configuration from a host over the local network. It would be better to use a router that uses a built-in floppy, an EPROM, or a flash PROM to store this data.

How often must the router be rebooted during a reconfiguration process? A number of routers must be restarted whenever a configuration parameter is modified. If a restart takes long enough to cause a perceptible interruption of service on the network connections, then this type of reconfiguration may have to be scheduled for off hours, incurring additional overtime costs or resulting in a postponement of needed changes. This is not an issue if the restart procedure is rapid enough to not cause disruption, or if restarts are not generally required.

7.7.17   Other Features

Vendors attempt to introduce further differentiation of their products by introducing special features, such as prioritizing the processing of different protocols, header compression on WAN or dial-up ports, and encapsulation support for "other" protocols, IBM's SNA for example. In some network installations, features of this sort may become a determining factor. This is particularly true when the new network is to replace an established bridged network. The users expect transparent reliable connectivity with the low latency inherent in many bridged networks.

7.7.18   Performance

Many aspects of router performance could become factors in device selection, but must be considered in relationship to the design of the network, the applications that will use it, and the number and type of nodes on each LAN segment. Three such factors are: the length of time that it takes for the device to process a packet, known as latency; the rate at which packets can be processed reliably, known as throughput; and the effect of offering the device a data rate that is greater than the throughput rate, known as overload. The effect of router latency is discussed in Chapter 15, IP Network Performance, and is not examined here.

RFC 1242 defines[4] throughput as "the maximum rate at which none of the offered frames are dropped by the device." This is an important measure, since even a single dropped packet will require that the communication on the affected virtual circuit be suspended until the higher level protocol recognizes that a packet is missing. This is usually accomplished by waiting a protocol-specific maximum time and then retransmitting the missing packet. A timeout can take a number of seconds, during which time no data is transferred. This can have a major effect on the effective data rate. A router that processes large packets at a reliable rate of 750 packets/sec could have a greater effective throughput than a router that can forward packets at a rate of 800 packets/sec but loses 1% of the frames at rates greater than 700 packets/sec. It is important to understand the methodol-

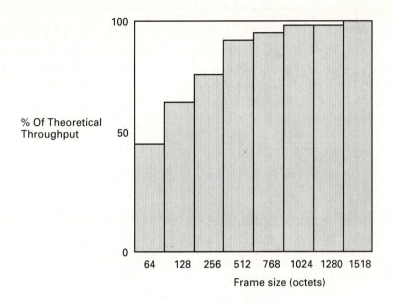

Figure 7.15   Throughput graph

ogy used to measure the "throughput" value that a vendor might provide for its router. If the measurement does not follow the *RFC 1242* definition for throughput, the resulting value is of little real meaning. (See Figure 7.15 for a sample throughput graph.)

The effects of overload on a routers' abilities to forward frames can very greatly. The internal architecture of many routers allows a fixed rate of packet processing. Offering a greater input packet rate results in no significant change in the rate at which frames are processed, just more frames are dropped. In a few routers, the processing rate actually goes up slightly as the input rate increases. Unfortunately, in some devices the processing rate drops precipitously as the input rate exceeds the router's processing capacity. *RFC 1242* defines the frame loss-rate parameter to help quantify the behavior of a device under overload conditions. This parameter is to be reported in a graph representing the ratio of offered versus processed packets at a number of input packet rates up to the maximum theoretical rate for a particular size packet on the media under test. (See Figure 7.16 for an example of a frame loss-rate graph.)

Performance evaluation tests like these should be performed over a range of frame sizes, for the transport protocols supported by the router, and with the addition of the filter functions, might be required for network management or security. With this information, a comparison can be made between various vendors' products or within a single vendor's product line, but this information by itself will not enable one to answer the basic network performance question, "How long will it take for me to load 1-2-3?" Performing the same tests while using a simulation of the actual network traffic on a specific set of LANs will get one a bit closer to an answer. Such a simulation would include intermixed packet sizes and

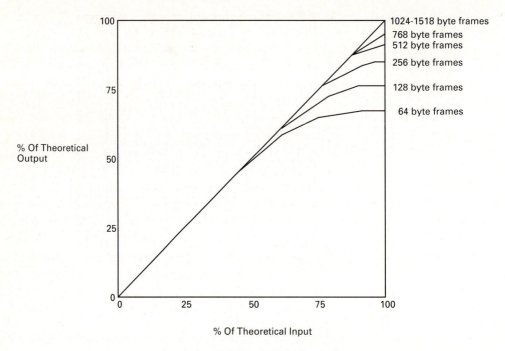

Figure 7.16   Frame loss-rate graph

protocols with pseudorandom interpacket gaps. Since major components of the amount of time it takes to load software or access files do not depend on the network (average disk latency and server congestion, for example), a real answer cannot come from an examination of only the network. These tests can help establish whether a particular router could become a determining factor in apparent network performance.

It is extremely unlikely that a single LAN could become saturated with small frame traffic. An Ethernet can support (theoretically) 14,880 64-octet frames per second. Even with only a few nodes on a net (to avoid the rate reduction inherent in the CSMA/CD scheme used in Ethernet), it is almost inconceivable that a frame rate anywhere near saturation could occur with small frames. It is far easier to encounter saturation on a LAN with large frames. On the other hand, an Ethernet can only support 812 1518-octet frames per second. Many of the current generation of high-speed LAN servers and workstations engaged in graphics-intensive applications, such as CAD/CAM, can easily cause bursts of several seconds duration at or near network saturation with large frames. Thus it is important to check that interconnection devices be able to process large frame traffic at rates approaching the maximum theoretical limit.

It is reasonable to expect that as long as a router joining two Ethernet LANs together is able to process more than 5,000 64-octet packets per second it will never become a hindrance to network-based applications, as long as it is also able to process packets at close to the theoretical maximum rate for packet lengths greater than 768 octets. Routers that are used in the hubs of star network topologies should have an aggregate packet handling ability in direct proportion to the number of ports. A router used to join ten Ethernet LANs should be able to process at least 25,000 64-octet packets per second to meet the same criteria.

Packet handling ability above this rate can give some assurance of router functionality even under catastrophic conditions, but will have little other effect unless the higher performance also ensures that interactive management functions will operate under the conditions of an overloaded network. There are few routers that fully separate the processing of management and control requests from the processing of routing information or the forwarding of packets. For all but these routers, an overloaded network could result in an inability to communicate with the router management functions just at the time when it would be most useful to be able to tell the router to shut down a port or to add a filter condition.

There is little differentiation between the ability of routers to communicate over most wide area links. With the exception of routers that offer some form of header compression, the packet transfer rate over WAN links is determined almost exclusively by the data rate of the link. The devices themselves are easily fast enough to keep up with the link. Device performance should not be an issue when linking two sites, each with a single LAN, via a link of T1 or slower speed. Performance could become an issue if the same router were required to support a large number of simultaneous WAN connections.

7.7.19 Future

New interconnect technologies, such as frame relay, SMDS, and ATM, as well as the ever-continuing evolution of transport and routing protocols, will prevent any significant consolidation in the proliferation of the vendors of interconnection devices like bridges and routers. Thus, the process of selecting a specific vendor is unlikely to become much easier, and, indeed, now that almost all of the major computer systems manufacturers are also offering routers, the trend is towards a more difficult choice.

REFERENCES

1   R. Braden, Ed., *Requirements for Internet Hosts–Communication Layers, RFC 1122,* 1989; and R. Braden, (Ed.), *Requirements for Internet Hosts–Application and Support, RFC 1123,* 1989.

2   P. Almquist, Ed., *Requirements for IP Routers,* Internet-Draft, 1991.

3   P. Holbrook and J. Reynolds, (Eds.), *Site Security Handbook, RFC 1244,* 1991.

4   S. Bradner, Ed., *Benchmarking Terminology for Networking Interconnection Devices, RFC 1242,* 1991.

CONTENTS   (Continued)

We now continue looking at the difference between "implementing the protocols" and "implementing a system." This time we look at the details an end-system implementor must be cognizant of in order to realize a production system that hosts applications.

8.1 INTRODUCTION

In October 1989, *RFC 1122* and *RFC 1123* were published.[1, 2] These two documents, *Requirements for Internet Hosts—Communications Layers* and *Requirements for Internet Hosts—Application and Support*, contain over two hundred pages of detailed information, the culmination of several years' work by many people. These documents represent a detailed analysis of the major standards used by hosts in the Internet, including the specifications for Internet Protocol (IP),[3] Internet Control Message Protocol (ICMP),[4] User Datagram Protocol (UDP),[5] Transmission Control Protocol (TCP),[6] Telnet,[7] File Transfer Protocol (FTP),[8] Trivial File Transfer Protocol (TFTP),[9] Simple Mail Transfer Protocol

(SMTP),[10] and the Domain Name System (DNS).[11] *RFC 1122* and *RFC 1123* contain additions, corrections, amendments, and references that clarify the original specifications.

It is important to be aware that *RFC 1122* and *RFC 1123* are, as their titles indicate, requirements for any host implementation of these protocols. The additions, corrections, amendments, and references in this pair of documents are now considered to be part of the referenced protocols, and must be followed by implementors of these protocols.

These documents are necessarily technical and specific at times, and one needs the context of the original specification of the protocol to fully understand what is being said. Many of the requirements contain discussion sections, explaining the motivation or discussion behind the requirements, especially for topics that caused heated discussion in the working group that wrote the documents.

The order of topics and subtopics in this chapter is roughly similar to that in *RFC 1122* and *RFC 1123*, which are mostly laid out in the same order as the protocol specifications that they update. Preserving this order should help to identify sections of this chapter with the corresponding section of the *Host Requirement* documents or the various protocol specifications.

8.2 INTERNET PROTOCOL

The Internet Protocol (IP) is the base on which many other protocols and applications are built. It provides the mechanism to move packets from a source host to a destination host, with intervening gateways. It provides for the ability to fragment packets as they traverse various networks, and to reassemble the fragments back into the original datagram at the final destination. It provides routing functionality, bounding on packet lifetimes (to terminate routing loops), and methods for specifying different types of service to be used in delivering datagrams.

8.2.1 Subnet Addressing

RFC 1122 makes the support of subnet addresses a requirement for all hosts. Subnetting allows a group of networks to be treated as a single network by hosts and routers not connected to those networks. Subnetting also makes the administration of local networks easier. That is, subnetwork numbers can be assigned locally as needed;, there is no need to go off someplace else to get new network numbers as new networks are added.

Before subnetting, each network needed to have a unique Class A, B, or C network number assigned to it. Network numbers are used in routing packets, and all the routers in the network had to know about all the network numbers in the network. As the number of networks in the Internet increased, the sizes of the routing tables got larger and larger. Subnetting allows a group of physical networks to be assigned a single Class A, B, or C network number, with the individual host addresses split up into groups that are assigned to each network. Routers within the subnetted network still have to know about all the individual subnetwork numbers, but routers outside of the subnetted network only need to have one routing entry for the entire network number.

Before subnetting, the system was similar to having a box of hosts for each network, and requiring that everyone know the location of every other box. With subnetting, groups of these boxes are put into larger boxes. Routers that are contained in a big box still have to know how the little boxes are arranged within it, but they only need to know where the other big boxes are, and not how the little boxes are arranged within them.

8.2.2 Fragmentation and Reassembly

IP datagrams can be no more than 65,535 bytes in length, including the IP header. This limit is due to the fact that the length field in the IP header is 16 bits long. However, very few networks can support datagrams of that size at the hardware level. Two common networks are Ethernet and FDDI, which can handle datagrams of about 1500 bytes and 4500 bytes, respectively. To allow the transmission of IP packets that are larger than is permitted on the media, the IP protocol includes a method to fragment packets into smaller segments, and reassemble them at the final destination.

The IP header contains several pieces of information to aid fragmentation and reassembly: a 13-bit Fragment Offset field; two flags, Don't Fragment (DF) and More Fragments (MF);, and an Identification field. The DF bit is set at the source if a packet is not allowed to be fragmented. If a gateway receives an IP packet with the DF flag set, and it is forwarding the packet to a network on which the packet will not fit without fragmentation, then the gateway will drop the packet, and send back an ICMP Destination Unreachable message, with the code set to 4 ("fragmentation needed and DF set"). Otherwise, the gateway would fragment the packet into two or more pieces. Each of these fragments would contain the same value in the Identification field, enabling the receiver to identify which fragments are to be reassembled.

When fragments are received, they are identified by having either the MF flag set, or a nonzero Fragment Offset. All fragments that have the same values in the Identification, Source Address, Destination Address, and Protocol fields are treated as being fragments of the same packet. It is important for a host to generate unique values for the Identification field of each packet sent, because for a given connection, the Source Address, Destination Address, and Protocol fields remain constant.

Every host must implement code to support the reassembly of IP fragments, and it may also implement code to fragment IP datagrams. *RFC 815, IP Datagram Reassembly Algorithms,*[12] contains an excellent design of a simple mechanism for implementing the reassembly of IP datagrams. It is highly recommended that anyone implementing IP reassembly code read this document. The only thing to be aware of is that *RFC 815* neglects to mention that when a fragment is received for a datagram of which no previous fragments have been received, the IP header of this fragment must be saved, whether or not it is the first fragment of the packet. This is because if the first fragment was lost and never arrives, an IP header is needed so that an ICMP Time Exceeded message can be sent back to the originating host.

8.2.3 Routing

For the most part, a host should not have to worry about routing. That is the function of gateways. However, a host has to be able to make some intelligent decisions about where to send packets that are destined for hosts that are not on networks to which it is directly attached. The procedure for accomplishing this is straightforward. Initially, the host needs to know the address of at least one gateway. It then sends all nonlocal traffic to that gateway. It is the responsibility of the gateway to determine whether a received packet should have been sent to another gateway. In this case, the gateway will forward the packet to the correct gateway, but also send an ICMP Redirect back to the originating host to inform it of the correct gateway to use. The host can record this information in its routing table, and use the information to send all future packets to the correct gateway. It should be noted that all routes that are dynamically added in this manner should just be host-level routes, even if the ICMP Redirect message was labeled as a network redirect, because some older gateways incorrectly send out network redirect messages for subnetworks, when they should just be sending out host redirects.

8.2.4 Type-Of-Service

The Host Requirements Working Group had many discussions about the Type-Of-Service field in the IP header, and whether to make its implementation a "must," "should," or "may." One view was that if the gateways didn't implement the Type-Of-Service field, then there wasn't any need for the hosts to implement it. Conversely, if the hosts didn't implement it, then there wouldn't be any need for the gateways to implement it. It's the classic chicken-and-egg problem. It was decided, to break this cycle, that hosts must implement a method for the transport layer to tell the IP layer what the Type-Of-Service field should contain for each packet that is sent out, and that the IP layer should pass back up to the transport layer the contents of the Type-Of-Service field of incoming datagrams.

   It should be noted, however, that the group recognized that without experience in using the Type-Of-Service field, it would not be possible to specify exactly what the various Type-Of-Service values meant. Also, the transport layer may not know the correct Type-Of-Service that should be used. It is the application that really knows what is needed. So, to have a robust implementation of Type-Of-Service, it would be wise for a host implementation to provide a mechanism for an application to set the Type-Of-Service value on a connection. This should include a configuration file that all the applications could use to find out their own default Type-Of-Service values, and some mechanism with which the user can override the application default values.

More recently, the definition of the Type-Of-Service field has been updated[13] by *RFC 1349*. Rather than being a bit field with 5 distinct bits (two of which were always 0), it is now a 4 bit field with enumerated values. (The fifth bit is still 0, but is no longer considered part of the Type-Of-Service field.) Only 5 bit patterns are currently defined; 1000—minimize delay, 0100—maximize throughput, 0010—maximize reliability, 0001—minimize monetary cost, and 0000—normal service. Note that the first three definitions match up exactly with the old bit value definitions, provided that only one bit is set.

RFC 1349 also covers IP routing based on the Type-Of Service field. A host may need to know about routing based on Type-Of-Service. If so, it should use what is called weak Type-Of-Service routing. If a packet has a nonzero Type-Of-Service value, then only one of two routes may be considered a match. The first is a route to the specified destination, with an exact match on the Type-Of-Service value. If such a route does not exist, then a route to the specified destination with normal service (TOS is zero) may be used. If neither case is satisfied, then the destination is unreachable.

8.2.5   IP Options

The fixed part of an IP header is 20 octets in length. In addition to the fields in the fixed part of the IP header, there is a variable-length section for IP options, which conveys additional information. This information, though possibly required in some situations (such as the Security option), is not needed in all instances to ensure correct operation of the IP protocol. Hence, it is only added to the IP header when needed.

8.2.5.1   *Security*

The IP Security option, as defined in *RFC 791* and revised in *RFC 1038*, is obsolete. *RFC 1108* specifies the proper format for using the Security option. It specifies two options, a Department of Defense (DOD) Basic Security option and a DOD Extended Security option. The Basic option specifies only the level, and under whose rules the level is to be interpreted. The Extended option is defined only as a framework. The actual placement and interpretation of the bits in the option are left up to the various government bodies, who will document their particular usage.

The IP Security option was defined only with US Government bodies specifically in mind. Because of this, there is an effort under way to define a Commercial IP Security Option, for use by commercial and non-US Government bodies that wish to be able to label IP packets with security information. This work was started as a working group of the Trusted Systems Interoperability Group (TSIG), and is now a dually chartered working group of both TSIG and the IETF.

When implementing security options, it may not be desirable to allow applications to directly specify the option; rather, it may be better to have another mechanism for the application to specify the security information in some internal format, and have the IP layer do the translation to the appropriate security option. In this situation, there is a question as to what to do if the application attempts to directly set a security option. There are three choices: always return an error, return an error only if the option doesn't match the current determined value, or silently ignore the option. Which method is best depends on the interface that is provided for the application to set IP options. A common implementation only allows the entire set of IP options to be replaced. In this situation, an application that wishes to modify or add an IP option would first get a copy of the current IP options, modify them, and then replace them. Because the IP option space is limited, it would make sense to provide the security option along with other options, so that the application can determine how large or how many IP options can be added. Hence, when the application modifies the current list and hands it back to the IP layer, the security option will be included, and should not cause an error.

8.2.5.2 Stream Identifier

The Stream Identifier option, originally designed to carry SATNET stream identifiers, is now obsolete. It should not be sent, and if received, it must be silently ignored.

8.2.5.3 Source Route

There are two source route options, Loose Source and Record Route (LSRR) and the Strict Source and Record Route (SSRR). The SSRR option specifies the exact list of gateways and hosts that the packet is to traverse, whereas the LSRR option specifies some, but not necessarily all, of the gateways and hosts that the packet is to traverse. Support for both sending and receiving packets with the source route options is required. When a packet is received at the final destination with a completed source route, the source route must be passed up to the transport layer, which will reverse the route and use it when sending replies. *RFC 1122* clarifies *RFC 791*, which has some ambiguity about what goes into the Source Route option when it is being generated. The correct format is that the source address of the originating host is not included in the source route option, since this information is already in the IP Source Address. In addition, the receiving host is responsible for turning around the route correctly, even if it receives a source route option that includes the source address.

8.2.5.4 Record Route

An IP packet may have at most 40 bytes of options. If no other IP options are used, this means that a Record Route option can record at most 9 IP addresses (the type, length, and pointer fields use up 3 bytes, leaving 37 bytes for the route data; each IP address is 4 bytes long). The most useful application of the RR option is with an ICMP Echo Request packet. When the packet is received at the destination, the RR option is copied over into the Echo Reply packet. This allows the entire round-trip path to be recorded. However, in the Internet today, the number of hops between two hosts can easily exceed five, thus reducing the usefulness of the Record Route option. Because of this, the Record Route is made optional by *RFC 1122*. A host is not required to be able to originate or process a

Record Route option. (Note that if an implementation chooses to not implement the Record Route option, it must still be able to properly ignore it if it is received.)

8.2.5.5   IP Timestamp

Each entry in the Timestamp option is 8 bytes long; thus at most it can contain only 4 entries. Unless the IP addresses are prespecified (in which case the sender of the option prespecifies the IP addresses of the gateways or hosts that should add timestamps), this makes the Timestamp option even less useful than the Record Route option. Hence, the Timestamp option is also made optional by *RFC 1122*.

8.2.5.6   Other and Unknown Options

If an IP option is received that is not implemented or is unknown, then that option must be silently ignored. Note that, except for the End of Option List and No Operation options, the second octet of every IP option contains the length of the option, and this will continue to be true for any future options. Thus, unknown options can be skipped over, and options after the unknown option can (and should) still be processed.

8.2.6   Internet Control Message Protocol

Even though it is defined as a separate protocol, ICMP is actually an integral part of IP, and must be part of any implementation of IP. ICMP provides the mechanism to communicate errors and control information between hosts. There are some rules that apply to the processing and sending of ICMP messages.

8.2.6.1   Error Messages

RFC 1122 lists several conditions under which ICMP error messages must never be sent. The main purpose of these rules is to prevent *broadcast storms*. Broadcast storms are caused when a single packet is broadcast on a network, and its reception causes most or all of the hosts on that network to respond in some manner. At best, this causes temporary congestion on the network. In the worst case, for example, if the originating packet had the broadcast address as its source, the responses to the original packet also would be broadcast, and cause additional responses from each host. In a situation such as this, the only recourse might be to unplug and reboot all the machines on the network. This condition is often referred to as *meltdown*.

The instances under which ICMP error messages must not be sent were developed from real experience in which the implementation of these rules would have prevented broadcast storms. *RFC 792* requires that ICMP error messages must never be generated in response to a packet that is itself an ICMP error message, or in response to a packet with a nonzero fragment offset. *RFC 1122* adds that if a packet is received with a destination address that is a broadcast or multicast address, as a link level broadcast, or with a source address that does not specify a host (e.g., broadcast, multicast, loopback, or Class E addresses), ICMP messages must not be generated. One implication of these additional rules is that the link layer has to inform the IP layer when a packet is received as a link layer broadcast packet.

Destination Unreachable

A Destination Unreachable error message is generated, either by a gateway or the final destination host, when an IP packet cannot be delivered. Codes 0 and 1, usually generated by some intervening gateway, indicate that either the network or the host itself is unreachable. These two codes, along with code 5 (which indicates that a source route failed), may be transient errors. Thus, when they are received, they must be treated as such. For example, when one of these codes is passed up to the TCP layer, the TCP layer must not make a decision to drop any existing connections based solely on the Destination Unreachable message.

Codes 2 and 3 are usually generated by the destination host, indicating that either the protocol specified in the IP header, or the port specified in the transport header, is not accessible. It should be noted that, depending on how the code is written, it may or may not be readily obvious whether a particular protocol is accessible. In this situation, a Port Unreachable message may be sent, since if the protocol is truly inaccessible, then any port within that protocol is also inaccessible.

RFC 1122 defines six additional codes. Codes 6 and 7 indicate that the destination network or host is unknown (as opposed to codes 0 and 1, which indicate that the destination is known, but unreachable). Code 8 indicates that the source host is isolated. Codes 9 and 10 indicate that communication with the destination network or host is administratively prohibited. Codes 11 and 12 indicate that the network or host is unreachable for the specified type of service.

When a Destination Unreachable message is received, the IP layer must communicate that information to the appropriate transport protocol. The transport protocol should use that information, and if it has its own mechanism for reporting such errors, it must treat the ICMP Destination Unreachable message for the same purpose.

Code 4, "fragmentation needed and DF set," is sent by a gateway when a packet with the DF bit set is received that is too large to be forwarded without IP fragmentation. It should be noted that *RFC 1191, Path MTU Discovery,*[14] makes use of, and modifies, the code 4 Destination Unreachable message. The 32-bit "unused" field is redefined by *RFC 1191* to have the upper 16 bits still unused, and the lower 16 bits must be the Maximum Transmission Unit (MTU) of the next-hop network to which the gateway could not forward the packet, due to the DF bit being set. The basic concept of path MTU discovery is that the originating host sends a packet equal to the MTU of the outgoing interface, with the DF bit set in the IP header. If the packet is too large, the host will receive back a Host Unreachable–fragmentation needed message, which will contain a new, smaller MTU. The host switches to this new MTU, and repeats the procedure. Eventually, the smallest MTU of all the networks traversed will be found, and all packets sent will be smaller than or equal to that value, eliminating the need for any gateway to fragment the packets.

detect and deal with all these conditions. Data packets must be acknowledged, and are retransmitted until that acknowledgment is received. Sequence numbers allow duplicate packets to be ignored, and out-of-sequence packets to be queued at the TCP layer until the missing packets are received, so that the data will be presented to the application in the correct order. Checksums over the TCP header and data protect the integrity of the data; packets received with a bad checksum are silently ignored.

TCP is the transport used by the FTP, Telnet, and SMTP, and most other connection-oriented applications.

8.4.1   The PUSH Bit

TCP is a protocol that provides a byte stream. It does not provide any form of "packetizing" data. A common error is to assume that the PUSH bit can be used for this purpose. An implementation of TCP may provide buffering on the sending, the receiving, or both sides of a connection. The push function is used to "push" the data through these internal buffers, and deliver them to the user process on the receiving side. When data are received, if the PUSH bit is set in the packet, then all data received prior to it, including the data in datagram with the PUSH bit, are made available to the user process. If the PUSH bit is not set, the data may be buffered to accumulate several datagrams for delivery to the user in a single data transfer.

On the sending side, a TCP implementation may choose to delay the sending of data to try sending larger packets. In this situation, TCP is required to either provide a mechanism for the user process to indicate when data need to be pushed out, or make sure that the data eventually go out and that the PUSH bit is set in a datagram, when the system does not have any additional data queued up for transmission. Another thing to keep in mind is that PUSH bits should be collapsed, when possible. The important thing about collapsing PUSH bits is that it guarantees that the PUSH bit cannot (and should not) be used as a record marker.

8.4.2   Urgent Pointer

Probably the most important thing to say about the TCP Urgent Pointer is that it is just that, a pointer. TCP does *not* provide out-of-band data, but rather a pointer to "interesting" data. The Urgent Pointer points to the last byte of the urgent data, so the byte following the Urgent Pointer is the first byte of the interesting data. (The description of the Urgent Pointer on page 17 of *RFC 793* is in error, and the description at the bottom of page 56 is correct.)

Implementors of TCP should be aware that the Urgent Pointer is not limited to data in the current packet, but may point not only beyond the current packet, but even beyond the current window.

8.4.3 TCP Options

All TCP implementations are required to handle TCP options in any TCP segment. Unrecognized options are to be ignored. To aid in the processing of unknown options, *RFC 1122* requires that any new TCP option contain a length field as the second octet. This means that the End of Options List and No Operation options will be the only TCP options without length fields. If an option is received with an invalid length (less than 2 octets or more than 60 octets), TCP must recognize and handle the error; *RFC 1122* suggests resetting any connection on which invalid TCP options are received.

8.4.3.1 *Maximum Segment Size*

The Maximum Segment Size (MSS) option, which is sent only in the SYN segment, is used to inform the remote side of the connection about the largest amount of data that can be received in a single TCP segment. Over the years, understanding of how to properly use the MSS option has been clarified and changed. *RFC 793* stated that in the absence of the MSS option, any segment size was allowed. Experience showed that in the absence of the MSS option, it was better to be conservative, and *RFC 8791* states[18] that in the absence of the MSS option, a default value of 536 must be assumed. *RFC 879* also further clarifies that the value in MSS option is the maximum IP datagram size minus 40 (the size of the IP and TCP headers without any options).

The decision as to what value to put into the MSS option is based on several pieces of information. Ideally, the MSS value would be the largest value that could be received, and would not require any IP-level fragmentation. This would be no bigger than the maximum size of datagrams allowed on the network to which the host is directly attached. Because there was no information available about the path to the remote host, early TCP implementations used the local network for determining the MSS value. This led to a problem when both hosts were attached to networks with larger MTUs than some network in the middle of the path; each host would be sending datagrams that would have to be fragmented in the middle of the path. To address this issue, hosts started doing two things. First, when sending to a host that was not on the directly attached network, an MSS of 536 was assumed, regardless of what was received in the SYN packet. Second, to keep remote hosts that did not have this logic from sending larger packets, if the remote host was not on the directly attached network, then an MSS value of 536 was sent, regardless of the MSS of the directly attached network. Today, most TCP implementations have this logic, so the need to send an MSS of 536 to distant hosts to keep the remote side from sending larger packets that would be fragmented is no longer needed. Continuing to use 536 for the MSS of distant hosts is now a burden, preventing the distant host from sending larger packets, even if it knows that it can do so without causing IP fragmentation.

A host should use the MTU of the directly attached network when determining the proper MSS value, whether or not the remote host is distant. When sending data, the sender should use an MSS of 536, regardless of the received MSS value, if the remote host is not on the directly attached network and if there is no other information available on which to base a better decision. Better information about the MTU of the path can be determined by using path MTU discovery, as mentioned above.

8.4.3.2   New TCP Options: Extensions for Long-Delay Paths

When TCP is used over a network that has a large delay-bandwidth product, limitations in TCP are exposed that are not problems over slow or local area networks, which typically have a small delay-bandwidth product. *RFC 1072* proposed several new TCP options to deal with these problems, and *RFC 1185* augmented and refined *RFC 1072* with additional information. These two documents were then merged, and after further refinement were published in 1992 as *RFC 1323*, a Proposed Internet standard.[19]

The problems with the original TCP specification are the TCP window size, cumulative acknowledgments, round-trip timing, and sequence wrap-around. Several new TCP options have been defined to address these issues. Prior to these new options, only the SYN packets have contained TCP options. The existence of options in non-SYN segments might cause problems for hosts that don't understand the new options: at best it will cause extra per-packet overhead; at worst it might cause connections to be dropped. To avoid as many problems as possible, the definitions of these new options include mechanisms by which the presence of these options in the SYN segments is used to determine whether the remote host understands the new options; thus it avoids sending any of the new options to hosts that don't understand them.

8.4.3.3   Window Shift Option

The TCP window is a 16-bit quantity, meaning that there can never be more than 65,535 bytes of outstanding, unacknowledged data. Once a host has sent a full window of data, it cannot send anything else until it receives an acknowledgment (ACK) and a window update from the remote hosts. This implies that to drive a network at full speed, the remote host must be able to advertise a window that is larger than the delay-bandwidth product of the path being used. For Ethernet speeds (10 Mbits/sec), a cross-country link with a 30-ms roundtrip delay only needs a 36-Kbyte window. However, a DS3 (4-Mbits/sec) cross-country link would require a window in excess of 164-Kbytes, more than double the maximum TCP window size.[20]

To allow larger windows, and to introduce a minimal amount of processing overhead, it should be noted that the TCP window does not have to be a precise value. Though it is described in bytes, the size of the window, and updates to the window, are usually done with a much larger granularity. So, without changing the size of the window field in the TCP header, if both sides agreed that the window was a description of 4 byte-units, then windows would be four times as large.

The Window Shift option allows the side sending it to inform the other side of the connection what size of unit it will be using when it sends window update information. The unit size is a power of 2, up to 2^{14}. The value sent is the exponent, so a window shift value of 4 would imply that the window will be in units of 16 bytes each. Multiplying a value by some power of 2^n is the same as doing a bitwise shift of n of that value, hence the name, the Window Shift option.

To determine if both sides of the connection understand it, the option is only sent in the SYN segment, and it is only used if it is both sent and received. This means that the option should be sent, even if the sender is not going to be shifting his window, in which case a value of 0 should be sent.

8.4.3.4 TCP Timestamps Option

The Timestamps option is used to address two problems, round-trip timing and sequence wrap-around. The option has two 32-bit fields: a timestamp, which is generated by the sender of the option, and a reply field for returning timestamps received from the other side of the connection. A typical TCP implementation gets round-trip timing information by noting the time when a particular data segment is sent, and then noting when the ACK is received. This method allows the round-trip time to be updated once per round-trip time. If the connection has a large delay-bandwidth product, this can imply that the round-trip time will only be updated every several hundred packets or more, due to the accounting needed to keep track of timing multiple segments. The Timestamps option can be used to accurately time round trips by putting the option into each datagram sent. When a Timestamps option arrives, the receiver need only compare the value in the reply field with the current timestamp to determine the round-trip time. With this option, every ACK received would then contain round-trip timing information.

An implementor should note that there will not be a one-to-one correspondence between the number of Timestamps options sent and the number of Timestamps options received. If the receiver is only sending an ACK for every other packet, then only half of the received timestamp values will be returned in Timestamps options. This is the normal mode of operation, and implementors must not depend on, or bother to try to send, a Timestamps option for every Timestamps option received.

The values put into the Timestamps option are measured in a system-dependent unit of time. The receiver of the Timestamps option doesn't need to know anything about what unit of measurement the received timestamps represent, since it just sends the values back in the reply field of its Timestamps options. However, since timestamps will represent a monotonically increasing sequence of numbers, that knowledge can be used to avoid TCP sequence wrap-around problems.

The TCP sequence space is 32 bits, and the window is used to signify what part of that sequence space is currently valid. If old packets show up, they will be outside of the window and will be discarded. However, once 4.3 million (2^{32}) bytes of information have been sent over a single TCP connection, values for the current window into the sequence space will be the same as when the connection was first started. This is not a problem, as long as there is some guarantee that by the time we wrap the sequence space, any old packets from the previous window sent into the same part of the sequence space will have gone away.

The maximum segment lifetime is two minutes, so everything is okay as long as it takes more than two minutes to wrap the sequence space. Any connection running in excess of 286 Mbps can wrap the sequence space in less than two minutes. One solution to this problem would be to increase the TCP sequence space beyond 32 bits, but this would require either modifying the TCP header or adding a new TCP option to contain the additional bits for the sequence and acknowledgment fields. Or, one could take advantage of the information present in the TCP Timestamps option to identify old packets.

A property of the values in the Timestamps option is that the sequence of these values, if all the packets are received in order, will be a monotonically increasing sequence. Hence, if a packet is received with a timestamp less than the previous timestamp, it can be identified as an old packet. However, packets can be reordered in transmission. By keeping track of the timestamp value from the last packet that advanced the left edge of the TCP window, and only comparing timestamp values when a packet is first received, the problem with reordered packets is avoided.

To avoid problems with interoperability, the Timestamps option may always be sent in the initial SYN packet, but should only be sent in later packets if the Timestamps option was received in the initial SYN packet.

8.4.3.5 *Selective Acknowledgment*

Although *RFC 1072* defined both a Selective Acknowledgment (SACK) option and a SACK-Permitted option, they were both removed before *RFC 1323* was published. It was generally felt that the semantics and definition of the SACK option were not understood well enough to be standardized, and their definition has been deferred to a later time. When a definition is agreed upon, it will be published as a separate *RFC,* and possibly will be merged back in with *RFC 1323* at a later time. An explanation of the SACK option is included here for informational purposes only.

When a connection with a high delay-bandwidth product is being used, and the individual packet size is relatively small, there may be hundreds of packets in transmission at any given time. TCP only allows for the receiver to notify the sender of the packets that have been received with no missing holes. Thus, if one packet is lost, the receiver may accumulate several hundred packets on a resequencing queue, waiting for the one lost packet to be retransmitted. The sender, however, does not know that only one packet was lost. It knows what sequence number it needs to start retransmitting from (the last acknowledgment number received), but not how many data need to be retransmitted. If the sender doesn't retransmit enough data to fill the missing hole, the connection will stall until another retransmission. If the sender is overzealous and retransmits all the unacknowledged data, bandwidth will be wasted sending data that has already been successfully received. The SACK option allows the receiver to inform the sender about packets that have been received after a missing segment. With this knowledge, the sender will know how many segments need to be retransmitted and will not waste bandwidth resending data that have already been successfully received.

8.4.4 Checksum

The checksum field in TCP is not optional. The sender must always generate a checksum, and the receiver must always verify the checksum, discarding any packets with bad checksums. Because the checksum routine is so heavily used, it is usually worth any effort spent optimizing the checksum routine. For a good discussion on techniques and algorithms for computing the checksum, see *RFC 1071*.[21]

8.4.5 Initial Sequence Number

RFC 793 specifies a clock-driven scheme for determining the Initial Sequence Number (ISN) when establishing a TCP connection, which must be used. An ISN generator is used to determine the ISN values. The generator drives a 32-bit value that is incremented approximately every four microseconds; thus it will take over four and a half hours for this value to wrap.

8.4.6 Simultaneous Opens

If two TCPs attempt to actively create a connection with the same port numbers, only one connection is created. This sometimes surprises developers, and is known as "crossing SYNs." Normally a three-way handshake is used to start up a TCP connection; one host sends a SYN packet, the other host sends back a SYN/ACK packet, and the original host sends back an ACK. In the case of a simultaneous open, both sides send a SYN packet. Upon receipt of the SYN, both sides then generate a SYN/ACK packet, and when these are then received, each side enters into the *established* state.

8.4.7 RST Segments

The TCP Reset packet (in which the RST bit is set) is used to reset a TCP connection that has been shut down abnormally for some reason. A typical example is when a host on one end of a TCP connection crashes, and comes back up before the other side drops the connection. The host that crashed no longer has any information about the TCP connection. When the other host sends a packet for the connection, the host that crashed sends a RST packet to inform the other side that the connection no longer exists.

A reset packet does not contain any user data, and one topic of discussion in the Host Requirements Working Group had to do with sending data in a reset packet. It was generally agreed that data in a reset packet could be used to contain a message to indicate the reason for the reset. No standard currently exists for this use of data in reset packets, but implementors of TCP should allow for the possibility that at some time in the future, reset packets may contain data.

8.4.8 Slow Start

One problem with the TCP window mechanism is that it tells the sender how many data can be sent, but does not tell the sender how fast the data can be sent. If the data being sent traverse a slow network, it is easy for the sender to overwhelm the gateway between the fast local network, and the slower long-haul network, causing packets to be dropped and increasing congestion. These problems and solutions for them are discussed in detail by Van Jacobson.[22] *RFC 1122* makes the transmission algorithm, which combines "slow start" and "congestion avoidance," mandatory for all TCP implementations.

The Slow Start algorithm is based on the principle that to maintain optimum performance, the connection should be in a steady state, in which new packets are injected into the network by the sender only as old packets are removed from the network by the receiver. It was noted that the ACK packets coming back from the receiver could work as a clocking mechanism for the sender. Once steady state is achieved, for each packet that is acknowledged, a new packet can be sent. The question is how to get to that steady state. One way to get this clocking mechanism going is to just dump a window's worth of data onto the network. This will work if the gateway has enough buffering to hold a full window's worth of data. Usually, though, the gateway doesn't have enough buffering and packets get lost. A more conservative method of starting the clocking mechanism is to use Slow Start. A new TCP state variable is added, the congestion window. When sending data, the sender uses the smaller of the advertised window and the congestion window to decide how much data to send. The congestion window is initially set to be the size of one packet's worth of data. Whenever a packet is acknowledged, the congestion window is opened further by one packet's worth of data. In the first round trip, one data packet is sent. When the ACK is received, the congestion window is opened to two packets, and two packets are sent. When the ACKs for both of those packets are received, the congestion window is opened by one packet for each ACK, allowing a total of four packets to be sent. As can be seen, the congestion window grows exponentially, as long as the ACKs keep coming back. If a packet is lost, which is indicated by the retransmission timer going off, then the congestion window is set back to one, and slow start begins again.

Using Slow Start alone is not enough. You can quickly see that if the receiver's window is large enough, it can lead to a situation where the connection starts off sending one packet, then it ramps up to sending more packets than the gateways can handle and something gets lost, and the connection goes back to sending one packet and repeating the cycle. What is needed is to avoid the congestion in the first place. This is done by decreasing the congestion window to a "safe" value whenever a loss is noticed, and then slowly increasing it. Jacobson recommends cutting the congestion window in half, and then increasing arithmetically by the inverse of the congestion window, in packets. So, the increase becomes "maxseg×maxseg/cwnd," where maxseg is the maximum segment size, and cwnd is the congestion window.

This means that there are two different algorithms. Slow Start allows the congestion window to start small, and quickly grow to the point where congestion causes packets to be lost. The second algorithm for congestion avoidance drops the congestion window back to a safe value, and then slowly opens it to avoid going beyond the congestion point. What is needed is some way to decide which algorithm to use. This is done by introducing a new variable, the *ssthresh*, or slow start threshold. If the congestion window is less than the ssthresh value, then the Slow Start algorithm is used. If the congestion window is larger than ssthresh, then the congestion avoidance algorithm is used. The ssthresh value is initially set to the advertised window. When the retransmit timer goes off, ssthresh is set to one-half of the congestion window, and then the congestion window is reset to one packet. Since the congestion window was growing exponentially due to the Slow Start code, and the current congestion window is what caused the congestion, taking one-half of the congestion window for the crossover point is a nice conservative value.

To get a much more detailed explanation of the Slow Start and Congestion Avoidance algorithms, along with discussion on determining the retransmit timer, consult the article by Van Jacobson.[22]

8.4.9 Zero-Window Probes

A receiver TCP advertises a window into which the sender is allowed to send data. Once the sender has sent that much data, it is not allowed to send any more data until a window update is received. If a window update is not received, then the window is closed, and no more data can be sent. However, because window updates are usually just sent in ACK packets, and because ACK packets are not reliably transmitted, if the window update is lost, it is possible to get into a situation where the sender believes that the window is closed, and the receiver is just waiting for new data.

To deal with this situation, the sender is always allowed to send one additional byte of data beyond the end of a closed window. This is called a Zero-Window probe. When the receiver gets the data, if the window was really open, it will acknowledge the single byte of data and send the current window. The sender gets the new window update, and the transfer continues. If the receiver really has a closed window (usually due to an application not reading the incoming data), then it will drop the data and send back an ACK indicating that the data were dropped, and that the window is still 0.

The sender must support the ability to probe zero windows, to avoid deadlock situations like the one indicated. The sender must also realize that the window may legitimately be closed for long periods of time, and as long as ACKs are being received in response to Zero-Window probes, the connection must be allowed to remain open. The first window probe should be sent after the normal retransmit interval. Successive window probes should then be backed off exponentially, similar to the TCP retransmission timer, and an implementation may combine probes and retransmissions into a single procedure.

8.4.10 TTL

RFC 793 specifies that if the lower layer is IP, then TCP should set the IP Time-To-Live (TTL) field to 60. Using a constant value is no longer correct; though a default value may be used for the TTL, this value must be configurable by the application.

8.5   TELNET

The Telnet protocol is probably one of the most widely implemented applications protocols. Its primary usage is to allow users to log into a remote host. Early implementations of Telnet tended to be simplistic; there was some option negotiation at the beginning of the session, and then it went into single-character, remote echo mode. In this mode, each character typed by the user is sent to the remote host without interpretation, and is not echoed to the user's screen. The terminal driver on the remote host does the input processing, and echoes back any necessary data to be displayed on the user's screen. On a local area network, where the round-trip time is small and the data rates are fast, this is not a major problem. However, if the remote host is thousands of miles away or on the other side of a slow link, things can start to become frustrating for the user while waiting for the characters typed to be echoed to the screen. Also, certain functions, like interrupting output, are not acted on promptly. Users can become annoyed when they type "^C" to interrupt the process on the remote machine, and then several more pages of output continue to be displayed before the output is finally aborted.

The current trend is to add new options and functionality to the Telnet protocol to allow as much input processing to happen on the local host as possible. This reduces the amount of packets injected into the network, provides users with more immediate feedback as they are typing, and provides a more seamless transition from the local environment to the remote environment.

8.5.1   The Go Ahead Function

The Telnet Go Ahead (GA) command was designed to support half-duplex, lockable terminals. This type of terminal does not allow the user to type input while output is being displayed, or vice versa. These terminals implicitly switch control from the user typing input to the display of output when the user finishes typing a line. However, the host system needs to inform the terminal when it is through displaying output, so that control can be given back to the user to type in more data. To provide for this functionality, GA was developed. When the Telnet server discovers that no more output will be forthcoming, and that the process is blocked waiting for user input, it sends the GA command, and when the client Telnet receives the GA command, it informs the terminal that control should be given back to the user keyboard. For systems that did not need to use the GA command, the Telnet Suppress Go Ahead (SGA) command was designed to allow both ends of the connection to disable the generation of the Go Ahead command. However, as with all Telnet options, either side could choose to disable, or refuse to enable, the SGA option.

In reality, many operating systems provide no way for the Telnet server process to reliably determine when output has terminated, and the process being executed is blocked waiting for more input. Also, these half-duplex, lockable terminals are, for the most part, not in use anymore. For these reasons, many implementations of Telnet would never generate the GA command, regardless of the state of the SGA option. The group that was working on the *Host Requirements* documents wanted to deprecate the GA command, relegating it to the status of a historical artifact. However, there was a contingent that claimed that GA was still needed for the use of Data Entry Terminals (DET). So, rather than outlaw the use of GA, it was decided that support of the SGA option would be mandatory; Telnet servers that do not generate GA must attempt to negotiate the SGA option (that is, they must send "WILL SGA"), and Telnet clients must accept the negotiation of the SGA option (when a "WILL SGA" is received, the client must send "DO SGA").

8.5.2 Control Function

RFC 885 defined a new Telnet command, IAC EOR.[23] The value for EOR is 239. When it was defined, there was concern that hosts that didn't understand the IAC EOR command would not properly ignore it, thus the Telnet End-of-Record option was added so that it could be determined whether or not the other side of the connection would understand the IAC EOR command. *RFC 1183* extends the list of IAC commands defined in the Telnet specification to include the EOR value. It also makes it mandatory that hosts properly receive and ignore any Telnet commands that are not understood.

All Telnet implementations must support the control functions Abort Output (AO), Are You There (AYT), Data Mark (DM), Interrupt Process (IP), No Operation (NOP), Subnegotiation (SB), and End Subnegotiation (SE). In addition, the End-of-Record (EOR), Erase Character (EC), Erase Line (EL), and Break (BRK) commands may be supported.

Since *RFC 1122* was issued, three more control functions have been defined. They are described[24] along with the LINEMODE option, in *RFC 1184*. The added functions are End-of-File (EOF), Suspend (SUSP), and Abort (ABORT). If a host supports the LINEMODE option, it must support these three additional control functions; hosts that do not support the LINEMODE option may also support these control functions.

8.5.3 Telnet Synch and Flushing Data

The Telnet Synch command is used to flush user data (but not Telnet commands) from the Telnet data stream. A Synch consists of a Data Mark command sent in TCP Urgent mode, with the TCP urgent pointer pointing to the octet containing the data mark command. When the receiving side receives notification that the TCP connection is in urgent mode, it

must then start reading the data stream, discarding all user data while retaining (and processing) all Telnet commands, until the Data Mark command is found and the TCP connection is no longer in urgent mode. If the connection is still in urgent mode after the
Data Mark command is found, then the flushing must continue until another Data Mark
command is found and the connection goes out of urgent mode.

When a server Telnet receives an Abort Output (AO) command, the output stream
must be flushed by sending a Synch back to the user. When the server Telnet receives an
Interrupt Process (IP) command, it may send a Synch back to the user; however, it should
only do this if it is consistent with what the host (on which the server is located) does when
it receives the equivalent of the Telnet Interrupt Process command.

One of the problems with relying on the remote side to decide when to flush the output
stream is that there is a delay between when the user types something that should cause the
output stream to be flushed (such as generating an Interrupt Process command), and when
the server side receives that information and sends back the Synch command. During that
interval, output continues to be presented to the user, which may be very annoying. There
is also no guarantee that the server will generate the Synch command.

The client Telnet may choose to send an Abort Output command after sending commands, such as Interrupt Process, that should flush the output stream. This will guarantee
that the server will generate the Synch command, but it does not solve the time delay problem. The client Telnet could just begin discarding output once the Abort Output command is sent, until the connection goes into and out of urgent mode and the Data Mark
command is received. The problem with this approach is that when dealing with older
servers that do not properly generate the Synch command, the client will be stuck in a loop
flushing all data.

The Telnet Timing-Mark option can be used much more reliably to flush output. After
sending the Interrupt Process command, a "DO TIMING-MARK" is sent, and output is
then flushed until either a "WILL TIMING-MARK" or "WONT TIMING-MARK" is
received. The TIMING-MARK option is special in that whenever a DO TIMING-MARK
is received, a response must always be sent, even if a WILL TIMING-MARK has already
been sent. Because the DO TIMING-MARK is sent right after the IP, the client can be
assured that when it receives the WILL/WONT TIMING-MARK, the IP has been processed and output can be safely resumed. The only potential problem with this scheme is
that if the host processes the IP and generates new output (such as a prompt), and the
server Telnet processes that new output before processing the incoming TIMING-MARK
option, the output that was processed before the WILL/WONT TIMING-MARK was
returned will be flushed by the client.

In reality, whether it is better to send an AO or a DO TIMING-MARK will depend on
the server. Therefore, the client Telnet should provide some mechanism for the user to
choose which of the two (or even both) schemes should be used.

8.5.4 Terminal Type Option

When the Terminal Type option is used, the side that is sending the terminal type names must use the terminal type names that are defined in the *Assigned Numbers RFC*[25] if they exist for the particular terminal type in question. The side that receives the terminal type names, however, must accept any names that are presented, and may not ignore names that it receives just because they are not in the *Assigned Numbers RFC*. These rules allow well-known terminal names to be used whenever possible, and still allow new names to be added as needed without having to rebuild Telnet applications.

The Terminal Type option, originally defined in *RFC 930*, was extended and reissued[26] as *RFC 1091*.[27] The original definition allowed the server Telnet to get a list of terminal names from the client Telnet. Once the client Telnet had sent its entire list of terminal names, it would continue to send the last terminal name to successive queries from the server. It was assumed that all the different terminal names were synonyms for the same terminal type, and the server would just pick the one that it liked best. With the advent of bit-mapped terminals, a "terminal" may actually be able to emulate several different terminal types, each requiring different processing characteristics. In this situation, it is necessary for the client to know which terminal type the server has picked. The extensions accomplish this by stating that as each terminal type is sent, the client switches to that terminal type. When the client has sent the entire list, it repeats the last terminal type once to indicate the end of the list, and then cycles back to the beginning of the list for successive queries from the server. The server, upon receiving the same terminal type twice, picks the terminal type that it likes best, and then continues to query the client until it presents that terminal type again, at which point both client and server will be in sync. However, if the server gets the last received terminal type a third time rather than the beginning of the list, it can assume that it is talking to an older *RFC 930* version, and should stop sending requests for additional terminal types.

8.5.5 LINEMODE Option

At the time that the *Host Requirements* document was published, the Telnet LINEMODE option[28] had also just been published. Because of the timing of the release of these documents, it was not possible to make any requirements in *RFC 1123* about the LINEMODE option; however, a discussion section was added to indicate that when the LINEMODE option became available, hosts should implement at least the client side of the option, and possibly also the server side. Since that time, additional implementation and usage experience has been gained. In fact, the original *RFC* for the LINEMODE option, *RFC 1116*, was made obsolete in October 1990 by a new revision, *RFC 1184*.

8.5.6 Echo Option

A host must make certain that the Echo option is not enabled in both directions on a Telnet connection. (i.e., If a WILL ECHO has been sent, a DO ECHO must not be sent
until a WONT ECHO has been sent, and if a DO ECHO has been sent, a WILL ECHO
must not be sent until a DONT ECHO has been sent.) Under normal circumstances, a
client should never send a WILL ECHO, as this would imply that the client would be
sending the terminal output back to remote machine as terminal input!

8.5.7 End-Of-Line Conventions

No discussion of the Telnet protocol would be complete without a discussion of the Telnet
End-of-Line conventions. Because this has been a continuing problem for implementors,
and because much time was spent getting the description of the issues in *RFC 1123* correct, the complete text from *RFC 1123* is included here:[29]

> The Telnet protocol defines the sequence CR LF to mean "end-of-line." For terminal
> input, this corresponds to a command-completion or "end-of-line" key being
> pressed on a user terminal; on an ASCII terminal, this is the CR key, but it may also
> be labelled "Return" or "Enter."
>
> When a Server Telnet receives the Telnet end-of-line sequence CR LF as input
> from a remote terminal, the effect MUST be the same as if the user had pressed the
> "end-of-line" key on a local terminal. On server hosts that use ASCII, in particular,
> receipt of the Telnet sequence CR LF must cause the same effect as a local user press-
> ing the CR key on a local terminal. Thus, CR LF and CR NUL MUST have the
> same effect on an ASCII server host when received as input over a Telnet connection.
>
> A User Telnet MUST be able to send any of the forms: CR LF, CR NUL, and LF.
> A User Telnet on an ASCII host SHOULD have a user-controllable mode to send
> either CR LF or CR NUL when the user presses the "end-of-line" key, and CR LF
> SHOULD be the default.
>
> The Telnet end-of-line sequence CR LF MUST be used to send Telnet data that is
> not terminal-to-computer (e.g., for Server Telnet sending output, or the Telnet pro-
> tocol incorporated another application protocol).

DISCUSSION:

To allow interoperability between arbitrary Telnet clients and servers, the Telnet protocol defined a standard representation for a line terminator. Since the ASCII character set includes no explicit end-of-line character, systems have chosen various
representations, e.g., CR, LF, and the sequence CR LF. The Telnet protocol chose the
CR LF sequence as the standard for network transmission.

Unfortunately, the Telnet protocol specification in RFC 854 has turned out to be
somewhat ambiguous on what character(s) should be sent from client to server for the
"end-of-line" key. The result has been a massive and continuing interoperability headache, made worse by various faulty implementations of both User and Server Telnets.

Although the Telnet protocol is based on a perfectly symmetric model, in a remote log-in session the role of the user at a terminal differs from the role of the server host. For example, RFC 854 defines the meaning of CR, LF, and CR LF as output from the server, but does not specify what the User Telnet should send when the user presses the "end-of-line" key on the terminal; this turns out to be the point at issue.

When a user presses the "end-of-line" key, some User Telnet implementations send CR LF, while others send CR NUL (based on a different interpretation of the same sentence in RFC 84). These will be equivalent for a correctly implemented ASCII server host, as discussed above. For other servers, a mode in the User Telnet is needed.

The existence of User Telnets that send only CR NUL when CR is pressed creates a dilemma for non-ASCII hosts: they can either treat CR NUL as equivalent to CR LF in input, thus precluding the possibility of entering a "bare" CR, or else lose complete interworking.

Suppose a user on host A uses Telnet to log into a server host B, and then execute B's User Telnet program to log into server host C. It is desirable for the Server/User Telnet combination on B to be as transparent as possible, i.e., to appear as if A were connected directly to C. In particular, correct implementation will make B transparent to Telnet end-of-line sequences, except that CR LF may be translated to CR NUL or vice versa.

IMPLEMENTATION:

To understand Telnet end-of-line issues, one must have at least a general model of the relationship of Telnet to the local operating system. The Server Telnet process is typically coupled into the terminal driver software of the operating system as a pseudo-terminal. A Telnet end-of-line sequence received by the Server Telnet must have the same effect as pressing the end-of-line key on a real locally-connected terminal.

Operating systems that support interactive character-at-a-time applications (e.g., editors) typically have two internal modes for their terminal I/O: a formatted mode, in which local conventions for end-of-line and other formatting rules have been applied to the data stream, and a "raw" mode, in which the application has direct access to every character as it is entered. A Server Telnet must be implemented in such a way that these modes have the same effect for remote as for local terminals. For example, suppose a CR LF or CR NUL is received by the Server Telnet on an ASCII host. In raw mode, a CR character is passed to the application; in formatted mode, the local system's end-of-line convention is used.

8.5.8 Data Entry Terminals

The rules for entering and leaving the data entry terminal (DET) mode are as follows:[2]

- The server uses the Terminal-Type option to learn that the client is a DET.

- It is conventional, but not required, that both ends negotiate the EOR option.

- Both ends negotiate the Binary option[30] to enter native DET mode.

- When either end negotiates out of binary mode, the other end does too, and the mode then reverts to normal NVT [Network Virtual Terminal].

8.6 FILE TRANSFER PROTOCOL

FTP is the primary protocol used in the Internet for file transfer. It is currently defined by *RFC 959*, as modified by *RFC 1123*.

8.6.1 Data Types

FTP allows for data to be transferred with one of four different data types: ASCII, EBCDIC, IMAGE, and LOCAL. The default data type is ASCII, and all FTP implementations must support it. The optional data type of EBCDIC is to allow efficient transfer of data between hosts that support EBCDIC as their internal character representation. The IMAGE type allows for efficient binary transfer of data, and although *RFC 959* recommends that the IMAGE type be supported, *RFC 1123* adds the requirement that all FTP implementations must support the IMAGE type.

   The LOCAL type is used to specify a logical byte size for the data being transferred. This may be different from the byte size used to transfer the data. The required argument with this type is the logical byte size. The most common use of the LOCAL type is with a size of 8, and must be supported; on an 8-bit byte machine, this is equivalent to the IMAGE type. When the logical byte size is different than transfer size of eight, the logical bytes are packed into the transfer bytes, without regard to the byte boundaries of the transfer bytes.

8.6.2 ASCII and EBCDIC Format Controls

Both of the ASCII and EBCDIC data types can be specified with an optional qualifier to indicate what type of vertical format control is associated with the data. There are three types: NON PRINT, TELNET FORMAT CONTROLS, and CARRIAGE CONTROL (ASA). Every implementation must support NON PRINT; it is the default format if none is specified. As its name implies, NON PRINT data are usually destined for storage or processing, and do not need to contain any vertical format information. TELNET FORMAT CONTROL data implies that the data contain appropriate vertical format controls that a printer process can interpret. The control characters are CR, LF, NL, VT and FF, plus the two-character sequence, CR LF, which denotes the end of a line. For hosts that do not make a distinction between NON PRINT and TELNET FORMAT CONTROLS, the latter should be implemented to be identical to NON PRINT. A host may also support CARRIAGE CONTROL, which specifies that the file contains ASA (FORTRAN) vertical format control characters.[31]

8.6.3   Data Structures

FTP defines three types of structures that may be imposed on the data being transferred: file-structure, record-structure, and page-structure. The default type, file-structure, implies that there is no internal structure to the file being transferred, and it must be supported by all FTP implementations. The second type, record-structure, which is used when a file is made up of sequential records, is required for systems that support an internal record format, and is optional for hosts that do not support records. The third type, page-structure, was designed specifically with TOPS-20 systems in mind. In general, this type is not recommended, but if an FTP needs to implement support of "holey" or "random access" files, it must use the page-structure, rather than invent some private FTP format.

RFC 959 talks about converting between file-structure and record-structure formats, and requires that there be strict invertability in the transformation. Unfortunately, it is not always possible to support the inversion and keep the data useful, so *RFC 1123* relaxes this requirement to say that an implementation should do the transformations in such a manner that they are invertible. *RFC 1123* cites a good example of when a transformation is not invertible:[32]

> Imagine a record-oriented operating system that requires some data files to have exactly 80 bytes in each record. While STORing a file on such a host, an FTP Server must be able to pad each line or record to 80 bytes; a later retrieval of such a file cannot be strictly invertible.

8.6.4   Creating TCP Connections for Data Transfer

When STREAM mode is being used to transfer files, a new TCP connection must be created for each data transfer. If several files are to be transferred, then several TCP connections will be used. Because TCP places a delay on when a socket pair can be reused, it would be good to use a different socket pair for each file transferred. This is accomplished by the client using the PORT command to specify a nondefault data port; it should be used before each transfer command is sent. When using a mode other than STREAM mode, the data connection can be left open and reused for successive file transfers, and there is no need to issue multiple PORT commands.

The PASV command is used to set up a data connection for a third-party data transfer. Normally, the client FTP does the passive TCP open when creating a data connection, and the server does an active TCP open. When doing a third-party transfer, one of the two FTP servers must do a passive TCP open instead of an active TCP open. The client issues a PASV command to one of the two servers, and the reply that is returned contains the address and port number that that server is using to do the passive TCP open. The client then issues a PORT command with this information to the other server, followed by the appropriate commands to each server to start the data transfer. The format of the address and port in the reply to the PASV command is not clearly defined in *RFC 959*. On page 40 it shows the format as (*h1, h2, h3, h4, p1, p2*), where *h1, h2, h3* ,and *h4* are the four bytes of the Internet address, and *p1* and *p2* are the two bytes of the TCP port number. On page 45, in Figure 3, it shows a similar format, but without the parentheses. A client FTP implementation must then be able to receive and interpret the host and port information with or without parentheses.

When a server creates a data connection using the default port (e.g., a PORT command was not received prior to the transfer command), and the host on which the server is running is a multihomed host, the server must use the same local IP address that is associated with the control connection.

8.6.5   Listing Files

FTP provides two methods for a client to get a list of files from the server. The two commands are LIST and NAME LIST (NLST). The LIST command is intended to return system specific information about a single file, group of files, or files in a directory. While the information may be very useful to the user, it is not useful for an automatic multiple file transfer mechanism. To get just a list of files that can be used by a program, the NLST command is used. The list of files returned from an NLST command must be legal pathnames that can be used as arguments to data transfer commands.

The data type used for transferring the data from a LIST or NLST command should be either ASCII or EBCDIC, with a further qualification of NON PRINT (the default).

8.6.6   Nonstandard Additions to FTP

Even though FTP provides a very rich command set, there will always be some functionality that implementors would like to have that is not covered. FTP allows for nonstandard extensions by using the SITE command. When adding nonstandard features to an FTP implementation, the SITE command should be used, rather than adding new private commands or making nonstandard extensions to the existing FTP command set. FTP servers that support additional commands through the SITE command should make their syntax available as the reply to a HELP SITE command.

Although not mentioned in either *RFC 959* or *RFC 1123*, a useful server implementation that supports the SITE command could also support a SITE HELP command. The client could then use HELP SITE command to get a list of local extensions and their syntax, and SITE HELP <local command> to get further information about a specific local command, much in the same manner that a HELP <command> is used to gain additional information about a specific standard FTP command.

8.6.7   The Store Unique Command

RFC 959 added several new commands to the FTP command set. One of them is Store Unique, or STOU. The Store Unique command is similar to the Store command, except that it stores the data in a filename that is unique to the current directory. *RFC 959* incorrectly states that the name of the file in which the data is stored is returned in a 250 reply message. *RFC 1123* replaces this with either a "125 Transfer Starting" or "150 Opening Data Connection" message, the exact format of which is:

FILE: *pppp*

FILE: *pppp*

where *pppp* represents the unique pathname of the file that will be written.

8.6.8 End-of-Line Conventions on the Command Socket

FTP commands are terminated by the Telnet End-of-Line sequence, CR LF. This is the only thing that should be used to determine when an entire FTP command has been received. More specifically, because the command connection is a TCP connection, and thus just a byte stream, the implementation must be prepared to receive partial commands, and continue reading from the command socket until the CRLF has been received. Conversely, it is also possible to receive more than a single FTP command on a single read from the command socket, and implementors must ensure that when multiple commands are received they are all processed in the order received.

8.6.9 FTP Replies

FTP commands are sent from the client FTP to the server FTP, and replies are sent from the server FTP to the client FTP. All FTP replies begin with a 3-digit number. The first digit, 1–5, specifies whether the command is: 1, in progress; 2, completed; 3, now waiting for another command; 4, failed due to transient errors; or 5, failed due to permanent errors. The second digit, 0–5, provides function groupings for: 0, syntax; 1, information; 2, connections; 3, authentication and accounting; 4, unspecified; and 5, file system. The third digit provides finer gradation of the groupings specified in the second digit.

The 3-digit code is followed by a space and one line of text. When the meaning of the reply being returned matches the definition in *RFC 959*, the server should use exactly the same text as listed in *RFC 959*. Multiple line responses are sent by following the 3-digit code with a hyphen (-), followed by two or more lines of text. The last line of text in a multiple line reply begins with the same 3-digit code as the first line, followed by a space and the final line of the multiple line reply message. All client FTP implementations must be able to handle multiple line reply messages. If the client has to place some restriction on the number of lines that it can handle in a reply message, then it must be able to continue to receive the rest of the lines in the reply, ignoring them until the final line of the reply is received. A FTP server must send only correctly formatted replies, and it should be noted that *RFC 959*, unlike earlier versions of the FTP specification, does not allow for the server to send spontaneous reply messages.

Server FTP implementations should use only the reply codes listed in *RFC 959*, but there may be times when the listed codes do not precisely define the correct response for a given situation. Because the server may send a different code than is listed in *RFC 959* in these cases, client FTP implementations should use only the first digit of the 3-digit response when using the reply code to make procedural decisions. Servers should also use the 4xy reply codes instead of the 5xy reply codes whenever it is reasonable to assume that if the command were done again in a few hours, there would be a good chance that it would succeed.

8.6.10   The FTP Control Connection

Although the control connection is defined to use the Telnet protocol, it is not intended to be a full-blown Telnet implementation. Specifically, the client FTP should be able to send the Telnet SYNC and Interrupt Process commands, but must not send any other Telnet commands. The server, although it should not get any Telnet option to negotiate, must be able to receive and refuse any Telnet options that might come over the command connection. Refusing a Telnet option means responding with a Telnet WONT or DONT command.

8.6.11   A Minimum FTP Implementation

Although *RFC 959* lists the requirements for a minimum FTP implementation, it was decided that it did not include enough of the FTP command set. The minimum FTP implementation, as defined in *RFC 1123*, is:[33]

> Type: ASCII non-print, IMAGE, LOCAL 8
>
> MODE: STREAM
> STRUCTURES FILE, RECORD*
> COMMANDS:
>
> USER, PASS, ACCT,
> PORT, PASV, TYPE, MODE,
> STRU, RETR, STOR, APPE,
> RNFR, RNTO, DELE, CWD,
> CDUP, RMD, MKD, PWD, LIST, NLST,
> SYST, STAT, HELP, NOOP, QUIT.

> *Record structure is REQUIRED only for hosts whose file systems support record structures.

Implementors of FTP are encouraged to implement more than just the required minimum implementation. There are many commands that provide useful functionality, but they will not be of much use if they are not implemented. Even though the record structure is only required for hosts whose file systems support record structures, other hosts may accept record structure data, storing it as a literal byte stream.

8.6.12 Experimental FTP Commands

The FTP protocol allows for experimental commands. Experimental commands are commands that begin with an X. If an experimental command becomes a standard command, it will be given another name, without the leading X. This poses a potential problem, because for a period of time there will be clients and servers that support the experimental command names, but not the new official names of these commands. To deal with this situation, servers should continue to recognize and support the experimental names, along with the official names. It is a bit more work for a client to deal with this situation, but it is still straightforward. The client should first send the official name of the command, and if the response it receives is either "500 Syntax error, command unrecognized" or "502 Command not implemented," the client should send the experimental form of the command.

8.6.13 Idle Timeout

A Server implementation of FTP should have an idle timer, to terminate the FTP server process if there is no transfer in progress, and no command has been received for a set period of time. The time-out period should be configurable, with the default value being at least 5 minutes.

At least one popular server FTP implementation has added a "SITE IDLE <time>" command to support this function. If the SITE IDLE is received without the argument <time>, the current idle timer value is returned in the reply "200 Current IDLE time is *nnn* seconds," where *nnn* is the number of seconds that the idle timer is currently set to. If received with the argument <time>, the idle timer is set to that value, and the reply "200 Maximum IDLE time set to *nnn* seconds" is returned, where *nnn* is the argument received, or if the <time> value is less than 30 seconds or more than a configured maximum value, the reply "501 Maximum IDLE time must be between 30 and *mmm* seconds" is returned, where *mmm* indicates the maximum number of seconds to which the idle timer may be set. This particular implementation uses a default idle period of 900 seconds (15 minutes), with a default maximum idle timer value of 7200 seconds (two hours).

8.6.14 FTP Restart Mechanism

The FTP specification contains a mechanism for restarting a data transfer if it is aborted after a partial transfer of the file. To take advantage of this feature, restart markers need to be inserted into the data stream by the sender of the data. The insertion of restart markers into the data stream requires that either Block or Compressed mode be used for data transfer. It is the responsibility of the client to keep track of the restart markers, for later use when restarting the file transfer. The information saved is a list of pairs of system dependent file information. The sender of the file inserts restart markers into the data stream. The receiver of the file, upon receiving a restart marker, writes all previous data to the disk, and encodes the current position in the file. If the receiver of the file is the client, then the client just writes the sender–receiver pair of markers to a file. If the receiver of the file is an FTP server, it also writes all previously received data to the disk, and encodes the current position in the file. It then returns the sender's restart marker, along with the just-calculated receiver's marker, in a 110 reply message. Note that if the client is transferring a file to the server, it will be receiving its own restart markers back in the 110 reply messages. If the client is doing a third-party transfer, then the sending server will be generating the restart markers, and the receiving server will be sending both restart marks as a pair back to the client in the 110 reply message. The description of the 110 reply message in *RFC 959* is incorrect. The correct format for the 110 reply message, as found in *RFC 1123*, is:[34]

> MARK ssss = rrrr

> Here,

> - ssss is a text string that appeared in a Restart Marker in the data stream and encodes a position in the sender's file system;

> - rrrr encodes the corresponding position in the receiver's file system.

> The encoding, which is specific to a particular file system and network implementation, is always generated and interpreted by the same system, either sender or receiver.

RFC 1123 also adds two new reply codes for dealing with errors encountered when using restart markers:[35]

> 554 Requested action not taken: invalid REST parameter.

> A 554 reply may result from a FTP service command that follows a REST command. The reply indicates that the existing file at the Server-FTP cannot be repositioned as specified in the REST.

> 555 Requested action not taken: type or stru mismatch.

> A 555 reply may result from an APPE command or from any FTP service command following a REST command. The reply indicates that there is some mismatch between the current transfer parameters (type and stru) and the attributes of the existing file.

Although *RFC 959* makes reference to returning the restart markers to the user, this should not be taken too seriously. A good implementation of the restart mechanism would save the restart markers in a file on the client, without bothering the user. This file would contain a record of restart marker pairs received, and allow all three types of file transfers to be restarted: client-to-server transfers, server-to-client transfers, and third-party, server-to-server transfers. Once the file is successfully transferred, the restart marker file should be removed.

When the client wishes to restart a transfer to a server that was aborted, it looks up the last (*ssss, rrrr*) pair in the restart file, repositions the file pointer of the file that is being sent to *ssss*, and sends a REST *rrrr* command to the server, followed by the appropriate transfer command.

When the client wishes to restart a transfer from a server that had been aborted, it looks up the last (*ssss, rrrr*) pair in the restart file, repositions the file pointer of the file that is being saved to *rrrr*, and sends a REST *ssss* command to the server, followed by the appropriate transfer command.

When the client wishes to restart a third-party transfer, it looks up the last (*ssss, rrrr*) pair in the restart file, sends a REST *ssss* command to the server that was sending the file, and a REST *rrrr* command to the server that was receiving the file, followed by the appropriate transfer commands to both servers.

When a client FTP is sending data with restart markers, it must not assume that the server will be sending 110 replies immediately upon receiving a restart marker. In other words, having sent a restart marker in the data stream, the client must not wait for the 110 reply before sending more data.

8.6.15   FTP User Interface

The FTP specification describes the format of commands and replies sent between the client and server FTP implementation. Normally, a protocol specification does not talk about a user interface. However, there are some parts of the FTP user interface that are not part of the protocol, but should be implemented to allow maximum flexibility.

Pathnames must not be limited to the character set supported by the local machines file system. Specifically, *RFC 959* allows any character, except a CR or LF, to be part of a pathname, and the user interface must allow these pathnames to be entered by the user. Note that this means that a space (ASCII 0x20) is a valid character in a pathname, and the user must be able to enter it in a pathname. This does not mean that the file system has to accept pathnames with characters outside of its supported character set, but that the user has to be able to enter them.

The user FTP interface will usually not be able to support all of the FTP commands, especially the SITE command. To allow the user to send commands to the server that the client FTP does not understand, the client FTP user interface should include a QUOTE command, to enable the user to pass arbitrary character strings to the server FTP. It should be noted that the FTP server will be sending back replies in response to these commands, so the client FTP implementation should take this into account.

When a client FTP receives error replies (4xy and 5xy codes), it should display the full text of the error reply for the user to see. The client FTP should also have a verbose mode. When verbose mode is enabled, the client FTP should display all commands sent to, and all replies received from the server FTP.

8.7   TRIVIAL FILE TRANSFER PROTOCOL

The Trivial File Transfer Protocol (TFTP) is a simple stop-and-wait protocol for transfer-ring files that runs on top of UDP. TFTP lacks many of the features of FTP, including security, access control, and directory services, and is much slower than FTP, due to a limit of 512 bytes per block and having to wait for an acknowledgment of each block before sending the next one; however, it is precisely this simplicity that makes TFTP useful in constrained situations, such as in EPROM, when used for booting.

8.7.1   Transfer Modes

The TFTP specification defines three transfer modes: netascii, octet, and mail. The mail mode is not used anymore, and should not be implemented.

8.7.2   UDP Header Length

In the appendix of the TFTP specification, the length field of the UDP header is incorrectly described. The UDP length field always includes the eight bytes of the UDP header itself.

8.7.3   Sorcerer's Apprentice Syndrome

The TFTP specification allows for the resending of the current packet, when a duplicate packet is received. The intention of this is that if machine A sends a packet and it does not receive a response, it does not know whether the packet was lost, or whether the response was lost, so it must resend the original packet. At machine B, if the original packet was lost, when the second one arrives it will look like a new packet, and everything will continue as normal. If the response from B to A is what was lost, then when the retransmitted packet arrives at B, it will be a duplicate, indicating that the response from B to A got lost and needs to be retransmitted.

In theory this works well, but in practice it can lead to unanticipated network load, especially when the path between the two machines is congested. Take the example again, but this time assume that no packets are being lost. Instead, machine A sends a DATA packet and either it or the ACK packet from B is delayed just long enough for machine A to decide that something was lost, so machine A retransmits its DATA packet. Machine B receives the first DATA packet, and sends an ACK back to A. It then receives the second DATA packet, and sends another ACK back to A. Meanwhile, back on A, the first ACK packet is received, and the next DATA packet is sent. Then the second ACK packet arrives, and the second DATA packet is sent again. Back on B, two DATA packets arrive, and another ACK is generated for each packet, which in turn will wind up causing A to send two copies of the next DATA packet, and so on. This situation is known as the "Sorcerer's Apprentice Syndrome." Note that the transfer can still be completed, and the transfer is done correctly. The problem is that all the data will have been sent twice, most likely adding to congestion that caused the situation to occur in the first place.

To fix this situation, the protocol must be modified. *RFC 1123* changes TFTP so that the side sending the DATA packets must never resend the current data packet in response to receiving a duplicate ACK packet. It must resend the current DATA packet only when its retransmit timer has expired. The other side, which is generating the ACK packets, must continue to generate ACK packets when duplicate DATA packets are received. With this change, generating duplicate ACKs will not cause anything to happen, and the implementation on the receiver side could be simplified by eliminating the retransmission timer. However, there still is value in having a retransmission timer on the ACKs, as it can help when an ACK is genuinely lost.

It should also be noted that the situation that leads to the Sorcerer's Apprentice Syndrome is due to a retransmission timer going off before a response is received. This timer could have gone off either because the initial retransmit time was too short, or because larger than expected round-trip times are being experienced. In either case, since the implementation probably doesn't have any information to give a good estimate of how long the initial retransmission timer should be, the implementation should be careful about how often retransmissions are done, especially when doing multiple retransmissions of the same packet. At a minimum, a TFTP implementation should have an exponential backoff algorithm for doing multiple retransmits of the same packet. The TCP retransmission algorithm is a good example to look at when designing a TFTP retransmission algorithm.

8.7.4   Extensions

Although the TFTP specification allows for other transfer modes, and versions of TFTP have been extended to allow secure operation by passing passwords or authentication information, currently there are no extensions beyond *RFC 783* that have been standardized.

8.7.5   Access Control

As mentioned earlier, TFTP does not provide any mechanism for authentication. Because of this, a server implementation of TFTP should provide some configurable mechanism for restricting access to files. At a minimum, the TFTP server should only allow the reading and writing of files that a totally unprivileged user would be able to read and write. The administrator should also be able to limit access to a specific set of directories or files, possibly with the additional restriction of only allowing read or write access (in addition to the protection mode of the file).

TFTP server implementations should also ignore TFTP requests that arrive with an IP destination address that is a directed broadcast address. Without this restriction, someone hoping to gather information or write to files that they shouldn't have access to, could send a TFTP read request as a directed broadcast and wait to see if anyone responds, to find the weak systems.

8.8 SIMPLE MAIL TRANSFER PROTOCOL

SMTP is defined in *RFC 821*. It describes the protocol used for exchanging mail between hosts in the Internet. The formats of the mail messages themselves are described in a companion document,[36] *Standards for the Format of ARPA Internet Text Messages, RFC 822*. The biggest change to the Internet mail system is the addition of the Domain Name System (DNS), which has caused changes in mail routing and address formats, even though SMTP itself has changed very little.

8.8.1 *RFC 821*

RFC 821 is a well-written document. It contains numerous examples, and should be easy for implementors to follow. *RFC 1123* mainly updates parts of SMTP to indicated current usage.

8.8.1.1 *MAIL and RCPT Commands*

The MAIL command is used to initiate a mail transaction, and specify the sender of the message. It is followed by one or more recipient (RCPT) commands, each of which specifies one recipient for the message. The names sent in both of these commands must be fully "canonicalized." This means that they are not nicknames, domain abbreviations, or CNAMEs; they either directly identify a host or are DNS mail exchange (MX) names.

   In the syntax section of the SMTP specification, the Mail command syntax is described as:

    MAIL <sp> FROM:<reverse-path> <CRLF>

neglecting to include the fact that <reverse-path> may be "<>" when sending notification messages, to ensure that if errors are found in the notification message, another notification message is not generated.

8.8.1.2 *Verifying and Expanding*

Two of the commands that SMTP provides are the Verify (VRFY) and Expand (EXPN) commands. The Verify command is used to verify a single mail address. The Expand command is used to get an expansion of a mailing list. Although *RFC 821* does not require either of these commands in a minimal implementation, they have become very useful to administrators for debugging mail delivery problems. Because of this, *RFC 1123* states that VRFY must be implemented, and that EXPN should be implemented.

   There has been concern that use of EXPN is a potential threat to privacy and security. Because of this, *RFC 1123* also states that an implementation may have a configuration option that allows VRFY and EXPN to be disabled. A robust implementation of this could also allow EXPN to be disabled on a per-mailing list basis.

RFC 1123 also defines a new reply code for the VRFY command:[37]

252   Cannot VRFY user (e.g., info is not local), but will take message for this user and attempt delivery.

8.8.1.3   SEND Commands

SMTP defines three commands that allow the data of a mail message to be delivered directly to a user's terminal. These are the SEND, Send Or Mail (SOML), and Send and Mail (SAML) commands. The SEND command requires that the mail data be delivered directly to the user's terminal. The SOML command allows the data to be delivered to the user's terminal, but if unable to (the user might not be logged in) it can deliver the message to the user's mailbox. The SAML command requires that the message be sent to both the terminal and mailbox. These commands are optional, and need not be implemented. If they are implemented, and they are received for a user to whose terminal the receiver-SMTP does not have write access (for example, when mail is being relayed through an MX record), the receiver-SMTP can return the reply "251 User Not Local" to the RCPT following a SEND.

8.8.1.4   HELO Command

The Hello (HELO) command is used at the beginning of a SMTP session to determine that the hosts are connected to whom they think they are. The HELO command takes one argument, the domain name of the client that is sending the HELO command. This value must be a valid principal host domain name so that the receiver-SMTP can validate the address without having to do DNS Mail Exchange address resolution. Since verifying the name against the IP address of the sender will require a DNS lookup, and may take considerable time, an implementation may choose not to do verification. If it chooses not to do verification, it must still verify that the name has a valid syntax, since the name is used in a Received: line. If it does do verification and the verification fails, however, the receiver - SMTP must not refuse to accept any messages. The fact that the verification failed can be inserted into the Received: line as described below.

8.8.1.5   Mail Relay

Three types of mail forwarding are identified in *RFC 1123*: a mail exchanger, a relay, and a gateway. Mail gateways pass messages between different environments; mail relays forward mail as the result of a source-routed mail message; and mail exchangers, or simple forwarders, use private information about the recipient to forward a mail message to the correct destination.

Unless a mailer is acting as a gateway, it should only add to the message header (for example, by adding a Received: line), and it should not alter any of the existing fields in the message header.

Source routes are now discouraged in the Internet environment. The DNS provides for global addressing, and MX records can handle most cases where source routing might be needed. Because of these architectural decisions, to discourage the use of source routes, a sender-SMTP should not use explicit source routes when sending a RCPT TO: command. All receiver-SMTPs must still be able to receive messages with explicit source routes, even if they don't support them. In this situation, the receiver-SMTP should try to deliver the message to the host specified by the rightmost @ sign, and should only return an error if that is unsuccessful. For example, assume a receiver-SMTP received a line like:

RCPT TO:<@hop1,@hop2:user@desthost>

If it did not support source routing, then rather than returning an error, it would attempt to deliver the message directly to *desthost*, using a RCPT line like:

RCPT TO:<user@desthost>

8.8.1.6   Recipient Command

Recipient (RCPT) commands may be verified as they are received, or they may be accepted and verified at a later time. If they are being verified as they are received, the responses to the Recipient commands must be sent within a reasonable time to keep the sender from timing out the connection (see below). Local names are usually quick to verify, and failing the Recipient command is preferred to accepting the message and then failing it, which wastes network bandwidth. Mailing lists can take a long time to verify, and thus are good candidates for deferred verification. Nonlocal names require a DNS lookup, and may also have their verification deferred. If they are verified immediately, and the DNS look-up returns a soft error, the address still must be accepted. All of implies that when the response "250 OK" is received after a Recipient command, there is no guarantee that the address specified is valid. Recipient errors found after the message is accepted will be reported back to the appropriate address with a notification message of the error. All receiver-SMTPs must support receiving messages sent to the reserved mailbox "postmaster."

8.8.1.7   DATA Command

RFC 821 states that "When the receiver-SMTP accepts a message either for relaying or for final delivery it inserts at the beginning of the mail data a timestamp line." This has to be interpreted to indicate that there are some situations when the timestamp line does not need to be added, which is wrong. Every receiver-SMTP must insert a timestamp line at the beginning of the message. A timestamp line is a Received: line. The syntax for the Received: line is:[38]

```
received =    "Received"  ":"           ; one per relay
              ["from" domain]           ; sending host
              ["by" domain]             ; receiving host
              ["via" atom]              ; physical path
        *     ("with" atom)             ; link/mail protocol
              ["id" msg-id]             ; receiver msg id
```

```
["for" addr-spec]          ; initial form
";" date-time              ; time received
```

A timestamp line indicates at least three items: the host that the message was received from ("from" domain), the host that received the message ("by" domain), and the date and time that the message was received (";" date–time). The "from" field should contain the name of the source from which the message was received, both as reported in the HELO command, and as a domain literal of the remote IP address of the connection. Including both of these can aid in the tracking of bogus or illicit mail. If multiple Recipient commands were received, this may be reflected in the "for" field by specifying a list of addr-specs. Though not required, *RFC 831* suggests that the "id" field may contain an @. The date–time field, as mentioned below, should contain a 4-digit representation of the year. All receiver SMTPs must make sure that they only insert Received: lines; that is, the Received: lines that were previously added to the message must not be modified.

8.8.1.8 SMTP Replies

SMTP replies, which are sent by the receiver SMTP in response to SMTP commands sent by the sender-SMTP, have a well-defined format. It is a 3-digit number, followed by a space and one line of text. A multiple line reply is generated by having each line start with the same 3-digit number, immediately followed by a hyphen (-) and the text. The last line of a multiple line reply is indicated by having the 3-digit code followed by a space, as in the 1-line reply message.

The first digit of the 3-digit reply code indicates the category of the reply code. It may be between 1 and 5. A 1 indicates that the command has been accepted, but the sender should wait for another reply before proceeding. A 2 indicates that the command has been successfully completed, and that a new request may be started. A 3 indicates that the command has been accepted, but another command is needed to continue the request. A 4 indicates that the command failed due to a temporary failure, and may succeed if retried at a later time (the receiver may have just run out of disk space). A 5 indicates that the command failed, and will probably not succeed if tried again at a later time (the mail may have been addressed to an unknown user).

The second digit of the reply code may be between 0 and 5. A 0 indicates something dealing with syntax, for example, "500 Syntax error, command unrecognized." A 1 indicates information, such as "211 System Status." A 2 indicates a reply that refers to the transmission channel, such as "220 <domain> Service Available." Both 3 and 4 are reserved. A 5 indicates something to do with the mail system, such as "250 Requested mail action okay, completed."

The third digit is used for an even finer-grained control. It is not generalized as the first and second digits are generalized.

Because the format of the reply messages is defined so well, it is easy for implementors to use define and reply codes that are not explicitly listed in *RFC 821*. This has led to interoperability problems, so receiver SMTPs should send only the reply codes that are explicitly listed in *RFC 821*, and should use the exact text shown in the examples in *RFC 821* whenever appropriate.

The sender-SMTP must use the 3-digit code only when making decisions about how to process reply messages, and should use only the first digit of the reply code whenever possible. The only exceptions are the 251 and 551 replies, whose texts contain information that the sender-SMTP may need:

> 251 User not local; will forward to <forward-path>

> 551 User not local; please try <forward-path>

In these instances, the exact text should be used, so that the sender-SMTP will be able to parse the text more easily.

8.8.1.9 Transparency

After the sender-SMTP sends a DATA command, all following lines, up to the end of text indicator, are the mail text. To indicate the end of mail text, a single period is sent (that is, the sequence <CRLF>.<CRLF>). To keep this from meaning that a mail message cannot contain a line with just a single period, provision is made for data transparency to allow any mail text. The sender-SMTP checks each line of mail text before sending it, and if it begins with a period, an additional period is inserted into the beginning of the line. When the receiver-SMTP receives a line that begins with a period that contains additional text, the leading period is deleted. If a line with a single period is received, the receiver-SMTP will know that it is the end of mail text indicator. To ensure message transparency, all implementations must add and delete periods to mail text in this manner.

8.8.1.10 WKS Use in MX Processing

Prior to the advent of DNS, the delivery of mail was fairly straightforward. When mail was addressed to a mailbox, an SMTP connection was opened to that machine and the mail was delivered. DNS allows mail to be delivered to a place other than the mailbox to which the message is addressed, through the use of MX records. The usage of MX records for mail routing is described[39] in *RFC 974*. One of the specific recommendations in *RFC 974* is that when processing MX records, a DNS Well-Known Service (WKS) query should be done to determine if the domain name listed in the MX record actually supports SMTP. Experience since then has shown that WKS records are not widely supported, and thus the WKS query should not be used in MX processing.

8.8.2 *RFC 822*

8.8.2.1 Message Specification

RFC 822, when specifying the syntax for the Return-path line, omits the ability to have a return path of "<>," which needs to be allowed to prevent error messages from generating further error messages if the original error message cannot be delivered. The correct syntax is:

```
return="Return-path""":"route-addr
        /"Return-path""":""<" ">"
```

RFC 1123 also adds another optional header field, the "Content-Type:" field. This new header field is described[40] in *RFC 1049*. It allows "mail reading systems to automatically identify the type of a structured message body and to process it for display accordingly." The syntax of this field is:

```
Content-Type    :=  type [";" ver-num [";" 1 # resources-ref]] [comment]
type            :=  "POSTSCRIPT" / "SCRIBE" / "SGML" / "TEX" / "TROFF" / "DVI" / "X-"atom
ver-num         :=  local-part
resources-ref   :=  local-part
```

The exact values for the "ver-num" and "resources-ref" fields depend on the value for "type," and are explained in *RFC 1049*.

Although not reflected in *RFC 1123*, *RFC 1341* more fully defines the Content-Type: field.

8.8.2.2 *Date and Time Specification*

The date specification in *RFC 822* only allowed for a 2-digit specification for the year. *RFC 1123* changes the syntax for the date to:

```
date = 1*2DIGIT month 2*4DIGIT
```

Though 2-digit year specifications are still legal, with the next century swiftly approaching, all mail software should be modified to use 4-digit year designations to ease the transition.

The time zone names specified in *RFC 822* list names for only the four main time zones in the US, and the military time zones are specified incorrectly. (The military time zones are specified with the signs reversed, and thus they contain no information in *RFC 822* headers.) Because the Internet is worldwide, there is a strong trend to use numeric time zone specifications, since they can be used to specify any time zone in the world. The definition of the time zone in *RFC 822* is listed twice; the definition in Appendix D is missing the last four lines of the definition; the main body of the document correctly defines time zones:[41]

```
zone  =           "UT"          /   "GMT"        ; Universal Time
                                    ; North American: UT
      /   "EST" /   "EDT"        ;    Eastern:      - 5/ - 4
      /   "CST" /   "CDT"        ;    Central:      - 6/ - 5
      /   "MST" /   "MDT"        ;    Mountain:     - 7/ - 6
      /   "PST" /   "PDT"        ;    Pacific:      - 8/ - 7
      /   1ALPHA                 ; Military: Z = UT;
```

```
        ;                   A:-1; (J not used)
        ;                   M:-12; N:+1; Y:+12
/ ( ( "+" / "-") 4DIGIT)  ; Local differential
        ;                   hours+min. (HHMM)
```

8.8.2.3   Mailbox Specification

According to the definition of "mailbox" in *RFC 822*, lines such as:

    From: <user@anymachine.anyplace>

are not valid, and would have to be of the form:

    From: some_phrase <user@anymachine.anyplace>

RFC 1123 changes the definition of "mailbox" to:[42]

```
mailbox  = addr-spec            ; simple address
         / [phrase] route-addr  ; name & addr-spec
```

which makes "phrase" optional, and legalizes addresses like that in the first example.

8.8.2.4   Local-Part

The addr-spec part of a mailbox is defined as:[43]

```
addr-spec = local-part "@" domain  ; global address
local-part = word *("." word)      ; uninterpreted
                                   ; case-preserved
```

As indicated, the local-part is uninterpreted, and case is preserved. To ensure this, when a message is being forwarded by a host that is not the destination host, the local-part of the address must be left exactly as received, with no interpretation.

The local-part may contain embedded routing information to gateway Internet mail to a foreign mail environment, which will be interpreted appropriately at the gateway into the foreign mail environment. A common routing operator is *!*, used as a left-binding routing operator in some foreign mail systems. The *%-hack* is a commonly known method of doing routing information, using the *%* as a right-binding routing operator. An address like *user%domain%relay2@relay1* is used to get a message to *relay1*, where the local-part, *user%domain%relay2*, is interpreted as *user%domain@relay2*. The message then goes to *relay2*, where the new local-part, *user%domain*, now becomes *user@domain*, and the message is delivered to *domain* for delivery to *user*. When the % operator is used in conjunction with other routing operators, it should have lowest precedence, hence an address like *host!user%relay* would be interpreted as *(host!user)%relay*.

8.8.2.5 Domain Literals

Though discouraged, an Internet-specific domain literal, which is an address specified in decimal dotted notation, must be recognized by all mailers. Even more important, hosts must recognize any domain literals that specify any of their own IP addresses so that mail can be delivered. Domain literals are defined as:[44]

```
domain-literal    ="[" *(dtext / quoted-pair) "]"
dtext             =<any CHAR excluding "["      ; -> may be folded
                    "]," "\" & CR, & including linear-white-space>
quoted-pair       =  "\" CHAR                   ; may quote any char
                                                ; (Octal,   Decimal.)
CHAR              =<any ASCII character>        ; (0-177,    0.-127.)
CR                =<ASCII CR, carriage return>  ; (15,           13.)
```

This definition is very broad; an Internet-specific domain literal refers to an address which is within the Internet; it is restricted to an IP address specified in dotted decimal notation:

```
                                          ; (Octal,Decimal.)
DIGIT                  =<any ASCII decimal digit>   ; (60- 71,48.- 57.)
internet-domain-literal = "[" 1*3DIGIT "." 1*3DIGIT  ; example: [10.0.120.4]
                          "." 1*3DIGIT "." 1*3DIGIT "]"
```

8.8.2.6 Common Address Formatting Errors

All implementations are required to accept all valid 822 address formats, and to generate only valid 822 addresses. Unfortunately, it is common for implementations to incur errors in generating or parsing 822 headers. These are some of the more common addressing errors, listed in *RFC 1123*. A group address is defined as:

```
group = phrase ":" [#mailbox] ";"
```

and a common error is to forget the trailing semicolon.

Failing to use fully qualified domain names at the right-hand side of an @ sign in header address fields is another common mistake. An example cited in *RFC 1183* is that if the From: address field is not fully qualified, then a "reply" may not be able to automatically construct the correct return address, especially if the message has crossed domain boundaries. Although *RFC 822* does allow addresses to be abbreviated within a single subdomain, this cannot be supported in the Internet mail environment, due to the requirement that header fields be passed without alteration.

Messages can be explicitly source routed by specifying the path to the mailbox, such as:

```
@hop1,@hop2,@hop3:user@final_destination
```

Some hosts do not properly parse explicit source routes. Elements of explicit source routes are removed from the left-hand side at hop1, hop2, and hop3, so that when the message is delivered from hop3 to final_destination, the address is just "user@final_destination."

Trailing dots on domain names in message addresses or ids is a violation of *RFC 822*. Some systems erroneously add trailing dots, which overqualifies the domain name.

8.8.2.7 *Explicit Source Routes*

Even though they are legal, explicit source routes, as described above, are strongly discouraged. They should not be generated, but they must be accepted for compatibility with earlier systems. Some of the reasons for discouraging explicit source routes were described above in the section on Mail Relay.

8.8.3   SMTP Queueing Strategies

Most SMTP implementations have mailboxes for incoming mail, queueing areas for outgoing mail, and daemon processes for receiving mail and retransmitting mail that is queued up for delivery. There are several optimizations that can be used when sending and receiving mail. A note for queueing strategies in general is that they need to have timeouts for all activities, and an implementation must never send error messages in response to error messages.

8.8.3.1   *Sending Strategy*

When a mail message is composed and sent, many typical sender SMTP implementations attempt to immediately deliver it. If this is unsuccessful, the message is queued up for later delivery by a process that attempts periodic retransmits of the queued-up mail. The mail queue must include not only the mail message, but the envelope information.

When there has been an error in attempting to deliver a mail message, an attempt to resend the message should be delayed by at least 30 minutes, in the absence of more sophisticated and accurate determinations for the nondelivery. It is usually good to try to retransmit the message a couple of times in the first hour, and then back off to 2 or 3 hours between attempts. This should continue for at least 4 or 5 days before giving up on delivering the message, or until it is successfully delivered.

The sender SMTP should keep a list of the hosts that it has been unable to reach. This list should detail when the last attempt was made, and provide a pointer to a list of messages that are destined for that host. When a retransmission is attempted, it need only be done for the first message queued up for that host. If the retransmission fails, there is no need to try sending the other messages. Whenever a message is received from a host for which there are queued-up messages, that is a good indication that the queued-up messages can probably be successfully sent, shortening the queueing delay.

If a message is destined for several users on the same remote host, the sender SMTP should make use of multiple RCPT commands to allow a single copy of the message to be sent, and let the receiver SMTP take care of making copies of the message for each recipient.

8.8.3.2 Receiving Strategy

A receiver SMTP should always keep a list pending for the SMTP port, which implies that the receiver SMTP will need to be able to handle multiple TCP connections at the same time. Though it is not encouraged, a receiver SMTP may place a limit on the number of simultaneous TCP connections that can be maintained.

8.8.4 Timeouts in SMTP

When an SMTP connection is established, there should be timers to determine when the other side of the connection has stopped responding. Two ways to implement the timers would be to either place a timer on each command that is sent, or have a timer that covers the entire transmission of one mail message. Because different commands can have different characteristics, based on how quickly they can be responded to, having one timer per mail message would require that the timer be very large to cover lots of possible conditions, such as very large messages or large mailing lists that require a large amount of time to expand. *RFC 1123* recommends that implementations take the former approach, that of applying separate timers for each command and each buffer of data that is sent. Experience with busy mail-relay hosts has provided much practice in determining appropriate minimum timeout values for sending commands and data blocks. The following list of recommended minimum timeout values is taken from *RFC 1123*:[45]

- Initial 220 Message: 5 minutes
  A sender-SMTP process needs to distinguish between a failed TCP connection and a delay in receiving the initial 220 greeting message. Many receiver-SMTPs will accept a TCP connection but delay delivery of the 220 message until their system load will permit more mail to be processed.

- MAIL Commands: 5 minutes

- RCPT Command: 5: minutes
  A longer timeout would be required if processing of mailing lists and aliases were not deferred until after the message was accepted.

- DATA Initiation: 2 minutes
  This is while awaiting the "354 Start Input" reply to a DATA command.

- Data Block: 3 minutes
  This is while awaiting the completion of each TCP SEND call transmitting a chunk of data.

- DATA Termination: 10 minutes.

    This is while awaiting the "250 OK" reply. When the receiver gets the final period terminating the message data, it typically performs processing to deliver the message to a user mailbox. A spurious timeout at this point would be very wasteful, since the message has been successfully sent.

    A receiver-SMTP SHOULD have a timeout of at least 5 minutes while it is awaiting the next command from the sender.

8.8.5 Reliable Mail Receipt

To maintain a reliable mail system, when a receiver-SMTP receives a 250 OK message in response to its DATA command, it must have some confidence that the receiver-SMTP will reliably deliver or forward the mail message. The receiver-SMTP must do its best to ensure that the mail message will not be lost. System crashes and running out of resources are not valid reasons for losing mail messages.

There are times when a mail message is accepted, and later it is determined that the message cannot be delivered for various reasons, for example, errors in mailing lists or "soft" domain system errors. When this happens, a mail notification message must be sent back to the originator, and the notification message must have a null reverse path (<>). The only exception to this rule is if the return address in the undeliverable message is also the null reverse path; in this case, the notification message must not be sent. When determining the address to which to send the notification message, explicit source routes should be simplified down to the final hop (e.g., if the mail arrived with a return address like *<@a,@b:user@d>*, the address for the notification message would be just *<user@d>*).

8.8.6 Reliable Mail Transmission

When transmitting a message, the sender-SMTP has to first translate the destination address into an IP address. This may fail due to soft errors, such as transient problems with the DNS. The sender-SMTP must queue the message for later delivery if it cannot resolve the destination address due to soft errors. Once the address is resolved, the sender SMTP may discover that rather than a single IP address, it has multiple IP addresses. This can happen when either there are multiple MX records in the DNS for the destination, or if the destination is a multihomed host. The sender-SMTP must be able to try (and retry) sending to each of these addresses until the message is delivered. The sender-SMTP may have a configurable limit on how many alternate addresses it is willing to try, but it should always try at least two addresses.

When multiple addresses are returned due to multiple MX records, each MX record will have a preference indication that can be used to sort the MX records, and hence IP addresses, in order of preference. After sorting the MX records, if multiple addresses are returned for a single MX record, due to the destination being multihomed, then the DNS should already have sorted the addresses in order of preference, and the sender-SMTP must not reorder those addresses.

8.8.7 Domain Name Support

The DNS is now an integral part of the Internet. All SMTP implementations must contain support for the DNS; specifically they must support MX records and the use of the DNS to translate host names into IP addresses. For more information, see the following section on the DNS.

8.8.8 Mailing Lists and Aliases

Aliases and mailing lists are important features that SMTP implementations should support. When everything is working properly, mailing lists and aliases provide the same functionality; they are pseudo-mailbox addresses that contain a list of destination addresses. When a message arrives destined for the pseudo-mailbox address, for each destination address in the list, the message is duplicated, the pseudo-mailbox address is replaced with the destination address, and the message is then sent on to the destination address. A mailing list differs from an alias in only one additional aspect; along with replacing the destination address in the envelope, the return address in the envelope is also replaced, but with the mailbox of the list maintainer. This difference is apparent when there is an error in the delivery of the message to one of the destination addresses in the list. With an alias, the notification message gets returned to the originator of the message; with a mail list the notification message is sent to the list maintainer.

8.8.9 Mail Gatewaying

Mail gatewaying is the term used to describe the process by which mail messages are relayed between different mail environments. The rules for doing mail gatewaying can become complex, and are very dependent on the mail environments through which the mail is being forwarded. *RFC 1123* describes six general rules that can be used when gatewaying mail between the Internet and other mail environments:

1   Header fields may be rewritten as necessary when crossing mail environment boundaries.

2   A new Received: line must be added when gatewaying in or out of the Internet environment, and any existing Received: lines must not be modified.

3   From the Internet side of the gateway, all valid address formats and all valid *RFC 822* messages should be accepted.

4   When forwarding a message into the Internet, the gateway must ensure that all header fields conform to the requirements for Internet mail. In particular, fields with addresses must satisfy *RFC 822* syntax.

5   When forwarding a message out from the Internet, the gateway should try to ensure
     that if an error message is generated in the foreign mail environment, it will be sent to
     the return path listed in the envelope information, not to the sender listed in the From:
     field of the message header.

6   Likewise, when forwarding a message into the Internet, if the incoming message has a
     distinct error message return address, that address should be put into the envelope
     return path so that any errors will be sent to the correct error address.

8.8.10 Maximum Message Size

SMTP does not impose a maximum message size. However, many SMTP implementations
impose limits on how large mail messages may be. For implementations that impose a
maximum message size, that value must be at least 64 Kbytes in length (including the message headers). Note that electronic mail is often used for purposes other than just sending
mail. Often entire documents or ASCII files are sent via electronic mail, and in these
instances a 64-Kbyte maximum message size may be much too small, as these mail messages often become 1 Mbyte or even larger.

8.9   DOMAIN NAME SYSTEM

8.9.1 Overview and Motivation

People do not like to refer to their computers as numbers. They prefer to give them names
that are easier to remember, or according to some standard scheme for a group of
machines. But IP addresses are 32-bit numbers. To support giving machines both names
and IP addresses, there needs to be some way to do a mapping between the two. A straightforward implementation was to use a file that contained a list of IP addresses,[46] with a
unique name for each address in the list, and library routines for looking up information in
the file. Applications could then use these routines to do name-to-address conversions.
This type of mechanism for handling name-to-address and address-to-name mappings
worked well when the Internet was small, even when it got up to several hundred
machines. However, the Internet was growing fast, and trying to keep copies of the name-
to-address translations up to date on every machine was quickly becoming a losing battle.
The master database was constantly changing, and local network administrators wanted to
take control and responsibility for updating the tables for their own machines.

   Out of the need to deal with this expanding database there arose several ideas. What
eventually evolved is now referred to as the Domain Name System, or DNS. *RFC 1123*
requires all hosts to implement a resolver for the DNS, and a mechanism using the DNS
resolver to convert host names to IP addresses and vice versa. An overview of the DNS is
best given by the following design goals, as stated in *RFC 1034*:[47]

- The primary goal is a consistent name space which will be used for referencing to resources. In order to avoid the problems caused by ad hoc encodings, names should not be required to contain network identifiers, addresses, routes, or similar information as part of the name.

- The sheer size of the database and frequency of updates suggest that it must be maintained in a distributed manner, with local caching to improve performance. Approaches that attempt to collect a consistent copy of the entire database will become more and more expensive and difficult, and hence should be avoided. The same principle holds for the structure of the name space, and in particular mechanisms for creating and deleting names; these should also be distributed.

- Where there (*sic*) tradeoffs between the cost of acquiring data, the speed of updates, and the accuracy of caches, the source of the data should control the tradeoff.

- The costs of implementing such a facility dictate that it be generally useful, and not restricted to a single application. We should be able to use names to retrieve host addresses, mailbox data, and other as yet undetermined information. All data associated with a name is tagged with a type, and queries can be limited to a single type.

- Because we want the name space to be useful in dissimilar networks and applications, we provide the ability to use the same name space with different protocol families or management. For example, host address formats differ between protocols, though all protocols have the notion of address. The DNS tags all data with a class as well as the type, so that we can allow parallel use of different formats for data of type address.

- We want name server transactions to be independent of the communications system that carries them. Some systems may wish to use datagrams for queries and responses, and only establish virtual circuits for transactions that need the reliability (e.g., database updates, long transactions); other systems will use virtual circuits exclusively.

- The system should be useful across a wide spectrum of host capabilities. Both personal computers and large time-shared hosts should be able to use the system, though perhaps in different ways.

8.9.2   Zero TTL

When a Resource Record is received with a Time-To-Live (TTL) value of 0, it must still be accepted and used to satisfy the current transaction, after which it should be discarded (e.g., not placed into the cache). This is very useful when the data contained in the Resource Record is constantly changing. For example, if a host has several interfaces, each with its own IP address, and it desires to distribute the incoming connections across the interfaces, the local name server could satisfy each query for a hostname-to-IP address translation by cycling through the list of interfaces. In this case, you would want each query to be used once and then discarded, so that each additional query would come back to the local name server. Using a zero TTL value accomplishes this.

8.9.3   Query Class Types

The DNS supports an arbitrary number of class types. While it is possible to specify the "QCLASS=* to indicate multiple classes, this should not be used unless the requestor really wants information for more than one class. If information from only one class is desired, then the QCLASS value should indicate the explicit class; e.g., QCLASS=IN is used to specify Internet datatypes.

8.9.4   Unused Fields

In both queries and responses, fields that are unused must be filled in with 0s. The place where the information is going may wish to look at the unused fields, and may do strange things if arbitrary data is put into them.

8.9.5   Message Compression

The DNS allows for message compression by providing a mechanism for eliminating duplication of domain names in the message by using pointers.[48] Rather than adding a complete domain name every time one occurs in the message, a pointer can be used to reference a domain name that has already been used. The pointer does not have to, but may point to the beginning of another domain name, or it can point to a trailing segment of another domain name. For example, if *foo.corp.com* is already listed, then *bar.corp.com* can be listed by specifying the first component, *bar*, followed by a pointer to the *corp.com* segment of *foo.corp.com*. Although *RFC 1035* says that programs need to be able to understand pointers only in incoming messages, *RFC 1123* requires that servers use compression in responses to avoid overflowing UDP datagrams.

8.9.6   Local Configuration Information

Local configuration information is just that, local information. Recursive and full-service name servers will usually have a local configuration file that can contain information like the location of other name servers. There is no guarantee that this information is accurate, so it must not be included in any responses that are sent out. In the past, serious problems have occurred in the Internet when servers have sent out their local configuration information, and the information was obsolete or just plain wrong.

8.9.7   Full Service and Stub Resolvers

Though a host may implement a resolver however it chooses (as long as it conforms to the specifications of the protocols), two different models are suggested in *RFC 1123*: the Full-Service Resolver and the Stub Resolver.

A full implementation of the resolver service is referred to as a Full-Service Resolver. It must be able to deal with and recover from errors, e.g., communication problems or failing name servers. A Full-Service Resolver must also implement a cache, so that successive requests for the same information can be satisfied out of the local cache. Of course, since there is a TTL value associated with each resource record, the cache keeps track of, and flushes, any Resource Record in which the TTL value has expired.

A Full-Service Resolver should also have local configuration information that identifies several of the root name servers and several local name servers. This information will allow the resolver to have good connectivity, and access to the entire name space. If there should happen to be communication failures, the hope is that having information about several root servers will allow the resolver to continue to get information. If the resolver is cut off from all the root servers, having the location of several local name servers will allow it to continue to resolve local information.

A Stub Resolver is one that contains just enough information to allow it to talk to a nearby recursive name server. In this case, much (but not all) of the burden of implementing a Full-Service Resolver is avoided. At a minimum, a Stub Resolver must be able to send requests to multiple recursive name servers in case some of them are not responding. A Stub Resolver is useful on less capable hosts, e.g., PCs. It also has the advantage that if there are several Stub Resolvers going through the same name server, that name server will be building up a richer cache of information, reducing the number of queries that need to be sent outside the local network. This is not to say that a Stub Resolver cannot implement a local cache. However, if it does choose to have a local cache, it must timeout the cached information, just like a Full-Service Resolver.

8.9.8 Transport Protocols

The DNS may use either UDP or TCP; both transport protocols use the well-known port number of 53. The trade-offs between the two transports are that the overhead associated with using UDP is lower than using TCP, but TCP provides more reliability than UDP and can handle larger amounts of data. Resolvers and servers must support UDP for DNS transactions, and should also support TCP.

All queries (except Zone Transfer queries) should first be sent via UDP. If the response comes back truncated, the query should then be retried using TCP. If it is not retried using TCP, then care must be taken to ensure that the truncated response is not cached for later use in a way that loses the fact that the response was truncated.

There are several instances when TCP may be preferred over UDP. Zone Transfer queries and responses require reliability, and must use TCP. A resolver and server may choose, by private agreement, to use TCP for all transactions between them. A program, knowing that it will be making several name server queries, may also choose to inform the resolver that it would prefer to use TCP when talking to the name server. Servers that support the use of TCP as a transport must ensure that they are able to continue to process incoming UDP queries while TCP connections are being serviced.

8.9.9   Broadcast and Multicast Queries

Sending a DNS query via UDP with an IP broadcast or multicast address may be used as a mechanism for determining where the local name servers are located. When the responses are received, the IP addresses should be cached so that later DNS queries can be sent directly to the name servers using their unicast addresses. Servers are not required to, but may choose to support queries that arrive with an IP broadcast or multicast address. There is a danger in responding to queries received via an IP broadcast or multicast address. If the Recursion Desired bit is set in the query and it is received by several name servers, and they all go off and try to resolve the request, it will wind up creating an unnecessary load on both the networks and the servers. To avoid this problem, the Recursion Desired bit must not be set in queries sent to an IP broadcast or multicast address, and if a server receives a query with a destination IP broadcast or multicast address, it must ignore the Recursion Desired bit if it is set.

8.9.10   Resource Usage

Because the use of the DNS is so vital to the Internet today, *RFC 1123* lists several rules for servers and resolvers to keep DNS, as a whole, healthy. These rules, taken from *RFC 1123*, are as follows:[49]

1   The Resolver MUST implement retransmission controls to insure that it does not waste communication bandwidth, and MUST impose finite bounds on the resources consumed to respond to a single request. See *RFC 1035*, pages 43-44 for specific recommendations.

2   After a query has been retransmitted several times without a response, an implementation MUST give up and return a soft error to the application.

3   All DNS name servers and resolvers SHOULD cache temporary failures, with a timeout period of the order of minutes.

   DISCUSSION:

   This will prevent applications that immediately retry soft failures (in violation of Section 2.2 of this document) from generating excessive DNS traffic.

4   All DNS name servers and resolvers SHOULD cache negative responses that indicate the specified name, or data of the specified type, does not exist, as described in *RFC 1035*.

5   When a DNS server or resolver retries a UDP query, the retry interval SHOULD be constrained by an exponential backoff algorithm, and SHOULD also have upper and lower bounds.

IMPLEMENTATION:

A measured RTT and variance (if available) should be used to calculate an initial retransmission interval. If this information is not available, a default of no less than 5 seconds should be used. Implementations may limit the retransmission interval, but this limit must exceed twice the Internet maximum segment lifetime plus service delay at the name server.

6   When a resolver or server receives a Source Quench for a query it has issued, it SHOULD take steps to reduce the rate of querying that server in the near future. A server MAY ignore a Source Quench that it receives as the result of sending a response datagram.

IMPLEMENTATION:

One recommended action to reduce the rate is to send the next query attempt to an alternate server, if there is one available. Another is to backoff the retry interval for the same server.

8.9.11   Multihomed Hosts

Multihomed hosts are hosts that have more than one IP address. The DNS allows all of these addresses to be returned in a single response to a name-to-address query. In this situation the question arises, "Should any significance be placed on the order of the addresses in the response?" The answer is that the addresses should be ranked according to preference. This preference may be based on various items, such as the network numbers of the directly connected networks, knowledge of performance or reliability characteristics, or even just administrative requirements. Because of this, there is no general algorithm for the DNS to use to sort a list of addresses.

One method that has been successful for sorting an address list is to have a list of preferred network numbers in order of preference in the DNS configuration data. The address list would then be sorted in the same order as this preference list, with addresses not listed in the preference list put at the end of the address list.

8.9.12   Extensibility

All of the well-known, class-independent formats must be supported by DNS software. However, because the DNS was designed to be extensible, the software should be written in such a way that as new well-known formats are defined and old ones are made obsolete, the new formats can be added or deleted with a minimal amount of impact, and that non-standard types can be added for local experimentation. The only limitations on new data types would be message compression, and translation between the internal Resource Record format and the external printable format.

Compression is a concern because it requires knowledge of the Resource Record data format. Using compression on non-well-known or class-dependent formats may not work, because the receiver of the query or reply does not understand that format. This implies that compression can be used only on well-known, class-independent formats.

The internal format for storing information must allow for the fact that resource records may be received (via a Zone Transfer) that are not understood, and hence cannot be translated into an external, printable format. This implies that the internal format for storing information cannot be textual.

8.10   SUMMARY

As you can see, *RFC 1122* and *RFC 1123* contain a wealth of information about the major protocols used in the Internet. If you have been reading this chapter just to get some idea of what is contained in these documents, the author hopes you have found it useful and did not have to go off to the *RFC* documents to understand most of the information. If you are an implementor, remember that while the information contained here should be accurate, the *RFC* documents are the official standards. If there is a discrepancy between this chapter and information contained in the *RFC* documents, the latter take precedence.

One may wonder if *RFC 1122* and *RFC 1123* will be the final word on *Host Requirements*. The answer to that is a resounding "No!" At some point in the next several years, a new IETF working group will probably be started to update *RFC 1122* and *RFC 1123*. There were several topics that the first working group did not come to consensus on, and either omitted or came to some sort of compromise on, and there were other topics that did not have enough experience at the time for something authoritative to be said.[50] As the Internet grows, and as new technology is developed, the requirements on a host, and possibly even the definition of what is a host, will be changing. As in the past, protocols will continue to be enhanced and improved to meet the changing needs of the world. What is a research topic today may become a requirement in a future revision of the *Host Requirements* documents.

REFERENCES

1   R. Braden, Ed., *Requirements for Internet Hosts—Communications Layer, RFC 1122*, Internet Engineering Task Force, October 1989.

2   R. Braden, Ed., *Requirements for Internet Hosts—Application and Support, RFC 1123*, Internet Engineering Task Force, October 1989.

3   J. Postel, *Internet Protocol, RFC 791*, Information Sciences Institute, September 1981.

4   J. Postel, *Internet Control Message Protocol, RFC 792*, Information Sciences Institute, September 1981.

5   J. Postel, *User Datagram Protocol, RFC 768*, Information Sciences Institute, August 28, 1980.

6   J. Postel, *Transmission Control Protocol, RFC 793*, Information Sciences Institute, September 1981.

7   J. Postel and J. Reynolds, *Telnet Protocol Specification, RFC 854*, Information Sciences Institute, May 1983.

8   J. Postel and J. Reynolds, *File Transfer Protocol (FTP), RFC 959*, Information Sciences Institute, October 1985.

9   K. Sollins, *The TFTP Protocol Revision 2, RFC 783*, MIT, June 1981.

10 J. Postel, *Simple Mail Transfer Protocol, RFC 821*, Information Sciences Institute, August 1982.

11 P. Mockapetris, *Domain Names—Concepts and Facilities, RFC 1034*, Information Sciences Institute, November 1987; and P. Mockapetris, *Domain Names—Implementation and Specification, RFC 1035*, Information Sciences Institute, November 1987.

12 D. Clark, *IP Datagram Reassembly Algorithms, RFC 815*, MIT Laboratory for Computer Science, July 1982.

13 P. Almquist, *Type-Of-Service in the Internet Protocol Suite, RFC 1349*, Consultant, July 1992.

14 J. Mogul and S. Deering, *Path MTU Discovery, RFC 1191*, Digital Equipment Corporation Western Research Laboratory, November 1990.

15 R. Braden and J. Postel, *Requirements for Internet Gateways, RFC 1009*, Information Sciences Institute, June 1987.

16 R. Finlayson, T. Mann, J. Mogul, and M. Theimer, *A Reverse Address Resolution Protocol, RFC 903*, Stanford University, June 1984; and B. Croft and J. Gilmore, *BOOTP—UDP Bootstrap Protocol, RFC 951*, Stanford University, August 1985.

17 J. Mogul and J. Postel, *Internet Standard Subnetting Procedure, RFC 950*, Stanford, August 1985.

18   J. Postel, *The TCP Maximum Segment Size and Related Topics, RFC 879*, Information Sciences Institute, November 1983.

19   V. Jacobson, R. Braden, and D. Borman, *TCP Extensions for High Performance, RFC 1323*, Lawrence Berkeley Laboratory, May 1992.

20   A. Nicholson et al., High Speed Networking at Cray Research, *ACM Computer Communications Review*, Vol. 21, No. 1, January 1991.

21   R. Braden, D. Borman, and C. Partridge, *Computing the Internet Checksum, RFC 1071*, Information Sciences Institute, September 1988.

22   V. Jacobson, *Congestion Avoidance and Control, ACM Computer Communications Review*, Vol. 18, No. 4, August 1988.

23   J. Postel, *Telnet End Of Record Option, RFC 885*, Information Sciences Institute, December 1983.

24   D. Borman, *Telnet Linemode Option, RFC 1184*, Cray Research, Inc., October 1990.

25   J. Reynolds and J. Postel, *Assigned Numbers, RFC 1340*, Information Sciences Institute, July 1992.

26   M. Solomon and E. Wimmers, *Telnet Terminal Type Option, RFC 930*, University of Wisconsin–Madison, January 1985.

27   J. VanBokkelen, *Telnet Terminal-Type Option, RFC 1091*, FTP Software, Inc., February 1989.

28   D. Borman, *Telnet Linemode Option, RFC 1116*, Cray Research, Inc., August 1989.

29   *RFC 1122*, pp. 21–23.

30   J. Postel and J. Reynolds, *Telnet Binary Transmission, RFC 855*, Information Sciences Institute, May 1983.

31   *RFC 959*, p.14; and *Communications of the ACM*, Vol. 7, No. 10, p. 606, October 1964.

32   *RFC 1123*, pp. 32–33.

33   *Ibid.*, pp. 34–35.

34   *Ibid.*, pp. 36–37.

35   *Ibid.*, p. 37.

36 D. Crocker, *Standard for the Format of ARPA Internet Text Messages*, *RFC 822*, Deptartment of Electrical Engineering, University of Delaware, August 13, 1982.

37 *RFC 1123*, p. 50.

38 *RFC 822*, pp. 17–18.

39 C. Partridge, *Mail Routing and the Domain System, RFC 974*, CSNET CIC BBN Laboratories Inc., January 1986.

40 M. Sirbu, *A Content-Type Header Field for Internet Messages, RFC 1049*, CMU, March 1988.

41 *RFC 822*, p.26.

42 *RFC 1123*, p. 56.

43 *RFC 822*, p. 27.

44 *RFC 822*, pp. 10–11.

45 *RFC 1123*, pp. 62–63.

46 K. Harrenstien, M. Stahl, and E. Feinler, *DOD Internet Host Table Specification,*, *RFC 952*, SRI International, October 1985; and K. Harrenstien, M. Stahl, and E. Feinler, *Hostname Server, RFC 953*, SRI International, October 1985.

47 *RFC 1034*, pp.2–3.

48 *RFC 1035*, p. 30.

49 *RFC 1123*, pp. 77–78.

50 R. Braden, *A Perspective on the Host Requirements RFCs, RFC 1127*, Information Sciences Institute, October 1989.

CHAPTER 9

Architectural Security

STEPHEN KENT

CONTENTS

369

As the new communities enter the Internet, new issues of security arise. When the core Internet technology was developed, network security was a largely undeveloped topic. Today, there are well-known principles of how networking technology should be designed with an eye towards security. For now, we begin with an introduction to the field and then see how the concepts introduced can be "retrofitted" into the existing architecture.

9.1   WHAT IS A NETWORK SECURITY ARCHITECTURE?

The term *network security architecture* is one which evokes varied connotations in the minds of different, knowledgeable individuals. At one end of the spectrum, a security architecture might consist primarily of concept and terminology definitions and fairly abstract guidance for protocol designers. The OSI security architecture, *ISO 7498-2*,[1] is of this flavor. Much of that standard is devoted to a tutorial on security, defining security services and mechanisms, and discussing generic threats in an open systems network environment.

Only a small portion of the document provides a framework to evaluate proposed security facilities in OSI protocols. The essence of the framework is captured in two tables and an accompanying (nonnormative) annex. One table provides guidance as to which security mechanisms can be utilized to provide particular security services. The second (and more controversial) table specifies which security services might be offered by protocols at each of the seven layers in the reference model. Nonetheless, considering the context in which *ISO 7498-2* exists, i.e., the companion documents specifying the OSI reference model and the management framework, *ISO 7498-2* is at an appropriately abstract level of architectural specification.

Many have expressed the view that an Internet security architecture should provide a more concrete set of guidelines for network designers and product developers, not just protocol designers. This suggests that an Internet security architecture should encompass not only the sort of concept definitions provided in *ISO 7498-2* and the tables contained therein, but also should provide more specific guidance about where to implement security services within the Internet protocol suite. (Annex B of *ISO 7498-2* presents the rationale used to guide the choices of which services are offered at given layers, but the resulting service-layer table is fairly nonrestrictive.) This view is in keeping with an Internet philosophy that emphasizes system interoperability, e.g., by producing standards that tend to be less generic than their OSI counterparts.

In the OSI (and CCITT) arena, the base standards typically are sufficiently generic to preclude the development of interoperable products by independent implementors based solely on these standards. This leads to "profiles" that fill in details, place restrictions on the size of data items, etc., so that independent, interoperable implementations are feasible. In the Internet environment, standards are typically more specific and thus usually do not require the addition of profiles. There is also a tendency in the Internet to develop standards for contexts that ISO might deem "local matters," to allow users greater "mix-and-match" flexibility in selecting equipment from vendors, e.g., the OSPF standard.[2] Given this orientation of Internet standards, an Internet security architecture should probably be less generic and more restrictive than its OSI counterpart.

For example, it might be argued that an Internet security architecture ought not to offer multiple approaches to providing a secure version of a common application, such as Telnet, since the result might be incompatible implementations of "secure" versions of Telnet. A network application, such as e-mail, that is ubiquitous in its connectivity, would be even less well served by an architecture that embraced multiple security solutions. Yet even architecturally specific security approaches for such applications tend to allow options in choices of algorithms, to preserve flexibility. Thus a security architecture must achieve a balance, permitting sufficient flexibility to accommodate constructs not envisioned by its authors while providing sufficient guidance to minimize the divergence that leads to incompatibility.

Unfortunately, at the time this book is being written, the Internet does not have a well-articulated security architecture of any form. This chapter does not remedy that situation, but it does attempt to make some progress. This chapter examines the OSI security architecture in detail because much of what has been defined therein is directly relevant to the Internet, and thus it provides a reasonable foundation for an Internet security architecture. The chapter also examines an internetwork security architecture that has existed, but which has not been well-articulated, for over a decade. That architecture derives from the US Department of Defense (DOD) roots of the TCP/IP protocol suite, and the focus of the architecture is on security properties that are compatible with the DOD view of computer security, e.g., as articulated in the *Trusted Computer System Evaluation Criteria* (TCSEC).[3]

Some aspects of this DOD Internet security architecture are sufficiently influenced by the DOD perspective on security so as to be generally inappropriate for today's Internet. Nonetheless, many of the precepts that underlie this architecture are more broadly applicable. Thus examining this architecture, in addition to the ISO security architecture, is a worthwhile step in developing a more broadly based Internet security architecture.

This chapter will also explore the factors that influence the development of a security architecture for the Internet of today, and tomorrow. Work is currently underway in the Privacy and Security Research Group (PSRG) of the Internet Research Task Force (IRTF) on the development of such an architecture, and the preliminary direction of that work is reflected in this chapter.

9.2 SECURITY SERVICES AND MECHANISMS: OSI AND BEYOND

ISO 7492-2 defines the security architecture for the OSI model, complementing the basic reference model defined in *ISO 7498-1*. This document is an excellent starting point for an

Internet security architecture. Layers 1–4 of the OSI reference model correspond directly to protocols used with the TCP/IP suite. The two protocol suites diverge in that the TCP/IP suite allocates to applications the communications services corresponding to layers 5–7 in the OSI suite. However, layer 5 has no security services associated with it, according to *ISO 7498-2*. The discussion of security services provided at the Presentation and Application Layers is easily related to TCP/IP applications. Thus the discussion of security services throughout this section, using OSI layer terminology, is entirely relevant to the TCP/IP suite.

The ISO security architecture addresses five major elements: definitions of security services, definitions of security mechanisms, principles of security service layering, a mapping of security services to layers, and a mapping of mechanisms to services. As noted above, a small but important portion of the standard is devoted to a discussion of the principles that underlie the decisions of which services are offered at each layer. There are other aspects to this standard, e.g., definitions of types of attacks, but these are more tutorial, than central to the architecture. Three annexes provide additional, informative background information on the architecture, further motivating the decisions expressed in the standard.

Security services are (abstract) concepts that can be employed to characterize security requirements. They differ from security mechanisms, which are concrete measures for implementing security services. The critical architectural element of this standard is the statement of which security services ought to be provided at each layer in the reference model. This statement is a guide to protocol designers, not to protocol implementors, nor to network designers.

One of the best known parts of *ISO 7498-2* is the table that maps security services to reference model layers. A table of this sort must be derived from a set of underlying principles. Prior to discussing security services and layering, it is appropriate to review these principles. In *ISO 7498-2*, seven security layering principles are described, which are paraphrased below:[*]

1 The number of alternative means of achieving a security service should be minimized. This is a sound principle that discourages diversity just for diversity's sake. The development and implementation of security technology is a complex task, and this principle argues for minimizing the number of times this task must be carried out. However, many would argue that the OSI security architecture does not adhere closely to this dictum; i.e., the architecture embodies many alternatives for providing security services at different layers.

2 Security services may be employed at more than one layer when building a secure system. This is undeniably true, and is illustrated in a discussion of hybrid security solu-

---

[*] *ISO 7498-2* adds an eighth statement that is not parallel to those listed here; i.e., the security architecture is applicable to end and intermediate systems.

tions in various contexts, e.g., in the DOD networks described below. This principle implies that a single service can legitimately appear at multiple layers in a services-layers table. Note the inherent tension between these first two principles; i.e., Principle 1 argues against offering a service at multiple layers, but Principle 2 argues for such an offering. Clearly a balance must be achieved. For example, often it is appropriate to offer a service at multiple layers because different layers are provided by different administrative entities.

3   Security functionality should not unnecessarily duplicate existing communications functionality. This suggests that, whenever possible, one should rely on existing communication services so that security mechanisms do not duplicate these functions. This is an excellent principle, but often one discovers that the base communication facility cannot be exploited to provide security without sacrificing security. For example, it is tempting to use sequencing or error detection facilities present in Transport Layer protocols as part of providing analogous security services. However, sequence numbers and error detection codes designed to deal with benign error conditions may not be adequate to withstand malicious attacks. If protocol designers were to consider security implications as part of the protocol design problem, it might more often be possible to avoid such duplication.

4   Layer independence should not be violated. This is an obvious principle and one that should be honored. A danger in not honoring this principle is that one might employ security mechanisms at a layer that, because of unwarranted assumptions about services provided at another layer, will fail when these assumptions prove false. This does not imply that protection at one layer cannot rely on security mechanisms at a lower layer, but rather that the relationship must be explicit and based on well-specified service interfaces. Another form of layer independence violation arises in routers and bridges that examine higher layer protocol information in an effort to provide finer granularity access control. These security facilities may fail when new (higher layer) protocols are introduced or when cryptography is employed at higher layers.

5   The amount of trusted functionality should be minimized. This principle is well represented in the *DOD* architecture, as described below. A corollary to this principle is that it is essential to understand what constitutes the trusted functionality in a security system; i.e., what the system relies upon for its secure operation. This principle motivates the provision of security services on an end-to-end basis, versus relying on trusted intermediaries. In turn, this argues for implementing security at higher layers. However, minimizing duplication (Principles 1 and 3) argues for not providing services on a per-application basis. These trade-offs motivate the provision of security services for a wide range of applications at the (inter-) Network or Transport Layers. However, as we shall observe later, use of the Network or Transport Layers often implies integration of security protocols into operating systems, and that poses its own set of real-world problems.

6   Whenever protection provided at one layer relies on security mechanisms at a lower
    layer, it is essential that no intervening layers violate this dependence. This is related to
    Principle 4, since a failure to maintain layer independence could easily violate inter-
    layer security assurances. This precept is related to several others. Minimizing trusted
    functionality (Principle 5) argues for moving security services to higher layers, but
    using security mechanisms at one layer to provide services at higher layers is supportive
    of efforts to avoid duplication (Principles 1 and 3).

7   Security services provided at a layer should be defined in a fashion that promotes mod-
    ular addition of the services to the base communication services. This has a very practi-
    cal focus; i.e., not all implementations of a layer will require or offer all possible
    security services, so modularity will simplify the design and implementation of such
    services. In the Internet, this is a very important precept as we are dealing with a large,
    installed base into which we will wish to retrofit security services.

Having briefly analyzed security service layering principles, we can now explore service
definitions and layer selections as specified by *ISO 7498-2*.

9.2.1   Security Services

The OSI security architecture defines five primary security services: confidentiality, authentication, integrity, access control, and nonrepudiation. For most of these services there are
also variants defined, e.g., for connectionless versus connection-oriented communications.
These choices of services are not intrinsic; i.e., alternative choices for fundamental security
services are possible, but the former are now well accepted, and form a good basis for discussion throughout this chapter. This section reviews each of these services and its variants
and relationships among the services. It also discusses where each service is to be offered
within the reference model, according to *ISO 7498-2*, and explores some of the motivations for layer-service choices.

9.2.1.1   Confidentiality

Confidentiality is defined in *ISO 7498-2* as "the property that information is not made
available or disclosed to unauthorized individuals, entities, or processes." This is the property that most often comes to mind when security is discussed, and it is of special concern
in networks where disclosure of information might occur at any of a variety of points in a
communication path.

Four versions of this service are described: connectionless, connection-oriented, selective
field, and traffic flow. The first two are the obvious characterizations of confidentiality
applied to connectionless and connection-oriented protocol environments. Connection-
oriented confidentiality can be offered at any layer, except Session or Presentation.* This is
consistent with the reference model, where connection-oriented communication services
are offered at all layers. Connectionless confidentiality may be offered at all but the

Physical, Session, and Presentation Layers, the former being excluded because of the perceived connection-oriented character of the Physical Layer.

The third version of confidentiality, selective field confidentiality, applies to both environments, but it requires that only selected portions (fields) within a packet be protected. This service is offered only for the Application Layer, where distinct fields might exhibit different protection requirements in a fashion meaningful to a user, i.e., where the fields being protected are other than just protocol control information. Mechanisms may be provided within the Presentation Layer in support of this service.

Traffic flow confidentiality is a service that serves to protect against "traffic analysis," by concealing origin-destination patterns, the quantity of data transmitted, and the frequency with which communication takes place. These external characteristics of communication can be visible to an attacker, even if the user data portion of a packet is concealed. For example, it would be easy to distinguish between Telnet and FTP traffic based on packet size, even if the TCP port fields and all data above the IP layer were concealed. This service is best provided at the Physical Layer, but partial service can be offered at the Network and Application Layers as well. In the latter layers, traffic padding (see below) is required to effect partial traffic flow confidentiality, but this technique is generally thought to be too costly to be practical.

9.2.1.2 *Authentication*

Two types of authentication services are defined in *ISO 7498-2*: data origin and peer-entity. Data origin authentication is defined as "the corroboration that the source of data received is as claimed." This service applies to connectionless communication, where each packet is independent of every other packet, and thus the most that can be guaranteed, from an authentication perspective, is that the source of each packet is as indicated in the packet header. This service is tightly coupled to connectionless data integrity (see section 2.3.1.3), in that it does not seem very useful to be assured of the source of data if its integrity cannot be established.

In a connection-oriented environment,[†] peer-entity authentication is the appropriate authentication service, defined as "the corroboration that a peer entity in an association is the one claimed." This form of authentication implies timeliness, which is not available from simple data origin authentication, because of the binding of the identity of the peer entity to a specific association. Thus, attacks involving the replay of data associated with

---

[*] This exclusion of the session layer is characteristic of all security services; i.e., none are offered at that layer. The rationale provided is that either the services could better be provided at other layers, or the security functionality offered is inconsistent with the communication functionality provided by the session layer. The exclusion of the presentation is different in that *ISO 7498-2* argues for providing facilities at that layer in support of a wide range of application layer services.

[†] *ISO 7498-2* cites peer-entity authentication as applicable to connectionless data transmission in one place (6.2.4), despite defining this service in a fashion that clearly ties it to connection-oriented transmission (5.2.1.1).

another association, even between the same peer entities, can be thwarted through reliance on this service. Here there is a natural coupling with connection-oriented integrity, for a rationale parallel to the one cited above for data origin authentication.

Both forms of authentication are defined for the Network, Transport, and Application Layers, where both connection-oriented and connectionless protocols are provided. There is disagreement between the OSI and IEEE standards communities with regard to the applicability of authentication services at the link layer. The IEEE 802.10 Secure Interoperable LAN Standards committee (SILS) has defined a Secure Data Exchange (SDE) protocol[4] that operates between the LLC Layer and the MAC Layer (part of the Link Layer) and provides the data origin authentication service.

Because SDE can be employed with a variety of high-layer protocols—OSI, TCP/IP, and proprietary—many see a significant benefit in provision of this security service at the MAC layer. The MAC layer is uniform across the family of IEEE/ISO LAN protocols (802.3, 802.5, and 802.6), so one can build network security devices that provide this service across a range of LAN technologies. This is one of several examples where the OSI security architecture clashes with current, expert analysis. Arguments also can be made for providing authentication at the Link Layer in circuit (versus LAN) environments, further calling into question the *ISO 7498-2* layer applicability guidelines for this service.

9.2.1.3   *Integrity*

According to *ISO 7498-2*, this security service is offered in two basic forms: connectionless and connection-oriented, either of which may also be provided on a selective field basis. Another consideration is whether the connection-oriented service includes a provision to attempt recovery if a violation of integrity is detected, a connotation apropos only in a connection-oriented protocol environment. The connection-oriented integrity service provides for the detection of "any modification, insertion, deletion, or replay of any data within a [packet] sequence." The use of connection-oriented integrity in conjunction with peer-entity authentication provides a high degree of protection against a wide range of active attacks. This service is offered at the Network, Transport, and Application Layers, with the recovery facility available only at the two higher layers.

Connectionless integrity addresses the modification of a single packet, but without regard to any larger context, e.g., an association. Thus, this service generally does not address deletion, insertion, or replay attacks. It is the natural complement to data origin authentication. This service also is offered at the Network, Transport, and Application layers. Here, too, the IEEE 802.10 SDE protocol diverges from the OSI architecture; it offers connectionless integrity at the link layer. There seems to be good justification for such an offering, as it can provide security services across a wide range of networks, irrespective of the higher layer protocols employed.

A hybrid service can be offered in communication contexts that require some protection against replay and reordering, but not strict sequencing. For example, applications like packet video or packet voice need to screen out duplicate packets, must not deliver a packet if any of its successors have already been delivered, and must not deliver damaged packets. However, these applications are prepared to deal with some packet loss. Thus, there are requirements for a service that provides more than connectionless integrity, but less than the connection-oriented integrity defined in *ISO 7498-2*. In the Internet environment, the integrity service employed with the secure version of SNMP[5] exhibits this hybrid requirement.[6]

The selective field variants for both connection-oriented and connectionless integrity provide corresponding functionality, but only for specified fields within each packet. Like the similarly named confidentiality service, these variants are offered only at the Application Layer, though they may rely on Presentation Layer mechanisms to support the service.

9.2.1.4   Access Control

Access control is defined in *ISO 7498-2* as "the prevention of unauthorized use of a resource, including the prevention of use of a resource in an unauthorized manner." The definition supports not only the notion of authorized versus unauthorized entities (users, processes, etc.), but also the concept that an authorized entity is granted only specified access rights to a resource. Thus, attempts by both "insiders" and "outsiders" to gain unauthorized access to resources are addressed by this security service.

Access control is sometimes confused with authentication because of the trivial access control policy "if I can authenticate the user, he is authorized." Sometimes there is also confusion between access control and confidentiality services. This arises in part from the fact that access control mechanisms can be used to prevent unauthorized access to data, hence preventing unauthorized disclosure. However, access control may encompass more than "read" access to data, and thus it may address more than just confidentiality. Conversely, some techniques for providing confidentiality do not control access to data, so the two services are not equivalent. Furthermore, some access control techniques do not address all of the threats that might result in unauthorized disclosure, so access control does not subsume confidentiality.

An access control service is used to enforce an access control policy. *ISO 7498-2* says relatively little about such policies from an architectural perspective, but does provide some useful definitions. It characterizes access control (or authorization) policies in two dimensions: the criteria for the access control decisions versus the means by which the controls are managed. The two types of policies, based on decision criteria, are referred to as identity-based and rule-based. The former type of policy typically relies on the authentication service to verify the identity of an accessor, prior to granting access to a resource. The identity may be that of a user, a process, an end or intermediate system, or a network. The form of identity that is used as input to the access control decision depends on the granularity of authentication and on the layer at which the service is provided. For example, user and process identities are appropriate inputs for access control at the Application Layer, but not at the Network Layer.

A rule-based policy may rely on associating some form of (identity-independent) authorization with each accessor and some form of (identity-independent) access rules with each protected resource. In such policies, an access control decision typically is driven by a set of rules that relate authorizations to sensitivities, but make no mention of identity. For example, a rule might be expressed in terms of the time and day at which an access is attempted, or the clearance that a user possesses, irrespective of the user's identity. This is in contrast to a policy in which the access control decision is based exclusively on the user's identity, irrespective of time, day, or clearance. Note, too, that the authorization of an accessor and the sensitivity of a resource need not be expressed using the same terms. For example, data may be marked "Company Proprietary," and the corresponding authorization may be "employee of company *X*."

Two types of access control policy management are described in *ISO 7498-2*: user-imposed and administratively-imposed policies. The former type of policy is well illustrated in most operating systems, wherein users are empowered to control access to their files (typically on an identity basis). In contrast, some operating systems and most networks provide access control facilities that may be manipulated only by administrators. For example, in X.25 networks, Closed User Groups (CUGs)[7] are identity-based, administratively-imposed access control facilities managed by network administrators. Real-world access control policies often are composites, including a mixture of identity and rule-based controls, some of which are user imposed and others of which are administratively-imposed.

Access control services may be offered at the Network, Transport, and Application Layers in the reference model. Here again, the IEEE 802.10 SDE protocol diverges from the standard, providing access control at the Link (MAC) Layer for LANs. Even in a point-to-point Link Layer context, it would seem that access control is a viable service to offer. For example, one can readily imagine providing access control at layer 2 for dynamically established circuits, e.g., dialup telephone lines. A major practical advantage of providing access control at this layer is the protocol independence offered.

9.2.1.5   *Nonrepudiation*

Nonrepudiation is a security service that is not so commonly discussed as the others. It is defined as preventing "denial by one of the entities involved in a communication of having participated in all or part of the communication." Two forms of nonrepudiation are defined: nonrepudiation with proof of origin and nonrepudiation with proof of delivery. Both forms are meaningful only at the Application Layer, largely because the concept of "denial" is meaningful only for users, not other entities. The two forms of the service are symmetric and complementary.

The former service provides the recipient of data with proof of the origin and integrity of the data, and protects against any subsequent attempt by the sender to (falsely) deny sending that data. The latter service provides the sender with proof of the delivery of data, protecting against any subsequent attempt by the recipient to (falsely) deny having received the data. Both services are more powerful than what can be achieved through the use of data origin authentication. The difference here is that the recipient (sender) can prove to a third party that the data in question was sent by the sender (received by the recipient), and has not been tampered with by anyone. Electronic messaging protocols are obvious candidates for these services, especially when used to support applications like Electronic Data Interchange.

In attempting to repudiate a communication, a sender or recipient may attempt various ploys, including constructing distinct messages that are equivalent relative to the nonrepudiation mechanisms. Also, if the nonrepudiation mechanisms are based on possession of some secret quantity (as most are), then intentional disclosure of that quantity is a means of attempting to repudiate a communication. This is analogous to purchasing some merchandise using one's own credit card, then reporting the card lost or stolen in an effort to avoid paying. Thus, nonrepudiation mechanisms must associate time with protected communications, and must incorporate some conventions for declaring possible disclosure of (secret) information employed by senders or recipients in providing this service.

9.2.1.6 Availability: The Missing Security Service?

Many of those who have studied *ISO 7498-2* have suggested that an important security service is not represented. The service, which might be called "availability," is defined as one that addresses attacks that would deny services to users. Some have suggested that concerns related to denial of service are properly addressed as "quality of service" guarantees, but this seems to divert attention from the security aspects of these concerns. Measures taken to implement various qualities of service to users, but which are not designed to deal with malicious attacks against such guarantees, are unlikely to provide adequate protection.

It can be argued that the access control service addresses denial of service concerns. The argument is based on the observation that denial of service occurs in one of two ways: an entity consumes resources in an unauthorized fashion by exceeding its resource allocation quotas, or an entity violates access controls on the management system and so as to disrupt communication in a global or selective fashion. However, analysis of the mechanisms cited in *ISO 7498-2* in support of the access control service calls into question this interpretation of the scope of the access control service.

Perhaps the best rationale for considering communications availability as an explicit, separate service arises from the standpoint of a prospective user of a system articulating security requirements in terms of the *ISO 7498-2* service definitions. Experience suggests that users are unlikely to make the connection between access control or other security services and a legitimate desire to express a requirement for availability.

If availability were to be added to the security service list, it is natural to ask at what layers it ought be provided, and what mechanisms would be used to provide the service. Access control mechanisms applied to communication resources, e.g., bandwidth, can play a role in ensuring availability, and those mechanisms are likely to be implemented at the Network Layer. An ability to invoke alternative routing to bypass network outages is another important means of addressing availability, and routing control mechanisms can be provided at the Network or Application Layer in support of this. Within a network composed of active switching elements, a variety of security mechanisms may be employed to secure the (internal) network management protocols from attacks that might result in denial of service. Thus, it would seem that the Network and Application Layers (including management entities) are the primary points at which an availability service could be provided, and that a wide range of mechanisms can be employed to implement this service.

9.2.2   Specific Security Mechanisms

ISO 7498-2 includes brief descriptions of a set of security mechanisms, and a table that relates these mechanisms to security services. This list of mechanisms is neither fundamental nor comprehensive. For example, technology for physically protecting circuits as a means of providing confidentiality at the physical layer is not included. Control of electromagnetic emanations from equipment processing sensitive data, a common concern in national security contexts, is similarly absent.

The characterization of mechanisms as *specific* or *pervasive* also seems somewhat arbitrary, at least in some cases.[*] For example, security labels are characterized as pervasive rather than specific, but with no explicit justification for this distinction. Still, the brief overview of security mechanisms provides useful background in *ISO 7498-2*, and the following discussion reviews the same set of mechanisms. The discussion of specific mechanisms, and the mapping of these mechanisms to services, is not really central to a security architecture, and so less attention is paid to mechanisms here than to services.

9.2.2.1   *Encipherment*

Encipherment refers to the use of cryptography to transform data, rendering the data unintelligible. (The term *encipherment* is used in lieu of *encryption* because in some languages, the latter connotes entombment.) Although the term *encipherment* is used here, in most cases the complementary function of decipherment (decryption) is also employed. Prior to encipherment (after decipherment), data is referred to as *plaintext*. After encipherment (before decipherment), data is referred to as *ciphertext*. Both symmetric (secret key) and asymmetric (public key) cryptography are cited as appropriate instances of this mechanism.

Encipherment typically is used to provide confidentiality, but also can support other security services. This support arises because some techniques for effecting encipherment have the property that any modification of ciphertext results in unpredictable modification of the underlying plaintext. When such techniques are employed, they provide a good basis for integrity and authentication mechanisms at the same or higher layers.[8] The

---

[*]   The intent is that the use of *specific* mechanisms supports individual security services at specific layers, while *pervasive* mechanisms are generally useful, and may not be specific to any particular security service.

generation, distribution, and storage of cryptographic keys used with encipherment are properly security management functions.

9.2.2.2 Traffic Padding

Traffic padding is a mechanism that can be used to offer some traffic flow confidentiality above the Physical Layer (e.g., at the Network or Application Layers). Traffic padding may involve the generation of spurious traffic, padding of legitimate packets, and transmission of packets to other than the intended destination. Both legitimate and spurious packets may be padded to a constant maximum length, or they may be padded to random, varying lengths. To conceal source-destination patterns, spurious traffic would have to be transmitted to a variety of destinations, making this a costly technique that is rarely employed. Of course, this mechanism is not effective unless packets are afforded (connection-oriented or connectionless) confidentiality.

9.2.2.3 Routing Control

Another mechanism in support of confidentiality is routing control. It is employed at the Network or Application Layer to constrain the paths that data (e.g., packets or messages) traverse from source to destination. Selection of routes may be explicitly under the control of end systems, e.g., source routing, or may be performed by intermediate systems, e.g., based on security labels applied to packets by end systems. This mechanism explicitly requires trust in intermediate systems, and thus is vulnerable to subversion at more places than encipherment between end systems. This mechanism might also be employed in support of the integrity with recovery service, e.g., to select alternative routes in light of attacks that disrupt communications.

9.2.2.4 Digital Signature

Digital signature mechanisms usually are implemented using asymmetric cryptography, although techniques based on the use of symmetric cryptography have been developed. A digital signature is generated by the originator of data, and is verified by the recipient. Using asymmetric (public key) cryptography, a signature may be generated by computing a checksum function on the data to be signed, and then enciphering the resulting value with the private component of the originator's asymmetric key pair. A recipient validates a signature by deciphering the signature value, using the public component of the originator's asymmetric key pair, and then comparing the result to the checkvalue computed on the data by the recipient.

Using asymmetric cryptography, the generation and validation of a digital signature involve cryptographic keys that are associated with the signer (the originator), but are not specific to the validator (the recipient). Thus, the signer need not be aware of the identity of any of those who may later verify the signature, making this mechanism especially well suited to broadcast or multicast applications. If the proper form of checkvalue (e.g., a one-way hash) is employed, this mechanism can support the nonrepudiation service. It can also support authentication and integrity services where identity of an entity that will validate signed data is not known in advance, or where multiple entities may need to validate the signature.

9.2.2.5 *Access Control Mechanisms*

Access control mechanisms are used to support the access control service. A wide range of such mechanisms have been defined over time, with most being inspired by computer security technology. The mechanisms are often closely related to the access control policies that are to be enforced. For example, to support an identity-based access control policy, it is common to employ a database that specifies access rights for entities with respect to resources. This database may be realized as access control lists, where a list is associated with each resource, specifying the identities and rights of each entity authorized to access the resource. Alternatively, the database may be realized through the use of capabilities (i.e., unforgeable tokens) where each authorized entity holds capabilities that stipulate its access rights with regard to various resources.

Many access control mechanisms use authentication mechanisms to establish the identity of an entity, or employ security labels to provide input to rule-based access control policy decisions. Rule-based access control policies may rely on other inputs, e.g., time and date, or access path, in making access control decisions.

9.2.2.6 *Data Integrity Mechanisms*

Integrity of an individual packet often is effected by appending to the packet some form of checkvalue, which is a function of the data in the packet. This checkvalue may be computed using a cryptographic function employing a secret key, or may be keyless, like an error detection code. If the checkvalue is used at or above a layer in which encipherment is applied, the latter form of function may suffice, whereas integrity mechanisms employed without the aid of such encipherment tend to be cryptographically based. Mechanisms of this form usually are used to support connectionless integrity, as well as data origin authentication. If the checkvalue applied by an originator can be verified by a recipient, then the recipient confirms not only the integrity of the packet but also its origin, e.g., based on the use of a symmetric key (available only to the originator and recipient) to compute the checkvalue. (Asymmetric cryptography also could be used here; however, the extra computation cost usually associated with such algorithms argues against their general use.)

If the integrity of a sequence of packets is required, then additional mechanisms are required to address packet reordering, replay, and deletion. Sequence numbers, used in conjunction with per-packet checkvalues, are the most common means of effecting connection-oriented integrity. Timestamps (and synchronized clocks) may be used in lieu of sequence numbers to detect replay, or may be used to provide a less stringent form of sequencing for some applications (e.g., packet video or packet voice).

9.2.2.7 Authentication Exchanges

As noted above, data origin authentication often is effected thorough the use of integrity mechanisms, in conjunction with cryptographic key management techniques. For multicast applications, digital signatures can provide the same capability. User authentication usually relies on passwords, but real-user authentication is outside the scope of the reference model, as human users are not properly application layer entities. (Fortunately, this perspective avoids the need for conformance testing of users.) However, passwords also might be used for interprocess authentication, although their use is highly questionable in an open networking environment.

Peer-entity authentication usually is effected via a two- or three-way handshake procedure, analogous to sequence number synchronization mechanisms used in some protocols. A one-way exchange provides only unilateral authentication, and cannot provide a timeliness guarantee without synchronized clocks. A two-way exchange can provide mutual authentication, but not mutual timeliness assurance without clock synchronization. A three-way exchange offers mutual peer-entity authentication without the need for synchronized clocks. Here, too, authentication usually relies on cryptographic key management mechanisms to associate the identity being authenticated with a key. The X.500 directory authentication framework (X.509)[9] provides examples of one-, two-, and three-way authentication exchanges for use with asymmetric key management techniques, although the specific protocols described in the standard contain some minor flaws.[10] Also, the one and two-way exchanges involve timestamps, and the implied reliance on synchronized clocks is potentially a problem in a distributed system environment.

9.2.2.8 Notarization

Notarization mechanisms involve the use of a third party, trusted by two or more communicating entities, to provide assurance about characteristics of data being communicated. The most commonly cited use for notarization is in conjunction with nonrepudiation services. For example, a notarization service might be used in conjunction with asymmetric digital signatures to provide a nonrepudiation with proof of origin or delivery service. Nonrepudiation services cannot be provided solely by a digital signature effected by an originator or recipient, because that mechanism does not embody a notion of time.

A notarization mechanism might be employed to provide a secure timestamp, attested to by a "time notary," as part of registering a signed document or message. This can be effected by having the time notary digitally sign data, with the signature consisting of the hash value for the message, the names of the originator and recipients, and the time and date at which the message is being registered. Note that in this example, the notary is not given access to the message itself, preserving message confidentiality. The signed data from the time notary could be provided, along with the message, to a third party to support claims of message authenticity, integrity, and time frame.

9.2.3   Pervasive Mechanisms

In principle, the security mechanisms listed under this heading are not specific to a particular security service, but rather provide an underpinning for services at various layers. As noted above, a mechanism like security labels, cited here, could just as well be considered a specific security mechanism. However, a mechanism like "trusted functionality" clearly belongs under this heading. The other rationale provided for grouping mechanisms under this title is their use in security management. One could imagine adding other mechanisms to this list, e.g., key management, which represents a somewhat higher level of integration. However, for the purposes of this chapter, we will review only those pervasive mechanisms examined in *ISO 7498-2*.

9.2.3.1   *Trusted Functionality*

Probably the best example of a pervasive security service is "trusted functionality." Trusted functionality encompasses a number of disciplines that can be employed to increase confidence that other security mechanisms function properly. For security-relevant software, rigorous specification and development techniques, independent or formal verification techniques, configuration management, and the use of secure distribution channels all add to the confidence that the software is performing its (security-relevant) functions properly. With regard to hardware, one can employ analogous specification, design, and verification techniques. Techniques for addressing concerns like compromising electromagnetic emanations and physical tampering are applicable here as well.

9.2.3.2   *Security Labels*

Security labels can be associated with individual packets, associations, etc., either explicitly or implicitly. Labels are typically employed in conjunction with enforcement of rule-based access control policies, although they may also be used with routing control in support of confidentiality. Some proposals have been made for using such labels to address not just sensitivity, but also integrity concerns in secure computer systems,[11] but the network environment has not given rise to comparable, comprehensive proposals. When a security label is explicit, it must be integrity protected, e.g., securely bound to the packet with which it is associated.

9.2.3.3   *Auditing*

A number of mechanisms fall under the general title of "auditing." Audit trails provide an important security facility, both for detecting attempts or successful examples of unauthorized access, and for "damage assessment," i.e., evaluating the extent of unauthorized access in the event of a security failure. There are two primary concerns with audit trails: knowing what to collect and knowing how to analyze what has been collected. If one collects too little data, then security-relevant events may be overlooked. If too much data is collected, it may impose performance penalties and storage problems. Analysis of audit trail data is

Table 19.1   Service applicability by layer adapted from *ISO 7498-2*

Services	Layer						
	1	2	3	4	5	6	7
Confidentiality (connection)	Y	Y	Y	Y			Y
Confidentiality (connectionless)		Y	Y	Y			Y
Confidentiality (selective field)							Y
Confidentiality (traffic flow)	Y		Y				Y
Authentication		?	Y	Y			Y
Integrity (connection)			Y	Y			Y
Integrity (connectionless)		?	Y	Y			Y
Integrity (selective field)							Y
Access Control		?	Y	Y			Y
Nonrepudiation (origin & delivery)							Y

often difficult in a network environment because of the need to gather data from various devices and coordinate it to provide a comprehensive picture of network activity. Analysis of this data to detect possible intrusion, versus damage assessment, is a complex task, but has been receiving increasing attention.[12]

One source of input to an audit trail is the detection of security events. Security events cover a range of activities, including failed authentication attempts, attempted access control violations, and integrity failures that cross thresholds normally associated with network residual error levels. An important aspect of detecting security events is setting thresholds that distinguish between benign errors and attacks, to avoid overloading audit trail analysis, and this is an iterative, adaptive procedure. A good event detection system must provide a network security administrator with significant latitude in selecting which events are to be monitored and logged, and in establishing thresholds on logging. In some circumstances, event detection should trigger not only an audit trail entry, but a real-time alarm for immediate attention of a network security administrator.

9.2.4   Services and Layers: A Closer Look

The discussion of security services in Section 9.2.2 noted where specific services were offered at different layers in the reference model. *ISO 7498-2* specifies service applicability (by layer) in commentary form in the body of the standard, with a table, and with an (informative) annex that provides rationale. A subset of the table is reproduced in Table 9.1. The rows correspond to services, the columns to layers in the reference model. In each cell, *Y* indicates that the service may be provided by a protocol operating at that layer in the model, whereas a blank cell indicates that the service ought not to be offered at that layer. This version of the table includes question marks (?) for entries where IEEE 802.10 offers services that are not offered by the OSI standard.

The remainder of this section explores in more detail the issues underlying the choices of offering security services at various layers. As noted at the beginning of Section 9.2, this layer-by-layer analysis is equally applicable to the TCP/IP suite of protocols, even though the OSI reference model layering terminology is employed. The correspondence between the two protocol suites for the bottom four layers is direct. In the TCP/IP suite, applications tend to incorporate functions from the Session, Presentation, and Application Layers, completing the correspondence.

9.2.4.1   *Physical Layer*

Security services offered at the Physical Layer typically provide protection on a point-to-point basis on circuits. (However, the use of suitably shielded coaxial cable might be cited as an example of a broadcast security (confidentiality) mechanism at this layer.) For example, security may be applied between a terminal and an end system, between an end system and an intermediate system, or between two intermediate systems. In each of these cases, the service is terminated at the processing or packet-switching points at the ends of a circuit, because they form the peers for the physical layer. (A circuit switch or smart multiplexor provides a means for switching circuits without terminating the circuit; hence, physical layer protection can be provided through circuit switches or multiplexors.) A major advantage of offering services at this layer is that the protection can be independent of higher layer protocols.

However, mechanisms and devices providing security at this layer are generally tied to a specific technology. For example, a frequency-hopping spread spectrum modulation technique used with radio communications for confidentiality would not be applicable to wireline communications. Moreover, physical layer security devices often incorporate the physical layer interface of a specific technology into the device, so as to make the device as transparent as possible and thus easily integrated into systems. In such circumstances, a given device may employ a generic security mechanism but may have a limited range of applicability because of the integration of the communication interface into the device. For example, one physical layer encipherment device may be limited to synchronous links at speeds up to 64 Kbits/sec or 128 Kbits/sec, while a similar but incompatible device might operate at T1 speeds and preserve T1 framing. Both may use the same cryptographic algorithm as the underlying mechanism, but each would have a limited range of applicability.

The utility of services at this layer is limited somewhat in an Internet environment because of inability to span packet network, much less Internet, paths. However, if traffic flow confidentiality is required, this is the only layer at which it can be provided in a thorough fashion without severe performance penalties. Another shortcoming of devices operating at this layer is the difficulty of managing them. In an effort to appear transparent to existing communication system components, and in support of backward compatibility with such components, devices providing security at the physical layer are usually unaddressable in a network context. Special provisions for out-of-band communication often are required to manage these devices in a fashion comparable to the way other network devices are managed.

Services offered at this layer are restricted to connection-oriented confidentiality and traffic flow confidentiality, according to *ISO 7498-2*. It is easy to imagine how confidentiality is provided at this layer, typically using encipherment on a bitwise basis. These services can be implemented in a highly transparent fashion, i.e., without the introduction of any additional data (except during connection establishment). Integrity and authentication generally are not feasible here because the bit-level interface of this layer typically makes no provision for the additional data that must be transported to provide these services.

However, use of appropriate encipherment techniques at this layer can support these services at higher layers. For example, cryptographic modes like the DES output feedback mode do not provide any unpredictable error extension in the event that ciphertext is modified, and so this mode would be a poor choice if more than confidentiality is desired. In contrast, a DES mode like 1-bit cipher feedback does provide the desired error characteristics, and thus provides a suitable basis for integrity and authentication.

9.2.4.2 Link Layer

In a circuit context, Link Layer security services are typically provided on a point-to-point basis, as with physical layer services. Again, the services must terminate at points where the link layer peers reside, e.g., end systems and switches. In a LAN (or MAN) environment, security services also may be offered on a multicast or broadcast basis, based on the underlying LAN technology, as well as on a point-to-point basis. In LANs adhering to the IEEE 802 series of standards, in which the Link Layer encompasses both the LLC and MAC sublayers, this service can cross bridge boundaries between LAN and MANs, so long as the bridged networks employ compatible MAC protocols. Thus, link layer security can be offered between end systems on the same or dissimilar LAN and MANs, if the end systems adhere to protocol standards.

An advantage of services offered at this layer is independence of higher layer protocols, making it possible to use link layer security devices with a variety of protocol suites. Devices implementing security services at the link layer are tied to a specific link technology, but also are likely to be specific to a given physical technology. Here, the major reason for a limited range of applicability is the tendency to provide devices that can be retrofitted into existing communication paths in a largely transparent fashion. An "inline" device of this sort necessarily embodies specific physical interfaces, and thus becomes restricted in its applicability. Even if this were not the case, other hardware considerations would probably impose similar constraints. For example, a link encipherment device that operates at speeds up to 10 Mbits/sec for use in an Ethernet or 802.3 environment probably employs cryptographic hardware that would not support an equivalent security capability for a 100 Mbits/sec FDDI interface.

According to *ISO 7498-2*, the services offered at the Link Layer are connection-oriented confidentiality and connectionless confidentiality. Because most link layer protocols, e.g., LAPB,[7] incorporate error detection and a sequencing facility to support retransmission, there would seem to be an opportunity to provide connection-oriented integrity with recovery. However, in a protocol like LAPB, the sequence number space is relatively small (up to 128 frames in the extended version of the protocol), and the error detection code (CRC32) has not been selected for security purposes.[*] Thus it may not be possible to provide a "high quality" connection-oriented integrity service at this layer without introducing an explicit security protocol. Introducing such a protocol would hinder transparency, which would otherwise be an attraction of security services at this layer. Data origin authentication can be provided, to the extent that the (native) link layer error detection code can be coupled with appropriate cryptographic mechanisms (e.g., employed for confidentiality).

In LAN and MAN environments defined by the IEEE 802 (ISO DIS 10039) standards series, most commonly used link layer protocols do not provide connection-oriented services, but provide error detection. This suggests that connectionless integrity (without recovery) is a feasible security service, and the SILS SDE protocol offers precisely this facility. LANs are often broadcast media, and the SILS committee wanted to create a security protocol that could be used in a LAN environment in which not all devices would implement it. Thus, the native error detection capability at this layer is not exploited in the SDE protocol; instead, the protocol introduces its own security-oriented integrity check. In this fashion the SDE protocol also offers data origin authentication, connectionless integrity, and access control services otherwise omitted from the *ISO 7498-2* table row for this layer.

In summary, there are significant differences in which security services can reasonably be offered at the link layer in circuit or LAN environments. A fundamental difference is that confidentiality can be offered in a circuit environment in a highly transparent fashion. In contrast, in a LAN and MAN environment, the richer set of services offered by SDE is not transparent; e.g., the SDE sublayer takes space away from the maximum link layer PDU, and this may be quite visible to end systems.

9.2.4.3 Network Layer

Network Layer security services can be provided between end systems across a network, independent of intervening switches: e.g., X.25 packet switches. *ISO 7498-2* cites several security services as appropriate for this layer: including connectionless, connection-oriented, and traffic flow confidentiality, integrity (connection oriented without recovery and connectionless), data origin and peer-entity authentication, and access control. If offered at the top of the Network Layer (IP or CLNP),[14] security can be provided to end systems

---

[*] A recent paper[13] describes how to modify enciphered data in a fashion invariant under CRC32 if the wrong cryptographic modes are selected.

across dissimilar networks connected to form an Internet. It is also possible to provide security services between an end system and an intermediate system (e.g., a router) when IP or CLNP security is employed. There are motivations for all three of these cases.

If network layer security is provided in a fashion that is specific to a given network technology, the security services offered can be independent of higher layer protocols. Thus, for example, X.25-specific security services can provide transparent protection for OSI, TCP/IP, or proprietary protocols at higher layers. Such services necessarily end at the termination of an X.25 virtual circuit, although such a virtual circuit might span multiple X.25 networks, connected via X.75 gateways.

ISO 7498-2 argues that the security services offered at any layer should be consistent with the communications services provided by that layer. In the context of network-specific security services, this dictum further restricts offered services. For example, the X.25 packet protocol provides sequenced delivery, but does not include any explicit packet integrity facilities. There are no security services comparable to these X.25 communication services. In such circumstances, it may be most appropriate to employ mechanisms at one layer that are supportive of security services effected at higher layers. For example, one can provide confidentiality, peer-entity authentication, and access control for X.25 virtual circuits using mechanisms that support connection-oriented integrity and authentication at the Transport Layer. Of course, devices implementing network-specific security services and mechanisms are intrinsically tied to the corresponding network technology.

Security services offered at the top of the Network Layer have the ability to span various intermediate network technologies, and to traverse routers. For example, in conjunction with CLNP or IP, one can offer data origin authentication, connectionless integrity, connectionless confidentiality, and access control. At this sublayer, the services and mechanisms can be implemented in a fashion that is independent of underlying network technology. The same protocols and mechanisms could be used to provide secure communication between two workstations on (incompatible) LANs, across a WAN, or between these workstations and a computer on yet another WAN (based on a different technology). However, devices that provide these services may be network-specific by virtue of their realization with specific lower (e.g., physical and link) layer interfaces. Thus, in the example above, if external physical devices are used to implement these security services, then the devices used on the two LAN workstations and the computer would all be different.

Historically, Physical and Link Layer security services are usually implemented in external hardware. It is much more feasible to implement network layer security internally to an end or intermediate system. An internal implementation avoids the lower layer specificity problems cited above. External implementations of Network Layer security services also are feasible, and offer the opportunity to retrofit, but at end systems such implementations are not capable of providing fine-grained services (as described below). Moreover, communication performance often suffers when using external Network Layer security devices, e.g., because of serialization delay across the added I/O interfaces. Finally, such devices are not completely transparent, and may interfere with network management (although the devices themselves may be quite amenable to network management).

Security services provided at the top of the Network Layer, e.g., in conjunction with CLNP or IP, can be employed at intermediate systems, not just end systems. There can be several advantages to offering security services at an intermediate system. In many network topologies, an intermediate system often acts as a portal between a LAN or a set of LANs and a WAN, at a boundary between a "local" administrative entity and some other administrative entity. Providing security services at such a boundary, i.e., at an intermediate system, is especially attractive from a security management perspective, in that only a small number of systems are affected, rather than all end systems. Also, protection can be afforded not only between intermediate systems at administrative boundaries, but also between such systems and end systems (using the same security protocols).

Security provided in the Network Layer can be viewed as a form of "bulk" protection between end or intermediate systems. Certainly, when protection is provided between intermediate systems, the granularity may be rather coarse, i.e., networks (versus end systems). However, it is possible for the intermediate systems to offer security services with the granularity of individual end systems "behind" them; i.e., the protection afforded to packets can vary, based on the end system address. Some intermediate systems provide even finer-grained protection, e.g., routers that provide primitive routing control with the granularity of protocol type, by examining TCP port addresses. This example violates layering principles and it fails to generalize; CLNP and TP4 do not provide an analogous "hook" for a router to provide protocol filtering.

When protection is provided between end systems, it might seem that the protection offered would be limited to the granularity of end systems. Here too, however, it is possible for processes at higher layers to request different security services through security quality-of-service parameters internal to the end systems. Facilities to provide network layer security services at these granularities are described in the draft OSI NLSP specification.[15] NLSP incorporates an architected means to request this finer granularity of security services within an end system.

Finally, implementation of network layer security services in end systems will tend to require modification of kernel software within operating systems. This is because operating systems often incorporate network layer protocol software in the kernel, for both performance and security reasons. This implies that the addition of (internal) network layer security services cannot be effected without an ability to effect kernel modifications. In such cases, provision of such services often is outside the purview of application developers and sophisticated end users, and requires commitment by vendors of end and intermediate systems.

9.2.4.4   Transport Layer

At the Transport Layer, *ISO 7498-2* identifies several security services: confidentiality (connectionless or connection-oriented), integrity (all but selective field), data origin and peer-entity authentication, and access control. There is only one significant difference between security services offered in support of connectionless Transport Layer communication and those offered in upper network layer communication. That difference is the ability to provide protection at intermediate systems (using upper Network Layer mechanisms) rather than only at end systems (using Transport Layer mechanisms).

Connection-oriented Transport Layer security services can, in principle, offer protection not available from connectionless upper network layer security, but the differences may be minimal in practice. The differences are ones that arise from the connection-oriented versus connectionless nature of the underlying communication services. However, a well-designed connection-oriented transport protocol can exploit connectionless integrity and data origin authentication provided at the network layer, plus security quality-of-service marking on a per-packet basis, to achieve much the same effect provided by connection-oriented transport layer security services. (To exploit this capability, a transport layer protocol would have to manage its sequence number space carefully to avoid duplication, which would result in replay vulnerabilities.) The residual security service differences here entail the granularity of authentication and access control provided, at the level of network addresses rather than processes.

Transport security mechanisms may suffer from the same problems as network layer security mechanisms in that transport layer protocols also may be implemented within operating system boundaries for many popular systems, e.g., UNIX. Here, too, the introduction of transport security mechanisms is not within the purview of users or application developers, but rather requires cooperation of end system vendors.

9.2.4.5   Session Layer

ISO 7498-2 does not permit security services to be offered at the Session Layer. This layer offers very little in the way of communication services, e.g., compared with the Transport or Application Layers. Based on the precept that one should not provide security services that do not correspond to underlying communication services, this argues against offering security services at the Session Layer. Rather, it is argued that security services can be better offered at the Transport, Presentation, or Application Layers.

9.2.4.6   Presentation Layer

The Presentation Layer often is cited as an ideal layer at which to provide protection because security services are viewed as data transformations, like the other Presentation Layer functions. This view probably is motivated by a perception that security equals encipherment, which is an oversimplification. *ISO 7498-2* adopts something of a schizophrenic attitude toward provision of security services at this layer. It states that "facilities will be provided by the presentation layer" in support of various forms of confidentiality, a stronger statement than is made for any service at any other layer. Note that this strong statement about "facilities" does not result in listing any "services" as being explicitly provided at this layer, although the encipherment mechanisms may be employed in support of a wide range of services at the application layer. The confidentiality facilities offered here can be in support of connection-oriented, connectionless, or selective field variants.

Because this layer is used to transform data between native and network representations, there is a significant advantage to enciphering data at this layer rather than at the application layer. If an application performs encipherment, it prevents the presentation layer from providing this function. This is a strong argument against employing application layer encipherment for applications where the peers engage in direct (versus staged) communication. The alternative is to duplicate presentation layer functionality in applications. Note that in the TCP/IP suite, since presentation functions are embodied within applications, as opposed to being in a separate layer, this potential conflict is avoided.

9.2.4.7   Application Layer

ISO 7498-2 declares that all security services may be offered at the Application Layer, and nonrepudiation may be offered only at this layer. However, offering some security services at this layer poses problems because of the conflict with presentation layer functionality. This conflict was alluded to above, with regard to confidentiality, and it applies equally well to most mechanisms employed to implement integrity and authentication services as well. This limitation is overcome in the context of staged delivery applications, e.g., messaging and directory services, by embedding presentation functions into the application (e.g., X.500 and X.400 specifications[9, 16]). The conflict also is avoided in the TCP/IP suite, where presentation functions are typically incorporated into applications.

In fact, applications like messaging and directory services can be secured only via Application Layer security. Messaging requires security services at this layer for several reasons. First, some security services employed in conjunction with messaging are apropos only at this layer, e.g., nonrepudiation. Second, messages are typically addressed to multiple recipients (application layer multicast), and delivery is staged through message switches. Lower layer protection often is offered only on a real-time, point-to-point basis. In the context of messaging, the use of lower layer security mechanisms could offer protection from an originator to a message switch (MTA), between MTAs, and between MTAs and recipients, but only on a step-by-step basis. To provide end-to-end, "writer-to-reader" security requires the use of techniques specific to messaging.

For directory services, similar problems prevent lower layer security services from adequately addressing application security requirements. For example, a query from a user to a directory server may have to be forwarded (*chained,* in X.500 parlance) to other directory servers as part of formulating a response. If a directory server which eventually receives the query is to make an access control decision based on the identity of the originator of the query, that access control decision cannot be effected by lower layer protocols. Moreover, without trusting the servers that have forwarded the query, the server that responds to it cannot be certain that the query is unmodified. Thus this application, like messaging, illustrates the best reason for providing security at the application layer, i.e., an inability to meet security requirements by relying on lower layer services.

For many, one of the most attractive reasons for providing security services at this layer is the ability to implement these services outside of operating systems. Thus application developers or suitably capable users can implement security mechanisms within applications, without relying on vendors of end systems to incorporate the mechanisms. The unfortunate aspect of application-specific security services and mechanisms is that they may be application-specific. Thus each implementation might serve only one application, which does a poor job of amortizing the underlying development effort, leading to duplicative efforts. Moreover, since the design and implementation of security mechanisms is a complex process, engineering protection on a per-application basis increases the risk that each application-specific design or implementation will be flawed.

A compromise entails the provision of security services using a generic Application Layer service element, to avoid duplicative implementation efforts. This avoids the problem of inserting the resulting security protocol into each operating system, while not requiring application-specific security solutions to be developed and implemented. Ongoing work in OSI, related to a revision of the upper three layers of the reference model, supports this approach, as does the existing TCP/IP protocol suite.

9.3 THE DOD INTERNET SECURITY ARCHITECTURE

9.3.1 Motivations

The TCP/IP protocol suite evolved from work funded by the Defense Advanced Research Projects Agency in the 1970s. This work had as a major goal the development of protocols that could be used by DOD in a wide range of network technologies, including strategic and tactical local and wide area networks. The intent was to provide standard protocols that could be employed independently of the underlying network technology, and in the face of varying network topology. The flexibility provided by such protocols would enable DOD network users to exploit a wide variety of network resources to establish and maintain computer communication, even if the network resources were not completely reliable or if the overall topology varied as a result of such unreliability.

These features were considered quite important for a protocol suite in a time when cold war concerns envisioned the need for DOD users to "reconstitute" communications that might be disrupted by malicious attacks on transmission or switching resources during a war. Such attacks might include the jamming of radio links in a tactical network or the destruction of packet switches or gateways in tactical or strategic networks. (Some DOD wags referred to the case of a bomb destroying a switch as an example of "ballistic jamming.") One popular notion was that non-DOD, e.g., public, networks could be employed in emergencies to reconstitute critical communication capabilities in wartime. Some aspects of these concerns apply in the face of terrorist and hacker threats, outside of wartime conditions.

Consistent with this goal of developing protocols that can be used with a variety of networks under less-than-ideal conditions, is the concept of being able to communicate securely under such circumstances. In such circumstances, network subscribers could not rely on the intervening networks being secure, e.g., if public networks were exploited in an emergency. Even in the context of stable, dedicated DOD networks, there is a strong motivation not to rely on the security of network components to provide security for subscribers. This motivation arises from what is referred to in security jargon as the "principle of least privilege" or "need-to-know." (This principle is analogous to "information hiding" precepts in object-oriented programming.)

The principle here is that only those elements of a system (a computer or a network) that have a legitimate requirement to process data should have access to that data. This principle has influenced the design of secure computer systems for over 20 years, and it is equally applicable to secure networks. In fact, the layered design of modern network protocols, e.g., TCP/IP and OSI, is especially supportive of this principle. With regard to networks, this principle argues for providing security for subscriber data by applying technology at the source and destination of communication, i.e., at the endpoints. This strategy minimizes reliance on intervening network components, and thus reduces the number of the points at which subscriber data can be compromised.

Note that the principles that motivate what is usually referred to as "end-to-end security" are consistent with protocol layering precepts as well. For example, in both the OSI and TCP/IP protocol suites, peer-to-peer communication between end systems takes place above network-specific protocols. This makes it possible to protect data transmitted between end systems in a fashion that is independent of the network technology employed by intervening networks and that is also unaffected by intermediate systems (e.g., routers).

9.3.2   The Computer and Communication Security Connection

Like networking, computer security had its origins in work funded by DOD,[17] and for many years, it has emphasized confidentiality as its principal goal. Many critics of the TCSEC contend that it focuses too much on this security service and ignores other services (e.g., integrity). When DOD developed a successor evaluation criterion for networks, the Trusted Network Interpretation of the TCSEC (TNI),[18] it continued to emphasize confidentiality at the expense of other network security services.

Another aspect of computer security in the DOD environment is a focus on "assurance" rather than functionality. Security functionality refers to the security features that are offered by a system. For example, if one system offers access control lists that provide entries for explicitly named users, that system exhibits greater security functionality than a system in which the list entries can refer only to the owner, a group, or world (the UNIX paradigm). However, the former system may offer increased functionality without assurance, or even with less assurance than the latter system.

In the DOD computer security environment, the emphasis has always been on assurance, often to the exclusion of functionality. This is exemplified by the TCSEC, where the focus is on confidentiality, and the primary distinction among various evaluation ratings is one of assurance, espe-cially at the higher rating levels. The paradigm for this computer security strategy is the development of secure operating systems that act as *reference monitors*. A reference monitor is a trusted mediator of access by *subjects* (e.g., users or processes operating on their behalf) to pro-tected resources called *objects* (e.g., files or processes) in a system. To be effective the reference mon-itor must mediate all accesses by subjects to the resources it protects, and it must protect itself against tampering (unauthorized access) by subjects.

Within the DOD environment, much emphasis has been placed on reference monitors that enforce a rule-based, administratively-imposed security policy model[19] that specifi-cally addresses the problem of malicious, untrusted application software (e.g., a Trojan Horse) attempting to disclose sensitive data in violation of this policy. This paradigm addresses not only overt attempts at such disclosure, e.g., a user attempting to access a file that contains data for which he is not "cleared," but also so-called "covert channels" in which a Trojan Horse indirectly signals information. The primary goal of this approach to computer security is to permit users having differing security authorizations, or processing different levels of sensitive data, to employ untrusted applications executing on top of a trusted operating system.

During the era when TCP/IP was primarily a DOD protocol suite, network security for these protocols correspondingly focused on assurance, rather than functionality, and emphasized confidentiality over other security services. DOD network security also addressed the problem of Trojan Horse software in a computer attempting to circumvent network security policy and disclose sensitive data. In essence, the paradigm for network security in the DOD environment has been that of the reference monitor. Here, instead of processes within computers being the subjects and files and other processes being the protected resources, the end systems are viewed as the subjects and the network elements, or other end systems, are the protected resources. Thus, there is a strong parallel between both paradigms, and the security policies that have been the focus of DOD computer and network security strategies.

Historically, communication security devices developed for the protection of classified information fit the reference monitor model perfectly. The devices were quite simple (lim-ited functionality) and built to very high standards of assurance. The primary security ser-vice they were engineered to provide was confidentiality. Despite these parallels between the computer security philosophy and the communication security philosophy in the DOD environment, there is a major difference between the two: hardware.

Secure communications devices employ very carefully designed, usually custom-built hardware to achieve high assurance. The software used in such devices was quite minimal, until the devices evolved to accommodate the protocols used in packet networks. In con-trast, the DOD computer security effort has been based largely on the use of commercial computer hardware, and relies on careful design and analysis of (a minimal set of) operat-ing system software for security. (There is a reliance on user-supervisor mode and memory protection facilities to support the security software, but CPUs have included such facilities for some time.) In the later half of the 1980s, these two disciplines began to merge, as the requirements for network (rather than communication) security devices have required greater functionality and very high assurance.

During the time when the development of TCP/IP was being funded by the DOD (the 1970s and most of the 1980s), there could be little doubt that the assurance offered by the software-based approach to computer security was much lower than that of the hardware-based communication security devices in use. (The only documented network security device that relies extensively on trusted software rather than on the more traditional, trusted hardware approach, is the BLACKER system.[20] However, this system involved a massive investment of time and money to develop, and the resulting equipment does not offer performance and interface capabilities in keeping with current WAN technology.)

More importantly, the population of computers in DOD had, and still has, very few systems that were "trusted" (high assurance). Thus the DOD approach to network security has been based on the need to introduce a high assurance device as a trusted intermediary (reference monitor) between a computer and the communication network to which the computer is attached. The alternative would require that one have a high degree of trust in the computer system, a requirement not in keeping with near-term reality.

9.3.3   The DOD Philosophy of Network Security

As explained above, DOD approaches to network security were motivated by three beliefs: confidentiality is the primary security service; high assurance is essential; and computers are generally untrusted. These factors, when combined with the principle of least privilege and the reference monitor paradigm, yield an architecture that relies on the use of very high assurance network security devices at the link, MAC, and IP layers in networks.

9.3.3.1   *Physical Layer Encipherment*

Physical layer devices (often referred to as *link encryptors*) are used in networks with little or no change from the ways in which they were used prior to packet network technology, representing a successful reuse of technology in a new context. The security features provided by such devices are precisely the ones described earlier in the discussion of the OSI security service and mechanism. Operating at the bottom of layer 2, these devices provide confidentiality, especially traffic flow confidentiality, on a point-to-point basis. Figure 9.1 illustrates several points at which physical layer encipherment devices might be employed in a typical network environment. These devices can be employed on leased and dialup access lines, and interswitch trunks. The specific devices used in each context may differ, e.g., because of differences in circuit bandwidth, but the technology is fundamentally common.

A network (WAN) protected with physical layer encipherment devices is vulnerable at each of the switches, where the packets are in plaintext (i.e., not enciphered). This clearly violates the principle of least privilege. A network that makes use of only link encipherment technology must rely on the switches to operate correctly; otherwise the misrouting

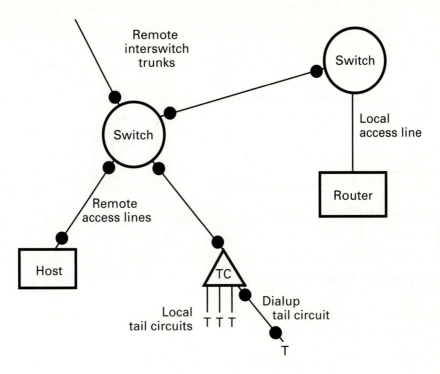

Figure 9.1   Physical layer encipherment

of a packet could violate security. As noted above, the assurance provided by computer security techniques generally does not match that provided by communication security devices; thus, there is considerable reluctance to mix data of different security levels (e.g., Secret and Top Secret) in a network that relies exclusively on link encipherment. Even if the switches employ high assurance technology, there is a valid concern that the least well-protected switch (in terms of physical, procedural, or personnel security) can compromise the entire network.

9.3.3.2   IP Layer Encipherment

To provide a network security solution that minimizes reliance on untrusted switches, DOD has spent considerable resources on the development of network layer security devices for use in TCP/IP networks over the last 15 years. Such devices can protect traffic from source to destination, independently of intervening switches. By operating at the IP layer, they can protect any application protocol, as well as both connection-oriented and connectionless transport protocols (e.g., TCP and UDP). Typically, these devices offer connectionless confidentiality and access control (effected via key distribution). They also provide data origin authentication and connectionless integrity, or offer support for these

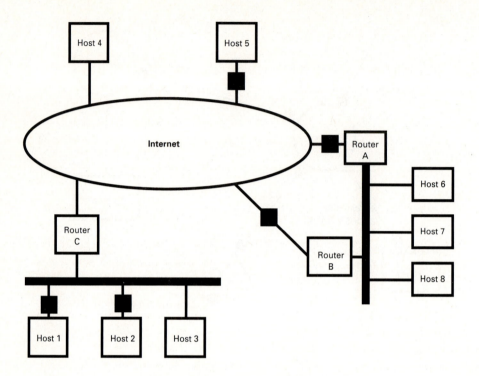

Figure 9.2   IP layer security devices

services at higher layers. Perhaps most importantly, implementation of security services at the IP layer makes it possible to develop network security devices that are external to computers and thus can be employed with the vast collection of untrusted computers in the inventory. Figure 9.2 illustrates points at which these devices can be employed in LAN and WAN environments.

A very useful feature of IP layer security devices is that they can be used either with an individual end system computer, or in conjunction with a router, as shown in Figure 9.2. In the latter configuration, the protection provided typically is for all of the devices on a LAN. If a LAN supports a collection of untrusted computers all processing data of the same sensitivity (typically referred to as a "system high" LAN), then this granularity of protection is appropriate. Unless the router is trusted and there is some reliable means of segregating data on the LAN (see below), this is the best that one can achieve in such an environment. In such circumstances, the network security devices are providing protection across the WAN, or a set of WANs.

This configuration does not meet the principle of least privilege articulated earlier. However, the cost of these devices has typically been so great (on the order of $10,000) that this is the common way in which they are employed. When these devices were conceived, in the late 1970s, time-sharing was the network computing paradigm and multiuser computers were directly connected to WANs (e.g., the ARPANET). Relative to the cost of a time-shared computer and the WAN attachment, these devices were reasonably priced at $10,000–$12,000. However the shift to PCs and workstations attached to LANs diverges significantly from the original model, and makes the cost of such devices unacceptably high relative to our current computing paradigm. Hence, there is a tendency to amortize the cost of such devices over the set of workstations attached to a LAN.

Recalling the Trojan Horse concern cited earlier, it is worth exploring how IP layer devices address the problem of protecting data transmitted by an untrusted computer. It is necessary for the IP header to be available in plaintext form for processing by routers between these devices, and for the network layer header to be available as well. In combination, these two headers provide substantial opportunities for "bypassing" data from a Trojan Horse within the end system around the high assurance network security device.[21] This problem is addressed in several ways. First, many of the optional fields in the IP and network layer headers are simply not bypassed. This robs the end system of ability to exploit a number of features provided by the network and the Internet, a trade-off consistent with the paradigm of "assurance first, functionality second."

Second, the addressing information need not simply be bypassed. These network security devices are used not only to protect against disclosure of data to unauthorized users (e.g., wiretappers), but also to restrict communication among the community of authorized users as well. Both administratively-imposed, rule-based (e.g., a Top Secret computer would not be authorized to send data to a Secret computer), and identity-based access controls (based on IP addresses) typically are provided. Hence, no packets are transmitted between two network security devices unless there has been explicit authorization. This significantly reduces the ability of a Trojan Horse to modulate the address fields in the IP header, though it does not eliminate this covert channel completely. Since the network header address is derived from the IP address (and selection of the appropriate next router hop), these functions can be performed by the network security device without reliance on the host protocol software.

One approach to minimizing the problem of bypassing addresses and other header information was adopted in DOD network security architecture in the late 1970s through the mid-1980s: the dual catenet model. (The term *catenet* derives from terminology used in the 1970s to describe the Internet as a concatenation of networks.) In the dual catenet model, an IP layer security device enforces a strict address space boundary, via IP layer encapsulation. Thus, the addresses used by end or intermediate systems on the protected (red) side of an IP layer security device are completely disjoint from those used by end or intermediate systems on the unprotected (black) side. This absolute barrier mitigates the covert channel concerns cited earlier, but at a price.

Figure 9.3 illustrates a sample configuration employing devices designed using this model. Note that because of the dual address space model, the red routers (*A* and *B*) and hosts (6, 7, and 8) cannot communicate with the black router (*C*). Conversely, hosts with-

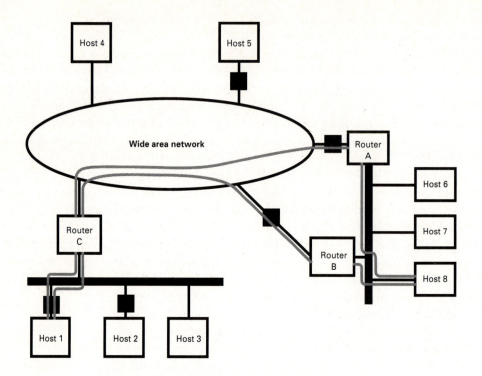

Figure 9.3   Single and dual catenet device examples

out these security devices (e.g., hosts 3 and 4) are not aware of the existence of the routers, and hence, the LAN, behind the devices. Thus the dual homing offered by this network topology cannot be fully exploited. This is because the IP address associated with a packet after it is encapsulated while passing through the device in front of host 1 will be that of one of the devices in front of routers A and B, not the address of the ultimate destination (host 8). Moreover, hosts 1, 2, 5, 6, 7, and 8 cannot communicate with router C, and thus engage in MTU discovery, which increases the likelihood of fragmentation.

If the WAN pictured here provides a facility like logical addressing, this too may not be available when these security devices are employed. The potential problem is that if logical addressing makes the WAN addresses for routers A and B identical, the security devices must be cognizant of this, and keys distributed to the security device associated with router A must also be available to the device associated with router B. Otherwise, packets enciphered and destined for one of the devices may be delivered to the other device and not be decipherable. Figure 9.3 illustrates this potential problem by indicating two paths a packet might traverse en route from host 1 to host 8, via two different IP layer security devices. Suitably sophisticated key management can alleviate this problem.

The alternative strategy, the single catenet model, attempts to avoid some of the shortfalls of the dual catenet model by not introducing an address space dichotomy. However, this model introduces its own potential problems, also illustrated in Figure 9.3. In an IP security system designed in accordance with this model, there is no division of the address space at the security device boundaries, even though encapsulation may still be employed to address covert channel concerns. However, because of the address transparency of the devices, it is possible for an enciphered packet to be routed to either of the devices sited at routers. In the example, packets from host 1 that are addressed to host 8 might arrive either at the device in front of router *A* or the device in front of router *B*. This imposes a requirement on the devices to be prepared to accommodate such routing, the same problem cited above for single catenet devices when used with logical addressing.

There is also the possibility that an enciphered packet might be fragmented, and the fragments might arrive at different devices, precluding the reassembly that is required prior to decipherment. Again, in Figure 9.3, a packet from host 1 addressed to host 8 might be fragmented at router *C*. Different fragments could arrive at the devices in front of routers *A* and *B*. Unless all the fragments can be collected at a single device, reassembly cannot take place, and communication will fail. Also note that a packet could be fragmented twice, prior to and after encipherment, and provision must be made to distinguish between the two types of fragments. Encapsulation can be employed here, in conjunction with a single address space, to preserve the distinction between the two types of fragments.[22]

Perhaps the most critical problem arising with such devices is the need to bypass (or simulate) interrouter communication protocols. In the example, routers *A* and *B* must communicate with router *C*, e.g., via EGP or BGP, across the security devices. Since trusted routers are generally not available, this poses a potentially severe security problem as the devices cannot be certain that the bypassed router packets do not contain sensitive information being communicated via covert signaling. If devices built on the single catenet model are employed only in simple network topologies, all of these problems can be avoided, but this constrains the utility of such devices. In principle, the devices could process the interrouter packets, simulating the interactions that would take place with the routers "behind" them but, in other than simple topologies, this simulation could rapidly become unworkable.

9.3.3.3 MAC Layer Encipherment

In principle, IP layer security devices can be deployed on LANs, with suitable LAN interfaces, on a per-workstation basis. However, as noted above, the high cost of such devices makes this generally prohibitive. Moreover, many of the IP layer security devices that have been developed for the DOD community do not provide LAN interfaces, but rather offer WAN (specifically X.25) interfaces, suited for use with router attachments to DOD WANs. To complement the WAN IP-layer devices, and to provide protection in mixed protocol environments, vendors have developed LAN security devices that operate above the MAC layer and below the LLC layer, typically for Ethernets and IEEE 802.3 networks.

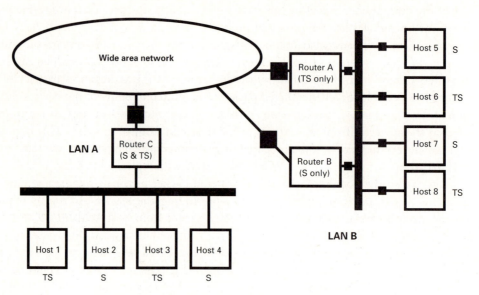

Figure 9.4   Multi-level LAN connectivity example

These devices fill an important niche, allowing DOD users to create multilevel secure LANs, which can then be connected to the multilevel WANs created by the use of IP layer security devices described above. For example, Figure 9.4 illustrates two ways of providing such a connection. LANs *A* and *B* are both multilevel, with a mixture of Secret and Top Secret workstations on each. LAN *A* relies on trusted software in the workstations to maintain the separation of data. LAN *B* makes use of external cryptographic devices to separate traffic on it. LAN *A* uses a single, trusted router to connect the LAN to a WAN security device, which is capable of maintaining the data separation through the use of security labels on the packets and cryptographic technology. LAN *B* uses two untrusted routers, one for each security level, and two WAN security devices, each restricted to a single level, to provide similar connectivity into the WAN environment. Both approaches are viable.

In the LAN environment, the same principles guide the design of devices, although several types of devices have arisen because of the different assumptions that may be appropriate for LANs. For example, many LAN security devices encipher data to provide connectionless confidentiality, provide or support data origin authentication and connectionless integrity, and employ key management to effect access control. Other devices do not employ encipherment for confidentiality (though they may employ cryptographic measures for data origin authentication and connectionless integrity), relying instead on trusted hardware and software to effect access control, and on physical and procedural security measures to effect confidentiality.

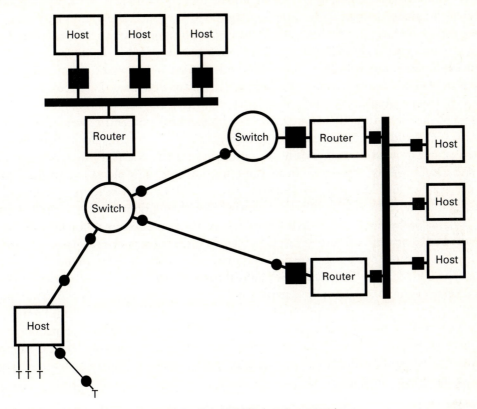

Figure 9.5 Hybrid DOD security example

9.3.3.4 Hybrid Systems

In practice, the DOD network security architecture relies on all three of the layer-specific systems described above to effect comprehensive security for sensitive data. Figure 9.5 illustrates how physical, IP, and MAC layer security devices can be used together to provide protection. In this example, the physical layer devices are employed to protect dial-up tail circuits, access lines to a WAN, and the trunks between the WAN switches. They provide confidentiality for user traffic on the tail circuits, and traffic flow security for user traffic on access lines and interswitch trunks. On one LAN, MAC layer devices provide confidentiality, access control, integrity, and authenticity (or support for these services at higher layers). On another LAN, and at router attachments to the WAN from the other LAN, IP layer devices provide connectionless confidentiality (not traffic flow confidentiality), access control, and connectionless integrity, and data origin authentication.

9.3.3.5 What's Missing from the DOD Model?

As noted above, considerable effort has been devoted to the development of security devices for use in the DOD Internet. These devices operate only at the three lowest layers in the protocol hierarchy (physical through network). In Section 9.2.4.7 it was observed that applications like messaging and directory services required application layer security mechanisms, yet there has been no mention of application layer security in the DOD architecture. This is no accident, but rather a natural effect of the time frame in which it arose and the security paradigm under which this architecture evolved.

The Domain Name System (DNS),[23] which today underlies IP directory services, evolved from a simple, centralized file model often referred to as *HOSTS.TXT,* from the name of the file at the NIC where name-to-address translation entries were maintained. In the 1970s and early 1980s, Internet directory services involved the maintenance of this file (via out-of-band means) and the acquisition of the file (via FTP) by hosts. Even in 1992, DOD WANs have yet to make the transition from this old model to the DNS, much less X.500. Thus, it is not surprising that the DOD network security architecture does not consider directory services as requiring special attention.

As noted in Section 9.3.2, the DOD network security architecture is heavily influenced by the DOD view of computer security. In that view, the concept of a reference monitor is central, and secure operating systems incorporate a reference monitor within the operating system kernel. The Physical, MAC, and IP Layer security devices described above act as reference monitors. Their implementation, as external devices in series with communication interfaces, reinforces the reference monitor precept of being safe from tampering (by untrusted software within an end or intermediate system) and capable of mediating all accesses. Provision of security services at the application layer runs counter to these precepts, in the same fashion that the DOD computer security model emphasizes secure operating systems over secure applications.

In fact, to effectively provide application layer security to the high standards set by DOD, one must start with a secure operating system as a base. One can imagine using the operating system security provisions to allow transmission of application data only after it has been processed through application layer security mechanisms. However, as noted earlier, secure operating systems, especially above the TCSEC C2 level (which have now become relatively commonplace), have been a long time in coming. To provide the requisite data separation alluded to above, a system must be rated at the TCSEC B1 level or above, and relatively few such systems exist even today. Thus it is not surprising that only in the late 1980s, as the DOD began planning for GOSIP (including X.400 and X.500) and as B-level systems began to appear, did the literature begin to point to the use of application-specific security as a viable mechanism within the DOD network security architecture.[22]

Another reason that application layer security has not been a high priority for the DOD architecture is the reliance on administratively-imposed, rule-based, access control. Most of DOD access control focuses on policies of this type, rather than identity-based policies. If identity, especially user identity, were more central to the policies that DOD has focused on, the application layer security would be more crucial, as user identities typically are available at this layer and not at the lowest three layers. However, with the exception of messaging, where the identities of the originator and recipients are considered critical, emphasis has been placed on rule-based policies that separate different levels of classified information and protect against Trojan Horse attacks that attempt to disclose information to unauthorized (less highly cleared) users or processes.

Given the orientation cited above, it is likely that the DOD security architecture will continue to emphasize lower layer security services. Application layer security will be pursued only where there is no means to meet security requirements at lower layers, and when the application is sufficiently common as to warrant the investment required for the development and implementation of security technology sufficient to meet DOD's high standards.

9.3.4 Security for the Open Internet

The preceding sections have analyzed the OSI security architecture in some detail, and examined the motivations that shaped the DOD IP security architecture. This section explores what an Internet security architecture might encompass, drawing on the discussions in the preceding sections. A multielement approach to describing an Internet security architecture seems appropriate. The OSI security architecture consisted of five major elements: security service definitions, security mechanisms definitions, security service layering principles, a mapping of services to layers, and a mapping of mechanisms to services. Each of these has a place in an Internet security architecture, though additional elements also may be appropriate, as noted below.

9.3.4.1 Security Service and Mechanism Definitions

Although one may quibble with details of the terminology defined for the OSI security architecture, for the most part it is quite serviceable, and is increasingly well accepted. This suggests that the Internet should begin by adopting that terminology to describe security services, mechanisms, and threats. It may be appropriate to incorporate additional security mechanism definitions, based on discussions in Section 9.2.3. Note that adopting the terminology used in *ISO 7498-2* does not require that one adopt the mapping of services to layers, or mechanisms to services, especially in light of the analysis provided throughout Section 9.2.

9.3.4.2 Security Principles

Section 9.2 presented and analyzed seven security layering principles that underlie the OSI security architecture. All of these are reasonable principles and probably should be included in an Internet security architecture. In addition to these principles, an Internet security architecture might add several principles, oriented toward choices of security mechanisms rather than security service layering. Among these principles might be the following:

1   Security mechanisms should be scaleable to encompass the entire Internet community. Today, the Internet architecture is being reexamined to expand the IP address space, so

as to accommodate more networks, and to alleviate the problems of routing to a very large number of networks (e.g., over a billion). With this experience in mind, it seems especially important to ensure that security mechanisms built for the Internet are capable of accommodating very large numbers of networks, computers, and human users. Thus, the names used in conjunction with authentication and access control mechanisms should accommodate such scope.

2   Security mechanisms should have the property that their security can be traced back to underlying technologies, e.g., algorithms and protocols, that are fundamentally secure. Thus the protocols and algorithms should exhibit no intrinsic flaws. This does not imply that such mechanisms are perfect, but rather that the imperfections result from implementation flaws or mismanagement, rather than fundamental weaknesses.

3   Security mechanisms should not constrain network topology. For example, a security mechanism would not be desirable if it could be used only in circumstances where a LAN or campus network is connected by only a single router to other networks.

4   Security mechanisms that are not subject to export control restrictions or patents, on both a national and an international basis, are preferred over mechanisms that are export-controlled or patented. However, no mechanism will be rejected as part of an Internet security standard merely because of export control or patent issues. In the security arena, the specter of export control looms very large, but many export control regulations also apply to other aspects of Internet technology as well. The Internet has a policy with regard to inclusion of patented technology into standards, consistent with that of ANSI and the IEEE.

5   There is a recognition that many security mechanisms require an infrastructure, the management of which may prove as expensive as the implementation of the security mechanisms. Thus there is a strong impetus to employ security technology that can exploit a common security infrastructure. For example, the PEM public-key certification system[24] is based on X.509, and its adoption is supportive of security services for X.500 directory systems and X.400 e-mail. Work on a common authentication technology that utilizes the directory naming scheme employed with certificates also is underway.

6   Cryptographic algorithms selected for standardization in the Internet must be publicly known, and preferably have withstood the test of time in the open literature. In the absence of formal proofs of the security of encipherment, hashing, signature, and similar algorithms, the best assurance available for such algorithms often arises from continued scrutiny in open publications. Proprietary algorithms are especially suspect as standards candidates, since the lack of disclosure of the algorithm makes broad-based scrutiny impossible. Such scrutiny does not, in and of itself, ensure that an algorithm is secure, but it is an essential part of the cultural assurance process.

9.3.4.3 Internet/DOD Security Architecture Differences

An Internet security architecture is expected to differ from the DOD architecture, in several important ways. It is useful to examine the bases for these differences and to understand the potential implications for an Internet security architecture.

The DOD architecture has focused extensively on confidentiality as its prime security service, with traffic flow confidentiality a major concern. As noted earlier, this focus results, in large part, from the concern about disclosure of sensitive (e.g., classified) information and from dealing with the threat posed by Trojan Horse software. These concerns can be countered by rigid adherence to a rule-based, administratively-imposed access control policy implemented in end systems and network security mechanisms. However, in the Internet environment, there is no widely adopted counterpart to this sort of access control policy, and so an emphasis on protection against the Trojan Horse threat is inappropriate.

In general, a strong requirement for traffic flow confidentiality has not been established in the Internet, although the user community may change its perception of this requirement over time, e.g., as the commercial user community grows. There are conflicting concerns here. For example, subscribers would generally expect that network management data on traffic flows would not be made public, yet they do not appear to expect a regional network provider to employ physical layer encipherment to protect interswitch trunks. Most subscribers probably perceive little or no threat from wiretapping these circuits, but do worry about inadvertent disclosure of data collected legitimately for management purposes.

Section 9.3.3 noted that the decision to focus on offering security services at lower layers is prompted mainly by the reference monitor security paradigm, adopted from computer security experience. By implementing security mechanisms in external devices at lower layers, DOD has been able to ensure the inviolability of these mechanisms, and ensure their role in mediating access. In contrast, in the Internet, there appears to be less demand for high-assurance security mechanisms and more for high functionality. For example, it is hard to imagine most Internet users paying a premium for external, per-computer cryptographic hardware versus using workstation software. Similarly, there has been no apparent demand by most Internet users for end or intermediate systems that are evaluated against security criteria (e.g., the TCSEC or INI). This is consistent with a model in which productive security mechanisms are prized over supportive mechanisms.

It also has been argued that the Internet community is concerned with a broad range of security services, i.e., more than just confidentiality. This is not entirely a fair contrast, since modern DOD security devices tend to provide or support connectionless integrity, peer-entity authentication, and access control, as well as connectionless confidentiality. However, the granularity at which these services are provided may tend to be finer in the Internet environment than in the DOD environment. For example, most DOD security devices, operating at lower layers, are able to provide these services only at the granularity of an individual end system or a LAN (or an ensemble of LANs). The access control provided emphasizes administratively-imposed user-imposed, rule- and identity-based policies at this granularity.

Today, a number of Internet subscribers employ packet filtering in routers to provide protocol-specific and direction-specific access control at the granularity of IP addresses. This packet filtering is spoofable, due to the lack of secure authentication for the Internet addresses on which the access control decisions are based. Many subscribers have expressed a desire to provide user and process granularity (identity-based) access control, a facility that requires use of higher layer security mechanisms. Thus the Internet community has, so far, opted for finer granularity, identity-based access controls, often provided with minimal assurance.

Finally, there are subtle differences in cryptographic key management between the two communities. The DOD security architecture, because of its affinity for high assurance and rule-based access controls, has tended to rely more on centralized key management systems. Part of the motivation here is that generation of very high quality keying material is a very difficult task, and is best effected under tightly controlled, very high security conditions. Moreover, if authorization data, e.g., for use with rule-based access control policies, is tightly bound to keying material, then the binding must be effected by a trusted authority.

In the Internet environment, it is likely that keys will be generated on a distributed basis, under very local control, e.g., on a per-user basis. Because the Internet is likely to make use of identity-based access control policies, the critical binding here is between keys and identities (versus keys and authorizations for use with rule-based policies). Use of an identity authentication system, such as X.509, permits this binding to be performed on a distributed basis, diminishing the need for a trusted central authority. Authorizations for use with identity-based access control policies can be managed either on an ACL basis, by using names, or by creating capabilities, e.g., the ECMA privilege attribute certificates.[25] In either case, the identity-based access control systems that seem likely to predominate in the Internet are well matched to distributed administration, in contrast to the more centralized key management schemes typically adopted in the DOD environment for use with lower layer security devices.

9.3.4.4 *Mappings: Services to Layers and Mechanisms to Services*

Another element that should be drawn from the OSI security architecture is the mapping of services to layers. Although preceding sections pointed out shortcomings in this mapping, the mapping is still a good starting point for an Internet security architecture. In fact, since the Internet is striving to encompass multiple protocols, it is almost required to incorporate a mapping that is at least as broad as that provided in *ISO 7498-2*. Given the analysis of Sections 9.2.1 and 9.2.4, it is appropriate to expand this mapping to include the layer 2 services proposed by the IEEE SILS committee (data origin authentication, connectionless integrity, and access control).

The OSI mapping of security mechanisms to services also has some shortcomings, as noted above, but for the most part the mapping is reasonable, and thus warrants adoption as well—at least as a starting point. Also, this is a much less important mapping than the services-to-layers mapping, and should probably be viewed more as an informative, than a normative part of a security architecture. For the Internet environment, the list of mechanisms should be made more specific, to provide concrete guidance to protocol developers. Mechanisms like Kerberos,[26] X.509 certificates, etc., should be explicitly cited as the preferred basis for implementing security services in the Internet, rather than the more generic mechanism discussions that appear in *ISO 7498-2*.

9.3.4.5 A Composite Mapping

The service-to-layer mapping often is viewed as the core of the OSI security architecture, and the mechanism-to-service mapping is often viewed as secondary. However, there are other mappings that one can envision incorporating into a security architecture, especially if the intent is to provide guidance that will promote interoperability. The Privacy and Security Research Group (PSRG) of the Internet Research Task Force is exploring one such additional mapping. This mapping focuses on network applications, usually as defined by a protocol or class of protocols. For each application, the security service requirements are characterized and a specific security technology, e.g., a set of security protocols and supporting infrastructure, is identified as appropriate to provide the requisite security services.

This mapping really is a refinement and composition of the OSI service-to-layer and mechanism-to-service mappings, and it captures what some have suggested should be the essence of an Internet security architecture. It should be clear, from discussions in previous sections, that such a mapping is only part of a security architecture, and it ought not to be developed in the absence of the definitions and other mappings described earlier. However, this composite mapping is useful in establishing standard options for securing various applications, maximizing the potential for interoperability.

In developing this mapping, the PSRG applied the OSI security layering principles and the Internet security mechanism principles elucidated above. In some cases, the mapping is based on examination of a specific protocol that provides a network service, but in most cases, it is based on the perceived requirements associated with any protocol offering the characteristic network service. Thus in some cases the mapping is protocol specific, while in other cases it is more generic. In some cases, specific protocols can be cited as appropriate to provide requisite security; in other cases a gap in available security functionality can be identified. The following is a sampling of this composite mapping, but it should not be construed as comprehensive nor as definitive. In each example, corresponding protocols from both the TCP/IP suite and the OSI suite are cited. This emphasizes how, in general, the same security approaches can be applied to classes of protocols irrespective of the protocol suite.

Electronic Mail

This is an especially common application—perhaps the most widely used application in the Internet. Today this service is provided primarily by a pair of protocols: *RFC 822,*[27] which defines message header formats, and SMTP, which defines a message transfer protocol. In the future the simple text messages of *RFC 822* will be joined by richer data types,[28] and the X.400 user population in the Internet is growing. The security service requirements for Internet e-mail are generally perceived to include connectionless confidentiality and integrity, data origin authentication, and nonrepudiation (by originator and recipient). These services provide protection for both message originators and recipients, but do not address the security concerns of e-mail service providers.

The Privacy Enhanced Mail (PEM) protocol is designed to provide (or support) these services in the *RFC 822* context. Future versions of PEM will accommodate Multipurpose Internet Mail Extensions (MIME) messages as well. PEM can also be carried as a body part in X.400. The 1988 version of X.411 incorporates a wide range of security mechanisms for messaging, encompassing not only the user-to-user services described above, but also a number of services involving mail relays, addressing the e-mail service provider concerns alluded to above. The Internet security architecture, in serving a multiprotocol environment, should encourage the use of these security mechanisms in conjunction with X.400, whenever appropriate to user security requirements. An Internet security architecture ought to encompass both the PEM and relevant X.411 security mechanisms.

Directory Services

There are two directory service models for the Internet: the Domain Name System (DNS) and X.500. Security service requirements are well defined for the latter, and X.500 incorporates an extensive set of protocol security mechanisms to implement these services. In contrast, there is no explicit characterization of security services for the DNS, and there is a corresponding lack of security mechanisms. Nonetheless, one can argue that, if the DNS were enhanced to incorporate security facilities, its service requirements would be quite similar to those defined for X.500, and that approach is adopted here.

There is a clear need for data origin authentication and connectionless integrity to protect directory queries and responses. Access control allows storage of data in a directory, with confidence that the data is modifiable only by authorized users or administrators, and that sensitive data is not disclosed to unauthorized users. It is expected that identity-based access control policies will be most relevant in the open Internet environment. All of these services are provided in X.500 via application layer protocol mechanisms. In addition, confidentiality for sensitive directory data may also be an important feature, but is most appropriately provided at the transport or network layer.

An Internet security architecture should recommend the use of the X.500 security facilities and corresponding lower layer (e.g., Network or Transport Layer) confidentiality mechanisms where needed. In the absence of DNS-specific security mechanisms, lower layer security mechanisms can be employed to provide authentication, integrity, and access control services; however, these will not provide functionality equivalent to that of X.500.

Network Management

In the open Internet, network management is provided primarily via SNMP. Recent enhancements to SNMP provide mechanisms in support of a set of perceived security requirements. The security services provided include connectionless confidentiality, connectionless integrity (with replay protection), data origin authentication, and identity-based access control. These services are intended to protect management communication against tampering, and to protect managed objects against attempts at unauthorized manipulation.

All of these services have been implemented in SNMP at the Application Layer, including a (symmetric) key distribution facility. It might appear that these services could be provided through the use of security mechanisms at lower layers. However, the integrity requirements here do not match the integrity services provided by connection-oriented or connectionless Network or Transport Layer protocols. At best, one could use such protocols to provide connectionless integrity and authenticity services, on top of which SNMP could add mechanisms to fulfill its requirements. This mismatch, plus the desire to engineer a comprehensive set of security mechanisms in a self-contained fashion and in advance of other (e.g., lower layer) security protocols, led to the development of the SNMP security enhancements.

It is reasonable to assume that a very similar set of security requirements is applicable to CMIP,[29] the corresponding OSI network management protocol, although CMIP does not yet incorporate equivalent security mechanisms. An Internet security architecture should embody the use of the security-enhanced SNMP (and a secure version of CMIP, should one become available).

Virtual Terminal and File Transfer

Virtual terminal applications are provided by protocols like Telnet and VT.[30] File transfer is supported by protocols such as FTP and FTAM.[31] For both types of protocols, obvious security requirements include connection-oriented confidentiality and integrity, peer-entity authentication, and (identity-based) access control. These requirements attempt to provide the security implicitly associated with a reliable, stream-oriented, point-to-point application protocol. One could provide these services via mechanisms implemented within these application protocols, but they also could be provided through the use of mechanisms at lower layers, e.g., at the transport or network layers. For example, a protocol like TLSP[30] could address these requirements, though the granularity of authentication provided at the Transport Layer may not be sufficient.

Relying on lower layer security mechanisms to support these security services for virtual terminal or file transfer protocols has the advantage of avoiding duplication of mechanisms, from both a development and an implementation standpoint. However, as noted earlier, there may be resistance to relying on mechanisms that require the introduction of new software into operating system kernels. For example, from a transition standpoint, it is easier to provide protection for these protocols if the security mechanisms are implemented at the application rather than at the Network or Transport Layers. Thus, for the moment, it isn't clear which approach should be preferred by an Internet security architecture.

File Servers

File servers are represented by protocols like Sun's NFS[32] and the Andrew File System (AFS) and are distinguished from file transfer protocols by providing a richer set of services, e.g., random access to files. Security service requirements here include connectionless confidentiality and integrity, peer-entity authentication, and (identity-based) access control. Some of these services (confidentiality and integrity) can be provided through reliance on Network or Transport Layer security protocols (e.g., NLSP or TLSP). However, the granularity at which access control must be provided, e.g., at the file or directory level, is clearly finer than can be offered via lower layer security services. None of these file service protocols are Internet or international standards, and no (strong) standard security protocols have been defined for these protocols. Thus, for now, it is difficult to make any concrete recommendation for an Internet security architecture with respect to file server protocols.

Interdomain and Intradomain Routing

Interdomain routing in the Internet may be effected via routers executing protocols like BGP, EGP, and IDRP.[33] Intradomain routing is effected via routers implementing protocols like OSPF and IS-IS.[34] Both types of protocols have similar security service requirements. Both require peer-entity authentication and connectionless integrity for the exchange of routing packets. It is conceivable that connectionless confidentiality also might be required in some circumstances, e.g., to conceal network topology information within a routing domain. Access control services might be employed to constrain neighbor connectivity.

Most of these security services can be provided using mechanisms at the Network or Transport Layers (e.g., via NSLP or TLSP), or can be engineered specifically for each routing protocol. (Some protocols, e.g., EGP, do not make use of a transport layer.) The granularity of authentication and access control is clearly well matched to the identification information provided at these layers. Some of these protocols may exhibit requirements that exceed connectionless integrity, but fall short of connection-oriented integrity. In such cases, it is possible to employ Network or Transport Layer connectionless integrity mechanisms, and then rely on additional, routing protocol sequencing facilities as necessary.

Alternatively, some of these protocols (e.g., BGP) incorporate syntactic place holders to support authentication and integrity. However, there are no matching security semantics (currently) specified for these routing protocols. Given the variety of routing protocols included in this class, there could be considerable benefit from utilizing common security mechanisms at the Network or Transport Layers.

A traffic flow confidentiality service may be offered by routers for subscriber packets on a point-to-point basis via Physical Layer mechanisms. However, a more subtle confidentiality requirement may arise in some circumstances. If some routers in a network are physically located in subscriber facilities, then other subscribers may desire confidentiality (connectionless and traffic flow) for their traffic as it transits these intermediate switches.

This could be provided by encapsulating (and protecting) the traffic at the entry router and at the exit router. This is clearly a Network Layer security service.

Other Protocol Classes

The preceding examples address only some of the most common protocol classes one encounters in the Internet. A partial list of other protocol classes that have been identified as having security requirements distinct from those above includes: time server protocols (e.g., NTP), news dissemination (e.g., NNTP), device-booting protocols (e.g., BOOTP), and print server protocols. In time, it is anticipated that these, and others, will be analyzed, and that recommended security techniques will be identified for each.

9.3.4.6 A Perimeter Security Approach

In exploring how to provide security for various network services, there often is a choice between developing an application-specific solution, or exploiting a common network or transport layer security technology. The former approach is essential for some applications, e.g., e-mail and directory services, if full security functionality is to be provided. However, for many applications, Network or Transport Layer security mechanisms would suffice. An alternative approach entails an application incorporating a few additional security mechanisms that rely on cryptographically enforced confidentiality, integrity, and authenticity from a Network or Transport Layer security protocol.

A specific motivation for adopting Network Layer security mechanisms arises from what might be termed a *perimeter* approach to security. A Network Layer security protocol such as NLSP offers the flexibility of implementation at either end systems or intermediate systems. Analysis of the DOD Internet security architecture indicated that this layering choice was motivated in large part because of the concern for high-assurance implementations, e.g., to address the threat of Trojan Horse software. The perceived threat in the open Internet appears to focus primarily on unauthorized access, but the concept of establishing a high-assurance security perimeter to counter that threat, and others, is still a valid strategy.

Today, many organizations' networks are not fully connected to the Internet. Instead, e-mail and DNS services are provided through a computer employed as a mail relay and DNS server. Any other access must be effected through an application layer gateway (often the same computer). This provides only very limited functionality to subscribers on the corporate network, losing much of the power and appeal of the Internet. This limited form of connectivity becomes unworkable if, for example, an organization wants to tie together sites at various locations via a shared network or via the Internet. Nonetheless, the concept of using an intermediate system to enforce a security perimeter (to act as a form of reference monitor) is well founded. An organization can devote resources to maintain a higher degree of security at the relay than can be effected at all the individual computers within the organization.

Another common approach to perimeter security is provided by routers incorporating *packet filtering*. This technique is used often in routers connecting corporate networks to the Internet. Here IP source and destination addresses, and well-known TCP and UDP ports, are used to make access control decisions. A common packet filtering policy permits two-way e-mail, DNS traffic, and outbound Telnet traffic, but all other traffic is barred. This filtering approach does not provide very fine-grained access control, is vulnerable to spoofing of IP addresses, and is not so effective when employed with OSI protocols. (Packet filtering does not work well with OSI protocols because the well-known port concept of TCP and UDP is not part of the OSI architecture.)

Packet filtering also fails to provide good protection for an organization should it attempt to create a "virtual private Internet" across the Internet or across a public network offering a service like frame relay or SMDS. In such circumstances, the lack of authentication for IP addresses significantly undermines the effectiveness of the mechanism. Other scenarios also are not well accommodated by this mechanism, e.g., authorized access to resources within the corporate network from a remote, nonaffiliated site by a traveling user. Even if a network administrator accepts the risks associated with the use of packet filtering as a security mechanism, there are likely to be growing administrative problems associated with this technique. The set of authorized applications will tend to grow over time, and will include more applications in which examination of TCP/UDP ports will not suffice to make access control decisions. For example, some applications may create ancillary connections using ports dynamically selected by the application, thus making the task of determining "authorized" port pairs unmanageable.

Packet filtering by a router is an example of a Network Layer security mechanism (it might be viewed as a form of routing control under the OSI mechanisms list). However, it violates the second security mechanism principle elucidated above; i.e., it is not based on a sound security foundation. Attempts to extend the concept to "peak at" higher layer protocol information, e.g., tracking connection establishment at the Transport Layer, are complex and probably violate the third security mechanism rule; i.e., they tend not to work in a situation where a LAN or campus network is multihomed. (In a multihomed environment not all packets associated with a connection may traverse the same gateway, making it very difficult to track connection establishment and termination exchanges at the Transport Layer.)

One can imagine alternative approaches to achieving the same perimeter security goals as packet filtering. For example, a hybrid strategy might use application relays for applications that entail relaying, and a router incorporating NLSP to secure real-time application communication. E-mail and directory services (especially X.500) are the obvious application relay candidates, and the security mechanisms developed for these applications specifically accommodate the staged delivery character that the use of an application relay embodies. Real-time applications, such as virtual terminal and file transfer, are easily accommodated by a security protocol like NLSP.

The traveling user scenario mentioned above, where the user employs a laptop or note-book computer equipped with NLSP, is easily accommodated using this approach. Use of NLSP among a set of routers connected to the Internet or a public packet network could provide a high-quality virtual private network and, via encapsulation, could even provide a level of traffic flow confidentiality. The major disadvantage of the scheme just described is that it cannot be effected unilaterally. Packet filtering can be introduced locally by an organization to provide some level of protection for access to its resources. Use of a net-work layer security protocol does not provide an analogous capability. Use of such a pro-tocol requires that the end systems (or designated intermediate systems) to which the corporate users wish to initiate connections must also implement the protocol. Thus the approach described here, although it offers additional security functionality and assur-ance, does not provide a complete replacement for packet filtering.

9.3.4.7   Security Infrastructure

Many of the security mechanisms that may find widespread use in the Internet require an infrastructure. The infrastructure provides management support for the security mecha-nisms, and may be viewed as a form of pervasive security mechanism. For example, secu-rity protocols like SILS, NLSP, and TLSP require some form of facility for the distribution of cryptographic keys. Even though these protocols operate at different layers in the protocol hierarchy, they all could be served by a single set of key management mechanisms. These mechanisms could encompass manual key management for very small, closed environments, and various forms of automated key management for larger, or more open, environments.

Work is underway in the Common Authentication Technology (CAT) working group to develop a hybrid system that would provide the automated key management alluded to above. This scheme would accommodate both symmetric key management, based on locally administered key distribution centers, and asymmetric (public-key) management using certificates. An important aspect of this hybrid system is that users of symmetric or asymmetric mechanisms could interoperate. The scheme is likely to be derived from ver-sion 5 of Kerberos (for symmetric key management), and a version of the scheme proposed in DEC's Distributed System Security Architecture.[35] This approach, using common infra-structure elements to support a variety of security protocols at various layers, is precisely the sort of architectural continuity that should be encouraged in the Internet.

Cryptographic key management is not the only security infrastructure problem to be addressed in the Internet. The certification system now being established for use with PEM provides a global, public-key certificate-based authentication technology that can be used in conjunction with key management of the sort alluded to above, or may be used independently. For example, this certification system is intended initially to serve PEM users who do not make use of the CAT mechanisms, because CAT mechanisms are restricted to real-time, point-to-point protocols. However, the PEM certification system can be used not only with PEM, but also with security mechanisms already built for X.400, X.500, and other protocols.

Additional common infrastructure mechanisms are required. For example, previous versions of Kerberos address authentication and key management, but try to be independent of access control mechanisms. The current version of Kerberos makes explicit provisions for certain access control functions, and the CAT-developed key management systems probably will incorporate similar functionality. This is appropriate, since there have been requests for a common access control technology that can be employed by developers of distributed applications. Audit collection and analysis mechanisms are also likely candidates for a common Internet security infrastructure.

9.4   ACKNOWLEDGMENTS

I would like to thank the members of the PSRG for their contributions to this chapter in the course of discussions at meetings in 1991 and 1992. Matt Bishop, Dave Gembeng, Russ Housley, Dan Nessett, and Cliff Neumann provided written comments, and Rob Shirey deserves special thanks for his very detailed review of this material. I also would like to thank those who have actively participated in the security working groups that were constituted in conjunction with two workshops on the future of the Internet architecture, in April 1991 and in January 1992. Finally, I would like to thank Dan Lynch, who persuaded me to write this chapter, despite my protestations that there was (and still is) no security architecture for the Internet.

REFERENCES

1   *Basic Reference Model-Part 2: Security Architecture, ISO 7498-2*, February 1989.

2   J. Moy, *OSPF Version 2, RFC 1247*, July 1991.

3   Department of Defense, *Trusted Computer System Evaluation Criteria, DOD 5200.28-STD*, December 1985.

4   *IEEE Standards for Interoperable Local Area Network (LAN) Security (SILS): Part B—Secure Data Exchange, IEEE 802.10B*, April 1992.

5   J.D. Case, M. Fedor, M.L. Schoffstall, and J. Davin, *Simple Network Management Protocol, RFC 1067*, August 1988.

6   J.M. Galvin, K. McCloghrie, and J.R. Davin, *SNMP Security Protocols*, *RFC 1352*, July 1992.

7   *Data Communication Networks: Services and Facilities, Interfaces*, Recommendations X.1-X.32, November, 1988.

8   V.L. Voydock and S.T. Kent, Security Mechanisms in High-Level Network Protocols, *ACM Computing Surveys*, Vol. 15, No. 2, 1983.

9   *Data Communication Networks: Directory*, Recommendations X.500-X.521, November 1988.

10 C. I'Anson and C. Mitchell, Security Defects in CCITT Recommendation X.509-The Directory Authentication Framework, *Computer Communication Review*, Vol. 20, No. 2, April 1990.

11 K.J. Biba, *Integrity Considerations for Security Computer Systems*, *ESD-TR-76-372*, Electronic Systems Division, Hanscom AFB, MA, April 1977; D.D. Clark, A Comparison of Commercial and Military Computer Security Policies, *Proceedings of the 1987 IEEE Symposium on Security and Privacy*, IEEE Computer Society, 1987.

12 T.F. Lunt, Automated Audit Trail Analysis and Intrusion Detection: A Survey, *Proceedings of the 11th National Computer Security Conference*, October 1988.

13 S.G. Stubblebine and V.D. Gligor, On Message Integrity in Cryptographic Protocols, *Proceedings of the IEEE Symposium on Research in Security and Privacy*, May 1992.

14 *Protocol for Providing the Connectionless—mode Network Service (Internetwork Protocol)*, *ISO 8473*, December 1988.

15 *Network Layer Security Protocol, ISO CD 11577* (under ballot), November 1991.

16 *Data Communication Networks: Message Handling Systems*, Recommendations X.400–X.420, November 1988.

17 J.P. Anderson, *Computer Security Technology Planning Study*, *ESD-TR-73-51*, Electronic Systems Division, Air Force Systems Command, October 1972.

18 National Computer Security Center, *Trusted Network Interpretation of the Trusted Computer System Evaluation Criteria*, *NCSC-TG-005*, July 1987.

19 D.E. Bell, and L.J. LaPadula, *Secure Computer Systems*, *ESD-TR-73-278*, Volumes I–III, The Mitre Corporation, Bedford, MA, November 1972–June 1974.

20   R. Shirey, Defense Data Network Security Architecture, *Computer Communication Review*, Vol. 20, No. 2, April 1990.

21   Encryption-Based Protection for Interactive User/Computer Communication, *Proceedings of the Fifth Data Communications Symposium*, September 1977.

22   R. Nelson, SDNS Services and Architecture, *Proceedings of the 10th National Computer Security Conference*, September 1987.

23   P.V. Mockapetris, *Domain Names—Implementation and Specification, RFC 1035*, November 1987.

24   J. Linn and S.T. Kent, *Privacy Enhancement for Internet Electronic Mail: Parts I–III, RFCs 1113–1115*, August 1989.

25   European Computer Manufacturers' Association, *Security in Open Systems: Data Elements and Service Definitions*, July 1989.

26   J. Kohn and B.C. Neuman, *Kerberos Version 5, Revision 5*, Project Athena, MIT, January 1992.

27   D. Crocker, *Standard for the Format of ARPA Internet Text Messages, RFC 822*, August 1982.

28   N. Borenstein, and N. Freed, *Multipurpose Internet Mail Extensions, RFC 1341*, June 1992.

29   *Common Management Information Protocol, ISO 9595*, July, 1990.

29   J.B. Postel and J.K. Reynolds, *Telnet Protocol Specification, RFC 854*, May 1983.

30   *Information Technology—Telecommunications and Information Exchange Between Systems—Transport Layer Security Protocol, ISO DIS 10736*, October, 1991; *Information Technology—Telecommunications and Information Exchange Between Systems—Virtual Terminal, ISO 904*1, 1990.

31   J.B. Postel, and J.K. Reynolds, *File Transfer Protocol, RFC 959*, October 1985; *File Transfer, Access, and Management (FTAM), ISO 8571*, October 1988.

32   Sun Microsystems, Inc., *NFS: Network File System Protocol Specification, RFC 1094*, March 1989.

33   K. Lougheed and Y. Rekhter, *Border Gateway Protocol 3 (BGP-3), RFC 1267*, October 1991; E.C. Rosen, *Exterior Gateway Protocol (EGP), RFC 827*, October 1982; *and Protocol for the Exchange of Inter-Domain Routing Information among Intermediate Systems to Support Forwarding of ISO 8473 PDUs, ISO CD 10747* (balloting completed December, 1991).

34 *Intermediate System to Intermediate System Routing Information Exchange Protocol for Use in Conjunction with ISO 8473, ISO 10589* (awaiting publication as an IS).

35 M. Gasser, A. Goldstein, C. Kaufman, and B. Lampson, The Digital Distributed System Security Architecture, *Proceedings of the 12th National Computer Security Conference*, October 1989.

CHAPTER 10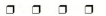

Creating New Applications

BARRY SHEIN

CONTENTS

A key strength of Internet technology is that many people implement new aspects of it—all the time! The Internet does not standardize on programmatic issues, per se. However, there are well-known programming environments. Rather than looking at the breadth of possibilities, we now focus on the facilities available to the implementor of a new application using one of the more common environments.

10.1   INTRODUCTION

To the programmer, the flexibility of network software is both a curse and a blessing. Conceptually, network applications are very simple: two or more programs pass data back and forth to accomplish some task. Simple applications are not much harder than this, but the opportunity for complexity can be vexing.

As with other objects in an operating system, such as files, the first chore is to name and address the object with which you wish to communicate. In a file system you would typically specify a file's name and its place in the file system hierarchy. Analogously, a networked application needs to address the host and specific application at the other end with which it wishes to communicate. To continue the analogy with files, a networked application must decide how the data stream is to be structured. This structure can be as simple as a stream of characters with no other order imposed, or it can be arbitrarily complex.

Several additional considerations are imposed on network applications that have no strong analogue with disk files. Networked communications operate in a time domain. When two applications communicate, the order of the communications is usually critical. Because networks can be unreliable in ways that file systems generally aren't, timers are often employed to avoid waiting forever for a response from the remote end. Network communications can be chosen to be reliable or unreliable, sequenced or not sequenced, and stream- or record-oriented. Typically, there are operating system calls that allow you to set or get information that is only loosely analogous to what is available with file systems, such as suppressing routing on a networked channel or using a broadcast address.

Even with this added complexity, writing network applications need not be difficult. As with any programming, you need to create a plan specifying what you wish to accomplish and to match that plan to the available facilities. To develop an effective plan you need to know what choices are before you. The purpose of this chapter will be to explain these choices, to show what sorts of problems they are used to solve, and to illustrate how to implement programs using these facilities.

10.2 A TAXONOMY OF NETWORK APPLICATIONS

10.2.1 Clients and Servers

There are several ways to classify network applications. The most common type of application is client-server. With client-server applications there are two or more programs, typically with one program acting as a master, or server, and the others acting as clients, or slaves. The hierarchical terminology of client-server or master-slave can be misleading, as if one side of the communication is more powerful or more important than the other. Another definition of a *server* is a program that serves up some resource. For example, a file server makes available files. A display server makes a bitmapped display (and keyboard and mouse) available to client programs. A client accesses these resources by connecting to a server and making requests.

Another common network applications architecture uses client-client or server-server structures. For example, consider a confederation of database servers. Each serves data, but together they might conspire among themselves to find the specific data being requested. None is particularly "client" or "server" when they speak to each other. This is also called a peer-to-peer application.

Finally, we have applications that don't quite fit into either of these categories. An example might be a program that makes no connections, but periodically broadcasts and receives broadcasts of information. There are many network routing managers that work in this manner. When they find a new route to a distant network they broadcast the information, so that every computer on the local network receives the update. Other routing daemons that are interested in the information catch the updates and squirrel them away. The interrelationship between these daemons is loose at best; none cares much if another goes away, except inasmuch as it might not get timely routing updates.

10.2.2 TCP or UDP?

The internet protocols impose another dimension of considerations on applications. The two most common protocols in an internet are TCP/IP and UDP/IP. TCP/IP is a reliable, stream protocol.[1] UDP/IP is an unreliable, datagram protocol.[2] TCP/IP guarantees that bytes sent will appear on the other end with no corruption and in exactly the order sent (it will mark the connection broken if this is not possible due to some network disruption). UDP/IP sends datagrams (i.e., blocks of data), with only an optional guarantee of the data being corruption-free and the possibility that the datagrams will arrive in a different order than they were sent. UDP/IP also provides no guarantee that the datagrams sent will arrive at all.

So why would an application designer ever choose UDP/IP? One reason is because there is an overhead incurred for the reliability and sequencing that TCP/IP provides.

Not all applications require that a datagram arrive in order, or even at all. Consider an application driving a slow-motion video image at 10 frames per second, or a continuous stream of sound, to a remote system. A low-probability mishap that causes some data to be lost or corrupted might only cause a $1/10$ second error in the displayed image, or a small crackle in the sound. But recovering that data would involve retransmitting it (as TCP/IP will do upon detecting any error). By the time the retransmitted data arrives it is probably too late to do anything with it in a real-time application like video or sound. In such a situation you are often better off just continuing with the next frame or sound bite rather than pausing while you inform the remote end that something wrong has occurred and asking it to retransmit. Similarly, you might have another way to recover from an error that is more efficient than TCP/IP's timeout and retransmission mechanism (such as having transmitted an error-correcting code with the data).

There is one pitfall to using UDP/IP. Some designers hear that it has lower overhead than TCP/IP, and struggle to use it in an inappropriate application. This often results in their simply reinventing TCP/IP, probably crudely, and now floating on the additional layer of UDP/IP.

For many applications, TCP/IP is likely to run faster than an application that imposes reliability and sequencing on top of UDP/IP. You might do some tests to convince yourself of this by comparing TFTP (a file transfer protocol that uses UDP/IP) and FTP (a file transfer protocol that uses TCP/IP) to see which is faster. In most implementations, FTP is much faster, mostly due to the asynchronous nature of TCP/IP. TCP/IP transmits in both directions almost simultaneously, receiving and verifying data, and thus keeping a channel very busy. TFTP, in contrast, sends a packet (block of data), waits for an acknowledgment, and then sends the next packet (or resends, on error). TFTP would show a lot of "dead-time" on the wire if you measured it; one side is usually waiting for the other side, rather than firing packets at each other simultaneously as occurs in TCP.

10.3 INTRODUCTION TO EXAMPLES

The best way to learn how to create new applications is to study annotated, working applications. In this chapter we will look at several working examples of increasing sophistication, each introducing new practical techniques in network programming.

The applications programming interface we will use is the Berkeley socket interface[3] under UNIX, or a C environment that provides an emulation of UNIX, and sockets, which are UNIX entities that are analogous to file descriptors. (Several such C environments exist for non-UNIX systems).

All of the examples below will use the following two convenience routines for reporting error messages and exiting with an error value:

```
extern char *prog;
extern FILE *errout;
```

```
/*
 * Error exit with our message
 */
fatal(msg) char *msg;
{
 if(errout)
      fprintf(errout,"%s: %s\n", prog, msg);
 exit(1);
 }

/*
 * Error exit with system message
 */
sysfatal(msg) char *msg;
{

      if(errout) {
           fprint(errout,"%s: ", prog);
           perror(msg);
      }
      exit(1);
}
```

10.4 COARSE STRUCTURE OF A CLIENT-SERVER APPLICATION

A skeletal structure for a server consists of the following:

1 Allocate a communication channel (socket).

2 Bind the socket to a port number that clients can address.

3 Inform the operating system of any relevant parameters needed.

4 Loop, waiting for incoming connections.

5 Process each connection.

A skeletal structure for a client consists of the following:

1 Allocate a communication channel (socket).

2 Connect the socket to a port number and host where the desired service resides.

3 Wait for the connection to complete and check for failure.

4 Perform the task.

5 Disconnect and clean up if necessary.

10.5   A WORKING EXAMPLE—TCP

Let's dissect and analyze a very simple client-server application using TCP/IP written in C on UNIX, or on any system that supports the Berkeley socket networking interface. The goal of the server will be to return system status information to the client. We will simply return the output of the finger command available on many systems.

10.5.1   A Simple Finger Server

10.5.1.1   Set Up

Our first problem is to specify the correct include (header) files. These are, minimally:

```
#include <stdio.h>
#include <sys/types.h>
#include <sys/socket.h>
#include <netinet/in.h>
#include <netdb.h>
#include <signal.h>
#include <errno.h>
```

The main() routine begins with some common and key declarations:

```
#ifdef TEST
#define TESTPORT 8888
#endif /* TEST */

#define FINGER "/usr/ucb/finger"

char *prog;

main(argc, argv) int argc; char **argv;
{
        struct servent *svp;   /* service entry      */
        struct protent *pp;    /* protocol entry     */
        int sock;              /* socket descriptor  */
        struct sockaddr_in sa;/* socket info         */
        extern int errno;

        prog = argv[0];
        errout = stderr;
```

10.5.1.2   Service Ports

The service entry from the system is filled in by a call to getservbyname(), which is a C library routine. Typically, but not necessarily, there is a file on UNIX systems (/etc/services) with entries describing well-known service ports and services. The entry for finger looks like:

```
finger          79/tcp
```

The entry says that finger is a TCP service assigned to port 79 (decimal). Many services have been preassigned to particular port numbers, either by being listed in the appropriate standards documents (*RFC* documents), or by prevailing convention.

We will use a test port number if the program has been compiled with either a –DTEST flag on the cc command line or if the line #define TEST has been added before the #ifdef. The reason is that low-numbered ports (under 1024), such as finger uses, are only available to super-users, and there may already be a server running on the public finger port on your system. The same port must be used in both the server and client. You can use the port returned by getservbyname() to try the client with the system's finger server; only servers are restricted from using low-numbered ports to prevent security problems.

The getservbyname() library subroutine will look this information up and return a servent structure with the following fields filled in (or a NULL pointer if the requested information can not be found):

```
struct servent {
  char *s_name;      /* official service name         */
  char **s_aliases;  /* other names for service, if any */
  ints_port;         /* well-known port for service    */
  char*s_proto;      /* protocol to use               */
};
```

The service name (s_name) for finger is simply *finger*. There are no aliases (s_aliases) for finger, typically, so this pointer will be empty. A port number (s_port) is called *well-known* if it is listed in an *RFC* as being assigned to a particular service.[4] Finger is assigned to port 79. You could skip this set up and just use port number 79, but it's generally good practice to get this information from the system, just in case it changes (not all services you may use will be as immutable as finger probably is by now). Finally, the protocol (s_proto) will be *tcp*.

10.5.1.3 Protocol Entries

The protocol entry is similar and is also retrieved from a file, in this case /etc/protocols. The entry in that file for tcp looks like:

```
tcp     6     TCP        # transmission control protocol
```

The protoent structure is filled in by a library call to getprotobyname(), and related calls. Its fields are:

```
struct protoent {
      char *p_name;          /* official protocol name   */
```

```
        char **p_aliases;       /* any aliases              */
        int p_proto;            /* protocol number          */
};
```

The official protocol name in this case will be the string *tcp*. If there were aliases and you gave one to getprotobyname(), this call could be used to translate back to the official name. The uppercase version is an alias (*TCP*), and will be listed in p_aliases. Finally, the protocol number expected by other system and library calls is in p_proto.

10.5.1.4 *Socket Addressing*

A socket, under UNIX, is an integer that is used within the kernel for I/O operations. Its address structure is the analogue to a file name, and is used to associate a socket with a particular host and service. You will fill it in with information obtained from the service entry and protocol calls, or other information coded into your program. The socket address structure is generically defined as:

```
struct sockaddr {
        ushort sa_family;
        char sa_data[14];
};
```

This is because it is used for all address families supported on the host, for example: Internet, UNIX (sockets in the file space), or ISO.

For each address family the address structures are generally redefined in a format convenient for that protocol. For the internet protocols this is defined in the file <netinet/in.h> as a sockaddr_in, containing:

```
struct sockaddr_in {
        short sin_family;          /* Address family (type)   */
        u_short sin_port;          /* Port to connect to      */
        struct in_addr sin_addr;   /* Host's address          */
        char sin_zero[8];          /* padding, ignored        */
}
```

The sin_family element is a short integer identifying which address type the subsequent information in the structure describes. Because it is the first element in the structure, the kernel can map it to a generic structure to decide how to interpret the information. The port number is the same as we have already discussed with the getservbyname() call and servent structure. We will simply copy that information, previously obtained, into this field.

The sin_addr is a fairly complicated structure containing a union that allows a programmer (typically, via library code) to break apart an internet address in various ways, such as treating it as a whole word or as 4 separate byte values. We will deal with this entity only indirectly via other library calls in these early examples.

Finally, the array sin_zero[] is just filled with 0s to make the internet version of this structure the same size as the generic version.

10.5.1.5 Numbers and Networking—A Slight Digression

At this point we should digress a little on numbers and networking. The internet protocols specify a format in which binary numbers are passed around between hosts.[4] This format is called network byte order. It does not apply to the application data—you can pass that around any way you like—but information that is used to establish the connection must be in the correct format.

At issue is whether the most significant byte is stored in the highest or lowest address in the word (which is multibyte, typically 4 bytes in length). Different processors store these bytes within a word differently. On DEC VAX and Intel x86 processors, the bytes are stored reversed relative to the order used in IBM 370, Motorola 68000, and most RISC architectures. Network byte order corresponds to how words are structured on the latter (e.g., IBM 370 and 68K) systems. When software is run on other architectures (e.g., VAX and Intel) the bytes must be swapped around within the word before they are introduced into the network.

To make this concept concrete, and to give you a way to investigate how your system stores bytes, the following very simple program can be run:

```
#include <stdio.h>
/*
 * byteorder.c
 */

main()
{
        char *p;
        long i;
        int j;

        p = (char *)&i;

        for(j=0; j < sizeof(i); j++)
                *p++ = j+1;
        printf(" 0x %lx\n", i);
        exit(0);
}
```

On an RS/6000, Sun/Sparc and other systems, the output is 0x01020304. This is network byte order. On a VAX, and other systems, the output is 0x4030201. The latter is not in network byte order, and must be converted.

Most systems provide subroutines (possibly implemented as macros) to swap these bytes. On architectures where no swapping is needed, these routines will have no effect, and often are implemented as simple macros that essentially disappear from the code during preprocessing, incurring no overhead at runtime. The relevant routines are:

- htons()   Host to network order, short word

- htonl()   Host to network order, long word

- ntohs()   Network to host order, short word

- ntohl()   Network to host order, long word

The numbers returned by getservbyname() and getprotobyname() are in network byte order. This means that if you wanted to print them out on a system with a different byte order you would need to correct for this, or else the numbers will appear strange, as in the following message:

```
printf("finger service port is %d/n",ntohs(svp->s_port));
```

Similarly, if you supplied your own port number, which is common when developing new services, rather than looking them up via the getservent() calls, you would need to correct for this:

```
#define MYPORT          8888
        port = htons(MYPORT);
```

Because the routines are guaranteed to do the right thing on any host, even if no reordering is necessary, it is a good idea to use them in all of your program code.

Now, on with the server code.

10.5.1.6   Network Database Library Calls

First, we need to look up the numeric port information corresponding to finger via TCP:

```
if((svp = getservbyname("finger","tcp")) == NULL)
    fatal("no service info for finger/tcp");
```

We have called getservbyname() with two arguments, the service name we want information about, and the protocol family we expect to use it on. Some services are defined for more than one protocol, such as the time service, which is TCP port number 37 and UDP port number 37 (the same port number in each case, but that is not required). If the routine returns a NULL (zero pointer), then no information could be found about the requested items. In that case we print an error message and exit with a nonzero error code.

Next we look up the information corresponding to the TCP protocol for use later in the program:

```
if((pp = getprotobyname("tcp")) == NULL)
    fatal("cannot get protocol entry for tcp");
```

This is very similar to the getservbyname() call in every way. It is important to note that for both calls, the area pointed at is statically allocated. This means that if you need to call the routines again, but wish to retain the results of previous calls, you must copy them somewhere else. In these particular usages this problem is not common, but it does come up with more complicated applications.

10.5.1.7   *Setting up the Socket Structure*

Next we fill in the socket address structure:

```
      bzero(&sa,sizeof(sa));
      sa.sin_family = AF_INET;
#ifdef TEST
      sa.sin_port = htons(TESTPORT);
#else
      sa.sin_port = svp->s_port;
#endif /* TEST */
      sa.sin_addr.s_addr = htonl(INADDR_ANY);
```

First we zero out the structure so that any areas not used (such as the padding at the end) are filled with 0s. Next we set the address family, which is AF_INET. Sin_family only communicates the address family information to the kernel, and so does not need to be corrected for byte order.

If we have defined TEST, then we can correct our constant TESTPORT for network byte order and copy it into the socket address structure. Otherwise, the port number for the finger service is copied out of the answer returned by getservbyname(). The port number was returned to us by that library call in network order, so there is no need to swap it again (in fact, doing so would be erroneous).

Finally, we address the s_addr element as a long word and set it to the system constant INADDR_ANY, which happens to be zero. However, we shouldn't rely on that, and we should use the predefined symbol converted to network byte order. INADDR_ANY is a wildcard, of sorts. It tells the system that we will take connections from anywhere.

Alternatively, we could set s_addr to the IP address of an interface for this machine. This is useful when there is more than one interface, as it tells the system we are only interested in connections coming in on that interface. One application of this might be a server that should only be used by hosts on our local network. Or we might start one copy of the server for each interface, to split up the work.

Next, we need to use the information just acquired to get a socket and bind it to the service we plan to provide.

```
  if((sock = socket(AF_INET,SOCK_STREAM,pp->p_proto)) < 0)
      sysfatal("socket");
```

10.5.1.8   Binding a Server's Socket to a Service

The constants AF_INET (Address Family Internet) and SOCK_STREAM (a stream socket) are defined in the system header file <sys/socket.c>. The pp->p_proto element in this case will be the value indicating a TCP socket is desired. It was filled in by our earlier call to getprotobyname().

```
if(bind(sock,&sa,sizeof(sa)) < 0)
    sysfatal("bind");
```

Bind() connects the information that we set up in the socket address structure to the actual socket just allocated. We need to tell bind() the size of the socket address structure because sizes may vary for different address families.

   The combination of these two calls, socket() and bind(), is analogous to the UNIX open() call. The socket() call allocates an object similar to a file descriptor, and bind() connects it to a particular object with which the operating system knows how to communicate.

Discussion

The immediate question that pops into mind is: Why not just use the UNIX open() call? Why were these new calls added to the 4.2 BSD version of UNIX? One reason is that open() already was widely in use, and took a string (a file path) as its first argument. Forcing it into double duty would have been clumsy. Another reason is that options can be set on a socket after the allocation but before the bind, which might affect its behavior later. The broad application of sockets to provide an interface to many different network protocols justified a design that allowed for great flexibility.

   Alternatively, one might speculate as to why we don't just simplify the interface and use a string, perhaps one that looks somewhat like a file name, and pass it to open()? This has been tried at least a few times, for example, in BBN's TCP/IP implementation for the TOPS-20 operating system. It generally has met with only modest success. In particular, options caused such a string to become quite bulky and to resemble a filename less and less. Unlike descending a directory tree, there can be many choice points in defining a network connection precisely.

   The reader is invited to write a routine—call it nopen()— that simulates such an interface, if you still find it compelling after reading this discussion. Rework the examples in this chapter using this simulation as a proof of concept.

10.5.1.9   Setting the Backlog

The listen() system call is used to set the *backlog*:

```
if(listen(sock,SOMAXCONN) < 0)
    sysfatal("listen");
```

Although calling listen() is not strictly necessary, it is common and expected in network server applications to set the maximum backlog permitted. Your server program might be bogged down servicing a request when, suddenly, another client tries to connect to you. The operating system is willing to make the client wait. But there are limits to how many clients it's reasonable to keep waiting. The operating system will impose some limit on how many clients may be queued up awaiting your acceptance of their connect attempt.

Using listen() you may set a limit for your server application that is equal to or less than the system-imposed limit. If your limit is more than SOMAXCONN, "excess" clients trying to get on the queue will receive an error that the connection has been refused. (Actually, in implementations I have looked at, the critical value is MIN (yourvalue, SOMAX-CONN)×$\frac{3}{2}$, for obscure reasons.) It is unfortunate that this is also the same error message received when there is no such service at this host. It is hard for a client to deduce that trying again in a few minutes might be successful.

We will design applications in a way such that if the queue ever gets very long, something is seriously wrong. Either the system itself is so busy that we are falling behind in our work hopelessly, or we are stuck in a loop or some other futile situation from which we may never return.

Discussion

There are two ways to ensure that the queue does not get very long. One is to fork() a copy of ourselves (or another program) that will actually do the work. That is, we will accept a connection, fork a child to do the work (passing the open socket down), and immediately return to accepting connections. The other way is to just not do very much work for each client (e.g., a server that has just returned the date probably does not have to make any special preparations to keep the conversation short). One could argue that a third method could be used—we could keep checking periodically for a new client (perhaps several times per second, based on timed software interrupt or some other event) no matter what we are doing. I will claim that this is just a form of multiprogramming—implementing the process scheduling loop within your application rather than using the one the operating system provides via fork().

10.5.1.10 The Main Loop

We now enter an infinite loop awaiting new connections:

```
for(;;) {
    int newsock;
    int sz;
    struct sockaddr_in newsa;

    sz = sizeof(newsa);
    if((newsock = accept(sock, &newsa, &sz)) < 0) {
    if(errno == EINTR)
```

```
                    continue;
              else
                    sysfatal("accept");
        }
        finger(newsock); /* finger() closes newsock */
  }
```

The accept() call blocks execution until a new client comes along, much like a read() call on a terminal causes the system to wait for the user to enter new input.

The return value of accept is a new socket for communicating with the newly arrived client. The socket address structure passed to accept () is filled in with host address information for the remote end of the connection.

Accept() might fail for any number of reasons. One reason, in which we are not interested, is if the call() is interrupted (such as by a timed interrupt elsewhere in the program, or a signal that a child process has exited). In that case, we will just ignore the error and proceed with the loop from the top. In any other case of accept() returning a negative value, we will assume that something serious has happened and exit after printing a suitable error message.

Finally, we call our finger() subroutine, passing the newly acquired socket, which will perform whatever chore we have promised. Other than the specifics of setting up the socket address and service port, you could replace the finger() routine with your own doit() routine and use this as a generic server for most simple applications.

10.5.1.11   The Simple Finger Service

A stream socket can generally be used like any UNIX file descriptor. The finger() routine implied above could be as simple as:

```
finger(sock) int sock;
{
      char buf[BUFSIZ];
      char cmd[BUFSIZ];
      FILE *pp;
      int i;

      switch(fork()) {

      case -1:                /* error      */
          sysfatal("fork");
      case 0:                 /* child      */
          break;
      default:                /* parent     */
          close(sock);
          return;
      }
```

```
        readline(sock, buf, BUFSIZ);
        sprintf(cmd, "%s %s", FINGER, buf);
        if((pp = popen(cmd, "r")) == NULL)
            fatal(cmd);
        while(fgets(buf, BUFSIZ,pp)) {
            hton_string(buf);
            if(write(sock, buf, strlen(buf)) < 0)
                    break;
        }
        pclose(pp);
        exit(0);
    }
```

If there is no error, the fork() call will return twice, once in the parent and once in the child. When fork() returns in the child, it returns 0. When fork() returns in the parent, it returns the system process id of the newly created child. On first glance this code is confusing; it is actually running twice after the fork call (unless some error has occurred).

When the parent is finished, it closes the socket and returns to the main routine, immediately ready to service a new client connection. This is how we avoid a backlog; i.e., we use multiprogramming to accomplish multiplexing.

The FINGER protocol[5] specifies that a finger server take at least a single text line to indicate a specific user or users, to limit the output. Our simple example will take exactly one line of text with, optionally, one username on it. We incorporate this argument into a command line buffer.

The popen() routine opens a read (or write) pipe to a command under UNIX. We echo the output of finger to the socket, converting the text to the network format.

10.5.1.12 Support Routines—Reading Text Across a Network

The child uses two routines, readline() and hton_string(), which have not been defined yet. Strings (or text lines) on an internet are passed in ASCII and are terminated with a carriage return and linefeed. UNIX text is in ASCII, but UNIX terminates text lines with just a linefeed, so the text has to be converted.

TCP does not guarantee that a block of bytes written to a socket will appear all at once in a single read call on the other end. All TCP guarantees is that they will all arrive correctly and in the order they were sent (else, an error will be reported). The readline() routine continues to read the socket until an entire internet format text line is seen (or until the function gives up and returns an empty buffer). The carriage return and linefeed pair is converted to the UNIX linefeed format:

```
/*
 * Reads up to a carriage return linefeed pair
 * and returns as null-terminated string in buf
 * (empty string on EOF or error).
 */
```

```
void
readline(sock, buf, max) int sock; char *buf; int max;
{
        int sawcr = 0;
        char *bp;


        for(bp=buf; (read(sock, bp, 1) == 1) && (max-- > 0) ; bp++)
            if(*bp == '\r')
                sawcr = 1;
            else if(sawcr && *bp == '\n') {
                bp[-1] = '\n';
                *bp = '\0';
                return;
            }
            else
                sawcr = 0;

        buf[0] = '\0';
        return;
}


/*
 * Convert UNIX text line to Internet text line.
 */
void
hton_string(bp) char *bp;
{
        int len;

        if((len = strlen(bp)) == 0)
                return;

        if(bp[len-1] == '\n') {
            bp[len-1] = '\r';
            bp[len] = '\n';
            bp[len+1] = '\0';
        }
        return;
}
```

Terminating the buffer with a null byte in hton_string() is not necessary, but it is convenient for use with routines that expect a C string.

10.5.1.13 Managing Child Processes

The astute reader will notice a few important details missing from this otherwise complete program. The most serious is that we have made no arrangement for waiting for exiting child processes. Under UNIX, child processes that exit and are not collected become zombies. These are processes that are mostly finished, but whose exit status is maintained because there is no practical way for the operating system to know whether or not another (parent) process will come along eventually and ask for it. Each zombie counts against the maximum number of processes you may have running at once, and against the maximum number of processes the system can have running at once. Not collecting child processes and putting them to rest properly is both rude and doomed to failure; eventually your fork() call will fail.

To correct this problem we can reap child processes using a software interrupt (signal). Toward the top of the program we add:

```
#include <signal.h>
#include <sys/wait.h>
```

and write a small interrupt handling routine to reap child processes:

```
reap()
{
    union wait s;

    while(wait3(&s, WNOHANG, NULL) > 0)
        ;
}
```

The wait3() system call waits for a child's exit, and informs the operating system that it is now alright to completely free any resources associated with that child process. If there are no child processes, then wait3() returns immediately with a −1. The exit status of the child and other information is returned in the first argument passed to wait3(). We are not interested in this, although it might be interrogated for errors or other conditions.

The wait3() call will wait for any active children to die, unless the WNOHANG flag is passed. With this flag, it returns immediately, either with a recently exited child's status; a −1, indicating that there are no children; or a 0, indicating that there are children but they are still active. We do not want to wait, we only want to collect children already exited. The third argument (in our example, NULL) can be a pointer to a resource usage structure and would, on successful return, contain the accounting information for the child process.

The routine loops just in case there is more than one child ready to be reaped; this is a harmless and occasionally helpful precaution.

In the main program, just before our accept() infinite loop, we set the signal to indicate that our reap() routine is to be called whenever a child exits:

```
signal(SIGCHLD, reap);
```

understands some variations, such as 18.1 (same as 18.0.0.1), and will cause your program to work like every other application, in ways users have come to expect. There's no sense in reinventing the wheel, as they say.

To look up a host we use the gethostbyname() or gethostbyaddr() library calls, which return a hostent structure containing the following elements:

```
struct hostent {
      char *h_name;          /* official name of host           */
      char **h_aliases;      /* alias list                      */
      int h_addrtype;        /* host address type               */
      int h_length;          /* length of address               */
      char **h_addr_list;    /* list of addresses from name server */
}
```

Hosts often have more than one name. The first element, h_name, is the official name of the host, and the h_aliases array will contain all its other names. You may pass gethostbyname() any name for the host that appears in either the h_name or h_aliases fields.

The address type is intended to distinguish between address families: Internet, ISO, DECnet, etc. The h_length field gives the length in bytes of the binary address. Finally the entity h_addr_list is an array of pointers to binary addresses for the host. Many hosts have more than one address, as they act as gateways between two or more networks. What is nearly impossible to know, from the application, is which of these addresses is the best to use. In some cases, only one address may even be reachable from the client's host. Our approach to this dilemma will be to simply try each address in turn until one works. This method does not guarantee choosing an optimal address (which would imply a route by which our packets travel). We could first check if any of the addresses provided are on the same network we are, which is usually a good indicator of a low-cost route:

```
if(((long)(addr.s_addr = inet_addr(host))) != -1) {

    if((hp = gethostbyaddr(&addr, sizeof(addr), AF_INET)) == NULL) {
          fprintf(stderr, "%s: host %s unknown\n", prog,host);
          exit(1);
    }
}
else if((hp = gethostbyname(host)) == NULL) {
          fprintf(stderr, "%s: host %s unknown\n", prog,host);
          exit(1);
}
/* Fill in the sockaddr structure */
bzero(&sa, sizeof(sa));
sa.sin_family = AF_INET;
#ifdef TEST
sa.sin_port = htons(TESTPORT);
#else
```

```
      sa.sin_port = svp->s_port;
#endif /* TEST */


    /* Get a stream (TCP) socket */
    if((sock = socket(AF_INET, SOCK_STREAM, pp->p_proto)) < 0)
        sysfatal("socket");
```

10.5.2.3 The Main Loop

Our main loop, modified to check all the addresses for the host, becomes:

```
    /* Loop through all addresses for host trying to connect */
    for(i=0; hp->h_addr_list[i] != NULL; i++) {
        /* Try next address in list */
        bcopy(hp->h_addr_list[i],
            &sa.sin_addr.s_addr, hp->h_length);

      if(connect(sock, & sa, sizeof(sa)) >= 0) {
          if((write(sock, user, strlen(user)) != strlen(user))
              || (write(sock, "\r\n", 2) != 2)) {
              fatal("write error");
          }
          /* Echo reply to standard output */
          while((i = read(sock, buf, BUFSIZ)) > 0) {
              buf[i] = '\0';
              ntoh_string(buf);
              fputs(buf, stdout);
          }
      }

      /* Done */
      close(sock);
      exit(0);
    }
  }

    fatal("could not connect to host");
  }
```

10.5.2.4 Connect

There is no bind() or listen() call in the client; these are normally only used by servers. Instead, the socket address is filled in with the next address and passed to connect(). Connect() is analogous to bind() for the client. A client makes an active connection; a server creates a passive socket. The active socket seeks out a server, or fails. The passive socket just sits and waits, even if it is impossible for some reason to be connected to a client. It seems intuitively backwards that the server is passive and the client is active, but when you understand the mechanisms, it makes perfect sense.

When connect() succeeds in returning a nonnegative value, the socket is connected through the network to a server. All that is left is to use ordinary UNIX I/O calls to read data from the socket and echo it to the user's standard output (probably, but not necessarily, the terminal). As with file I/O, returning from a read with the value 0 indicates that there is no more data to be read. We close the socket (not strictly necessary, in this example) and exit.

10.5.3   Servers Running Under inetd

Early in UNIX's networking history it occurred to some clever systems programmer that it was neither necessary nor desirable to have a server (or daemon) started at system boot for each service the system offers. There might be dozens of servers, and only a few of them might be used in a given day. The new idea was to start a sort of super-server which would listen on the port of every service the system offered. When a client connected, the super-server would start the appropriate server program and pass the connection down. The super-server is called *inetd*, and is started on system boot. It reads a configuration file telling it which services the system offers, and sits waiting for connections on all ports mentioned.

The inetd configuration file is a simple text file containing one entry per line, describing the services that inetd will manage. The entries in the file will vary a little from system to system, but they basically look like:

```
ftp   stream   cp   nowait   root   /usr/etc/ftpd   tpd
```

There are seven fields in each entry: the name of the service, the socket type, the protocol, whether inetd should wait for the server to exit before resuming listening on the socket, the user under which the server should run, the path of the server program, and the command line arguments (including the zeroth argument, usually but not necessarily, the command's filename).

When inetd starts a server, the newly connected socket is passed to it on file descriptor 0 (standard input, although it's bidirectional in this case). This greatly simplifies the coding of a server. In fact, the entire main() routine described above reduces to:

```
main()
{
      finger(0);
      exit(0);
}
```

All we are missing in a server started by inetd is the address information for the remote side of the connection, which we would otherwise get from the accept() call. This can be obtained from the getpeername() call, if we are interested:

```
main()
{
        struct sockaddr_in newsa;
        int sz;

        sz = sizeof(newsa);
        if(getpeername(0, &newsa, &sz) < 0)
            sysfatal("getperrname");
        finger(0);
        exit(0);
}
```

In this example, we do not use the information returned by getpeername() in any way. Something we might do with that information is to record in the system log that a connection has arrived, and where it has arrived from. Adding the following line right after the call to getpeername() accomplishes this.

```
syslog(LOG_INFO,"finger: from %s",
                        inet_ntoa(newsa.sin_addr));
```

You will also need to include the <syslog.h> header file at the top of your program file.

10.6 A WORKING EXAMPLE—UDP

A very simple UDP protocol, daytime,[6] is defined in *RFC 867*. A client sends a UDP packet, which is responded to with a human-readable (text) time string. The contents of the client's packet are not defined, it is only used to indicate the request. Normally this simple service, as well as several others, are handled directly by the inetd program. To test our server, we will need to use a UDP port other than the well-known port number, although we can try our client against any system running inetd.

10.6.1 The Daytime Server

10.6.1.1 Setup

The main() routine of the server is similar to the previous example. One variation is that we will use an optional test port number to let us run it without needing to modify our system's daytime facilities. The port I've chosen, 8888, is completely arbitrary, other than its being above 1024 (out of the range of well-known ports), and, as far as I know, is unused by any systems software. You can use another if the choice causes a problem on your system:

10.6.2   The Daytime Client

The daytime client is similar to the TCP client in our previous example. One important difference is that there might be no response to a request sent via UDP. The packet might be lost, for example, or hopelessly corrupted. UDP provides no method for dealing with these errors.

The example client will provide for this possibility by using a timeout. We will wait only 30 seconds for a response (the value is easily modified in the program), and when the alarm rings we'll assume a response will never arrive. There's no certainty to this method: a response might very well arrive 31 seconds after the request is made. The operating system knows to throw such a packet away if it's not claimed, so there's no harm done other than missing an opportunity.

Another approach, which might be more successful in some situations, would be to resend the request every few seconds until someone (perhaps the user waiting for a response) gives up. The motivation for resending the request would be that it might be our request that was lost, rather than the response.

Even more vexing is that not all servers support daytime requests, and UDP does not inform you explicitly when this is the problem. When a TCP client attempts to connect to a nonexistent service an error (ECONNREFUSED) is returned, so we at least know something has gone wrong (although it could also be that the backlog is full). When a UDP packet is sent to a nonexistent server the packet is just thrown away without response.

Consequently, there is little you can conclude from a timeout in a UDP client. There may be no appropriate server at the remote site; your request may have not made it through; the response may not have made it through; or everything might be fine and the network is slow, so you thought you had waited long enough but, in fact, the response was on its way! All you really know when a timeout failure occurs is that you set up some expectations (that a response would return within 30 seconds), and those expectations were not met.

10.6.2.1   Daytime Client Setup

First, some header files and other boilerplate:

```
#include <stdio.h>
#include <sys/types.h>
#include <sys/param.h>
#include <sys/socket.h>
#include <netinet/in.h>
#include <netdb.h>
#include <setjmp.h>
#include <signal.h>

#ifdef TEST
#define TESTPORT 8888
#endif
```

```
#define TIMEOUT    30
#define MSGSIZ     256

jmp_buf jbuf;

char *prog;
FILE *errout;

onalarm()
{
     signal(SIGALRM, onalarm);
     longjmp(jbuf, 1);
}
```

After the header files we have added a conditionalized constant TESTPORT to match the server. To use the test port you would compile with a flag, –DTEST, or its equivalent. The timeout has been set to 30 seconds; the choice is arbitrary, and is based more on a person's patience to wait for a response than on any deep knowledge of the correct value to use.

The message size, MSGSIZ, is also fairly arbitrary, although there are some considerations. UDP is packet-oriented and there are two limits on packet sizes. One is protocol-related: 64 Kbytes. A UDP packet has only a 16-bit field length, so at most 65,536 8-bit bytes may appear in the data portion of a UDP message. It is not very difficult for a programmer to break up a message into small parcels and reassemble them at the other end, but UDP will not do this for you (TCP will). The second limit is system-imposed. It is not guaranteed that a particular implementation of UDP will support a 64-Kbytes limit on a single UDP message; it might be considerably less.

Some investigation on various systems I have used reveals that the situation with practical length limitations under UDP is less than ideal. One system refuses to send a UDP packet more than 8 Kbytes in length, and returns an error when the sendto() is attempted (EMSG-SIZE). Then, when an 8-Kbytes packet is sent from that system successfully, to another vendor's system on which a server is running, it refuses to hear any packet larger than 4 Kbytes. No error is returned in that case, but the request is consistently ignored until the packet size is reduced. These variations are all on the same Ethernet.

Consequently, we try to keep UDP packets comfortably small; in our example, 256 bytes should do the job. The packet we are sending from the client contains no information, so most any size will do. For receiving, there is nothing in the specification[6] about a maximum, or even a suggested length for the textual reply. We will assume that common sense dictates that a date returned for human consumption will be less than 256 characters in length, likely much less. For simplicity's sake we will use this as the length for both the sent and received packets (it allows us to easily reuse the same buffer, as well).

The onalrm() routine is an interrupt handler for the SIGALRM timeout interrupt provided by UNIX. We use the setjmp() and longjmp() facilities, which provide for a nonlocal go to. A trap is set with setjmp(), which returns 0 on its first call. What setjmp() actually does is squirrel away the information needed to do a later longjmp() in the jbuf variable. Later, when longjmp() is called, setjmp() will appear to have returned again, almost magically. However, when setjmp() returns due to a longjmp() call, the return value will be nonzero, so we can distinguish this event in the code with a simple if() statement.

The following set-up code is similar to our previous TCP client example:

```
main(argc, argv) int argc; char **argv;
{
 struct servent *svp;
 struct protoent *pp;
 struct hostent *hp;
 int sock;
 struct sockaddr_in sa;
 int i;
 char buffer[MSGSIZ];
 char *host;
 struct in_addr addr;

 prog = argv[0];
 errout = stderr;

     if(argc != 2) {
     fprintf(stderr, "Usage: %s hostname\n", prog);
     exit(1);
 }
 else
     host = argv[1];


 if(((long)(addr.s_addr = inet_addr(host))) != -1) {

     if((hp = gethostbyaddr(&addr, sizeof(addr), AF_INET)) == NULL) {
             fprintf(stderr, "%s: host %s unknown\n", prog,host);
             exit(1);
     }
 }
 else if((hp = gethostbyname(host)) == NULL) {
     fprintf(stderr," %s: host %s unknown\n", prog,host);
     exit(1);
 }

 if((svp = getservbyname("daytime", "udp")) == NULL)
     fatal("no service entry for daytime/udp");

 if((pp = getprotobyname("udp")) == NULL)
     fatal("no udp protocol info");
```

We retrieve the host to query for the time from the command line; the person running the program provides the host name. We then look up the appropriate host, service, and protocol information as before.

10.6.2.2 Socket Setup

For this UDP example we use the following code to set up the socket:

```
        bzero(&sa, sizeof(sa));
        sa.sin_family = AF_INET;
 #ifdef TEST
        sa.sin_port = htons(TESTPORT);
 #else
        sa.sin_port = svp->s_port;
 #endif

        if((sock = socket(AF_INET, SOCK_DGRAM, pp->p_proto)) < 0)
                sysfatal("socket");
```

The only major variations from the TCP example are the use of a test port (which we could have done with our finger example, and is a recommended way to test code), and the use of SOCK_DGRAM in the socket call, which together with the AF_INET flag and pp->p_proto information tells the operating system that we want a UDP socket. Some systems implement another protocol, RDP (Reliable Datagram Protocol). To obtain an RDP socket, the first two arguments to socket() would also be AF_INET and SOCK_DGRAM, but the pp->p_proto flag would be different. Other combinations are possible, even if not common.

10.6.2.3 The Main Loop

The following is the working section of the code:

```
    signal(SIGALRM, onalarm);

    for(i=0; hp->h_addr_list[i] != NULL; i++) {
        int sz, ret;
        struct sockaddr_in newsa;

        if(setjmp(jbuf) != 0) {
            printf("timeout.\n");
            continue;
        }

        bcopy(hp->h_addr_list[i], &sa.sin_addr.s_addr, hp->h_length);
```

```
printf("Trying [%s]...", inet_ntoa(sa.sin_addr));
fflush(stdout);

if(sendto(sock, buffer, sizeof(buffer),0, & sa, sizeof(sa)) < 0)
    sysfatal("sendto");

alarm(TIMEOUT);

sz = sizeof(newsa);
ret = recvfrom(sock, buffer, sizeof(buffer), 0, &newsa, &sz);
alarm(0);
if(ret < 0) {
    printf("error\n");
    perror("recvfrom");
}
else {
    printf("ok\n");
    write(1, buffer, ret);
    exit(0);
}
    }
  }
```

Note that this code is different from the earlier TCP client example. First, we inform the operating system that if a SIGALRM (timed) interrupt should occur, our routine onalarm() will handle it. We then enter a loop trying every address for the requested host until we succeed (or run out of addresses to try).

The setjmp() is set for a later longjmp() from the onalarm() routine, as previously described. When a timeout occurs we print a message on the user's standard output, and proceed with the next address.

The address is copied to the partially filled-in socket address structure, we inform the user of the internet numeric address we are trying, and use sendto() to actually send the buffer. The alarm() is set, and we enter recvfrom(), hoping for a response. When we return from recvfrom() for any reason, success or failure, we immediately cancel the alarm() by passing it a 0-second timeout, a convention in UNIX that means "cancel any currently running alarms." At this point either we have detected some error by the recvfrom() call (not likely, unless there's been a programmer error), or we have received a successful response, so we can print the date received to the standard output, and we're done. Notice that there is no connect() call done in the client. UDP is connectionless; we merely fling a packet out onto the network via sendto(). Similarly, there was no accept() call in the UDP daytime server.

10.6.2.4 *Connect and UDP*

We can use connect() with UDP sockets. However, it has no networking effect as it would with TCP. Its only effect with a UDP socket, under UNIX, is to set the address for future sends and receives so we may use read() and write()—or send() and recv()—which don't specify a socket address on each call. Here is the same loop using the connect() approach and ordinary read() and write() calls. We will only use the first interface address from the hostent structure, to simplify the example:

```
bcopy(hp->h_addr_list[0],&sa.sin_addr.s_addr,hp->h_length);

if(connect(sock, &sa, sizeof(sa)) < 0)
        sysfatal("connect");

if(setjmp(jbuf) != 0)
        fatal("timeout");

printf("Trying [%s]...", inet_ntoa(sa.sin_addr));
fflush(stdout);

if(write(sock, buffer, sizeof(buffer)) != sizeof(buffer))
        sysfatal("write");

alarm(TIMEOUT);

ret = read(sock, buffer, sizeof(buffer));

alarm(0);

if(ret < 0) {
        printf("error\n");
        perror("write");
}
else {
        printf("ok\n");
        write(1, buffer, ret);
        exit(0);
}
```

Another way to exploit the relatively lightweight, connectionless approach in UDP would be to send off requests to addresses of more than one host, by just modifying the socket address structure repeatedly and firing off a sendto() with no intervening recvfrom() call. Then you could issue one recvfrom() call, and whoever returns an answer "wins;" the rest are ignored. Print the response and exit. You can identify who answered the request, if interested, by printing the information returned by recvfrom() in the newsa socket address structure.

10.6.3   UDP Broadcasts

Another common facility used in internetworking is broadcasting. When a program sends a broadcast packet, the packet is sent to every host on the network simultaneously. How this is accomplished depends upon the underlying network technology. On an Ethernet it is relatively easy; Ethernet supports its own broadcast protocol (by sending to an address of all 1s); the IP-to-device layer will just translate to the underlying device technology. Many network technologies don't support broadcasts at all.

Even on a local area, network broadcasts should be used sparingly. Broadcasts cause every machine on the network to at least glance at the broadcast packet, even if it's discarded (due to the lack of an appropriate service or protocol). Worse, badly designed applications have been known to engage in broadcast storms. This occurs when a host receives a broadcast, decides it needs to be responded to, and blindly sends the response back out to the destination address, resulting in another broadcast. A few hosts doing this, perhaps infinitely as they respond to the new broadcasts with more broadcasts, can cause the network to freeze up entirely. Most modern network implementations try to protect against this behavior, but a rogue application could still be a culprit.

A good use of broadcasts (some would say there are no good uses) would be to provide or request information very occasionally either when the application is sure many systems on the network are interested (such as a new resource coming on-line), or when it is very hard to determine the correct host to which to send a request (such as when a diskless workstation calls out for its disk server during a system startup).

10.6.3.1   Resource Location Protocol Broadcast Example

RFC 887 describes a protocol, Resource Location Protocol (RLP),[7] that has a broadcast option. The idea is that we want a particular service we believe is on our network but we don't know which host provides it, e.g., who is a printer server? Let's look at an example that implements a part of this protocol.

10.6.3.2   RLP Setup

The basic RLP protocol uses a data structure for requests that looks like:

```
#define MAXID 128

struct res_list {
      unsigned char protocol;
      unsigned char idlength;
      char          resource_id[MAXID];
};

struct rlp_request {
      unsigned char type;
      unsigned char flags;
      short msgid;
      struct res_list res; };
  /*
   * Types
```

```
   */
#define WHOPROVIDES 0
#define DOYOUPROVIDE 1
#define WHOANYWHERE 2
#define ANYONEPROVIDE 3
#define IPROVIDE 4
#define THEYPROVIDE 5
```

We'll put these definitions into a header file, rlp.h, along with a few service definitions:

```
#define PRINTER "Low-Res Printer"
#define HPRINTER "Hi-Res Printer"
#define CPRINTER "Color Printer"
#define FAXGATEWAY "Fax Gateway"
#define FACESERVER "Face Server"
```

The server will sit and listen for a broadcast request, check if it provides the requested service, and if it does, it will respond to the requester. If the server does not provide the requested service it will be silent, and ignore the request.

The client will be human-oriented, and will just print out the list of servers found for a requested service. It would not be hard to modify the client to be used as part of a larger software project.

We will skip the header *include* statements and get right to the server code:

```
#define MAXSERVICES 16

main(argc, argv) int argc; char **argv;
{
        char *services[MAXSERVICES];
        int nservices;
        int c, i;
        struct sockaddr_in sa;
        struct protoent *pp;
        int sock;

        prog = argv[0];
        errout = stderr;

        nservices = 0;
        while((c = getopt(argc, argv, "cfhpx")) != EOF) {

                switch(c) {
                case 'c':
                    services[nservices++] = CPRINTER;
                    break;
                case 'f':
                    services[nservices++] = FACESERVER;
```

```
                    break;
                case 'h':
                services[nservices++] = HPRINTER;
                    break;
                case 'p':
                    services[nservices++] = PRINTER;
                    break;
                case 'x':
                    services[nservices++] = FAXGATEWAY;
                    break;
                default:
                    fprintf(stderr,"%s: bad option: '%c'\n",prog,c);
                    exit(1);
                }
        }


    if(nservices == 0)
            fatal("no services?");
```

10.6.3.3   *Socket Setup And Binding*

This user interface is very simple, perhaps too simple. We expect flags, such as -c for Color Printer and -x for Fax Server, on the command line, and use the getopt() routine to set up the table of services for which the server will respond positively.

```
        if((pp = getprotobyname("udp")) == NULL)
            fatal("no protocol entry for udp");

        bzero(&sa, sizeof(sa));

        sa.sin_family = AF_INET;
#ifdef TEST
        sa.sin_port = htons(RLP_TEST);
#else
        sa.sin_port = htons(RLP_PORT);     /* port 39 */
#endif
        sa.sin_addr.s_addr = htonl(INADDR_ANY);

        if((sock = socket(AF_INET,SOCK_DGRAM,pp->p_proto)) < 0)
            sysfatal("socket");

        if(bind(sock,&sa,sizeof(sa)) < 0)
            sysfatal("bind");
```

All of this section should be familiar by now to the reader. Because few systems have the service rlp defined in their /etc/services files, we will define the constant value RLP_PORT (39) in rlp.h, or conditionally, use a test port RLP_TEST (8888) also defined in rlp.h. Alternatively, you could make sure there is an entry in the /etc/services file and use get-servbyname(), as with our previous examples.

10.6.3.4 *The Main Loop*

The main loop for our UDP resource server is:

```
for(;;) {
    int sz;
    struct sockaddr_in newsa;
    struct rlp_request rlpreq;

    sz = sizeof(newsa);
    if(recvfrom(sock, &rlpreq, sizeof(rlpreq), 0, &newsa, &sz) < 0)
        continue;

    if(rlpreq.type == WHOPROVIDES) {
        for(i=0; i < nservices; i++)
            if(strcmp(rlpreq.res.resource_id, services[i]) == 0)
{
                rlpreq.type = IPROVIDE;
                if(sendto(sock, &rlpreq, sizeof(rlpreq),
                              0, &newsa,sz) < 0)
                    sysfatal("sendto");
            }
    }
}
```

We use recvfrom() to receive the next broadcasted request. No special setup is required in the server to receive broadcasts on a particular port. If the request type is WHOPROVIDES, the only part of the protocol we are supporting in this example, we search through our services table to see if this is a service we provide and, if found, respond positively as specified in the *RFC*.

10.6.3.5 *Finding the Broadcast Address*

The client is more complicated, and represents most of the new material in this example. There is one shortcut taken: the broadcast address for the network is specified on the command line via a –b flag. You can determine network broadcast interfaces by using the SIO-CIFADDR flag and the ioctl() call.

To manually determine the broadcast address of an interface, you need its name. Typically, this is a three-character name, such as ie0, le0, or en0 (or ie1, etc.). There may be more than one interface on your system. The correct name for the interface can generally be determined by investigating the rc start-up files run at boot time to find where the system uses the ifconfig command to set the system's address:

```
grep ifconfig /etc/rc*
```

This might turn it up. If not, you may need to ask someone or consult the manual (or even watch the system's messages as it boots—it will usually report the network interfaces as part of the normal startup).

Given the correct name for the interface, the following command should yield the broadcast address we need:

```
/etc/ifconfig interface
```

A typical output would be:

```
en0: flags=2000063<UP,BROADCAST,NOTRAILERS,RUNNING,NOECHO>
                        inet 192.74.137.9 netmask 0xffffff00 broadcast 192.74.137.255
```

The number just after the word *broadcast* is what we are looking for.

Another approach to getting the system's broadcast addresses is to use the following script. It should work on most UNIX or compatible systems. Note that the script can be called from within a program via the popen() library call to obtain all broadcast addresses for the host we are running on:

```sh
#!/bin/sh
  for i in `netstat -i | awk \
      '{ if(($1 != "Name") && ($1 != "lo0")) print $1 }''
  do
      echo `/etc/ifconfig $i` | \
          awk '{ if($(NF-1) == "broadcast") print $(NF) }'
  done
```

10.6.4 The RLP Client

Similar to the previous UDP example, we will use a timed interrupt to know when to stop waiting for an answer:

```c
#define MAXSERVICES     16
#define TIMEOUT         10

jmp_buf jbuf;

char *inet_ntoa();

onalarm()
{
      longjmp(jbuf,1);
}
```

The reason for doing this includes all the reasons in the previous example (e.g., a lost request or other error), as well as a new concern: we are going to broadcast for services across the entire (local) network. We will then loop, looking for responses. How will we know when we have received all the responses that were sent to us? We won't, so we will loop until we timeout, printing any responses we get to the standard output.

```
main(argc,argv) int argc; char **argv;
{
        char *services[MAXSERVICES];
        int nservices;
        int c, i;
        struct sockaddr_in sa, sin;
        struct protoent *pp;
        struct rlp_request rlpreq;
        int sock;
        extern char *optarg;
        char *broadcast = NULL;

        prog = argv[0];
        errout = stderr;

        nservices = 0;
        while((c = getopt(argc,argv,"b:cfhpx")) != EOF) {

                switch(c) {
                case 'b':
                        broadcast = optarg;
                        break;
                case 'c':
                        services[nservices++] = CPRINTER;
                        break;
                case 'f':
                                services[nservices++] = FACESERVER;
                        break;
                case 'h':
                services[nservices++] = HPRINTER;
                        break;
                case 'p':
                        services[nservices++] = PRINTER;
                        break;
                case 'x':
                        services[nservices++] = FAXGATEWAY;
                        break;
                default:
                        fprintf(stderr,"%s: bad option: '%c'\n",prog,c);
                        exit(1);
                }

}
```

```
        if(nservices == 0)
                fatal("no services?");

        if(broadcast == NULL)
                fatal("must specify -b broadcast-addr\n");

        if((pp = getprotobyname("udp")) == NULL)
                fatal("no protocol entry for udp");

            bzero(&sa, sizeof(sa));
```

By now, the following portion of a client should be routine for you.

```
        sa.sin_family = AF_INET;
#ifdef TEST
        sa.sin_port = htons(RLP_TEST);
#else
        sa.sin_port = htons(RLP_PORT);  /* port 39 */
#endif
        sa.sin_addr.s_addr = inet_addr(broadcast);
```

10.6.4.1 Socket Setup and Binding

The broadcast variable will be set to a string looking like 192.74.137.255. The routine int_addr() will convert this to a binary address from the string.

```
        if((sock = socket(AF_INET, SOCK_DGRAM, pp->p_proto)) < 0) {
            perror("socket");
            exit(1);
        }

        bzero(&sin, sizeof(sin));
        sin.sin_family = AF_INET;
        sin.sin_port = htons(RLP_REPLY);
        sin.sin_addr.s_addr = htonl(INADDR_ANY);
        if(bind(sock, &sin, sizeof(sin)) < 0) {
            perror("bind");
            exit(1);
        }
```

The socket() call is the same as we have used previously. We next set up another socket address structure. UDP packets have a source port and a destination port. The destination port we set earlier to RLP_PORT. If we don't set a source port, the system will choose one for us. The server needs a port on which to send back the response. We need to know what that port is, so we can listen for the response. We set the source port to RLP_REPLY (chosen arbitrarily to be RLP_TEST+1), and will later use recvfrom() to receive messages on our own source port. Unlike previous examples, we use bind() in the client to prepare for this. The test setup is as follows:

```
i = 1;
if(setsockopt(sock, SOL_SOCKET, SO_BROADCAST, &i, sizeof(i)) < 0)
      sysfatal("setsockopt");
```

You can set socket options with setsockopt(). Several options are available. In this example, we are enabling broadcasts on the socket. Earlier versions of the Berkeley networking code allowed only super-users to send broadcasts. That limitation may apply to the system you are using; if you have problems, check the manual pages.

10.6.4.2 The Main Loop

The main loop is:

```
for(i=0; i < nservices; i++) {
      rlpreq.type = WHOPROVIDES;
      rlpreq.flags = 0;
      rlpreq.msgid = i;
      rlpreq.res.protocol = 0;
      rlpreq.res.idlength = strlen(services[i]);
      strcpy(rlpreq.res.resource_id, services[i]);

      if(sendto(sock, &rlpreq, sizeof(rlpreq), 0, &sa, sizeof(sa)) < 0)
            sysfatal("sendto");
}
```

We loop through the services requested on the command line by using sendto() for each service type. Technically, we should set the rlpreq.res.protocol element to an appropriate protocol (e.g., TCP, as returned by getprotobyname() in the p_proto element). See the *RFC* for details. The loop is

```
signal(SIGALRM,onalarm);

if(setjmp(jbuf) != 0)
      exit(0);

for(;;) {
      struct sockaddr_in newsa;
      int sz;
      struct hostent *hp;

      alarm(TIMEOUT);
```

```
        sz = sizeof(newsa);
        if(recvfrom(sock, &rlpreq, sizeof(rlpreq), 0, &newsa,&sz) < 0)
            sysfatal("recvfrom");
        alarm(0);

        if((hp = gethostbyaddr(&newsa.sin_addr,
             sizeof(newsa.sin_addr), AF_INET)) == NULL)
            printf("%s: ", inet_ntoa(newsa.sin_addr));
        else
            printf("%s: ", hp->h_name);
            printf("%s\n", rlpreq.res.resource_id);
    }
}
```

After setting up the signal handler SIGALRM and setjmp(), we loop and wait for responses. If recvfrom() returns a response, we turn off the timeout and print out the name of the host who responded and the service requested. The library call gethostbyaddr() will try to turn the binary address into the host's official name, or else will return NULL. If it returns NULL, then we can't do the translation, and we will print out the dotted-decimal address instead.

10.6.4.3   Compiling the RLP Example

Remember to use the –DTEST flag when compiling the server and client to use the test ports. To run the RLP server you use:

    rlpd -c -p -x -h

Otherwise, use whatever flag combination you want to test. Run the server on two or more clients, with different flags on each invocation. Then run the client with something like:

    rlp -b broadcast-address -c -p

You should get output from each server you are running.

10.6.4.4   Another Digression—Server Setup

Servers are usually started either via inetd or from the systems boot command files (typically, /etc/rc.local). When a server starts at boot time you need to do some housekeeping in the main() routine. The chores are to dissociate our program from the system console and fork() the server into the background. To report errors or other events you will want to use the UNIX system logging facility syslog(), rather than the standard error output.

The following skeleton code demonstrates this startup:

```
#include <syslog.h>
#include <ioctl.h>
#include <sys/file.h>

main(argc,argv) int argc; char **argv;
{
    char *prog = argv[0];
    int devnull;

    switch(fork()) {

    case -1:
        fprintf(stderr,"%s: could not fork\n", prog);
        exit(1);
    case 0:
        break;
    default:
        exit(0);
    }

    if((devnull = open("/dev/null", O_RDWR)) != -1) {
        dup2(devnull,0);
        dup2(devnull,1);
        dup2(devnull,2);
        if(devnull > 2)
            close(devnull);
    }
    else
        exit(1);

    openlog(prog,LOG_CONS|LOG_NOWAIT|LOG_PID,LOG_DAEMON);
    syslog(LOG_INFO,"%s started",prog);
}
```

The daemon forks, the child copy continues, and the parent exits. We then open the null device and duplicate it onto the standard input, output, and error file descriptors. From this point on, we can no longer use routines like printf(), unless we open a file or device to which they can send their output. You might also call chdir("/"); to change to the root (or some other) directory. If your system is POSIX-compliant you should call setsid() before the open() call.

The syslog facility sends output to a location specified in your system's setup (/etc./syslog.conf), typically one or more log files in either /var/log or /usr/adm. By modifying syslog.conf, you can also arrange to have certain types of messages sent to the console, other files, or can even contact terminals of a specified set of logged-in system administrators on local or remote systems.

The LOG_CONS option to openlog() indicates that if there is any problem in sending messages to the normal place (such as to a log file), then send the messages to the system console to avoid losing them. The LOG_NOWAIT option is not strictly necessary, but is used in servers that reap their own children via the SIGCHLD software interrupt. LOG_PID tells syslog to add the process id number to each message; this information is sometimes useful. The last argument to openlog(), LOG_DAEMON, tells syslog that we are a server. Finally, we send an initial message to the log recording our startup.

From this point on, your server would only use syslog() to record errors. Replace all calls to fprintf() and perror() appropriately.

10.7   OTHER ISSUES

10.7.1   FTP, SMTP, Text-Based Protocols

There are many other design elements used in internet programming. One that we did not touch on is prevalent in common protocols, such as FTP and SMTP. These involve a back-and-forth conversation, and then data transfers. For example, SMTP passes simple text lines like "HELO world.std.com\r\n" to which is replied, "250 Hello world.std.com\r\n" and so on.

10.7.2   Portability Versus Interoperability

Another issue is the distinction between portability and interoperability. A portable application will compile and run on many different systems. An interoperable application will interoperate with other applications on many different systems. A portable application uses a common language and library routines to make it possible to recompile on disparate systems. An interoperable application uses a common (standardized) protocol to communicate with other applications.

Judging by its success, TCP/IP and the IP suite are highly interoperable. Machines with very different architectures and internal models communicate easily with each other within an internet. A particular TCP/IP application, such as an implementation of FTP, may or may not be portable. But if it can talk to other FTP implementations successfully, then it is interoperable. The distinction is very important.

Even beyond basic interoperability, data transparency is another key issue. We touched on this topic when we talked about network and host byte order. But that was primarily constrained to small objects (words), which are used in the low-level protocols. What about your data?

Text—The Good, the Bad, and the Ugly

Text tends to be reasonably easy to move between systems. This is one reason that textual (string) messages are often used in applications protocols like SMTP and FTP. However, even textual data can present problems. For example, IBM mainframes use a text encoding called EBCDIC. Most other systems use ASCII. Although ASCII is specified for protocols like FTP, the data you want to transfer may be encoded in any way. Fortunately, FTP provides for a text mode transfer that will convert between (most) formats. Even so, ASCII-to-EBCDIC translations are not entirely well-defined; some characters just don't correspond between the two sets, and there are at least two translation tables in common use.

Another problem with text involves how records are stored on a particular machine. Common ways to separate lines of text are with a linefeed (in UNIX parlance, *newline*) or with a carriage return–linefeed pair at the end of each line (DOS and other systems). Mainframes often don't use line terminators; instead they store text as either fixed-length records padded with blanks, or variable length records with a count followed by the characters. Again, a protocol like FTP specifies a standard for the transmission of text using carriage return–linefeed pairs. FTP server programs are responsible for converting to the standardized text format; FTP client programs are responsible for converting from the standardized text format to whatever the local host prefers to see.

10.7.3 Binary and Structured Data

FTP can handle text very well, but binary or structured data is beyond its capabilities, other than to just transfer it, bit for bit, from one host to another (there are some small adjustments for 36-bit machines, but that's a special case).

Even a file as simple as an array of binary integers or floating point numbers will not transfer properly across various architectures. The target machine will not recognize the bits in the same way as the host machine, when read into a program later. One simple solution is to require a program that needs to share data to convert them to ASCII text strings, and transfer them to the other host, and to require that host to convert them back. This is simple and frequently used, because it is easy to write a program to do this conversion if the format is known beforehand.

10.7.3.1 XDR

More dynamic shared data environments, such as with a distributed database system, require more sophisticated approaches to the problem. One such approach is XDR (eXternal Data Representation) developed by Sun Microsystems.[8] XDR is a library of routines that allow one to describe a format for scalar or aggregate objects and then transfer them across the network interoperably.[9] For example, you could transfer floating point numbers between two hosts with the following code:

```
#include <stdio.h>
#include <rpc/rpc.h>
/*
 * Writer
 */ main()
```

```
{
        XDR xdrs;
        double dnum;
        FILE *fp;
        int sock;

        /*
         * ...socket and connection setup...
         */

        if((fp = fdopen(sock,"w")) == NULL)
            fatal("fdopen");

        xdrstdio_create(&xdrs, fp, XDR_ENCODE);

        /*
         * some time later
         */

        if(!xdr_double(&xdrs, &dnum))
            fatal("xdr_double");
}
```

After establishing a socket connection, we attach the socket to a stdio stream and use xdrstdio_create() to make it a XDR stream in the encode direction (for passing across the network). Other than omitting code to set up the other application's socket, the reader code is similar, except that you replace XDR_ENCODE with XDR_DECODE and create a read stdio stream. To read and write between applications you can use dup() to create a duplicate of the socket and set it up with fdopen() and xdrstdio_create() in the other direction.

You can write your own XDR routines to handle arbitrarily complex data objects by combining XDR primitives. If you had a structure that looked like:

```
struct record {
    long  amount;
    double percent;
};
```

You could create a new routine:

```
xdr_record(xp,rp) XDR *xp; struct record *rp;
{
    return(xdr_long(xp, rp->amount)
        && xdr_double(xp, rp->percent));
}
```

There are several primitives for basic data types. With these you should be able to transmit arbitrarily complex objects across a network transparently.

10.7.4 RPC

Another tool is Sun's RPC (Remote Procedure Call) package, which helps you develop programs that can transmit data across networks in a very transparent way.[10] They provide a tool, rpcgen, which translates an RPC program into a C program. The basic idea is that most of the network details are hidden, and RPC's underlying mechanisms let you make procedure calls on other machines on the network. XDR is handled within the RPC package. For more information, consult the *Sun Network Programming Guide*.

10.7.5 NFS

With these two tools, RPC and XDR, Sun built their very successful NFS (Network File System) protocol,[11] which is perhaps one of the most widely used applications on local networks. NFS lets you mount file systems from other computers on the network and use them as if they were local. The architecture involves an NFS server, client, and a mount daemon that knows how to honor mount requests on the server. Other processes are also used to improve throughput between the systems.

NFS abstracted the basic input, output and other file-oriented routines so that system file calls made from programs would instead be passed across the network and executed by the remote system. This is done via a virtual file system interface, which is basically a structure of function pointers and state data that replace the standard UNIX file I/O routines. All of this is transparent to the program. In fact, it is difficult for a program to distinguish whether it is working with a remote file or a local file.

REFERENCES

1 J.B. Postel, *Transmission Control Protocol, RFC 793*, September 1981.

2 J.B. Postel, *User Datagram Protocol, RFC 768*, August 28, 1980.

3 S.J. Leffler, M.K. McKusick, M.J. Karels, and J.S. Quarterman, *The Design and Implementation of the 4.3BSD UNIX Operating System*, Addison-Wesley, Reading, MA, 1989.

4 D. Cohen, *On Holy Wars and a Plea for Peace, IEN 137*, April 1, 1980.

5 D. Zimmerman, *The Finger User Information Protocol, RFC 1288*, December 1991.

6   J.B. Postel, *Daytime Protocol, RFC 867*, May 1983.

7   M. Accetta, *Resource Location Protocol, RFC 887*, December 1983.

8   Sun Microsystems, Inc., *XDR: External Data Representation, RFC 1014*, June 1987.

9   Sun Microsystems, *Network Programming Guide*, March 1990.

10 Sun Microsystems, *RPC: Remote Procedure Call Protocol Specification Version 2, RFC 1057*, June 1988.

11 R. Sandberg, D. Goldberg, S. Kleiman, D. Walsh, and B. Lyon, Design and Implementation of the Sun Network File System, *USENIX Conference Proceedings*, Summer 1985.

PART III ⬚ ⬚ ⬚ ⬚ ⬚

INFRASTRUCTURE

CHAPTER 11

Directory Services

PAUL V. MOCKAPETRIS

CONTENTS

As the Internet grows, more resources are available, but paradoxically, they are also harder to locate. The Internet uses a large number of naming and directory services, which we will now briefly survey.

11.1   INTRODUCTION

Directory services allow users to locate and identify network objects. In practice, the network objects that are of interest to the majority of Internet users are hosts, mailboxes, and other Internet users. However, many more types of network objects are used behind the scenes by network software, and new user-level applications for bibliographic searches, resource location, etc., are approaching widespread use and providing new user-visible network objects.

These services come into play as soon as a user leaves a local machine and accesses the Internet. If the user wants to log-in or ftp to a remote machine, that machine must be identified via a name. For example, the UNIX commands

```
%  telnet a.isi.edu

or

%  ftp nic.ddn.mil
```

ask that the user be logged onto a machine identified by the name a.isi.edu or ftp to a machine called nic.ddn.mil. Mail sent to

Hostmaster@NIC.DDN.MIL

uses the mailbox name Hostmaster@NIC.DDN.MIL to identify a mail destination. By convention, the mailbox name is composed of two component names: *Hostmaster* identifies a local mailbox at the domain, which is identified by *NIC.DDN.MIL*.

Other directory services allow a user to ask, for example, for the mailbox names of all users whose family name sounds like "MacPeters," or for the numbers of all *RFC* documents that contain the key phrase "X.500" in the title.

These services have evolved with the Internet, expanding with it in size and power. As yet, no single system has emerged that can satisfy all user requirements, which range from simple and fast lookups for host names, to address translations, to almost arbitrarily complex bibliographic searches. Despite the claims of various proponents, no single system is ever likely to do so.

The systems discussed include:

FINGER,   a simple service with distributed but disconnected servers

WHOIS,   a simple single-host database

DNS,   a distributed, integrated name service with simple primitives

NETFIND,   an information service built on top of FINGER, DNS, etc.

X.500,   a tremendously powerful and complicated service based on an incomplete international standard

WAIS,   a fully distributed database.

These are roughly listed in a spectrum that starts with the simplest services (FINGER) and goes toward the most database-like (WAIS). Purists will argue that FINGER is too simple to be called a directory service, that WAIS is too database-oriented, and that DNS is really a name service. A sophisticated Internet user will use most or all of these to get the "directory service" job done.

11.2 CONCEPTUAL EVOLUTION

Many systems can be traced to the basic need to support naming of network hosts and mailboxes. As computing evolved away from multiple disconnected machines toward networks, users needed some way to identify hosts of interest and their corresponding network addresses. This led to some basic terminology due to Shoch:[1]

> The name of a resource indicates what we seek,
> an address indicates where it is,
> and a route tells us how to get there.

Thus, in the Internet, a resource might be a host; its name might be nic.ddn.mil; its IP address might be 192.112.36.5; and the route would be a sequence of networks, links, and switches taken to reach it from a specific origin. Route calculations have always been highly dynamic and usually have been handled (at least in the Internet) by special routing protocols. The mapping of host names (typically character strings) to addresses (typically integers) motivated the first name services dedicated to this task. Of course, good designers immediately seized the opportunity to generalize, and built name services that are extensible to mailboxes, various servers, users, etc. The Clearinghouse system of XEROX PARC[2] was an early system that still compares favorably with most systems in use today.

In the ARPANET, which later became the DARPANET, and then led to the Internet, the whole issue seemed moot for the early years: a four-host ARPANET clearly needed no system for name service, since all of the names and addresses could be written on one punch card with room to spare! Later, larger populations were handled via a well-known file, HOSTS.TXT, which listed all of the known hosts, network numbers, their addresses, etc. The file was maintained by the Network Information Center (NIC), then at SRI. Names were unstructured character strings of up to 30 characters, though short names, such as "UCLA" and "NIC," were common. Administrators around the network would send HOSTS.TXT change requests to the NIC for processing, and would periodically "poll" the NIC for new versions of HOSTS.TXT.

However, by the early 1980s, the scalability of the HOSTS.TXT system began to be a concern. Intuitively, the total "work" implied by the HOSTS.TXT scheme is related to the product of three factors:

- The number of copies of HOSTS.TXT needed

- The size of each copy

- The rate of change of the file.

While the last factor may be only weakly related to the number of entries in HOSTS.TXT, the other factors are directly proportional, so the work is proportional to the square of the number of hosts (or worse).

The administrative problems are also significant: while local network technology allows, even requires, every system administrator to manage and allocate network and host addresses, the latency implied by a centralized NIC is always present, and all problem corrections also require NIC intervention. Local empowerment over most of these choices is essential.

The existing technology for replacing HOSTS.TXT in the Internet consisted of the XEROX Clearinghouse work, and a name system described in *IEN 116*.[3] The Clearinghouse system would have required agreement with Xerox and the import of supporting components from the Xerox protocol architecture; in any case, the fixed three-level hierarchy and caching style of the Clearinghouse system seemed ill-suited to the chaotic Internet. *IEN 116* was too limited in terms of functionality and scalability for serious consideration. As a result, a new scheme called the Domain Name System (DNS) was created for use in the Internet.

The primary features of the DNS include:

- Variable depth hierarchy for names. Name hierarchies are almost universal in naming systems, since they provide the minimal structure that allows structured distributed control, as well as an abstraction similar to that used in filenames. The DNS name space allows essentially limitless levels and uses the familiar period (.) as the level delimiter in printed names.

- Distribution controlled by the database itself. The current DNS database is divided into thousands of separately managed zones, which are managed by separate administrators. The distribution is controlled by data in the database.

- Connectionless service using UDP. This is a somewhat controversial choice but does provide low overhead service.

- Features for caching, and cache aging and removal. These are essential for efficient operation. Caching features are always discussed and frequently implemented in other systems, but the DNS is unique in using a single simple strategy for all data.

Measure	ARPANET 1969	IP/TCP 1983	Today 1992	Future 1996
Trunk speed	56 Kbps	56 Kbps	1–45 Mbps	2–10 Gbps
Interface speed	56 Kbps	10 Mbps	10 Mbps	1 Gbps
Computers	4	200	725,000	10,000,000
Cooperating net managers	1	64	5,000	100,000

Figure 11.1 Internet evolution

- Spartan features for database update, and data structuring. The DNS features in this area were selected to provide a relatively simple implementation at the cost of reduced functionality. Although the DNS data types are extensible, they cannot be easily extended without systemwide cooperation.

Figure 11.1 illustrates the magnitude of the growth trends that motivated the development of the DNS. From the first days of the ARPANET to an estimate for 1996, the number of hosts grew by a factor of several hundred thousand; over the same period, the number of separately administered organizations grew by a factor of several thousand.

The DNS, Clearinghouse, and other name services use a model that enables the distributed creation and maintenance of a simply structured database, with an emphasis on queries that typically know the name of interest; the primary benefit is what computer scientists call "delayed binding." That is, instead of using the address of a host, or an explicit mail exchange for a domain, the user specifies a name that is used to locate the address or mail exchange just before it is used. While this costs a lookup at runtime, it also means that the addresses and mail exchanges can change and the names will still work—so long as changes are reflected in the name service database. The ultimate goal is that system configuration changes would need to be reflected only in the name service for all applications to continue to run.

However, this still leaves the question of how the user learns the name of a host or a mailbox for a user in the first place. This type of service is oriented toward much less frequent, but much more complex requests. Here the typical operation is a search with some arguments that will eventually be used to derive a name for a name service. In the Internet, this type of service evolved in parallel with name service. Early service was provided by FINGER and WHOIS.

FINGER is a simple service in which a host or site provides information for local users. The system is distributed in that each site provides its own FINGER servers; however, the different servers do not share information, so that the user must know which server to ask. In effect, if you don't already know the site, or at least have a good way to figure it out, FINGER can't help much by itself. Using FINGER, it is trivial to find out which users are logged onto a specific machine and impossible to find out which machines a specific user is logged into.

WHOIS takes the opposite approach; it puts the data for all users in a single centralized database. The advantage is that searches can take place without network latency; the disadvantage is that the centralized site must maintain the database. As the user community grows, strains are created. Users see more of a need for quality in data they want to use than in data they maintain. A typical user will complain about the quality of data in the database and will also be quite lax about making sure that his or her own data is correct. Similarly, the user community will decry the need for larger, faster, and more accurate data, but will resent any attempt by the central database to recover costs.

11.3 FINGER

The FINGER protocol predates the Internet, having first been described in *RFC 742* in 1977. The current document[4] and protocol are an attempt to update the specification in light of security concerns and the *de facto* standard set by UNIX implementations.

The protocol is based upon TCP, and is simplicity itself. The client opens a TCP connection to a specified machine, and then sends a one-line query over the connection. The server at the other end of the connection reads the query, generates a response, and closes the TCP connection, completing the transaction.

This protocol is made still simpler by FINGER programs that scan off the query from a command line, along with the name of the host to be queried (defaulting to the local host if the argument is omitted).

The simplest use of FINGER has a null query (no arguments at all), for example:

```
% finger
Login    Name              TTY   Idle  When            Office
opr      Operations        co    1d    Thu 14:04 x144  1203M; SYSTEM
opr      Operations        a7    1d    Fri 23:49 x144  1203M; SYSTEM
pvm      Paul Mockapetris  c1          Sun 11:40 1102S  x285;DIV7
```

Here the finger command returns the log-in names of all users on the local machine, together with full names, phone extensions, idle time, etc.

If the query names a user, more detailed information is made available:

```
% finger pvm
Login name: pvm                 In real life: Paul Mockapetris
Office: 1102S, x285;DIV7
Directory: /nfs/u5/pvm          Shell: /bin/tcsh
On since Jan 16 11:40:36 on ttyc1
Plan:
Buy low, sell high, not necessarily in that order.
```

Most of this information is self-explanatory; the "Plan" is a file created by the user to be passed out in the event of a finger query, and often contains the network equivalent of a bumper sticker or manifesto.

FINGER queries can also be directed at foreign hosts, for example:

```
% finger @nic.ddn.mil
[nic.ddn.mil]
Login     Name            TTY    Idle  When          Where
nicguest  NICGUEST USER   p4           Sun 15:38     CHN3B201.AF.MIL
nicguest  NICGUEST USER   p0     39    Sun 15:03     144.75.3.144
nicguest  NICGUEST USER   p1           Sun 15:48     oz.plymouth.edu
```

Here the query is directed at the host nic.ddn.mil, and the users are all guest accounts using ftp to access files. Numerous standard options and switches exist for queries, as well as numerous extensions to FINGER to provide greater services.

FINGER is a security concern for two reasons. The first is the existence of a bad implementation, which played a part in the Morris worm incident. This isn't an issue with FINGER per se, but with any server that does not take adequate steps to protect itself from accidentally or maliciously malformed inputs. The second concern deals with the sensitivity of the information provided by a normally operating FINGER, and is a dilemma shared by all information sources. FINGER provides user names; these are helpful to an attacking hacker. FINGER can also be used to provide surveillance of a user's log-in time, and in some versions, the system can even be used to keep track of a user's electronic mail correspondents. As a result, many sites disable FINGER entirely, or restrict its use.

11.4 WHOIS

The WHOIS system uses the same simple TCP exchange as FINGER to query a single database on a specific machine. This is typically the host NIC.DDN.MIL, which keeps track of thousands of users and all of the domains, network numbers, and similar objects registered by the NIC. This tends to provide very good coverage for all top-level domains and the like, as well as DDN users and assorted network luminaries, but it misses millions of users.

As with FINGER, there is a defined query syntax with a lot of options. For casual use the only argument need be the name, network number, or other string of interest; WHOIS does a rough match and returns a brief summary of available items. You can zero into a single item by specifying its "handle," which is a unique identifier. Another way to narrow WHOIS behavior is to precede the argument with a keyword that limits the types of objects that are interesting: for example, PE for person, DO for domain, etc. (A full list of these can be had by sending a WHOIS query consisting solely of a question mark.)

To find out about ISO, we might try:

```
% whois iso
   ISO Central Secretariat (NET-ISO-CS)
   1 Rue de Varembe
   CH-1211 Geneva 20
   SWITZERLAND

      Netname: ISO-CS Netnumber: 138.81.0.0
```

```
      Coordinator:
      Henigsen, Brian (BH196) [No mailbox]
      +41 22 734 12 40

      Record last updated on 15-Feb-91.
```

To see this host record with registered users, repeat the command with a star ('*') before the name; or, use '%' to show JUST the registered users.

This entry reflects an IP network reservation. To find a user named Cerf you use the command line:

```
% whois cerf
Cerf, Vinton G. (VGC)       CERF@NRI.RESTON.VA.US
   Corporation for National Research Initiatives
   1895 Preston White Drive, Suite 100
   Reston, VA 22091
   (703) 620-8990 FAX: (703) 620-0913
   MILNET TAC user

   IAB Chairman

    Record last updated on 15-Jul-91.
```

Note that WHOIS doesn't know or care that we were looking for a person, it just matches keywords. To find out about the ISI.EDU domain, we might try:

```
% whois isi.edu
University of Southern California (ISI-VENERA) VENERA.ISI.EDU 128.9.0.32
University of Southern California, Information Sciences Institute (ISI-DOM)
                                                ISI.EDU
```

To single out one record, look it up with "!xxx", where xxx is the handle, shown in parenthesis following the name, which comes first.

Here, WHOIS has found two matches: a host named VENERA.ISI.EDU and the domain named ISI.EDU. To refine the search we could either specify a handle:

```
% whois \!isi-dom
University of Southern California, Information Sciences Institute (ISI-DOM)
   4676 Admiralty Way, Suite 1001
   Marina del Rey, CA 90292-6695

   Domain Name: ISI.EDU

   Administrative Contact, Technical Contact, Zone Contact:
   Bates, Ray (RB5) RBATES@ISI.EDU
   (213) 822-1511 or FAX: (213) 823-6714

Record last updated on 24-Oct-90.

Domain servers in listed order:
```

```
VENERA.ISI.EDU            128.9.0.32
VAXA.ISI.EDU              128.9.0.33
VAX.DARPA.MIL             192.5.18.99,192.48.218.99
```

To see this host record with registered users, repeat the command with a star ('*') before the name; or, use '%' to show JUST the registered users.

or use

```
% whois "DO ISI.EDU"
```

Note that the backslash in the first example is just a "UNIX-ism," as are the double quotes on the second call. (Your shell may vary.) Despite its limitations, WHOIS is a valuable asset.

11.5 THE DNS

The DNS[5] differs from WHOIS and FINGER in two significant ways: First, it is almost never used directly by users, but rather in an indirect manner by applications. Second, it is truly a distributed system, with thousands of cooperating servers.

The model of the system that most users and applications designers need consists of the name space, data values, and query functions, without knowledge of the database distribution and error recovery properties. Put differently, the "DNS abstract database" is the database we would see if it were possible to combine snapshots of all of the distributed portions in a single instant.

Database distribution deals with methods for dividing up the database into distributed sections and, more importantly, being able to locate any desired part in a timely and reliable way.

The abstract database and database distribution facilities of the DNS form the technical basis of the existing system; equally important to these is an understanding of the administrative and cultural traditions that shape the way the system is actually used.

11.5.1 The DNS Abstract Database—The Name Space

The DNS database follows a very simple model: a name space tree (called the hierarchy) with data items attached to its leaves and interior nodes. A sample tree is shown in Figure 11.2. (Note that this example, and those that follow, are for instructional purposes only; the real name space has nearly a million nodes.)

The name space has identifiers called *labels* on every node and leaf. A label is a string of 0 to 63 octets. (An octet is an 8-bit byte.) One label, the zero-length or null label, is reserved for the root of the tree. Labels need not be printable ASCII characters, although these are typically the easiest to work with.

The same label can be used on an unlimited number of nodes, with the provision that sibling nodes can't have the same label. (A recent survey found 384 uses of the word *venus* across the Internet, making it the most popular label.) Since label comparisons are case insensitive for the ASCII values corresponding to A–Z, this also means that sibling nodes cannot have labels that differ only in case. Whichever is entered first becomes the established case setting.

The domain name of a node in the tree is an ordered list, starting at the node, of all labels on the path to the root node. Since the root node has a unique label, its name is unique. Since siblings must have unique labels, all direct descendants of the root node are unique, and so on.

A domain is the subtree included under a particular domain name. Thus in Figure 11.2, all of the tree under the MIT.EDU. domain name is known as the MIT.EDU domain. Domains can be as small as a single node or as large as the whole name space. Although different parts of the tree are structured differently, the general concept is that the structure of the portion of the name space should parallel the administrative organization using it. This is partly a consequence of the distribution scheme, and partly a desire to use a familiar hierarchical organization, such as that used for files, addresses, and the like.

Domains closer to the root encompass those below, and leaf nodes are the most common places for hostnames and other primitive objects. The top levels usually correspond to countries or very broad generic groups, with increasing refinement as one goes down the tree. Thus MIT.EDU is a subdomain of EDU, LCS.MIT.EDU is a subdomain of MIT.EDU, and we would expect that XX.LCS.MIT.EDU might be a machine name.

The labels and domain names in DNS packets use a binary encoding, but the standard method of printing domain names is to separate each label with a dot. (The backslash is used to quote naturally occurring dots and other unprintable characters.) Thus in the sample tree shown in Figure 11.2, the node with the label XX has a domain name of XX.LCS.MIT.EDU.

This rule produces a trailing dot on every domain name. By convention, the trailing dot is used to signify complete, absolute domain names. Domain names that do not end in a trailing dot are assumed to be in need of completion. Completion algorithms vary, but the most popular algorithm uses the following steps:

1   If the name is long enough so that it might be complete (two or more labels) try it as is.

2   Failing that, try adding one or more well-known local origins. The local origins are usually the name of the local parent domain or domains.

When *venus* is used by a user at MIT, the completion convention might be to add the suffix MIT.EDU and see if a valid name has been generated; similarly a user at an IBM.COM site could use *venus* to mean venus.IBM.COM. If the name Venera.ISI.EDU is used at either site, it will be seen as long enough so that it may be complete, and will be tried as if it were Venera.ISI.EDU., which is identified as absolute by the trailing dot.

While this shorthand is an important labor saver in the local domain, absolute names (sometimes called fully qualified domain names, or FQDNs) must be used when the name

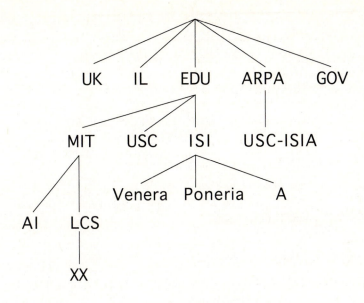

Figure 11.2   Sample domain tree

will be passed to another organization where it would be completed differently. This requirement is most often heard in connection with the use of domain names to specify mail destinations.

11.5.2   The DNS Abstract Database—The Data Associated with Names

The name space rules of the DNS create a hierarchical set of names, but a name does not describe the type or properties of the named object—merely its name. Information about a name is stored in a set of zero or more associated resource records (RRs). In reality, neither names nor RRs by themselves have much significance, so we usually deal with combinations of the two. The internal format for these is shown in Figure 11.3.

All RRs start with a fixed header that includes a type, a class, and a TTL. The type is a 16-bit integer that encodes a well-known abstract information type, such as a network address (A), a name server (NS) reference, etc. There are approximately 20 types defined and in various stages of standardization. The most well-known types are shown in Figure 11.4.

The class field was intended to be used to form separate but parallel name spaces for different protocol suites or instances of use. For example, the class field might distinguish an Internet-style address from a Chaos-style address, or even multiple internets using the same protocols. In reality, the Internet (IN) class is the only one used to any significant extent.

16	16	32	16	Variable
Type	Class	TTL	RDlength	RData

Type	An encoded value which specifies an abstract type for the RR. For example, address data uses mnemonic "A" or value 1.
Class	An encoded value which specifies a protocol family or instance of use. For example, IN for the DARPA Internet, CH for Chaos.
TTL	A 32-bit Time-To-Live value (seconds). Discussed later, but basically it is how long the data should be valid.
RDlength	Specifies the size of the RDATA field.
RData	The format and content of RDATA always depend on TYPE and also, for some TYPES, CLASS.

Figure 11.3   Resource record internal format

"TTL" stands for "Time-To-Live," and the field is a 32-bit integer. This value is used to limit the caching of data external to the DNS, and represents a length of time that the data in the RR can be kept before it should be reacquired from the DNS. For example, if an application retrieved data with a TTL of 120, it can legitimately use it for 120 seconds before the data should be reacquired. The value is selected by the system administrator who

Standardized	
A	Host address
NS	Name server identification
CNAME	Pointer to a canonical name alias
SOA	Start of authority information
MB	Mailbox (experimental)
MR	Mail relay pointer (experimental)
NULL	Null (experimental)
WKS	Well known service mask
PTR	General purpose pointer
HINFO	Host information
MINFO	Mail information
MX	Mail exchange
TXT	General purpose text strings
New from RFC 1183	
RP	Responsible person
AFSDB	AFS server identification
X25	X.121 address
ISDN	ISDN numbers
RT	Route through

Figure 11.4   Well-known types

```
Venera.ISI.EDU.                    86400 IN A 128.9.0.32
where
Venera.ISI.EDU.            =   owner name
86400                      =   the TTL of 60×60×24 secs, or 1 day
IN                         =   the class (Internet)
A                          =   the type (Address)
128.9.0.32                 =   dotted-decimal IP address
```

Figure 11.5   Sample printed resource record

creates the data, and presumably knows how volatile it is. Typical values for host addresses and the like are measured in days or weeks, but smaller values are used for special situations. An administrator can disable external caching of data by setting the TTL to 0.

The simple timer-based caching method can be augmented by more clever caching algorithms that also invalidate data, based on problems or other status information.

In addition to the standard type, class, and TTL fields, RRs include a length field that specifies the length of the actual typed data carried in the field RData. The content of the length field varies, depending on the type and class of the RR. For example, for Type = A and Class IN, the RData field contains a 4-octet IP address; for Type = NS, the RData field will contain a variable length domain name.

In normal applications, RRs are always kept in a binary form, but standardized printed forms exist for use in master files that contain the data as entered into name servers by systems administrators, and for use in diagnostics as well. A sample printed RR is shown in Figure 11.5. This example represents an address RR associated with the name Venera.ISI.EDU. Since the owner name, class, and TTL are often repeated in series of RRs, the normal notation is to omit repetitions and assume the last explicitly stated value. An example is shown in Figure 11.6, where all of the data associated with Venera.ISI.EDU is shown.

```
Venera.ISI.EDU.       A       128.9.0.32
                      MX      0  Venera.ISI.EDU.
                      HINFO   VAX–8650        UNIX
                      WKS     (128.9.0.32       UDP   ECHO
                              DISCARD DOMAIN TFTP
                              SUNRPC)
                      WKS     (128.9.0.32       TCP   ECHO
                              DISCARD DAYTIME NETSTAT
                              FTP TELNET SMTP TIME
                              DOMAIN FINGER POP
                              SUNRPC)
```

Figure 11.6   Sample resource record

11.5.3   The DNS Abstract Database—Queries

When an application wants information from the DNS, it supplies three arguments:

1   A query name, which specifies the name of interest

2   A query type, which specifies the types of RR desired

3   A query class, which specifies the classes of RR desired.

The query types and classes are supersets of the RR types and classes, with special values that match multiple types or classes. The best example is the query type denoted by an (*) or ANY, which matches any RR type and is used to retrieve all of the information stored at a particular name.

When a user enters an ftp request to host NIC.DDN.MIL, the ftp command queries the DNS for the query name NIC.DDN.MIL, with query class IN, and query type A. This asks for all Internet address RRs associated with the name.

Query responses normally take one of the following forms:

1   A set of answering RRs (zero or more)

2   An error indication stating that the name does not exist

3   A temporary error indicating that the answer cannot be determined now.

The first response indicates that the name was found and returns either the matching RRs or processed forms of the RR data, depending on the system details. Note that an empty response here is not an error; it merely indicates that although the name exists, no RRs at the name match the query specification.

Though undesirable, the temporary error is a condition that must be anticipated by applications and must be handled as a possible outcome. It cannot be totally avoided, since it may be caused by network disconnection rather then a DNS problem per se. Shortcuts, such as immediately retrying the request or assuming a hard failure, are unacceptable; immediate retries can result in a tight retry loop that saturates the network with useless traffic, while the latter approach aborts requests that could be successfully completed later.

11.5.4   Database Distribution

The DNS rules for database distribution can be easily understood in terms of the complete name space: starting with the complete tree, a "cut" can be made between any two nodes in the tree, dividing the tree into separately administered fragments called zones. As many cuts as required can be made. Theoretically speaking, the whole name space could be a single zone, or cuts could be made between all nodes, resulting in as many zones as there are names or nodes in the name space. This is illustrated in Figure 11.7, which shows how our sample name space might be divided with five cuts.

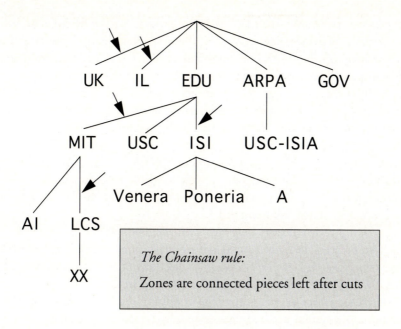

The Chainsaw rule:

Zones are connected pieces left after cuts

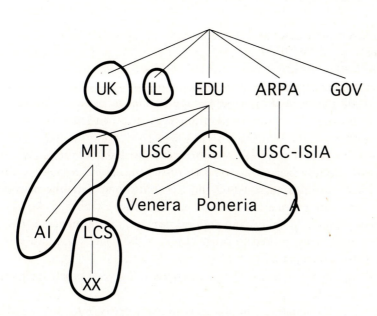

Figure 11.7   A sample database distribution

In practice, we don't start with a complete tree and divide it up. Instead, when an administration wants to control a part of the name space, it gets the owner of an existing zone to create a new name, cut the new name off into a separate zone, and hand control over. Once the new owners have control of the new zone, they are free to add new entries, and even to hand off the control of zones they create. Thus in our sample name space, if a new university, say Miskatonic University, wanted to join the system, it would persuade the existing administrator for the EDU domain to create a new name, for example, Miskatonic.EDU, and then turn control over to the Miskatonic University authorities.

Administrators create and cut zones by adding names and RRs to their existing databases in a fairly straightforward manner. Distribution of administrative control carries with it the responsibility for maintaining the master files for the new zone, and the responsibility for making sure that the zone data is made available by redundant name servers. (The administration that controls a zone will typically make data available via its own servers, but this is not a technical requirement.)

Good design practice dictates that every zone be distributed to at least two independent and redundant servers, to make sure its availability is not limited by the reliability of a single server or its attached network. Important sections of the name space, such as the top levels, are distributed to multiple servers distributed over the Internet.

An interesting aspect of this is that the distribution management was one of the first users of the DNS system and requires essentially no external configuration information; this isn't the case with some more sophisticated systems.

11.5.5 Name Space Structure and Administration

The DNS design attempted to maximize the number of choices available for the size and character set of names, distribution of control, and organization of the name space. While this freedom is still present and available for applications to use, administrative conventions govern the use of the upper portions of the name space, and practical concerns influence name choices.

The DNS was lucky in that a choice was made for the design of the upper levels of the name space well before this became an important issue and subject to politics. The choices made in 1984 and documented in Postel and Reynolds,[6] grandfathered names from the existing ARPA name space into a top level named ARPA, but established two sorts of other top-level domains: generic domains and country domains. Since then, the grandfathered domains under ARPA have moved to other places in the name space and various other reorganizations have taken place.

Top-level generic domains divide the name space into several broad categories, which are shown in Table 11.1.

In addition to these domains, one top-level domain per country was reserved, based upon the ISO 3166 two-letter country code. For example:

```
US              The United States
CA              Canada
CH              Switzerland
```

Table 11.1 Catagories of generic domains

Domain	Contents	Example
COM	Commercial	Sun.COM
EDU	Educational	MIT.EDU
NET	NICs and NOCs	ES.NET
MIL	US military	DARPA.MIL
GOV	Other US government	NASA.GOV
ORG	Other organizations	SFLOVERS.ORG

Each of these domains is typically a separate zone, and control of per-country domains is allocated to a responsible party in that country. (Determining what is a country and who is responsible has become much more difficult recently, and the procedures are still being refined.) The top-level generic domains are managed by the DDN NIC.

To create a new domain, an organization must first decide where it wants to be in the domain tree, and get permission from the owner of that zone. For example, a university could apply to the owner of the EDU domain, a company to the owner of the COM domain, etc. Of course, since the generic divisions are functional and the country divisions geographical, all applicants have at least two choices to consider.

Determining the authority for the zones you wish to join is fairly simple, since that information can be obtained from information files maintained by the DDN NIC or by queries to the DNS itself. Determining its policies may be simple or difficult. Since the essence of the domain system is distribution of authority, owners are free to set their own policies for the domains they manage. The generic domains admit virtually any organization that "fits" the description.

An important refinement is that an organization is allocated only one domain under the top level domains. For example, if the Physics and Classics departments of Miskatonic University each sought a separate domain under EDU, say Miskatonic-Physics.EDU and Miskatonic-Classics.EDU, they would be told to apply jointly for Miskatonic.EDU and then to internally subdivide that into Classics.Miskatonic.EDU and Physics.Miskatonic.EDU. This policy helps to reduce the load on the managers of the top-level domains and makes searching the space somewhat easier.

Countries set their own policies for their own domains. Some are more enlightened than others. For example, country domain authorities have occasionally restricted domain registration based on political considerations or the allowed mail protocols. Some countries enforce their policies by means outside of the DNS rules and prohibit registration in the generic domains.

The pattern of registration in the top-level domains and the data stored in them provide one of the most direct ways of measuring Internet growth. Figure 11.8 shows the growth in registration for domains under the top-level domains. Note that this is not the number of names, but the number of delegations under the top-level domains. While these charts seem to suggest that commercial domains are now the fastest growing segment, it should

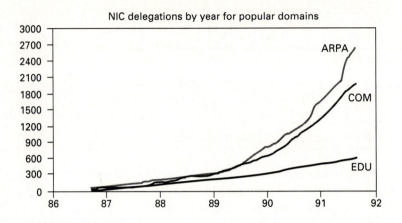

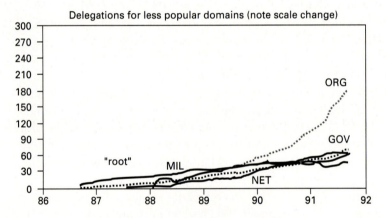

Figure 11.8   Registration for domains

also be noted that commercial organizations are more likely to accept registration under the top-level EDU domain, while educational institutions often register under country codes.

Lottor[7] describes results of a program called ZONE that attempts to collect all of the data in all of the zones that make up the domain space. In January 1992, it found approximately 727,000 hosts scattered through 17,000 zones. This substantially understates the real population, since many organizations disallow external access to data in their domains. Growth in DNS registration continues on an exponential path, with substantial new growth coming from new countries joining the Internet.

Despite the vote of confidence implied by registration, virtually every person on the Internet has an objection to all or some part of the scheme, but no consensus has ever been developed on a replacement and a transition plan. The most common objections are that the generic domains are all US-centric; indeed, an administrator for one country's network was heard to say "I won't allow organizations in my country to join these domains since they are US-only."

11.6 NETFIND

One of the (few) truly innovative ideas in directory services has been developed by Mike Schwartz at the University of Colorado.[8] The system, called NETFIND, locates users through a two-step process. First, user input in the form of a name, and possibly location information, is used to search a database, where the database is constructed off-line by observing public e-mail and other sources. The result of the database lookup is a list of "hints" where the user is likely to be found.

Second, using the hint list, FINGER, DNS, and SMTP VRFY probes are used to validate or refute the hints, and get up-to-the-minute information about mail address, log-in status, etc.

This system has many interesting qualities. A user can "register" by sending mail to one of the mail groups monitored by the NETFIND database gatherer (one hopes to the smallest group, to avoid flooding large lists with "Hi there!" messages). Analysis of messages could also hint at a user's protocol stack, language, or even work hours. Some find the "big brother" possibilities unfortunate.

Since the probe phase is efficiently performed in parallel, resource usage on the network can be a problem. The Colorado researchers have been quite careful, and the approach needs this care.

Last, some administrators disallow FINGER, SMTP VRFY, and other queries used by NETFIND on security grounds, and even view such probing as reason to suspect an attack in progress.

11.7 X.500

The international standard for directory services is known as X.500 (its CCITT name), although the same work is occasionally referred to as 9594 (its ISO name). The X.500 system was based on work from the IFIP and other communities, and rose to international standard status in 1988. It is based upon the rest of the OSI standards stack, including ASN.1, ROS, and ACSE.

The goals of X.500 are nothing less than a single, unified, worldwide system that completely describes all OSI resources and contains all manner of tools to search, authenticate, replicate, and formalize. The reality is that the 1988 standard described an all-encompassing vision, but made specifications only for parts of that vision, omitting important parts of the design. While this infuriated individuals who had trouble understanding the concept of an incomplete international standard, it created a challenging opportunity to fill in the holes.

In the Internet, an early implementation of X.500, called QUIPU, was done at University College London (UCL). A long-term X.500 implementation plan was recommended by Sollins[9] in 1989 but was never implemented, perhaps because of the start of the PSI white pages pilot (WPP) and the later DARPA field operational X.500 (FOX) project, both of which stressed immediate deployment. The QUIPU implementation has been joined by others over time. Due to efforts in the IETF and other communities, many of the holes have been filled in, and X.500 is starting to fulfill some of its promises. Rose[10] has a good description of X.500 and the WPP.

11.7.1 Conceptual Model

The overall model of the X.500 Directory Information Tree (DIT) and the Directory Information Base (DIB), i.e., the name space and data in it, are generalizations of the same ideas used in Clearinghouse and the DNS. However, X.500 adds an interesting twist by unifying the names and data in the tree into a single concept called an *attribute*. An attribute consists of a type and one or more values; attributes can be used either to simply store data at a node in the tree or to create an arc to a child node.

X.500 features a class inheritance system for typing data at nodes, and a comprehensive system for representing new data types, as well as rules called schema for specifying the attributes required in object classes, which classes can be subordinate to others, etc. Curiously enough, X.500 doesn't mandate or describe methods for carrying most of the definitions in X.500 itself. X.500 is intended to provide a completely distributed system, where applications access the globally distributed DIT though the services of a local Directory User Agent (DUA), which then communicates with the Directory System Agents (DSAs) that store the information.

Although this might seem fairly similar to the name servers and resolvers of the DNS, there is significant extra power and complexity.

X.500 communications are connection-, not datagram-oriented. The DUA identifies itself at the start of a connection using either the strong (certificates) or weak (password) authentication facilities of X.500. DSAs use this information to implement access control. (Most of the mechanism is absent from the specifications, but acceptable constructs have been created by the QUIPU community.)

X.500 operations can be as simple as a request for a certain type of information from a specific name, or can be as complicated as a request to search for various types of information in specified subtrees using "fuzzy" matching rules and given upper bounds on the cost of the query. As a result, a query operation can result in multiple subqueries to multiple DSAs, with the results being merged before a reply is returned to the user.

Replication and automatic location of DSAs with the desired information is another area in which the standard is curiously mute, but acceptable extensions have been defined and are in use.

Dynamic modification of the DIT is also provided for in the specification, but only in a limited sense. Manipulation on leaf nodes is allowed, but manipulations on interior nodes is restricted.

11.7.2 X.500 Name Space Administration and Applications

The importance of X.500 has led to repeated episodes of gridlock on a number of important issues related to name space administration, control, and structure. One hopes that the efforts from the pilots and the North American Directory Forum (NADF)[11] will result in early standardization, while preserving opportunities for experimentation. The services are becoming widespread enough that concerns for the public are under consideration.[12]

Applications of X.500 in the Internet are varied. The best demos are directory assistance programs, which flash up pictures of users and track their favorite beverages. Other uses include a WHOIS-like service based on the real WHOIS database and some distributed alternatives. A searchable directory of *RFC* documents is another application.

11.8 WAIS

Wide Area Information Services (WAIS) target the more general problem of coordinated access to information from a variety of bibliographic, news, quote, and library services. An early experimental service, combining the expertise of Thinking Machines Co., Dow Jones & Co., KPMG Peat Marwick, and Apple Computer, illustrates some of the possibilities and techniques that may eventually find their way into more ubiquitous use.

The WAIS system, like conventional directory services, has client programs that talk to servers using a standard protocol. The WAIS protocol is a publicly available extension.[13] The user describes the information of interest, selects probable sources, and launches the query. Multimedia documents are returned, and the user can peruse them.

An interesting innovation takes place at this point, called "relevance feedback." The user marks documents that are of interest, and the system will then look for others with similar content. The matching for similar content currently involves shared common words; however, there is no bar to future, more sophisticated algorithms.

WAIS users may also build rudimentary personalized newspapers by running a predefined query composed of the user's interests each evening, and combining all of the material that arrived in the previous day.

11.9 THE FUTURE OF NAMING AND DIRECTORY SERVICES

The gains realized in the evolution of services from Clearinghouse to X.500 have been essentially those that are realized from refinement, distribution of function, and wide availability of technology, rather than from revolutionary ideas or concepts. Some of these systems have been better than others in various ways: X.500 will always be more powerful than the Clearinghouse and DNS, but it will also be more expensive and slower.

However, there are indications that several new systems will provide new ideas that will fuel the next generation of directory services. As discussed above, the WAIS prototype provides new types of query refinement through feedback. The Archie system, developed at McGill University, is a combination of resource discovery tools that provide a directory of resources on the Internet. The system currently provides directories for anonymous ftp sites scattered across the Internet, together with the names and descriptions of software packages and similar resources. The active search and continuous maintenance have proven practical over intercontinental-scale systems. The resource discovery work at University of Colorado has illustrated the power of a system that builds a database using combinations of observation of news flows and active queries. Knowbots, a concept popularized by researchers at CNRI, proposes semiautonomous agents that cruise the Internet seeking answers to queries for their owners.

REFERENCES

1 J.F. Shoch, Inter-Network Naming, Addressing, and Routing, In *Proceedings COMPCON*, 1978.

2 D.C. Oppen and Y.K. Dalal, The Clearinghouse: A decentralized agent for locating named objects in a distributed environment, *ACM Transactions on Office Information Systems*, 1983.

3 J. Postel, *Internet Name Server, IEN 116*, USC Information Sciences Institute, August 1979.

4 D. Zimmerman, *The Finger User Information Protocol, RFC 1288*, 1991.

5 P. Mockapetris, *Domain names—Concepts and Facilities*, *RFC 1034*, USC/Information Sciences Institute, November 1987; *Domain names—Implementation and Specification, RFC 1035*, USC/Information Sciences Institute, November 1987.

6 J. Postel and J. Reynolds, *Domain Requirements*, 1984.

7 M. Lottor, *Internet Growth (1981–1991), RFC 1296*, 1992.

8 M.F. Schwartz and P.G. Tsirigotis, Experience with a Semantically Cognizant Internet White Pages Directory Tool, *Journal of Internetworking: Research and Experience*, March 1991.

9 K.R. Sollings, *Plan for Internet Directory Services, RFC 1107*, 1989.

10 M.T. Rose, *The Little Black Book: Mail-Bonding with OSI Directory Services*, Prentice Hall, 1991.

11 The North American Directory Forum, *Naming Scheme for c=US*, *RFC 1218*, 1991.

12 The North American Directory Forum, *User Bill of Rights for Entries and Listings in the Public Directory*, 1992.

13 National Information Standards Organization (NISO), *Z39.50-1988: Information Retrieval Service Definition Protocol Specification for Library Applications*.

CHAPTER 12

Network Management

JEFFREY D. CASE

CONTENTS

493

Because of its highly-decentralized nature, the Internet is managed by large numbers of autonomous entities. Despite this, there must be a common technology used by operators and devices in order to manage the components of the Internet. As with so many other technologies, the Internet community pioneered this work out of sheer necessity; and also with many Internet technologies, the technology found its way into many non-Internet environments!

12.1   INTRODUCTION

Until recently, network management lagged behind the technical advances in other areas of networking based on open standards; to some extent, it still does. Proprietary tools failed to meet the needs of users and managers of networks based on open protocols, such as the TCP/IP suite and those defined by ISO. This created a void. The dearth of management solutions for open networking protocols is one of the many reasons cited by computer and network hardware and software vendors for continuing to market proprietary networking products. Similarly, the absence to date of viable and interoperable management solutions for open networks based on OSI/ISO protocols has been one of the factors that has limited growth of the market.

One of the several reasons why network management has lagged behind in other areas of open networking is that there is a lack of agreement about what network management is. While there is no shortage of literature offering platitudes about the five functional areas of network management: fault—configuration, accounting, performance, and security management—the body of literature offering practical details about managing real open networks has, until recently, been virtually nonexistent.

Part of the problem is that "everyone knows" what *network management* is. However, the term means different things to different people. They often give widely varying answers to questions such as:

"What does a network manager do?"
"What questions do network managers need to be able to answer?"
"What problems do network managers need to solve?"
"What reports do network managers need to generate?"

Consequently, it is difficult to achieve consensus on what information is required to accomplish these tasks. As a result, it is difficult to obtain agreement on what data are required to generate needed information, what applications are needed to transform the data into information, and what mechanisms should be designed, implemented, and deployed for collecting and moving those data.

That is, while there are many individual personal opinions about what network management is, in general, there is no common, shared view. It is difficult, if not impossible, to engineer solutions to the problem, which is, as a result, ill-defined.

As a result, there have been several fundamentally different approaches to the network management problem. Some of the approaches have been found to be practical, and have attained widespread acceptance for portions of the problem of managing networks based on open networking protocols.

The Simple Network Management Protocol (SNMP)[1] is a key part of the operational, open, standard, network management framework. The SNMP management framework was originally envisioned for use in TCP/IP networks, but it is finding application in areas far afield of the original expectations. The SNMP management framework constitutes an open standard for network management, as established by the IAB. Consequently, the SNMP management framework can be said to be a declared or *de jure* standard. The relevant standards documents were elevated to full Standard protocols for the Internet community, with the status *Recommended* in May 1990. This affords the management framework the same standardization status as TCP.

Declared standards that are not deployed are of little use. However, this is certainly not the case with the SNMP management framework. Vendors have implemented it, customers have purchased it, network implementors have deployed it, and network managers are actively using it.

Users have driven the demand for SNMP-based systems. Because of user demands, its affordability, and its capabilities, SNMP went from a concept to a *de facto* standard in less than two years. No other protocol in the history of the TCP/IP suite has seen this rapid a rate of acceptance.

12.1.1 History and Motivation

The SNMP management framework is a descendant of the successful Simple Gateway Monitoring Protocol (SGMP).[2] The authors of SNMP were also the authors of SGMP. These individuals had a practical focus due to their active involvement in the design, management, and research of internets. The resulting design reflects the practical focus of the group. These same individuals, who were university researchers, users and managers of networks, and communications vendors, coded the initial implementations of the protocol. Their collective knowledge and experience, and their common, shared view of network management made it possible to design, implement, and deploy SNMP in just a few months. This team was augmented by a committee that contributed to the design of the protocol, and by other teams, which designed the SMI and MIB portions of the management framework.

SGMP was designed primarily for the monitoring of IP gateways in wide-area networks, and was widely implemented and deployed in that application. However, the success of the protocol led to its deployment in other areas as well, which led to increasing demands for changes in the protocol.

Some of these changes were improvements to the protocol, based on existing needs and the experience gained through operational use. The specification was altered to strengthen and extend the protocol in the area of management capabilities, and to reflect application in new areas beyond IP gateways.

Other changes were made, based on anticipated needs and political considerations. These changes led to increased use of a few OSI-style network management concepts. It was hoped that this would ease the eventual transition to management systems based on those concepts, when they become defined and implemented. These changes were not backwardly compatible with SGMP, but were necessary for SNMP to be allowed to become an endorsed standard. The changes included the definition and adoption of an OSI-style Structure of Management Information (SMI)[3] and Management Information Base (MIB).[4]

The early plan for the transition from SGMP to SNMP[5] called for the development of a common basis for network management that could be shared by multiple management protocols. In the original plan, the rules for how structuring information would be defined in a protocol-independent SMI, and the information to be managed would be specified in the MIB in a protocol-independent manner. Other documents would define specifications for the protocols: SNMP and the Common Management Information Protocol over the Transmission Control Protocol (CMIP over TCP/IP, or CMOT). It was anticipated that SNMP would accommodate the pressing short-term needs for management solutions, and that the longer term needs of the Internet would be met using the ISO CMIS/CMIP framework as a basis. The SNMP framework and CMOT frameworks would share the (hopefully) protocol-independent SMI and MIB. It was hoped that use of a common SMI and MIB would at some point in the future allow one protocol to be exchanged for another with little or no disruption, and with minimal impact on applications.

The good news that resulted from these efforts is that SNMP was defined, implemented, and deployed on a timely basis. The availability of multiple, independent, interoperable reference implementations accelerated progress. The Internet became manageable, and SNMP became a *de facto* standard. In recognition of this, SNMP's official standardization status was elevated by the IAB.

The bad news is that protocol wars resulted from the IAB's identification of dual standards. Sharing a single SMI and MIB was more difficult than originally thought. MIB standardization efforts were unable to reach agreement on extensions to the MIB, although operational requirements were adding pressure for needed extensions. The failure to reach agreement caused at least two efforts to define a standard protocol-independent applications programming interface (API) to be abandoned. In general, standardization progress stalled.

A second plan emerged as a result of the meeting of the Second Ad Hoc Network Management Review Group.[6] It was decided to decouple the SNMP and CMOT frameworks, allowing them to evolve independently, including allowing CMOT to diverge from the Internet Standard SMI in order to bring CMOT into closer alignment with the OSI CMIS design.

Under this plan, the SNMP community has flourished. It successfully developed MIB-II, the second Internet Standard MIB. Numerous other MIB specifications for transmission layer devices, additional protocol families, and new applications areas have similarly been developed. Acceptance of the SNMP framework has continued to increase, and the growth continues. In the meantime, CMOT standardization efforts have faded, and the relevant committee has ceased to meet.

12.1.2 Requirements

Modern network management poses several important requirements. First, the management framework must support both monitoring and control. Monitoring is required to determine the current state of the network. Control functions are necessary to effect changes in the network. For example, a fault management application might be able to monitor the network to detect and diagnose a fault, then take control actions to isolate, bypass, or repair it.

Second, modern network management requires the ability to manage all ten layers of implementation of the OSI seven-layer model, i.e., to provide top-to-bottom network management. This should include visibility to the physical level whenever possible.

Third, to the maximum extent possible and economically feasible, the scope of network management should be end-to-end. It should encompass all systems in the network. Of course, this level of ubiquity will never be reached, but if it is to be approached, there are important constraints on the range of acceptable design decisions, and implications for the management framework. For example, the agent portion of the framework must have a low implementation cost, low runtime cost, be scalable over the entire range of hardware and software systems (down to the resource-poor and up to the resource-rich), and be easily developed by a large number of implementors with a wide range of implementation skills and strategies.

Finally, the impact of the network management framework on the network should not be obtrusive. The bandwidth consumed by the network management function should be within acceptable limits.

12.2 THE SNMP FRAMEWORK

12.2.1 Architecture

The SNMP management framework is built upon an architecture consisting of four components: management agents in network elements, network management stations, a common protocol that joins the management stations and agents, and network management information.

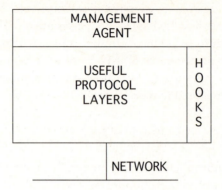

Figure 12.1   Conceptualization of a managed network element

12.2.1.1 Network Elements

Figure 12.1 depicts the architecture of a typical managed network element.

The first component of the SNMP framework is the network management agent. Network management agents are found in network elements, which are the devices that make up the network. They include end systems, such as hosts, workstations, file servers, print servers, and terminal servers, as well as intermediate systems, such as gateways, routers, bridges, repeaters, and supporting devices and media. Some of the network devices will be manageable. Manageable network elements will have a management agent that listens for and responds to network management queries and commands on its behalf.

A management agent listens for queries and commands from its network management station or stations. The SNMP protocol engine in the agent peers with SNMP applications in management stations. In general, the agent passively listens for a query or command, acts upon it, returns a response, and resumes listening passively.

The agent communicates with its network management station or stations via the "useful protocol layers." That is, the SNMP management framework is typically configured for "in-band" virtual peer-to-peer communications. Usually, although not always, the useful protocol layers consist of the relevant portions of the TCP/IP protocol suite, as shown in Figure 12.2, i.e., the User Datagram Protocol (UDP)[7] at the transport layer, IP[8] and Inter-

SNMP Protocol Data Unit
SNMP Header (Authentication)
Transport (UDP)
Network (IP)
Data Link / LLC / MAC

Figure 12.2   Encapsulation and layering

net Control Message Protocol (ICMP)[9] at the network layer, one or more link, media access control (MAC) layer, and the physical layer interfaces.

In some devices, the useful protocol layers serve other applications in addition to management, whereas in other systems, the useful protocol layers are present only to support the management function. In either case, the useful protocol layers almost always include instrumentation to keep track of the values of network management information of interest. For example, the instrumentation of the ICMP layer might include counters of the quantity of each type of ICMP message sent and received by the system. These ICMP layer statistics might be helpful to network managers diagnosing faults or analyzing performance.

To some extent, the SNMP protocol engine forms just another useful protocol layer, and may itself include instrumentation of the SNMP layers. This provides a measure of meta-management.

In addition to network management agents and instrumented useful protocol layers, the network elements also typically include an interlayer communications mechanism. This mechanism provides read or read-write access to the instrumentation located in the useful protocol layers. The interlayer communications mechanism is simply a purposeful violation of layering. The formal term used in OSI literature for this mechanism is *Layer Management Entity* (LME), but SNMP literature often simply calls them *hooks*.

Network elements are increasingly multiprotocol, supporting multiple protocol families, such as TCP/IP and OSI or DECnet simultaneously. In general, these systems pose no significant new challenges for the management framework. The existence of multiple sets of useful protocol layers requires multiple sets of instrumentation and multiple sets of hooks. It is simply a matter of more management variables.

Some systems do not provide native support for the SNMP protocol, yet still are able to participate in the SNMP management framework via a mechanism known as *proxy*. A proxy in the legal sense is one who is authorized and empowered to act or vote on behalf of another. A proxy agent in the SNMP management framework is an agent that has the resources and authorization to respond to queries and commands on behalf of another managed system. To accomplish this function, the proxy agent communicates with the target managed system via some private mechanism. This mechanism might take any number of forms, and might itself include use of SNMP, perhaps over alternative transports and encapsulation schemes.

There are several reasons why systems might want to participate in the SNMP management framework via proxy. Some systems fail to have the relatively modest hardware and software assets required to support SNMP. Other systems were implemented before support of SNMP became a practical and economic necessity for success in the marketplace.

12.2.1.2 Network Management Stations

The second component of the architecture is the network management station.

In the SNMP framework, one or more network management stations execute applications that monitor and control network elements. Management applications executing in the network management stations formulate and transmit appropriate requests, then wait for and process responses returned from agents.

Network management applications may have a variety of user interfaces. They may be command-line based, use a graphical user interface, such as the X Window System[10] or Microsoft Windows, or may be based on scripts and have no user interface at all. They may be fancy or useful. They are usually based on a popular operating system, such as UNIX, System V, VAX/VMS, or MS DOS.

The management stations sometimes reside in a Network Operations Center (NOC). There are almost always many network elements per NOC. There may be one or many NOCs for a given network element. For example, in larger networks, the behavior of a single network element might be monitored by NOCs on the desks of the manager of the facility, the network systems programmers, the network operators, and at the help desk, with a smaller number of these configured and authorized to exert control functions. Of course, in smaller networks, all of these responsibilities might be performed by a single individual using a single station.

In some networks, there may be multiple NOCs for a given network element. For example, some networks are configured with dual NOCs for redundancy and disaster recovery, with both NOCs monitoring and controlling the entire network. Networks that span large geographical areas may use redundant NOCs for time zone coverage and multilingual support. Finally, some networks discussed are jointly administered, for example the border gateways between two administrative domains, such as between a national backbone network and a state network.

All of these management station possibilities are permitted within the SNMP management framework.

12.2.1.3 Network Management Protocol

The third component of the architecture is the network management protocol, which is implemented by the protocol engines in the network management application entities. These are located in the management agents within the managed network elements and in the network management applications within the management stations.

SNMP supports two types of transactions. The transfer of information is primarily accomplished via synchronous query-response or request-response messages through a mechanism called *polling*. The SNMP management framework also includes the use of asynchronous messages called *traps* sent from agents to managers.

Every SNMP message consists of an authentication wrapper and an enclosed SNMP Protocol Data Unit (PDU). The authentication wrapper consists of a version number; a community string to convey authentication; authorization; and access control information; followed by one of five PDUs (get request PDU, get-next request PDU, set request PDU, get response PDU, and trap PDU).

Most communications in the SNMP management framework are based on the request-response PDU types. In retrospect, get response probably should have been simply named *response*, for it is sent in response to all requests, including get, get-next, and set.

When polling with the request-response PDUs, the management stations send appropriate queries and commands to the network management agents in the managed network elements. When an agent in a network element receives a request, it is examined for correctness, and a suitable error message is returned, if appropriate. If the sender is deemed authentic and suitably authorized, the agent acts upon the request.

The management application formulates an appropriate request by naming the variable or variables to be inspected (retrieved) or altered (set). SNMP queries, commands, responses, and traps may contain multiple variable bindings, or *varbinds*. A varbind is a pairing of a variable name and a variable value. By this mechanism, a single request may include the names of zero, one, or many variables. As a result, the management station may request or convey several pieces of information in a single message.

Each "request-let" in the request results in exactly one "response-let" in the response. That is, there is always a one-to-one mapping between the varbinds contained in the request and the varbinds contained in the corresponding response; i.e., there will be exactly the same number of varbinds in the request and the resulting response.

The get and get-next operators are used for network monitoring. The so called *powerful* get-next operator is able to perform all of the functions of the get operator, plus more. In addition, the get-next operator is able to traverse tables by retrieving the lexicographical antecedent of the requested variable. Finally, the get-next operator is far more robust than the get operator in the presence of errors, such as those caused by incomplete agent implementations. Consequently, it is strongly recommended that all new applications be written using the get-next operator rather than the get operator. The get operator was included in the design because it was believed to ease the support of proxy. SGMP, the predecessor of SNMP, did not have the get operator, and demonstrated that the get-next operator was more than sufficient.

The set request is used for network control. Network management stations may use it to modify network management information, create new instances of information (i.e., add new rows to lists and tables), and delete information (i.e., delete rows from lists and tables). Set requests can be used to replace the need for imperative commands, also known as *actions* in ISO network management literature. In SNMP, actions are accomplished as side effects of the alteration of management variables. The task of creating new verbs then becomes protocol-independent and is reduced to the definition of new information elements, and the semantics associated with setting them to particular values. This considerably decreases the complexity of the protocol, and significantly increases the generality of the framework.

While multiple request-lets may be transmitted in a single PDU within a single SNMP message, each information item retrieved or altered in the SNMP framework is named individually. No support for the retrieval or alteration of objects as aggregates, such as tables of variables, is realized by SNMP. Aggregate objects such as lists and tables of related information can be and are supported by SNMP as individual components. For example, while it is not possible to request four pieces of information about an interface by retrieving a single object, it is possible to retrieve four pieces of information about that interface by retrieving four objects, i.e., requesting the interface's speed, type, description, and status.

Similarly, the management station may convey several pieces of information in a single set request. Once again, these pieces of information may be related, such as several columns of a particular row in a table, or may be unrelated, such as several scalars and portions of rows from multiple tables. However, in practice, few management station applications exploit this capability (of setting unrelated things). Nearly all set requests sent by real network management station applications contain only single or related variable bindings.

SNMP defines a fifth message type, the trap message. Traps are sent asynchronously by agents to management stations to indicate occurrences of unusual events. Various bodies of literature use different terms for this type of indication. ISO literature uses the term *event*. Literature from IBM uses the term *alert*. Hardware developers and bus designers often associate the term *interrupt* with similar concepts. Operating systems literature often calls it a *trap*, as in *arithmetic exception trap*. The SNMP literature adopts this convention. The agent may emit a trap message to indicate an exceptional condition, perhaps with arguments that play a role similar to that of a trap vector. The management stations receiving the trap message may then use the trap notification (with or without additional arguments) to guide the timing and focus of its polling in a strategy known as *trap-directed polling*.

The delivery of traps cannot be guaranteed in failing networks, and this cannot be changed; hence traps are not and cannot be reliable. As a result, the SNMP management framework primarily utilizes polling, and traps are relegated to a secondary role.

12.2.1.4 *Network Management Information*

The fourth component of the architecture is the network management information, which is communicated between managers and agents via the shared network management protocol. That is, copies of the current values for network management variables of interest may be retrieved from an agent by the management station, or management stations may write new values into managed agents.

Network management information can take several forms in the SNMP management framework. Some variables are integers, such as counters, gauges, timer values, and state variables. Some are octet strings or strings of bytes, such as Internet addresses, physical addresses, system names, and descriptive text strings. Some are object identifiers, which are used to name object classes and object instances within classes.

These generic information types are defined, along with their semantics, in the SMI.[3] The SMI also defines how information is structured, describes a suitable object information model, and specifies the rules for describing current objects in the MIB, as well as defining new objects in the MIB.

The MIB is now distributed among several MIB documents, such as MIB-II.[11] These documents describe what information is managed, and define the syntax and semantics of the objects to be instrumented in the useful protocol layers. Finally, they place each MIB variable in the object tree, which is defined as a part of the object information model specified in the SMI document.

In summary, the SMI document specifies the common structures and the identification scheme for the definition of management information, including descriptions of an object information model and a set of generic types used to describe management information. The MIB document specifies the objects that are managed, including their naming, syntax, definitions, access, and status. Programmers familiar with C and similar languages will recognize the SMI as providing the type definitions, and the MIB documents as defining variables in terms of the defined types. The SNMP document specifies the protocols used to manage the objects.

Reading and understanding these documents requires familiarity with the ISO/OSI presentation layer standard *Abstract Syntax Notation One* (ASN.1)[12] language and syntax and the corresponding *Basic Encoding Rules* (BER).[13]

12.2.2 Abstract Syntax Notation One

SNMP makes heavy use of ASN.1. ASN.1 was originally designed for use as a part of the X.400 electronic mail message handling system,[14] but has since been adopted with minimal modifications and extensions by ISO as a standard presentation layer component. ASN.1 now is at the core of many ISO protocols, and is used in many applications far beyond its original design center.

12.2.2.1 The ASN.1 Goal

ASN.1 consists of two major parts. The first part[12] is a specification of a grammar or notation, which is used in defining portions of the Internet Standard SMI, all of the MIB documents, and in SNMP itself. A second ASN.1 document[13] part defines encoding rules. These completely specify the encodings for each data type and value, including how they should appear in messages.

The rules specify the transfer syntax. The encoding rules define the translation from the sending machine's internal representation into a machine-independent external representation, or intermediate syntax; the decoding rules define the translation of data from the external representation into the receiving system's internal representation. The transfer syntax allows the protocol data on the network to be represented in a machine-independent, widely understood, and widely accepted form.

12.2.2.2 Use of a Subset

ASN.1 is a very rich grammar, and therefore has a very rich set of encoding rules. However, the designers of the SNMP management framework elected to use only a well-engineered subset of the ASN.1 grammar, thereby bypassing much of the unnecessary complexity and overhead resulting from ASN.1's more elaborate features. Consequently, the set of applicable encoding rules is concomitantly reduced. Furthermore, where ASN.1 allows multiple choices, the SNMP designers made additional restrictions on the use of allowed encodings in the interest of simplicity. For example, the ASN.1 Basic Encoding Rules allow the use of both definite length and indefinite length encodings. While the use of indefinite length encodings makes it slightly easier to send data, it makes it considerably more difficult to receive data. Furthermore, it is unnecessary and wasteful to support two ways to accomplish a given low-level task within a protocol. Consequently, the designers prohibited the use of indefinite length encodings in the SNMP management framework.

12.2.2.3 Selection of ASN.1

ASN.1 was chosen for use in the SNMP management framework because it had become the *lingua franca* of network management, even though at least one of the SNMP authors thought that X.409, and thereby ASN.1, was some kind of "industrial strength window cleaning formula." Many standards bodies, including ANSI, IEEE, and ISO, use ASN.1 in defining their management standards. SGMP, the predecessor of SNMP, used a subset of ASN.1, and SNMP makes use of a larger subset. The first widespread use of ASN.1 in the Internet came with its adoption and use in the SNMP management framework. More traditional Internet applications used Sun Microsystems' eXternal Data Representation (XDR)[15] to meet the requirements of the presentation layer.

In retrospect, the use of ASN.1 in Internet management was a good choice based on political criteria, even if it was a poor choice based on technical criteria. The selection of ASN.1 was politically correct because without this choice, it is unlikely that SGMP, and subsequently, the SNMP would have had sufficient political acceptability to obtain high levels of acceptance in the standards community and market penetration. However, the use of ASN.1 in the SNMP management framework has several technical deficiencies. First, ASN.1 is unnecessarily complex, leading to unnecessarily large code sizes and slower execution. ASN.1 packs data into the smallest possible number of bytes on the network. As a result, data is neither word- nor longword-aligned, resulting in poorer performance and the trading of CPU cycles for media bandwidth. While this engineering trade-off may have been appropriate for electronic mail and messaging applications in the 1980s when large CPUs were interconnected via relatively slow serial lines, it is inappropriate for the network management tasks of the 1990s and beyond, when managed nodes frequently are small microprocessor-based systems interconnected via high-speed media. Furthermore, the use of ASN.1 in OSI, anchored by the Common Management Information Protocol (CMIP),[16] and the use of a subset of ASN.1 in the SNMP management frameworks have led to confusion among the naive, including the promulgation of the myth that SNMP is a subset of CMIP.

SNMP Message									
Auth Header		Protocol Data Unit							
						Variable Bindings List			
Version Number	Community String	PDU type	Req ID	Error Status	Error Index	name1:value1	name2:value2	...	namen:valuen

Figure 12.3   Request-response PDU format

12.2.3 The Protocol

The format of the four request-response PDUs is shown in Figure 12.3—all four have the same format. Only the trap PDU format is different, and the SNMP designers agree that, in retrospect, it should not have been different. The designers of SNMP opted to make the request-response formats identical in the interest of simplicity. As a consequence of this decision, some fields in some messages will not have meaningful contents. For example, a manager station application preparing to send a get request or get-next request will not know the values of the variable value portion of the varbinds of the request. If it already knew the requested values, there would be no need to ask for them. The variable value portion of the varbinds of get requests and get-next requests are ignored by the receiving agent. However, these fields must be present and must contain valid ASN.1 syntax. The protocol specification allows implementors to place any valid SNMP data value in those fields. It is strongly recommended that the ASN.1 value for NULL be used to fill these fields with "nothing," and many real management station implementations follow this recommendation in practice. Agents, of course, must be prepared to accept and ignore any value that might be sent in this position in compliance with the specification.

12.2.3.1 Message Size Limitations

The number of varbinds in a PDU within an SNMP message is limited only by the maximum message sizes supported by the communicating implementations. However, in practice, some implementations (in conflict with the specification) place artificial upper limits on the number of varbinds that they can produce or consume in a single message.

The largest SNMP message size that an SNMP implementation must support is 484 bytes. SNMP implementations are encouraged to support larger sizes whenever possible. However, to achieve the greatest amount of interoperability, management station applications are wise to limit their message sizes to 484 bytes unless they learn, perhaps through experimentation, that the target agent can support larger message sizes.

The value 484 was selected to provide implementors with a concrete lower bound on the maximum message size, and to minimize the amount of IP layer fragmentation that is likely to occur. The value 484 is the result of subtracting 20 (the size of the IP header without options) and 8 (the size of the UDP header) from 512, a popular lower bound for the maximum transmission unit size at the IP layer.

Having a message size, including IP and UDP headers, of at most 512 bytes does not guarantee that fragmentation of network management messages will not occur. However, fragmentation is expected to be rare in practice in real networks. The designers of SNMP were aware of the conventional wisdom that avoiding fragmentation is generally "a good thing." In addition, they thought it to be especially important to avoid fragmentation of messages used by network management applications whenever possible. Networks in failure modes often exhibit lossy characteristics, dropping many packets. Normally, an SNMP transaction consists of a single pair of request-response packets. Fragmentation spreads the management communications over multiple packets, and the probability that all fragments of a message will be received and reassembled drops rapidly. Consequently, the impact of fragmentation on management communications is that it greatly reduces the probability of success of the management communication in networks with failure modes causing high rates of packet loss. It is most important that the network management communications be successful in precisely these types of failure modes, so that faults may be detected, diagnosed, and bypassed or repaired.

12.2.3.2 *Error Handling*

SNMP has mechanisms for conveying a limited amount of error information in the response returned to the manager station when certain errors are detected. The ErrorStatus field communicates the type of error, if any. The ErrorIndex field indicates which varbind, if any, was found to be offensive.

The get and get-next operators can result in one of three values of ErrorStatus. The value *noError* indicates that all request-lets were processed successfully, without exception. The value *noSuchName* is generated when a request attempts to access a variable instance that does not exist, and when a manager station attempts to retrieve a variable for which it does not have sufficient authorization to access. The value *tooBig* indicates that the request was received successfully but that the response was too large, and exceeded a resource limitation on the agent. The ErrorIndex may be examined by the manager station, and the request can potentially be retried with fewer varbinds in the varbind list. Note that no error is generated and no response will be received if the request was too large for the agent to handle. The manager station application will time out.

The set operator can result in one of several values of ErrorStatus. The values noError, tooBig, and noSuchName have the same meaning as for the retrieval operators, except that it would be very unusual (but not impossible) for a manager to receive a tooBig in response to a set request. The value *badValue* is generated whenever a value received by the agent is not consistent with type, length, and range required for the variable. The value *genErr* (general error) can be generated for other errors that do not fall in any of these categories.

12.2.4 Variable Naming

In the SNMP management framework, the network management objects or variables are named using ASN.1 constructs termed *object identifiers*. The management objects are organized conceptually in the form of a tree.

The tree consists of an unnamed root connected to a number of subnodes via edges (also known as branches). Each subnode may, in turn, have an arbitrary number of children of its own. This process may continue to an arbitrary level of depth. Each arc forming a portion of a branch of the tree is labeled with a brief textual description and an integer.

The object identifier associated with a particular management object corresponds to the path through the tree from the root to the object. The object identifier is a sequence of integers from the labels along the path of traversal through the tree. As a result, each information element is uniquely named.

Object identifiers may be expressed in one of four forms: number, name, prefixed number, and name and number. For example, an ASCII string that contains a description of the location of a managed system has the synonymous names:

name form	sysLocation number form
number form	1.3.6.1.2.1.1.6
name and number form	{iso org(3) dod(6) internet(1) mgmt(2) mib(1) system(1) 6}
prefixed number form	{system 6}

Network management variables are identified by variable names. The variable name information is conveyed in SNMP PDUs in the variable name portion of the varbinds.

For example, the amount of time that a network management system has been operational may be found in the variable whose name is 1.3.6.1.2.1.1.3. However, this naming is not often considered to be "user friendly." Consequently, each variable also is named via a mnemonic textual string termed the *object descriptor*; in this example, it is *sysUpTime*.

An object identifier is an administratively-assigned name in that the authority to define variables is delegated to various groups for different subtrees of the tree. As a result, the position of a MIB variable in the tree is determined by the group defining the variable.

Object identifiers may be used to name objects other than management variables. For example, object identifiers can be and have been used to name standards documents, network elements, and the like.

12.2.5 The Management Information Base

The Internet Standard MIB was defined by the MIB Working Group of the IETF, under the auspices of the IAB. The Internet Standard MIB defines a number of variables that are to be implemented by all systems that contain the TCP/IP protocol suite. Provisions are made for the inclusion of additional enterprise-specific or vendor-specific extensions to the MIB, to allow vendors to differentiate their products in standard ways, or to provide for unanticipated needs. Provisions are also made for extensions as new standard variables are defined by the appropriate standards bodies.

All SNMP MIB variables are part of a global naming tree, as specified by the SMI. This is the same tree used for registration by other standards bodies, but SNMP uses a simplified version of the naming schemes used by other management frameworks.

Use of the subtree below the node identified by the object identifier 1.3.6.1 has been delegated to the IAB, and is administered by the Internet Assigned Numbers Authority on their behalf. There are four subtrees under this node.

The first subtree is reserved for future use; that is, its use will be defined in a future standards document that will describe how the OSI Directory may be used in the Internet.

The second subtree is used to identify objects defined in IAB-approved standards documents. This subtree consists of the Internet Standard MIB, plus many other IAB-approved standard MIB documents. These documents define the syntax, semantics, naming, and position of each data element in that portion of the tree.

Experimental MIBs

The third subtree is used to identify objects that are under experimental development, typically by a working group of the IETF. A portion of these variables will eventually become part of standard documents, at which time they will be relocated to the subtree for standard MIB variables.

For example, the authority and responsibility for naming and defining variables concerning the SNMP management of systems that implement FDDI was delegated to the FDDI MIB Working Group of the IETF. The FDDI MIB Working Group was allocated a particular subtree of the naming tree for that purpose, and no other group should name and define variables in that subtree.

Enterprise Specific MIBs

The fourth subtree is for the private definition of MIB variables and other network management objects. The private subtree has one subtree, the enterprises subtree. Vendors may request from the IANA a subtree under enterprises for their organization's use. Upon receiving a subtree, the enterprise may, for example, define new MIB objects in it. In addition, it is strongly recommended that the enterprise also register its networking subsystems under this subtree, to provide an unambiguous identification mechanism for use in management protocols. As of mid-1992, over 450 enterprises had been assigned subtrees in this area. However, it is known that not nearly all of these organizations have developed vendor-specific MIBs. Many have, to date, used these subtrees for registering their working subsystems.

While the fourth subtree is labeled "private," the MIBs in this portion of the tree are not necessarily private. They are often developed and controlled privately, but are made publicly available. Vendors are encouraged to publish their MIB definitions in standard MIB format in several media, but there is no requirement for them to do so. First, they should publish their MIBs as a part of their system documentation, perhaps as an appendix to their user guides. Second, they should publish their MIBs in machine-readable format, preferably through the Internet MIB Repository, as well as on the universal media, an MS-DOS diskette. This publication process, in standard MIB format, facilitates the loading of tables into table-driven management stations that can then be used to monitor and control agents that implement the private MIBs.

12.2.6 Security Model

The SNMP protocol design initially specified only "trivial" authentication mechanisms. These mechanisms are found in almost all of today's SNMP agent and manager station implementations. Stronger mechanisms have recently been proposed.

12.2.6.1 *Trivial Authentication*

Trivial authentication is based on a shared secret between the manager station and the agent. The agent receiving a query or command may determine that a message is from someone who knows the shared secret, and thereby infer that the message is authentic. It can then consult local tables to determine if the requested operation is authorized.

These mechanisms are subject to multiple types of attack: the shared secret is potentially more shared than secret, because the community information that conveys the authentication information appears in plain text in every SNMP message. SNMP transactions using trivial authentication are subject to several types of attack. For example, illicitly captured packets can be replayed at a later time or can be modified while in transit. In addition, eavesdropping on the network can compromise data confidentiality. In many networked environments, network management information obtained through monitoring is somewhat sensitive, but maintaining these data in strict confidence is not a requirement. However, in many networked environments, it is a requirement that network control operations be strictly limited to those personnel who are sufficiently authorized to perform them. Managers of the networks require standard authentication mechanisms, which provide more protection from these attacks than is provided by the trivial authentication mechanisms.

Fortunately, the SNMP designers anticipated this requirement for stronger authentication mechanisms. The original design would have included stronger mechanisms had there been sufficient implementation experience and consensus within the standards committees. However, timely consensus was not forthcoming, so the architects provided means within the protocol design for the inclusion of new mechanisms for authentication, authorization, and privacy, in anticipation of their definition and approval by the relevant standards-setting bodies.

Progress is being made on defining such new mechanisms. Three new documents define extensions to the security architecture, protocol mechanisms to support the new security model, and new "Party MIB" variables to support SNMP security. These new mechanisms will allow an SNMP agent implementation to determine with confidence whether any given request or response is coming from an authorized source, i.e., to determine if the message is authentic.

12.2.6.2 Goals and Threats

The proposed security enhancements are designed to provide authentication, integrity, access control, and the cooperation of multiple protocol entities. Four threats must be overcome to attain these goals: masquerade, modification of information, message stream modification, and disclosure via eavesdropping.

First, operation of the framework depends on protocol entities (agents and managers) being able to unambiguously determine that the source of a received message is authentic, i.e., the receiver needs to be able to determine who sent a message. This is necessary so that appropriate access controls can be instituted. The threat is that an unauthorized protocol entity might attempt a masquerade by assuming the identity of another protocol entity (that has the appropriate authorizations) and thereby attempt to gain unauthorized access to data.

Second, data integrity depends upon thwarting the threat of modification of information wherein messages are modified while in transit between a sender and a receiver. Alteration of messages from an agent to a manager could be used to deceive the manager. Alteration of messages sent from a manager to an agent could be used to convert a desired control operation (set request) into an undesired control operation.

The third threat is message stream modification. A malicious attacker could reorder, delay, or replay legitimate messages to effect an unauthorized result.

The fourth threat is disclosure via eavesdropping. This is particularly important when the SNMP is used as a mechanism for transferring information that should be kept secret, such as is the case when private keys are being distributed, or at other times when local requirements dictate secrecy.

12.2.6.3 Message Formats

The protocol separates SNMP messages into two independent components. The SNMP PDUs define the elements of operation, and convey the management information. The authentication wrapper conveys the authentication, authorization, and access control information. As a result, the wrapper can be redefined without changes to the syntax and semantics of the SNMP PDUs.

This feature is being utilized by the new emerging standards for mechanisms that elaborate on the SNMP authentication and privacy mechanisms. Additional SNMP message formats are being defined without changing the PDU syntax and semantics.

The new framework supports three new message formats. An administrator can configure which format to use:

- No authentication with no privacy

- Authentication with no privacy

- Authentication with privacy.

It is expected that most network administrators will configure their devices to the first format when monitoring, and to the second format for control operations. It is expected that in most networks, authentication with privacy will rarely, if ever, be used.

12.2.6.4 *Mechanisms*

The new proposals specify the use of the MD5 message-digest algorithm,[17] the US Federal Data Encryption Standard (DES),[18] and loosely synchronized clocks. Both MD5 and DES are used as "symmetric," i.e., they are private key mechanisms. The framework document provides the opportunity to define mechanisms based on "asymmetric" cryptography, i.e., public key technology, but none are initially defined.

The mechanisms utilize the concept of the SNMP "party." A SNMP party is defined as an execution context of a SNMP protocol implementation. Whenever a SNMP protocol implementation processes a message, it does so by acting in the role of one of the SNMP parties configured for it. Each SNMP party executes at a specific transport address, and has specific authentication parameters, privacy parameters, proxy information, and a MIB view. The authentication parameters include an algorithm, a secret, and the state information needed to maintain its clock and ensure proper message ordering. The privacy parameters include an algorithm and a secret. The proxy information either indicates no-proxy, or "points" to another SNMP party, where the real agent executes. The MIB view specifies the subset of an agent's management information (i.e., the MIB objects) that the party can access.

Thus, an SNMP Security message is sent from one party to another party. The message is authenticated (or not), according to the authentication parameters of the source party. The message is encrypted (or not), according to the privacy parameters of the destination party. Access control specifies that a source party is allowed to originate a particular set of SNMP operations (e.g., get requests and set requests, or just get requests) to a given destination party. The destination party's MIB view provides the limitation on which MIB objects the message can access.

The authentication mechanism is based on the MD5 message-digest algorithm and the use of loosely synchronized clocks. The sender of an authenticated message constructs the message to be sent, a secret authentication key, and clock information as a block of data. The MD5 algorithm is applied to the data, resulting in a 16-byte checksum called the *digest*. The digest is then made a part of the message, obliterating the secret authentication key. The message is forwarded to the destination, with or without encryption, depending upon the configuration set by the network administrator.

Upon receipt, the message is decrypted (or not), depending upon the configuration set by the network administrator. The received digest is saved temporarily and replaced in the received message by the receiver's value for the sending party's secret authentication key. The MD5 algorithm is then applied, yielding a digest value. If the resulting digest value matches the one saved from the incoming message, the receiver can be reasonably confident that the message originated from an entity with knowledge of the secret key, thereby providing authentication of the data's origin. Furthermore, the receiver can be reasonably confident that the message contents were not altered in transit, thereby protecting against data modification attacks.

Loosely synchronized monotonically-increasing clock values protect against message stream modification attacks. Messages that are "old," messages that arrive out-of-order, and duplicate messages are discarded.

The privacy mechanism uses the cipher block chaining mode of the DES to encrypt SNMP messages that the network administrator desires to protect from disclosure. An appropriate portion of the message is encrypted according to a secret key associated with the destination of the message. The message is decrypted at the destination using the same secret key value. Successful decryption requires the use of the secret key. Consequently, the message is protected from disclosure to the extent that the keys in use are kept secret.

The access control mechanism is refined slightly from the access control mechanisms found in the original SNMP design. The original SNMP design includes mechanisms for *MIB views*, whereby different management station populations are allowed different views of the MIB data. Through various MIB views, some manager stations might be given read-write access to all of the data, while other manager stations might be allowed read-only access to all of the data, or might be allowed read-write access to only certain subsets of the data. Most existing SNMP implementations implement MIB views, and therefore access control on an all-or-none basis, i.e., with extremely coarse granularity. A few SNMP implementations implement MIB views by group.

Some emerging SNMP applications pose requirements for MIB views with very fine granularity, i.e., at the instance level. While these requirements can be addressed using the trivial authentication mechanisms, it is anticipated that the applications will be implemented using the proposals for new standard mechanisms for authentication. As a result, managers of these systems will gain the additional benefit of being able to utilize the new party MIB to configure the MIB views.

12.2.6.5 Caveats

It is worth mentioning that these enhanced security features do not come without cost. First, while every effort was made to retain compatibility with the older security mechanisms whenever possible, differences are unavoidable. Second, the mechanisms have been shown to slow throughput and increase agent processor utilization by between 100% and 500%, depending upon the specifics of the operation.[19] Clock synchronization will produce additional network traffic and other overhead. Party management will be problematic. Some devices that support SNMP today will be unable to support the new mechanisms because they do not have sufficient hardware assets for the nonvolatile storage of secrets. Finally, the impact of export restrictions on vendors from the US is unclear but fearsome. Security is expensive.

12.2.6.6 Other Features

The new security documents provide new features in addition to those already listed. They further define proxy naming, addressing an issue that has been problematic in the past. Finally, they are perfectly general, including support for non-TCP/IP networks. These two aspects address the requirements for the cooperation of multiple protocol entities.

12.3 STANDARDIZATION STATUS

The documents that specify the SNMP management framework have been afforded Standard status by the IAB. Declaration as Internet Standards has followed specification in the IETF, the standards setting suborganization of the IAB, and implementation and testing by interested parties, followed by review and comment within the IETF.

12.3.1 SNMP

SNMP was initially defined in May 1988, and published as a Proposed Standard for the Internet in August 1988. It was reissued in April 1989 as a Draft Standard. In May 1990, the IAB elevated the status of the SNMP to that of a recommended full Internet Standard, affording SNMP the very same standardization status as that of TCP.

While it is significant that the IAB has embraced SNMP as a *de jure* standard, it is perhaps even more important that SNMP has become the *de facto* standard for network management. SNMP is the open protocol most often implemented by vendors, purchased by their customers, and used by managers to monitor and control their networks.

The SNMP specification is very stable. While the specification document and the related standards have been republished several times to elevate their standards status, there have been no substantive technical changes to the documents since 1988. This stability is one reason for SNMP's rapid growth of support and widespread success.

12.3.2 SMI

Like the SNMP protocol specification, the Structure of Management Information,[3] was initially defined in May 1988 and published in August 1988. It too, was elevated to become a *Recommended* full Internet Standard in May 1990.

In March 1991, a document describing a new concise MIB format was published,[20] which amplified and clarified some of the SMI rules for the definition of MIB variables. The new ASN.1 macro described therein for specifying MIB variables resulted in MIB documents that were approximately 40% smaller. These more concise documents also contained less redundant information, which had previously bred the opportunity for inconsistencies. Another important contribution was that the new format is more easily parsed by machine, which facilitates the automatic or semi-automatic loading of MIB information by manager stations, and to a lesser extent, by agent implementors.

As of this writing, the document defining the concise MIB format is a recommended Draft Standard for the Internet, and will likely be advanced to a recommended full Internet Standard in 1992. The use of this new MIB document format led to more concise and unambiguous MIB definitions; hence, transition to its use was almost universal and instantaneous.

Another related document was published in March 1991,[21] which defined a convention for specifying trap messages in a way similar to that found in the concise MIB documents. However, its use, and that of traps in general, is somewhat controversial; the document has not been proposed as a Standard, but is merely available for informational purposes. The document states, "Practitioners who do not employ traps can safely ignore this document," and most have.

12.3.3   MIBs

The original plan for MIB evolution specified in the SMI called for a rigorous MIB versioning process. This design was flawed, in part, because it failed to anticipate the success of the SNMP framework, leading to hundreds of engineers working to define standard MIB variables and perhaps an order of magnitude more engineers working to define private enterprise-specific MIB variables.

The original plan called for the publication of a single series of small, but growing monolithic MIB documents, each of which would supersede its predecessor. That is, MIB-I would be replaced by MIB-II, which would be replaced by MIB-III, and so on. This design was scrapped with MIB-II, and replaced by plans for many smaller and more or less self-contained MIBs to be developed independently.

12.3.3.1   MIB-I

The first Internet Standard MIB, or MIB-I, was first published in August 1988 as a Proposed Standard. It was reissued in May 1990, when it was elevated to a full Internet Standard. Finally, MIB-I was made obsolete when MIB-II was elevated to full Standard, and now has Historical status.

The current specification[11] of MIB-II is found in *RFC 1213*. It specifies approximately 180 MIB variable types, and is therefore approximately 50% larger than MIB-I. For the most part, MIB-II is a superset of MIB-I. It was first published in May 1990 as a Proposed Standard, and was elevated to Draft Standard in March 1991. MIB-II was advanced to full Standard in August 1991, thereby making MIB-I completely obsolete.

12.3.3.2   Other Standards Track MIB Documents

There are many other MIB documents presently on the standards track. Because the status of these documents changes almost daily, it is inappropriate to report on them in detail here. (A good source for up-to-date information in this area is *The Simple Times: The Bi-Monthly*

Newsletter of SNMP Technology, Comment, and Events. The Simple Times is distributed via electronic mail. Send a note to the electronic mail address st-subscriptions@dbc.mtview.ca.us for subscription information.)

However, it is reasonable to conclude that MIBs are being developed to provide instrumentation of almost all popular facets of computer networking and data communications, for there is much activity in these areas. Some of these activities are to create instrumentation in new areas of technology such as the Fiber Distributed Data Interface (FDDI), the Switched Multimegabit Data Service (SMDS), T3, and frame relay.

Some efforts are producing standard MIB variables in areas that had previously been relegated to vendor-specific MIBs. Examples include terminal servers, bridges, and physical layer hubs.

Sometimes, these MIB definitions are based on the previous work of other standards organizations. In such cases, the management information they have defined is transformed into SMI-compliant variables for use with the SNMP. Examples include the ANSI FDDI MIB and IEEE 802 LAN (802.3, 803.4, and 802.5) MIBs.

12.4 THE FUTURE, AND EVOLUTION OF THE INTERNET MANAGEMENT FRAMEWORK

While the future is not perfectly clear, there are at least three areas in which it is appropriate to make observations about the future, and the evolution of the SNMP framework. It is almost certain that the spate of MIB extensions will continue. There are proposals to enhance the security of the Internet standard management framework. As the Internet becomes increasingly multiprotocol, and as support for the ISO/OSI suite becomes more widespread, there will be management implications.

12.4.1 Refinement of Managed Object Definitions (MIB Extensions)

The frenzied pace at which MIB objects are being defined is expected to continue for the foreseeable future. The rapid MIB development is driven by three primary forces.

First, customers are requesting that vendors support new areas of technology and support management of existing areas of technology. That is, they have made it a requirement for the systems they purchase.

Second, engineers in the vendor community often propose working groups to define MIBs in new areas. One possible explanation for this is that it is relatively easy for engineers to obtain personal satisfaction and recognition from being able to make positive and lasting contributions to the art and science of networking. That is, it is "fun."

Finally, rules within the IETF standards organization require that all new protocols be instrumented with appropriate MIBs before they are allowed to enter the standards track.

12.4.2   Enhanced Security of the Internet Standard Management Framework

The perceived weaknesses of the SNMP management framework in the areas of authentication, authorization, access control, and privacy described earlier in this chapter are expected to be addressed in the near future. The three documents that collectively propose extensions to address these weaknesses should be published in the near term as *RFC* documents with the status of Proposed Standards. The path to standardization status has been long and tortuous, lasting more than three years, and is not yet completed.

Implementations of these proposals already exist. Two commercial implementations and two freely available implementations are known to interoperate. It is expected that these implementations will form the core of many future products, just as the early reference implementations of the SNMP framework are the basis of many of today's products.

12.4.3   Increased Use in Control Applications

SNMP is used widely for monitoring, but has not yet reached its potential in the area of control. This is due, in part, to the failure of some vendors to fully implement the protocol, including *set* functions, and in part, to the weaknesses of the initial security framework.

However, it is anticipated that the new security proposals will erase the excuses that many vendors have used for not implementing SNMP-based control functions via sets. This will be an important, if costly, benefit.

12.4.4   OSI Management

As the Internet and internets become increasingly multiprotocol, there will be management implications. In many cases, the support of new network, transport, and other layers is simply a matter of more MIB variables. The instrumentation in these layers can be accessed via SNMP over conventional mechanisms. MIB definitions for this instrumentation are already available for DECnet Phase IV and OSI CLNP. This allows a single SNMP agent on a multiprotocol device, such as a multiprotocol router, to manage multiple sets of useful protocol layers.

Some systems will support only a single protocol family, such as OSI. In such cases, there are at least two viable options.

One option is to implement the OSI management framework anchored by the Common Management Information Service (CMIS),[22] and the Common Management Information Protocol (CMIP).[16] However, this is problematic today for three reasons. First, the overhead of implementing CMIS and CMIP on resource-limited systems may be too expensive. Second, these protocols have little market share today, so vendors choose to implement SNMP instead, and as a result, their market share remains low. Finally, while CMIS and CMIP are well-defined international standards, much of the supporting infrastructure, such as the ISO equivalents of the SMI, MIBs, and transport profiles, have not reached the same level of standardization or stability. As a result, migration to the international standard CMIP management framework is problematic at this time because there are at least nine different standard CMIP management frameworks, which unfortunately do not interoperate. Fortunately, the standards bodies are cooperating, and with time may reach convergence. In the meantime, there are too many specifications but not enough implementations, and too many profiles but not enough code.

12.4.5 Conclusion

The SNMP management framework has enjoyed phenomenal growth and success because it meets today's network management requirements. SNMP's simple, yet elegant protocol operations, variable naming scheme, and provisions for MIB extensibility have made it popular among network equipment vendors and network managers alike. They have made SNMP the *de facto* standard for open management through market forces, and the relevant standards organizations have embraced SNMP and the related specifications as *de jure* standards.

The growth continues as the SNMP management framework is applied in new areas beyond its roots in managing wide area TCP/IP packet switches. SNMP is not just for gateways, but is being utilized for monitoring and controlling many kinds of networking systems, from MAC layer devices to host applications. SNMP isn't just for networks, but also is being used for system administration and other non-network management applications. SNMP isn't just for TCP/IP networks anymore, but is being applied to all kinds of networking technology, including other protocol families, such as DECnet and OSI, or in cases where there is no internetworking protocol already present (including UDP and IP), only to support networking management. The popularity of SNMP is international.

As a result of this unanticipated growth and success, the SNMP management framework, the so called "short-term" standard for open network management isn't short term anymore, but will continue to grow and prosper as long as it continues to meet the needs of its constituents.

SNMP is not perfect. However, the ability to exploit extensibility mechanisms designed into the framework—such as the provisions to accommodate the definition of new MIB variables and to enhance the security provisions—will help the framework meet the evolving requirements of network managers. These mechanisms will help ensure that SNMP will continue to hold an important place in the art and science of open heterogeneous network management for many years to come.

12.5 ACKNOWLEDGMENTS

Portions of this chapter are adapted from *The Simple Network Management Protocol for Internet Network Management*, by Jeffrey D. Case, © 1991, Jeffrey D. Case, and multiple publications of SNMP Research, Incorporated, © 1991. Used by permission.

Portions of the section on the security model are adapted from the "Security and Protocols" column by Keith McCloghrie from *The Simple Times: The Bi-Monthly Newsletter of SNMP Technology, Comment, and Events*, Volume 1, Numbers 1–3. (Send a note to the electronic mail address st-subscriptions@dbc.mtview.ca.us for subscription information.) ISSN 1060-6068. Used by permission.

REFERENCES

1   J.D. Case, M.S. Fedor, M.L. Schoffstall, and J.R. Davin, *A Simple Network Management Protocol, RFC 1157*, DDN Network Information Center, SRI International, May 1990.

2   J.R. Davin, J.D. Case, M.S. Fedor, and M.L. Schoffstall, *A Simple Gateway Monitoring Protocol, RFC 1028*, DDN Network Information Center, SRI International, November 1987.

3   M.T. Rose and K. McCloghrie, *Structure and Identification of Management Information for TCP/IP-Based Internets, RFC 1155*, DDN Network Information Center, SRI International, May 1990.

4   K. McCloghrie and M.T. Rose, *Management Information Base for Network Management of TCP/IP-Based Internets, RFC 1156*, DDN Network Information Center, SRI International, May 1990.

5   V. Cerf, *IAB Recommendations for the Development of Internet Network Management Standards, RFC 1052*, DDN Network Information Center, SRI International, April 1988.

6   V. Cerf, *Report of the Second Ad Hoc Network Management Review Group, RFC 1109*, DDN Network Information Center, SRI International, August 1989.

7   J. Postel, *User Datagram Protocol, RFC 768*, DDN Network Information Center, SRI International, August 1980.

8   *DDN Protocol Handbook, Volume One: DOD Military Standard Protocols*, DDN Network Information Center, MIL-STD 1777 (also available as ARPA Internet *RFC 791*), SRI International, September 1981.

9   J. Postel, *Internet Control Message Protocol, RFC 792*, DDN Network Information Center, SRI International, September 1981.

10 R.W. Scheifler and J. Gettys, The X Window System, *ACM Transactions on Graphics*, Vol. 5, No. 2, pp. 79–109, 1986. Special issue on user interface software.

11   K. McCloghrie and M.T. Rose, *Management Information Base for Network Management of TCP/IP-Based Internets: MIB-II, RFC 1213*, DDN Network Information Center, SRI International, March 1991.

12   *Information Processing—Open Systems Interconnection—Specification of Abstract Syntax Notation One (ASN.1)*, International Standard 8824, International Organization for Standardization, 1987.

13   *Information Processing—Open Systems Interconnection—Specification of Basic Encoding Rules for Abstract Syntax Notation One (ASN.1)*, International Standard 8825, International Organization for Standardization, 1987.

14   *Message Handling Systems: Presentation Transfer Syntax and Notation*, Recommendation X.409, International Telegraph and Telephone Consultative Committee, October 1984.

15   Sun Microsystems Inc., *XDR: External Data Representation Standard, RFC 1014*, DDN Network Information Center, SRI International, June 1987.

16   *Information Processing Systems—Open Systems Interconnection—Management Information Protocol Definition. Part 2: Common Management Information Protocol*, Draft International Standard 9596-2, International Organization for Standardization, 1988.

17   R. Rivest, *The MD5 Message-Digest Algorithm, RFC 1321*, DDN Network Information Center, SRI International, April 1992.

18   *Data Encryption Standard*, Federal Information Processing Standard (FIPS) Publication 46-1, National Institute of Standards and Technology, January 1988.

19   D.L. Partain, *Security Extensions to the SNMP Management Framework*, Master's thesis, The University of Tennessee at Knoxville, January 1992.

20   M.T. Rose and K. McCloghrie, *Concise MIB Definitions, RFC 1212*, DDN Network Information Center, SRI International, March 1991.

21   M.T. Rose, *A Convention for Defining Traps for Use with the SNMP, RFC 1215*, DDN Network Information Center, SRI International, March 1991.

22   *Information Processing Systems—Open Systems Interconnection—Management Information Service Definition-Part 2: Common Management Information Service*, Draft International Standard 9595-2, International Organization for Standardization, 1988.

CHAPTER 13 ❏ ❏ ❏ ❏

Tools for an Internet Backbone

HANS-WERNER BRAUN AND ELISE GERICH

CONTENTS

Although it is difficult to characterize any hierarchy in the Internet, it is often useful to view networks as being either backbone or regional. A backbone (or transit) network interconnects regionals, and regionals connect sites. We begin looking at operational tools, by considering them from the perspective of a backbone network.

13.1 OVERVIEW

The widespread growth of the currently deployed Internet infrastructure poses serious challenges to effective network management. The establishment of the NSFNET backbone several years ago as a means to connect the tens of mid-level networks, which themselves may connect to hundreds of campus networks, necessitated a distribution of responsibility among these multiple layers, imposing additional complexity on the task of network maintenance and operation.

Each group is responsible for only its own Internet component. Inevitably, the quality of service provided by one component has a direct impact on the larger Internet infrastructure, and, of course, on the other component networks. Given the necessity of robust operation of a still-developing infrastructure, the existing state of technology suggests that an environment of solely competing network providers would not be as effective as a cooperative undertaking. The provider of the NSFNET backbone network has already realized that any feasible approach would involve collaboration with the mid-level networks, and the mid-level networks have in turn recognized the need for similar cooperation with each other, as well as with their attached campus clients.

As a cooperative step, the NSF-funded supercomputing centers, with their vested interest in the continuation and evolution of the initial 56-Kbits/sec NSFNET backbone, created the Federation of American Research Networks (FARNET). Although initially composed of only the NSF supercomputer centers, FARNET was subsequently expanded to include all mid-level networks, and even some other networking organizations, such as commercial providers. FARNET outlined goals for the entire network community, such as the instrumentation of individual network operations centers with tools to monitor the large-scale Internet. Establishing communication channels for the rapid exchange of information regarding the health of Internet components not only allows the provision of network status information to end users in a timely manner, but also constitutes an important step toward alleviating and eventually repairing network problems.

As the networking industry grew more competitive, but not more standardized, component networks strove for a greater share of the infrastructure, and also for the right to provide "commercial" Internet services. We find ourselves today in an intermediate stage, where multiple national backbones connect to numerous mid-level service providers, which themselves connect to an even greater number of local sites, such as universities, research institutions, federal installations, and private commercial organizations.

It is essential to find a balance where service providers have an incentive to maintain collaboration, but still are able to independently pursue individual interests. Unfortunately, we are still only learning initial lessons about the possible steps in this development process; in the meantime, the networking community desperately needs the Internet fabric to remain intact. A cooperative spirit is imperative, requiring well-designed tools at local and global levels, addressing long- and short-term behavior, drawing on human and technical means, to maintain and manage the global Internet.

13.2 THE NSFNET BACKBONE MANAGEMENT AND OPERATION

The National Science Foundation originally granted Merit Network, Inc. an award to engineer, build, and manage the T1 backbone network among 13 NSF-sponsored mid-level networks. The original 1987 award project now includes a 14th node on the T1 backbone, and an amended award provides for the engineering and implementation of a T3 network to 16 NSF-sponsored sites, which include the 14 T1 sites. The original 14-circuit, 13-node T1 backbone was completed in July 1988. Merit redesigned the T1 backbone in the summer of 1989 to provide multiple paths to each of the 13 nodes, and installed the 14th node in the fall of 1990. Figure 13.1 illustrates the NSFNET T1 network as of 1991.

In January 1991, Merit installed the first phase of the T3 backbone connecting the 16 NSF-sponsored locations; it completed the project in September 1991. Figure 13.2 includes detailed information about the T3 network, including T1 backup links, as of early 1992.

IBM, through a joint study agreement with Merit, has provided the hardware and software for nodes on both backbones. The T1 hardware is PC/RT-based: the switching node architecture consists of multiple processors dedicated to separate functions and connected by a common token ring. In the T3 backbone nodes, which are based on the IBM RS6000, a single processor handles all of the distributed packet-switching functions mentioned above. Accommodating this new routing architecture has required the redesign of some of the T1 network tools, particularly those concerning statistics gathering.

13.2.1 Daily Management and Operations

The Merit Network Operations Center monitors the T1 and T3 networks, and is responsible for initiating appropriate actions to resolve all troublesome occurrences on the backbone. To provide this first level of support for accurate and reliable network status, the Network Operations Center (NOC) is staffed 24 hours per day, seven days per week. The responsibilities of this continual coverage are to acknowledge alerts concerning the networks, track identified and reported problems, and initiate appropriate responses to the alerts.

The NOC identifies problems primarily in three ways: machine alerts, electronic mail, and phone calls. The NOC relies heavily on a tool developed by Merit staff, called Internet

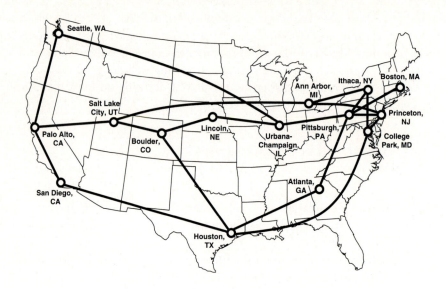

Figure 13.1   NSFNET T1 network (1991) (Courtesy of Merit Network, Inc.)

Rover, to generate alerts that are projected onto large screens in the operations center. Each operator can also have the Internet Rover displayed in a window on a workstation. Current problems are displayed, as well as comments concerning the status of a problem.

When a problem first appears on the display, an operator signs up to take ownership of it, and enters a comment on the screen noting the problem is being addressed. This avoids any duplication of effort. Having taken responsibility for an alert, the operator opens a trouble ticket to record the ensuing activity to resolve the problem.

The trouble ticket system is critical to the entire process because it permits the documentation of problems, so that trends and recurring trouble areas can be identified. It is also necessary to accurately document activity, because the original operator may have to hand the problem over to another operator when the work shift changes. This permits continuity in problem resolution.

Some problems may be resolved immediately by the network operator, but in other cases the operators complete their preliminary investigations and then contact the appropriate second-level support group. Depending on the initial analysis completed by an operator, the problem may be referred to IBM service, MCI network support, or the Merit engineering staff. This is where good documentation in the trouble ticketing system is invaluable, so that the next level of support has all the information needed to further the investigation.

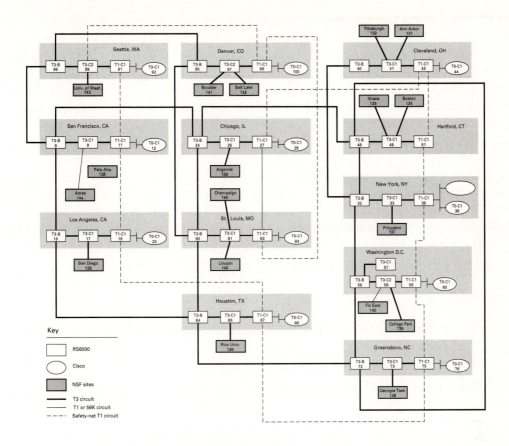

Figure 13.2   ANSNET/NSFNET T3 topology

Even when the NOC has referred a problem to the next level of support, its responsibility has not ended. The NOC still tracks the progress of the problem by requesting updates from the appropriate support group, and by notifying the management structure of problems that exceed certain time periods in the process of their resolution. This notification process provides a good communication channel between the operations group and the management group, so that both are aware of the status of the networks.

Response to electronic messages and telephone calls follows an identical process to that of machine-generated alerts. However, there is the added responsibility to work with the individual or organization that reports the problem. The NOC acknowledges all reported problems, and opens a trouble ticket to track activity concerning each report. It continues to track the problem and communicate with the client until the trouble ticket is closed. The NOC provides the first level of support for network problems, and is responsible for the day-to-day health of the network.

13.2.2   Trouble Ticket Systems

A trouble ticket system is essential to the successful management and operation of a network; it is a mechanism for logging, tracing, following through, and resolving specific network problems. The NSFNET Backbone Network Operation Center currently uses IBM's Information Management product to record network trouble tickets, with a customized format to reflect the needs and requirements of the NSFNET operations staff at Merit in Michigan.

The NSFNET staff also developed a TCP/IP server that allows querying of the Network Information Management Trouble Ticket system from outside client systems, allowing rapid access to information. The TCP/IP server runs on an IBM MVS mainframe; clients run on local UNIX systems. Other features of the trouble ticket server include the ability to read an individual ticket or to search for all tickets matching specified criteria. The objective is to provide timely, accurate, and consistent information on a problem's status to people involved in the daily operations of the network. This distributed system allows for collaboration among many people at geographically distant locations.

13.2.3   Network Information Services

The nature of the routing architecture of the NSFNET backbone requires the maintenance of configuration files reflecting characteristics of the network environment, in particular the connectivity of client networks. Data records include entries for IP network numbers, preference values for certain paths, associated Autonomous System numbers, network location, and contact information, as well as cross references among information sets. Maintaining the database originally only required attending to records for just a few hundred IP network numbers. The set of registered network numbers for the NSFNET Backbone Network has now grown to over six thousand and shows no sign of abatement. With the enormous growth of the number of networks known to the Internet at large, the manual process of maintaining the data on these networks has become unwieldy. Since this information is critical to the smooth operation of the T1 and T3 backbones, the automation of this process must be foolproof. Any misinterpretations of the information by a program can cause major disruptions to smooth communication between networks.

To relieve the manual intervention needed to maintain configuration files, and to avoid misinterpretations of electronically submitted updates, Merit staff have been working on a NOC configuration tool that will improve the efficiency with which the NOC can process electronic mid-level network configuration requests. Currently this tool is still under development, and is being run in parallel with the manual process. It is anticipated that eventually this will permit more efficient and less resource-intensive management of the maintenance of the information associated with network numbers and routing configuration files.

The network routing database system allows the generation and maintenance of routing configuration files for each NSFNET backbone node, updates the information approximately twice weekly, and propagates new routing configuration tables to backbone nodes.

The information related to routing configuration tables and other data sets is available via direct file access on a network information services host, as well as via a SPIRES mail-based query of the NSFNET database. The NSFNET information services host also provides a library of other information: various documents and articles on other network topics; lists of addresses and contacts for specific mid-level networks or individual IP networks; and traffic statistics for the NSFNET Backbone.

The NSFNET project designed and implemented a scheme where the mid-level networks could use the backbone to provide redundant paths to destinations that were multiply connected. As the number of networks known to the NSFNET has increased, the complexity of maintaining up-to-date and consistent routing tables on the backbone routers has also grown. Because of the growing complexity, Merit has redesigned the configuration database using the Informix system, and is developing some additional tools that will automatically parse incoming routing requests and updates, among other tasks. Merit has also developed a prototype client that can query the database. This is an initial step toward making routing configuration information available to operators at other network operations centers. Such a client would be useful in debugging routing problems.

The NSFNET project staff initially chose the Stanford Public Information and Retrieval System (SPIRES) for use as the trouble ticket and database management system on which to base their information services and network routing configuration requirements. There have been some new developments with the configuration database. The project is now moving from SPIRES to Informix for its database support system.

13.2.4   Data Collection

Data collection, for the purposes of monitoring, measuring, and analyzing performance characteristics, is a fundamental requirement for the operation and management of any large-scale network, such as the NSFNET Backbone. A large source of information about network usage is retrieved from the network nodes via the Simple Network Monitoring Protocol (SNMP). The NSFNET Nodal Switching Subsystems (NSSs) run SNMP servers that respond to queries regarding standard SNMP Management Information Base (MIB) variables.

The statistics information is collected at 15-minute intervals. In particular, information on 6 variables from the SNMP server on each node is collected for each network interface:

- Interface in-octets

- Interface out-octets

- In errors

- Out errors

- In packets

- Out packets.

The SNMP server stores a month's worth of data on its local disk before moving the data to another machine for processing. Specific utilities collect the data from the server, sort it by Timestamp and interface identifier, aggregate the counter readings, and then provide a summary of the daily counts for these variables. The collected statistics allow the collation of a wide variety of traffic reports, including a daily summary of traffic at each interface that connects to exterior backbone clients, and monthly summaries of aggregated values for each counter. The daily traffic aggregations are available in reports via anonymous FTP from the Internet host nis.nsf.net. Graphical representations of traffic statistics are also being used for network analysis, planning, and presentations.

The day-to-day SNMP statistics gathering of the NSFNET Backbone is augmented by a software package, NNStat, which allows further insight into specific traffic characteristics. NNStat, a set of programs and utilities developed by the Information Sciences Institute of the University of Southern California, provides a method for the collection and aggregation of traffic statistics, as well as remote access to the collection process.

Each NSFNET packet switch includes a dedicated processor to run the Statistics Acquisition Agent (SAA). The SAA listens to data on the token rings interconnecting the processors of a backbone node, and then builds statistical objects based on the collected information. It is possible to define the granularity of data gathering. For example, relatively modest traffic conditions allow the collection of every packet traversing a node, but as the load increases, it becomes necessary to revert to statistical sampling of the nodal traffic.

A central collection agent running the Statistics Collection Host (SCH) software periodically calls out to each of the backbone SAAs, logs their statistical objects, and resets the objects. The collection agent is an IBM RS/6000, and it collects approximately 55 million bytes of raw statistics daily, at a 15-minute granularity. Although mostly source and destination IP network number pairs, the data also include distributions of TCP and UDP applications traffic, and a distribution of packet sizes.

After collecting the data, a specialized software package compiles a matrix of network number-to-network number traffic counts, which forms the basis for the following publicly-available files characterizing traffic across the NSFNET backbone:

- Traffic distribution for network numbers by packets and bytes

- Port distribution by packets and bytes

- Traffic itemized by individual countries.

13.3   TOOLS FOR NETWORK MANAGEMENT AND OPERATION

As important as traffic totals and the reports characterizing traffic characteristics are, it is also necessary to have tools that analyze traffic patterns and apply this information to future network planning. This section focuses on such tools for effective network management.

We differentiate network tools into two major categories: tools in support of real-time work and non-real-time tools for analyzing a collected data set. Real-time network management tools are typically needed during general operation of the network, such as to retrieve error information from the environment and then react to it. Other real-time tools allow for specific performance tests on existing networks. Non–real-time tools allow for the analysis of network behavior following the collection of network information, and include simulation facilities. Both analysis and simulation are important requirements for successful network planning.

Statistics collection tools may be either intrusive or nonintrusive. Intrusive tools typically conform to some request-response function, where a networking entity responds to a request or query. Ping, an ICMP Echo Request–Reply tool, is an example of a real-time, intrusive tool frequently used to determine reachability, latency, and the quality of connectivity. Nonintrusive tools passively monitor traffic without disturbing the networking environment. Examples include Ethernet monitors (e.g., Netwatch), NNStat, iptrace, and tcpdump, all of which run on collection processors that do not introduce queries as part of the monitoring activity.

Many of these tools are described in more detail in *RFC 1147*: *FYI on a Network Management Tool Catalog: Tools for Monitoring and Debugging TCP/IP Internets and Interconnected Devices*, R. Stine, Editor.

13.3.1 Tools Available for Real-Time Network Management and Operation

13.3.1.1 *Cylink Network Management System (CNMS)*

The Cylink Network Management system is a PC/DOS-based application that uses out-of-band lines to access the Advanced Channel Service Units (ACSUs) that terminate a T1 circuit. This system has permitted the NOC to diagnose problems remotely, and to take corrective actions at remote and unstaffed sites. Some of the actions that the operators can perform using CNMS include checking the Extended Super Frame (ESF) registers, selecting network clocking, obtaining internally stored alarms and performance data, reconfiguring the ACSUs, and putting the T1 line in loopback.

13.3.1.2 *Internet Rover*

The Internet Rover, a software tool written by NSFNET staff, is one of the primary tools used by the Merit NOC to monitor the NSFNET backbone. The Internet Rover program (InetRoverd) consists of a collection and a display module.

InetRoverd reads a configuration file that contains a list of network nodes and associated monitoring tests to perform on those nodes. If a test fails, the program adds an entry to a file that is used for problem reporting. If a test corresponding to an existing problem entry subsequently succeeds, the entry is removed. All entry additions and deletions are logged.

A display utility displays the list of current problem situations. This program periodically polls and reads the problem file. Operators can update a problem entry, using the display program, and can insert comments that will be visible to all instantiations of the display program.

The InetRoverd utility is used to monitor both the T1 and T3 NSFNET backbones. It discovers the backbone topologies, and stores the state of the network nodes and links in a file. The Network Status File contains a list of objects that names specific nodes and links. The node class includes ASs (Autonomous Systems) and NSSs (Nodal Switching Systems). The link class contains ISISLinks (interior routing) and ASLinks (exterior routing).

Upon start-up, InetRoverd requires 30 seconds to determine the state of the network. State transitions and node discovery are subsequently logged to files.

The graphical front end to the data collector displays nodes and links, colored to reflect their state as seen in the network status file. As the program discovers new node and link objects in the network, it updates the map to show the new objects. A mouse-driven interface allows the operator to decide the placement of a node, and the program automatically saves the resulting map.

Figure 13.3 illustrates a sample screen of the rover tool, as it would appear in the NSFNET Network Operations Center.

13.3.1.3   NNStat

NNStat is a collection of programs, developed at USC-ISI, that provides an Internet statistic collecting capability. NNStat collects traffic statistics via an Ethernet tap on the local network, rather than instrumentation on the gateways. If all traffic entering or leaving a network or set of networks traverses a local Ethernet, then stationing a statistic gathering agent on that local network allows the gathering of a profile of the wider-scale traffic. Statistical data is retrieved from the local agents by a global manager.

A program called *statspy* performs the data gathering function. Essentially, *statspy* reads all packets on an Ethernet interface and records all information of interest. The program examines each packet to determine whether the source or destination IP address (typically a gateway address), is one that is being monitored, and if so, examines the packet further to see if it matches the collection criteria.

A program called *collect* performs global data collection, by periodically polling various *statspy* processes in the domain of interest to retrieve locally-logged statistical data. For single data retrieval requests an *rspy* utility can be used.

13.3.1.4   nslookup

The program *nslookup* is used for interactive query of Internet domain servers. This tool is essentially a database front end that converts user queries into domain name queries. Although specific servers can be specified, nslookup queries the local domain name server

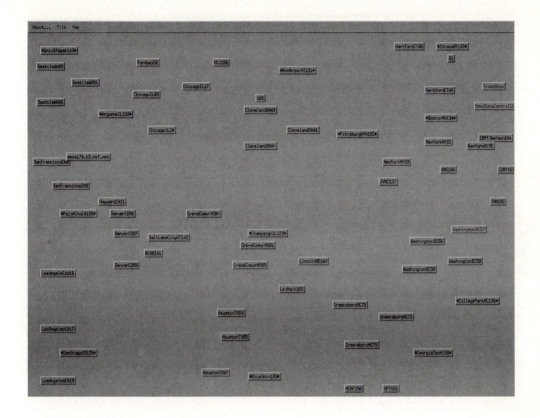

Figure 13.3   Rover tool sample screen

by default. The NSFNET operations to determine IP name-to-address mappings for client machines use *nslookup*.

13.3.1.5   netstat

The program *netstat* accesses network-related data structures within the kernel of an operating system, then provides an ASCII format at the terminal. It can provide reports on the routing table, TCP connections, TCP and UDP listens, and protocol memory management. It accesses operating system memory to read the kernel routing tables. NSFNET operators use *netstat* extensively to verify routing tables.

13.3.1.6   ping

The program *ping* sends an ICMP Echo Request to obtain an ICMP Echo Response from a host or gateway. The *ping* command is useful for determining the status of the network and various foreign hosts, tracking and isolating hardware and software problems, and testing, measuring, and managing networks. The *ping* command sends one datagram per second, and prints one line of output for every response received.

If the host is operational and on the network, it responds to the Echo. Each Echo Request contains an IP and ICMP header, followed by a *timeval* structure, and enough bytes to fill the rest of the packet. Primary results of *ping* queries are delay, delay jitter, and general connectivity.

13.3.1.7   Tcpdump

Tcpdump is a utility that allows for the passive collection of packet headers on a broadcast medium, like an Ethernet, while also allowing the specification of filters to capture only packets that match certain criteria. Interpretation of the packet headers can either happen in real time, by displaying a result on a requester's terminal, or by writing the data into a binary file, with an off-line parsing at some later time.

13.3.1.8   Traceroute

Traceroute is a tool that allows the route taken by packets from source to destination to be discovered. It can be used for situations where the IP record route option would fail, such as intermediate gateways discarding packets, routes that exceed the capacity of an datagram, or intermediate IP implementations that don't support record route. Round trip delays between the source and intermediate gateways are also reported, allowing the determination of an individual gateway's contribution to end-to-end delay. Other options include loose source routing, which allows one to investigate the return path from remote machines back to the local host.

Traceroute relies on the ICMP time-exceeded error-reporting mechanism. When an IP packet is received by a gateway with a Time-To-Live value of 0, an ICMP packet is sent to the host that generated the packet. By sending packets to a destination with a TTL of 0, the next hop can be identified as the source of the time-exceeded message. By incrementing the TTL field, subsequent hops can be identified. Each packet sent out is also time-stamped. The Timestamp is returned as part of the ICMP packet so a round trip delay can be calculated.

Some IP implementations forward packets with a TTL of 0, thus escaping identification. Others use the TTL field in the arriving packet as the TTL for the ICMP error reply, which delays identification. Sending datagrams with the source route option will cause some gateways to crash. It is considered poor form to repeat this behavior.

13.3.1.9   xgmon

The *xgmon* program, initially developed by IBM for the NSFNET backbone project, is a network management system that supports monitoring data collection via SNMP. It pro-

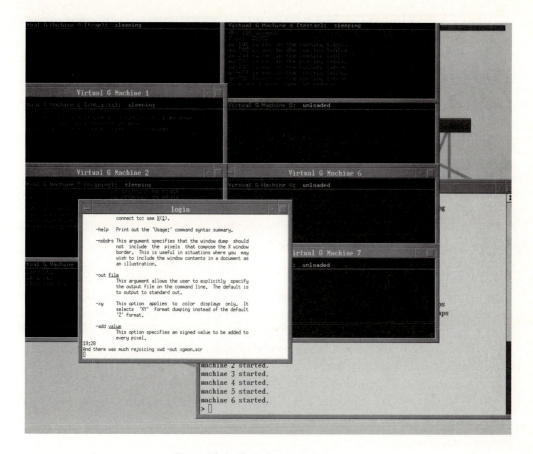

Figure 13.4   Sample xgmon screen

vides an extendible environment that includes a rich command language, simultaneous execution of multiple, independent queries, and an X-Windows-based graphical interpretation of several status variables. The *xgmon* program uses X11 by default. Figure 13.4 shows multiple text windows in a sample *xgmon* screen dump.

13.3.2   Tools for Performance Experiments

13.3.2.1   *NCNS*

This performance measurement package, initially developed at Carnegie Mellon University, allows for throughput measurements based on UDP services. The implementation consists of a server and a client site, with the server expecting UDP traffic from the client site. The traffic must follow a specific model, however, consisting of a start packet, multiple data packets, and one or more stop packets. Both the server and the client can then determine the amount of time the transaction required, as well as an estimate of the throughput. The server site can also determine how many packets were received out of sequence.

13.3.2.2   Spray

Spray is a traffic generation tool for a Sun that generates RPC or UDP packets, or ICMP Echo Requests. The packets are sent to a remote procedure call application at the destination host. The count of received packets is retrieved from the remote application after a certain number of packets have been transmitted. The difference in packets received versus packets sent represents, on a LAN, the packets that the destination host had to drop due to overflowing queues. This allows one to obtain a measure of throughput relative to system speed and network load.

13.3.2.3   TTCP

TTCP is a traffic generator that can be used for testing end-to-end throughput of TCP/IP implementations. Cooperating processes are started on two hosts. One side opens a TCP connection and transfers a high volume of data, and the delay and throughput are calculated. Execution of this utility greatly increases the system load. The source for this tool under BSD UNIX is available via anonymous FTP from vgr.brl.mil, in file ftp/pub/ttcp.c, and from sgi.com, in file sgi/src/ttcp.c.

13.3.3   Tools for Network Analysis

13.3.3.1   Merit NNam

The NSFNET Backbone effort included some development work on a network analysis facility. The resulting tool, NNam, was designed for, but not restricted to, a study of the NSFNET Backbone network. Built on a UNIX platform with an X-Window/Motif graphical front end, the tool offers an (TCP/IP) interface that enables multiple remote clients to access a common data set.

A built-in route computation component allows the tool to construct optimal routes (shortest paths) between nodes in a network, using the same Dijkstra shortest path function (SPF) algorithm used in the NSFNET Backbone itself.

The tool accepts network-derived node-node traffic flow data as input, and uses an IP traffic matrix to compute resource usage for all components of the network. It produces a comprehensive analysis of resulting traffic patterns and load points. It also provides a delay-based analysis of the network, including charts of average hop counts, and packet delay. NNam can produce a spectrum of network characteristics from a combination of input traffic or weights assigned to links in the network. Characteristics of outbound traffic can also be easily analyzed to facilitate optimal routing.

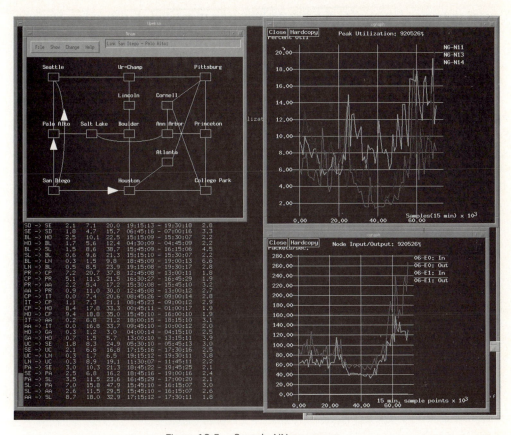

Figure 13.5   Sample NNam screen

Most results appear in mouse-driven graphical form, which helps users quickly identify trends and the combined influence of different network parameters.

It is expected that this tool will continue to evolve. Enhancements should include the following functions:

- Support the construction and subsequent analysis of optimal network topologies based on given traffic matrices and optimization criteria.

- Allow multiple simultaneous interactions among users so that, for example, the actions of one user appear on other users' workstations.

- Represent a geographical network to aid in choosing locations for new nodes and links based on geographical proximity, as well as traffic and reliability characteristics.

The interactive graphical interface to NNam accepts input from several sources, including data derived by SNMP, NNStat, and other special applications. It aggregates and analyzes the data, returning the results to the user interface. Figure 13.5 shows a sample NNam screen, showing selections for network analysis evaluations and corresponding windows, both text- and graphics-based.

13.4 ACKNOWLEDGMENTS

The authors would like to thank Kimberly Claffy of SDSC for her great help in editing this section, and John Labbe of Merit for his help for providing screen images of tools that the NSFNET NOC uses. The authors acknowledge the support received from the National Science Foundation (NCR-9119473 (SDSC) and NCR-8720904 (Merit)).

CHAPTER 14

Tools for an Internet Component

RAMAN KHANNA, BRIAN LLOYD, AND WILLIAM YUNDT

CONTENTS

We now continue looking at operational tools, but this time from the perspective of a regional network. These networks often have a tight coupling with their subscriber sites, so their tools and procedures often require a high degree of integration with their subscriber infrastructure.

14.1 SCOPE AND DEFINITIONS

The influence of the National Science Foundation (NSF) in the evolution of the Internet over the last six years has produced a three-tiered logical structure: first-tier backbones, second-tier mid-level networks (regional networks, multisite organizations, or other wide area connectivity groups), and third-tier (end-user) sites (e.g., campus, building, office, or laboratory networks). This chapter will focus on the management and operation of the mid-level second-tier network, with a view both "upward" to the backbone tier and "outward" to the third tier. End-user sites use many of the same operational tools as mid-level networks, so the discussion and examples throughout this chapter may refer to either context.

The organizational infrastructure of today's Internet is more complex than the three-tiered logical view. Some Internet service providers are focused on a single logical tier, while others operate both backbone and mid-level networks. Some providers also offer services other than interconnection of networks, such as individual host computer connection services for a customer site, or dial-in access in multiple cities for users on the move. Multitier providers may employ a broader set of operational tools than will be covered here, but few of the tools are exclusive to a particular logical tier. The term *mid-level service provider* (MSP) will be used in this chapter to mean any organization that provides connection services between an end-user site and one or more Internet backbone systems, though an MSP may provide many other services, including services in other tiers.

Much of the experience in building and applying tools to mid-level network operation and management has flowed from campus networks, principally at large universities, into the regional and other mid-level network organizations. SRI, BBN, Mitre, and other commercial and nonprofit networking organizations have also contributed much to the tools and know-how. Many network operational tools and much of the underlying technology originated in the ARPANET era, with TCP/IP development that predates the current three-tiered Internet structure. Additional tools and methods have been developed, some to address the problems of management and operation peculiar to the mid-level networks that had no direct analog in the ARPANET era, and others to deal with more generalized needs and problems.

Though each mid-level network has evolved unique tools, policies, methods, and practices, there is much in common among them. We will discuss generic needs and tools, but will use examples that are best known to us from the operation of the mid-level networks with which we are most familiar, or which have provided some examples for our use.

In this chapter, we shall construe the term *operational tools* in the broad sense; i.e., to include practices, methods, and organizational models, in addition to the technological tools that support network operation and service delivery. The discussion is divided into two areas: operations, and services and support. Operations is the focal area in which technology-based tools are discussed with specific examples. Other chapters deal in greater depth with some of these tools and their underlying protocols, which will not be discussed here.

The reader should be aware that the tools for operation and management of an Internet component, whether a connected office, campus, or regional network, are still primitive. The development of operational tools is in its infancy, but the rate of improvement in scope, power, and versatility is increasing rapidly. The size and complexity of today's Internet and the service expectations of the growing user population demand operational stability, service reliability, performance predictability, and, essentially, utility-like delivery and support. The "production" Internet is rising to these expectations, but the rate of change in the underlying technologies is great and the industry is young. Like the early days of the automobile or telephone industry, there are many suppliers, and much innovation, competition, and excitement in the rush to improve products and meet demand. Compatibility across suppliers and standards for service delivery and operational tools are difficult to develop and maintain in this climate. But the suppliers recognize that the most fundamental needs of the marketplace cannot be satisfied without these elements, and there is much cooperative activity underway to these ends. There is little doubt that the material in this chapter will become rapidly out moded, or that the number and power of tools will grow to fill books on this subject. The authors have confidence in that future.

14.2 NETWORK OPERATIONS

MSPs and other Internet components use a variety of tools for operational planning and management. A definitive treatise on this subject is beyond the scope of this chapter. The intent here is to describe the elements involved, some of the issues, and examples of the tools employed.

14.2.1 Operational Planning

Operational planning for an Internet component must, at a minimum, cover capacity and performance, reliability, and service objectives, including the cost of service delivery. This section will focus upon the capacity and reliability aspects in MSP operational planning with some cost implications. The general state of simulation and modeling tools will be briefly discussed, and selected services and support aspects will be discussed.

data processed on a remote supercomputer), it may be critical to test the product with real data at multimegabit speeds only available via a T3 connection.

Should an organization pay for a redundant link to the MSP hub site? The answer in this case may depend on the cost of network failure to the organization. For example, an organization that sells access to information may elect to pay for a redundant link if the expected value of lost business from a link failure exceeds the cost of a second link.

In general, it is easier to justify fault-tolerant design for the MSP backbone and its connection to first-tier backbones because any failure at this level impacts all sites connected to the MSP. However, the decision to stock complete spares at each hub site may depend on the service level promised to customers. Because many MSPs require customers to pay for the link from their site to the closest hub site and the associated equipment costs, the decision to have a redundant link from a customer site to the MSP backbone has to be made by the customer. Further, few end-user sites have the ability to establish a redundant link with "path diversity" (i.e., two links with separate physical paths between the end-user site and the hub site), so the redundancy does not eliminate single points of failure on the path.

MSPs have developed tools of various kinds, commonly based upon spreadsheet models, to analyze the cost impact of alternative capacity and service levels. In the case of the NSF regional networks, these models may be used to derive the distribution of costs among the membership base. Additional alternatives to MSP service delivery, such as substitution of SMDS and Frame Relay services for dedicated leased-line backbones, will require more sophistication of the cost-modeling tools.

14.2.1.4   Network Modeling and Simulation

As more organizations are realizing the importance of access to the Internet and corporate internetworking, the customer base of most MSPs has been increasing at a phenomenal rate. To deliver consistent service in the face of increasing traffic and changing traffic flow patterns, network managers need modeling and simulation tools. The network managers' ability to anticipate bandwidth needs is critical for effectively managing the growth of MSPs because capacity and topology adjustments may require weeks or months to accomplish.

Sophisticated network managers are using data captured from network analyzers such as Network General's Sniffer,™ to obtain better understanding of the traffic generated on a particular network segment. Monitoring the changes in traffic over a long period of time can provide useful information. For example, consider traffic patterns on an MSP backbone connecting MSP customer networks to the NSFNET backbone. The increase in traffic on this segment over a two-year period, during which the number of end-user sites increased from 20 to 100, can be used to roughly predict the traffic on this segment as more end-user sites are added. Linear extrapolation based on numbers of sites, however, can have a wide margin for error because the traffic generated by individual sites increases significantly due to:

- The number of nodes within network sites increasing rapidly. For example, during the last three years the number of nodes on the Stanford University Network (SUNet) has increased at an annual rate of about 40%.

- More client-server, distributed computing, and multimedia applications becoming available, driving up the bandwidth consumed per user.

An MSP, however, is impacted by the intersite traffic. Changes in traffic patterns on site networks are not necessarily predictive of traffic on MSP backbones. Network analyzers can be used to monitor the traffic and performance on the MSP backbone, but for predicting traffic in the future, network modeling and simulation tools can be used to examine differing load scenarios and performance results. Simulation tools can also be used for evaluating the comparative performance of various network design options. Over the years many network modeling and simulation tools have been used by network managers. However, easy-to-use tools that can be effectively used by someone with limited background in network simulation have not been available until recently. Some of the factors that make a simulation tool more attractive to network managers are:

- The ability to model a network complex (i.e., multipath, multichannel, endomixis bandwidth) topology easily

- The ability to characterize and parameterize the behavior of network components. For example, traffic levels presented by a site network to an MSP backbone are important to predict the performance of the backbone; so is the proper characterization of the router performance at the boundary between the site and the MSP backbone.

- The ability to predict end-to-end throughput, delays, and bottlenecks.

Our survey of network managers for various MSPs and site networks showed that only a small number are currently using or planning to use network simulation tools. As a result, most network managers deal with network performance and capacity issues in a reactive rather than a proactive mode.

14.2.2 Network Operations Center (NOC)

A well-functioning NOC is critical to successful operation of a network, whether at an end-user site, MSP, or backbone network. Even though all NOCs have to provide certain basic services, such as fault detection, isolation, and recovery, it is important to realize that the role of a NOC in an MSP is different than the role of a NOC for an end-user site or backbone network. For example, it may be reasonable for a campus or enterprise NOC to support end users who may not be able to identify whether a problem they are experiencing is due to network failure or failure of the server they are trying to access. On the other hand, a NOC for an MSP Network is generally expected to provide support to the network support staff at end-user sites. Another example is that in a end-user site environ-

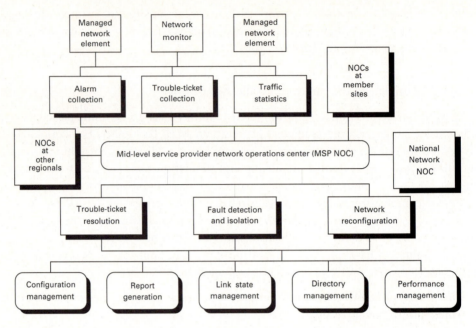

Figure 14.2   Diagram of a Mid-level Service Provider Network Operations Center (MSP NOC)

ment, all internetworking resources are generally managed by the same administrative entity, whereas in the case of an MSP, multiple administrative entities and service providers may be involved. Most MSP NOCs monitor and troubleshoot problems related to the transport only (through TCP or layers 1 through 4 of the OSI model), with a focus on the network (routing) layer functions, whereas end-user site NOCs may have to support the diagnosis of problems at higher layers as well. The NOCs of the MSPs and the end-user sites must effectively coordinate their activities to be responsive to end-user problems that may be caused by one or more contributing problems at any location in the Internet paths between end nodes. Figure 14.2 is a sample functional block diagram of an MSP NOC.

14.2.2.1   NOC Tools

Increasing numbers of universities, research institutes, and corporations are relying on Internet connectivity for day-to-day business. For example, many universities have decided to use remote supercomputing centers operated by the NSF rather than operating one locally. Thousands of researchers rely on access to these supercomputing centers from their workstations. This requires that all three tiers of the Internet operate reliably. However, it puts the most burden on MSP NOCs for rapid fault detection, isolation, and resolution. Network managers responsible for NOCs have realized that to do a reasonable job, more effective tools are needed. A number of working groups under the auspices of the IETF are addressing issues related to managing NOCs and providing tools for managing large networks. *RFC 1147* provides a tutorial on network management and a catalog of network management tools. Tools mentioned in the catalog range from *ping* to protocol analyzers. This section describes major categories of NOC tools and selected examples.

14.2.2.2 *Distributed Administration Tools*

Network administration involves tasks like registering network nodes, the generation of host tables for domain name services and BOOTP tables, inventory management, and accounting management. Distributed administration tools are essential for the operation of an MSP, as hundreds of administrative entities are involved. It is generally neither convenient nor cost-effective for MSP NOC staff to be involved in the administration of networks connected to the MSP backbone. NetDB is an example of a tool intended to support distributed network administration. Developed at Stanford University, NetDB is a key element in the operation of the Stanford University Network (SUNet) and BARRNet.

NetDB is built around a relational database that contains information about network components (hosts, routers, bridges, etc.) and their relationships; for example, identification of all the bridges related to a specific subnetwork.

NetDB provides a way of registering a unique host name, within a defined domain, and the IP address for each networked computer. A wide range of additional information, such as networking software, location of the computer, and the systems administrator responsible for the computer, is also included. For example, Stanford uses network operating systems information to keep track of the number of personal computer users with TCP/IP packages from specific vendors.

NetDB provides input to various network software services, such as the Domain Name System (DNS), the Bootstrap Protocol (BOOTP), AppleTalk™ tables, IP routing, and information for the network management database.

NetDB is used at Stanford to keep an on-line database of all faculty, students, and staff. WHOIS (or other directory server) records can be updated through the NetDB database facilities by individuals, and provide information ranging from e-mail addresses, office and residence phone numbers, job titles, and office addresses.

NetDB provides the facility to divide the Stanford.edu domain into logical subdomains based on subnet addresses or other address grouping criteria. This allows the central organization to delegate to local network administrators the authority for maintaining records about the computers for which they are responsible.

NetDB makes it very easy for network administrators to generate a wide range of reports. Commonly generated reports include: the total number of computers connected to a network or subnetwork, a breakdown of these computers by CPU type and by operating system, and the change in numbers of various types of computers from previous months or years. NetDB is also used with other monitoring data (e.g., collected ARP cache data) to provide reports that help network administrators maintain the address spaces for which they have responsibility. For example, addresses in use on each subnet are tracked and compared with NetDB-registered host addresses to produce reports of unused addresses and unregistered hosts, and to help manage address assignment. Below are two simple NetDB-generated reports taken 6 months apart that show the addition of 11 subnets and 1,214 IP host addresses:

NetDB: SUNet Summary, generated Wed Jan 1 22:30:01 PST 1992		
Summary:	Defined IP Subnets:	156
	Active IP Subnets:	111
	Registered Nodes:	6733
	Assigned IP Addresses:	11157

NetDB: SUNet Summary, generated Mon Jun 1 22:30:01 PDT 1992		
Summary:	Defined IP Subnets:	161
	Active IP Subnets:	122
	Registered Nodes:	7947
	Assigned IP Addresses:	12667

The growth is broken down according to the following categories:

- Defined IP Subnets: The number of distinctly numbered IP subnets within SUNet

- Active IP Subnets: A crude measure of subnets that are doing useful work, obtained by not counting those with 2 or fewer addresses

- Registered Nodes: A count of all NetDB entries that have one or more IP addresses

- Assigned IP Addresses: A count of all the IP addresses that have been assigned in NetDB.

NetDB automates a number of network operational administrative tasks by generating configuration and control tables for the network. For example, it generates configuration files for DNS, AppleTalk™ Routers (K-Box), and BOOTP. In addition to these configuration files, NetDB also feeds its data to the WHOIS database. *Cron*, a UNIX daemon that automatically runs pre-scheduled jobs, initiates jobs on the NetDB server each night precisely at 8:00 PM and 10:00 PM to extract data from the NetDB database. The extraction process is run twice to increase the robustness of the system. The data is then processed by a combination of *shell*, *awk*, and *perl* scripts to produce DNS and AppleTalk Router configuration files. The total time taken to run the entire generation process is on the order of a few minutes. The DNS configuration files are distributed to other DNS server machines via a *rdist* UNIX utility program. The *rdist* program makes certain that the DNS configuration files are current on these servers. Three DNS servers are geographically dispersed at key locations to ensure name resolution service survives single location failures. Once the DNS configuration files are distributed to these servers, another *cron* job is run on each of these servers to reinitialize the DNS server processes with the new information. The Apple-

Talk router configuration files generated on a NetDB server are distributed to various hosts that serve as the AppleTalk Internet servers. Once the files are properly updated on these server machines, a cron job scheduled on these machines starts the AppleTalk router reinitialization process.

The New England Academic and Research Network (NEARnet) uses a membership database and a DNS support system to provide functions similar to NetDB. NEARnet maintains information about each of their member sites in a networked database for ready access by the staff. This database contains both administrative and operational information, such as connection types, designated contacts, travel directions to the site, access procedures, and billing information. NEARnet has developed tools that periodically mail this information to each site for verification, and that allow members to easily confirm their entry over the network. Thanks to the membership database, many of NEARnet's operation and administrative activities have been automated and require little or no staff intervention. For example, mailing lists are generated directly from the database each morning; such lists automatically contain the latest changes for each site, including the current designated site contacts.

The membership database[2] is built upon a commercial UNIX database product, using standard forms and SQL routines. Simple reports are generated directly from the database, while final-form outputs (such as invoices) are formatted via *troff* for printing.

NEARnet provides primary or secondary domain name services for almost all of its members. Due to their large membership, this has resulted in over 300 domains that must be administered. These domains are handled via a set of tools designed to minimize staff intervention at each phase of the process. First, a zone database is maintained which identifies all of the domains and relevant information, such as the primary and secondary name servers to provide the name service. Another database is kept that tracks all of the hosts in those domains for which NEARnet is the primary name server. Each evening these databases are used to build the necessary configuration for the name daemon program (*named*). This includes the automatic generation of the SOA, NS, and PTR records for those domains for which NEARnet is the primary server. In the case of secondary domains, nightly tools confirm that the primary server is running, and that the necessary name server records are in place. If anything is amiss with the primary, electronic mail is automatically sent to the responsible person describing the problem and the recommended changes. These tools have dramatically reduced the amount of hands-on involvement that was previously required.

Since the domain name services that NEARnet provides to its members rely upon accurate information in the WHOIS database, they monitor the database for any changes and compare it nightly with the last valid version to detect changes that would affect their members. Any discrepancies are reported to the appropriate staff members for resolution. This monitoring detects changes when they occur, and gives NEARnet time to respond before a member site is impacted.

14.2.2.3 Configuration Management

ISO network management architecture identifies configuration as one of the five key elements of network management. Configuration management functions include the ability to identify network elements and to query network elements for their configuration information; maintaining and updating this information; and maintaining relationships among network elements.

Vendors of data communication equipment are getting pressure from their customers to make their devices "plug-and-play" simple to minimize configuration requirements. At the same time, customers are asking them to make their devices "flexible" to deal with the wide range of requirements. As a result, despite the progress made by the data communication vendors toward easier configuration procedures, device configuration continues to be a tedious task. Network devices are becoming more complex to keep up with emerging standards and technologies while continuing to support existing standards. For example, a router may have to support three or four network protocols (e.g., IP, DECnet, IPX, and Apple-Talk), two or three IP routing protocols (e.g., RIP, EGP, IS-IS, and OSPF), and three different types of media connections (e.g., Ethernet/802.3, synchronous serial for T1/T3, FDDI, and token ring/802.5). Supporting a large number of such devices and multiple protocols requires sophisticated configuration management for which few tools are currently available.

The key tool for configuration management is a central (relational) database of all the configuration information. The main requirement is convenient and flexible mechanisms for the comparison or update of configuration information.[3] For an MSP with distributed administration, a central database is critical for maintaining this information. This allows NOC staff, as well as the network engineers at a customer site, to access the same information and to make changes to a single database. Of course, operational procedures requiring that the central database be kept up-to-date are very important. Many managers of large networks can recall network failures caused by someone changing the configuration of a device without updating the configuration database. A typical scenario is that a network technician changes the network number and reconfigures a router interface card to reflect the new interface number without bothering to update the information in the configuration database. During the next couple of days that router requires rebooting. It will generally access the central database to obtain the configuration information, including addresses of all its interfaces. The missing update will result in a mismatch between the network address on a router interface for a subnet and the addresses of the hosts on that subnet. As a result, no host on that subnet will be able to communicate over the network. This situation can be prevented in two ways:

- Allow only a small number of authorized network administrators to change configurations, and clearly document the procedures for making such changes. For the reliable operation of a network, this must be a requirement.

- Periodically verify the database configuration information of all critical network elements, such as routers and bridges, and notify NOC staff if there is a mismatch. This provides reasonable protection against occasional human errors.

Configuration management tools are also critical for managing major changes in topology and network configuration. For example, consider a situation requiring that the network number of an MSP backbone, to which dozens or hundreds of routers are connected, be changed. With a database, a network administrator can make a global change in reflecting the new network number and then issue a command that causes the configuration information on all routers to be reloaded from the central database.

NEARnet uses a tool called Equipment and Gateway Management to perform a combination of inventory and configuration management.[2] Due to the size of NEARnet, it is necessary to track the circuits, equipment, and routers with automated tools. The network currently has over 1400 components that must be tracked and maintained. The Equipment and Gateway Management system consists of two databases, which contain the name, location, property tags, software, and access information (such as IP addresses and dialup phone numbers) for all of the devices that make up the network. The information in these databases is entered manually when the site is installed, and is updated whenever the device is changed. This information is used to confirm actual service costs, to generate monitoring software configuration files, and to assist operations by providing configuration details and related maintenance information during problem resolution.

Route filtering, the selective filtering of routing protocol updates received by routers, is typically used in three ways by MSPs:

1   To provide a simple policy mechanism for preferring routing information received from multiple external peers. For example, BARRNet filters everything believed to have originated on the CSUNET peer network, and uses the filters to preferentially assign internal CSUNET paths to northern California destinations and T3-NSFNET paths (which have a higher bandwidth over the long-haul) to CSUNET southern California destinations.

2   To prevent incorrect routing information from end-user sites from being learned and propagated within the region. An MSP may explicitly filter all routing information learned from its end-user sites so that bad information known to the end-user sites cannot be learned and propagated across the MSP backbone. This has prevented the occurrence of serious problems within an MSP network on more than one occasion.

3   To limit the amount of bandwidth consumed by routing updates. To this end, the MSP may filter all updates sent to "stub" end-user sites so that only the minimum information need be sent over low-capacity (e.g., 56-Kbps) serial lines. Typically, this means only "default" information is advertised to those sites.

In certain scenarios, where there exists a high degree of trust between the sender and receiver of routing information, filters may also be applied by the sender when it is more convenient to do so. For example, BARRNet does not filter routing updates received from the NASA Science Internet (NSI), nor does NSI filter what is received from BARRNet. Because of the routing technology used in these two networks (OSPF, used internally by both networks), the amount of configuration is greatly reduced for this peering arrangement. While normally it is necessary to explicitly list each and every network number to be advertised or believed, a feature of OSPF allows the selection of routes to be advertised based on a *tag* associated with the routes when they are first learned by the system. This allows, for example, all of the more than 200 BARRNet routes to be described by a small list of around 6 tag values. Needless to say, this sort of reduction in configuration information greatly simplifies network management.

Traffic filtering, the selective forwarding of user data packets based on some criteria, is typically used to implement a measure of security at the point where a router connects the end-user site to an MSP network. It should be strongly emphasized, however, that such filtering provides a very weak level of security, since any security based on knowing IP addresses or TCP/UDP port (service) numbers is inherently weak. With this caveat in mind, MSPs provide traffic filtering on the router equipment installed at end-user sites.

Typically, sites will request traffic (packet) filtering to restrict (by IP address) either the machines at the site that are allowed to send packets (and by virtue of TCP and UDP's generally symmetric nature, receive packets) from the rest of the Internet, or to restrict (by TCP or UDP port or service number ranges) the services that are allowed to connect from the "outside" Internet into their machines. A common example would be a site that wishes to allow all of its machines to initiate any TCP connections outbound but only wishes SMTP mail and domain service connections inbound. It should be noted that the ability to filter on the basis of both the TCP/UDP service and the direction in which the service is initiated is limited, given that such filtering depends on the assignment of TCP and UDP "well-known service" numbers, which are not always used by all services. One notorious example is the Network File System (NFS), which is widely known to be very vulnerable to attack, and therefore is typically denied across router boundaries to the end-user site. NFS uses a UDP port number (2049) that is not in the well-known service range normally assigned to server processes. The existence of such special-case port numbers complicates the configuration, and may lead to compromised security if all special port numbers are not known to the network manager. In addition, since the concept of *well- known service* is merely a convention that is not enforced by the network, the assignment of special security semantics to these port numbers is potentially dangerous. All this said, however, it remains the case that many end-user sites request their MSP to provide this sort of traffic filtering by IP addresses or TCP/UDP port numbers.[*]

14.2.2.4 Fault Management

To provide reliable service to its customers, an MSP must have adequate facilities to detect, diagnose, and resolve faults. Fault management is one of the five network management components defined by OSI, and its primary objective is to ensure maximum network

---

[*]   Information on route and packet filtering was provided by Vincent Fuller, Bay Area Regional Research Network.

availability. Network monitoring, alarm threshold definition, alarm generation, alarm processing, trouble ticketing, remote diagnosis, and remote device control capabilities are the key elements of fault management.

Network monitoring, which is dealt with in more detail below, includes the display of the status of all links, critical network components, and network traffic on various segments. This is accomplished with a combination of polling management agents in various devices, such as routers and bridges, and of polling dedicated network monitoring devices placed on critical network segments. The display has to be easy to understand and capable of allowing network managers to zoom in on segments to study them in detail.

Alarm threshold definition is critical for proactive management. It is tightly coupled to performance management, as network thresholds are generally set to warn network managers about performance degradation rather than the failure of a device. Selection of appropriate alarm thresholds for various parameters is important for effective alarm management. Alarm generation and processing is supported by most network monitors and management stations. Alarm processing is generally coupled with trouble-ticketing, so that selected alarms automatically generate a trouble ticket. Of course, a trouble ticket can be generated by an end user at a site, or by the NOC staff as well. The real challenge is timely diagnosis and resolution of detected faults. In MSPs, where multiple entities, such as MSP NOCs, end-user site NOCs, National Network NOCs, and the local phone company, may be involved in fault isolation and resolution, it is important to have alarm generation and processing coupled with a trouble-ticketing system.

Various MSPs are using a combination of tools to ensure quick resolution of network faults. Even today, most MSP NOCs are not staffed by fully qualified diagnostic network engineers 24 hours a day, and as a result, pagers are being used extensively for informing engineers about network-related problems. Key BARRNet engineers are provided with an X-terminal connected via 56-kbps digital lines to the network management station. This allows engineers to monitor the network from their residences, and sometimes resolve problems without having to travel into the field. To ensure the high availability sought by the membership, NEARnet utilizes an automated network monitoring and response system known as *Ping_Page*.[2] *Ping_Page* continuously checks the availability of each member's network, and initiates corrective action if a given site should become unavailable for any reason. In most cases, the corrective action is to select and page the appropriate network technician via display pagers. The technician has a limited amount of time to acknowledge the problem before *Ping_*page moves on to the designated backup and operations manager. NEARnet is responsible for maintaining all of the components of a member's connection, and as a result can often resolve a situation before the site has detected the problem.

Carnegie Mellon University (CMU) has developed a network management tool,[4] SNMPCon, to provide automated fault detection, diagnosis, correlation, and reporting for a variety of fault domains. A color Motif interface presents reports generated by the system which also supports trouble-ticket tracking. These fault reports are also stored in a Sybase database for historical analysis and report generation.

The strength of the CMU system lies in its distributed architecture, which allows the easy integration of many diagnostic modules. These diagnostic modules analyze data from various sources, and channel the fault information to the system user. Diagnostic modules have been written to monitor general network connectivity and device status, routing anomalies, Domain Name System operation and consistency, network server operation (DNS, BOOTP, and so on), and AppleTalk network operation and consistency. SNMPCon has proven that intelligent diagnosis can be performed by traditional technology without waiting for expert system technology to become available.

14.2.2.5 *Trouble-Ticketing and Tracking*

For an MSP network serving hundreds of customers, a trouble-ticketing system is an essential tool. In addition to controlling the trouble resolution process, trouble tickets are useful for building a knowledge base to support future expert systems, supervising service-level agreements, and calculating network availability.[5] Dale Johnson has described desirable features, competing uses, and architecture of an integrated trouble-ticket system for a NOC in *RFC 1297*. Most MSPs we contacted are either currently using a trouble-ticketing system or are planning to use one in the near future. At this stage most trouble-ticketing systems being used in MSPs were developed in-house, though virtually every telephone company or large PBX operating organization has sophisticated systems. Recently, some commercially developed trouble-ticketing systems, specifically designed with computer networks in mind, are becoming available (e.g., Action Request System from Remedy Corp.), and are likely to gain popularity. CMU and NEARnet have developed their own trouble-ticketing systems. Trouble-ticket exchange standards are under discussion and development in the IETF and will eventually permit much better hand-off and tracking of problems across and among MSP and backbone service providers, with a potential for tracking of resolution across the entire Internet from the end-user site. A brief description of the trouble-ticketing system used by NEARnet follows.[2]

> This system allows problems to be tracked from initial report to satisfactory resolution. As the NEARnet staff work to resolve problems, the current status is always entered into the trouble-ticket system. The system automatically distributes such updates to affected NEARnet members via electronic mail. The system also has a finger interface which allows interested parties to remotely query the status of tickets in the database. For those problems which involve sensitive information, the system supports private tickets which have a limited distribution.
>
> NEARnet is committed to providing end-to-end problem resolution for their members and in this role NEARnet has found the trouble-ticket system invaluable. NEARnet members may report problems via their hotline phone number or electronic mail, and NEARnet will open a ticket and begin work on resolution. When the source of a problem appears to be located outside of NEARnet, the NEARnet Operations Staff will provide the necessary information to the appropriate NOC for resolution. NEARnet will continue to monitor the status of the problem

and report progress via their trouble-ticket system. Once the problem is resolved and the member reports that they are satisfied, the ticket is closed. Closed tickets are retained in the database and are used to produce trend reports showing problematic equipment and services.

14.2.2.6 Performance Management

There seems to be an interesting race going on between people involved in delivering packet-switching equipment and people involved in developing network-based applications. As soon as network managers implement networks based on the next generation of high-speed network standards (e.g., FDDI), developers create new applications that can easily overload the new network and generate performance problems. As a result, network managers are always looking forward to installing the emerging standard that will increase the bandwidth of their network by an order of magnitude. A common myth among the network-naive is that most network performance problems can be solved by increasing the network's bandwidth. End-to-end performance seen by the network user is the combined result of the performance of the user workstations, the network that connects clients and server systems, and the servers. From users' perspective, response time, throughput, and availability are the three most important network performance criteria. Poor response time may be caused by overloaded servers or misconfigured devices rather than an inadequate bandwidth. Similarly, throughput problems are sometimes caused by disk I/O bottlenecks or inadequate buffers on a server. Of course, performance problems may be caused by congestion on the MSP backbone or the links from end-user sites to the MSP. LANs on end-user sites generally have more capacity than the links that connect end-user sites to MSPs. For example, an end-user site using a FDDI backbone may be connected to an MSP using a T1 link and the MSP may only be using an Ethernet backbone. The T1 link, can be swamped by a single session between two high-performance RISC workstations, or a single workstation and server, without significantly loading the enterprise backbone or the MSP backbone. Alternatively, 20 or 30 concurrent file transfer sessions between PC-class machines and remote file servers can easily overload the MSP Ethernet backbone. If the routers linking end-user sites to the MSP have insufficient buffers, packets will be dropped, resulting in poor response time for interactive traffic. MSP networks are generally engineered in such a way that these occurrences are bound to happen, but only for short intervals and will occur with a sufficiently low frequency to be acceptable to users.

Performance management involves three activities: monitoring the network and servers to gather statistics; analyzing these statistics to detect network, router, or server bottlenecks; adjusting network topology or controlling key parameters in network devices or servers to remove the bottlenecks. Rates of change and absolute levels of parameters, such as the number of collisions, retransmissions, broadcasts, etc., are useful metrics for indicating network performance. *Baselining* is used to establish metrics and associated values for a desirable performance level. Having established the baseline values for a level of performance, network managers can set thresholds for various parameters. For example, if it is determined that users do not experience performance problems as long as the total number of collisions on Ethernet segments is under 0.5% of the total traffic, the network manager may set the collision threshold at 0.5%. If the number of collisions on an Ethernet segment exceeds this threshold, an alarm is sent to the management station. Network technicians can then use other tools to analyze the segment that generated the alarm to isolate the causes of the collisions. Similarly, network and systems managers can set thresholds for queues on a file server to indicate a greater-than-normal load on that file server. Many network managers use an Internet Control Messaging Protocol (ICMP) echo facility called *ping* to estimate response time and packet loss on a path. It should be noted that the response time for *ping* packets is determined by the delay caused by the networks, as well as the delay introduced by the system responding to *ping* packets. *Ping* and other monitoring and diagnostic tools are further discussed below.

The third and most important aspect of network performance, from the viewpoint of most users, is network availability or *up-time*. It is easy to monitor and report availability from the manager's "global outage" viewpoint (i.e., all service is disrupted), but difficult to define, monitor, and report availability from the network user's viewpoint, particularly if your purview is only the MSP between users at either end of the Internet. Network managers determine the average availability of their networks over a period of a month, and express it in percentage up-time. Many MSPs would be able to claim essentially 100% availability on this basis because the built-in redundancy in their topologies and equipment guarantees that multiple failures are required to produce a global outage. To the user, however, it is irrelevant that the MSP has 100% up-time if they suffer poor availability because the network, the router, or the power to equipment connecting to the MSP at their site is unreliable. Meaningful availability information is the subject of discussion among MSP members of the Federation of American Research Networks, within the IETF, and in other forums. Standards for availability reporting will help allow comparison among MSPs so they have a better basis for relative evaluation of their own performance. Collaborative trouble-ticketing should provide data to help correlate end-to-end availability information with causal locations. But, all in all, availability information and analysis has a long way to go before it will provide the desired results for end users.

14.2.2.7 Operational Management Reports

Some MSPs provide regular summary reports of their operational performance. These reports are important to management, acting both as a tool for comparing on-going operational results and as a communication tool between the MSP and its end-user sites. CERFnet produces an informative weekly operational report, an abbreviated example of which is shown in Figure 14.3. The report is divided into sections covering CERFnet's overall description, outage incidents, network operational activities, communication link utilization, and equipment (router) up-time (the time elapsed since the last reboot). The timeliness of this report permits sites to understand what has affected their network use, and to assess the responsiveness of the MSP. It lets the MSP management track the relative

Date: Mon, 24 Feb 92 13:15:47 PST
From: Donna Bigley <donnab@CERF.NET>
Subject: CERFnet Weekly Report for the week of Monday, February 23, 1992.
###
This is the CERFnet weekly activity report for the period of Monday, February 17th through Sunday, February 23rd, 1992.
This report is also available through anonymous FTP from NIC.CERF.NET [192.102.249.3] in the cerfnet/cerfnet_stats
subdirectory. The filename is: 23-february-92.txt
All times are in Pacific Standard Time, and in the 24-hour format.
Please direct any questions or comments to:
donnab@cerf.net or help@cerf.net
****
NETWORK OUTAGES:

SITE:	McDonnell Douglas
SITES AFFECTED:	McDonnell Douglas
TIME STARTED:	MON. 2-17-92 15:55
TIME ENDED:	MON. 2-17-92 16:30
TIME ELAPSED:	35 min.
REASON:	Site Scheduled Maintenance
SITE:	McDonnell Douglas
SITES AFFECTED:	McDonnell Douglas
TIME STARTED:	MON. 2-17-92 20:30
TIME ENDED:	WED. 2-19-92 13:33
TIME ELAPSED:	1 day 17 hours 3 min. (Intermittent Access)
REASON:	Equipment Trouble
SITE:	SERI/KOREA
SITES AFFECTED:	SERI/KOREA
TIME STARTED:	WED. 2-19-92 04:42
TIME ENDED:	WED. 2-19-92 08:48
TIME ELAPSED:	4 hours 6 min.
REASON:	Unknown

⋮

(remaining entries deleted)

⋮

NETWORK ACTIVITY:

A heavy load on the CERFnet stub on Thursday, February 20th, affected routing; however, the load has
been brought down and routing stabilized.

On Friday, February 21st, all T1 networks announced out of San Diego were not getting announced
into any of the T3 gateways on the NSFnet. After NSFnet reloaded the new configurations, the T1
hosts were reachable through the T3 side.

On Saturday, February 22nd, between 10:0 –11:30, and on Monday, February 24th, between 04:00–
04:30, there was intermittent access due to new NSFnet routing. CERFnet split into a separate AS # for
routing to and from the NSFnet.

Figure 14.3   CERFnet sample operational report

CERFNET TRAFFIC CAPACITY USAGE AT EACH CIRCUIT LINK

LINK	SPEED	CAPACITY	PEAK HOUR (PDT)
SDSC/CALTECH	1.544 mbps	12.1%	17:00
SDSC/UCI	1.544 mbps	05.7%	12:00
SDSC/UCLA	1.544 mbps	04.9%	12:00
SDSC/UCOP	1.544 mbps	04.6%	11:00
UCI/UCLA	1.544 mbps	00.6%	17:00
SDSC/UCR	512 kbps	01.5%	13:00
UCLA/UCSB	512 kbps	06.5%	14:00
SDSC/AGI	1.544 mbps	00.2%	20:00
⋮	⋮	⋮	⋮
CALTECH/CADAM	56 kbps	00.6%	17:00
CALTECH/CLAREMONT	56 kbps	15.3%	15:00
CALTECH/DISNEY	56 kbps	04.3%	17:00

⋮

(remaining entries deleted)

⋮

SITE CISCO BOX UPTIME SINCE LAST REBOOT (as of 00:15 PST on Feb. 24, 1992):
CERFnet BACKBONE

CALTECH [131.215.139.253]	Up: 04 days 15 hours 51 minutes [CERFnet Scheduled Maintenance]
SDSC Drzog [132.249.16.13]	Up: 01 days 13 hours 52 minutes [Software Changes]
SDSC Hang10 [132.249.16.15]	Up: 00 days 00 hours 35 minutes [Software Changes]
UCI [128.200.1.101]	Up: 45 days 16 hours 07 minutes
UCLA [128.97.130.10]	Up: 16 days 13 hours 42 minutes
UCOP [134.24.52.112]	STILL DOWN [Equipment Trouble]
UCR [134.24.108.105]	Up: 100 days 12 hours 36 minutes

CERF 1544

AGI [134.24.202.110]	Up: 10 days 13 hours 54 minutes
APPLE [134.24.70.200]	Up: 119 days 06 hours 15 minutes
BIOSYM [134.24.57.200]	Up: 21 days 06 hours 48 minutes
CISCO Systems [134.24.54.200]	Up: 82 days 14 hours 09 minutes
CSUCO/SWRL [130.150.102.200]	Up: 40 days 12 hours 46 minutes
GA [134.24.221.200]	Up: 01 days 04 hours 41 minutes [Unscheduled Site Maintenance]
GD [134.24.60.200]	Up: 53 days 04 hours 14 minutes
LLUMC [134.24.208.200]	Up: 96 days 12 hours 22 minutes
SAIC [134.24.53.208]	Up: 50 days 08 hours 34 minutes
SCAQMD [134.24.234.200]	Up: 66 days 14 hours 27 minutes
SDSU [192.77.100.101]	Up: 76 days 16 hours 31 minutes
UCSB [134.24.107.107]	Up: 96 days 07 hours 38 minutes

CERF 56

AJS [134.24.225.101]	Up: 37 days 14 hours 17 minutes
CADAM [134.24.229.200]	Up: 19 days 13 hours 01 minutes
CLAREMONT [134.24.206.109]	Up: 10 days 14 hours 02 minutes

⋮

(remaining entries deleted)

⋮

Figure 14.3 (Continued)   CERFnet sample operational report

reliability of the mid-level connectivity services with a small investment in time and analysis. Further, by performing time series analyses of the utilization statistics, the managers can watch for growth trends and identify links in which capacity changes should be evaluated.

14.2.3 Operational Monitoring and Troubleshooting Tools and Methods

The previous sections described the elements of network operation and management. With proper design, network monitoring and management can identify and isolate problems so that they may be corrected before they become apparent to the users.

14.2.3.1 *What and How to Monitor*

The key to effective monitoring is knowing what and how to monitor. In a wide area regional network based on current technology there are usually many point-to-point links and interconnecting routers. Therefore, awareness of the status of every link and router is important, and the monitoring mechanism must be able to deduce the state of every router and link in the network. This is the lowest level of monitoring. The MSP also needs to collect information about error rates on the links so as to be able to identify links that are gradually failing or providing degraded service. Lastly, there needs to be a method to collect utilization statistics so that the network designer can forecast future demand and can add additional backbone capacity as necessary.

14.2.3.2 *Tools for Management and Monitoring*

As recently as two years ago, there were no coherent tools for monitoring and managing a network. The primary tool was the user who would use the telephone to call and complain about a problem. Someone at the NOC would then use tools like *ping, traceroute,* and TELNET to identify, isolate, and correct the problem. (These tools are discussed in more detail in the section below.) The problem with these tools is that they are effectively manual tools and require a good bit of manual input to extract the necessary information.

If a network outage were sufficiently advanced (advanced beyond the, "hey, it's broken," telephone call stage) monitoring consisted of using *ping* (sending ICMP echo requests) to probe all of the devices being monitored, e.g., routers, interfaces, and hosts, and ensuring that the responses came back. Lack of response from a device indicated that a problem existed somewhere in the network, but manual intervention was still required to isolate the fault.

The great beauty of SNMP is the simplicity of the agent used in devices being monitored. The agent is able only to respond to queries for information and to set pre-defined, preformatted variables. It makes no attempt to format or interpret any of the data being requested or set. The task of interpreting and formatting is left to the monitoring device (the client), usually a relatively powerful processor dedicated to the task.

SNMP monitoring devices are usually high-performance workstations with good graphics capability. Most SNMP monitoring software makes use of the graphics capability to present network status in a form that may be interpreted at a glance, which is a significant advantage in large networks.

14.2.3.3 Operational Limitations of SNMP

Simplicity can also be a liability. Monitoring the current state of the network with SNMP is virtually identical to the *ping* approach described earlier. The management station sends queries to all the devices in the network, and assumes that they are working properly as long as the monitoring station continues to receive appropriate responses. Lack of a response from a particular device indicates only that a problem exists, not that there is necessarily a problem with the unresponsive device.

In addition, the polling nature of SNMP adds a load to the network. The administrator can extract more detail at the expense of a greater load on the network, a difficult trade-off to have to make. A network whose links are running close to capacity may be overloaded to the point of collapse by increasing the monitoring load.

SNMP includes a mechanism to provide more timely information and to notify the management station of significant events. This mechanism is called trapping. A trap is an unsolicited message sent by the agent to the client in response to a significant event in the device being monitored, i.e., a link failure, a reboot, etc. However, there is a fly in the ointment; traps are based on unreliable datagrams (UDP) so that just when you desperately want to get this information through ("Hi, the network is melting down and routers are dropping like flies."), the likelihood is that the packet will be lost and the management station will be none the wiser. On the other hand, reliable datagram delivery mechanisms are likely to fail as well when the network is in trouble. An out-of-band channel through a separate, healthy network may provide a solution, if the cost is justifiable.

14.2.3.4 Monitoring Link State Rather than Reachability

Monitoring the reachability of a device in the network with SNMP or *ping* is extremely useful but it has its limitations. For example, assume that you have a network with little or no redundancy and a critical link fails. In this case the monitoring station or device will show all of the devices on the far side of the failed link as being unresponsive. The result is a map displaying many failed devices. The flood of erroneous information can mask the real problem.

Now let us examine the case of a network that is rich in redundancy. If the network has a link state-based interior routing protocol, such as OSPF or IS-IS, that can converge very rapidly, it is possible for the network to discover the link failure and reroute the traffic between SNMP or *ping* polls to the affected area of the network. The result is that your monitoring station fails to report the outage. (This is not absolutely true if you are querying for state information of every link and the interface of every device, but then you are back to the problem of overloading your network with monitoring queries—especially during outages where network capacity may be significantly reduced.)

If we examine this scenario more closely, it is clear that the link state-based routing protocol can detect an outage and its cause far more rapidly than can SNMP or *ping*. Since the link-state information is propagated very rapidly through the network in response to changes in the network topology, it is possible to use this information as an adjunct to SNMP monitoring, to reduce the monitoring traffic and to provide more timely information about the internal state of the network. A much more efficient network monitoring scheme could make use of SNMP polling to monitor singly connected leaf devices and the presence of the routers, and use the link-state information from the routing protocol to monitor the state of the internal network core. Please note that this will only work with link state routing protocols like OSPF and IS-IS. It will not work with Bellman-Ford (distance vector) routing protocols like RIP or IGRP.

14.2.3.5 XNETDB—An Example of an Integrated Network Monitoring and Management System

Developed by Ohio Academic Resources Network (OARnet), XNETDB is an example of a network monitoring and management system based on X-Windows and MIT's SNMP, with integrated database and statistics viewing capability. In addition to acquiring and displaying information about the state of routers and their connected circuits for continuous monitoring and alarm annunciation, XNETDB has integrated database facilities that support map-based site selection by the user to display:

1   Site equipment configuration information

2   Circuit identification, contact, and specification

3   Technical contact names, addresses, telephone numbers, and other descriptive information.

Differing line speeds are displayed in different colors, or line thicknesses for monochrome displays. A status message displays special alarm information from monitoring of selected router state information. For example, loss of a default route may be a condition that is explicitly trapped and displayed on the XNETDB monitor.

Seven state and statistic information choices are provided for each router in a pull-down menu invoked by mouse-cursor clicking on the desired router (see Figure 14.4). *Information, Interfaces, Contacts, Shell, Routes, Stats,* and *Route-Report* were the router menu titles available in the 1991 implementation discussed here. Menu item *Information* provides router board IDs, serial numbers, out-of-band control port access numbers, and router models and version information. Menu item *Interfaces* details specific interface information, IP addresses, line speeds, and state information. Menu item *Contacts* displays information used to contact the people responsible for the site liaison. Menu item *Shell* opens a Telnet session log-in window to the router. Menu item *Routes* displays the current routing table: destination network, next hops, routing metric, and protocol source. The integrated database stores daily statistics logged via SNMP traps, including the routing changes and

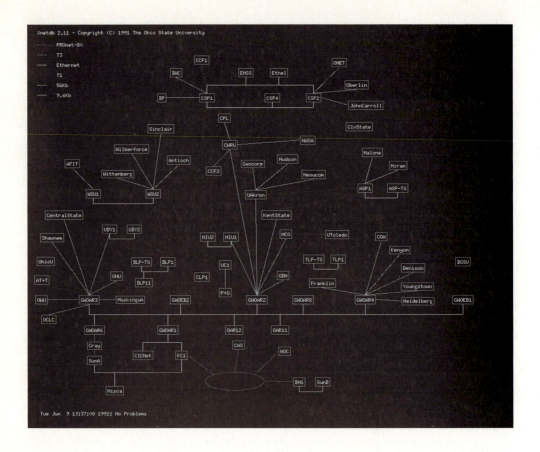

Figure 14.4   Sample screen from the XNETDB monitor

traffic data. Menu item *Stats* provides the traffic statistics to and from the site over an inter-face, and local network traffic for a specified historical time interval (i.e., a day). Menu item *Route-Report* provides the routing changes for the requested day.

A second pull-down menu is opened by clicking on a circuit. It has two choices; *Information* and *Contacts.* The database contains static information for each circuit (carrier, des-ignation, type and DSU/CSU information for both ends), and contact information (usually the telephone company names and numbers associated with the ordering and repair of a leased line), displayed by selecting one of the two choices.

A high-level summary pull-down menu provides the operations center with network-wide information about all the known circuits (source, destination, number, and carrier), CSU/DSUs (listed with location, manufacturer, model, rev level, and serial numbers), and sites (listed with official domain names). Three other summary menu selections display peak utilization statistics for a selected day for all hub and leaf nodes, other summary utilization data, and link down-time statistics.

Among the principal operational advantages of a system like XNETDB over some other SNMP-based network management system is the ease with which an operator can move from the detection of a fault condition to corrective action by use of the integrated database information.

By coupling the contact, configuration, and other descriptive information into the same SNMP map-based object-oriented display, the operator need not search for matching information in multiple files or databases for devices, circuits, and other network objects associated with the possible fault sources. "Point, select, and click" is all that is required, using the object pull-down menus, to bring the related information together without need for further lookup.

The global information makes it easy to determine how many objects on the network satisfy a particular criterion. For example, if it is necessary to upgrade router configurations to support a new software release or added functionality, the global configuration information allows a rapid determination of the number of upgrades required and the locations of the units matching particular configuration parameters. The provision of SNMP trap data that provide information about routing changes is another valuable function of this system, which helps identify routing problems and anomalies that may otherwise go undetected and cause end-to-end failures to the network users for no obvious reason.

It is also true, however, that every tool has its limitations. The integrated database is only as good as the procedures implemented to keep it up to date. SNMP fault isolation is subject to the same limitations of in-band (common channel) signaling with this system as it is with any other. Recognizing the latter limitation, the XNETDB database includes the out-of-band access numbers for routers and other network device console ports, where available. OARnet is continuing to improve and add to the system. There is potential for further integration with trouble-ticketing, RMON monitoring, and other operational tools and systems.

14.2.4 Common Tools for Troubleshooting

There are a number of levels of troubleshooting techniques, some requiring substantial hardware investment (e.g., dedicated protocol analyzers) and others that depend upon the particular troubleshooting capabilities embodied in a network device, such as a router. The former are not available at many network locations, and the latter are most often proprietary and unique to the implementation supplied by a specific equipment manufacturer. There are some tools, however, that are widely available and used universally by Internet engineers and technicians (see *RFC 1147*). The following discussion elaborates on two such tools.

At the first level, that of deducing basic router and link states, there are a couple of tools that are useful in detecting and isolating problems. The simplest of these tools is the program called *ping*, discussed briefly above, that generates ICMP echo requests. (Note that Echo Requests and Echo Responses are only two of the many kinds of ICMP messages.) The *ping* program sends an ICMP echo request to the remote device and listens for a response to return. If the response is returned, *ping* reports the round-trip time. By periodically sending ICMP Echo Requests to all the devices, e.g., routers, interfaces, and hosts, the manager can deduce from a positive response that all the devices along the path from the source to the destination are working, and, from the round-trip time, something of the load on the different paths. Here is a sample of output from *ping* taken from a Sun workstation:

```
ray:brian 14 > ping -s angband.stanford.edu ping angband.stanford.edu: 56 data bytes
64 bytes from Angband.Stanford.EDU (36.98.0.21): icmp_seq=0. time=60. ms
64 bytes from Angband.Stanford.EDU (36.98.0.21): icmp_seq=1. time=60. ms
64 bytes from Angband.Stanford.EDU (36.98.0.21): icmp_seq=2. time=60. ms
64 bytes from Angband.Stanford.EDU (36.98.0.21): icmp_seq=3. time=60. ms
64 bytes from Angband.Stanford.EDU (36.98.0.21): icmp_seq=4. time=80. ms
64 bytes from Angband.Stanford.EDU (36.98.0.21): icmp_seq=5. time=60. ms

—Angband.Stanford.EDU ping Statistics—

6 packets transmitted, 6 packets received, 0% packet loss
round-trip (ms) min/avg/max = 60/63/80
```

Ping displays the sequence number and round-trip time of each response. A gap in the sequence number (Icmp_seq) denotes a lost packet. When the operator terminates the *ping*, the program also displays the total number of echo requests sent, the number of responses received, and the minimum, average, and maximum round-trip times. The minimum, average, and maximum round-trip times are useful in determining performance trends for the path to a particular destination. To gain even more information, the size of the *ping* packets and the *ping* interval may be varied.

For quite some time, monitoring a network consisted of writing a script that ran periodically and used *ping* to determine the reachability of all the devices. This technique is still useful. It can be used to determine if all the components are working. SNMP also uses the same conceptual technique (i.e., send a query and wait for a response) to determine if the specified device or interface is still "alive."

But what if there is a problem reaching a remote device, or even just a problem of poor performance? How can you locate the problem? Neither *ping* nor SNMP are designed to provide this information. Fortunately there is another tool called *traceroute* that will return information from intermediate systems or routers that lie on the path from the source to the destination.

Traceroute is a variation on the *ping* theme that permits the collection of information about intermediate nodes along the way to the destination. *Traceroute* takes advantage of the Time-To- Live(TTL) feature of IP. (See Chapter 4 for information on the TTL field.) *Traceroute* sends out a packet (usually a UDP packet to a port with no server waiting) with the TTL set to 1. This causes the nearest device to send back an ICMP TTL-exceeded message. *Traceroute* also times the round-trip time for the packet. With subsequent packets the TTL is increased so that the ICMP TTL-exceeded message comes from subsequent intermediate routers. This permits the user of *traceroute* to determine the exact path taken by packets going to the destination, the latency of each sucessive hop (indicated by comparing the round-trip times of each hop), and where connectivity finally fails (indicated by the reception of ICMP unreachable messages or by a total lack of response). Here is a sample of *traceroute* output:

```
ray:brian 16 > traceroute angband.stanford.edu
traceroute to angband.stanford.edu (36.98.0.21), 30 hops max, 38 byte packets
```

1	arthur.lloyd.COM (158.222.1.1)	0 ms	0 ms	20 ms
2	USBR-C1.BARRNET.NET (131.119.111.1)	20 ms	40 ms	20 ms
3	USBR.BARRNET.NET (131.119.245.1)	20 ms	40 ms	40 ms
4	UCD.BARRNET.NET (131.119.12.1)	40 ms	40 ms	40 ms
5	131.119.9.6 (131.119.9.6)	60 ms	60 ms	60 ms
6	SU-A.BARRNET.NET (131.119.254.200)	60 ms	80 ms	60 ms
7	SU-CAMPUS.BARRNET.NET (131.119.252.100)	60 ms	60 ms	80 ms
8	forsythe-gateway.Stanford.EDU (36.56.0.2)	60 ms	60 ms	60 ms
9	Angband.Stanford.EDU (36.98.0.21)	60 ms	80 ms	60 ms

Note that *traceroute* provides the name and address of each router along the way to the destination, as well as three round-trip times for each hop along the way. Three probes per hop gives the operator a rough indication of the average round-trip time to a particular router or host in the path to the destination. This information is quite useful in determining bottlenecks and other performance problems.

Let us now assume that there is a problem. First, *ping* is reporting that a particular destination is unreachable. Here is the output from *ping*:

```
% ping ray.lloyd.com
PING ray.lloyd.com (192.124.48.2): 56 data bytes
^C
—ray.lloyd.com PING Statistics—
4 packets transmitted, 0 packets received, 100% packet loss
```

Since there are many routers/links between the source and destination, *ping* can only verify that a problem exists. It provides no information about where the problem is. At this point the *traceroute* is brought into play to determine where the problem actually lies. Here is the output from *traceroute*:

```
% traceroute ray.lloyd.com
traceroute to ray.lloyd.com (192.124.48.2), 30 hops max, 40 byte packets
```

1	SU-CAMPUS.BARRNET.NET (36.56.0.200)	4 ms	0 ms	4 ms
2	SU-B.BARRNET.NET (131.119.252.201)	4 ms	4 ms	0 ms
3	SU2.BARRNET.NET (131.119.254.6)	4 ms	0 ms	4 ms

4	UCD.BARRNET.NET (131.119.9.1)	27 ms	27 ms	27 ms
5	USBR.BARRNET.NET (131.119.12.12)	35 ms	39 ms	39 ms
6	USBR-C1.BARRNET.NET (131.119.245.101)	39 ms	35 ms	35 ms
7	LLOYD.BARRNET.NET (131.119.111.2)	62 ms	62 ms	74 ms
8	LLOYD.BARRNET.NET (131.119.111.2)	82 ms !H	74 ms !H	70 ms !H

In this example the problem exists at the router LLOYD.BARRNET.NET. The symbol !H means that the router returned an ICMP host-unreachable message, indicating that it has no route to the destination system.

The following example demonstrates how a routing loop appears to *traceroute*.

% traceroute jessica.stanford.edu traceroute to jessica.stanford.edu (36.21.0.20), 30 hops max, 40 byte packets

1	ietf-term.ietf.cerf.net (134.24.249.31)	3 ms	3 ms	3 ms
2	sdsc-ietf.cerf.net (134.24.79.100)	9 ms	43 ms	4 ms
3	longboard-sdsc.cerf.net (134.24.99.254)	63 ms	5 ms	6 ms
4	hang-sdsc.cerf.net (134.24.99.2)	11 ms	5 ms	8 ms
5	longboard-sdsc.cerf.net (134.24.99.254)	7 ms	8 ms	7 ms
6	hang-sdsc.cerf.net (134.24.99.2)	8 ms	7 ms	8 ms
7	longboard-sdsc.cerf.net (134.24.99.254)	24 ms	10 ms	9 ms
8	hang-sdsc.cerf.net (134.24.99.2)	10 ms	10 ms	13 ms
9	longboard-sdsc.cerf.net (134.24.99.254)	19 ms	13 ms	14 ms
10	hang-sdsc.cerf.net (134.24.99.2)	14 ms	16 ms	13 ms
11	longboard-sdsc.cerf.net (134.24.99.254)	90 ms	51 ms	39 ms
12	hang-sdsc.cerf.net (134.24.99.2)	23 ms	15 ms	16 ms

Note that the responses alternate between two routers, hang-sdsc.cerf.net and long-board-sdsc.cerf.net. These two routers have conflicting routes to Stanford that point at each other. This kind of problem can occur if there is a connectivity failure somewhere in the network and the routing protocol has not converged upon a new route, or it can indicate misconfiguration of one or both of the routers. In any case, it is worthwhile for the network administrator to examine the routing information contained in the offending routers.

14.3   NETWORK SERVICES AND SUPPORT

14.3.1   Connection Services

MSPs must offer a variety of connection services to support the range of end-user sites requesting Internet access. The conventional connection services for the last five years have been predominantly based on 56-Kbps and 1.544-Mbps telephone company leased lines connecting routers for switching packets between the end-user site and the MSP backbone. The tools and methods for establishing and maintaining connectivity with these facilities are well understood and service is generally manageable, though subject to the problems and limitations described in earlier sections.

More recently, lower cost and performance modes of connection have become standard offerings of most if not all MSPs. Dial-in service is now commonplace, and mobile service is on the way. These connection services bring with them different problems and limitations. They require different levels of support and application services, different monitoring and troubleshooting tools, and a different level of control (e.g., access and security) than the conventional leased line services. Dial-in service is further discussed below.

In the near future, higher speed T3, SMDS, and SONET services will become available in increasing quantity, first in major metropolitan areas and long-haul networks, permitting deployment in limited numbers of end-user sites, MSPs, and national backbones. This deployment will require further enhancement and addition to the tool kits of the MSPs and end-user sites, on which we will not speculate.

Dial-in Networking

Internetworking has become commonplace, and a moderate and growing number of users need access to the Internet regardless of their location. For the purposes of low-cost connection and mobile computing, this implies access through the General Switched Telephone Network (GSTN).

Until recently dial-in access was typified by connection of dumb terminals or terminal emulators to terminal servers in the MSP or end-user site network. While a great deal may be accomplished with terminal access, more and more people are demanding full dial-in host and network access. The arrival of the dialup IP router now makes this possible.

Most dialup routers transmit IP datagrams encapsulated within the Serial Line Internet Protocol (SLIP) or the Point-to-Point Protocol (PPP). SLIP is the simpler of the two protocols, but it is much more limited. With SLIP, only IP datagrams may be transmitted. An MSP considering offering support for other protocol stacks, i.e., OSI/CLNP, DECnet, Novell Netware/IPX, Appletalk, etc., will find SLIP to be too limiting. In addition, both ends of the SLIP link must be completely preconfigured, making support for mobile hosts very labor intensive. Also, SLIP provides no mechanism for authentication of the incoming connection. The MSP must provide some other external mechanism to authenticate the incoming connection.

On the other hand, PPP provides the necessary features. It supports multiple protocols on the same link. At the time of this writing the IETF PPP working group has written documents describing IP, DECnet, IPX, Appletalk, OSI/CLNP, and MAC-layer bridging over synchronous and asynchronous links.

PPP also provides a mechanism to assign an IP address to a remote device. This feature allows mobile hosts to connect to the nearest point-of-presence, regardless of where it exists in the network. When the host connects using PPP, the PPP address negotiation will permit the dialup router in the point-of-presence to assign an IP address to the host from a pool of addresses. The host then uses that address for the duration of the session. When the session is over and the connection is broken, the dialup router de-allocates the address and returns it to the pool. Since mobile hosts do not need permanently assigned addresses, routing is simplified and address space is conserved.

In spite of the advances, there are still some remaining problems with dialup routing. First, there are no official centralized services to provide authentication and authorization information to the dialup router. This leads to duplication of all user information in all the dialup routers, and the concomitant problems of maintaining duplicated information. Second, there is no official mechanism for the collection of accounting and usage information. Management of dial-in modem pools and router ports presents new challenges for MSPs and end-user networks alike; few tools are currently available to make the task easier, but they are on the way. One of the significant challenges for method and tool development is service management for large populations of dial-in users as our organizations engage more seriously in the support of telecommuting and Internet access from residences. Performance Systems International, Inc., an MSP and backbone service provider, has been a leader in developing dial-in services and management tools deployed on a national scale.

14.3.2   Other Network Services

Providing basic connectivity is necessary but not sufficient today. The model of the typical new end-user Internet site has shifted from the large enterprise or university, capable of providing its own support for base network applications and user services, to a much smaller, less self-sufficient scale of enterprise, such as a small college or business. The new clients of the MSP most often want and minimally need the following services: domain name service, mail and mail spooling, network news, time synchronization, and consulting services. Responsibility for the provision, coordination and management of these services requires an understanding of their operational requirements, their standardized methods, and the tools needed to support them.

14.3.2.1   *Domain Name Service*

All of an MSP's subscribers require domain name service (DNS). They need access to the root name servers to find other hosts in the network, and the root name servers require access to a name server that provides information about the subscriber's domain. In addition, every subscriber requires at least two servers for his or her domain; a primary name server, usually kept locally, and one that is not part of the subscriber's network.

The primary name server is usually a UNIX system running the Berkeley *bind* program sometimes known as *named* (pronounced *name-dee*). The subscriber configures one or more systems running *named*. These systems become the name servers for the subscriber's network. In addition the subscriber needs to arrange for some other network to provide secondary or backup name service should the primary name servers become unreachable. The MSP should provide this service to the subscriber.

Subscribers that have only mobile hosts cannot provide their own name services. In this case the MSP should provide the primary, as well as secondary, name services.

The Berkeley *bind* program is very common and virtually all domain name servers are based on it. This has the advantage of using the same configuration file format regardless of the platform upon which the program is running. The common-base allows the MSP to provide preformatted configuration files as an additional service to the subscriber. With the tremendous growth of internetworking, the average technical experience of subscribers is decreasing. Providing preformatted configuration files for *named* is helpful in getting new subscribers up and running in a timely fashion.

14.3.2.2 Mail

In most cases (note the exception discussed below), the MSP does not need to provide any special service (other than reliable connectivity) to the subscriber to support network mail service. Mail is usually delivered directly to one or more of the subscriber's systems.

On the other hand, the configuration of electronic mail can be quite difficult. There are many different electronic mail programs that implement the Simple Mail Transfer Protocol (SMTP) used throughout the Internet. The two most popular are sendmail and the Multi-channel Memo Distribution Facility (MMDF). Most systems come with one or the other of these packages.

Sendmail is clearly the most common electronic mail program used on the Internet. The program supports both SMTP and UNIX-to-UNIX Copy (UUCP) mail. There are two major problems with sendmail that make it worthwhile for the MSP to provide configuration assistance to its clients:

1   There are several versions of sendmail in use, all slightly different. The version of send-mail distributed by Sun Microsystems is very close to, but not 100% compatible with, the version currently being distributed by the University of California at Berkeley.

2   The format for the sendmail configuration file (sendmail.cf) is very cryptic, making it easy for the administrator lacking experience with sendmail to make mistakes.

To simplify this problem, the MSP should provide a repository of preconfigured send-mail.cf files for at least, but not limited to, the following system configurations:

1   Stand-alone hosts running Berkeley sendmail

2   Stand-alone hosts running Sun sendmail

3   Unsecure hosts running Berkeley sendmail that attach to a part of the client's network outside of a firewall, and forward mail to an internal system for redistribution

4   Same as Case #3, but for a host running Sun sendmail.

These four configuration files should be sufficiently generic to permit most subscribers to use one or more of them without change.

MMDF is an alternative to sendmail. Unlike sendmail, which is a single, very large program that does all of the mail handling, MMDF is a collection of smaller programs, each of which performs a different function. MMDF also uses many, understandable configuration files, instead of a single, cryptic one. Generally speaking, MMDF is considered to be more secure than sendmail by virtue of having multiple, smaller, more understandable programs.

The MSP should make available to its subscribers a set of logically preconfigured configuration files for MMDF users. This is not as critical as it is with sendmail because the MMDF distribution comes with good documentation that will walk the system administrator through setting up a working system.

More end-user sites, including individuals working from home, are beginning to make use of dialup service. Dialup service implies that the subscriber will not be connected to the network at all times. Other end-user sites have permanent connections but no computers that are both continuously operational and suitable as mail hosts. This makes SMTP generally unsuitable for mail delivery to these sites because SMTP assumes that the recipient system is on the network at all times. What is needed is a mail spooling system, a machine that will store mail until the subscriber's system connects to the network and downloads mail.

For mail spooling there are basically two protocols that will meet the need of store-and-forward mail delivery: the Post Office Protocol (POP) and the UUCP-over-TCP daemon (UUCPD). POP is designed for individual users who wish to pick up their mail from a central mail repository. When the user's system connects to the network, the POP client connects to the POP server on the mail repository. The client sends the user's ID and password, and the server then downloads the mail into the user's system. POP is ideal for mobile hosts that support only one user (laptop computers come to mind here).

For systems that support multiple users and that only occasionally connect to the network, UUCPD is a more efficient mechanism. UUCPD works like UUCP, and allows all the mail for a remote system to be delivered when the remote system connects and requests its mail. Configuration of UUCPD is virtually identical to configuration of ordinary UUCP.

To support these "mail on demand" subscribers, the MSP needs to set up a system to act as a mail repository. This system should support both POP and UUCPD. The mail exchange (MX) records in the DNS database for systems that are not connected to the network full-time should point to the mail repository or mail spooling system. That way, mail from other systems in the Internet destined for an occasionally connected system finds its way to the mail spooling system. Trouble shooting lost or misdirected mail requires that the MSP designate a postmaster, operate file backup and recovery facilities, and provide other mail delivery and support functions normally found in a computer center.

14.3.2.3   Network News

Another important application, probably second in popularity only to electronic mail, is network news (sometimes called USENET news). In the Internet news is delivered to systems using the Network News Transfer Protocol (NNTP). An NNTP server acts as a repository for news in much the same fashion that a mail repository works for mail. Getting news from another system is called "getting a news feed." When a remote system wants to receive news, it connects to the NNTP server and downloads all news articles that it does not already have.

The MSP should maintain a system that will act as an NNTP server. It makes sense for the mail spooling system and the NNTP server to be the same system.

14.3.2.4   Network Time

Another useful service is the Network Time Protocol (NTP). NTP is a mechanism for synchronizing the clocks in most computer systems to a reference standard with a high degree of accuracy (errors of only a few milliseconds between the reference standard and client systems).

There are a number of ways that an MSP can provide this service. The best way is to provide a primary reference system, known in NTP parlance as a *stratum 1 server*, to which client systems can slave their clocks. There are several reference standards, including atomic clocks, and GPS satellites, but the most cost-effective standards are radio-based devices that synchronize to radio stations WWV or WWVB. The National Institute of Standards and Technology (NIST) operates a set of reference standard clocks. The timing information from these reference clocks is transmitted over WWVB at 60 KHz and over WWV at 2.5 MHz, 5 MHz, 10 MHz, and 15 MHz. Since the distance from the WWVB and WWVB stations to the receiving system may be known with great accuracy, the time presented by the reference may be corrected for the propagation time of the time signals. The MSP should provide a *stratum 1* time standard for the subscribers.

14.3.2.5   Consulting Services and Tools

Pre-configuration of mail, news, and NTP is fine, but there will always be subscribers who need more assistance. For these people, the MSP needs to provide consulting services.

It is not necessary for the MSP to provide consulting services directly. The MSP may maintain a list of local consultants, or it may retain the consultants to solve subscriber problems on a case-by-case basis. It may be more convenient for the subscriber if he or she can get all the services in one place. That implies that the MSP should make the services available directly to the subscriber. The methods and tools for providing network application consulting include automated call director systems, the well-known anonymous FTP service for programs and documents, and a wide range of other techniques. Little is yet available in the way of automated or computer-assisted consulting, or expert systems consultants for end-user sites, but the growth in the marketplace is likely to produce opportunities for such products.

14.3.2.6   Documentation and Training

Documentation and training tools have traditionally been the responsibility of the third-tier, end-user site because much of the information important to network users is site-specific. Enterprise networking applications and services vary widely from industry to industry and from business to business, so these require documentation and training tailored to the

CHAPTER 15 ❏ ❏ ❏ ❏

IP Network Performance

JEFFREY C. MOGUL

CONTENTS

CONTENTS   (Continued)

Even when a network appears to be operating correctly, it may often require significant tuning in order to achieve optimal performance. This tuning occurs at all levels of the protocol stack. As such, the topics involved are quite varied.

15.1 INTRODUCTION

One of the trickiest problems in the design and operation of a computer system is to assure its adequate performance. Nowhere is this more of a problem than when the computer system is a network. Network performance is hard to define, hard to measure, and hard to improve. Improvement is not impossible, however, and the purpose of this chapter is to provide some guidance for this.

Obtaining optimal performance from a network implementation requires a far deeper understanding of the technology, and especially of the environment and applications, than is required for simply creating or configuring a correctly operating network. Many books, journals, and conference proceedings have been filled with attempts to understand and improve network performance, and much remains unknown. In a single book, let alone a single chapter, it is impossible to cover all there is to know about the topic, and what is known changes daily. My approach will, instead, be to explain some of the basics of network performance, and to communicate some of the more important specific lessons that have been learned about the performance of IP-family protocols.

To make sense of the discussions in this chapter, you will have to be familiar with the IP-family protocols, with the configuration and use of IP networks, and with the basic concepts of operating systems. Other chapters in this book will serve as a good starting point, but you may need to have the IP specifications (also known as *RFC* documents) available if you aren't already familiar with them. In most cases, practical work in network performance does not require mathematical sophistication, although you might find it helpful if you want to read the theoretical and scientific literature.

15.1.1 Other Reading

The best basic reference on IP technology is the two-volume set *Internetworking with TCP/IP,* by Douglas Comer and David Stevens.[1] Many of the issues discussed in this chapter are covered more completely in these books, the second of which describes an actual implementation in great detail. It may be useful to refer to these books if you are confused by one of my explanations.

Each IP protocol is specified in one or more *RFC* documents. Experience often reveals that an *RFC* is flawed, incomplete, out of date, or ambiguous. The IETF therefore established a working group to review the state of the art and provide expert guidance on what host software should (or should not) do; the results are *Requirements for Internet Hosts—Communication Layers* (*RFC 1122*), and *Requirements for Internet Hosts—Application and Support* (*RFC 1123*).[2] These are more conveniently referred to as the *Host Requirements* documents.

Useful information on practical issues, primarily for managers of UNIX systems, may be found in *System Performance Tuning* by Mike Loukides.[3]

Network performance is the subject of active research. The state of the art can change, literally, from month to month, no doubt making some of what I've written here obsolete before it is printed. If you want to keep up with current research on network performance, these are some of the most interesting publications:

- *Proceedings of the SIGCOMM Symposia on Communications Architecture and Protocols.* The preeminent conference on computer networking, the annual ACM SIGCOMM

(Special Interest Group on Data Communication) Symposium is the traditional venue for presenting recent research results.

- *Computer Communications Review*: SIGCOMM's quarterly newsletter, while not as selective as the SIGCOMM conference, often publishes high-quality research, and on a shorter publication cycle.

- *Internetworking: Research and Experience*: A relatively new journal devoted to issues in internetworking.

- *IEEE Transactions on Communications*, *ACM Transactions on Computer Systems*: These "archival" journals carry more formal, and often more abstract, papers than the SIG-COMM publications. The publication lead times are longer, because the review process is more stringent. Relatively few of these papers are specific to IP, perhaps because IP researchers would rather see their work in print quickly than in the more prestigious journals.

15.2   GENERAL ISSUES

15.2.1   What is "Performance?"

What do we mean when we talk about the performance of a car or a stereo system? A high-performance car is one that "goes fast;" a high-performance stereo is one that "sounds good." But the terms *goes fast* and *sounds good* are not as simply defined as they might seem. Do we call a car faster if it has a higher top speed, or if it accelerates quicker? Do we call a stereo better if it has a higher top volume, or if it can pick up a weaker FM station without static? And what about the performance of, say, a city bus? We only care about the performance of the bus when it becomes inadequate (say, when it can't reach the top of a steep hill).

In short, the definition of a system's performance depends intimately on how we are using the system. It is no different for networks: for some applications, we care mostly about how many bits per second we can move from end to end, and for other applications we care about how long it takes to get a single bit from one place to another. In many cases, we don't really care at all about the network's performance, as long as it isn't acting as a bottleneck. So sometimes we care more about maximizing bandwidth, sometimes about minimizing latency, and sometimes we only care that both are "good enough."

15.2.2   The Curse of Graceful Degradation

We design our network protocols and implementations to be robust in the face of failures. That means that a temporary failure (such as a corrupted packet) at one layer is reflected in higher layers, not as a failure, but as a decrease in performance. Such *graceful degradation* is a valuable property, but it can mask the symptoms of problems in the network; a network

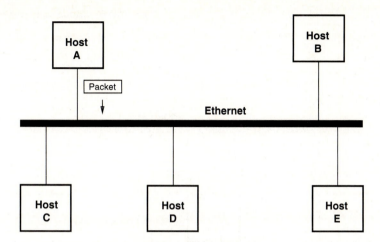

Figure 15.1 One host trying to send a packet

manager has to look for these problems before the users complain, lest another low-level failure result in complete malfunction.

Graceful degradation also means that the performance of a system can "rot" without any apparent cause. For example, if a terminator is left off the end of a section of thinwire Ethernet, resulting in the loss of, say, half of all packets, nothing on the network will necessarily fail, but performance may go down by an order of magnitude. Since the problem results in no immediate failure, it might not be noticed for hours, or even days, by which time it will be hard to remember who was working on which section of cable.

Sometimes the problem masked by graceful degradation is not a fault, but simply an unavoidable aspect of the underlying network. A user might have unwittingly mounted an NFS file system from a server at the other end of a slow link, or a router might be dropping packets because it is congested. In such cases, while it may be possible to solve the underlying problem, it is also important that the upper layers adapt to changes in the parameters of the network (or that users adapt their expectations of what can be accomplished).

Network performance is thus entangled with network reliability, which itself is the topic of entire books. I will have to avoid a detailed discussion of reliability, but one should note that many issues in network performance arise because our networks are not entirely reliable at all levels. When errors occur or when expectations are unmet, performance may suffer: reliable network protocols are a way to turn errors into delays.[*]

15.2.3 Bandwidth, Latency, and Queueing Delays

Consider the simplified network shown in Figure 15.1. Five hosts are attached to an Ethernet, and Host *A* is about to send a packet (perhaps to Host *B*). Let us suppose that the

---

[*] Thanks to Brian Reid for this aphorism.

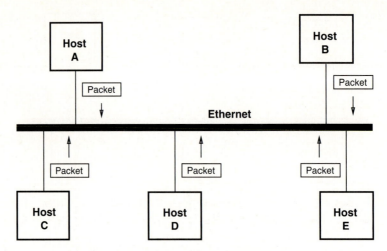

Figure 15.2   Five hosts, each trying to send a packet

packet contains 1212 bytes of data (because this means that it takes exactly 1 millisecond to transmit this packet on an Ethernet). Let us also assume that all the hosts are infinitely fast; that is, that almost no CPU time is required to send or receive a packet.

How long will it be before Host *B* has received the packet and can use its contents? In this case, the only delay is the time it takes to move the bits over the Ethernet, so Host *B* will have the packet exactly 1 millisecond after Host *A* decides to send it.

Now consider the situation in Figure 15.2. All five hosts simultaneously try to send a packet of 1212 bytes, but the Ethernet can only accept one packet at a time. What is the delay between Host *A* and Host *B* in this case?

To see what is going on, we can abstract the picture in Figure 15.2 to depict a queue of packets waiting to be transmitted, as in Figure 15.3. Since the Ethernet is probabilistic, we don't know the order in which the hosts will be able to send their packets, so let us assume the worst case for Host *A*. It will then have to wait for the other four hosts to complete sending their packets before it gets a chance to transmit, so the net delay will be 5 milliseconds rather than 1 millisecond. (This ignores the additional delay imposed by contention for the Ethernet; if we assume that the cable is quite short, the contention delay will be negligible.)

But the situation is even worse than this. Suppose that the applications on each host think they can get the full bandwidth of the Ethernet, and each tell their systems to send a packet once per millisecond. Since this is five times the load that the network can absorb, the queue will grow arbitrarily large, and the transmit delays will become arbitrarily long. This situation is known as *congestion*. Because queues never have infinite storage available, at some point packets will have to be dropped.[*]

---

[*]   And if the queues could grow to infinite length, so would the delays.[4]

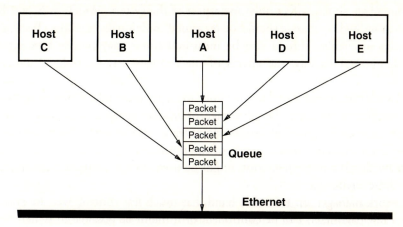

Figure 15.3   Queue abstraction of Figure 15.2

Congestion thus leads to increased delays, and sometimes to packet loss; so an important aspect of network design is how one manages to avoid congestion. Since one cannot always afford to engineer an entire network with excess capacity, one theme of this chapter will be how to avoid or recover from congestion when the offered load is more than the network can handle.

15.2.4   Measurement Methods

Accurate measurements of network behavior are necessary when trying to tune or predict network performance. What one expects to be happening on a network is not always what is actually going on, and direct observation is required to ensure that one's theoretical understanding is aligned with reality. Network implementors, as well as network managers, need to pay constant attention to various measures of network performance. In Section 15.3, I will discuss some common tools and techniques for network performance analysis.

15.2.5   Tuning Methods

When measurement reveals that performance goals are not being met, some aspect of the network must be tuned to improve things. This is an iterative process, consisting of the following cycle:

- Measure the network.

- Analyze and understand the results.

- Change something.

Repeat until performance is adequate.

in Boston and do a remote procedure call on a server in San Francisco, you will have to wait at least 30 milliseconds no matter how fast your computers and network are.

Round-trip delays are one of the most important limiting factors in protocol performance. Even a transport protocol that can exchange many data packets during each round-trip delay, such as TCP, must wait for an entire round-trip delay when doing such tasks as connection establishment and termination, and when discovering and responding to errors.

Bigger packets are better

When sending a given amount of data, it is better to break it into a small number of large packets rather than into a large number of small packets. Each packet imposes overhead on the network (packet headers), routers (routing decisions), and end hosts (protocol processing and device interrupts). These per-packet overheads are in addition to any per-byte overheads, and so the fewer the packets, the lower the total overhead.

There are times when large packets are not appropriate. Use of excessively large IP packets may cause fragmentation, which is bad (see Section 15.7.5). Also, when a large packet is transmitted over a slow link, it delays the transmission of small packets, and so may harm interactive response time (*RFC 1144*).[5]

Avoid timeouts and retransmissions

The datagram model behind the design of IP means that low-level packet transport is unreliable, and so to provide reliable services higher layers must detect packet loss by using timeouts. Timeouts are bad for performance, because each time one occurs it means that network resources have been idle for a lengthy period, almost certainly at least one round-trip delay.

This may make throughput unbearably slow. For example, suppose that when a connection is operating properly, it can move 100 packets per second. Let us also suppose that the appropriate timeout interval for this connection is 1 second. If just 1% of the packets are lost, then after every 99 packets (on the average) the connection will pause for a second, thus halving the total throughput. If one out of ten packets is lost, the total throughput will drop by almost 90%. As the probability of timeout increases, throughput drops precipitously.

Congestion avoidance is better than congestion recovery

When a network is congested, packets are lost. To avoid congestion, it may be necessary to reduce the rate at which connections send data, but a network operating just below the point of congestion will be more efficient than if it is congested. Each packet that is lost due to congestion is wasted effort, work that will have to be done twice. The network bandwidth and router resources consumed by lost packets are most precious during congestion, when they are in short supply.

Congestion avoidance is like insurance: you pay a little up front (reducing transmission rate) to avoid a disaster later on (packet loss caused by congestion).

Fewer hops is better

Each time a packet passes through a router, it is delayed at least briefly. Other things being equal, the packet will arrive sooner at its destination if it traverses fewer hops.

Of course, other things are not always equal. A low-hop route might be more congested, or use lower-bandwidth links, than a route with more hops. But hop count is a reasonable metric for measuring the cost of a path, in the absence of other information.

CPU speed is more important than LAN speed

Experience has shown that it is hard to get an end-host to take full advantage of a high-speed network link. The bottleneck in local-area networking is often the speed of the CPU, not the speed of the LAN.

The important aspect of CPU speed is not how fast a CPU can do a floating-point multiplication (TCP can be implemented without *any* floating-point operations), but rather how fast it can move bytes from one place to another. The most expensive part of handling a TCP packet is not the protocol header processing, but the checksum computation, and most of this cost comes from moving the data.[6]

Use a fast path for the common cases

Network protocols must be designed to deal with all sorts of error conditions and exceptions. These special cases can make the code quite complex and inefficient, yet may occur infrequently. By identifying the common case, coding an efficient implementation for that case, and then finding a cheap way to detect when a special case has occurred, one can improve the performance for the common case without affecting the correctness of the implementation. The performance in the exceptional case might be slightly worse, but since this is infrequent nobody will notice.

Performance issues cross layer boundaries

Many people view layered architectures as a magical solution to problems in networking. Get the layer-to-layer interfaces right, they say, and you can safely implement each layer without thinking about the messy details of the other ones.

People who make networks work pay no attention to such nonsense. True, layered architectures provide valuable structure, and layered implementations are usually easier to get right, but there are times when strict adherence to layering gets in the way of making things work or making them work well.

For example, it simply is not possible to produce a good implementation of a transport protocol, such as TCP or Sun's RPC, without considering the size of the packets that can be carried at the data link layer. It may be possible to get something to work, but it won't work well. Crowcroft et al. relate a horror story about the performance of an oblivious layering of RPC over TCP.[7]

When queues get long, the system must become more efficient

Many systems tend to work less efficiently when they become overloaded. This is terrible, because it reduces throughput at precisely the time when it is most important to drain the queue as fast as possible, causing the queue to grow instead of shrink. A positive feedback loop of this sort results in congestive collapse. Solutions include the use of algorithms that are linear, or better, in the size of the queue (instead of quadratic or exponential), and algorithms that batch multiple tasks together so as to amortize overhead costs.

Batching has the nice property that throughput actually rises with increasing load. For example, an X Window System server that can read many X requests in one system call will perform fewer system calls per request under heavy loads than under light loads, when it might have to do one call to receive each request.

15.3 MEASUREMENT TOOLS AND METHODS

There are many kinds of tools available for measuring network performance, which is another way of saying that no one tool is really satisfactory. Performance problems come in various forms, and different approaches must be used for each form.

Measurements of real systems can be made in several ways. One might do direct measurement of the time it takes to complete a task, such as transferring a file from one host to another. One might examine the counters maintained by a router to determine the amount of traffic that it handles, and how often it has to drop packets because of overload. One might use a network monitor to measure the load on a LAN, or trace a connection to find out how long it takes for one host to acknowledge the packets sent by another.

15.3.1 Fundamentals of Performance Analysis

The field of computer systems performance analysis is yet another topic worthy of entire books. Few people are truly expert at it, but it isn't that hard to at least be honest about your skills, and so understand the limitations of the results you get.

Some of the fundamentals of good performance analysis, as described in Raj Jain's book *The Art of Computer Systems Performance Analysis*,[8] are:

- Select appropriate evaluation techniques, performance metrics, and workloads.

- Conduct performance measurements or simulations correctly.

- Use proper statistical techniques.

- Design experiments to provide the most information with the least effort.

- Use simple queuing models when appropriate.

Rather than go into detail about the field, since I don't have enough space (and I'm not an expert), I will list a few pitfalls to avoid:

Make sure you have a big enough sample

One measurement is usually not enough to provide accurate information about how well a system performs. Network software isn't always deterministic, and pure luck may cause sizable variations in your measurements. Also, network loads change from second to second, and from day to day, and what takes 5 seconds when the load is low might take 60 seconds when the load is high.

Compensate for poor clock resolution

If you are measuring short operations, such as the time it takes to transfer one packet, you must also be careful about the time resolution of your measurements. Many operating systems provide timing facilities that are incapable of resolving events less than a few milliseconds apart. For example, if your system's clock ticks at 100 Hz, and you are measuring the time it takes to *ping* a nearby host that is actually 1 millisecond away, you might discover that the round-trip time reported for most of the packets is zero (because the clock will not have ticked during the 2-millisecond round trip). To avoid this problem, you may have to repeat the operation many times and measure the total elapsed time, then divide that by the repetition count.

Make sure your samples are characteristic

A common mistake is to measure one mode of use when the system is sometimes used in a different way. For example, if you only measure during working hours, because you believe that is the busiest part of the day, you might not discover that the highest load takes place at 1:00 AM when all your workstations' disks are backed up over the network.

Are you controlling all the variables?

Sometimes a series of measurements may show variation due to causes irrelevant to what you are trying to measure. For example, if you are measuring the time it takes to transfer a file from one system to another, you might find a lot of variation arises because the disk on the target system is in heavy use during some samples and not during others. You might be able to avoid this by obtaining stand-alone access to the systems under test, or perhaps by bypassing irrelevant stages of the transfer. For example, users of UNIX systems could store files to `/dev/null`, to avoid doing any disk writes.

Watch out for caching effects

Caching is one of the most important techniques used to improve performance, but it can also complicate the measurement of performance. You should understand where caches exist in the system, and decide if you want to measure the performance of the caches, or of the uncached operations.

For example, if you are measuring file transfer performance, and you want to avoid measuring the cost of disk reads, you can use caching to your advantage, if the file being transferred fits into the file system cache on the source machine. The first time you do the transfer, the file might not be resident in the cache (this is called a *cold-cache* measurement) but if subsequent transfers are done right away, and no other large files replace your file in the cache, then these *warm-cache* measurements will omit most of the cost of disk-reading, and will better reflect the actual network performance.

If, on the other hand, you want to measure the cold-cache performance, you may be able to ensure that the source file is not preloaded in the file-system cache, by reading a different, large file before performing your measurement.

Either way, taking advantage of the cache behavior requires some understanding of how the cache works. It may be difficult to guarantee that a file is entirely preloaded into (or entirely absent from) the cache.

You might be more concerned with the performance of a cache than with the performance of the rest of the network. For example, you may want to know how well the name-resolution cache performs in an implementation of the Domain Name System. To "measure" this performance, you will need to know the costs of a cache hit and a cache miss (and you will need to know how variable those costs are), as well as the cache hit rate for a properly chosen workload. Without those three values, you cannot properly characterize the actual cache performance.

It can be difficult to measure cold-cache performance (or cache-miss cost) when the operation being measured is quite brief. As I noted earlier, accurate timing of brief operations is hard unless you do them repetitively, but repetitive operations, by their nature, may cause warm-cache behavior.

For example, to measure the cost of an ARP-cache miss, which might be on the order of a millisecond or less, one cannot simply *ping* the same host over and over (since this would reflect warm-cache behavior), and it might not be practical to invoke an explicit cache-flush command (because this might take so much longer than the cache-miss that it would overwhelm your measurements of the cache-miss time). However, if you know that there are 200 hosts on your network and you *ping* each of them once (after first flushing the ARP cache) then you will end up with 200 cold-cache measurements in a row, probably a large enough sample to measure with a low-resolution clock.

Measure the right thing

Since it's impossible to measure everything, one has to make decisions about what to measure based on assumptions about a network and its workload. One should be careful not to make fragile assumptions, lest they be wrong and result in useless measurements.

For example, when you measure the time it takes to transfer a file across a network, are you measuring the speed of the network, or are you actually measuring the speed of a badly designed interface that may not run at full network speed?

Or, if you measure the time it takes to transfer a megabyte, but the dominant use of your network is to transfer 1-Kbyte files, you may be misled about the usable performance. The performance of long connections should be dominated by the available bandwidth; the performance of short connections is usually dominated by the cost of connection setup, which depends more on end-to-end latency than on bandwidth.

For example, to transfer 1 Kbyte over a T3 (45 Mbits/sec) network takes about 180 microseconds for network occupancy. Even though transfer may take only a single exchange of packets, if the hosts are more than about 25 km apart, the speed of light imposes more latency than the network bandwidth. Measuring the bulk-transfer bandwidth would be misleading if the main use of this network is for short, RPC-style transfers.

Be careful when extrapolating

It is often necessary to predict system performance from a set of measurements taken under different conditions. This has to be done carefully, because the measurements may not scale linearly, or because they may not be applicable when the parameters change. A well-tuned system may become more efficient under increasing load, although it might collapse when completely overloaded. A badly tuned system may become less efficient as the load increases. Either way, measuring performance at one load level does not allow you to extrapolate its performance at another load.

Beware of the dangers of inappropriate summarization of data. Many people want to reduce a complex set of measurements to a single number, so that they can say that one system is better than another without actually having to think. (Some people do this to hide the fact that one system is worse than another.) For example, it would be wrong to consider solely the maximum performance of a system if all alternatives provide adequate performance, and one is a lot cheaper. On the other hand, price/performance ratios are worthless if only one of the alternatives is capable of doing the job. (What good is a system that uses Monday's data to provide a forecast of Tuesday's weather, if the result won't be available until Wednesday?)

If you are interested in pursuing the topic of performance analysis in more detail, you might want to read *Telecommunications Networks: Protocols, Modeling and Analysis* by Mischa Schwartz.[9]

15.3.2   Simulation and Modeling

It is not always possible to obtain measurements of the actual system under actual loads. You might be trying to predict system response to future loads, to choose between several alternatives, or to measure something that cannot directly be observed in the real system. In such circumstances, it may be more appropriate to measure a simulation of the network, or to devise an abstract model, which can then be used to calculate the desired information.

Good simulations depend on an accurate description of the network and workload, and simulation software can be complex. (Such software, some of it designed specifically for analyzing networks, can be purchased from a number of vendors, and there are also some free simulators available from research institutions.) On the other hand, if the right parameters are chosen, it takes relatively little mathematical sophistication to use a simulation to analyze the performance of complex systems. A simulator even lets you measure some things, such as queue lengths, that may be impossible to measure in a real system.

To use a model, you don't need any fancy software or a lot of computer time; you just need a good understanding of the system and some mathematical skills. The idea is to capture the essential behavior of the system in an abstraction that is mathematically tractable. Queueing models are quite common, since the nature of network performance often boils down to the behavior of the various queues in the system. The requirement for tractability usually means that drastic simplifications must be made, both in the design of the model and in the shape of the workload. While it is not impossible to come up with correct simplifications, it is easy to get them wrong, and so the predictions of a model should always be validated against as many real-system measurements as possible.

More information on the use of queueing models may be found in *Quantitative System Performance: Computer Systems Analysis Using Queueing Network Models* by Lazowska, Zahorjan, Graham, and Sevcik.[10]

15.3.3 Benchmarking

Benchmark results are often a critical part of the decision to purchase one system instead of another. While it might be possible to decide between simple components, such as disk drives or memory, based solely on their specifications, for more complex systems one cannot easily derive performance from specifications, and benchmarking is necessary to discover performance under typical loads.

The problem with benchmarks is that they are open to manipulation and misinterpretation. (It has been said that there are lies, damned lies, and benchmarks.) System vendors often report benchmark results in their sales literature, and because competition over performance is so stiff, vendors use every possible trick to make their results look as good as possible. Even if the benchmark tests themselves are honest, the pressure to do well on benchmarks sometimes drives a vendor to design a system specifically for its performance on well-known benchmarks, and perhaps to ignore the consequences for other workloads.

Since some vendors would rather compete on the basis of honest performance, consortia have been formed to create useful benchmarks, designed to be hard to manipulate. For example, the TPC/A transaction-processing benchmark[11] requires that the number of (simulated) users for a benchmark run scale with the speed of the system. (Actual high-performance transaction systems have lots of users, and so this rule ensures that the performance will be properly balanced.) As of this writing, relatively few benchmark consortia have been formed in the networking area; one notable example is the NFS benchmark developed by the LADDIS consortium.

In spite of the pitfalls, benchmark results can still be valuable if employed with care. You should consider whether the workload used by the benchmark is similar to the way you will be using the system, and you should make sure that the system configuration used by the benchmark is similar to what you can afford. The best benchmark is to measure the system in question in your actual environment; many vendors are willing to lend you equipment for you to run tests on, if you intend to make a major purchase.

15.3.4 Network Management Systems

The advent of SNMP-based network management systems has made it a lot easier to perform network measurements on IP networks. Although in some cases, SNMP has encouraged implementors to provide more performance information, mostly it was already available, and SNMP has simply made it easier to obtain. Virtually all vendors of IP systems now support SNMP, and there are many SNMP-based management stations on the market. (See Chapter 12, Network Management, for a more complete discussion of SNMP.)

Some SNMP Management Information Base (MIB) variables provide event rates, but more typically they provide performance information in the form of counter values. A counter might show the number of packets passed, or the number of errors encountered; to turn these values into rates requires that the management station sample the counter more than once, at known intervals, and divide the difference in counter value by the length of the time interval.

SNMP is best suited to provide long-term performance information about a network, such as might be used for capacity planning. It is less useful for doing short-term performance measurements.

SNMP (or any network management protocol) works by interacting with a host, router, bridge, etc., to obtain the value of predefined variables. This has several drawbacks:

- The system being measured must support SNMP. While most network resources with embedded processing power can or do support SNMP, not all resources have a CPU. For example, an Ethernet is simply a piece of cable, so there is no way for an SNMP management station to ask an Ethernet for performance information.

- The network must be functional. Although SNMP interactions are "simple," they require a minimal level of functionality from the network. If the network is suffering from serious congestion, for example, it may not be possible to use SNMP to discover what is causing the congestion if the congestion makes it too hard to exchange SNMP packets. It is also possible that a failing system could provide wrong values to SNMP, thus misleading the network manager as to the cause of a performance problem.

- The information required must be defined in a MIB. The variables returned by SNMP are part of a tree-structured database. Portions of this database, called MIBs, exist for various kinds of network entities. To support multivendor interoperability, the structure of each MIB must be agreed upon, a process that can take years of committee work. Information not described in a MIB implemented by the system being queried is unavailable to SNMP, so at times SNMP will not be able to provide the detail that you need.

- The SNMP interaction may change what is being measured. When an SNMP management station fetches a value from a network resource, it uses the network to do so, and thus puts a load on both the network and the resource being queried. On a slow network link, or on an overloaded host (especially if SNMP authentication is used) the SNMP load could be a significant fraction of the total load. SNMP thus cannot provide an exact picture of what the network would be doing if you weren't watching it.

15.3.5 Network Monitors

One way of avoiding the problems associated with using SNMP for performance measurement is to use network monitoring. Network monitoring is the collection of packets on a broadcast LAN by a host other than their destination without the active involvement of source and destination hosts, and presentation of packet information in a useful form.

Because network monitoring is a passive approach, it can avoid the problems of SNMP. For example, if you want to know the average utilization of an Ethernet during a given period of time, a monitor can capture all the packets sent during that period, counting them and the number of bytes they contain; applying a simple formula then provides the average utilization. None of the hosts have to "support" this activity, and it places no added load on the network. It even works when the network is overloaded (although to get an accurate measure of Ethernet load, as opposed to utilization, the monitor also has to measure the number and size of Ethernet collision fragments).

Typical performance-related functions of network monitors include:

- Measurement of LAN load averages

- Measurement of load peaks

- Identification of most-active packet sources

- Measurement of LAN error rates.

Most network monitors also are able to parse protocol headers at various levels of the protocol stack, usually up to TCP, and sometimes NFS. This allows them to report more complex information, such as the rate of TCP retransmissions, the rate at which new connections are made, or the breakdown of NFS requests by operation type or file system.

Network monitors can also be used as performance debugging tools, because they can be used to trace the packets exchanged as part of a specific network interaction. For example, if you are having trouble with TCP connections between a pair of hosts, a packet trace made with a network monitor may reveal excessive retransmissions, or the wrong choice of packet size.

Network monitoring is not a perfect solution. While the approach is quite flexible in theory, in practice if you want to measure some obscure aspect of network performance you may have to write the monitoring software yourself. This is often easier than trying to modify existing host software to report novel information, but it does require some effort and skill.

Because a network monitor must examine every packet on the network, even though it may decide to ignore most of them, the monitor system has to meet stringent performance requirements. Some systems can only keep up with the network if the load is below a certain threshold, which may limit their utility during conditions of heavy load. When you purchase or configure a monitoring system, you should find out if it will have adequate performance. Nowadays, it is not hard to design a monitor that can keep up with an Ethernet, but it may be a while before affordable monitors can capture all the packets from a heavily loaded FDDI network.

When using a network monitor to obtain packet traces, it may be necessary to store thousands or even millions of packet headers for later examination. Some stand-alone monitors have limited storage capacity; monitors based on high-performance workstations may be able to store traces into disk files at a sufficient rate to keep up with the network.

For more information about network monitoring, you might want to read the book *Network Monitoring Explained*, by Chiu and Sudama.[12]

15.3.5.1 *Monitoring Mesh-connected LANs*

Most current LANs are shared-channel networks, meaning that only one packet can be in transit at any given time, and at any point on the network one can see all the packets go by (at least, on segments without an intervening router or bridge). This makes network monitoring simple; you can attach a monitor anywhere on the LAN, and it will see all the packets. Because many shared-channel systems do not scale well, and because their aggregate capacity is limited to what can be carried over the single shared channel, future LANs may be built as meshes of point-to-point links connected by active switches.[13] Mesh-connected LANs can carry many packets at once, which is good for the users but makes network monitoring much harder. They also do not provide a single point where one can attach a network monitor and hope to see all the packets. Innovations in the design of mesh-connected LANs and LAN monitors may solve this problem.

15.3.5.2 *Commercial Network Monitors*

Many vendors sell network monitors that support IP-family protocols; most of these products also support other protocol families, such as AppleTalk, DECnet, OSI, and various PC-LAN protocols. Each product has its own features and drawbacks, and new products or revisions show up all the time. I will list a selection here, but I cannot possibly be comprehensive or up to date. Trade publications, such as *Data Communications*, often run articles surveying the market.

Commercial monitors range in price from about $1000 to more than ten times that much. They come in three basic categories: software-only packages, to run on existing systems; PC-based turnkey (hardware and software) packages; and special-purpose hardware designs.

The cheapest are the software-only packages. These include:

- LANWatch™ from FTP Software, for MS DOS

- NetMatrix from Matrix Computer Systems, for SPARC systems

- Protolyzer from ProTools, for OS/2

- NetVisualize™ from Silicon Graphics, for SGI IRIX systems

- NetScope from Qualix, for SPARC systems.

The bulk of the products are turnkey systems based on PC hardware, but often incorporating special-purpose network interfaces and packaging. These include:

- LANview from Cabletron Systems

- Sniffer from Network General

- LANalyzer from Novell

- ChameLAN from Tekelec

- DA-30 from Wandel & Goltermann.

Some vendors produce special-purpose hardware, in order to obtain the best possible performance. These include:

- TRAKKER™ from Concord Communications

- LAN Traffic Monitor from Digital Equipment Corporation

- Ether Meter® from Network Application Technology

- LanProbe from Hewlett-Packard

- The Network Professor® from Technically Elite Concepts

- SpiderProbe from Spider Systems.

Many network monitoring products can be used in a "remote" mode, allowing a network manager to place one on each LAN segment of a large network and then to collect their data from a central monitoring point. Some remote monitors communicate over the network; others use dedicated serial links, which adds complexity but may be more useful when the network is inoperable.

15.3.5.3 Free Network Monitors

Several useful network monitoring programs for use on general-purpose workstations or PCs are publicly available. You can consult the NOCTools catalog (*RFC 1147*)[14] for a lengthy list, but I will describe three of the most useful ones here.

The program[15] tcpdump captures, filters, and prints packet headers for many IP protocols, as well as for some popular LAN protocols and a few non-IP protocols. Its filtering mechanism, while somewhat confusing at first, is extremely flexible and can be used to find tiny needles in large haystacks. For example, this tcpdump command:

    tcpdump ip host nic.ddn.mil and tcp port 20

asks for all the tcp packets to or from host NIC.DDN.MIL on port 20 (which is the FTP-DATA) port. When a host on the local LAN (Jove) then does an FTP transfer of a short file, the following trace shows the entire connection:

```
15:31:06.876 NIC.DDN.MIL.20 > Jove.1413: S 155968:155968(0) win 24576
15:31:06.884 Jove.1413 > NIC.DDN.MIL.20: S 124019:124019(0) ack 155969 win 4096
15:31:07.013 NIC.DDN.MIL.20 > Jove.1413:. ack 1 win 24576
15:31:07.048 NIC.DDN.MIL.20 > Jove.1413:. 1:513(512) ack 1 win 24576
15:31:07.059 Jove.1413 > NIC.DDN.MIL.20:. ack 513 win 3584
15:31:07.188 NIC.DDN.MIL.20 > Jove.1413:. 513:1025(512) ack 1 win 24576
15:31:07.192 Jove.1413 > NIC.DDN.MIL.20:. ack 1025 win 4096
15:31:07.196 NIC.DDN.MIL.20 > Jove.1413:. 1025:1537(512) ack 1 win 24576
15:31:07.259 Jove.1413 > NIC.DDN.MIL.20:. ack 1537 win 4096
15:31:07.321 NIC.DDN.MIL.20 > Jove.1413:. 1537:2049(512) ack 1 win 24576
15:31:07.325 NIC.DDN.MIL.20 > Jove.1413:. 2049:2561(512) ack 1 win 24576
15:31:07.333 Jove.1413 > NIC.DDN.MIL.20:. ack 2561 win 4096
15:31:07.388 NIC.DDN.MIL.20 > Jove.1413:. 2561:3073(512) ack 1 win 24576
15:31:07.388 NIC.DDN.MIL.20 > Jove.1413: FP 3073:3145(72) ack 1 win 24576
15:31:07.395 Jove.1413 > NIC.DDN.MIL.20:. ack 3146 win 3512
15:31:07.403 Jove.1413 > NIC.DDN.MIL.20: F 1:1(0) ack 3146 win 4096
15:31:07.501 NIC.DDN.MIL.20 > Jove.1413:. ack 2 win 24576
```

The columns from left to right give the time the packet was captured; the source host; and port number; a greater-than symbol, indicating the direction of packet flow; the destination host and port number; symbols abbreviating the TCP Flags field; and an indication of the relative sequence numbers, amount of data transferred, the relative acknowledgement number, and the advertised window size.

From this trace one can discover a few things such as the effective window size (NIC.DDN.MIL seems to transmit 1024 bytes at a time, even though Jove is advertising a window of 4096 bytes), and the approximate round-trip time (about 110 milliseconds, as measured from the receipt of the first FIN packet to the receipt of the acknowledgment for the second FIN packet).

Using a similar tcpdump command while transferring a 327-Kbyte file produces a much longer trace, which would be tedious to analyze by hand. Instead, we can process the trace

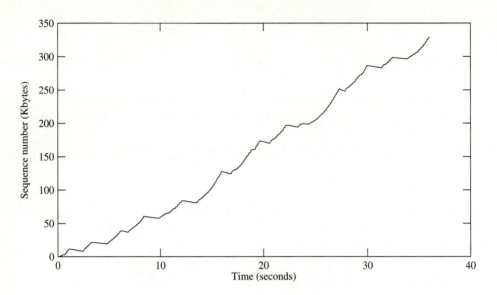

Figure 15.4   Plot of sequence number versus time

to produce a graph of sequence number versus time, as shown in Figure 15.4. We will return to analyze the meaning of such plots in Section 15.8.

While tcpdump concentrates on displaying information about individual connections, a software package called NNStat[16] is designed to collect statistics about the IP traffic flowing on a LAN. NNStat uses a powerful language to describe which packets should be counted, and in what form the counts should be maintained. You can obtain the relative frequencies of certain kinds of packets, a histogram on a particular value, or a matrix showing traffic flows between all known sources and destinations, and several other kinds of statistical measures.

For example, using this parameter file:

```
## Enumerations for certain label values are defined elsewhere
##
include parm.enum

## Create statistical objects and attach them to fields ##
attach {
  record ICMP.type in ICMP freq-all; # Frequency of ICMP types
  record IP.protocol in IP.protos freq-all; # Frequency of IPprotocols
record IP.length in IP.lens hist-pwr2(10); # Histogram of IP datagram sizes
  }
```

after a few minutes of gathering statistics, I obtained this report (I've put boxes around the interesting stuff):

OBJECT: IP.lens Class= hist-pwr2 [Created: 16:34:52 01-09-92] ReadTime: 16:41:14 01-09-92, ClearTime: 16:34:52 01-09-92 (@-382sec)
Total Count= 71117 (+0 orphans)
Avg= 146 Min= 39 Max= 1500

```
[0-9]= 0
[10-19]= 0
[20-39]= 2
[40-79]= 41043
[80-159]= 22146
[160-319]= 4091
[320-639]= 1327
[640-1279]= 550
[1280-2559]= 1958
[2560-5119]= 0
```

OBJECT: IP.protos Class= freq-all [Created: 16:34:52 01-09-92]
ReadTime: 16:41:14 01-09-92, ClearTime: 16:34:52 01-09-92 (@-382sec)
Total Count= 71117 (+0 orphans)
#bins = 3

```
[17 "UDP"]= 38348 (53.9%) @-0sec
[6 "TCP"]= 32653 (45.9%) @-0sec
[1 "ICMP"]= 116 (0.2%) @-1sec
```

OBJECT: ICMP Class= freq-all [Created: 16:34:52 01-09-92]
ReadTime: 16:41:14 01-09-92, ClearTime: 16:34:52 01-09-92 (@-382sec)
Total Count= 116 (+0 orphans)
#bins = 3

```
[8 "Echo Req"]= 53 (45.7%) @-13sec
[0 "Echo Rep"]= 42 (36.2%) @-13sec
[3 "Dest Unreach"]= 21 (18.1%) @-1sec
```

We can see from IP.lens that most IP packets carry under 160 bytes (although there is a small peak above 1280 bytes, from IP.protos, that the traffic is pretty evenly split between UDP and TCP packets, and that most of the few ICMP packets sent during this period were Echo Requests or Replies.

My final example is a program called nfswatch,[17] which provides a dynamic display of NFS activity on a character-cell terminal. nfswatch understands enough about the arcana of NFS and the kernel that it is able to delve into the NFS RPC messages and extract information about what operations are being performed on what files. (This means that porting nfswatch to a new system requires some understanding of kernel data structures.)

Several different displays can be produced. This one

gnomea.pa.dec.com	Thu Jan 9 17:00:54 1992	Elapsed time: 00:01:30	
Interval packets:	2470 (network)	658 (to host)	0 (dropped)
Total packets:	29083 (network)	1314 (to host)	1039(dropped)

Monitoring packets from interface ln0

	int	pct	total		int	pct	total
ND Read	0	0%	0	TCP Packets	3	0%	26
ND Write	0	0%	0	UDP Packets	638	97%	1159
NFS Read	624	95%	983	ICMP Packets	0	0%	0
NFS Write	0	0%	0	Routing Control	11	2%	75
NFS Mount	0	0%	1	Address Resolution	5	1%	35
Yellow Pages/NIS	0	0%	0	Reverse Addr Reso	0	0%	0
RPC Authorization	0	0%	0	Ethernet Broadcas	18	3%	154
Other RPC Packets	0	0%	2	Other Packets	12	2%	94

4 file systems

File Sys	int	pct	total	File Sys	int	pct	total
/	0	0%	0				
/gnomea_a1	624	100%	983				
/usr	0	0%	0				
/var	0	0%	0				

shows that for the server being monitored (gnomea.pa.dec.com), during the monitoring interval all the NFS operations were done on file system /gnomea_a1. This next example, somewhat abbreviated:

37 client hosts[13 not displayed]   more->

Client host	int	pct	total	Client host	int	pct	total
eustace	9	4%	259	jdion	7	3%	278
nemesis	9	4%	220	loinaz	7	3%	260
evans	8	4%	288	menon	7	3%	237
sutter	8	4%	273	dinosaur	7	3%	223
fitch	8	4%	265	jennifer	7	3%	222
ouster	8	4%	263	augustus	7	3%	221
tadpole	8	4%	261	emanon	7	3%	221
turrini	8	4%	259	haddad	7	3%	220
acevedo	8	4%	221	mcfarling	7	3%	220
pluto	8	4%	220	norm	7	3%	219
morbo	8	4%	219	russell	7	3%	219
chief	8	4%	218	wrl463	7	3%	218

shows the activity (for a different server) broken down by client host, in declining order of operation rate. A final abbreviated example:

22 file systems

File Sys	int	pct	total	File Sys	int	pct	total
wrl(21,24)	268	86%	1795	donald(21,18)	1	0%	1
borg(21,3)	10	3%	69	nsl(23,18)	1	0%	1
wrl(21,34)	7	2%	56	vlsi(21,5)	1	0%	1

nsl(23,10)	6	2%	6	torrey(21,43)	1	0%	1
borg(21,5)	5	2%	41	gilroy(9,39)	1	0%	1
jove(9,26)	5	2%	5	jove(9,50)	1	0%	1
gatekeeper(23,10)	1	0%	3	wrl(21,27)	0	0%	65
gilroy(9,50)	1	0%	1	jove(9,4)	0	0%	7
gilroy(9,178)	1	0%	1	gnomea(21,5)	0	0%	5
wrl(21,16)	1	0%	1	jove(9,42)	0	0%	1
vlsi(21,26)	1	0%	1	mayo(21,5)	1	0%	1

shows all the NFS activity on the local network, broken down by server host name and file system ID.

A tool such as nfswatch can be extremely useful when tracking down NFS performance problems, such as why a given NFS server is overloaded, by revealing which clients are responsible for the server load, and what operations are being performed.

15.4 NETWORK INTERFACE HARDWARE

Computers connect to networks through their network interface hardware. A network interface deals with the lowest layers of the protocol stack, starting with the physical details of signaling, the collection of bits into frames or packets, and (in shared-access technologies like CSMA/CD or token ring) the channel access protocol. The job of the interface is to off load some processing tasks from the main CPU, to provide a level of data integrity and perhaps reliable transmission, to perform some filtering on the incoming packet stream, and to move data back and forth between the host and the network as fast as possible.

The design of a network interface significantly affects the performance of the system. As CPUs and networks become faster, the role of the interface becomes progressively more important, because modern CPUs achieve much of their speed through the use of caching, and network exchanges invariably require uncachable accesses. Lots of research is being done into the design of better network interfaces. I will cover just a few points related to the use of IP.

15.4.1 Data Alignment

Modern CPUs load and store data far more efficiently when that data is aligned on memory-system word boundaries. Most fast machines use 32-bit words, although 64-bit CPU chips are now hitting the market. When such a CPU must load or store misaligned data, it may take many more instructions than it does to reference properly aligned data.

Most of the fields in IP-family protocol headers are "naturally" aligned. Thirty-two-bit values, such as IP addresses and TCP sequence numbers, are aligned on 32-bit boundaries, and headers are padded so that subsequent header or data fields start on 32-bit boundaries. Some small fields are not naturally aligned on both ends, which makes it harder to process them on little-endian systems, but they do not cross 32-bit alignment boundaries. (Values in IP header options sometimes straddle such boundaries, but options are not widely used.)

Other protocol designers have not been so thoughtful. Some protocols, such as Ethernet,[18] use headers that are not multiples of 32 bits in length. Even worse, some protocols use variable-width fields, in a misguided attempt to save network bandwidth in exchange for CPU cycles.

If a network interface requires the host to send and receive link-level packets that are aligned on word boundaries, this may force the host to deal with IP headers that are misaligned. The IP layers would then either have to play complicated games to load and store packet fields, or the entire packet would have to be copied so that protocol processing could take place on a properly aligned copy.

A simple change to the network interface can eliminate such inefficiencies. If the interface allows the start of the data-link packet to be misaligned, then the host can arrange for the start of the IP header to be properly aligned. For example, an Ethernet interface can be told to buffer packets, starting at an address 2 bytes past a 32-bit word boundary. Since the Ethernet header is 14 bytes long, this means that the IP header will start 16 bytes after this boundary, and so it will be properly aligned. Such a design might add some slight complexity to the Ethernet interface, but it eliminates a tremendous source of overhead in IP, TCP, UDP, and NFS processing.

15.4.2 Outboard Protocol Processors

One might ask, if the job of the network interface is to offload the task of processing lower-layer protocols from the host, why it should not also offload the higher-layer protocols. Several vendors did, in fact, introduce "outboard" protocol processors that incorporated IP/TCP support into the network interface hardware. While these interfaces were probably bought mostly by customers who could not obtain native IP/TCP software for their CPUs, many people treated them as a means of improving performance: "Why waste valuable host CPU cycles doing something that the interface board could do?"

This is a mistake. Outboard protocol processors have numerous disadvantages (they may use slower CPUs than the main host, and it may be hard to upgrade their TCP implementation when necessary), and they fail to solve the problems that actually reduce performance. Processing the IP and TCP headers is not generally that expensive (see Section 15.10.2). Multiplexing multiple connections, and moving the data to and from the application, are expensive,[19] and are not ameliorated by the use of an outboard processor.

The current trend in research on network interfaces is in the opposite direction. A network interface should make it possible for a protocol layer to send and receive data as fast as possible; it should not try to modify the data by itself, since anything it does will probably be of little use and will simply add latency to the delivery of packets.

15.4.3 Outboard Encryption Processors

Unlike protocol processing, encryption might well be done better on an outboard processor. Encryption algorithms, such as DES, are hard to implement efficiently on a general-purpose CPU, yet special-purpose DES chips achieve remarkably good performance. (The DES algorithm allows for significant parallelism, which a special-purpose chip can exploit more easily than a normal CPU.)

Since we want to limit the number of times packet data must be copied over a bus, the obvious place to put an encryption engine is on the network interface board. This requires the higher level software to tell the interface board which part of a packet should be encrypted (or decrypted), and with what key. (Some part of the packet must be in clear text, such as the IP header, so that the receiver can know what to do with it.)

For transmitted packets, this specification is easy: the driver provides encryption parameters to the interface along with the outgoing packet. For incoming packets, this is harder; the host software does not know which key to use on which packet until after the packet has arrived. The host software could read enough of the cleartext packet headers to decide how to decrypt the packet, and then ask the interface to decrypt the rest of the packet. Or, the packet might carry (say, in an IP header option) enough information to allow the interface to choose the proper decryption key.

15.5 LAN ISSUES

Most IP packets travel over local area networks. Local-area network (LAN) technology is an area of active research, not to mention acrimonious debate among the vendors of competing technologies. Many aspects of LAN design influence network performance, but only a few of these issues are specific to IP, so I will resist the temptation to enter the debate myself.

15.5.1 MTU

All LAN technologies used for IP transmit data in packets. Each technology places limits on the minimum and maximum length of a packet. The maximum length limit is called the Maximum Transmission Unit (MTU), and is central to IP performance.

A LAN designer might follow several criteria in choosing an MTU. First, the MTU limits the amount of buffering that an interface will need to store a packet for transmission or reception. Second, the MTU limits the amount of time that the LAN can be tied up with any one packet. For example, if the LAN bandwidth is 100 Kbits/sec, and if the MTU were 125 Kbytes, then a single packet could tie up the LAN for an entire second. This would make interactive response terrible. Even if the LAN is perfectly fair to all hosts (in the sense that no host could send two packets while another host was waiting to send just one), on a network with N hosts one host might have to wait N seconds to send a packet.

It has been suggested that the MTU should be chosen to keep the host-access delay below 200 milliseconds.[5] Since a single LAN might connect on the order of a hundred hosts (more than this and it gets too hard to manage), this implies that the single-packet delay should be on the order of a millisecond or two. The MTU therefore should be about a thousandth of the 1-second bandwidth of the network. For example, on the 10 Mbits/sec Ethernet, its 1500-byte MTU imposes a per-packet delay of 1.2 msec.

15.5.2 Trailer Encapsulations

Since copying packets around in memory is expensive, it is sometimes profitable to use implementation techniques that "move" packets using page-table manipulation instead of memory copies. To use page-flipping, it may be necessary to ensure that packet data is aligned on page boundaries.

One alignment technique is to arrange for the packets to be read into memory via DMA so that the TCP data portion starts exactly on a page boundary. This means that the start of the packet buffer must be arranged so that the headers appear at the end of the previous page, and it also suggests that variable-length headers should be avoided. It might be reasonable to "optimize for the common case," and assume that the incoming packets are, say, TCP packets with no header options. If the DMA buffer start address is properly chosen, then most packets will arrive with the TCP data area properly aligned.

A different approach was taken with 4.2BSD, that of using a special Ethernet *trailer encapsulation* (*RFC 893*)[20] for IP packets whose transport-level data areas are exactly paged-sized on the sending host. In a trailer encapsulation, the Ethernet packet type encodes the length (in 512-byte blocks) of the data pages, and the data pages immediately follow the Ethernet header. The IP and TCP headers then follow the data pages—hence the term *trailer.* Although the use of trailers must now be negotiated between the peer hosts (using a variation on ARP), the original 4.2BSD code did not do this negotiation, and might not interoperate with all implementations.

Trailers might have provided a small performance improvement when they were first introduced. They now do more harm than good, first because they force the use of more packets than would be required if the entire 1500-byte payload of an Ethernet packet were used, and second because many modern CPUs use a page size that is much larger than an Ethernet packet, which makes page-flipping useless. (While FDDI can carry 4096-byte pages, and the FDDI MTU is close to this value, the use of trailers on FDDI is explicitly banned by *RFC 1188*.)[21] Thus, it is probably best to disable the use of trailers.

Because the BSD code was optimized to use trailers, some versions will not exploit the entire 1500 byte Ethernet MTU even when trailers are disabled. Fixing this bug in the TCP code will yield modest, but measurable improvements in TCP throughput over Ethernet.

15.6 WAN ISSUES

When IP was designed, local area networks were a novelty. The primary goal of IP was to support the interconnection of networks, mostly for long-distance communication. While many LAN-based protocol families compete successfully in the marketplace, today only IP provides vendor-independent, multiorganizational wide area network (WAN) service to a significant user population.

IP owes much of its continued success to its ability to solve WAN problems. Many of these problems (scaling, routing, management, and security) indirectly affect performance, and are covered elsewhere in this book. I will concentrate in this section on those issues most directly related to IP performance.

15.6.1 Congestion

When an IP host sends a datagram, it expects the network to make a *best-effort* attempt at delivery. The sender has no direct information about the state of the network; in particular, it does not know if the network is so congested that it lacks sufficient resources to deliver the packet.

Not all network technologies have this problem; some use admission controls to prevent a packet from entering the network unless the necessary resources are available. Similarly, the telephone system might give you a busy signal when you try to place a call, but once the connection is made you know that it will not be displaced by other traffic.

Admission controls have several drawbacks: bursty traffic may underutilize the reserved resources; a network with admission controls is harder to engineer than a best-effort network; and a best-effort network might be more resilient when an intermediate node fails, since it does not require routing nodes to maintain connection state. During the design of IP, it was thought that the benefits of a simple, stateless datagram network outweighed the costs.*

The success of IP and the Internet leaves no doubt that this choice paid off, but it does leave us with the problem of congestion. Since the network cannot defend itself against excess traffic, IP hosts must cooperate to avoid congesting the network. They do this by reducing the load they offer in response to signals from the network. These signals might be explicit, such as ICMP Source Quench messages sometimes sent by routers, or they might be implicit, such as the timeout caused by a packet dropped due to congestion.

In the IP model, responsibility for dealing with congestion lies not with the IP layer, but with the higher layers already responsible for reliability, sequencing, and flow control. In Sections 15.8.10 and 15.8.11 I will describe the methods now used by TCP to avoid and recover from congestion. Other transport layers, such as UDP, may depend on the good behavior of applications to avoid congesting the network.

Note that most LAN technologies provide some sort of admission control, at least to the point of providing fairness. For example, the *binary exponential backoff* mechanism used by Ethernet allocates bandwidth fairly among the hosts on the LAN, to a first approximation. These limiting mechanisms do not extend across routers, which is why congestion becomes

---

* The design arguments are more subtle and complex than I have described. David Clark does a much better job of explaining the IP design philosophy.[22]

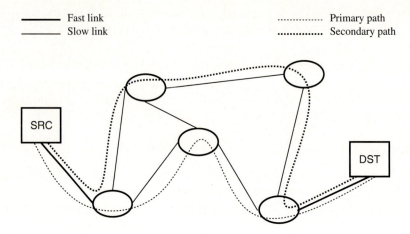

Figure 15.5   Path-splitting to obtain more bandwidth

more important in the WAN case. Even LAN-level mechanisms cannot always protect a LAN from congestive collapse, so IP implementations must be sensitive to congestion even when used in a LAN-only environment.

15.6.2   Path-Splitting

One virtue of IP's stateless-router approach is that a sequence of datagrams from Host *A* to Host *B* need not all follow the same path (that is, the same sequence of routers). This is most valued because it insulates the end hosts from failures in routers or links, by allowing the network to reroute around failure. It also allows the network to route a set of packets in parallel along several paths, which in principle can provide more end-to-end bandwidth than a host could obtain if all its packets were constrained to follow a single path.

For example, Figure 15.5 shows a simple network of five routers, connected by slow links (say, 56 Kbits/sec). Two hosts, SRC and DST, are attached to nearby routers via fast links. If packets from SRC to DST are constrained to follow only the primary path, then at best 56 Kbits/sec can flow from SRC to DST. If the network can simultaneously route packets over the secondary path, then twice the end-to-end bandwidth is available, or 112 Kbits/sec. In a real network, there may be competition for both paths, but at times there may be enough idle bandwidth to make this pay off.

Path-splitting has drawbacks. In Figure 15.5 we can see that the secondary path travels one more hop than the primary path. This may increase the variability in end-to-end delay, which will cause problems for TCP round-trip-time estimation (see Section 15.8.9), NTP delay estimation, and applications depending on low "jitter." Moreover, it may cause packets to arrive out of order. Although out-of-order delivery is explicitly allowed for IP packets, some implementations might not have been adequately tested in this situation, and may become confused.

15.6.3 Serial Line Protocols

It has been said that IP and TCP were designed to run over any network technology, including a pair of paper cups connected with string. About the closest that people actually come to this is the use of IP over low-speed serial lines, such as dial-up connections through the telephone network.[*]

Unlike LANs and packet-switched WANs, serial connections (as they come from the phone company) do not directly supply the packet-oriented link layer that IP expects. One must employ an encapsulation protocol to provide framing and other desirable services. Two encapsulation protocols, SLIP and PPP, have been specified for the use of IP over serial lines.

15.6.3.1   Serial Line IP

Serial Line IP (SLIP, *RFC 1055*)[23] is widely used today, although it is quite explicitly not an official "standard." SLIP simply provides framing. It is not meant to provide packet type identification or addressing, because it is used only for IP packets and only on single-drop point-to-point links. It provides no error detection, so upper layers must use checksums (serial lines are notoriously noisy).

Packets are framed by a single END byte at the end of the packet. (Good practice suggests sending an END at the beginning of each packet, to make sure that line noise does not add extra bytes to the front of a packet.) An ESC byte can be sent in the middle of the packet to protect a data byte that matches the END value. This means that packets that contain lots of END or ESC bytes take longer to send; a packet consisting entirely of N END bytes takes $2N$ bytes to transmit over SLIP. The ESC and END bytes do not match any printing ASCII characters, so (for English-speaking users, at least) they are unlikely to appear in interactive traffic.

Most applications of low-speed links can benefit from compression techniques, which trade CPU cycles for reduced packet sizes. SLIP provides no general-purpose compression mechanism, but some implementations support a TCP-specific compression scheme that can be quite effective (see Section 15.8.14).

15.6.3.2   Point-to-Point Protocol

Although SLIP serves quite nicely in some situations, it fails to solve many of the problems with point-to-point links. The Point-to-Point Protocol (PPP, *RFC 1171*)[24] provides a more flexible mechanism for transmitting packets over these links. It supports the simultaneous use of several protocol families (such as IP, DECnet, and OSI), error detection, and link configuration, and provides negotiation mechanisms to support capabilities like data compression and end-point address discovery.

---

[*]   Some might argue that amateur packet radio connections are even more tenuous, but hams enjoy that sort of thing.

Because PPP is more complex and robust than SLIP, it adds more per-packet overhead to each datagram. While SLIP gets by with 1 extra byte per packet, PPP by default adds at least 8. SLIP does not transmit any link-level packets besides the encapsulated IP packets, whereas PPP's Link Configuration Protocol (LCP) involves several packet exchanges that must be done before a link can be used.

These differences mean that PPP is slightly less efficient than SLIP. PPP, however, allows the link endpoints to negotiate changes in the encapsulation format. The LCP can be used to eliminate 3 of the 8 overhead bytes, and invoke one or more compression schemes (*RFC 1172*).[25]

PPP provides a framework for continued protocol evolution. For example, PPP may be used on the connection between the two halves of a long-distance bridge between two Ethernets. Ethernet imposes a minimum frame size of 60 octets, so smaller datagrams must be padded to this length. The PPP Extensions for Bridging (*RFC 1220*)[26] provides a means to compress these pad bytes, to improve the efficiency of PPP in this application. Additional extensions to PPP are likely.

15.6.4   Path MTU

WAN data links have MTUs, just as LANs do (see Section 15.5.1), but in a wide area network the interesting quantity is not the MTU of any particular link. Rather, the minimum MTU over a given path (between a source host and a destination host), known as the *Path MTU*, governs the size of the largest IP packet that can be sent across the path without fragmentation.

The Path MTU between two hosts is not necessarily a constant. The routing topology in a WAN might change during the lifetime of a connection, shifting the packets to a different sequence of links and thus a different set of MTUs. Path MTUs may also be asymmetric; the path from Host *B* to Host *A* may not be the reverse of the path from Host *A* to Host *B*.

15.6.5   Today's Internet

The Internet arose from what were, in retrospect, humble beginnings. The ARPANET, with its 56-Kbits/sec links, provided almost all of the long-distance connectivity. With so little available bandwidth, we were lucky that the Internet comprised only a few hundred hosts, and slow ones at that.

Soon, if not already, there will be more than a million hosts on the Internet. Many of these, for security reasons, cannot directly inject IP packets into the WAN, but almost all can send electronic mail messages, and the net effect is a tremendous traffic load. Individual routing sites now handle more than a gigabyte each day, and the US national backbone includes many T3 (45-Mbits/sec) links. Overseas paths and US regional networks are probably not far behind. A number of commercial providers have entered the market, selling WAN Internet bandwidth to customers unable to get the government to pay their network bills.

Hosts are getting faster, too, and will be demanding more network bandwidth (and better latencies) than is needed to simply carry electronic mail messages. Multimedia workstations can display full-speed video and (using data compression technology) transmit it over the Internet. Some people believe that long-distance interactive multimedia will change human interactions as dramatically as they were changed by electronic mail. Meeting the performance requirements for such applications, while simultaneously scaling the Internet to include more hosts (by several orders of magnitude), is going to be an interesting challenge.

15.7 THE IP, ICMP, AND ARP LAYERS

IP (*RFC 791*) is a datagram protocol.[27] That means that there is no attempt made to guarantee reliable delivery, and so performance issues related to IP are fairly simple: does a packet arrive at all, and if so, how long does it take?

15.7.1 Routing Protocols

As an IP packet travels along its path, each router along the way must decide how to forward the packet. One approach is to use one of the source routing IP header options, by which the source host picks an explicit path and instructs the routers how to follow it. Although it might be the wave of the future, source routing is not often used now (there isn't enough room in the IP header to carry an entire route for many important paths through the Internet). Instead, we use hop-by-hop routing, and so the routers need to have up-to-date routing tables.

Routers communicate routing table information using routing information protocols, which are discussed in more detail in Chapter 5, Routing Protocols. The design of routing protocols can be quite complex; among the requirements for a good routing protocol is that it respond quickly to changes in the network topology, without requiring a lot of network bandwidth, router CPU power, or router memory. Older routing protocols required little CPU power or memory, but tended to perform badly in large or frequently changing networks. Newer IP routing protocols are more stable and efficient of network bandwidth, although they are only practical now that routers are faster and have a good deal of RAM.

For more information on the design and analysis of routing protocols, you might want to read *Interconnections: Bridges and Routers*, by Radia Perlman.[28]

15.7.2 Routing Issues

The route chosen to get a packet from its source to its destination can have a significant effect on communications performance. In an internet, there may be several possible paths, with varying performance parameters, including:

- End-to-end bandwidth

- End-to-end delay

- Number of hops

- Minimum MTU

- Congestion.

The variability in these parameters is sometimes more important than their actual values.

There is no one "best" route for all applications, but rather one must consider the requirements of an application when choosing a route for its packets. This is the concept of *policy routing*. Policy routing also covers issues like security, acceptable use, and service charges,[29] but support for performance-related policies is more mature and more generally available.

Suppose there are two routes from Host A to Host B; one route minimizes delay, while the other maximizes bandwidth. If a user on Host A wishes to transfer a large file to Host B, using the route that maximizes bandwidth might be appropriate. If the user instead wishes to do a remote login to Host B, then the route minimizing delay may be more desirable. And, if the application is real-time packet voice, the route that minimizes the variability in delay may be the best, but only if it provides sufficient bandwidth for a conversation.

The ability of current IP implementations (hosts and routers) to support varying performance metrics is limited, at best. Few host implementations allow applications to specify a Type-Of-Service (TOS) value for the IP header, and routers do not always pay attention to the Type-Of-Service field. Instead, routing protocols tend to disseminate metrics that are chosen to provide good performance in general.

The simplest routing metric is the hop count, since delay is usually minimized by minimizing hop count. In some cases, it may be appropriate to bias the routing metrics to prefer the use of high-speed networks (such as Ethernet or T1) instead of a path with fewer hops over much slower networks (such as DS0 or SLIP links). When configuring a router, it is usually possible to bias the hop count to favor a fast router over a slower one.

Getting these biases right is an art, and one cannot always guarantee the best possible performance. One sometimes finds two hosts in adjacent buildings communicating via a router in a foreign country. This is especially likely to happen when a link in the network fails, and the routing algorithms automatically choose a new route that hadn't been considered when the biases were set.

15.7.3   Router Performance

Although in WANs performance is often limited by link speeds and queueing delay, in regions of interconnected high-speed LANs (such as might be found in a campus network) the routers may limit performance. Routers can decrease end-to-end bandwidth and increase end-to-end delay. Poorly designed routers that drop packets even when uncongested significantly reduce performance by causing timeouts and retransmissions.

Routers impose additional delay in several ways:

Queueing delay

Queueing delay is not directly the fault of a router. However, when a router delays packets for other reasons, it (or perhaps an upstream router) will suffer longer queues and thus more queueing delay.

Channel access delay

Channel access delay is also not the fault of a router. When a packet must traverse multiple links, however, it may have to pay a channel access delay on each hop, so the use of routers does impose additional channel access delays.

Store-and-forward delay

Simple routers follow a store-and-forward model. When a packet arrives at one interface, it is buffered in its entirety. Once the entire packet is received, a forwarding decision is made and the packet is then transmitted on the outgoing interface. This means that the best-case total delay from the arrival of the last byte of the packet, to the departure of the last byte of the packet, is at least the packet transmission time. For example, if the router connects two Ethernets and the packet takes 1 millisecond to transmit at 10 Mbits/sec, it will be delayed an additional millisecond by store-and-forward delay.

An alternative to store-and-forward is cut-through routing. In this model, the router buffers just enough of the packet to determine its destination, and then (if the outgoing channel is free) copies the rest of the packet directly from the input to the output. The delay imposed is thus proportional to the length of the IP header, instead of to the length of the entire packet. Cut-through routing is more difficult because it requires multiple data paths through the system, and because the router must make forwarding decisions and IP header modifications "in real time."

IP is amenable to cut-through routing, because it is possible to make a routing decision based only on the first few bytes of a long packet. (This would not be true if trailer encapsulations [see Section 15.5.2] were used, since then the addressing information is at the end of the packet; but routers generally do not negotiate the use of trailers.)

There is a catch, though: while in IP there is no checksum over the entire packet that must be computed before forwarding, it is possible that the incoming packet may have a bad link-layer checksum. A cut-through router would not realize this until the end of the received packet, by which time most of the outgoing packet would already have been sent. Since there may be no way to mark the outgoing packet as corrupt, the cut-through router has, in effect, turned a detected error into an undetected error. The error should still be caught by TCP or UDP data checksums, but not everyone is careful enough to use UDP checksums.

Decision-making delay

Once the IP header has been received, the router can make a forwarding decision (even a store-and-forward system can overlap this decision with reception of the rest of the packet). The main cost is doing a routing-table lookup, which can often be ameliorated through the use of a cache.[30] IP addresses are fairly easy to parse (compared to, say, OSI's variable-length addresses) but the routing table may be quite large.

Some routers provide datagram-level access controls, allowing a system manager to specify rules about which packets will or will not be forwarded. For example, the router may be told to forward all SMTP packets and discard all Telnet packets. Doing these checks may require the router to examine higher level headers (such as TCP or UDP), and may also require a complex table lookup.

Checksum calculations

A router must check the IP header checksum of all received packets, and discard those that appear to be damaged. Computing the header checksum is relatively cheap (if there are no IP header options, this should take under two dozen instructions). An IP router is required to decrement the TTL field in the IP header, so the checksum must be adjusted before the header is transmitted. Because the IP checksum is just a 1's-complement sum, it is not necessary to recompute it from scratch; instead, the old checksum is adjusted by the change in the value of the TTL field (and any other changes, if required by IP header options).

Options processing

Processing of IP header options can be quite expensive. They turn the IP header into a variable-length object, which complicates checksum calculation. They are not of a fixed format, which means that parsing them is expensive. Finally, since an option may specify source routing, routing and security decisions must be postponed until after option processing. All of these facts conspire to push options-laden packets off of the "fast path" through the router code, so this also increases delay.

In my experience, few IP packets carry IP header options. This is likely to change in the future, as several new developments in IP protocol design may require the regular use of options.

Routing protocol and management overhead

An IP router does more than just forward packets. It must also participate in one or more routing information protocols, and probably in a network management protocol. Time spent processing packets for these protocols means added delay for the packets being forwarded. This suggests that implementors and network managers should consider these costs when choosing a routing protocol or deciding how often to poll a router for network management information.

The factors contributing to router bandwidth are simpler. The primary issue is how fast bits can be moved from the input interface to the output interface. A cut-through router may require the bits to pass just once over some sort of interconnect (such as a DMA bus). A store-and-forward router probably requires two DMA transfers. In either case, the performance of the memory or DMA path is a major contributor to the effective bandwidth of the router. Some store-and-forward routers use a modified form of cut-through, where the packet is buffered in a memory pool which is "close" to both interfaces. The IP header is copied into CPU memory, but once the forwarding decision is made, the CPU instructs the interfaces to transfer the bits directly.

A technique commonly used to increase throughput is called *pipelining*. The progress of a packet through a router may go through several stages, which may have to be done sequentially for a given packet but which may operate in parallel on separate packets. Once a packet has progressed from stage 1 into stage 2, another packet can start on stage 1. For example, in a store-and-forward router, an outgoing packet can be moved via DMA out of the buffer pool while an incoming packet is being moved via DMA into the buffer pool. When the pipeline is full, the net throughput of a router with N pipeline stages can be N times the throughput of the slowest stage.

Measurement of router performance requires some care, to avoid being mislead by meaningless numbers and confusing definitions (*RFC 1242*).[31] For more information on router performance measurements, see Chapter 5, Routing Protocols. Measurements of currently available routers are published periodically.[32]

15.7.4 Redirects

The accepted model for IP end hosts is that they should not participate in routing information protocols. Rather, they should determine the set of adjacent routers (perhaps by using the Router Discovery Protocol (*RFC 1256*),[33] and for each new destination, choose an arbitrary router from this list. If the router happens not to be on the path to the destination, it will forward the packet to the correct router and also send an ICMP Host Redirect message to the source host, which should then update its routing table entry for the destination.

An IP host that fails to process Host Redirect messages will continue to function, but network performance will be impaired because every packet that it sends to the wrong router will appear twice on the local LAN, and will also cause another ICMP message.

15.7.5 Fragmentation and How to Avoid It

When an IP packet is larger than the MTU of a link over which it is about to be sent, the sending host (source host or router) must *fragment* the packet into several pieces, each with its own copy of the IP header, and send the pieces individually. Once all the fragments are received at the destination host, that host reassembles them into a complete datagram. Fragmentation thus allows the use of varying MTUs throughout the Internet without requiring an end host to know the minimal MTU that its packets may encounter.

Fragmentation can lead to severe performance problems, due to a phenomenon called *deterministic fragment loss* (DFL).[34] DFL occurs when each time a given packet is fragmented, one of the fragments is unusually likely to be lost. For example, if the destination host (or an intermediate router) cannot handle two packets in quick succession, the second fragment of a datagram may be lost almost every time an attempt is made to send the datagram.

IP has no facility for selective retransmission of fragments; if one fragment is lost then the whole packet must be retransmitted. Therefore, DFL means that it may be nearly impossible to get an intact IP datagram through, even if the network is delivering most of the fragments successfully. Since IP has no negative-acknowledgement mechanism, retransmission is only triggered by a higher level timeout, and so the throughput of a connection suffering from DFL may drop by many orders of magnitude.

The best way to avoid DFL is to avoid fragmentation. This means sending IP datagrams that are small enough to pass without fragmentation through the lowest-MTU link on the path to the destination. The trick is to guess what this size is, because sending packets that are smaller than necessary increases overhead and can decrease throughput (albeit more gradually than does DFL).

One approach is to assume that if the destination is not locally connected (i.e., if a router is used to get to the destination) then the path may traverse low-MTU links. Following this reasoning, it has been recommended (*RFC 1122*)[2] that for non-local hosts, an MTU of 576 bytes should be assumed. This is not small enough to prevent fragmentation on every possible path, but at the time the recommendation was made it was a good compromise between DFL effects and per-packet overhead.

The current Internet is a different situation. Most of the long-distance connectivity is over links with MTUs of 1500 bytes or higher, and the spread in link MTUs is larger than it used to be. Therefore, using a fixed packet size of 576 bytes can waste a moderate amount of the available performance. For this reason, the Path MTU Discovery (PMTUD) mechanism (*RFC 1191*)[35] was developed (see Section 15.10.7). PMTUD allows a source host to learn the actual worst-case MTU on the current path, and so optimize the choice of packet size. While PMTUD support in routers is quite simple and may soon be ubiquitous, PMTUD support in end-hosts is not generally available (as of this writing).

Many BSD-based systems assume that all subnets of a given IP network are "local" to each other, and thus that it is safe to send larger datagrams. This is true for campus-style networks composed of high-speed (and hence high-MTU) links, but some organizations have built nationwide networks using low-MTU links. The assumption is inappropriate in these cases, and can lead to DFL. If this causes problems, one can disable the assumption by setting the `subnetsarelocal` kernel global variable to zero.

15.7.5.1   *Buffering Issues in Fragment Reassembly*

IP fragmentation can also lead to problems in the reassembly process at the destination host, by causing various forms of temporary deadlock. Deadlocks occur when there are cir-

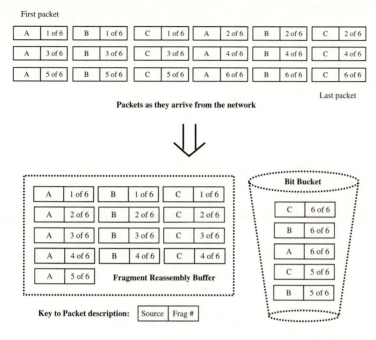

First packet

A	1 of 6	B	1 of 6	C	1 of 6	A	2 of 6	B	2 of 6	C	2 of 6
A	3 of 6	B	3 of 6	C	3 of 6	A	4 of 6	B	4 of 6	C	4 of 6
A	5 of 6	B	5 of 6	C	5 of 6	A	6 of 6	B	6 of 6	C	6 of 6

Last packet

Packets as they arrive from the network

Fragment Reassembly Buffer

Bit Bucket

Key to Packet description: | Source | Frag # |

Figure 15.6 Fragment reassembly deadlock from lack of buffer space

cular dependencies among multiple consumers of a limited resource. When the IP fragment reassembly process deadlocks, progress halts until the reassembly timeout on a fragment expires, at least 60 seconds after the fragment was received. At this point, it is unlikely that any of the other buffered fragments will be worth saving. The cycle of fragmentation and deadlock may repeat *ad infinitum.*

Fragment reassembly deadlock can occur simply because of insufficient buffer space. For example, suppose that there is space for 20 Kbytes of fragments, and each of three hosts sends a 8 Kbyte datagram as six separate 1500-byte fragments. If the fragments arrive neatly interleaved, the situation illustrated in Figure 15.6 might arise: the fragment buffer fills up with parts of all three packets, and some fragments from each packet are discarded.

Fragment reassembly deadlock can occur in some systems because of a more subtle circular dependency.[36] Consider a system that allocates both large and small buffers from the same pool of memory, and which requires that when a large buffer is used, a small buffer must also be used to contain a pointer to the large buffer. (This corresponds to the 4.2BSD *mbuf* mechanism.) It may be the case that when a fragment arrives, there are sufficient large buffers to hold it, but no small buffers to refer to the large buffer. This causes the reassembly process to deadlock.

The problem can be ameliorated by ensuring that a reasonable number of small buffers are kept free, even if the memory allocator could potentially aggregate some of them to create more large buffers.

15.7.6 Identification Wrap-Around

When an IP packet is fragmented, the receiving host needs some way to match up the fragments to reassemble them. The IP header includes a 16-bit Identification field. Each IP datagram sent by a host is supposed to carry a unique Identification, so that if it is fragmented, it can be reassembled. Sixteen bits of Identification allows the receiver to distinguish between 2^{16}, or 65536, different datagrams. Many connections transfer far more packets than this, so the IP Identification field will wrap around sooner or later. If this is not to cause confusion among fragmented packets, possibly leading to checksum errors or worse, we must ensure that an Identification value is not used for one packet while a previous packet with the same value is still in existence.

The lifetime of an IP packet is not infinite; the 8-bit Time-To-Live (TTL) field in the IP header is supposed to be decremented at least once per second. This yields a maximum lifetime *in transit* of 255 seconds, although TCP packets are not supposed to live more than the Maximum Segment Lifetime (MSL) of 120 seconds (*RFC 793*).[37] Once a fragment has arrived at an end-host, regardless of the remaining TTL value, it might be retained for as long as 120 seconds (*RFC 1122*).[2] Therefore, a fragment might exist, either in the network or in a reassembly queue, for as long as 375 seconds.

To avoid Identification wrap-around, on the face of it, a host cannot generate 16 fragmentable datagrams at a rate faster than $2^{16}/375 = 174$ packets/second. If the host uses a smaller initial TTL value, such as 60, the limiting rate increases to 364 packets/second, which is almost acceptable. (With 512-byte segments, this is approximately the rate of a T1 connection.) Even if the initial TTL were reduced to 1 (it must not be zero), the limiting rate would still be under 550 packets/second. (Note that the Identification field need not be unique over all the connections to which the host is a party, but rather only over those with a given destination host.)

We obviously cannot accept such limits on our packet rates. Most implementations, including those derived from 4.2BSD, live dangerously, in the hope that data checksums will catch attempts to reassemble an IP packet from mismatched fragments. (I know of no implementation that monitors the IP packet rate and throttles it if necessary, but with a lot of overhead it could be done.) A better approach is to simply avoid fragmentation, through the use of the Path MTU Discovery mechanism (see Section 15.10.7). PMTUD ensures that no packet is ever fragmented, which means that the IP Identification is never used and so wrap-around is irrelevant.

15.7.7 Checksums

The IP header checksum serves to detect corruption of the fields in the IP header; it does not protect the data portion of the packet. This allows routers and the IP layer in host software to be reasonably sure that their part of the packet is intact, without forcing them to touch every byte in the packet. The IP checksum algorithm, also used by ICMP, TCP, and

UDP to protect their headers and data, is designed to be relatively inexpensive to compute, yet catch certain classes of errors common to communications systems. The IP checksum provides no protection at all against certain other kinds of errors, such as reordering of the 16-bit words in a packet.

Higher layers might have data integrity requirements that demand different forms of protection. For example, an application that can tolerate a few bad bits but is sensitive to packet delay may find the cost of any whole-data checksum not worth the benefits. On the other hand, an application demanding high levels of reliability and security may require a much stronger checksum than the one used by IP.

Checksum errors usually result in subsequent retransmission of the corrupted packet. One form of checksum error, caused by a common error in implementing the checksum algorithm, can silently degrade performance without always halting communication altogether. The problem is that IP checksums are calculated in 1's-complement arithmetic, which has two representations for zero (known as 0 and –0).

A host that improperly deals with such values may cause a spurious checksum error on certain packets. If the error is in the calculation of the IP header checksum, the error will probably disappear on the retransmitted packet, since the IP Identification value for the new packet will be different from the old one. If the error is made when calculating ICMP, TCP, or UDP checksums, it may persist through many (or infinite) retransmissions, since data in the retransmitted packet may not change at all.

15.7.8 Broadcast Storms

A *broadcast storm* arises when many hosts on a LAN simultaneously attempt to broadcast a packet, usually for no good reason. This is wasteful of LAN and end-host resources, and in the worst cases can completely disrupt communications for long periods.

There are several ways to cause broadcast storms, and so even though precautions are usually taken to avoid them, it is unlikely that they are entirely a thing of the past.

One precaution against broadcast storms is to ban the transmission of an ICMP error message in response to any broadcast packet. For example, if a host broadcasts a UDP packet to a nonexistent UDP port, we do not want hundreds of hosts to send an ICMP Destination Unreachable message in response.

Another source of past broadcast storms has been confusion over the IP broadcast address. Over the years people have used a variety of patterns for defining IP broadcast addresses (*RFC 919*).[38] Consider what might happen if a host was misconfigured so that it fails to recognize a particular address as meaning "broadcast" when seen in incoming packets, but does manage to broadcast outgoing packets with that destination. (This could happen if some well-intentioned dimwit decided to "publish" an ARP translation for the broadcast address.)

Host *A* starts by sending a packet to its broadcast address, X. The broadcast is received by Host *B*, which thinks it is a non-broadcast packet for the local network and obviously not for Host *B*, so Host *B* decides to forward the packet. Host *B*'s IP output routines manage to send the packet as a broadcast, however, so the process repeats until the packet's Time-To-Live field decrements to zero.

It gets worse. Suppose that there are *N* hosts on the LAN configured like Host *B*. After the first cycle, there will now be *N* copies of the packet floating around. After two cycles, there will be $2N$ copies floating around. If the original Time-To-Live value is *T,* by the end of this process there could be N^T copies of the packet...but it is likely that by that point, many will have been dropped due to complete congestion of the network.

To protect against this kind of broadcast storm, it has been decreed that no IP packet that was received as a link-layer broadcast may ever be forwarded (*RFC 1122*).[2]

15.7.9 Synchronized Overloads

Related to the broadcast storm is a phenomenon called *synchronized overload.* This occurs when many hosts try to do something useful, all at the same time. For example, when power returns after a power failure, a large group of diskless machines may simultaneously start trying to bootload over the network. Or, if lots of diskless machines are running the RWHO protocol, they might all try to write their *rwhod* data files to their NFS servers at precisely the same time when they receive an RWHO broadcast. (If the RWHO broadcasters have nicely synchronized clocks, they may compound the problem by causing each client to do many such NFS writes in short order.)

While these overloads, unlike broadcast storms, may be the result of useful work, they may still cause problems. Such synchronization of load will cause congestion, which leads to queueing delays, and prolongs the disruption. It is more efficient to spread the workload evenly over time. The best solution is to slightly randomize the time when certain operations (such as BOOTP requests or RWHO broadcasts) are performed, so that they are unlikely to happen in synchrony.

It has been suggested that synchronized overload might also occur through a process called *self-synchronization,* in which some form of feedback causes processes on separate hosts to accidentally synchronize their behavior.[39] This might happen, for example, if a number of distributed clients with nearly identical service periods were forced to share a lock. Once a queue of clients builds up for this lock, the same clients may again compete at the end of the next service cycle.

15.7.10 Address Resolution Protocol

The Address Resolution Protocol (ARP, *RFC 826*)[40] is used to map IP addresses to link-level addresses for many popular data link layers. ARP is quite simple, and most implementations observe the specified optimizations that allow one exchange of ARP packets to fill in the necessary ARP-table entries for both parties to the exchange.

A host's ARP table is usually managed as a cache. That means that it may not be large enough to hold translations for every host on the LAN, so when space runs out, entries may be removed (preferably using a least-recently-used algorithm). If a host is only communicating with a few local peers, it is not likely to run out of ARP table space.

If, however, a host (such as a router, or file server) communicates with lots of hosts on a busy LAN, it might encounter thrashing in its ARP table. That is, entries may be replaced while they are still needed. The result of thrashing is that many IP packet transmissions are preceded by ARP exchanges, potentially tripling the packet rate on the network and the delay encountered in sending small packets.

The BSD implementation of ARP uses a hash table, consisting of an array of linked lists of entries. The length of each list is limited to a relatively small value, so with an unlucky set of peer IP addresses, thrashing may occur long before the table is full. It is also possible for a program to make "permanent" entries in the ARP table, which reduces the threshold at which thrashing takes place.

The best solution for potential thrashing is to make sure that your ARP tables are sized for a reasonably large LAN population. Unfortunately, the BSD ARP implementation does not maintain statistics that would allow the direct detection of thrashing, so this might only be discovered by observing poor server or router performance, or because the ARP rate is much higher than expected.

15.7.11 ARP and FDDI-Ethernet Bridges

We saw in Section 15.7.5 that IP fragmentation can cause problems. In Section 15.10.7 I will describe the Path MTU Discovery (PMTUD) mechanism for preventing fragmentation. PMTUD works best when a sending host knows the MTU of the LAN to which it is connected. This value is normally implied by the type of LAN used, but when an FDDI network is connected to an Ethernet via a bridge, the picture becomes foggier.

Some FDDI-to-Ethernet bridges fragment IP packets that are too large to forward, and respect the IP header's Don't-Fragment flag (necessary to make PMTUD work), but one cannot rely on all bridges to do so. It is possible, instead, for an FDDI host to detect when a packet has been forwarded from an Ethernet, and to use that information to avoid sending large packets to Ethernet hosts.[41]

FDDI packet headers start with a Frame Control (FC) octet, which defines various packet formats. In the Logical Link Control (LLC) format, which is used to carry IP and ARP packets, the FC octet also carries a priority field. Packets originating at an FDDI host carry a nonzero priority. FDDI bridges are required to preserve the priority on packets forwarded between FDDI networks, and to set the priority to 0 if the packet is forwarded from an Ethernet.[42] Thus, if the packet crosses any Ethernet before being forwarded onto an FDDI ring, no matter how many more forwarding steps follow, the receiver can detect this.

Before any IP packets can be exchanged between hosts on the same (bridged) LAN, the hosts must first exchange ARP packets. ARP packets are always small enough to fit into an

Ethernet packet, so they will pass safely through any bridge. An ARP packet arriving at an FDDI host will therefore convey not only the host address information, but also a guaranteed indicator of the Path MTU to the sending host.[*] Thus, the MTU information is available before any IP packets are sent.

The topology of a bridged LAN might change after the initial packet exchange, which means that an FDDI host must constantly monitor incoming packets to detect those hosts reached via a path that uses an Ethernet. One might implement this by having the FDDI device driver keep a table of host addresses and MTUs. If the MTU changes, the driver must inform the IP layer (or the IP layer must ask the driver for the MTU to a given destination, each time it sends a packet).

Table entries must have timeouts, on the order of several minutes, and when a packet is sent to host for which no entry exists (perhaps because it has timed out), the MTU must default to the Ethernet MTU. Otherwise, a TCP connection could deadlock: a host could continually try to send a 4-Kbyte segment across an Ethernet, and (because TCP has no negative acknowledgement mechanism) there may be no flow of packets in the opposite direction that could signal an MTU change.

15.8   THE TCP LAYER

The TCP protocol (*RFC 793*)[37] is the most important transport protocol in the IP family. It is also the most complex, and we have far from a complete understanding of its behavior under all but the simplest circumstances. A great deal of experience with TCP, some of it painful, is slowly leading us toward robust implementations with optimal performance. Meanwhile, researchers are considering ways to evolve TCP for better performance in future networks. (Other researchers are trying to find ways to replace TCP, but that is not the topic of this section.)

15.8.1   Understanding TCP Performance

TCP can be summarized as a sliding-window protocol without selective or negative acknowledgments. Most of the interesting performance issues for TCP derive from managing the use of the window, so it is worth spending a little time to understand how it works.

First consider the behavior of a much simpler protocol, the Trivial File Transfer Protocol, or TFTP (*RFC 1350*).[43] TFTP is a stop-and-wait protocol: once the sender has sent one packet, it must wait for an acknowledgement packet from the receiver before sending the next packet.[†] This makes implementing TFTP (nearly) trivial, but it also means that TFTP will not perform very well.

---

[*]   We assume that the path between the hosts on a bridged LAN is symmetric; i.e., if a packet from Host *A* to Host *B* crosses only FDDI rings, then a packet from Host *B* to Host *A* will not cross an Ethernet. This is, in fact, guaranteed by the spanning-tree algorithm used to route packets in bridged LANs. (During a topology change, the path may be asymmetric, but only briefly.)

We can calculate the best-case performance for a TFTP connection, knowing only the end-to-end delay D between the sender and the receiver (and assuming that the network is uncongested). Once the sender has sent a data packet, it must wait for a full round-trip time (RTT) of $2D$ before it can send the next packet. The maximum data size in a TFTP packet is 512 bytes, so TFTP can transfer 512 bytes every $2D$ seconds, or $256/D$ bytes per second. Between Boston and San Francisco, the speed-of-light delay is about 15 milliseconds, so at best one could transfer about 18 Kbytes per second between these two cities using TFTP. Note that this is true no matter how "fast" the nationwide network is.

TCP avoids this limit by using a sliding window. That means that rather than sending just one packet before waiting for acknowledgement, a sender keeps track of the amount of unacknowledged data, and can keep transmitting as long as this quantity does not exceed a specified *window size*. The window size is provided by the receiver with each acknowledgement; that is, the receiver indicates how much more data the sender can send. If the sender is sending too fast, the window size reported by the receiver will shrink, thus throttling the sender. This is known as *flow control*.

More precisely, the value that the receiver transmits to the sender is known as the *offered window*. The difference, computed by the sender, between the most recently received offered window and the amount of outstanding unacknowledged data is known as the *usable window*. The usable window governs how much more data the sender can inject into the connection.

The maximum TCP window size is 65535 bytes. This means that TCP can support a much higher bandwidth over a high-delay path (also known as a high delay-bandwidth product) than a stop-and-wait protocol like TFTP. Between Boston and San Francisco, the best TCP can do is about 2.3 Mbytes per second. The relative performance advantage of 128:1 applies at lower RTTs as well, although on LANs other bottlenecks might begin to dominate.

A TCP acknowledgement refers to the last byte that has been received in an uninterrupted sequence. That is, if segments have been dropped or have arrived out of order, the receiver can only acknowledge the range of sequence numbers received without any gaps, and not the extra packets that have arrived but are not yet "useful." Since TCP lacks selective or negative acknowledgements (i.e., those that would indicate gaps in the received sequence), a dropped segment may cause retransmission of a large range of segments that have actually been received. Thus, TCP performance is quite vulnerable to lost segments, and much of the work on improving TCP has been devoted to avoiding segment loss.

15.8.2 The Self-Clocking Model of TCP

One way to look at TCP, or a similar sliding-window protocol, is that it automatically adjusts its use of the network to match the available bandwidth. The user doesn't have to

---

† The terms *sender* and *receiver* are conventionally used with respect to the data packets, unless further qualified. That is, acknowledgements are sent from the *receiver* to the *sender*.

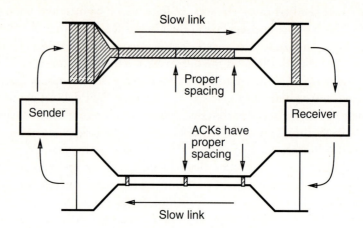

Figure 15.7   TCP self-clocking behavior

set any parameters to tell TCP how fast to send data if the bandwidth of the network is lower than what is implied by the end-to-end delay and window size. This is referred to as *self-clocking* behavior.

To get an idea of how this works, refer to Figure 15.7. We will assume that all the data packets are large and of the same size, and that the acknowledgement packets are all fairly small. The horizontal dimension represents time, and the shaded area is proportional to packet size.[44] We see data packets leaving the sender, and at some point reaching the bottleneck along the path to the receiver (the link that has the lowest bandwidth). The data packets are spaced out along this link by the link's transmission latency, and so their spacing when they arrive at the sender corresponds to their spacing on this link. In fact, it corresponds to the fastest rate at which the link can accept packets of this size.

The receiver acknowledges each packet as it arrives (provided that its buffer does not fill up), and so the acknowledgements (ACKs) leave the receiver with the same spacing (in time) as they arrived. If all goes well, the acknowledgements also arrive at the sender with this spacing, because they are "small" and so are not delayed by the bottleneck link.

If the sender then launches a new data packet every time it receives an ACK, it will be delivering data packets to the bottleneck link exactly with the spacing that the link is willing to accept. Therefore, no queue (or not much of a queue) will build up at the head of the bottleneck, and the TCP connection will proceed at the most efficient possible rate.

This is, of course, an idealized model of what really happens. Many of the techniques covered in the sections that follow are aimed at preserving this behavior in the face of possible disruptions, but there may be circumstances when this isn't possible. Section 15.8.13 discusses what happens then.

15.8.3   Window Size Effects

Not surprisingly, the choice of window size can have a significant effect on TCP performance. Many older implementations, possibly in an attempt to save memory, limit the

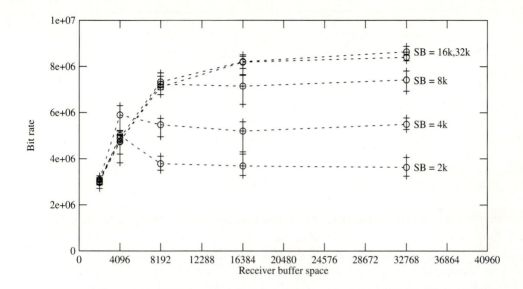

Figure 15.8   TCP performance as a function of receiver and sender buffer sizes

advertised window size to 4 Kbytes. Even in more recent implementations, the most common window size seems to be 16 Kbytes, and I have not seen anyone use a window size above 32 Kbytes. Perhaps this is because it is too easy to get bitten by sign-extension bugs when using a value with the high-order bit set. At any rate, as our WANs move from T1 rates (1.5 Mbits/sec, less than the Boston-to-San Francisco rate limit) to T3 rates (45 Mbits/sec, more than the rate limit on that path) we will need to use the largest possible windows to fully exploit these links. Fortunately, memory is more than 16 times cheaper than it was when the 4-Kbyte window size was chosen, so we should not have to worry about running out of space.

A simple test, transferring 4 Mbytes between processes on two hosts, shows the value of a reasonably large receiver buffer size. I measured the average process-to-process TCP data rate, in bits/sec, as the receiver and sender buffer sizes are varied. The end systems were identical high-performance workstations, connected over an Ethernet. Note that the best process-to-process TCP rate will be somewhat less than 10 Mbits/sec, because some of the bandwidth is taken up by packet headers.

Figure 15.8 shows the results for 10 trials at each combination of buffer sizes. The circles, connected by dotted lines corresponding to a fixed sender buffer size (SB), show the mean values for each buffer size combination. The vertical bars show the range of transfer rates achieved. There is a strong relationship between buffer size and throughput, and the typical default of 4096 bytes is clearly suboptimal.

On BSD-based systems, an application can change the receiver buffer size of an open socket using the following code:

```
int bufsize = desired_buffer_size;
setsockopt(open_socket, IPPROTO_TCP,SO_RCVBUF,
            &bufsize, sizeof(bufsize));
```

Similarly, an application can change the send buffer size using this code:

```
int bufsize = desired_buffer_size;
setsockopt(open_socket, IPPROTO_TCP, SO_SNDBUF,
            &bufsize, sizeof(bufsize));
```

15.8.4 Segment Size Effects

All other things being equal, use of larger segments (TCP packets) should result in better performance. Larger segments should mean fewer segments, and thus less protocol over-head. TCP segments that are exactly the length of a memory-system page allow the use of page-flipping techniques, and page sizes are getting larger.

Bigger is not always better, alas. The danger of Deterministic Fragment Loss (DFL), as described in Section 15.7.5, means that once the TCP segment size is increased beyond the worst-case MTU, performance may drop dramatically. (In some cases, throughput may drop to zero.) To avoid fragmentation, a TCP implementation can use the "576 if non-local" rule, or could use the Path MTU Discovery (PMTUD) mechanism (*RFC 1191*).[35] The latter approach is preferable, since it both prevents fragmentation when very low MTUs are encountered, and it allows the use of much larger segments when that is feasible.

If the PMTUD approach is taken, the TCP per-connection data structures need to include an additional field, so that TCP can separately record both the Maximum Segment Size (MSS) value provided by the peer host, and the effective MSS imposed by MTU limits. Otherwise, the TCP implementation would be unable to take advantage of MTU improvements during the lifetime of a connection, if the route changes to one with a larger worst-case MTU.

As mentioned in Section 15.5.2, one unnecessary limit on segment size is the predisposition of BSD-based TCP implementations to set the segment size to a multiple of 512 bytes (even when trailers are not actually in use). On an Ethernet, with an MTU of just under three times 512 bytes, these implementations send 1024-byte segments, which increases the number of segments sent by about 50%. Fixing this bug can improve performance by a modest, yet measurable, amount.

15.8.5 Silly-Window Syndrome

Early TCP implementations often suffered from something called *Silly-Window Syndrome* (SWS), which could cause performance to drop by several orders of magnitude (*RFC 813*).[45] SWS occurs when the receiver offers a nonzero window even when it would lead to a tiny usable window, and when the sender then takes advantage of this "silly window" to send a tiny packet. The result can be a continual stream of tiny packets, each caus-ing the receiver to offer another silly window, and we know that tiny packets cause poor performance.

For example, suppose that the receiver can buffer 2048 bytes, and the sender is using a 512-byte segment size. The sender fills the pipe with four segments, and the receiver acknowledges the first segment immediately after receiving it (so that it offers a 2048-byte window). The sender sees this acknowledgement, and computes the usable window as 512 bytes (since it has sent 1536 bytes that are still unacknowledged).

Now suppose that the application asks to send 64 bytes with the PUSH flag sent, fol-lowed by another large buffer. The sender sends one segment of 64 bytes with the PUSH bit set, followed by a 448-byte segment (to use up the usable window).

When the 64-byte segment arrives at the receiver, it immediately acknowledges the seg-ment and offers a 2048-byte window. This acknowledgement arrives at the sender, which knows it has sent 1984 bytes that are still unacknowledged. Thus, the usable window is only 64 bytes, and if there is more data available the sender will launch another tiny packet into the network, continuing the cycle *ad nauseum*.

In other words, each time the application PUSHes a buffer that happens not to be on a nice segment boundary, a new silly-sized burp will appear in the packet stream, never to disappear until the application stops sending data for at least one round-trip time.

The astute reader will have realized that the actions of the sender and receiver in this example, while perfectly legal according to the TCP specification (*RFC 793*),[37] unnecessar-ily compound the problem. Simple algorithms have been developed to avoid SWS, and the current state of the art is described in the *Host Requirements* document (*RFC 1122*).[2] The vicious cycle can be broken at either the sender or the receiver; implementing SWS avoid-ance algorithms at both ends protects you even where your peer doesn't do so.

On the receiver side, the solution is to delay advancing the offered window unless the advance is at least half the available buffer space, or big enough to fill a "reasonably large" segment. In other words, even if the receiver has infinite buffer space, it should not offer space to the sender until doing so would cause a hefty increase in the usable window size, or until delaying to do so would cause a significant decrease in throughput.

On the sender side, the solution is to delay sending data (for a short timeout period, related to the round-trip time) unless one of the following conditions holds:

1 A maximum-sized segment can be sent (i.e., the usable window is patently not silly).

2 The data is PUSHed by the application, and there is enough usable window to send all the PUSHed data (i.e., the offered window does not split the PUSHed data into two packets).

3 The amount of data to be sent is at least half of an estimate of the receiver's total buffer size.

One should read the *Host Requirements* document (*RFC 1122*)[2] for a more precise descrip-tion of SWS-avoidance algorithms and their interaction with other aspects of TCP.

15.8.6 Delaying Acknowledgements

Sending and processing TCP acknowledgements has a cost, both in network resources and in end-host CPU time. While the TCP specification allows a host to acknowledge immediately the receipt of every packet, this is a bad idea. For example, if the receiver is a Telnet server, each incoming keystroke packet could generate three responses: an acknowledgement of the incoming packet (but with no change in offered window), an acknowledgement that changes the offered window (when the Telnet server reads the byte), and a packet containing an echoed character. (The second ACK should be suppressed by the SWS-avoidance algorithm.)

The current recommendation (*RFC 1122*)[2] is that TCP receivers should delay sending an acknowledgement until one of these conditions holds:

1   A packet carrying data is being sent in the reverse direction.

2   A significant amount of data can be acknowledged (the recommendation is that there should be an ACK for at least every second full-sized segment).

3   A significant increase in the offered window is available.

4   A timer expires (the delay must be no more than half a second).

These conditions are designed to give the receiver a chance to increase the spacing between acknowledgement-only packets without delaying them so much as to decrease the performance of the sliding-window mechanism.

It is also required that if a receiver has a number of incoming segments queued, it must process them all before generating the next ACK. That is, if the receiver knows that it can aggregate the ACKs for several received packets, it must do so.

Note that if the sender's window is less than twice its segment size, the receiver will delay after every data packet (waiting for a second full-sized segment, which is not going to arrive) and net throughput might drop as low as two packets per second. This suggests that the sender's buffer should never be smaller than twice the MSS used on the local network.[*]

15.8.7 "Tinygram" Suppression

TCP is typically used in one of two modes: sending large quantities of bulk data, or sending many tiny packets at high rates. It is necessary, and possible, to implement TCP in such a way as to provide good service in both modes. It is best if this can be done with a minimum of "knob twisting" by the applications, since if there are parameters to be adjusted, then some people will get them wrong.

---

[*]   The sender's window might also be reduced by the congestion control mechanisms described in Sections 15.8.10 and 15.8.11, but if congestion window gets below two segments then the network is probably badly congested, and the extra delay imposed by the receiver might be desirable.

Applications that send lots of short packets, such as Telnet, can potentially waste a lot of network and CPU performance. If a TCP packet on an Ethernet carries but a single character, that character is effectively surrounded by 64 bytes of overhead (including TCP, IP, and Ethernet headers, and the required Ethernet preamble and spacing). Only 1.6% of the Ethernet bandwidth would be carrying useful information, and the end hosts might spend all of their time processing interrupts and protocol headers.

A sending TCP could simply wait until a reasonable number of bytes are buffered before sending them. This would not be acceptable for interactive applications, such as Telnet: when I hit a key on my keyboard, I usually want an immediate response from the remote system. Interactive applications want PUSHed data to be sent as soon as possible, and Telnet tends to PUSH every keystroke.

This dilemma is solved by the use of *Nagle's algorithm* (*RFC 896*),[46] which tries to coalesce short segments without introducing much extra delay. The algorithm, as described in the *Host Requirements* document (*RFC 1122*),[2] is to delay sending new data if there is outstanding unacknowledged data until either of these conditions holds:

- The outstanding data has been acknowledged.

- A full-sized segment can be sent.

For an application such as Telnet, this has the effect of clumping together small groups of keystrokes, which are sent once per round-trip time; this is only really noticeable if the RTT is so high that using Telnet would be painful in any case. Essentially, it means that if you can type faster than the network can carry your keystrokes, then TCP will start clumping your keystrokes together in groups large enough to allow the network to keep up.

Certain applications, such as the X Window System, must send lots of small chunks of data over TCP at high rates. These chunks must be sent synchronously (i.e., with PUSH set), because the application is interactive. The Nagle algorithm is inappropriate in this case, because the exchange must be as fast as possible. Therefore, TCP implementations are required to provide a way to disable the Nagle algorithm; in BSD-based systems, the `TCP_NODELAY` socket option is used for this purpose.

15.8.8 Repacketization

When an application has handed TCP data to be sent, the sending TCP must keep that data buffered for possible retransmission. If retransmission is required, the sender has two choices: it can send the buffered data in the same-sized chunks as it was sent before, or it can "repacketize" the data so as to send larger (and thus fewer) packets. Repacketization is only possible, of course, if the original transmissions were not done in maximal-sized packets, and should not be necessary if all possible steps are taken to avoid packet loss.

If repacketization is not done, then it is possible to retransmit exactly the same IP datagram as was sent before, including the original packet's IP Identification field. This could be important if the original packet has been fragmented, because even if fragments are lost on the second attempt, it may be possible for the receiver to patch together one intact packet from the fragments of several partial packets. However, as described in Section 15.7.5, Deterministic Fragment Loss often causes the same fragment to be lost each time, and so nullifies the value of reusing the IP Identifier. It is better to simply avoid fragmentation than to go through contortions attempting to reuse the IP Identifier value.

15.8.9 Round-Trip Time Estimation

Accurate estimates of the round-trip time (RTT) are crucial to TCP performance. If the RTT estimate is much too high, then packet loss will not be detected as soon as it might be, and the performance of TCP in lossy situations will suffer. If the RTT is the slightest bit too low, however, retransmission will occur even when packets are not being lost, and net throughput will become terrible as each packet is transmitted (and acknowledged) two (or three or ninety-nine) times. Clearly the estimate must not be too low, but it also should not be far too high.

The original TCP specification (*RFC 793*)[37] described a simple algorithm for estimating the RTT and computing a retransmission delay. This algorithm is no longer considered acceptable, because it incorrectly measures the RTT when retransmissions are taking place, and because it fails to deal with situations where the RTT has a high variance.

Two new algorithms have been specified (*RFC 1122*)[2] for estimating the RTT: Van Jacobson's algorithm for computing a "smoothed RTT" that handles variance properly,[44] and Phil Karn's algorithm for removing the ambiguity in RTT measurements when retransmissions are taking place.[47]

15.8.9.1 Jacobson's RTT Estimation Algorithm

The basic TCP retransmission timeout algorithm is to compute a mean RTT using

```
SRTT = αSRTT + (1−α)MRTT
```

where *SRTT* is the smoothed RTT estimate, and *MRTT* is the most recent RTT measurement, and α is a decay constant (whose recommended value is 0.9) so that older samples are forgotten with an exponential decay. Given SRTT, the retransmit timeout period is calculated by

```
RTO = βSRTT
```

where β is meant to account for variation in the actual RTT.

The original TCP specification used a constant value for β, which was wrong in most cases. Jacobson's algorithm estimates the actual variance by computing the average error in the SRTT value. That is, if *SRTT* is treated as a prediction of the next round-trip time, which turns out to be MRTT, then the error *Err* is computed using

```
Err = MRTT-SRTT
```

and a smoothed estimate of the error *RTTVAR* can be computed using an exponential decay.

Jacobson combines the calculation of SRTT and RTTVAR, as expressed in the equations:[1]

```
delta = MRTT-RTT
new_SRTT = SRTT-(Gain_1 * delta)
new_RTTVAR = RTTVAR + Gain_2 * (|delta|-RTTVAR)
```

where Gain_1 and Gain_2 are factors between 0 and 1 that control how fast new samples affect the calculated values.

Since floating-point operations are expensive, and in some CPU architectures forbidden entirely in kernel mode, Jacobson converted these calculations to use scaled integer arithmetic:

```
delta = (MRTT - 1) - (SRTT / 8)
SRTT = SRTT + delta
if SRTT < 0 then SRTT = 1
if delta < 0 then delta = -delta
delta = delta - (RTTVAR / 4)
RTTVAR = RTTVAR + delta
if RTTVAR < 0 then RTTVAR = 1
```

The initial retransmit timeout interval *RTO* is then set to

```
RTO = (SRTT / 8) + (RTTVAR / 2)
```

See Jacobson's paper for an explanation of why this actually works.

If retransmission occurs more than once in a row, this is a good indication that the calculated RTO was too small. Packets are probably being lost due to congestion, and when the network is congested the worst thing to do is to inject additional packets too rapidly. Subsequent retransmissions should be made using a *binary exponential backoff* algorithm, similar to the one used with Ethernet, except that the delay is not randomized. The RTO value is simply doubled at each stage, until a set maximum is reached. Theoretical analysis, as well as simulation and practical experience, shows that exponential backoff is probably the only method that stabilizes the congestion in the network. Effectively, it provides the sender with an estimate of its fair share of the total load on the network.

15.8.9.2 Karn's RTT Measurement Algorithm

Accurate estimation of the RTT and its variance requires proper measurements of individual RTTs. An individual RTT is measured from the time a packet is sent until the time an acknowledgement is received for that packet.

Early TCP implementations simply measured the time from the first transmission of a packet until the reception of an acknowledgement for that packet. This would work fine if packets were never retransmitted, but if a packet is lost and retransmitted, the RTT measurement will be high (it will probably be almost twice the real RTT plus the RTO interval), and so the SRTT and RTO will be set too high. Not only will this reduce performance by unnecessarily delaying retransmission on the next packet loss, but there will be a positive feedback (because the RTT measurement for the next retransmitted packet will include a larger RTO interval).

One approach that was suggested to avoid this problem was to time from the last transmission of a retransmitted packet until an ACK is received. This is a terrible idea. The reason is that if the original SRTT estimate was too small, the packet was not actually lost, and the retransmission occurred just before the arrival of the acknowledgement, the measured RTT could be tiny (because TCP cannot tell if the ACK is for the original packet or the retransmitted version). This too-low RTT value will further decrease the SRTT, again causing a positive feedback. The consequences of underestimating the RTT are much worse than those of overestimating it, since many more packets are injected into a network that may already be congested.

Karn's algorithm[47] resolves the ambiguity of measuring the RTT for a retransmitted packet, by simply not measuring it at all. That is, if a packet must be retransmitted, the SRTT value is not updated when its ACK arrives. This ensures that only unambiguous samples will be fed into the SRTT calculation, which should thus converge to the correct value.

Since the need for retransmission indicates that the SRTT might be too low, we need a way of delaying retransmission of subsequent packets even though we have not updated the SRTT. The second part of Karn's algorithm is to keep the backed-off value for RTO (once a retransmitted packet has been successfully acknowledged), since this value is likely to be longer than the actual RTT. Only when the SRTT is recalculated from a new, unambiguous sample do we recalculate the RTO interval from the SRTT and RTTVAR values.

Measurement of round-trip time may cost the sender significant amounts of CPU time and state-storage space. For this reason, many TCP implementations (such as 4.3BSD) do not measure the RTT of every segment, but rather measure it only once per RTT. That is, when a segment is sent and no measurement is currently in progress, the sequence number of that segment is remembered and a timer is started. When the acknowledgement for that segment is received, the value of the timer is used as the RTT measurement, and a new measurement may be initiated.

15.8.10 Slow-Start

In normal operation, TCP may send several packets at once to transmit a large usable window's worth of data. Once packet loss and retransmission has occurred, however, this may be a bad idea. Since packet loss is often caused by congestion, it is a good indication that the network is overloaded, and the sender should reduce its load on the network.

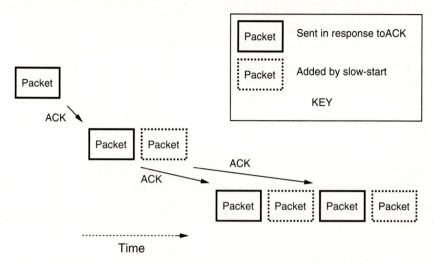

Figure 15.9   Exponential growth of congestion window

How much should the sender reduce its load? Van Jacobson's and Mike Karel's slow-start algorithm[44] is a simple approach that works pretty well, and is now required for TCP implementations. A TCP sender initiates a slow-start phase at the beginning of a connection, and whenever packet loss implies that the network may be congested.

The key to the slow-start algorithm is the introduction of an additional window concept, known as the *congestion window*. A TCP sender is limited to send no more data than is allowed by the congestion window (and is also still limited by the usable window). The size of the congestion window is an estimate of how much data can be sent without congesting the network.

At the beginning of a slow-start phase, the congestion window is set equal to the maximum segment size (MSS). Thus, only one packet can be sent. Then, each time an ACK is received, the congestion window is increased by the MSS value. This can cause an exponential growth in the size of the congestion window, and thus in the number of packets sent, as shown in Figure 15.9.

It may seem paradoxical that adding a constant to the congestion window on each ACK can cause exponential growth in the window size, but remember that (unless ACKs are coalesced at the receiver) each packet sent results in the return of an ACK. So, if the congestion window was N, then one RTT later N ACKs will be received, causing the MSS to be added to the congestion window N times. The new congestion window will be $2N$, and so after each RTT the window size will double.

Of course, if we continue to grow the congestion window exponentially, then pretty soon it will be really large and we will overload the network again. This is not what we want! We need a way to decide when to stop this exponential growth phase, and Jacobson and Karels suggest doing so at half the window size that got us into trouble in the first place. In other words, when we encounter packet loss, we record one-half the current congestion window size in a variable, called the *slow-start threshold*, and during the subsequent slow-start phase we stop growing the congestion window once it reaches this threshold.

If we simply left the congestion window there, each time we encountered any sort of packet loss we would cut the window in half. Pretty soon, the window size would be stuck at one packet, TCP would become a stop-and-wait protocol, and (although the network would be much less congested) the end-to-end performance would be lousy. How to grow the window after the slow-start phase is the topic of Section 15.8.11.

Some routers will send an ICMP Source Quench message when they wish to reduce the incoming packet rate. It is not clear that this is a useful thing to do, because it is hard to define the right time to send a Source Quench or the right host to send it to, but if a TCP sender does receive such a message, it should enter a slow-start phase for the connection in question.

15.8.11 Congestion Avoidance

Congestion causes packet loss, and packet loss ruins TCP performance. While exponential RTO backoff and slow-start allow TCP to recover from congestion (once it is detected through packet loss), it is better to avoid congestion in the first place. Since we cannot continue the exponential growth of the congestion window indefinitely, but we don't want to leave it stuck at the slow-start threshold, we need a different mechanism once slow-start is done. The algorithm now specified is what Van Jacobson and Mike Karels call *congestion avoidance*,[44] but it should really be thought of as a scheme for determining how much bandwidth is available.[*]

The concept behind congestion avoidance is that the TCP sender has no way to discover the available bandwidth except by direct experiment. That is, the sender increases its use of the network until something indicates that it is using the right amount. There are two possible indications:

1   A packet is lost due to congestion. This means that the sender has overdone things, and will have to back off and try again.

2   The pipeline becomes full; the flow of acknowledgements back from the receiver (the usable window) limits the sender, and the system becomes self-clocking.

We would dearly like to see the second signal, rather than the first, since the first signal (a lost packet) indicates that our attempt at congestion avoidance has failed. The dividing line between the two operation regions (fast enough or too fast) might be quite small, so the

---

[*]   Note that there have been several schemes proposed for congestion avoidance mechanisms, both for TCP and for other protocol families. These include explicit feedback from congested routers[48], and rate-based schemes that explicitly control how fast a host is allowed to send.[49]

safest approach is to increase the congestion window by tiny amounts in the hope that we reach "fast enough" and stop there.

The tiniest amount by which we should increase the congestion window is "one packet." (If we increased it by a smaller amount, we would still have to send an additional packet, and routers drop stuff in units of packets.[*]) We cannot simply increase it by one packet per ACK, though, since (as we saw in Figure 15.9) this actually leads to exponential growth. Instead, we should increase it by one packet per round-trip time. This can be accomplished through increasing it by the reciprocal of the current congestion window, each time an ACK is received.

If you think about the congestion window as counting the number of packets in flight, and suppose that there are N packets currently in the pipeline, then for each ACK it will be increased by $1/N$, for a total increase of N/N or 1. (Of course, the math doesn't work out like this, but if you think about the instantaneous effect on the pipeline, it makes more sense.)

The combined implementation in TCP of slow-start and congestion-avoidance is quite simple. Assume that the congestion window is stored in the variable `cwnd`, the slow-start threshold has been stored in `ssthresh`, and the MSS value is kept in `mss`. Then this code will update the congestion window upon the receipt of an ACK (adapted from Jacobson):[44]

```
if (cwnd < ssthresh)
  cwnd += mss;
else
  cwnd += (1/cwnd);
```

When a packet loss is detected, we have to store the slow-start threshold and enter a new slow-start phase (adapted from Zhang et al.):[50]

```
ssthresh = MAX(MIN(cwnd / 2, maxwnd), 2 * mss);
cwnd = mss;
```

Here, `maxwnd` is the estimate of the receiver's total buffer size, as used in the Silly-Window-Syndrome avoidance algorithm.

One potential problem with this congestion avoidance scheme is that if the network is populated with some hosts that implement it, and some that do not, then one might expect that the "bad" hosts would get more than their fair share of the network bandwidth. The key to fairness in this situation is the behavior of a router when it gets congested and has to discard a packet. Whose packet does it discard?

If the router could somehow sense which source was cheating and preferentially drop its packets, then for at least one round-trip time (until the sender times out and starts retransmitting) the "good hosts," slowly but steadily, will evenly divide up the remaining bandwidth. The original proposal for such a scheme, called "Fair Queueing" (*RFC 970*)[4, 51] has

---

[*]   A slightly more formal argument is given by Van Jacobson.[44]

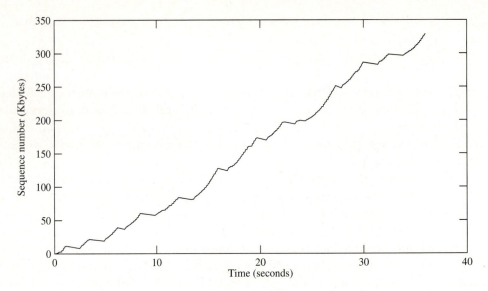

Figure 15.10   Plot of sequence number versus time

been the subject of much research and some controversy (*RFC 1254*),[52] and perhaps some variant of this approach will be adopted in the future.

One might ask why, in the absence of some mechanism that enforces fairness, would anyone want to use congestion avoidance and thereby put themselves at a disadvantage to people who don't? The answer is that congestion avoidance is necessary even in the absence of competition, because it is quite possible for one connection to cause congestion in an otherwise unused network. Congestion avoidance can save your TCP from itself.

15.8.12   Slow-Start and Congestion Avoidance in Action

In Section 15.3.5.3, I showed how the tcpdump program could be used to obtain plots of the TCP sequence number versus time. For the reader's convenience, I have reproduced Figure 15.4 as Figure 15.10, which shows the sender's sequence numbers for a transfer of 327 Kbytes across a relatively low-bandwidth path.

The curve shows a generally smooth slope, which is good, but occasionally displays "teeth" characteristic of the slow-start algorithm. To see this in more detail, I have graphed just the first three seconds of the connection in Figure 15.11. Each packet transmission is marked with a triangle.

We can see that the sender starts by transmitting just one packet, followed by bursts of two, three, and five packets. At about this point, we seem to reach the capacity of the network, because the packets with sequence numbers of about 8K and above, sent at about one second after the start of the connection, are not acknowledged. About 1.5 seconds

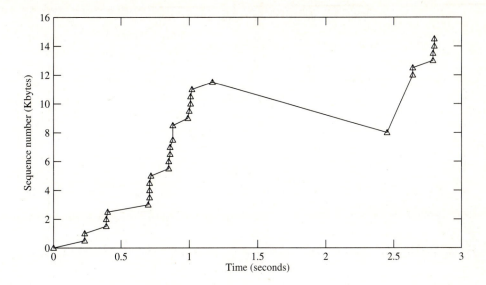

Figure 15.11   First 3 seconds of Figure 15.10

later, the sender times out and retransmits them; note the subsequent doubling of the congestion window (one, two, and four packets) characteristic of slow-start.

Note that not all the unacknowledged packets were lost; the sender only retransmits one of those segments, so the receiver presumably had the others ready for acknowledgement once the gap in the sequence number space was repaired.

Continuing our detailed look at the connection in Figure 15.12, we see that it subsequently encounters additional packet losses but appears to have been chastened by the result of its exponential increase in the congestion window. The slow-start phase that starts about 4.9 seconds into the connection ends after only one doubling, after which the congestion window increases by one segment per round trip time. We still see packet losses, but they become less frequent after the first few events.

15.8.13   Problems with the Self-Clocking Model

In the nice picture in Figure 15.7, showing TCP neatly self-clocking, the acknowledgments arrive at the sender with the spacing that they were given by the receiver. This is a shaky assumption, since any queueing along the return path will cause some of the ACKs to be delayed. The later ACKs may catch up with the slower ones, causing the sender to receive a burst of ACKs all clumped together (Figure 15.13). This is known as *ACK-compression*[50] (or sometimes *ACK-smashing*). The sender may respond to a clump of compressed ACKs with a clump of data packets, sent at a rate faster than the network can tolerate.

While ACK-compression does not change the long-term average rate of data-packet generation, it may cause the instantaneous rate to increase significantly. If one of the rout-

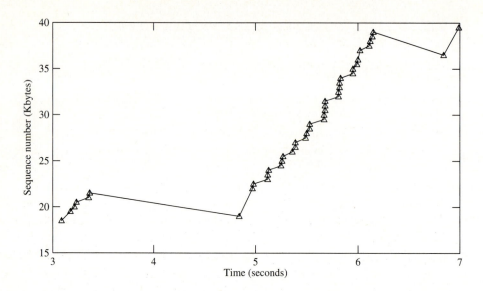

Figure 15.12   Next 4 seconds of Figure 15.10

ers along the path is nearly congested, this could push it over the precipice, resulting in packet loss for either the ACK-compressed connection or some innocent bystander.

ACK-compression takes place only under certain conditions. First, the return path must be carrying enough data traffic to cause ACKs to be queued; this is normal in the Internet. Second, the ACKs and the interfering data traffic must not be neatly interleaved (or the ACK spacing would tend to be increased, if anything) but rather segregated into clusters (first a bunch of data packets, then a bunch of ACKs). This behavior has been observed in simulations and simple test networks.[53] Finally, unless the receiver's maximum window is

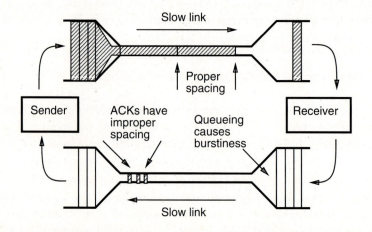

Figure 15.13   TCP ACK-compression (compare to Figure 15.7)

large enough, the total number of ACKs in transit may not be enough to render the effect observable. A trace-based study of connections through the Internet shows that ACK-compression does indeed occur, although it rarely seems to lead to congestion.[54]

15.8.14 Header Compression

People sometimes use TCP over low-speed lines, perhaps using a link protocol such as SLIP or PPP (see Section 15.6.3). The overhead of TCP and IP headers may often dominate the actual amount of data transferred, especially for single keystroke exchanges in Telnet. For each byte of keystroke data sent, at least 40 bytes of IP and TCP header are required.

Van Jacobson observed that, if a slow link is being used for a small number of TCP connections, most of the fields in the IP and TCP headers do not change from packet to packet. Those fields that do change, such as the TCP sequence number, change only by a small amount. In fact, the difference between the headers in two successive small packets can be encoded in just 5 bytes, or in just 3 bytes if one makes some assumptions about typical uses of TCP (*RFC 1144*).[5] This makes interactive use of TCP over low-speed lines far more pleasant.

The original implementation of this technique was for use with the SLIP framing protocol (see Section 15.6.3) and is called CSLIP. The new PPP protocol also supports IP/TCP header compression.

15.8.15 Future Protocol Plans

The telecommunications industry is installing long-distance links of incredible bandwidth. While TCP performs admirably in most existing networks, it will have some obvious problems over such *long fat networks* (LFNs). Several proposals have been made to fix these problems. As of this writing they are controversial, and have not been fully implemented, but they illustrate the nature of possible solutions.

15.8.15.1 *Scaling the Window Size*

In Section 15.8.1 we saw how TCP's performance over paths with high delay-bandwidth products is limited by the relatively small window size. Since physicists have been unable to increase the speed of light, the only way to improve TCP performance over such paths is to increase the window size.

The obvious solution would be to expand the 16-bit window size field in the TCP header to, say, 32 bits. This won't work because a TCP implementation using the new packet format would not interoperate with one using the old format, and it is unrealistic to expect that all TCP installations would immediately be upgraded to the new scheme.

Instead, researchers have proposed defining a new TCP header option that would apply a scale factor to the window field (*RFC 1323*).[55] That is, if the scale factor is, say, 4, then the receiver would divide its remaining buffer size by 4 before inserting it into the TCP window field, and the sender would multiply the offered window by 4 before computing the usable window. In order that the receiver not employ this scheme unless the sender will understand it, neither side will send scaled window values until it has received a Window Scale Option from its peer.[*]

15.8.15.2   *Selective Acknowledgements*

When a packet is lost on a long fat network, many other packets will be in the pipeline, and are likely to arrive intact at the receiver. However, the receiver has no way to inform the sender that the packet was probably lost, since TCP acknowledgements indicate only the last sequence number received without a gap. The sender will only discover the packet loss after it times out waiting for an acknowledgement, wasting more than one entire round-trip time. The sender will then have to retransmit not only the lost packet, but all the subsequent ones that the receiver already possesses, thus wasting almost half a round-trip time's worth of bandwidth.

Along with the Window Scale Option, therefore, a new Selective Acknowledgement (SACK) Option has been proposed (*RFC 1072*).[56] A receiver would send a SACK option to advise the sender that it has received certain ranges of sequence numbers, beyond the end of the properly acknowledged window. The sender could then avoid redundant retransmissions. To maintain compatibility with existing implementations, some of which may not be able to process TCP option on non-SYN segments, the transmission of SACK options must be preauthorized by the sender, using a SACK-Permitted Option on its SYN segment.

Use of SACK may complicate the slow-start algorithm. Further research may reveal when TCP can safely retransmit a dropped packet, as requested by a SACK option, without having to commence a slow-start phase. As of this writing, the SACK mechanism defined in *RFC 1072* is not recommended for use.

15.8.15.3   *Round-trip Time Measurement with the TCP Timestamps Option*

Since (as we noted in Section 15.8.9.2) it is typical to measure the round-trip time only once per RTT, on a high delay-bandwidth network RTT measurements will be made quite infrequently relative to the rate of packet transmission. This makes it more likely that during an RTT measurement, some packets will be lost, causing a retransmission and invalidating the RTT measurement. Thus, on such networks it may be quite difficult to estimate the smoothed RTT, and performance will suffer.

To decouple the measurement of RTT from the fate of individual data segments, it would be nice to have an unambiguous method for measuring the RTT. The TCP Timestamps Option has been proposed for this purpose (*RFC 1323*).[55] The Timestamps Option includes two timestamp fields, one called *TS Value* and one called *TS Echo Reply.* The idea is that each TCP packet carries a Timestamps Option, with the TS Value field indicating

---

[*]   An added complication requires that the Window Scale Option appear only in SYN segments; this imposes the mild restriction that the scale cannot be changed once the connection is under way.

when the packet was sent. The receiver remembers the TS Value, and copies it into the TS Echo Reply field on the next TCP packet it transmits. Upon receiving an acknowledgement, therefore, the sender merely subtracts the TS Echo Reply timestamp from the current time to get a measurement of the RTT.

Because this so-called Retransmission Time Measurement (RTTM) mechanism is simpler and more accurate than the RTT estimation methods originally specified for TCP, it might well be worth using, even for low-delay connections.

Use of the Timestamps Option is only allowed if one was received from the peer TCP on a SYN segment. The receiver may collect several timestamp values before it has a chance to echo one back to the sender; rules have been proposed for how the receiver chooses, from among these timestamps, which one to echo.

15.8.15.4 *Protection Against Wrapped Sequence Numbers*

TCP sequence number calculations are done using modular arithmetic; if an increment to the sequence number causes it to overflow the 32-bit representation, it is possible to continue the connection because the difference between two sequence numbers can still be calculated unambiguously. This is because the TCP specification includes the concept of a Maximum Segment Lifetime (MSL), which limits the persistence in the network of any segment and thus of its associated sequence numbers. The TCP sequence number calculation will be unambiguous, but only if it takes longer than an MSL for the current sequence number to wrap around.

The TCP specification sets the MSL to two minutes, or 120 seconds. The size of the sequence number space is 2^{32} bytes, or 2^{35} bits. This means that TCP cannot consume sequence number space (send data) faster than

2^{35} bits / 120 seconds = 286 million bits/sec

without running the risk of accepting a stale duplicate packet due to sequence number wrap-around. TCP implementations have already achieved rates of at least 700 Mbits/sec between two machines, and 800 Mbits/sec over a software loopback.[57] Because of the danger of wrap-around, such high-speed implementations cannot send more than four billion bytes before pausing to let stale segments expire.

The TCP Timestamps Option (*RFC 1185*)[58] can also be used to support the Protection Against Wrapped Sequence Numbers (PAWS) mechanism. Since the timestamp values are monotonically increasing (in modular arithmetic), the receiver can reject any segment that arrives with an out-of-order timestamp. This might occasionally result in the loss of a good packet, but it will prevent any stale duplicates from creeping in. In effect, the timestamp values act as the high-order bits of an extended sequence number.

The "clock" used to generate the values for the Timestamps Option need not tick at a standard rate, so long as it is monotonic and ticks at a "reasonable rate." The recommended rate is somewhere between 1 msec and 1 second per 12 tick; at 1 msec per tick, the PAWS mechanism supports bandwidths up to 8×10^{12} bits/sec, and segment lifetimes of over 24 days.

15.8.15.5 *Controversy*

The TCP extensions described in this section are not without their flaws. All proposals that depend upon new TCP header options will be of little use until they are relatively widely implemented, since both ends of a connection must support them. Further, the implementation of some of these options, such as Selective Acknowledgement, are moderately complex, so there may not be sufficient incentive for vendors to support them.

It may be that it is time to replace TCP with a new protocol that preserves the best features of TCP without repeating its shortcomings, since it would be almost as easy to negotiate the optional use of a new transport protocol as it would be to negotiate the use of a slew of options (*RFC 1263*).[59]

15.9   THE UDP LAYER

UDP (*RFC 768*)[60] is a datagram protocol; that is, it makes no attempt at reliable delivery. This means that the performance effects of graceful degradation do not arise in the UDP layer, although they may well be a problem at higher layers. All UDP must do is to convey datagrams as fast as possible. Section 15.10 discusses general issues in the implementation of transport protocols, and many of these apply to UDP.

The performance of higher layers that depend on UDP, if they try to provide reliable communication, is, of course, affected by the reliability of UDP and lower layers. Thus, any phenomenon, such as congestion or Deterministic Fragment Loss, that causes packet loss will reduce performance. There is not much that can be done about this at the UDP layer, so its clients must solve these problems.

15.9.1 Checksums

The UDP checksum, unlike the IP header or TCP checksums, is optional. A host may send a distinguished "no checksum" value instead of taking the time to compute a checksum over the entire UDP data region. In BSD-based systems, a kernel global flag (udpcksum) controls whether checksums are sent or not. The *Host Requirements* document (*RFC 1122*)[2] specifies that UDP packets with bad checksums *must* be discarded by the receiver, but in the BSD-based systems if udpcksum is false, then the received checksum is not checked.[*]

Checksum calculation is expensive, to be sure, and benchmarks will look a lot better if they are done with UDP checksums turned off. This is dishonest, because it is generally not safe to operate this way. Most applications that use UDP packets assume that UDP, while unreliable, does not deliver corrupted data, and so they do not bother to compute

---

[*]   The historical impetus for this behavior is that some early UDP implementations incorrectly calculated the UDP checksum, and it was easier to disable it in the receiver than to fix it in the transmitter.

their own checksums (which may be foolish,[61] but the UDP checksum is normally good enough). When UDP checksums are disabled, instead of causing graceful degradation, data errors cause graceless disaster.

UDP checksum errors are rare, perhaps one in a few hundred thousand or so, but if one should corrupt the contents of the file you had just spent a day editing, you would not feel so happy about having saved a little CPU time by not calculating checksums.

15.10   IMPLEMENTATION OF TRANSPORT PROTOCOLS

Although most of the interesting research on protocol performance has addressed the design of the protocols themselves (that is, what packets appear on the network and when), the actual performance of a system also depends on many hidden details of the implementations. These details do not change the observed characteristics of the packets on the network, but rather change the speed with which the packets are processed.

That these are *details* does not make them unimportant. A suboptimal implementation can easily fritter away much of the performance available on a high-speed network. Indeed, minimization of protocol processing overhead may be the single most important factor in performance at FDDI speeds and above.

Although there are processing costs for each layer, the transport layer tends to be the most expensive, for two reasons. First, this is often the most complex layer. Second, and progressively more crucial, transport layer processing may require the host to handle every byte. This is especially painful on the fastest CPUs, whose speed depends on cache performance, because such data-handling normally runs at cache-miss speeds rather than cache-hit speeds.

Implementations of the two important IP transport protocols, TCP and UDP, have both been subjected to scrutiny. David Clark et al. have analyzed[19] the factors affecting TCP processing. Craig Partridge and Stephen Pink[62] have analyzed some of the factors affecting UDP processing. These issues have also driven proposals for new IP transport-level protocols, such as NETBLT (*RFC 998*),[63] that intend to avoid imposing unnecessarily large overheads on the end hosts.

15.10.1   State Lookup

When a TCP packet arrives at a host, the first step in TCP processing is to figure out which connection it belongs to, and then to find the state record associated with that connection. This record, often called the TCP Control Block (TCB) or Protocol Control Block (PCB), contains information, such as sequence numbers, acknowledgement numbers, window sizes, round-trip timers, etc.

On a small system, such as a workstation, there may be relatively few PCBs, and a simple linear search will be sufficiently fast. On a time-sharing system with many logged-in users, there may be several hundred PCBs, and the linear search might cost more than all the other costs of handling a short TCP packet.

One simple trick is to use a small cache of recent successful matches, to bypass the cost of a full search. This caching works because locality tends to be high; that is, when a packet arrives at a host, it is likely to be for the same connection as the previous packet.[64]

The 4.3BSD-Reno release incorporated a *one-behind* cache, which keeps track of the PCB for the most recent arrival. Subsequent research has shown that the 4.3BSD-Reno implementation was faulty, and also that some additional gains could be achieved by remembering as well the PCB of the most recently transmitted packet.[62] Transmission is a good indication that a connection is active and will probably receive a packet soon. Such simple caching schemes do well for workstations and time-sharing systems of moderate size, because both kinds of system tend to exhibit high locality on arriving packets.

A large transaction processing system, however, has relatively low locality. Packets on hundreds or even thousands of connections may be evenly interleaved, thus negating the value of any caching strategy, no matter how sophisticated. The cost of searching for the right PCB becomes unbearably high.[65] The obvious answer is to use a more sophisticated data structure, such as a hash table, which (combined with careful coding of the search routines) will significantly reduce the PCB lookup overhead.

15.10.2 Header Prediction

Once the appropriate TCB has been located, the next step in processing a TCP packet is to determine where in the sequence number spaces its sequence and acknowledgement numbers lie, and what response should be made to the packet. These decisions can be quite complex, because TCP is a duplex protocol and because all sorts of special cases intrude. This complexity leads to long, slow code paths, and limits performance.

One of the rules of thumb proposed in Section 15.2.8 is "use a fast path for the common cases." Van Jacobson applied this principle to TCP processing, calling his changes to the 4.3BSD code "header prediction."[66] The idea is that when a TCP connection is moving bulk data, the same kind of packet is sent repetitively, with predictable changes in sequence number and no changes in most header fields. We can "predict" what the next packet will look like, and so set up a fast path to handle it.

The first step is to check that the packet contains nothing unusual. This means that the TCP flags should not contain SYN, FIN, RST, or URG; that the sequence number be the one we are expecting (i.e., the segment is not received out of order); and that the offered window has not changed. These checks can be made using a total of three integer comparisons. If any check fails, the packet must be handled on the "slow path."

Although TCP is a full-duplex protocol, during high-speed transfer data is usually flowing in only one direction. Therefore, an incoming TCP packet usually falls into one of two cases:

1   Receiver processing.   The packet contains new data, does not acknowledge anything new, arrives in order, and we have buffer space to hold it. These tests can be done in

three more integer comparisons, plus a little more arithmetic to calculate the available buffer space.

2 Sender processing.   The packet carries no data, acknowledges our in-transit data, and our congestion window is full size (i.e., we are not in the middle of slow-start or congestion avoidance). These tests require two subtractions and three integer comparisons.

In other words, after a total of six integer comparisons and a couple of subtractions, the TCP header prediction algorithm either gives up (and puts the packet on the slow path) or has decided exactly what needs to be done with the packet. These fast paths can be streamlined as well, since each fast path is designed for a specific case and can ignore the subtleties that complicate the slow path (such as congestion avoidance). The fast path for receiver processing is about seven lines of C code; for sender processing, about twice that.

15.10.3 Checksums

IP transport protocols checksum the entire data region of each segment, because the IP layer itself provides no guarantee of data integrity. If it were not for the data checksum, however, the transport protocols would not in theory have to touch any of the packet bytes beyond the headers. In practice, it might be necessary to copy the data from one buffer to another, especially in the UNIX I/O model, in which an application specifies where in its virtual address space the kernel must store received data.

Most implementations of UDP and TCP, therefore, touch each data byte twice: once to move it from user space to kernel space (or vice versa), and once to checksum it. With some reorganization of the code, these two operations may be combined into a joint checksum-and-copy operation, with a resulting decrease in per-byte overhead.[6, 19]

On incoming packets, this trick may expose a multithreaded user process to temporarily corrupt buffers: one thread may read a buffer that another thread is using for TCP input, during the interval when corrupt data has not been repaired by the normal TCP retransmission mechanism. Such nonserializable interactions between two threads are foolish in any event, so the problem is of little concern.

Although the cost of data motion can dominate the cost of checksum calculation on a fast machine, it is still necessary to do the calculations efficiently. The IP checksum (used for IP header checksums, as well as for TCP and UDP data checksums) is a 1's complement sum over the 16-bit quantities in the packet, padded if the packet contains an odd number of bytes. One's-complement arithmetic is somewhat tricky, since most CPUs use 2's complement arithmetic, but it is not difficult to find significant optimizations. Such techniques include loop-unrolling and deferred end-around carries (*RFC 1071*).[67] It is also worth noting that since the IP checksum is insensitive to byte ordering, the checksum routine never needs to do any byte-swapping.

15.10.4 Timer Implementation

A TCP sender must ensure that its retransmission timer is set each time it sends a segment, and must clear the timer when the corresponding acknowledgement is received. A TCP receiver may need to manipulate a timer on each segment reception, to implement delayed-acknowledgement and Silly-Window-Avoidance. This means that the cost of setting and clearing timers must be small. Other transport protocols, such as the Sun RPC protocol (*RFC 1057*),[68] also require frequent timer manipulation.

A host may have hundreds or thousands of TCP connections in progress. This means that one cannot simply shift the burden of work onto the code that updates the timers once per clock tick, or else this process would be too expensive.

So that these overheads do not dominate the cost of protocol processing, a good protocol implementation depends on a highly tuned timer package. The 4.2BSD TCP system includes its own timer package, which allows per-packet timer manipulations to be done in just a few instructions. However, the code that checks to see if a timer has expired is linear in the number of active TCP connections, and runs (effectively) seven times a second. It is not clear if this will scale well, or if periodic timer maintenance will consume excessive resources on a system with many active TCP connections. It might be necessary, on such a system, to adopt a more efficient algorithm for timer maintenance, such as the one proposed by Varghese and Lauck.[69]

15.10.5 Internal Queueing and Scheduling Issues

Many protocol implementations have resource allocation limits to make sure that no single process uses up all the buffer space. For example, in 4.2BSD, between each protocol layer there is a queue for waiting packets, and the length of each queue is limited. In some circumstances, these queue limits can interact in unforeseen ways.

When layer A cannot place a packet on the input queue of layer B, it can either drop the packet or it can wait for the queue to become available. In the latter case, the input queue for layer A might become full, causing the problem to cascade back to a point where some layer, such as the network interface hardware, will be forced to drop a packet.

At times, one cannot avoid dropping packets due to host resource exhaustion. A poorly designed network implementation, however, may drop packets for no good reason, or it might drop the wrong packets.

15.10.5.1 Scheduling the Layers

Network implementations based on 4.2BSD, and probably many others, tend to give more priority to input processing than to output processing, and more priority to lower layers rather than higher ones. The goal of such a policy is to prevent running out of network interface buffers, which are often scarce, and thereby dropping incoming packets. The policy goes too far, however, and can contribute to collapse in the face of overload when coupled with a queue scheme that limits the length of upper-layer input queues.

Consider what happens to a host receiving a steady stream of incoming datagrams faster than it is able to process them. Since the lower layers of input processing take priority over other processing phases, packets will build up in an upper-layer input queue until that queue hits its limit. From then on, the system will happily continue to receive packets and process them through several layers, before discarding them when they reach the full queue.

This is precisely the wrong behavior for an overloaded host. If CPU time is scarce, the host should be discarding excess packets as early as possible, rather than wasting the time to process them up through a few layers before throwing them away.

If input processing is given strict priority over output processing, when a host becomes overloaded the input side may hog all the CPU resources. This starves the output side, preventing the transmission of packets. As a result, applications on other hosts may time out and retransmit their packets. This further overloads the host, leading to continued output starvation and "livelock."

The combination of limited-length queues and static priorities effectively gains memory efficiency and simplifies scheduling in exchange for wasting CPU time. Host memories are far larger (and cheaper) than they were when this design was done, and the trade-off causes problems for high-bandwidth networking.

One simple solution is to increase the queue-length limits, or to remove them entirely. It might be wise to limit the total amount of memory allocated to network buffers, but once a packet has entered a host it should be allowed to reach its final destination.

The scheduling system should also allow a queue-consumer to run often enough to drain its input queue, at an average rate matching the rate at which the queue is being filled. Otherwise, the queues will get unnecessarily long, increasing the associated queueing delays. The consumer need not be started each time a new packet is available; this might eliminate the efficiency obtained by batching the processing of several packets.

One should not ignore the problem of conserving the network interface's input buffers, since these are probably a more precious resource than CPU memory. Beyond this, however, the scheduling system should strive for fair allocation of CPU resources among the various layers. A kernel architecture based on threads can provide fairness, if one can limit the amount of time that each thread is allowed to run before ceding the processor.[70]

One might also consider eliminating the queueing and scheduling mechanisms entirely, and run through the entire protocol stack (as a series of procedure calls) for each packet. If this could be done fast enough to avoid dropping packets at the network interface, it would bypass a lot of overhead and would guarantee that each received packet gets to the end of the line.

15.10.5.2 Output Flow Control

The queueing design in 4.2BSD-based systems has another problem: a sending layer cannot know if the interface driver fails to successfully transmit a packet. For example, an Ethernet interface may drop a packet after encountering too many collisions. When an Ethernet is heavily loaded, this may cause many packets to disappear.

This problem is most conspicuous when one tries to measure the rate at which a host can send packets. If an application writes packets as fast it can, the operating system might discard some of them without telling the application, once the packet rate begins to saturate the LAN (and hence causes transmission failures). A benchmark application that simply counts the number of "successfully" transmitted packets will be misled about the true performance of the system. Instead, one must design complex benchmarks that count the packets after they are transmitted on the network, a technique prone to failure because many systems can send packets faster than they can receive them.

15.10.6   TCP Buffer Management Strategies

As I mentioned in Section 15.8.3, the choice of TCP window size (the receiver's buffer size) has a direct effect on throughput (see Figure 15.8). Much less obvious, but no less important, is the effect of choice of the sender's buffer size, and how the sender's buffer is managed.

15.10.6.1   *Filling the Sender's Buffer*

In TCP implementations based on 4.2BSD, data is not sent directly from the application's buffer. Instead, associated with each connection is a pair of *socket buffers* (one for input data, one for output data). A socket layer routine named *sosend*() is responsible for moving data from the application buffer to the output socket buffer.

To avoid tying up all of a system's memory with buffered output data, the size of the output socket buffer is limited. This means that the socket buffer may become full of unacknowledged, already-transmitted data, forcing the TCP sender to stop transmitting packets even when the application buffer contains additional data and space remains in the usable window. Even when some untransmitted data remains in the socket buffer, the rules of the Silly-Window Syndrome (SWS) avoidance algorithm (see Section 15.8.5) may prevent the TCP sender from transmitting.

The policy followed by *sosend*() to decide when to move data from the application buffer to the output socket buffer may thus be crucial to good TCP performance, especially on a LAN. Depending on the amount of data in each of the buffers, *sosend*() must choose between moving data or blocking until more space is available.

The original 4.2BSD version simply moved as much data as possible whenever there was any space in the output socket buffer, but apparently this policy caused excessive fragmentation of buffers (somewhat like the Silly-Window Syndrome). The 4.3BSD version blocks if all three of these conditions hold simultaneously:

1   At least one page of data remains in the application buffer.

2   Less than one page of free space remains in the output socket buffer.

3   At least one page of unacknowledged, transmitted data is already in the output socket buffer.

As Crowcroft et al. point out,[7] this scheme can still cause fragmentation, especially for RPC-style interactions, in which the application transmits relatively small buffers.

For example, suppose that we have a half page of data in the application buffer, but only a quarter page of free space in the output socket buffer. The 4.3BSD scheme would allow *sosend*() to move the data into the socket buffer, thus causing the remaining buffer to be sent in two TCP packets.

The 4.3BSD-Reno version of this code fixes the problem by using a different test; it blocks if both of these conditions hold:

1   The remaining space in the output socket buffer is not enough to hold the remaining application data.

2   The remaining space in the socket buffer is less than a low-water mark threshold.

It seems reasonable to set the low-water mark to be the TCP connection's MSS; this means that *sosend*() will transfer new data into the output socket buffer only if it can either use up the rest of the application data, or if the amount transferred is enough to send a full-sized TCP packet. Alternatively, one might set the threshold to be equal to the page size, which (on BSD-derived systems) allows socket data to be kept in page-size "clusters" rather than in chains of small "mbuf" buffers. (Section 15.10.6.4 explains how to resolve this apparent dilemma.)

15.10.6.2 Choosing the TCP Send Buffer Size

TCP throughput, as discussed in Section 15.8.1, cannot be faster than one window-full per round-trip time. In a system with a limited send buffer size, such as those based on 4.2BSD, throughput is further reduced if the sender's buffer is smaller than the receiver's window. The sender effectively forfeits its right to use some of that window, and so the number of packets it can inject into the pipeline is artificially limited.

When using high-delay paths, therefore, one should make sure that the TCP send buffer size is as large as possible, as long as this does not overcommit the available buffer memory on the sending host.

Even on low-delay paths, small send buffers can cause serious throughput problems. As I mentioned in Section 15.8.6, when the send buffer size is less than 2MSS, the receiver's delayed-acknowledgement mechanism may stall the connection every few packets. Since there is no reason to limit the send buffer size except to conserve a little host memory, a system that is not memory-starved should probably prevent the TCP send buffer size from being set below 2MSS. That is, any attempt by an application to do so should be ignored.

15.10.6.3 Shrinking the Receiver Buffer Size

One can also cause throughput to drop by shrinking the receiver buffer size (i.e., the maximum window size), after the connection has started, to a value below the MSS. The sender-side SWS-avoidance rules require the sender to postpone sending a packet if the amount of data to be sent is less than the MSS and also less than half the receiver's estimated buffer size. This estimate is usually based on the largest advertised window size during the connection, and the sender has no way of knowing if the receiver's buffer shrinks. From the sender's point of view, after the receiver has shrunk its window, the available window might always look "silly."

Implementations based on 4.2BSD exacerbate this problem in two ways:

1   It is impossible to change the receiver's buffer size before the connection has been fully established, so any attempt to set a size smaller than the default will appear to shrink the window.

2   Although the SWS-avoidance algorithm (*RFC 1122*)[2] specifies that the sender should delay for a period "in the range 0.1–1.0 seconds," these implementations actually delay for five seconds before using a silly window.

At the receiver's side, the best solution is to prevent an application from shrinking the window below the initial value. On the sender's side, it might pay to age the estimate of the receiver's buffer size; that is, once the SWS-avoidance delay has been triggered, the current estimate would be discarded, on the assumption that the window might have shrunk.

On an Ethernet, with an MSS of 1460 bytes, it would be strange to see a receiver's buffer size set below the MSS, although some implementations for small machines apparently do use a 512-byte window. On FDDI, where the MSS may be as high as 4312 bytes, even a 4096-byte receiver buffer is too small. Many hosts now default to 16 Kbytes, but it is not inconceivable that some older applications explicitly set the window to 4 Kbytes (believing that they may be increasing, rather than decreasing, the buffer size). Such applications might actually perform far worse when moved from Ethernet to FDDI.

15.10.6.4   Setting the TCP MSS

The TCP MSS (Maximum Segment Size) is usually calculated by subtracting the default IP and TCP header lengths from the MTU in effect over the path in question. For example, two hosts communicating directly over an Ethernet would set their MSS to 1500 − (20 + 20), or 1460 bytes.

On some LANs, this may not be appropriate. Consider FDDI, with an MTU of 4352 bytes. By the straightforward calculation, the TCP MSS would be 4312 bytes. This is an unfortunate choice, however, for two reasons:

1   If the send buffer size is set to 8 Kbytes (not an unreasonable value for use on Ethernet), it will be less than 2MSS (8624 bytes), and so performance will be significantly reduced because of the receiver's acknowledgement policy. For example, if the receiver's delay is 0.2 seconds, the throughput will drop to 8 Kbytes/0.2 seconds, or 328 kbits/sec: not a particularly effective use of a 100-Mbits/sec medium.

2   Even when the send buffer is more than 8 Kbytes, it is likely to be a multiple of a large power of 2: 16 Kbytes, 32 Kbytes, etc. These sizes are not integer multiples of 4312;

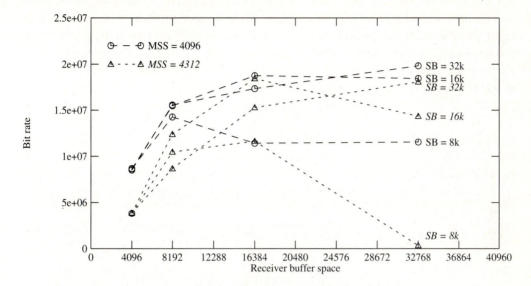

Figure 15.14   Effect of MSS choice on FDDI performance

thus, the TCP output engine will occasionally leave a small remainder at the end of a buffer, resulting in poor utilization of the network (and perhaps even in acknowledgement delays).

It makes sense to modify the MSS calculation, to round the result down to a "nice" value when this does not reduce the value "too much." For FDDI, setting the MSS to 4096 instead of 4312 reduces the payload of a packet by only 5%, and actually improves performance in all cases; see Figure 15.14. For Ethernet, on the other hand, setting the MSS to 1024 instead of 1460 dramatically decreases performance; see Figure 15.15.

15.10.7   Path MTU Discovery

Fragmentation of IP packets, while not invariably harmful, can cause such pathological problems as Deterministic Fragment Loss (see Section 15.7.5) or IP Identification wraparound (see Section 15.7.6). On the principle that an ounce of prevention is worth a pound of cure,[*] a consensus is developing that fragmentation should be avoided.

The Path MTU Discovery (PMTUD) mechanism (*RFC 1191*)[35] proposes a guaranteed way to avoid fragmentation: set the Don't Fragment (DF) bit in the IP header on every datagram. If the datagram reaches a router that cannot forward it, because of its length, the router must drop the packet and return an ICMP "Destination Unreachable/Fragmentation Needed and DF Set" message. (I'll call this a *TooBig message*.)

---

[*]   In metric countries, the ratio is 28.3 g to 0.454 kg.

Clearly the sending host must do something clever with a TooBig message, or else communication will cease. The PMTUD mechanism allows the host to infer the size of a datagram that the offending router would be able to forward without fragmentation; the host reduces its packet size to that estimate and tries again. While the process may have to repeat several times (if the MTU shrinks more than once along the path) it should converge fairly quickly.

PMTUD is not implemented in a single layer; it communicates information between all the layers in the IP protocol stack, up through the layer that chooses what size of packet to send. This is called the *packetization layer*. TCP is a packetization layer, but UDP is not, because a layer above UDP (such as the Domain Name System or Sun RPC) must choose the UDP packet size.

Path MTU estimates for each destination are stored in a table, usually the IP routing table. The initial estimate for a destination is the first-hop MTU; that is, the packet size that could be sent on the host's own network interface without fragmentation. A packetization layer using PMTUD sets its packet size from the current estimate, and asks the IP layer to set the DF flag on outgoing packets.

If there is no link along the path that forces fragmentation of the packet, the DF flag has no effect and everything proceeds without a hitch. If, however, a router must reject the packet, it returns a TooBig message to the sender. This is received by the ICMP layer, which must use the information in the TooBig message to estimate a new MTU.

The router that rejects the packet knows how large a packet it would have been able to forward, but the original specification for TooBig messages (*RFC 792*)[71] does not provide a way for the router to pass this information back to the sending host. The PMTUD specifi-

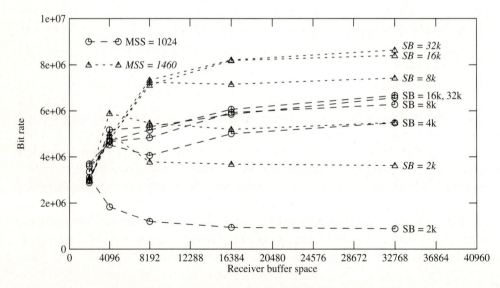

Figure 15.15   Effect of MSS choice on Ethernet performance

cation steals a previously unused field in the TooBig message for this purpose. Some router vendors have already implemented this change, but because not all routers have been updated, the PMTUD mechanism provides a fallback.

Although an IP link MTU may in theory be anywhere between 68 bytes and 64 Kbytes, in practice there are only about ten different MTUs in use. Equipped with a table of these values, called the *plateau table*, the ICMP layer can make a new estimate of the correct MTU by choosing the first plateau smaller than the size of the failing datagram. For example, if we tried to send a 1500-byte datagram and got a TooBig message, we would reduce our estimate to 1006 bytes (the MTU used on SLIP and ARPANET technology); a subsequent TooBig message would reduce the estimate to 508 bytes. We expect the process to arrive at the right estimate after only a couple of wasted round trips.

Once communication has been established, a subsequent change in routing topology might change the actual Path MTU. Reaction to a decrease will be swift, since a router will generate a TooBig message as soon as a packet crosses the new threshold. We would like the estimate to respond to increases in the actual Path MTU, as well, and to do this we time out our stored estimates after a few minutes. When an estimate times out, we increase it by one level in the plateau table, until we reach the MTU of the first hop link. This gradual increase means that if the actual Path MTU has not changed (the usual case) we will only waste one round trip returning to the proper plateau.

When the ICMP layer decides on a new PMTU estimate, it updates the value stored in the IP routing table and then notifies all the transport-layer entities using this destination. The transport layer may, in turn, have to pass the notification up until it reaches the packetization layer.

15.10.7.1 TCP and PMTUD

When TCP learns of a new PMTU estimate, it must modify the size of the segments that it sends. If the estimate has increased, TCP must avoid sending segments larger than the limit imposed by the peer host using a TCP MSS option. This means that the TCP control block must contain not only the current MSS value, but also the MSS limit.

If the PMTU decreases, this means that a TCP packet was dropped by some router. TCP could simply wait for its retransmission timer to expire, but it may be much more efficient to retransmit the dropped segment immediately. TCP must not retransmit more than once per decrease in the PMTU estimate; in particular, it should not retransmit in response to every TooBig message, since several of these may be generated in response to a burst of packets. Retransmissions triggered by TooBig messages should trigger slow-start behavior, but should not change the slow-start threshold.

Before the development of PMTUD, the best way for IP to avoid fragmentation was to limit the packet size to 576 bytes if the destination is non-local. Many BSD-based TCP implementations also use this rule to limit the MSS value that they send to their peers. This was useful back when few hosts voluntarily limited the size of the packets they sent, since it forced such hosts to send small datagrams. With PMTUD, however, the artificial limit on the MSS option is unfortunate, because it means that packets will generally be much smaller than the Path MTU would allow. Today, the proper value for the MSS option should be the MTU of the host's network interface. Sending a smaller value would reduce performance by preventing the use of large packets; sending a larger value would reduce performance by encouraging the use of packets that could not be forwarded onto the last-hop link without fragmentation.

15.11   THE DOMAIN NAME SYSTEM

IP protocols at the transport layer and below refer to hosts using IP addresses. Higher layers (including human users, the highest layer of all) use names rather than addresses. Not only are names easier to remember, they also add a layer of indirection that makes it possible to modify an IP host's address without confusing software (or humans) that don't particularly care what its address is.

The original mechanism for Internet naming required that all names be registered with a central site, and all hosts periodically retrieved a host table from that site. This almost worked when the Internet had a few hundred names; there are now over 700,000 known names (*RFC 1296*),[72] and the number appears to be growing exponentially. Even if the longest host name were only 5 bytes (the minimum size that would allow that many permutations of alphabetic characters), a host table holding 700,000 host names and their addresses would be 6.3 Mbytes long. If a central site had to distribute a copy of the table to each host, it would take almost 9 months to transmit all those bytes over a T1 connection.

Naming in the Internet is now done using the Domain Name System (DNS). The DNS names are hierarchical, which allows both distributed name service and distributed namespace management. Levels in the hierarchy are known as *domains*, and each domain may be managed by a separate organization and served by a separate server. A domain must be served by several servers, each with a replica of that domain's name database, to help ensure availability and to spread out the load.

Although the basic philosophy behind the DNS is quite simple, its successful implementation and operation involves a tremendous amount of attention to detail. In some ways, the DNS is more complex than TCP; TCP is simply a protocol, while DNS is an entire distributed system, not just a protocol. I will try to summarize the aspects of the DNS that affect performance, but for the subtle details you should consult the specification (*RFC 1034, RFC 1035*)[73] and the *Host Requirements* document (*RFC 1123*)[2] and Chapter 11.

15.11.1   Resource Record Types

The DNS database contains more than just the names of hosts. Associated with each DNS name is a set of *resource records* (RRs). The most useful RR types include:

A   Host address record.

MX   Mail-exchange record (*RFC 974*).[74] These are used to provide a level of indi-
           rection in the mail system, so that a mail server can accept mail for hosts that
           may not be directly reachable via the Internet.

CNAME   Canonical name for a host. This allows the DNS to translate nicknames for a
           host to the host's primary name.

PTR   Pointer record. This is most useful when one is doing an inverse lookup, trans-
           lating an IP address back to a host name.

These are the RR types most often used by higher level applications. Several other RR
types are defined, mostly for the internal workings of the DNS.

DNS tags all data with a *class* code, such as *IN* (Internet). This allows the DNS to map
from a single name to addresses in several different protocol families. Almost all existing
DNS entries are of class IN.

15.11.2 Name Resolution

Applications use name *resolvers* to contact one or more name servers, as necessary, to translate a name. Each resolver and name server, except for those at the root of the tree, must be
preconfigured with the addresses of at least one higher-level server.

Consider the name CS.STANFORD.EDU. We start by sending this name in a query to
one of the *root* name servers, such as NS.NIC.DDN.MIL. This server will translate as
much a suffix of the name as possible, and then refer us to the servers for that subtree. In
this case, we would get a list of the STANFORD.EDU servers. From this list we choose
JESSICA.STANFORD.EDU, which tells us that CS.STANFORD.EDU has IP address
36.8.0.7, so we have the result after two steps. Other name resolutions may require queries
to three or more name servers.

15.11.3 Caching in the DNS

If a resolver followed this procedure every time it had to translate a host name, the root
servers would be swamped. (If each of 700,000 hosts did just one name translation per
hour this way, the root servers would handle almost 200 requests per second.) Also, each
translation would take several round-trip times across the network. The DNS avoids these
problems through the use of caches in the resolvers. DNS also supports the use of *full-service resolvers*, which provide shared caches for use by large numbers of hosts.

A full-service resolver accepts requests to resolve domain names. If the requested name is
found in its cache, then it can return an answer without bothering any servers. Otherwise,
if a suffix of the requested name is cached, then the resolver can contact the appropriate
server for that suffix without bothering the root or other high-level servers. Since it may

take some time to obtain the reply to a forwarded request, a full-service resolver should be able to service many requests concurrently.

In most cases, name resolution requests are for hosts that are "nearby" in the domain hierarchy. For example, hosts at Stanford are far more likely to ask for translations of STANFORD.EDU names than MIT.EDU names. This locality of reference means that most name translations can be satisfied either from nearby caches or nearby servers, and so the higher-level name servers need not participate in most translations. Otherwise, the performance of the DNS would be pitifully slow.

Caches should be used not only for storing successful translations, but also for storing unsuccessful ones. Consider what would happen if a malfunctioning host were to repeatedly try to translate the name THIS.DOES.NOT.EXIST. If failures were not cached, each attempt would create useless work for the high-level name servers. A resolver that caches failures can short-circuit these attempts, limiting their effect on performance.

There are two kinds of failures in the DNS. Temporary, or *soft*, failures are those resulting from a problem in the lookup mechanism, such as a dead server or a network problem. Permanent, or *hard*, failures are authoritative negative responses, indicating that the name requested is known not to exist.

Name servers provide timeout information along with negative responses, so a resolver knows how long it can cache a hard failure. After a soft failure, the resolver should at some point be willing to retry the lookup, but there is no point in doing it too soon; network and host failures usually last for several seconds, at least. Even if an end-host (or "stub") resolver is foolish enough to retry immediately after a soft failure, a full-service resolver should short-circuit such a retry by returning the cached error indication.

15.11.4 DNS Time-To-Live Values

DNS caching has one drawback: if the true value for a name is changed at its primary server, there is no feasible way to invalidate all the cached copies. Because caching is so fundamental to the performance of the DNS, a compromise is made between cache performance and cache consistency: associated with each RR is a Time-To-Live (TTL) value, governing how long it may be cached. TTL values limit the duration of any inconsistent cached copies, so that the system eventually corrects all inconsistencies.

TTL values range from zero, which means "don't cache this RR," up to several days. Entries whose RRs are not expected to change should have long TTLs, to increase the likelihood of a cache hit. Entries whose RRs are volatile should have short TTLs, to decrease the likelihood inconsistency.

Network managers often have some advance warning before having to change type A (IP address) record values. For example, it may be known several days in advance that a host is being moved from one subnet to another, or that a subnet number is being changed (which causes all the host addresses on that subnet to change). In such a situation, it is useful to temporarily reduce the TTL values of the addresses that are about to be modified.

Suppose you are planning on changing the address for host X.Y.Z, whose TTL is currently 3 days. If, at least 3 days in advance of changing the A record value, you had changed its TTL to (say) 10 minutes, then when the address change is made, you know that after 10 minutes nobody in the Internet will have a cached copy of the old A record. Once the change is made, you can set the TTL back to 3 days, and the load on your name server will return to normal.

15.11.5 Choice of Transport Protocol

While DNS servers are supposed to respond to TCP requests, DNS requests are normally done using UDP packets. A minimal TCP connection requires at least six packets, whereas a UDP exchange requires just two, and end-host protocol processing for TCP costs somewhat more than for UDP.

In some cases, TCP may be more appropriate. Because there is no restriction on the size of DNS database entries, some responses might be too big to fit into a single UDP packet.[*] In such cases, the resolver might retry the request using TCP instead of UDP. Also, if a resolver is making heavy use of the same name server, it might be preferable to configure the resolver to use TCP instead of UDP. This is most useful when the path between the resolver and server is unreliable or congested, since TCP can adjust to such problems, reducing the number of transport-level retransmissions, and eliminating the need for DNS-level retries (which place a heavy load on the database lookup server).

15.11.6 Timing of Query Retransmissions

When DNS queries are done using UDP, they will sometimes fail due to communication errors or server overload. The principle of graceful degradation requires that resolvers retry failed queries, but it would be a mistake to reissue a request too quickly. This would simply increase network congestion or server overload, resulting in congestive collapse and reduced performance. It is recommended (*RFC 1123*)[2] that the retry interval be no less than the round-trip time or five seconds, whichever is greater. Subsequent retransmission timeouts should follow an exponential backoff pattern (for example, doubling on each retry) and the number of retransmissions should be limited.

15.11.7 Message Compression

If a DNS response is too large to fit into a UDP datagram, and the resolver retries the request using TCP, lots of effort is wasted. Not only are many more packets exchanged than necessary, but the server is forced to do the database lookup twice. To reduce the chances

---

[*]   Database administrators are encouraged to avoid creating entries that would not fit in a UDP packet
      (*RFC 1123*).[2]

that this will be necessary, the DNS uses a message-compression scheme to eliminate redundancy in a message. If two names passed in a message contain the same suffix, only the first instance is passed as an ASCII string. The second instance of the suffix is simply a pointer to the first. Pointers take up only two octets, quite a bit less than the names they replace.

For example, MX records often contain the names of several possible mail servers. Usually, all the servers accepting mail for a host will be "near" that host in the hierarchy; that is, they will be in the same higher-level domains. Thus, the various names in an MX record usually have a long common suffix, which can be replaced by a pointer in all but the first occurrence.

15.11.8   Translation of Numeric Addresses

Once in a while, a user will be forced to refer to a host with its IP address instead of its name. This might be because the name is not known, or because some name server is down and the name cannot be translated.

Applications normally accept IP addresses, in the normal A.B.C.D notation (e.g., 10.1.0.11). Many applications try to translate such names using the DNS, and only parse them as numeric addresses once the DNS returns an indication of failure. This use of the DNS is unnecessary, since a host name will never be composed entirely of numeric fields, and so the host can parse such strings immediately as addresses.

Even when the DNS is working, parsing numeric addresses locally saves network exchanges and reduces resolver load. When the DNS is not working, the unnecessary DNS request may turn into a long delay. Since this is the time when one is most likely to use a numeric address instead of a name, it is particularly unwise to make the useless DNS request.

15.11.9   Replication and the Effect of a Dead Server

Resolvers are usually configured to know about more than one higher-level server or full-service resolver. This replication means that even when one DNS server is down, hosts can still do name translations. A resolver may encounter a timeout when it attempts to contact the dead server, but by rotating subsequent retries among the other servers it knows about, it can fulfill the request as long as at least one server is available.

When only one address needs to be translated, the delay introduced by a dead server is usually negligible. Sometimes, however, a large number of names must be translated in order to perform a higher level function. For example, an *rlogin* server may need to translate many of the host names in its /etc/hosts.equiv file before it finds one whose address matches the calling host. If it does a dozen such translations, and each time starts by asking the first DNS server in its list of servers, when that server is dead it may take over a minute before the *rlogin* server can verify the client address.

This kind of performance bug can be especially painful to users. A dead name server someplace in their network may make interactive operations, such as remote command execution, take minutes instead of seconds, without providing any direct evidence of a problem.

The solution is for name resolvers to cache information about dead servers. Once a request times out and the resolver then succeeds in contacting a secondary server, the next time the resolver needs to translate a name it should first try the server that successfully responded to the previous request. If this attempt times out, the resolver can then run through its entire list of servers, but in most cases the cached server will reply immediately and DNS delays will again be negligible.

15.12 APPLICATION LAYERS

Real users never employ TCP or UDP directly. They run an application program, which almost always layers additional protocols above the transport level. Not infrequently, the performance bottlenecks lie here. Bottlenecks above the transport layer tend to fall into a few categories:

- Buffering issues.   Does the application buffer its output so that the transport layer can send large enough packets? Does the buffering strategy of the transport layer confound the application by failing to meet delay requirements?

- Presentation layer.   Does the cost of presentation processing (converting data from one format to another) overwhelm other costs?

- Timeouts.   Applications use timeouts to detect failures, just as the transport layers do. An application-layer timeout must be chosen with knowledge of how the underlying layers perform, to avoid unnecessary retries.

IP defines several "Type-Of-Service" (TOS) values, which are intended to allow applications to favor either low delay or high bandwidth, if a choice must be made. Little support for TOS exists in current hosts and routers, so few applications specify a TOS. Future WANs may provide much more TOS support, so application implementors should consider what TOS best serves their purposes.

15.12.1   Telnet and rlogin

The Telnet protocol (*RFC 854*),[75] which is used for remote terminal access, typifies the class of highly interactive, low data rate applications. Humans like to see fast responses to their keystrokes, and notice if the delay is more than a few hundred milliseconds. On the other hand, in most cases a Telnet connection has suitable bandwidth if it can update a screenful of information in a similarly short interval; this implies a data rate on the order of 10 Kbytes/sec.

If the speed of light were the only limit to good latency, we should be able to use Telnet between any two points on Earth without suffering unreasonable delays. Since other issues, such as nongeodesic routes and congested links, conspire to make long-distance delays quite a bit worse than this, we may need to work around such delays.

Telnet clients and servers should certainly use the IP Type-Of-Service mechanism to specify Low Delay (and not High Throughput, since that isn't necessary). This may not do much good, since the existing Internet is usually not able to select special low-delay routes, but some day it might pay off.

15.12.1.1   Improving Latency

Since we cannot always eliminate latency in the network, we can instead reduce interactive delay by performing certain "interactive" functions at the client end of the connection.

One such function is *flow control*, which here means the use of special characters (such as CTRL/S and CTRL/Q) to suspend or resume a stream of terminal output. While long delays in keystroke echoing may be irritating, long delays in flow-control processing may render it useless. Suppose that your are logged into a system over a high-bandwidth network with a round-trip delay of 1 second, and your screen is being filled with output at the rate of one screen every 100 milliseconds. If you type CTRL/S to suspend the output, you will miss ten screens of information before the flow pauses.

The Berkeley *rlogin* protocol (*RFC 1282*),[76] which was developed for 4.2BSD but is now commonly used in other systems, lets the server host do most of the interactive processing (such as keystroke echoing) but allows the client host to do flow control. Since some interactive programs, such as text editors, redefine the flow control characters to have other functions, the rlogin protocol allows the server to inform the client when the connection should be in "raw" mode. In this mode, all character processing is done at the server.

The Telnet Linemode Option (*RFC 1116*)[77] takes a more comprehensive approach to client-side character processing. The Linemode Option allows the server to negotiate with the client the handling of many special characters, for such functions as flow control and line editing (e.g., erasing a typed character). The server can also tell the client which characters must be handled at the server end, which allows the client to do local echoing of all other keystrokes. Not only does this make typing a lot more pleasant, but it reduces the number of packet exchanges from one per character to one per line (in the normal case).

The Linemode Option is quite a bit more complex than most other Telnet options, and has not yet been universally implemented. It may be longer still before applications with idiosyncratic character-set interpretations, such as text editors, are able to negotiate these with the Telnet server. This means that if a user enters one of these applications, most likely the Telnet layer will revert to remote character-at-a-time behavior, with the consequent exposure to high network latency.

15.12.1.2   Improving Throughput

A single Telnet or rlogin user only hits a few keystrokes each second, and probably needs at most a few thousand characters of output per second. This does not take much processing power by itself, but when a single host (such as a terminal server, transaction processing, or timesharing system) must handle tens or hundreds of active Telnet connections at once, the requirements pile up. Fortunately, Telnet traffic is usually quite bursty, as users spend most of their time sitting and thinking (or just sitting), so the peak load generated by N users will be much less than N times the peak load generated by a single user.

Telnet processing time can be divided into per-packet and per-byte processing. For keystroke processing, the per-packet costs dominate. Use of Telnet-level aggregation techniques like the Linemode Option, and TCP-level techniques such as the Nagle tinygram-suppression algorithm (see Section 15.8.7), can help reduce the per-packet costs and the associated costs of transport-level processing. It may also be prudent to use an efficient TCB-lookup mechanism (see Section 15.10.1) since a large timesharing system may have lots of active connections in progress.

Per-byte costs for Telnet are high because every byte must be scanned for presentation-layer processing. Although most data bytes turn out to be plain text, any byte can potentially introduce a command sequence. Telnet command sequences, used for functions such as option negotiation and flow control, are preceded by the Interpret-as-Command (IAC) character. Commands can flow in either direction, so both client and server must check every byte to see if it is an IAC character.

Presentation processing within Telnet must also deal with the variation in end-of-line sequences between various operating systems. For example, UNIX systems use LF to end a line of text, while VMS systems use CR-LF. The Telnet protocol settles this by converting host-specific conventions into a standard end-of-line sequence (which, however, was ambiguously specified at first (*RFC 1123*).[67] Both client and server must examine every character in order to implement this convention. If the Linemode Option is in use, the client must check every input character to see if it should be processed locally or forwarded to the server.

15.12.2 FTP and *rcp*

The IP File Transfer Protocol, FTP (*RFC 959*),[78] is the primary way to transfer files between systems. FTP supports a wide range of file types and provides not only file-copying commands, but also commands for manipulating directories. My discussion of FTP performance will concentrate on the speed at which it moves file data, since the other commands usually do not cause performance problems.

An FTP connection starts with a control connection that uses a Telnet-like protocol, although the full Telnet command set is not available. The control connection is used by the client (FTP user) to issue commands to the server, and the server to issue responses to the client. All data transfer takes place on separate data connections, one for each file (or directory listing) transferred. Since the control connection is used only for short commands and responses, its performance is not particularly important. It will tend to be limited by network latency, and the latency of the end-host file system operations.

FTP data transfers can be done with various combinations of data types, data structures, and transfer modes. Some of these combinations can make presentation processing expensive.

The FTP data types are:

1   ASCII is used for transferring text files. As in the Telnet protocol, presentation processing involves maintaining the end-of-line convention, which means that both client and server must scan every byte. Optionally, a printer format control subtype may be specified, which further complicates presentation processing (this is not widely implemented).

2   EBCDIC is similar to ASCII; when used on an ASCII client or server this requires presentation processing to translate the character sets.

3   Image is used for transferring binary data in 8-bit bytes. This type normally requires no presentation processing, unless one of the end hosts uses a different byte size.

4   Local is used for transferring binary data between hosts with differing byte sizes. This inherently requires expensive presentation processing on at least one end.

When the client and server use the same representation for all file types, Image mode is safe to use and will provide by far the fastest service, often by a factor of two or more. Image mode may also be necessary to preserve the content of binary data. Some FTP user programs therefore attempt to recognize if the server is compatible, and automatically set the data type to "image."

The FTP data structures are:

1   File.   The file is treated as a continuous sequence of bytes and no internal structure appears on the data connection.

2   Record.   The file (which must be type ASCII or EBCDIC) is divided into a sequence of records. The boundaries between records are identified by special marks in the data connection, and so may require additional presentation-level processing.

3   Page.   Similar to Record but each "page" is transmitted with addressing information that allows the receiver to deposit the data units in random order rather than strict sequence. Page structure also adds presentation-processing costs, but because it can be used to transfer "holey files" (sparse files for which only certain blocks are stored on disk) it may improve performance by avoiding the transfer of large "holes" over the network. Page structure makes sense only for the Image and Local data types.

The FTP transmission modes are:

1   Stream. The data structures are transmitted as a simple stream of bytes. For File structure, this means that no additional presentation processing is necessary. Record structures are separated by special end-of-record (EOR) control codes, so if records are used the receiver must examine every data byte to check for control codes.

2 Block. The data structures are transmitted as blocks, each preceded by a header saying how long the block is. The header also contains flags indicating, among other things, if the block is the last in a record. When Record structures are used, this is more efficient than Stream mode because the receiver need not scan every data byte looking for EOR codes.

3 Compressed. Similar to Block mode, allows compression of the data through a simple run-length encoding. For data which contains long runs of a single byte value, this can reduce network transmission costs, but for random data the number of bytes transferred may well be worse. When compression is successful, it requires more presentation-layer processing than Block mode on both client and server ends, so it might not be worthwhile in any case.

The 4.2BSD FTP implementation supports only File structure and Stream mode. This reduces the incentive for adding support for other structures and modes to an FTP implementation, since it would not be able to make use of these modes when interoperating with BSD-based FTP software. Even if widely implemented, these options would not be all that useful because of the cost of additional presentation processing, and because the increasing homogeneity among file systems makes the simplest combination (Image/-File/Stream) usable in most situations.

There is one potential payoff for using Block or Compressed mode, and that is their support of "restart" processing. Consider an FTP transfer of a large file that is continually interrupted by communications failure or host crashes. If the file takes, say, 24 hours to transmit and the server host crashes every 10 hours or so, then the probability of getting the file across in one piece is near zero. The system does not degrade gracefully.

The user might be able to solve the problem by breaking the file up into 1-hour chunks, and transferring them with individual FTP connections, thus allowing partial retransmission of the file. This may not always be possible (say, if the file is being read from a server where the user has no direct access). It also requires the user to do extra work that should have been done by the communications system.

The FTP protocol therefore allows the sender of a file to insert *restart markers* into the data, as long as the transfer is not being done using Stream mode. The FTP user program stores these markers as they arrive from the server (for a *retrieve* command) or as the server echoes them (for a *store* command). If the transfer should fail, the client can restart it at the right position by issuing a *restart* command using the information in the most recently stored marker.

Since FTP is often used to transfer large files, and since no reverse traffic flows along the data connection, FTP performance can suffer more than that of other applications from complex interactions between buffer sizes and TCP's delayed-acknowledgement mechanism. When FTP performs poorly, and the bottleneck is not in the file system at either end, it might be wise to examine a trace of the TCP packets to see if the connection is pausing from time to time. This might indicate a faulty buffering policy at the sender,

connection has been established the server can search its queues for all the messages destined for that host, and transfer them all on the same connection.

A server which must deliver the *same* message to several recipients on the same host, perhaps as the result of a mailing list expansion, can do even better. The SMTP protocol allows the sender to issue multiple RCPT ("recipient") commands for the same message body, which then need be transferred only once. This saves packets and network overhead, and is especially useful when the body is lengthy.

An SMTP receiver, once it has accepted a message, is obligated to make a serious effort to deliver or relay the message without losing it. The server cannot guarantee that a severe hardware failure, such as a disk-head crash, will not wipe out the message, but it should at least protect against power failures and software crashes by committing the message to stable storage before acknowledging receipt.

Synchronous disk operations are usually quite slow compared to network delays and can limit SMTP performance in much the same way that they limit NFS write performance. Typical SMTP receivers, such as the Berkeley sendmail program, store each message in a separate file. This not only means that the data and meta-data must be stored synchronously, but that each new message also involves a directory update, which is usually done synchronously as well.

The synchronous-write delays encountered by SMTP can be ameliorated by the use of nonvolatile RAM (NVRAM), such as Legato's PrestoServe™ product. NVRAM allows parallelism between the receiver's disk activity and the other phases of an SMTP conversation. It may also reduce disk load by making possible many "dirty block" cache hits, since the directory used to store the queue may be used for several message deliveries before the NVRAM contents are written to the disk.

While use of the file system's directory as a way to organize the queue of pending messages simplifies the implementation of an SMTP server, it can cause performance problems when the queue gets large. Many operating systems use directory-search algorithms whose running time is linear in the number of entries; this means that the directory-search costs for processing all N entries in a queue of messages is proportional to N^2. When processing time increases as the queue length gets worse, throughput drops even lower and an unstable feedback loop results; once a server enters this trap it may not recover for a long time.

The solution, if one cannot modify the algorithm used for directory searches, is to break up the directory used for message queueing into several pieces. One natural division is to keep a separate queue for each concurrent processing stream, and divide up new messages among the queues as evenly as possible. If there are ten such queue directories, the directory search costs will be a hundred times lower than if only one directory were used.

15.12.3.3 *Avoiding Duplicate Deliveries*

Between the time that an SMTP receiver has committed a message to stable storage, and the time that the SMTP sender receives the subsequent acknowledgement and removes the message from its own queues, there is a finite interval during which the connection may fail. (Perhaps one of the hosts crashes, or perhaps the network fails and the sender times out the connection.) If a failure occurs, both hosts will be left holding a copy of the message, and when the failure is repaired, both copies will be delivered. Duplicate deliveries waste network resources and, if the chances of failure are high (because of flaky networks or systems, or an unusual message) the process may repeat *ad infinitum*. Since a flaky network generally slows down delivery of many messages, it might become increasingly bogged down processing duplicates instead of delivering new mail.

To minimize the probability of message duplication, SMTP implementations must make this interval as short as possible. On the receiver side, that means acknowledging a message as soon as it is stored, even if some header processing must be done later on. (If subsequent processing fails, perhaps because of an invalid recipient, the receiver can always return an error message in a separate piece of mail.) On the sender side, it means removing the message from the stable-storage queue as soon as the acknowledgement arrives.

The window of vulnerability cannot be entirely eliminated, so duplicate messages do sneak through. A server can suppress duplicate messages by logging the Message-ID field appearing in most mail headers (*RFC 822*).[82] Upon receipt of a message, the server checks this log to see if the same Message-ID has already been received; if so, the message is a duplicate and can be dropped.

The log must be kept in a data structure that allows both efficient update and efficient lookup; otherwise, the server might waste more time managing the log (which must be done on every message) than handling the occasional duplicate (which should happen rarely). The log might grow to be quite large on a busy server; entries need not be retained forever, but it is probably wise to retain them for three to five days, since typical SMTP senders will retry for that long before giving up.

15.12.3.4 *Avoiding Network Round Trips*

A typical SMTP conversation involves many round trips between the sender and receiver, as each of the sender's commands is acknowledged in turn. A minimal exchange consists of a HELO command, a MAIL FROM command, a RCPT TO command, a DATA command, the body of the message, and a QUIT command. The shortest message thus requires six round trips across the network.

This lockstep behavior may also cause problems when sending longer messages. Remember that the TCP slow-start algorithm (see Section 15.8.10) increases the congestion window by one packet for each acknowledgement received. At the beginning of an SMTP conversation, the connection places only a tiny load on the network, so packets are unlikely to be dropped even if the network is nearly congested. This means that the sender's congestion window will be fairly large by the time it starts to send the message body, and it might well overrun the available network capacity. Packets will be lost, and the proper operating point will not be discovered until several round-trip times later.

Van Jacobson, Craig Partridge, and Phil Karn[83] have observed that there is no intrinsic reason for the SMTP sender to wait for each command to be acknowledged before sending the next one. Almost all of the time, the acknowledgements will be positive, and even if something goes wrong (such as an incorrect destination address) no harm would be done if the sender did not discover this immediately. As long as the acknowledgements are checked before the sender dequeues its copy of the message, all would be well. An SMTP using this "fast-send" trick would eliminate several round-trip times from the conversation; the entire exchange might be compressed into as few as seven TCP packets. It would prevent the slow-start algorithm from being fooled.

In practice, alas, this does not work. The problem is that some SMTP receivers assume that commands will arrive one at a time, and after parsing one command they clear their input buffers. The subsequent commands are lost, or garbled, and the sender will probably time out. The effort wasted when this happens wipes out the savings achieved when the fast-send trick works.

15.12.3.5   Type-Of-Service for SMTP

Since most SMTP connections transfer fairly short messages, bandwidth is usually not the issue. The multiple–round trip problem implies that SMTP senders should specify Low Latency service. In those rare cases where a large message is being sent, High Bandwidth might be specified instead. I see no obvious message-length threshold for making the latency-versus-bandwidth decision; perhaps this will be more obvious once we have some experience with real networks that support TOS.

15.12.4   SNMP

Network managers have worn out too many pairs of shoes running between the consoles of their computers. Networks have grown far too large to be managed except via network management protocols, which allow a manager sitting at one console to view and adjust parameters at hosts and switching nodes spread over wide areas.

The network management protocol used in today's Internet is called the Simple Network Management Protocol (SNMP, *RFC 1157*).[84] SNMP, a packet exchange protocol, allows a "manager" program to query an "agent" process running at a remote site. For example, an SNMP manager might periodically ask a router to return the number of errors encountered on a specific data link.

The data kept by SNMP agents is called the *Management Information Base*, or MIB. The MIB is a tree-structured database, containing subtrees for various IP protocols, hardware devices, functional divisions (such as routing tables), and the like. For more information about SNMP and MIBs, see Chapter 12, Network Management.

Network management should not get in the way of normal, productive use of the network. This means that SNMP should not consume excessive network resources or CPU cycles. Several aspects of the SNMP protocol have been problematic in this respect, and I will summarize the issues in this section.

15.12.4.1 ASN.1 BER Processing

Each object in the MIB has a name, a type, and a value. An ObjectName is a sequence of integers, describing the position of the object in the MIB tree. For example, the object `ifOperStatus.1`, which refers to the current operational status of the first network interface on a given system, has the ObjectName 1.3.6.1.2.1.2.2.1.8.1.

Objects in the MIB are defined using Abstract Syntax Notation One (ASN.1).[85] Object-Names and values, when transmitted in SNMP messages, are encoded using the ASN.1 Basic Encoding Rules (BER).[86] The Basic Encoding Rules were designed to minimize data size, at the expense of extra CPU cycles for encoding and decoding. The specification requires, for example, that data be transmitted in the most compact form possible; this means that integers of different values might have different sizes in the data stream. The use of a variable-width format means that the decoding procedure must scan every byte in the encoded message, which can be quite costly.

When an integer is located in a BER stream, it will probably not be the size of a natural integer on the receiving host. It is also not likely to be aligned on an integer boundary. This forces the decoding procedure to perform expensive extractions and expansions to convert the data into a useful form.

One could implement a BER decoder by feeding a formal grammar to a compiler-generator, such as YACC,[87] but this turns out to produce a slow decoder. Faster BER decoders require hand-coding, because the data manipulations are so expensive. Even with careful programming, BER decoding might still be the CPU bottleneck for processing SNMP messages.

15.12.4.2 Access to Tables

Managed hosts often maintain tables of interesting information. For example, a router might contain a table listing its network interfaces, a routing table, and an ARP table. SNMP includes a simple but powerful GetNext operator that allows a manager to do an in-order walk over the leaves of a subtree of the agent's MIB. Since a table is by definition a subtree whose children are its table entries, repeated application of GetNext allows the manager to retrieve all of the table entries.

Table entries in SNMP are identified by their ObjectNames, rather than by a compact set of indices. This means that the manager does not necessarily know the complete set of table entries before traversing the table. Therefore, the GetNext operation takes as an input parameter the ObjectName of the previous tree node. To walk through a table, one first obtains the ObjectName of the table itself, applies GetNext with that ObjectName to get the first entry in the table, and then repeatedly applies GetNext with the ObjectName of an entry to get the successor entry. When what GetNext returns is not a child of the table's ObjectName, the traversal has been completed.

Since the manager cannot issue a new GetNext request until it knows the result of the previous one, each GetNext request must be sent in a separate SNMP message, and the issue rate is limited to once per round-trip time. This makes table retrieval slow, especially over high-delay networks and especially for large tables.

One trick that can help is to traverse several different parts of a table in parallel. In a single SNMP message, the manager can request the successor to several different table entries. To initiate the parallel traversal, the manager either must know the ObjectNames of several intermediate entries in the table, or it must guess them using a heuristic search. Once the manager knows a set of subtrees, it can then traverse several in parallel by issuing a message containing one GetNext for each of the subtrees (*RFC 1187*).[88]

The SNMP protocol requires that GetNext return ObjectNames in lexicographic order; that is, the agent must (in effect) sort the tables. The underlying table may not be kept in sorted order (a routing table, for example, might be stored as a hash table) which means that the agent must either maintain a sorted index into each table, or it must recreate the sort order each time the GetNext operator is used. The latter is incredibly wasteful of CPU time; the former consumes some memory space on a system that may not have much to spare.

15.12.4.3 *Packet Size Limits*

SNMP provides no mechanism to negotiate the use of UDP packets larger than the default size, which limits the size of SNMP messages to 484 bytes. Unlike the Domain Name System (see Section 15.11.7), SNMP does not support compression of repeated ObjectName prefixes in a message. That is, if a message contains references to objects 1.23.45.67.1, 1.23.45.67.2, 1.23.45.67.3, and 1.23.45.67.4, the prefix 1.23.45.67 must be transmitted four times. This limits the number of SNMP requests per UDP message, causing the use of more packets than might be necessary, as well as more network round trips.[*]

15.12.4.4 *Error Handling*

Although an SNMP manager may make multiple requests in one message, only one error code may be returned in each reply. While the error message does identify which request went wrong, SNMP does not specify what the agent should do with the other requests, and in fact various agent implementations have taken several approaches. This means that the manager must repeat the original message, with the offending request removed, to ensure that the results of the other requests are valid. If several of the original requests are erroneous, the retransmission cycle may have to be repeated several times.

It may seem strange to worry about the performance of SNMP on erroneous requests, since errors should be rare events. SNMP, however, does not have another way to indicate that a requested variable does not exist; since some variables are not always present, this forces the manager to request their value "experimentally" and so causes frequent errors. The continued evolution of the MIB, with the addition of new variables to existing groups, means that queries from a newer manager to an older agent will routinely evoke "noSuch-Name" errors.

---

[*]   It might be possible to issue one SNMP request message before receiving a reply for the previous one, but this might cause problems with the authentication mechanism.

15.12.4.5 *Authentication*

The SNMP protocol includes a Set message that allows a manager to change the value of a variable on an agent. For example, the network manager may want to adjust a timeout parameter, change a routing table entry, or turn off routing over a given link. The uncontrolled use of Set would expose SNMP-managed systems to security threats, in the form of malicious or misconfigured changes.

SNMP therefore includes hooks for the use of authentication mechanisms, to ensure that the manager making a request is in fact allowed to do so. (Authentication also ensures that the responses seen by a manager do indeed come from the right agent, rather than an interloper.) Since secure SNMP authentication mechanisms have only recently been defined (*RFC 1351, RFC 1352, RFC 1353*),[89, 90, 91] few current implementations provide true authentication and most agents simply prohibit Set messages.

Authentication is normally accomplished through the use of a *shared secret*; that is, the manager and agent both know a key, which is not (one hopes) known to potential intruders. An SNMP message is authenticated by using the key to compute a *message digest*, a compact value that (if the message digest algorithm is secure) can only be computed if one knows both the message content and the secret key. The digest value is then transmitted with the message, proving to the recipient that the message was generated by an entity that possesses the secret key. Timestamp values or sequence numbers can be included in the message to ensure that intruders do not "replay" old messages that they have copied from the network.

The choice of message digest algorithm is central to the success of the authentication scheme. A good algorithm should be cryptographically sound, and yet should not require too much CPU time to compute. For example, the MD5 algorithm (*RFC 1321*)[92] can process over a megabyte per second on a fast workstation, which corresponds to at least a thousand SNMP exchanges per second: more than one would expect the network software to handle.

On the other hand, MD5 might only be able to process several dozen SNMP requests per second on a slower CPU, such as might be used in a low-cost router or terminal server. This may well limit the utility of authenticated SNMP for managing such "small" systems, since many SNMP exchanges might be needed to perform a relatively simple task.

15.13 ACKNOWLEDGMENTS

I could not have put together this chapter without the help of many generous people. My employer, Digital Equipment Corporation, allowed me to spend time (and computer resources) writing this instead of doing my normal duties. Floyd Backes, Dave Borman, Jim Gettys, Chet Juszczak, Paul Koning, K. K. Ramakrishnan, Craig Partridge, Matt Thomas, Win Treese, Glenn Trewitt, and Paul Vixie all went out of their way to help me understand things that I really didn't know that much about.

REFERENCES

1 D.E. Comer, *Internetworking with TCP/IP: Volume I: Principles, Protocols, and Architecture*, Prentice Hall, Englewood Cliffs, 1991; and D.E. Comer and D.L. Stevens, *Internetworking with TCP/IP: Volume II: Design, Implementation, and Internals*, Prentice Hall, Englewood Cliffs, 1991.

2 R. Braden, *Requirements for Internet Hosts—Communication Layers. RFC 1122*, Network Information Center, October 1989; and R. Braden, *Requirements for Internet Hosts—Application and Suppor, RFC 1123*, Network Information Center, October 1989.

3 M. Loukides, *System Performance Tuning*, O'Reilly & Associates, Sebastopol, 1991.

4 J. Nagle, On Packet Switches With Infinite Storage, *IEEE Transactions on Communications*, Vol. COM-35, No. 4, pp. 435–438, April 1987.

5 V. Jacobson, *Compressing TCP/IP Headers for Low-Speed Serial Links, RFC 1144*, Network Information Center, February 1990.

6 D.D. Clark and D.L. Tennenhouse, Architectural Considerations for a New Generation of Protocols, in *Proc. SIGCOMM'90 Symposium on Communications Architectures and Protocols*, pp. 200–208. Philadelphia, September 1990.

7 J. Crowcroft, I. Wakeman, Z. Wang, and D. Sirovica, Is Layering Harmful? *IEEE Network Magazine*, Vol. 6, No. 1, pp. 20–24, January 1992.

8 R. Jain, *The Art of Computer Systems Performance Analysis*, John Wiley & Sons, New York, 1991.

9 M. Schwartz, *Telecommunications Networks: Protocols, Modeling and Analysis*, Addison-Wesley, Reading, 1987.

10 E.D. Lazowska, J. Zahorjan, G.S. Graham, and K.C. Sevcik, *Quantitative System Performance: Computer System Analysis Using Queueing Network Models*, Prentice Hall, Englewood Cliffs, 1984.

11 J. Gray, Ed., *The Benchmark Handbook for Database and Transaction Processing Systems*, Morgan Kaufmann Publishers, Inc., San Mateo, 1991.

12 Dah-Ming Chiu and Ram Sudama, *Network Monitoring Explained: Design and Applications*, Ellis Horwood Ltd., Chichester, England, 1992.

13 E.A. Arnould, F.J. Bitz, E.C. Cooper, H.T. Kung, R.D. Sansom, and P.A. Steenkiste, The Design of Nectar: a Network Backplane for Heterogeneous Multicomputers, in *Proc. 3rd International Conference on Architec-*

tural Support for Programming Languages and Operating Systems, pp. 205–216, ACM, Boston, April 1989; and M.D. Schroeder, A.D. Birrell, Michael Burrows, H. Murray, R.M. Needham, T.L. Rodeheffer, E.H. Satterthwaite, and C.P. Thacker, *Autonet: a High-speed, Self-configuring Local Area Network Using Point-to-Point Links*, Research Report 59, Digital Equipment Corporation Systems Research Center, April 1990.

14 R. Stine, *FYI on a Network Management Tool Catalog: Tools for Monitoring and Debugging TCP/IP Internets and Interconnected Devices*, RFC 1147, Network Information Center, April 1990.

15 S. McCanne and V. Jacobson, *An Efficient, Extensible, and Portable Network Monitor*, 1992, in preparation.

16 R.T. Braden, A Pseudo-Machine for Packet Monitoring and Statistics, in *Proc. SIGCOMM '88 Symposium on Communications Architectures and Protocols*, pp. 200–209, Stanford, CA, August 1988; and R.T. Braden and A.L. DeSchon, *NNStat: Internet Statistics Collection Package—Introduction and User Guide*, Release 2.3 edition, USC/Information Sciences Institute, Marina del Rey, 1989.

17 D. Curry, *nfswatch*, 1991.

18 *The Ethernet, A Local Area Network: Data Link Layer and Physical Layer Specifications (Version 1.0)*, Digital Equipment Corporation, Intel, Xerox, 1980.

19 D.D. Clark, V. Jacobson, J. Romkey, and H. Salwen, An Analysis of TCP Processing Overhead, *IEEE Communications Magazine*, Vol. 27, No. 6, pp. 23–29, June 1989.

20 S.J. Leffler and M.J. Karels, *Trailer Encapsulations*, RFC 893, Network Information Center, April 1984.

21 D. Katz, *A Proposed Standard for the Transmission of IP Datagrams over FDDI Networks*, RFC 1188, Network Information Center, October 1990.

22 D.D. Clark, The Design Philosophy of the DARPA Internet Protocols, in *Proc. SIGCOMM '88 Symposium on Communications Architectures and Protocols*, pp. 106–114, Stanford, August 1988.

23 J. Romkey, *A Nonstandard for Transmission of IP Datagrams Over Serial Lines: SLIP*, RFC 1055, Network Information Center, June 1988.

24 D.D. Perkins, *The Point-to-Point Protocol for the Transmission of Multi-Protocol Datagrams Over Point-to-Point Links*, RFC 1171, Network Information Center, July 1990.

25   D.D. Perkins and R.Hobby, *The Point-to-Point Protocol (PPP) Initial Configuration Option, RFC 1172*, Network Information Center, July 1990.

26   F. Baker, *Point-to-Point Protocol Extensions for Bridging, RFC 1220*, Network Information Center, April 1991.

27   J.B. Postel, *Internet Protocol, RFC 791*, Network Information Center, September 1981.

28   R. Perlman, *Interconnections: Bridges and Routers*, Addison-Wesley, Reading, 1992.

29   D. Estrin, *Policy Requirements for Inter Administrative Domain Routing, RFC 1125*, Department of Computer Science, University of Southern California, November 1989.

30   D.C. Feldmeier, Improving Gateway Performance with a Routing-Table Cache, in *Proceedings of IEEE INFOCOM '88*, pp. 298–307, New Orleans, March 1988.

31   S.O. Bradner, *Benchmarking Terminology for Network Interconnection Devices, RFC 1242*, Harvard University, July 1991.

32   S.O. Bradner, Testing Multi-Protocol Routers: How Fast Is Fast Enough? *Data Communications Magazine*, Vol. 20, No. 2, pp. 70–86, February 1991; and S.O. Bradner, Ethernet Bridges and Routers: Faster Than Fast Enough, *Data Communications*, Vol. 20, No. 3, 58–69, February 1992.

33   S.E. Deering, *ICMP Router Discovery Messages, RFC 1256*, Network Information Center, September 1991.

34   C.A. Kent and J.C. Mogul, Fragmentation Considered Harmful, in *Proc. SIGCOMM '87 Workshop on Frontiers in Computer Communications Technology*, pp. 390–401, Stowe, August 1987.

35   J.C. Mogul and S. Deering, *Path MTU Discovery, RFC 1191*, Network Information Center, November 1990.

36   D. Ting, J. Forecast, K.K. Ramakrishnan, and D. Flower, *Buffer Management Issues in Host Networking Software: Fragmentation and Reassembly*, 1992, in preparation.

37   J.B. Postel, *Transmission Control Protocol, RFC 793*, Network Information Center, September 1981.

38   J.C. Mogul, *Broadcasting Internet Datagrams, RFC 919*, Network Information Center, October 1984.

39   J.D. Spragins, J.L. Hammond and K. Pawlikowski, *Telecommunications: Protocols and Design*, Addison-Wesley, Reading, 1991.

40   D.C. Plummer, *An Ethernet Address Resolution Protocol, RFC 826*, Network Information Center, November 1982.

41   P.Koning, FDDI, Bridging, and the Internet Protocol Family, 1989, Presentation at the Interop '89 Birds-of-a-Feather session on FDDI.

42   IEEE, *Local Area Network MAC Bridges—Fiber Distributed Data Interface (FDDI) Supplement*, Draft Standard P802.1i/D2, IEEE, July 1990.

43   K.R. Sollins, *The TFTP Protocol (Revision 2), RFC 1350*, Network Information Center, July 1992.

44   V. Jacobson, Congestion Avoidance and Control, in *Proc. SIGCOMM '88 Symposium on Communications Architectures and Protocols*, pp. 314–329, Stanford, August 1988.

45   D.D. Clark, *Window and Acknowledgement Strategy in TCP, RFC 813*, Network Information Center, July 1982.

46   J. Nagle, *Congestion Control in IP/TCP Internetworks, RFC 896*, Network Information Center, January 1984.

47   P. Karn and C. Partridge, Improving Round-Trip Time Estimates in Reliable Transport Protocols, *ACM Transactions on Computer Systems*, Vol. 6, No. 4, pp. 364–373, November 1991.

48   K.K. Ramakrishnan and R. Jain, A Binary Feedback Scheme for Congestion Avoidance in Computer Networks with a Connectionless Network Layer, in *Proc. SIGCOMM '88 Symposium on Communications Architectures and Protocols*, pp. 303–313, Stanford, August 1988.

49   L. Zhang, VirtualClock: A New Traffic Control Algorithm for Packet Switching Networks, in *Proc. SIGCOMM '90 Symposium on Communications Architectures and Protocols*, pp. 19–29, Philadelphia, September 1990.

50   L. Zhang, S. Shenker, and D.D. Clark, Observations on the Dynamics of a Congestion Control Algorithm: The Effects of Two-Way Traffic, in *Proc. SIGCOMM '91 Symposium on Communications Architectures and Protocols*, pp. 133–147, Zurich, September 1991.

51   J. Nagle, *On Packet Switches with Infinite Storage, RFC 970*, Network Information Center, December 1985.

52   A. Mankin and K.K. Ramakrishnan, *Gateway Congestion Control Survey, RFC 1254*, Network Information Center, August 1991.

53 S. Shenker, L. Zhang, and D.D. Clark, Some Observations on the Dynamics of a Congestion Control Algorithm, *Computer Communication Review* Vol. 20, No. 5, pp. 30–39, October 1990; and R. Wilder, K.K. Ramakrishnan, and A. Mankin, Dynamics of Congestion Control and Avoidance of Two-Way Traffic in an OSI Testbed, *Computer Communication Review* Vol. 21, No. 5, pp. 43–58, April 1991.

54 J.C. Mogul, Observing TCP Dynamics in Real Networks, in *Proc. SIGCOMM '92 Symposium on Communications Architectures and Protocols*, pp. 305–317, Baltimore, August 1992.

55 V. Jacobson, R. Braden, and D. Borman, *TCP Extensions for High Performance, RFC 1323*, Network Information Center, May 1992.

56 V. Jacobson and R. Braden, *TCP Extensions for Long-Delay Paths, RFC 1072*, Network Information Center, October 1988.

57 A. Nicholson, J. Golio, D.A. Borman, J. Young, and W. Roiger, High Speed Networking at Cray Research, *Computer Communication Review*, Vol. 21, No. 1, pp. 99–110, January 1991; and D.A. Borman, private communication, 1992.

58 V. Jacobson, R. Braden, and L. Zhang, *TCP Extension for High-Speed Paths, RFC 1185*, Network Information Center, October 1990.

59 S. O'Malley and L.L. Peterson, *TCP Extensions Considered Harmful, RFC 1263*, Network Information Center, October 1991.

60 J.B. Postel, *User Datagram Protocol, RFC 768*, Network Information Center, August 1980.

61 J.H. Saltzer, D.P. Reed, and D.D. Clark, End-To-End Arguments in System Design, *ACM Transactions on Computer Systems*, Vol. 2, No. 4, pp. 277–288, November 1984.

62 C. Partridge and S. Pink. A Faster UDP, in *Proc. 2nd MultiG Workshop*, pp. 57–64, Stockholm, June 1991.

63 D.D. Clark, M.L. Lambert, and L. Zhang, *NETBLT: A Bulk Data Transfer Protocol, RFC 998*, Network Information Center, March 1987; D.D. Clark, M.L. Lambert, and L. Zhang, NETBLT: A High Throughput Transport Protocol, in *Proc. SIGCOMM '87 Workshop on Frontiers in Computer Communications Technology*, pp. 353–359, Stowe, VT, August 1987.

64   J.C. Mogul, Network Locality at the Scale of Processes, in *Proc. SIG-COMM '91 Symposium on Communications Architectures and Protocols*, pp. 273–284, Zurich, September 1991.

65   P.E. McKenney and K.F. Dove, Efficient Demultiplexing of Incoming TCP Packets, in *Proc. SIGCOMM '92 Symposium on Communications Architectures and Protocols*, pp. 269–280, Baltimore, August 1992.

66   V. Jacobson, 4BSD TCP "Header Prediction," *Computer Communication Review*, Vol. 20, No. 2, pp. 13–15, April 1990.

67   R. Braden, D. Borman, and C. Partridge, *Computing the Internet Checksum, RFC 1071*, Network Information Center, September 1988.

68   Sun Microsystems, Inc., *RPC: Remote Procedure Call Protocol Specification Version 2, RFC 1057*, Network Information Center, June 1988.

69   G. Varghese and T. Lauck, Hashed and Hierarchical Timing Wheels: Data Structures for the Efficient Implementation of a Timer Facility, in *Proc. 11th Symposium on Operating Systems Principles*, pp. 25–38, Austin, November 1987.

70   K.K. Ramakrishnan and W.R. Hawe, The Workstation on the Network: Performance Considerations for the Communications Interface, in *Proc. of the Second Workshop on Workstation Operating Systems (WWOS-II)*, pp. 105–108, Pacific Grove, CA, September 1989.

71   J.B. Postel, *Internet Control Message Protocol, RFC 792*, Network Information Center, September 1981.

72   M. Lottor, *Internet Growth (1981–1991), RFC 1296*, Network Information Center, January 1992.

73   P. Mockapetris, *Domain Names—Concepts and Facilities, RFC 1034*, Network Information Center, November 1987; and P. Mockapetris, *Domain Names—Implementation and Specification, RFC 1035*, Network Information Center, November 1987.

74   C. Partridge, *Mail Routing and the Domain System, RFC 974*, Network Information Center, January 1986.

75   J.B. Postel and J. Reynolds, *Telnet Protocol Specification, RFC 854*, Network Information Center, May 1983.

76   B. Kantor, *BSD Rlogin, RFC 1282*, Network Information Center, December 1991.

77   D. Borman, *Telnet Linemode Option*, *RFC 1116*, Network Information Center, August 1989.

78   J.B. Postel and J. Reynolds, *File Transfer Protocol (FTP)*, *RFC 959*, Network Information Center, October 1985.

79   S. Garfinkel and G. Spafford, *Practical UNIX Security*, O'Reilly & Associates, Sebastopol, 1991.

80   R. Caceres, P.B. Danzig, S. Jamin, and D.J. Mitzel, Characteristics of Wide-Area TCP/IP Conversations, in *Proc. SIGCOMM '91 Symposium on Communications Architectures and Protocols*, pp. 101–112, Zurich, September 1991.

81   J.B. Postel, *Simple Mail Transfer Protocol*, *RFC 821*, Network Information Center, August 1982.

82   D.H. Crocker, *Stanford for the Format of ARPA Internet Text Messages*, *RFC 822*, Network Information Center, August 1982.

83   C. Partridge, private communication, 1992.

84   J.D. Case, M. Fedor, M.L. Schoffstall, and J.R. Davin, *A Simple Network Management Protocol (SNMP)*, *RFC 1157*, Network Information Center, May 1990.

85   Information Processing Systems—Open Systems Interconnection, *Specification of Abstract Syntax Notation One (ASN.1)*, International Standard 8824, International Organization for Standardization, December 1987.

86   Information Processing Systems—Open Systems Interconnection, *Specification of Basic Encoding Rules for Abstract Notation One (ASN.1)*, International Standard 8825, International Organization for Standardization, December 1987.

87   S.C. Johnson, *YACC–Yet Another Compiler-Compiler*, Technical Report 32, Bell Laboratories, Murray Hill, July 1975.

88   M.T. Rose, K. McCloghrie, and J.R. Davin, *Bulk Table Retrieval with the SNMP*, *RFC 1187*, Network Information Center, October 1990.

89   J.R. Davin, K. McCloghrie, and J.M. Galvin, *SNMP Administrative Model*, *RFC 1351*, Network Information Center, July 1992.

90   J.M. Galvin, K. McCloghrie, and J.R. Davin, *SNMP Security Protocols*, *RFC 1352*, Network Information Center, July 1992.

91   K. McCloghrie, J.R. Davin, and J.M. Galvin, *Definitions of Managed Objects for Administration of SNMP Parties, RFC 1353*, Network Information Center, July 1992.

92   R.L. Rivest, *The MD5 Message Digest Algorithm, RFC 1321*, Network Information Center, April 1992.

CHAPTER 16

Operational Security

STEPHEN D. CROCKER

CONTENTS

Despite its lack of a formal security architecture, there is considerable effort being spent to make the Internet a more "secure" place. Not surprisingly, much of this work is spent on human factors. But, there are also new technologies being developed and deployed which may very well usher in a new era of "secure services."

16.1 INTRODUCTION

This chapter focuses on the operational aspects of network security. We will examine network security from the perspective of operators and system administrators. Inevitably, a discussion on this topic becomes a "how-to" exposition; e.g., a system administrator asks, "How do I configure my network so as to protect our resources, while permitting our people to do their work?"

The specific answer to this question depends, of course, on a number of things, including the possible threats of concern, the equipment in use, the organization of people, and the policies of the organization. However, there are some general concepts that apply broadly to most organizations, and the aim of this chapter is to review the basic ideas and provide guidance and pointers to additional information for system administrators and network operators.

Much of the information in this chapter is expanded upon in the *Site Security Handbook*,[1] which provides more than a hundred pages of extensive advice to site and network managers. It also contains a comprehensive annotated bibliography. For anyone contemplating setting up or operating a network, this is a "must read" document. (And in typical Internet style, it is available free of charge from any *RFC* repository.)

16.2 BACKGROUND

Probably no single event in the annals of network security is as important as the Internet worm incident,[2] which began on November 2, 1988. The worm, a program that propagated itself from machine to machine, was installed on only one machine and then proceeded to move copies of itself to thousands of others throughout the Internet. It gained access to these machines by exploiting flaws in the *finger* and *sendmail* programs on the Berkeley UNIX Operating System, and by testing accounts for easy-to-guess passwords. Once it gained entry to a machine, it usually consumed most of the machine's computing time. (The worm was not intended to be so intrusive. The author, Robert Morris Jr., claims he intended for the worm to run in background mode and remain undetected for a long time. As with most programs being tested, this one had a bug, and the result was runaway execution.)

The worm did little direct, malicious harm, except to consume machine resources and propagate itself to other machines. Had the author intended, the worm could have erased user files, altered files in subtle ways, or collected and distributed vast quantities of private information. Even though the worm was relatively benign, the impact was dramatic and costly. Considerable resources were consumed. For several days, operations were disrupted throughout the Internet, and system administrators and system programmers struggled to understand the worm and eradicate it. The major damage of the worm was the staff time lost in dealing with it. See Spafford[2] for a detailed chronology of the worm incident.)

The immediate effect of the worm was dramatic, but the direct damage was modest compared to the lasting indirect effect. After the worm, the level of trust throughout the Internet decreased markedly. In many quarters, the Internet is viewed as a hostile environment, and quite a few organizations have refused to be attached to it, or have imposed technical barriers in the form of *gateways* and *firewalls*.

The Internet worm incident also served as a wake-up call for the network security community. One immediate result was the creation of the Computer Emergency Response Team (CERT) at the Software Engineering Institute of Carnegie-Mellon University in Pittsburgh, PA. The CERT is a clearinghouse for information, and a source of advice and help whenever someone reports an incident. Similar groups have formed since then, each focused on providing rapid response to a particular community.

Yet another institutional response was the commissioning of a major study by the National Research Council. The result was an excellent report,[3] *Computers at Risk*, published in 1991. This report presented a comprehensive assessment of key computer and communications security issues, and recommended both short- and long-term actions for enhancing the security of the US computer and communications infrastructure. This report forms the basis for a number of government and private sector plans currently being formulated and implemented.

Despite these strong institutional responses, the network security problem is not amenable to any quick fixes. The Internet evolved in an environment that stressed openness, experimentation, connectivity, and flexibility. Little attention was given to security. As a result, security throughout the Internet is uneven. No uniform standards or controls exist, and each host is separately at risk. Further, the traditions of openness and ease-of-use continue to be prized by both the vendor and user communities. Where security and ease of use conflict, ease of use often prevails. For example, some vendors continue to ship operating systems that are "unsafe out of the box," i.e., whose initial state once they are attached to the Internet permits anyone to access any user's information from anywhere on the Internet.

Because of the uneven state of security throughout the Internet, it is incumbent on all users, administrators, service providers, and vendors to strengthen the security of the systems they use, administer, sell, or build. There are far too many aspects to cover in one small chapter, so we will focus on a few key points that address the majority of the operational security problems found in the Internet today.

The most important principle in this area is that effective operational network security depends on both administrative and technical controls. Neither is adequate without the other. A network that has in place strong technical controls, but which is not administered properly, is not well protected. Administrative procedures make no sense unless they are tied to the proper use of available technical controls. Therefore, this chapter focuses on both administrative and technical issues, rather than on just one or the other.

16.3   ADMINISTRATIVE ISSUES

The administrative side of operational network security can be viewed as addressing the following questions.

- What are the assets being protected? Against which threats? From whom?

- What is the organization's policy regarding network security?

- Who is assigned responsibility and authority for network security administration? For training? What is the policy for dealing with security incidents? What procedures are in place?

We will deal with each of these questions in turn.

16.3.1   Identifying the Assets and Threats

In general, an organization knows what assets it needs to protect, but it is helpful to be explicit. Standard principles of risk management should be applied. An organization should perform a risk analysis that identifies the assets and analyzes the security threats or risks. The most important result of such an analysis is a better understanding of the value of the assets, the probability of attacks occurring, and the ultimate losses that can occur. This is essential to determining the level of security controls that should be applied to protect the assets.

A full treatment of risk analysis is beyond the scope of this chapter. See Fites et al.[4] and Pfleeger[5] for a more complete treatment of the subject.

The assets usually fall into two classes, information and systems. Information assets are the files and data that users generate and use. The security risks to information assets are unauthorized disclosure (viz., someone steals the information), and unauthorized modification or destruction. System assets are the computers and networks that process the information. The security risks to system assets are disruption and theft of services.

Although the protection of these types of assets is often intertwined, some aspects are distinct. For example, a network may be vulnerable to disruption, thereby causing a denial of service. The disruption might not lead to the destruction or disclosure of any sensitive information, but it would interrupt the flow of work.

A key element in forming any security plan is understanding where the risks are. For any network that is connected to the global Internet, one obvious risk is that "intruders" from far away might penetrate the network, and disrupt services or alter or steal sensitive information. This threat is real, as Cliff Stoll's epic encounter documents,[6] but it is not the only threat. Insider threats may be even more important. Insider threats are directly related to the size of the system. Large-scale corporate, government, or academic networks will have a diverse set of users, not all of whom are equally trustworthy. Dividing the world into "inside" and "outside," with the intent of trusting no one on the outside and trusting everyone (equally) on the inside, makes no sense if there are, say, 10,000 people on the inside. Moreover, individual trustworthiness may be related to the information involved. In the appropriate environment, it may be reasonable to permit hundreds or even thousands of people to have access to selected sensitive technical information, but inappropriate to permit any of those same people to have access to personnel information.

A proper risk assessment helps an organization define the assets it needs to protect and the source of its threats. Most often it is helpful to view the assets in terms of perimeters of protection. There is often one perimeter around the entire set of assets, and then additional perimeters around selected assets within. Once the perimeters have been identified, an organization can select and put in place the administrative and technical controls that are matched to the value of the assets and the threats that have been identified.

16.3.2 Policy Statements

One of the first things an organization should do to protect its information and its information processing systems is to establish a formal security policy, put it in writing, and promulgate it to all concerned. A policy document serves two purposes. It provides an explicit declaration of the organization's interest in protecting its information and information processing resources, and it sets forth the priorities and terms of reference for its organizational and technical procedures.

A typical security policy should be relatively short, usually only a few pages. It serves only as a top-level statement of the issues. More detailed procedural documents are often written to support and implement the policy.

Policy statements vary with the size and nature of the organization. The policy statement for network service providers may be different from the policy statement for users of network services.

A network provider needs a policy statement that speaks to its employees and its customers. In addressing its customers, the network provider must state both what it expects from the customers, and what protections it provides to its customers. The statement need not be detailed, but it should provide the basis for whatever specific procedures or rules it puts into effect. For example, if a network provider reserves the right to suspend service to a customer if there is evidence that the customer is a source of attacks on other sites, the service provider should say so in a policy statement. In addition to notifying customers of their responsibilities and potential consequences for breaches, such statements also provide a degree of assurance to other customers. In this sense, a policy statement is both a legal foundation for the service provider's procedures, and a marketing and customer relations tool.

The network provider's policy statement must also speak to its employees. It must set forth the posture of the provider with respect to protection of the provider's resources and the protection of the customers. Again, such statements need not be detailed; they serve primarily to provide notice to the employees of the provider's posture and a legal foundation for whatever internal rules and procedures are put in place.

An organization that is a consumer of network services, or which provides network services only internally, also needs a policy statement, but the emphasis is usually on stating the organization's rules for handling information and protecting the information processing resources. Often an organization will have a more general policy in place related to handling sensitive information, irrespective of automation. For example, a business enterprise may state that personnel and financial information is deemed to be "company sensitive," and that only designated employees may be given such information. Special restrictions may be placed on this information, such as prohibitions against processing the information on systems that are connected to external networks. Similarly, a university may have a policy that explicitly prohibits plagiarism and other forms of misuse of research results. In these cases, the organization's network security policy should be written in terms of the overall information handling policy.

16.3.2.1 The Internet Security Guidelines

To foster the development of policy statements, the Internet Architecture Board (IAB) has issued the *Internet Security Guidelines*.[7] The IAB does not have operational responsibility for the Internet or any of its constituent networks, so the thrust of this document is to set forth the general set of ethics and concerns common throughout the Internet. This document is also a starting point for network operators, site administrators, vendors, and users who wish to develop their own policy statements. It is reprinted at the end of this chapter.

16.3.3 Security Administration and Incident Handling

The preliminary steps in protecting a network consist of developing a clear analysis of what needs to be protected and from whom, defining how the information and systems fit into the larger context of the organization, and promulgating a network security policy. With these in place, the real work begins. The job of protecting information and computing resources falls to some extent on every user, operator, and administrator. System administrators are responsible for setting up the controls, and educating the users and operators as to how to use them. Users and operators are responsible for understanding and employing the available controls.

16.3.3.1 Incident Handling

In almost any organization, there are likely to be security incidents, either real or imagined. What is a security incident? The definition will vary from group to group, but the general notion is that a security incident is any event that results in interference with the correct operation of the systems, violates the security policy of the organization, or even appears to do so.

The three main issues in handling an incident are deciding how serious it is, deciding what to do about it, and marshalling the resources to handle it. It is common for the first report of an incident to come in the middle of the night or some other inconvenient time. It is also common for the incident to be reported to someone who is not in a position to handle it correctly. Whenever an incident occurs, it is important for all concerned to know how to react. This requires defining the procedures in advance and promulgating them to all users and operators.

It is recommended that sufficiently large organizations organize an incident response team that is available for consultation and action whenever it is needed. The team needs to have sufficient technical expertise to deal with the system issues, and it needs to have sufficient management maturity and authority to deal with the people and business issues that may be involved.

The notion of establishing a response team is good practice even for very small organizations. It may amount to little more than having the chief network operator know how to contact the president of the company, but it is nonetheless important for the chief network operator to know that it is appropriate to make the call, and to have the phone number.

Having the authority to act is useless unless there is also sufficient knowledge of what actions to take. Sometimes the actions taken in response to an incident can be worse than the incident itself. A typical overreaction to a network security incident might be to shut down the network. In addition to the obvious disruption of the entire network, this action may also shut off the communications necessary to find and fix the problems in the first place. Jon Rochlis and Mark Eichin comment[8] that during the Internet worm incident:

> Sites which disconnected themselves from the network at the first sign of trouble hurt themselves and the community. Not only could they not report their experiences and findings, but they could not get timely bug fixes. Furthermore, other sites using them as mail relays were crippled, thus delaying delivery of important mail until after the crisis had passed. Sites like MIT and Berkeley were able to collaborate in a meaningful manner because they never took themselves off the network.

For further information on establishing and operating a computer security incident response capability, see Wack.[9] While this publication is written primarily for federal agencies, it is also intended for other governmental, commercial, and academic organizations. It describes organizational, technical, and legal issues connected with establishing and operating an incident response capability.

16.3.3.2   Outside Help

As noted in the introduction, one of the institutional responses to the Internet worm was the establishment of the CERT. (The CERT was established at DARPA's initiative. It was in operation two weeks after the worm incident, setting a record for efficient government action.) The CERT operates around the clock, and provides a focal point for a wide variety of network security problems. The staff of the CERT is fairly small, but its members have considerable expertise, as well as access to a wide range of experts. They can solve problems themselves, or provide pointers to additional help. Another important function of the CERT is to filter out rumors and misinformation pertaining either to alleged holes and attacks, or pertaining to alleged fixes. Contact information for the CERT is listed below.

Since the CERT was established, a number of similar organizations have come into existence, each aimed at serving a specific community. These organizations maintain regular contact with each other, and hold annual workshops to compare techniques and developments. Recently, these organizations have begun to engage in active educational efforts, in addition to their original reactive mission.

The CERT and similar organizations observe a strict code of confidentiality. To attain the confidence of the network and host operators who report incidents to them, these organizations are very careful about giving out information about other sites unless the site involved specifically authorizes them to disclose details. The CERT does not report incidents to the FBI or other law enforcement agencies, but it will cooperate with these agencies if the affected sites ask it to.

As part of setting up an internal response team, it is entirely appropriate to make contact with the CERT or other external incident handling organizations, and to learn what kinds of actions should and should not be taken. See Scherlis et al.[10] and Fraser and Pethia[11] for additional material on the background and operation of the CERT.

16.4   HOST-LEVEL TECHNICAL CONTROLS

The preceding section focused entirely on administrative and organizational security controls. None of these controls will make a difference in security if the network or hosts attached to the network are technically unsound. Unfortunately, current systems come with many vulnerabilities. In this section we will examine ways to protect hosts and networks. The focus here is primarily on protection against external attacks, i.e., attacks from people who do not have valid accounts on the machines being protected, but some of these strategies also aid in reducing the ease of attack from insiders.

With respect to protecting hosts from an outside attack, there are generally three approaches. The first is to strengthen each host so that it is able to withstand attacks from the outside. The second is to isolate the majority of hosts, and limit access to them from the outside. The third is to log system access to help determine if and when an attack is occurring or has occurred. All of these strategies are appropriate and recommended.

Within the category of strengthening individual hosts, experience has shown that the two largest sources of vulnerabilities are poorly chosen passwords and configuration errors. Together, these two sources of vulnerabilities account for the overwhelming majority of penetrations.

16.4.1 Password Management

Using passwords on individual user accounts has been the principal mode of protection in shared computer systems for three decades. Passwords have always been a source of problems because they are frequently chosen by users to be easy to remember. A very significant fraction of the passwords in use even today is chosen to be the user's first name, the name of a spouse, or a simple word. These choices are easy for the user to remember, but they are also easy for an intruder to guess.

In the early days, the only sharing was within a small work community, and the threat of penetration came only from others who had physical access to the computer. Although password attacks existed in those days, the risk was usually far less than it is in today's highly networked environment. In the early 1960s, a typical time-shared computer might have had 30 to 100 users, and was accessible only to them. In the current Internet environment, each host that is fully connected to the Internet is accessible to millions of people. Thus, over the past 30 years, there has been a ten-thousandfold increase in the number of people who can potentially connect to each computer. Moreover, password guessing has become highly automated. Dictionaries of common words are a standard tool of a would-be penetrator, and even an ordinary personal computer may be fast enough to permit searching of hundreds of thousands of possible choices.

Since the use of passwords has been the principal line of defense against unauthorized access, it is obviously essential that they be chosen properly or replaced with stronger defenses. There are two general approaches to choosing strong passwords, and there are also techniques available that replace traditional passwords with much stronger means.

The two general strategies for choosing strong passwords are to restrict the password that the user is allowed to choose, or to look for poorly chosen passwords after the fact. Two techniques exist for restricting passwords. One is to let the user choose a candidate password. The system then checks whether the password meets several conditions, all of which are designed to weed out weak passwords. Typical criteria are the minimum length of the password, whether the password is on a list of poor password choices, and often some requirement that the password contain digits, punctuation, or intermixing of capital and lowercase letters. When a minimum length is set, it is usually at least six characters, and eight is far preferable. The lists of poor password choices are usually dictionaries containing large numbers of the words in the native language; these are often augmented with other likely combinations of characters.

Another strategy that is sometimes used to restrict passwords is to have the system assign them. This method is less common because most users find a system-chosen password is hard to remember, although algorithmic tricks can produce effective passwords that are relatively mnemonic and hence easier to remember. When a system assigns passwords to its users, there is a far greater likelihood that the users will write down their passwords to remember them. Writing down a password has always been considered a hazardous act because it increases the chance that someone will find the written password and have access to the account.

The inhibition against carrying around a written password is probably still appropriate, but it can be argued that it is time to reexamine the relative risks. In a highly networked environment, relatively few potential intruders will have direct physical contact with the legitimate users, and it may be appropriate to strengthen the passwords even at the expense of creating a vulnerability from written passwords. This point of view is debatable, and there is not enough data to argue either side convincingly at this time.

Restricting the user's choice of passwords is a good idea, but it usually requires changing the system. The second approach to choosing string passwords is to test passwords after they have been selected. In most systems today, passwords are stored in an encrypted form. When the user logs onto the system, he or she types the password in the clear. The system then encrypts the offered password and compares the encrypted form against the entry in the password table. If it matches, access is permitted. Password-guessing programs work by generating possible passwords, encrypting them and then checking them against the entries in the password file. There are various strategies for speeding up the guessing process, and counter strategies for making it harder to guess passwords.

Several tools have been written to check for bad passwords. One of the most common is called *Crack*; (see below).

Reports by NIST and the Antinodal Computer Security Center offer further guidance[12] on the use of passwords. Also see Garfinkel and Spafford,[13] or the standard references[14] for a more detailed discussion of password guessing and counter strategies, including particularly the notion of "salts."

Any discussion of passwords must also include more modern access control techniques, which use challenge-response systems instead of ordinary passwords. In a challenge-response system, when the user initiates the log-in process, the system presents a "challenge." This challenge is different each time the user initiates the log-in sequence, and the user is required to supply the response that matches the challenge. Challenge-response systems are very attractive because they are robust against wiretaps. Even if an eavesdropper copies the log-in sequence, the data will not be usable in the future because the system will ask for a different response.

There are three general forms of challenge-response systems in use, two which require the user to carry a computational device or *token*, and one which requires the user to carry a list of one-time passwords. In the systems that require the user to carry a token, both the system and the token contain the same shared secret quantity. When the log-in process is initiated, the system asks the user to identify himself or herself, typically by keying in a secret Personal Identification Number (PIN). The system then generates a random challenge and the user is required to return a response that is keyed to this challenge. In most of these systems, the challenge is in the form of a several-digit number. The user keys this number into the token, and the token displays a response, which the user returns to the system. The system carries out the same computation in parallel, and if the system's computation matches the user's response, access is granted. This idea is used in a number of existing products.

Another existing product uses a variation on the theme. This product is a time-based system. Instead of presenting the user with an explicit challenge, the challenge is implicit in the time of day. Each token is constantly computing a unique next response, usually every 30 or 60 seconds, and the user simply supplies the current value along with his or her secret PIN.

A variation on the challenge-response scheme that does not require the user to carry a token is based on the use of one-time passwords. The user carries a table of responses, say 25 or so, that are generated by the host system in advance. Each time the user logs into the system, the system requests the user to supply a particular response from the table. Once supplied, the response is considered to be "consumed," and the system does not ask for it again.

Challenge-response systems are in use on only a small minority of Internet systems today, but they can be reasonably low in cost, and their use is growing.

16.4.2 System Configuration

The second largest source of vulnerabilities is *poor system configuration*, which means the system has been configured with an exploitable security flaw. There are several common kinds of configuration errors, particularly accounts with no passwords, versions of security-critical programs with known holes, and access control files that permit unauthorized users to access the system.

In the discussion on password management, the implicit assumption was that every account has a password, and that each password is under the control of a particular user. However, it is not uncommon for systems to be unnecessarily configured with accounts that require no password at all. Sometimes these are *guest* or *demo* accounts, sometimes they are intended to be used by maintenance personnel, and sometimes they are intended to be used by system utilities, e.g., *uucp*. In these cases, the unprotected account is a gaping hole and an open invitation to any penetrator. In most systems, it is easy to check whether any accounts are not protected by passwords, but often there is no one with the expertise, time, or responsibility to do the check or secure any unprotected accounts.

There are a limited number of situations in which an account may not be protected by a password. For example, to provide public services, such as the WHOIS service on the NIC, an account may not require the user to provide a password. Other examples are the widespread and ever popular anonymous FTP services, which typically accept any password or the password *guest*, though many FTP servers now request that the user provide his username to facilitate logging. In any case, systems that support unprotected accounts should not be used to process sensitive information, and the programs run on these accounts need to be scrutinized and carefully configured.

Other common sources of vulnerabilities are old versions of security-relevant software with known security holes. What is security-relevant software? It is any software that forms part of the security perimeter of the system. In a typical system, network service programs usually run with system privileges. If there is a bug in such a program, it is possible for the attacker to take over the program and penetrate the system. The Internet worm exploited two such holes, one in the sendmail program and one in the finger program. The most common version of the sendmail program was compiled with a debug option turned on. The debug option enabled the sendmail program to accept commands, as well as mail, from other sites. This was a useful feature for debugging the mail software during a test period, but the option was unintentionally left on and distributed to thousands of machines for many years. Today, most UNIX Operating Systems have been upgraded to newer versions of sendmail that do not have the debug option—or any of the several other bugs that were discovered subsequently—but there remain some computers on the Internet that have not been fully upgraded.

Other sources of vulnerabilities are access controls that are set to permit wide open access. For many computer systems, access to each account is settable by the user. And for those systems, the default access is to permit the account to be accessed from any site that claims to have the same user. This initial configuration facilitates setting up a local network with several machines that are shared by the same group of people, but it opens up a very wide hole when the same machines are accessible outside of the intended group.

Much of the vulnerability in these configuration problems is that the security of a system depends on a large number of separate details, each of which is unrelated to the others. This problem is endemic in current computer system designs; future designs may be better. In the meantime, one of the strongest approaches to improving the configuration security of current systems is the use of tools that check the configuration. COPS is one of the most widely used tools. It checks for accounts without passwords, internal permissions that are loose enough to permit someone to overwrite configuration files, the existence of old versions of security-relevant software with known holes, and a variety of other details. COPS is an evolving tool that is updated as new bugs and configuration vulnerabilities are discovered. Tools like COPS are a good adjunct to sound security administration. (More information on COPS is given below.)

16.4.3 Auditing

The next line of defense after proper password management and system configuration is intrusion detection. The establishment and use of an auditing mechanism to log important system access provides a means to determine if an attack is occurring, or if an attack has already occurred.

All standard network services permitted to run on an externally accessible machine should employ some form of logging. Many operating systems and standard system programs include built-in logging facilities. For example, the UNIX Operating System includes the *syslog* facility. These facilities should be turned on, and the resulting audit trails should be reviewed on a regular basis. An unusually large number of failed log-in attempts, log-in attempts at odd times of the day, or other unusual events may be signs of an attack.

Examples of important events that can and should be logged and reviewed include the following:

- Attempts to connect to and "log-in" to a machine via standard network services, such as Telnet and FTP

- Mail transactions (at least the control information and mail headers)

- Attempts to invoke "root" privileges

Log-in attempts and other attempts to connect to a machine, whether successful or unsuccessful, should be logged. The audit record should include essential information, such as usernames, system names or network addresses, line or port numbers, and timestamps.

Special precautions should be taken to ensure that audit trails cannot be modified or destroyed. For example, the logs may be shipped to and stored on a separate machine that accepts audit records but is otherwise unaccessible because it does not accept Telnet, FTP, or mail connections. Alternatively, logs may be directed to hardcopy devices that are physically protected.

16.5 NETWORK-LEVEL ACCESS CONTROLS

The preceding section focused on the security controls at the level of an individual host. In this section we will examine a form of security control that protects an entire local network using IP access controls.

One of the ways to protect a collection of hosts within a site is to control IP access from outside the site. The general idea is to identify a "choke point" through which all traffic passes between an internal network and the general Internet. The choke point may be a router, a special gateway machine, or a collection of gateway machines that form a firewall.

The term *gateway* is often used with at least two related but different meanings. Sometimes a gateway refers to a host that is physically in the path between the outside network and all interior networks. In these cases, the local topology consists of two or more local networks, one of which connects the gateway host to the external router, and the others of which connect the gateway host to internal hosts. The term *gateway* is also used to mean a specially designated host that is accessible to the outside network, unlike other internal hosts that are not accessible to the outside. In these cases, the accessibility is controlled by the router and not by the physical topology.

Irrespective of the means used to implement the control, the basic idea is the same. Network traffic is restricted based on three properties—the origin of the traffic, the destination of the traffic, and the protocol or service. For example, a site may designate a particular host as the only one that may receive connections from the outside, but other hosts within the site may initiate connections to the outside. Usually the designated host will be operated with a high degree of attention to host security, with specially trained and tasked staff. The main focus of this idea is to prevent attacks from *outside* of the local environment. A point not to be lost, however, is that this approach prevents only outsider attacks. It does not prevent insider attacks unless the internal environment is subdivided and walled off into smaller units.

To implement such controls, the network administrator sets up a matrix describing the traffic that is permitted between each member of a pair of hosts. Limitations on specific services—e.g., electronic mail is allowed but Telnet is not—may be specified by listing which ports are allowable destinations, since each service has a well-known port associated with it that is used to initiate the service. These are usually privileged ports on most hosts, which means that connections initiated to these ports are always under the control of the operating system and privileged programs, such as the Telnet or SMTP servers. A typical set of services that might be accessible from outside the site, and a typical access control matrix for these services, are listed in Tables 16.1 and 16.2, respectively.

Table 16.1 "Well-known" ports and protocols for several services

Service	Port	Protocol
FTP Data	20	TCP
FTP Control	21	TCP
Telnet	23	TCP
Mail Transfer (SMTP)	25	TCP
Host Name Service	42	UDP
Domain Name Service (DNS)	53	TCP or UDP
Network News Transfer Protocol (NNTP)	119	TCP
Echo/Echo Reply	*n/a*	ICMP

Table 16.2 Typical access control matrix

Source	Destination		
	Outside	Gateway	Inside
Outside	*n/a*	Selected privileged ports	nonprivileged ports only
Gateway	all	*n/a*	*n/a*
Inside	all	*n/a*	*n/a*

The choke point controls only traffic into or out of the local site, but does not control traffic between hosts within the same site. The gateway is a specially designated host that may or may not be physically in the path between the outside and other interior hosts. Not all "nonprivileged" ports are safe. NFS and X11 contain known holes, and are accessible via ports above 2048.

One way to implement these controls is to depend on controls within the router that connects a site to the external Internet. Modern routers contain abilities to filter traffic based on access control lists.

A different and somewhat stronger means to implement these controls is to interpose a gateway host in the path between the outside and all other interior hosts. In such a configuration the gateway is connected to two (or more) different local networks. One local network is connected to the external router. The other local networks are connected only to interior hosts. This form of gateway provides very strong isolation between the outside Internet and the interior hosts, but usually at a cost of severely restricting what forms of service are available to users within the site. Gateways are useful in implementing highly restrictive policies, such as permitting mail to move in and out of a site, but prohibiting all other access. A variation on this policy is to permit inside users to initiate Telnet or FTP connections to the outside only from the gateway host.

Cheswick[15] has developed a gateway that provides both strong isolation and controlled access between internal and external hosts by substituting application connectivity in place of IP connectivity. Several commercial vendors have developed similar systems for the Internet.

Sometimes a single gateway is not enough. For very large sites or organizations that are geographically dispersed, several gateways may be needed between the internal hosts and outside connections. The collection of these gateways forms a firewall.

16.6 FUTURE DEVELOPMENTS

It is evident that the current state of security in the Internet is far from adequate. Fortunately, there are several developments under way that will materially improve security throughout the Internet. Three of the most important are Privacy Enhanced Mail (PEM), distributed authentication using Kerberos and Common Authentication Technology (CAT), and the Secure Simple Network Management Protocol (Secure SNMP). All of these developments make use of cryptography, a technology that has not been widely used within the Internet to date.

In recent years, licenses for public key cryptography have become available, and various standards bodies, such as CCITT and the IAB, have begun to include it as a means of providing the key management and authentication services needed within an overall security architecture. For example, *The Directory-Authentication Framework* (CCITT Recommendation X.509)[16] sets forth the notion of public keys and certificates that is employed in both PEM and CAT.

16.6.1   Privacy Enhanced Mail

Privacy Enhanced Mail (PEM) entails the addition of the following security services to the Internet electronic mail messages (i.e., *RFC 822*):

- Message integrity. The message has not been altered or destroyed in an unauthorized manner.

- Message origin authentication. Identity of the originator of a message is corroborated.

- Message confidentiality (optional). The message is not made available or disclosed to unauthorized individuals, entities, or processes.

- Nonrepudiation of origin. The originator cannot deny having sent the message.

These services are implemented using a combination of asymmetric ("public key") and symmetric ("secret key") cryptography in particular:

- A cryptographically strong "message digest" is computed by the sender on the contents of the message. This value is transported with the message, and compared to a new value recomputed by the recipient to verify the integrity of the message.

- The message digest is sealed with an asymmetric algorithm using the sender's private key to form a "digital signature," the computer equivalent of a written signature. The signature is verified by the recipient using the sender's public key. This provides for the authentication of the sender of the message.

- If desired, the text of the message is encrypted with a symmetric encryption algorithm, for example DES. The key used for the encryption is generated for each new message, encrypted once for each intended recipient using their respective public key, and is transported, along with any other parameters required by the symmetric algorithm, with the message to enable the authorized recipients to recover the original message.

- When an asymmetric signature algorithm is employed, use of the sender's private key to sign the message digest provides for nonrepudiation of origin, and allows for the authenticated message to be forwarded to additional recipients with the authentication intact.

To make this system work, there has to be a way to convey each user's public key to all other users. Further, this method has to resist false advertising of someone's public key. The scheme adopted for PEM is to make use of the certificate structure contained in CCITT Recommendation X.509. A certificate is a cryptographically sealed document that contains a user's "distinguished name" and his public key. The distinguished name is intended to contain enough information so the reader can tell whether it really refers to the person he or she thinks it does. A distinguished name will usually contain a person's name and place of employment, but there can be other forms of distinguished names as well.

PEM will be deployed throughout the Internet during the last half of 1992 and early 1993. The original specifications[17] have been moved to Historic Standard status, since they no longer reflect current practice. New specifications[18] now exist as Internet Drafts and are targeted to become Proposed Standards in the near term. Consult the current IAB Official Protocols *RFC* to determine the current status and *RFC* numbers for the PEM specifications.

16.6.2 Distributed Authentication

Kerberos[19] is a distributed authentication system intended to be used within a large environment. It gives a means for providing service to users from unattended, and hence untrusted, workstations. In the Kerberos environment there are three types of hosts: clients, servers, and Kerberos key distribution hosts (KDCs). Kerberos provides a means for users to initiate service from an arbitrary workstation whose physical security while unattended cannot be trusted. Initiating a service request, the user establishes a connection with a KDC and identifies himself or herself. The KDC provides temporary tokens of identification known as *tickets*, which are kept within the workstation and used by the client software to authenticate the user to the desired server.

Kerberos was developed at MIT as part of Project Athena, and is used in a number of sites around the Internet. However, it is not yet widespread or commonplace, although some vendors are considering supporting it in their product lines. Possible limitations of Kerberos are discussed in *Limitations of the Kerberos Authentication System.*[20]

Kerberos uses DES, a symmetric encryption system. Kerberos was developed before public key cryptography became easily available. Public key systems have the advantage that it is easier to manage large sets of users using public key cryptography than by using symmetric key systems.

In light of the availability of public key cryptography, Digital Equipment Corporation initiated the development of a Distributed Authentication Security Service (DASS) that is based on public key cryptography, and makes use of the certificate structure contained in CCITT Recommendation X.509. This work has been made available to the IAB, and has formed the basis for development of a new standard for a Common Authentication Technology (CAT), which embraces either a public key infrastructure or a Kerberos secret key infrastructure. The plan is that individual client and server programs that need authentication services will make service calls to a common interface. Underneath that interface will be either DASS or Kerberos. Both the client and the server must be using the same services, i.e., either DASS, Kerberos, or possible hybrid authentication technologies, but neither has to know which is there. This means that the choice of DASS or Kerberos can be made within a site, and that individual software packages do not have to be tailored at development time to one or the other.

The overview of CAT is contained in Linn.[21] The CAT application program interface is further documented in Wray.[22] The specific implementations of DASS under CAT and Kerberos under CAT are documented in Kaufman[23] and Kohl and Neuman,[24] respectively.

16.6.3　Secure SNMP

The Simple Network Management Protocol (SNMP) specification[25] allows for the protection of network management operations by a variety of security protocols. The SNMP administrative model described in Davin et al.[26] provides a framework for securing SNMP network management. In the context of that framework, Galvin et al.[27] define protocols to support the following three security services:

- Data integrity

- Data origin authentication

- Data confidentiality

The model described in Davin et al. is an elaboration of the model set forth in the SNMP specification, departing from the community-based administrative model by unambiguously identifying the originator and intended recipient of each SNMP message. Each identity is represented by a SNMP party—a conceptual, virtual execution context whose operation is restricted (for security or other purposes) to an administratively defined subset of all possible operations—that architecturally comprises the following:

- A single, unique identity

- A single authentication protocol and associated parameters by which all messages originated by the party are authenticated as to origin and integrity (where no authentication is a valid option)

- A single privacy protocol and associated parameters by which all protocol messages received by the party are protected from disclosure (where no privacy is a valid option)

- A single Management Information Base (MIB) view to which all management operations performed by the party are restricted

- A logical network location at which the party executes

The addition of unique identities improves on the historical community scheme by supporting a more convenient access control model and allowing for effective use of asymmetric (public key) security protocols in the future.

　　The Digest Authentication Protocol[27] provides a data integrity service by transmitting a message digest—computed by the originator and verified by the recipient—with each SNMP message. The data origin authentication service is provided by prefixing the message with a secret value known only to the originator and the recipient, prior to computing the digest. Thus, data integrity is supported explicitly, while data origin authentication is supported implicitly in the verification of the digest.

　　The Symmetric Privacy Protocol[27] protects messages from disclosure by encrypting their contents according to a secret cryptographic key known only to the originator and the recipient. The additional functionality afforded by this protocol is assumed to justify its additional computational cost.

The Digest Authentication Protocol depends on the existence of loosely synchronized clocks between the originator and the recipient of a message. The protocol specification makes no assumptions about the strategy by which such clocks are synchronized, although one strategy that is particularly suited to the demands of SNMP network management is included.

Both protocols require the sharing of secret information between the originator of a message and its recipient. The protocol specifications assume the existence of the necessary secrets. The selection of such secrets and their secure distribution to appropriate parties may be accomplished by a variety of strategies; one strategy that is particularly suited to the demands of SNMP network management is included.

A MIB view is a subset of the set of all instances of all objects that may be supported by an SNMP protocol entity. When an SNMP protocol entity is processing an SNMP message on behalf of an SNMP party, it must verify that the requested operation is a member of the set of operations permitted for the party, and that the object to be accessed by the operation is within the MIB view for the party.

The logical network location for an SNMP party is characterized by a transport protocol domain and transport addressing information; for example, SNMP over UDP is a transport domain in which the addressing information would be an IP address. Together they represent the kind of transport service and the transport service address by which the party receives network management traffic.

To manage the information needed by the security protocols a MIB is specified in McCloghrie et al.[28] This allows the security protocols to manage themselves. In this way, the SNMP security protocols are not dependent on any other network service, a crucial feature during times of network stress.

SNMP security will be deployed throughout the Internet during the last quarter of 1992 and early 1993. The specifications now exist as Proposed Standards and are defined in *RFCs* 25-27.

16.7 FURTHER INFORMATION

This section contains pointers to further information in the form of books and papers to read, organizations to contact, and files and programs that are accessible via the Internet.

16.7.1 Further Reading

Garfinkel and Spafford's book, *Practical Network Security*,[13] Curry's report, *Improving the Security of Your UNIX System*, and his book, *UNIX System Security: A Guide for Users and System Administrators*,[29] which is an expansion of his report, are all excellent sources for information on the security of UNIX Operating Systems. They also contain material that is likely to be relevant to many other operating systems as well, although they present everything in terms of the UNIX Operating System.

RFC 1244, the *Site Security Handbook*,[1] is a compilation of advice that greatly expands on the material of this chapter. It is essential reading for anyone setting up or administering a site.

Fite's book, *Control and Security of Computer Information Systems*,[4] is a good guide to the issues encountered in forming computer security policies and procedures, and was one of the basic building blocks for the *Site Security Handbook*.

In addition to Cliff Stoll's epic tale in *The Cuckoo's Egg*,[6] his technical article,[30] "Stalking the Wily Hacker," adds some details. See also Bill Cheswick's paper,[31] "An Evening with Berferd in Which a Cracker is Lured, Endured, and Studied," and Steve Bellovin's paper "There Be Dragons."[32]

Collections of contemporary papers, including the landmark papers on the Internet worm and related matters, are contained in Lance Hoffman's book, *Rogue Programs: Viruses, Worms and Trojan Horses*,[33] and Peter Denning's book, *Computers Under Attack: Intruders, Worms and Viruses*,[34] and Steve Bellovin's paper "There Be Dragons.[32]

Excellent textbooks on basic issues in computer security and required reading for serious practitioners include Dorothy Denning's book, *Cryptography and Data Security*,[35] Morrie Gasser's book, *Building a Secure Computer System*,[36] and Charles Pfleeger's book, *Security in Computing.*[5]

16.7.2   Organizations

The CERT is available for both emergency and nonemergency consultation:

Electronic mail: cert@cert.org
For emergencies: (412) 268-7090
For information: (412) 268-7080
FAX:(412) 268-6989

US Mail:CERT/CC
Software Engineering Institute
Carnegie-Mellon University
Pittsburgh, PA 15213-3890
USA

In addition to the CERT, there are several other incident response and security teams. These are all members of FIRST, the Forum of Incident Response and Security Teams. A complete, up-to-date list of FIRST members is available via anonymous FTP at csrc.ncsl.nist.gov (129.6.54.11) in the file pub/first/first-contacts. The list is also available by sending electronic mail to docserver@csrc.ncsl.nist.gov, and including the message send *first-contacts*.

The FIRST secretariat can be contacted at (301) 975-5200 or by sending electronic mail to first-sec@first.org.

16.7.3 Tools

Two of the most useful security-related tools presently in circulation are *COPS* and *Crack*. Both tools have been announced on the *cert-tools* electronic mailing list. (Send subscription requests for the cert-tools mailing list to cert-tools-request@cert.org.)

COPS (Computerized Oracle and Password System)[37] is a set of programs and shell scripts that enable system administrators to check for possible security holes in their UNIX Operating Systems. The programs essentially take a snapshot of the system and provide a report on potential security flaws. They check for the improper configuration of system start-up and configuration files, user start-up files, and other important system files, programs, directories, and devices. COPS also includes a program that checks for easy-to-guess passwords.

COPS was written by Dan Farmer while he was at Purdue University. He completed it when he was at the CERT, and he has continued to maintain it after moving to Sun Microsystems. The COPS system has been posted to various USENET newsgroups, including alt.sources, and is available via anonymous FTP from various Internet sites, including archive.cis.ohio-state.edu and cert.org.

Crack (The UNIX Password Cracker) is a suite of programs designed to quickly and efficiently find easily guessable passwords in standard crypt() encrypted password files on UNIX Operating Systems. According to its author, "[Crack] is not meant to solve the problem of having easily guessable passwords (there are other packages for that) but it is meant as an administrator's tool to aid in building 'better secured' systems, and it is best used alongside other security packages, such as COPS."

The Crack system has been posted to various USENET newsgroups, including comp.sources.misc, and is available via anonymous FTP from various Internet sites, such as ftp.uu.net (where it can be found in Volume 28 of the comp.sources.misc archives).

REFERENCES

1 P. Holbrook and J. Reynolds, Eds., *Site Security Handbook, RFC 1244*, CICNet, July 1991. Also *FYI 8*.

2 E. H. Spafford, The Internet Worm Incident, in *Proceedings of the 1989 European Software Engineering Conference (ESEC 89)*, Springer-Verlag, 1989. Also reprinted in Hoffman's Rogue Programs.

3   D.D. Clark, *Computers at Risk: Safe Computing in the Information Age*, National Academy Press, Washington, DC, 1990. Results from the Systems Security Study Committee, Computer and Telecommunications Board, Commission on Physical Sciences, Mathematics and Applications, National Research Council.

4   M. Fites, P. Kratz and A. Brebner; *Control and Security of Computer Information Systems*, Computer Science Press, Rockville, MD, 1989.

5   C.P. Pfleeger, *Security in Computing*, Prentice Hall, Englewood Cliffs, 1989.

6   C. Stoll, *The Cuckoo's Egg, Tracking a Spy through the Maze of Computer Espionage*, Doubleday, New York, 1989.

7   R. Pethia S. Crocker and B. Fraser, *Guidelines for the Secure Operation of the Internet, RFC 1281*, 1991.

8   J.A. Rochlis and M.W. Eichin, With a Microscope and a Tweezers: The Worm from MIT's Perspective,*Communications of the ACM*, Vol. 32, No. 6, June 1989. Also reprinted in Hoffman's *Rogue Programs*.

9   J.P. Wack, *Establishing a Computer Security Incident Response Capability (CSIRC)*, NIST Special Publication 800-3, National Institute of Standards and Technology, Gaithersburg, 1991.

10   W.L. Scherlis S.L. Squires and R.D. Pethia, Computer Emergency Response, in *Computers Under Attack: Intruders, Worms, and Viruses* (P.J. Denning, Ed.) ACM Press/Addison-Wesley, Reading, 1990.

11   B.Y. Fraser and R.D. Pethia, The CERT/CC Experience: Past, Present, and Future, in *Proceedings of INET 92*, Internet Society, Reston, VA, 1992.

12   *Standard on Password Usage*, Federal Information Processing Standard (FIPS) Publication 112, National Institute of Standards and Technology, Gaithersburg, MD, 1985; and *Department of Defense Password Management Guideline*, Technical Report CSC-STD-002-85, National Computer Security Center, Fort George G. Meade, 1985.

13   S. Garfinkel and G. Spafford, *Practical UNIX Security*, O'Reilly & Associates, Inc., 1991.

14   R. Morris and K. Thompson, Password Security: A Case History, *Communications of the ACM*, Vol. 22, No. 11, 1979; D.C. Feldmeier and P.R. Karn, UNIX Password Security—Ten Years Later, in *Proceedings Crypto'89*, 1989; D.V. Klein, "Foiling the Cracker" Survey of, and Improvements to, Password Security," in *Proceedings USENIX UNIX*

Security Workshop, 1990; and P. Leong and C. Tham, UNIX Password Encryption Considered Insecure, in *Proceedings Winter USENIX Conference*, USENIX Association, Berkeley, CA, 1991.

15   W.R. Cheswick, The Design of a Secure Internet Gateway, in *Proceedings Summer USENIX Conference*, 1990. USENIX Association, Berkeley, CA.

16   *The Directory-Authentication Framework*, Recommendation X.509, The International Telegraph and Telephone Consultative Committee (CCITT), 1988. Developed in collaboration, and technically aligned, with ISO 9594-8.

17   J. Linn, *Privacy Enhancement for Internet Electronic Mail: Part I—Message Encipherment and Authentication Procedures*, RFC *1113*, 1989, makes *RFC 1040* obsolete; S. Kent and J. Linn, *Privacy Enhancement for Internet Electronic Mail: Part II—Certificate-Based Key Management*, RFC *1114*, 1989; and J. Linn, *Privacy Enhancement for Internet Electronic Mail: Part III—Algorithms, Modes, and Identifiers*, RFC *1115*, 1989.

18   J. Linn, *Privacy Enhancement for Internet Electronic Mail: Part I—Message Encipherment and Authentication Procedures*, Internet Draft, 1992, *RFC* in progress, will make *RFC 1113* obsolete; D. Balenson, *Privacy Enhancement for Internet Electronic Mail: Part III—Algorithms, Modes, and Identifiers*, Internet Draft, 1992, *RFC* in progress, will make *RFC 1115* obsolete; B. Kaliski; *Privacy Enhancement for Internet Electronic Mail: Part IV—Key Certification and Related Services*, Internet Draft, 1992, *RFC* in progress, and S. Kent, *Privacy Enhancement for Internet Electronic Mail: Part II—Certificate-Based Key Management*, Internet Draft, 1992, *RFC* in progress, will make *RFC 1114* obsolete

19   J.G. Steiner B.C. Neuman and J.I. Schiller, Kerberos: An Authentication Service for Open Network Systems, in *USENIX Conference Proceedings*, 1988; and S. P. Miller C.C. Neuman J.I. Schiller and J. H. Saltzer, Section E.2.1: Kerberos Authentication and Authorization System, Project Athena Technical Plan, MIT, 1988 USENIX Association, Berkeley, CA.

20   S.M. Bellovin and M. Merritt, *Limitations of the Kerberos Authentication System*, Proc. Winter USENIX, Dallas, TX, January 1992, pp. 253–267, USENIX Association, Berkeley, CA.

21   J.Linn, *Generic Security Service API*, Internet Draft, 1991, *RFC* in progress.

22   J.Wray, *Generic Security Service Application Program Interface: Overview and C Bindings*, Internet Draft, 1991, *RFC* in progress.

23 C.Kaufman, *DASS: Distributed Authentication Security Service*, Internet Draft, 1991, *RFC* in progress.

24 J.Kohl and B.C. Neuman, *The Kerberos Network Authentication Service*, Internet Draft, 1992, *RFC* in progress.

25 J. Case M. Fedor M. Schoffstall and J. Davin, *A Simple Network Management Protocol (SNMP)*, *RFC 1157*, 1990, makes *RFC 1098* obsolete.

26 J.R. Davin J.M. Galvin and K. McCloghrie, *SNMP Administrative Model. RFC 1351*, July 1992.

27 J.M. Galvin K. McCloghrie and J.R. Davin, *SNMP Security Protocols. RFC 1352*, July, 1992.

28 K. McCloghrie J.R. Davin and J.M. Galvin, *Definitions of Managed Objects for Administration of SNMP Parties. RFC 1353*, July, 1992.

29 D.A. Curry, *Improving the Security of Your UNIX System*, technical report ITSDT-721-FR-90-21, SRI International, 1990; and *UNIX System Security: A Guide for Users and System Administrators*, Addison-Wesley, Reading, 1992.

30 C. Stoll, Stalking the Wily Hacker, *Communications of the ACM*, Vol. 31 No. 5, May 1988.

31 W.R. Cheswick, An Evening with Berferd, In Which a Cracker Is Lured, Endured, and Studied, in *Proceedings Winter USENIX Conference*, 1992. USENIX Association, Berkeley, CA.

32 S.M. Bellovin, *There Be Dragons*, Third UNIX Security Symposium, Baltimore, September, 1992, to appear, USENIX Association, Berkeley, CA.

33 L.J. Hoffman, Ed. *Rogue Programs: Viruses, Worms, and Trojan Horses*, Van Nostrand Reinhold, New York, 1990.

34 P.J. Denning, *Computers Under Attack: Intruders, Worms and Viruses*, ACM Press/Addition-Wesley, Reading, 1990.

35 D.E.R. Denning, *Cryptography and Data Security*, Addison-Wesley, Reading, 1983.

36 M. Gasser, *Building a Secure Computer System*, Van Nostrand Reinhold, New York, 1988.

37 D. Farmer and E.H. Spafford, The COPS Security Checker System, in *Proceedings USENIX Summer Conference*, 1990. USENIX Association, Berkeley, CA.

APPENDIX: GUIDELINES FOR THE SECURE OPERATION OF THE INTERNET

This appendix presents the bulk of *Guidelines for the Secure Operation of the Internet*; the appendix and bibliography from the original are not included here.

Preamble

The purpose of this document is to provide a set of guidelines to aid in the secure operation of the Internet. During its history, the Internet has grown significantly and is now quite diverse. Its participants include government institutions and agencies, academic and research institutions, commercial network and electronic mail carriers, non-profit research centers and an increasing array of industrial organizations who are primarily users of the technology. Despite this dramatic growth, the system is still operated on a purely collaborative basis. Each participating network takes responsibility for its own operation. Service providers, private network operators, users and vendors all cooperate to keep the system functioning. It is important to recognize that the voluntary nature of the Internet system is both its strength and, perhaps, its most fragile aspect. Rules of operation, like the rules of etiquette, are voluntary and, largely, unenforceable, except where they happen to coincide with national laws, violation of which can lead to prosecution. A common set of rules for the successful and increasingly secure operation of the Internet can, at best, be voluntary, since the laws of various countries are not uniform regarding data networking. Indeed, the guidelines outlined below also can be only voluntary. However, since joining the Internet is optional, it is also fair to argue that any Internet rules of behavior are part of the bargain for joining and that failure to observe them, apart from any legal infrastructure available, are grounds for sanctions.

Introduction

These guidelines address the entire Internet community, consisting of users, hosts, local, regional, domestic and international backbone networks, and vendors who supply operating systems, routers, network management tools, workstations and other network components. Security is understood to include protection of the privacy of information, protection of information against unauthorized modification, protection of systems against denial of service, and protection of systems against unauthorized access. These guidelines encompass six main points. These points are repeated and elaborated in the next section. In addition, a bibliography of computer and network related references has been provided at the end of this document for use by the reader.

Security Guidelines

1   Users are individually responsible for understanding and respecting the security policies of the systems (computers and networks) they are using. Users are individually accountable for their own behavior.

2   Users have a responsibility to employ available security mechanisms and procedures for protecting their own data. They also have a responsibility for assisting in the protection of the systems they use.

3   Computer and network service providers are responsible for maintaining the security of the systems they operate. They are further responsible for notifying users of their security policies and any changes to these policies.

4   Vendors and system developers are responsible for providing systems which are sound and which embody adequate security controls.

5   Users, service providers, and hardware and software vendors are responsible for cooperating to provide security.

6   Technical improvements in Internet security protocols should be sought on a continuing basis. At the same time, personnel developing new protocols, hardware or software for the Internet are expected to include security considerations as part of the design and development process.

Elaboration

1   Users are individually responsible for understanding and respecting the security policies of the systems (computers and networks) they are using. Users are individually accountable for their own behavior. Users are responsible for their own behavior. Weaknesses in the security of a system are not a license to penetrate or abuse a system. Users are expected to be aware of the security policies of computers and networks which they access and to adhere to these policies. One clear consequence of this guideline is that unauthorized access to a computer or use of a network is explicitly a violation of Internet rules of conduct, no matter how weak the protection of those computers or networks. There is growing international attention to legal prohibition against unauthorized access to computer systems, and several countries have recently passed legislation that addresses the area (e.g., United Kingdom, Australia). In the United States, the Computer Fraud and Abuse Act of 1986, Title 18 U.S.C. Section 1030 makes it a crime, in certain situations, to access a federal interest computer (federal government computers, financial institution computers, and a computer which is one of two or more computers used in committing the offense, not all of which are located in the same state) without authorization. Most of the 50 states in the US have similar laws.

2   Another aspect of this part of the policy is that users are individually responsible for all use of resources assigned to them, and hence sharing of accounts and access to resources is strongly discouraged. However, since access to resources is assigned by individual sites and network operators, the specific rules governing sharing of accounts and protection of access is necessarily a local matter. Users have a responsibility to employ available

security mechanisms and procedures for protecting their own data. They also have a responsibility for assisting in the protection of the systems they use. Users are expected to handle account privileges in a responsible manner and to follow site procedures for the security of their data as well as that of the system. For systems which rely upon password protection, users should select good passwords and periodically change them. Proper use of file protection mechanisms (e.g., access control lists) so as to define and maintain appropriate file access control is also part of this responsibility.

3   Computer and network service providers are responsible for maintaining the security of the systems they operate. They are further responsible for notifying users of their security policies and any changes to these policies. A computer or network service provider may manage resources on behalf of users within an organization (e.g., provision of network and computer services within a university) or it may provide services to a larger, external community (e.g., a regional network provider). These resources may include host computers employed by users, routers, terminal servers, personal computers or other devices that have access to the Internet. Because the Internet itself is neither centrally managed nor operated, responsibility for security rests with the owners and operators of the subscriber components of the Internet. Moreover, even if there were a central authority for this infrastructure, security necessarily is the responsibility of the owners and operators of the systems which are the primary data and processing resources of the Internet. There are trade-offs between stringent security measures at a site and ease of use of systems (e.g., stringent security measures may complicate user access to the Internet). If a site elects to operate an unprotected, open system, it may be providing a platform for attacks on other Internet hosts while concealing the attacker's identity. Sites which do operate open systems are nonetheless responsible for the behavior of the systems' users and should be prepared to render assistance to other sites when needed. Whenever possible, sites should try to ensure authenticated Internet access. Sites (including network service providers) are encouraged to develop security policies. These policies should be clearly communicated to users and subscribers. The Site Security Handbook provides useful information and guidance on developing good security policies and procedures at both the site and network level.

4   Vendors and system developers are responsible for providing systems which are sound and which embody adequate security controls. A vendor or system developer should evaluate each system in terms of security controls prior to the introduction of the system into the Internet community. Each product (whether offered for sale or freely distributed) should describe the security features it incorporates. Vendors and system developers have an obligation to repair flaws in the security-relevant portions of the systems they sell (or freely provide) for use in the Internet. They are expected to cooperate with the Internet community in establishing mechanisms for the reporting of security flaws and in making security-related fixes available to the community in a timely fashion. Users, service providers, and hardware and software vendors are responsible for cooperating to provide security.

5   The Internet is a cooperative venture. The culture and practice in the Internet is to render assistance in security matters to other sites and networks. Each site is expected to notify other sites if it detects a penetration in progress at the other sites, and all sites are expected to help one another respond to security violations. This assistance may include tracing connections, tracking violators and assisting law enforcement efforts.

6   There is a growing appreciation within the Internet community that security violators should be identified and held accountable. This means that once a violation has been detected, sites are encouraged to cooperate in finding the violator and assisting in enforcement efforts. It is recognized that many sites will face a trade-off between securing their sites as rapidly as possible versus leaving their site open in the hopes of identifying the violator. Sites will also be faced with the dilemma of limiting the knowledge of a penetration versus exposing the fact that a penetration has occurred. This policy does not dictate that a site must expose either its system or its reputation if it decides not to, but sites are encouraged to render as much assistance as they can.

7   Technical improvements in Internet security protocols should be sought on a continuing basis. At the same time, personnel developing new protocols, hardware or software for the Internet are expected to include security considerations as part of the design and development process. The points discussed above are all administrative in nature, but technical advances are also important. Existing protocols and operating systems do not provide the level of security that is desired and feasible today. Three types of advances are encouraged:

   a   Improvements should be made in the basic security mechanisms already in place. Password security is generally poor throughout the Internet and can be improved markedly through the use of tools to administer password assignment and through the use of better authentication technology. At the same time, the Internet user population is expanding to include a larger percentage of technically unsophisticated users. Security defaults on delivered systems and the controls for administering security must be geared to this growing population.

   b   Security extensions to the protocol suite are needed. Candidate protocols which should be augmented to improve security include network management, routing, file transfer, Telnet, and mail.

   c   The design and implementation of operating systems should be improved to place more emphasis on security and pay more attention to the quality of the implementation of security within systems on the Internet.

PART IV   ❏   ❏   ❏   ❏   ❏

DIRECTIONS

CHAPTER 17   ❏

The Billion-Node

A. LYMAN CHAPIN

CONTENTS

The term "explosive Internet growth" is now a cliché. However, it is instructive to look at the problems being caused by the current round of growth in the Internet. Once again, we see our old friends addressing and routing causing the most concern.

17.1   THE SUCCESS OF THE INTERNET

From its beginnings in 1969 as a four-node experimental network, the Internet has grown to a size and scope that would have been inconceivable to the UCLA graduate students who connected the first host computer to the first ARPANET IMP. Today the Internet reaches over a million end users in at least 107 countries, and is growing so rapidly that estimates of the "size of the Internet" are obsolete long before they can be published. The Internet is surely one of the most successful large-scale distributed enterprises ever undertaken.

This degree of success was clearly not anticipated by the original architects of the Internet and its protocols, who imagined that a successful outcome of the experiment begun in 1969 might result in an Internet with, at most, 256 networks:[1]

> TCP addressing is intimately bound up in routing issues, since a HOST or GATEWAY must choose a suitable destination HOST or GATEWAY for an outgoing internetwork packet. Let us postulate the following address format for the TCP address. The choice of network identification (8 bits) allows up to 256 distinct networks. This size seems sufficient for the foreseeable future. Similarly, the TCP identifier field permits up to 65,536 distinct TCPs to be addressed, which seems more than sufficient for any given network.

The Internet has gone well beyond this "foreseeable future," and is growing so fast that reasonable projections of its size early in the 21st century show a billion-node Internet as pervasive—and indispensable—as the telephone network.

Success on this scale does not come without a price. To paraphrase Tom Robbins: "It is a fact of life that success eliminates as many options as failure. It is questionable, for that matter, whether complete success is always preferable to its alternatives." In the case of the Internet, success has brought the system within range of a number of fundamental architectural and operational limits, that were anticipated[2] as long ago as 1978:

> As N (the number of nodes in a network) grows, the cost of creating the topological design of such a network behaves like N^E where E is typically in the range from 3 to 6. Thus we see that topological design quickly becomes unmanageable. Secondly, we note that as N grows, the size of the routing table in each IMP in the network grows linearly with N and this too places an unacceptable burden on the storage requirements within an IMP. In addition, the transmission and processing costs for

updating such large tables is prohibitive. Third, even were the design possible, the cost of the lines connecting this huge number of nodes together grows very quickly unless extreme care is taken in that design. In all three cases just mentioned, one finds that the use of hierarchical structures saves the day. In the design case, one may decompose the network into a cluster of nodes, supercluster of clusters, etc., designing each level cluster separately. The same approach may be used in routing, where names of distant clusters, rather than names of distant nodes, are used in each routing table, thereby reducing the table length down from N to a number as small as $e^{\ln N}$ giving a significant reduction.

In very simple terms, the most immediate problems faced by the Internet as a result of its dramatic growth are (a) running out of IP network numbers, and (b) having too many routes. There are other problems on the horizon as well, among them the need to evolve the Internet routing architecture to accommodate the calculation and use of policy-based routes, and the current lack of mechanisms (such as path and resource preallocation) to bound end-to-end transit delay and transit delay variance. Here we will be concerned only with the scaling problems that are directly caused by the rapidly increasing size and extent of the Internet.

17.2 IP NETWORK NUMBER EXHAUSTION

Given the fixed 32-bit size of the IP address, there is an obvious upper bound on the number of IP hosts that can be identified. At first glance, this seems to be a very large number of hosts; a 32-bit address space, after all, is potentially capable of being used to identify over 4.2 billion (2^{32}) hosts. A flat address space—one with no visible internal structure—could in fact be used in that way. However, a flat address space in an Internet containing even a small fraction of 2^{32} hosts would make routing effectively impossible, since every router would have to store routes to every single host in the Internet.

The actual IP addressing scheme deals with this problem by defining a two-level hierarchy, dividing the address between a high-order network number part and a low-order host number part. The distribution of bits—how many form the network number, and how many are therefore left for the host number—can be done in one of three different ways, giving three classes of IP addresses:

1   8-bit network numbers, class A IP address:

0aaaaaaa	*bbbbbbbb*	*ccccccc*	*ddddddddd*

2   16-bit network number, class B IP address:

10aaaaaa	*bbbbbbbb*	*ccccccc*	*ddddddddd*

3   24-bit network number, class C IP address:

110*aaaaa*	*bbbbbbbb*	*ccccccc*	*dddddddd*

The class structure greatly alleviates the problem of routing, since routers can store one route to each network instead of one route to each host. Routing efficiency is gained, however, at the expense of address-assignment efficiency: unless there are precisely as many actual hosts in each network as it would be possible to identify, given the number of bits in the "host" part of the addresses with that network's prefix (network number), the unused addresses are wasted. That is, they can't be given to hosts that are not part of that network. In practice, therefore, what's important is not how many host (IP) numbers there are, but how many network numbers exist—and there are far fewer network numbers than host numbers.

To make matters worse, network number assignment in the Internet is plagued by the "3 bears problem." For most networks, a class A network number (which accommodates 2^{24} hosts) is "too big"; a class C number (256 hosts) is "too small"; but a class B number (about 65,000 hosts) is "just right." About 16,000 class B network numbers are available, and of those about 5,000 had already been assigned at the end of 1991. Although several techniques are available to either manage the assignment of the remaining network numbers more carefully, so as to improve the efficiency with which numbers are assigned to new networks, or reclaim numbers that have already been assigned, but are not being used by their "owners," a simple extrapolation of the current trend projects complete exhaustion of the class B network number space some time in 1994.

It is possible to deal with this problem by fiddling with the class structure so as to bring more of the available address space into the range that is "just right" for the majority of networks in the Internet (see the description of the CIDR scheme, below). However, eventually there will be more Internet endpoints than can be identified uniquely by a 32-bit IP address, no matter how creatively it is structured. Two radically different solutions have been proposed for this problem: make the addresses bigger, or allow the same IP address to be assigned to more than one Internet host. These alternatives are discussed later in this chapter.

17.3   ROUTING INFORMATION EXPLOSION

The greater the number of networks connected to the Internet, the more routing information that must be passed around among routers, and stored in tables in those routers, to maintain connectivity among all possible Internet endpoints. New routing protocols for the Internet are designed so that the amount of information that must be passed around among routers grows much less than linearly with the number of attached networks. New routers with more memory can probably keep up with the storage demands, but existing protocols (such as EGP and RIP) and routers (which in 1992, at the high end, are capable of storing on the order of 16,000 routes, and will very shortly be capable of storing on the order of 64,000 routes) will not necessarily be replaced fast enough to eliminate this problem. There is also a human dimension to the explosion of routing information in a rapidly expanding Internet, since network operators must perform a significant amount of configuration (and, in turn, a significant amount of monitoring to ensure that the configuration has been done correctly) to augment current and even next-generation interdomain routing protocols, which lack sufficient support for the policies and operational preferences of the network operators.

The root of the routing problem is the fact that the current IP address structure supports only a two-level routing hierarchy.[*] Interdomain routing operates on a flat network number, which means that every network is visible throughout the Internet (discounting local policy controls), and interdomain routers must maintain routes to each individual network. The only solution to this problem is to introduce additional structure in the internetwork address, to support routing based on the aggregation of individual networks into groups (and groups of groups, etc.).

It is important to recognize that the routing information explosion is a consequence of the two-level hierarchy built into the current IP address structure; it will still be a problem even if (actually, especially if) it is somehow possible to increase the number of usable IP addresses. A solution to the problem of running out of class B addresses described in the previous section, therefore, does nothing to solve the problem of having too many individual routes if it does not provide a basis for additional route aggregation.

17.4 SOLVING THE PROBLEM

The current IP-centered Internet architecture has persisted, essentially unchanged, for over 20 years, during which time the communication technologies on which the Internet is built, and the applications and services that it supports, have changed dramatically. Most of the people involved in internetworking research believe that the current Internet architecture has reached its limit, and that fundamental changes will be necessary to enable the Internet to evolve. Although there is little agreement on when this "sea change" is likely to take place, that it eventually will take place is seldom disputed.

As recently as 1990, it seemed that the Internet would be able to continue in its present course—perhaps with the help of some clever engineering, with which the Internet community is amply supplied—until the next-generation architecture appeared (with support for multigigabit network bandwidth, sophisticated policy-based routing, and end-to-end latency control, among other things), like the proverbial white knight, to carry the Internet into the (glorious) future. By mid-1991, it was apparent that the accelerating growth of the Internet had created the distinct possibility (though, as yet, by no means the certainty) that

---

[*] At this level of detail, subnetting within a network—although it is tremendously useful in the context of intra-AS routing—is ignored.

success would kill the Internet before its "white knight" arrived. Recognizing this possibility, the IAB asked a number of routing experts to form a task group to develop a strategic plan for the evolution of routing and addressing in the Internet, and to suggest ways in which the Internet could effectively hedge its bet that the future would arrive before it was overwhelmed by the burgeoning present.

This group formed in November 1991 after an IETF meeting in Santa Fe, New Mexico, and quickly named itself the ROAD group (for "routing and addressing"). By the following March, the group had prepared a report of its work, which showed that:

1   The potential for the Internet to be overwhelmed by its own success was quite real.

2   It would be possible to prevent this from happening without inflicting massive upheaval on the community.

3   Doing so would require vigorous and concerted pursuit, in parallel, of significant engineering and architectural initiatives that would be effective only if begun immediately.

The three most important of proposed initiatives are described below.

The Internet could move to a larger address space. In principle, the limitations of the current 32-bit IP address could be removed either by replacing it with a larger address, or by eliminating the requirement that IP addresses be uniquely assigned.

The latter approach would involve the mapping of local IP addresses to and from global IP addresses at the boundaries of addressing domains, permitting the existing 32-bit IP address space to be reused within each individual addressing domain, and reserving some portion of the address space for use as global addresses that could be passed between domains. This address-mapping-and-reuse concept, also referred to as *network address translation* (NAT), would involve the Internet directory (the DNS) in the translation of IP addresses between local and global representations at domain boundaries, and is unlikely to be adopted for at least the following reasons:

• Many widely used Internet applications exchange IP addresses as names in their application protocol; these applications (including FTP, NFS, and the Sun and OSF RPCs) will not work in the presence of nonunique IP addresses.[†]

• Since NAT deliberately "spoofs" the network addresses seen by two communicating hosts that are not in the same addressing domain, it disables any end-to-end security scheme that relies on a unique endpoint identifier; and since the IP address is part of

---

[*]   The road metaphor captured the imagination of the group, which quickly dubbed the two main threats of class B address exhaustion and routing information explosion, respectively, "truck 1" and "truck 2"; many of their discussions could easily have been outtakes from "Night of the Crash Test Dummies."

[†]   This is bad enough in the case of simple symmetric protocol exchanges (e.g., the FTP PORT command), but it is even worse in the case of (for example) the Sun and OSF RPC protocols, in which data structures containing IP addresses can be passed to third parties as well.

the TCP checksum, NAT also interferes with any security scheme that detects (and objects to) in-transit modification of the checksum.

- NAT involves the DNS in a passive monitoring role to trap IP address references that must be translated at border gateways. Leaving aside the practical difficulties of configuring the DNS for such a role, doing so necessarily constrains the way in which the DNS can evolve in its primary role as the Internet directory system.

The alternative is to adopt an addressing scheme with "more bits." The ROAD group identified two reasonable approaches: using the CLNP[*] internetwork packet format and NSAP[†] addressing scheme as a replacement for IP; or encapsulating IP packets within IP packets for interdomain routing, thereby gaining an additional 32 bits of IP address.

The CLNP approach is to gradually introduce CLNP alongside IP in Internet hosts and routers, with the goal of an eventual transition to a worldwide Internet that operates in much the same way as the current Internet, but with CLNP replacing IP, and NSAP addresses replacing IP addresses. It involves no encapsulation, translation, or address mapping in hosts or routers; during the period of transition (which, in practice, would almost certainly never reach a point at which there were no IP-only systems in the Internet), IP addresses and NSAP addresses could be assigned and used independently, and the routing and forwarding of IP and CLNP packets could be done independently. The attraction of the CLNP approach is the size and multitier hierarchical structure of the NSAP address, which would immediately solve the "too few addresses" problem and facilitate a solution to the "too many routes" problem (pending the deployment of routing protocols that can take advantage of the richer hierarchy). It also would take advantage of the considerable work that has already been done on CLNP in the Internet, and on host operating system interfaces that deal with NSAP addresses. However, it would require that all host software eventually change to support CLNP rather than (or, more likely, in addition to) IP; modifying TCP and UDP to run over CLNP (so as to preserve the existing installed base of TCP/IP applications); and adding new resource record types to the DNS for storing domain name-to-NSAP mappings. These are not trivial undertakings.

The IP-over-IP approach (also called ENCAPS) involves wrapping another partial or complete IP header around an IP packet when it leaves an autonomous domain (AD), and using the additional 32 bits of IP address gained thereby as an autonomous domain address, that would serve as the basis for interdomain routing. ENCAPS would reserve a small number of class A and class B network numbers to be used to form AD addresses; the network number would indicate that the address is an AD address, and the remainder of the address would contain the actual AD identifier. This greatly improves the scaling prop-

---

[*] CLNP is the acronym for the Connectionless Network Layer Protocol, which is the internetwork protocol defined by ISO standard 8473 (1988).

[†] NSAP is the acronym for Network Service Access Point; it refers to the addressing scheme that is used by CLNP—defined by ISO standard 8348 (1986)—which defines a 20-byte hierarchically-structured address.

erties of the existing Internet routing architecture, since AD identifiers (unlike IP addresses) can be structured to support almost any route aggregation scheme. Additional attractions of ENCAPS are that its impact would initially be on AD border routers only, leaving the intradomain routing of IP packets intact; and that it is an IP-only solution, which relies on widely deployed and well-understood IP technology and expertise. However, since IP addresses would still be globally unique (unless ENCAPS were augmented with a NAT), this scheme would not do anything about the "too few addresses" problem. (The ENCAPS proponents believe that classless interdomain routing (see below) will extend the life of the existing IP address space long enough that it will not be necessary to adopt a replacement.) Unless all hosts are modified to handle both encapsulated and unencapsulated IP, there will be a close coupling of interdomain routing and the DNS, since some router in each AD would have to query the DNS with the destination IP address to get the destination AD number to put in the encapsulating IP header. If hosts are modified, they can presumably obtain the necessary destination AD information from the DNS as part of the normal query to obtain the destination IP address from a host name; in this case, the host-changes issue for ENCAPS is the same as it is for the CLNP approach, except that the network/OS software interfaces for IP+AD addresses are not yet defined.

The Internet could adopt classless interdomain routing (CIDR). Regardless of whether "move to a larger address space" means CLNP, ENCAPS, or something else, it is possible to add several years (possibly many years) to the life of the existing 32-bit IP addressing scheme by breaking the rigidly fixed byte boundaries that define the three classes of IP address, and using more flexible bit-level masks to distinguish the network number. The classless CIDR scheme would permit blocks of contiguous class C addresses to be assigned to sites that would ordinarily need a class B network number (to accommodate more than 256 hosts, which is the maximum number that can be identified with a single class C network number). The ROAD group proposes that this will solve the immediate "running out of class B addresses" problem, although it clearly does not increase the available supply of IP addresses in general.

By itself, the assignment of a block of class C addresses rather than a single class B address creates a problem that is potentially much worse than the problem it attempts to solve: if routers must advertise each of the class C network numbers individually, the "too few addresses" problem has been solved at the (dramatic) expense of the "too many routes" problem. CIDR requires the development and deployment of interdomain routing protocols that summarize (aggregate) routing advertisements to single route entries (an IP prefix) for networks that share a common prefix and routing information. Sites with multiple contiguous class C network numbers would then be routed in the interdomain system with a single route entry, rather than an entry for each network number (as would be the case with current interdomain protocols).

In fact, it is necessary for this aggregation to occur recursively at the "next level up"—at transit routing domain boundaries (for example, the boundaries between NSFNET and the NSFNET regionals; between NSFNET and EBONE; or between NORDUnet and

Alternet)—to prevent unacceptable growth rates of routing tables in transit domain routers. This requires an additional degree of coordination in the management of network number assignments: sites that are topologically "close" with respect to transit domain routing must be allocated network number blocks with adjacent prefixes. Making "good choices" when assigning network numbers in this way is likely to be possible (if at all) only if the assignment authority is delegated to the organizations that are responsible for coordinating international and interorganizational routing. CIDR may not be possible if network number assignment remains centralized.

CIDR will require Internet network operators to use either BGP4 (an extension to BGP that supports, among other things, the variable-length subnet masks that are required by CIDR) or IDRP (the ISO standard interdomain routing protocol (ISO/IEC 10747), which also supports variable-length subnet masks) in place of EGP or EGP2. Networks that do not default external routes to a major transit network will not be able to continue using an intra-domain routing protocol (such as RIP) that does not support variable-length subnet masks, because incoming route advertisements representing aggregated sets of network addresses would have to be expanded, resulting in what would eventually be unsupportable increases in the amount of router memory required to store all of the routes individually.

The expected "time to impact" for CIDR is 2–3 years, given the time it takes to implement and deploy a new routing protocol, and the network operational adjustments that CIDR will require. Reasonable routing experts differ on whether CIDR buys enough time to wait for the "white knight" jump to a new Internet architecture, or only breathing room for the deployment of CLNP or ENCAPS. However, there is general agreement that CIDR is worth doing in either case.

The Internet could plan now for its future interdomain routing architecture. None of the initiatives analyzed by the ROAD group will buy an unlimited amount of time for the Internet. Possibly the most important observation in the ROAD report is that the high level of cooperation among the many members of the Internet community that will be necessary for any interim measure to succeed is unlikely to be obtained in the absence of a credible plan for the future routing architecture of the Internet. Most of the near-term initiatives are the networking equivalent of blind alleys. To escape an oncoming truck, one is perhaps willing to enter a blind alley—as long as there is a hole in the wall at the far end.

17.5 CONCLUSION

Throughout this chapter, we have assumed that there is a future architecture toward which the Internet is inexorably headed. Currently, the characteristics of that architecture are the subject of intense speculation and research, but eventually (according to the premise) their outline will become clear, and the Internet will undergo a quantum shift to a new networking paradigm (gradually, of course—nothing like this happens overnight). In that case, the question comes down to one of timing. If we must be prepared for a billion-node Internet based on the current architecture, then one of the proposals from the ROAD group (or an equally viable proposal that is not yet on the table) must be entrained as soon as possible. If, however, the billion-node Internet is not likely to arrive until after the architectural rules have changed, then our efforts would be better spent on sharpening the focus with which we perceive the characteristics of the new architecture, and searching for solutions to the problems of Internet size and extent in that context.

With respect to the anticipated new architecture, both CLNP and ENCAPS are steps sideways, rather than forward. A decision to deploy either would commit a significant amount of time, effort, and money to an enterprise that represents no forward progress toward the postulated goal of a "new Internet." However, betting everything on the arrival of the "white knight" before the viability of the current Internet architecture expires is a high-risk posture, both with respect to the potential consequences of misjudging the actual time horizon (disastrous), and with respect to the confidence with which today's network users and vendors are willing to invest, long-term, in the Internet and its technology. The fact that many of those users and vendors are seriously evaluating a paper tiger (OSI) as a long-term network technology foundation is appalling, and suggests the extent to which they doubt the ability of the Internet community to get its act together in time. It may very well be that a credible near-term solution to the routing and addressing problems of the current Internet architecture is essential, and must be aggressively pursued, regardless of when the millennium is expected.

REFERENCES

1 V.G. Cerf and R.E. Kahn, A Protocol for Packet Network Intercommunication, *IEEE Transactions on Communications*, Vol. COM-22, No. 5, 1974.

2 L. Kleinrock, Principles and Lessons in Packet Communications, *Proc. of the IEEE*, Vol. 66 No, 11, 1978.

CHAPTER 18   ❑ ❑ ❑ ❑

Internet Evolution and Future Directions

CHARLES E. CATLETT

CONTENTS

Finally, we return to the larger perspective and look at new challenges which the Internet must face as it grows larger and faster. It is beyond the scope of the *Internet System Handbook* to detail these challenges for all parts of the Internet community. Instead, we will focus primarily on scientific computing.

18.1 INTRODUCTION

The Internet is not about communications and computer technology, baud rates and megaflops; it is about enabling people to work with each other and with resources (data, computers, and instruments) without regard to time or space. Rather than focusing on what networks can do and what they might do in the future, this chapter will focus on what people do with networks and what they might do with networks in the future. From this, we will look at some of the capabilities that are being developed to enable people not only to take advantage of new uses of the Internet but to construct their own uses as well. How will this affect the Internet? What might Internet folk do to prepare?

Predictions of the future are often made based on extrapolations of present and past trends and conditions. In the past, the Internet was used for remote logins, bulk data transfers, and electronic mail. Currently, the Internet is used for these things, as well as extrapolations of them. Remote login is augmented by remote visualization. Bulk data transfer has evolved to, well, faster and bigger bulk data transfer. Electronic mail is evolving to multimedia network conferencing. So what might the future Internet give us? More people doing more of the same thing at the same time? Sure. Faster, bigger bulk data transfer? You bet—an entire encyclopedia in a second, to use a hackneyed illustration. Stereoscopic, high-definition video teleconferencing? Yes, that too.

A major driver behind the establishment of the ARPANET in the late 1960s was time-sharing of computing resources. A network that would interconnect computers in several time zones would allow users in one time zone to take advantage of the idle time of computers in time zones whose work day had not yet begun or had already ended. An interesting thing happened with the ARPANET, though. Certainly the main driver of time-shared computing across time zones was enabled, but other capabilities, not anticipated, soon became the primary use of the network. One of those capabilities was electronic mail. The network allowed researchers to exchange information in the form of text files in a way more convenient than either the postal system or the telephone. Electronic mail did not require that the information be printed, sealed in an envelope, stamped, and mailed—everything could be done from the terminal. Electronic mail also did not have the disadvantages of the telephone, such as "telephone tag," busy signals, or interruptions. Today electronic mail is pervasive not only in the academic community but in business and government as well. The ability to communicate rapidly and accurately using electronic mail was not a capability anticipated by ARPANET researchers, but it was a significant benefit brought about by the network.

What new capabilities might be enabled as the Internet reaches more and more communities, as computing technology grows from gigaflops to teraflops, and as Internet capabilities grow from megabits to gigabits?

This chapter looks at three ways that the Internet is changing. First, many more users are being added to the Internet in the US and internationally. Second, as end systems continue to increase in capacity and capabilities, the services that will be supported over the Internet will expand as users devise new ways to use it. Third, as networking technology moves from megabits, to multimegabits, to gigabits, even greater capabilities of the end systems and new modalities of network use will begin to appear on the Internet.

18.2 CHANGES IN SIZE

The ARPANET began as a research project in packet switching and the provision of time-shared services via networks. One of the most significant results of the project, however, was the establishment of a community of people—a result not of the technology itself but of capabilities enabled by the technology. What began as a research project resulted in something much larger in scope. In the same way, the NSFNET project began as an effort to interconnect supercomputer centers and their users. The result was more than supercomputer access. The NSFNET brought about an enormous expansion of the Internet infrastructure, and equally significant, of the Internet community.

A lot of people are crashing the Internet party. The immigration of noncomputer science researchers into the Internet community began with the NSFNET providing services to the university community at large. Corporations, community colleges, K–12 schools, and even private citizens are beginning to access the Internet, both in the US and abroad. These new groups of users include noncomputer scientists, as well as noncomputer literates, and they treat the Internet as a service, not necessarily as a shared community resource. They may or may not comply with established rules of Internet etiquette and acceptable use of the Internet as a strictly noncommercial research facility. Indeed, the applicability of the old rules of acceptable use becomes less clear when service providers market Internet access and when service providers like on-line databases provide access to their commercial services over the Internet.

Along with increases in user population there will be an increase in the amount of information available to users. With the large number of available electronic mail distribution lists and newsgroups, some users are employing software packages that filter through incoming information and automatically file it based on the topic, the sender, the distribution list, etc.

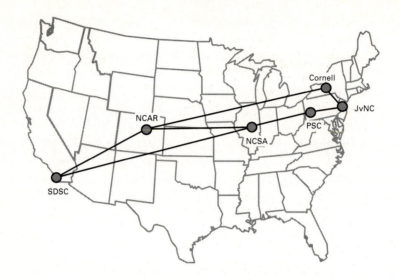

Figure 18.1   The NSFNET backbone network interconnected 6 NSF supercomputer centers in March
              1986. Each supercomputer center also established a mid-level network to interconnect
              sites with large concentrations of supercomputer users

The Internet has undergone many changes in size and scope, and these changes are only beginning to be seen and felt. These changes are discussed in terms of the number of participants in the Internet and the addition of new and different communities of users.

18.2.1   Growth in Numbers

To provide access to its newly established supercomputer centers, the National Science Foundation developed a three-tiered network architecture involving a national backbone, regional mid-level networks, and local campus networks. By 1986, when the NSFNET backbone (see Figure 18.1) was installed, the Internet had reached roughly 100 academic research sites, primarily in the US, but with several foreign sites connected via satellite.

Between 1986 and 1991 the NSFNET backbone grew from 6 nodes interconnected at 56 Kbits/sec to 16 nodes interconnected at 45 Mbits/sec (see Figures 18.2, and 18.3). The number of individual network sites grew from roughly 100 to over 3000 in this same period, and the number of foreign sites grew from several to several hundred. Along with the growth in connectivity, the traffic being carried by the NSFNET backbone alone has shown an approximate 10% increase compounded monthly for the past three years (see Figure 18.4).

In the early 1980s, the Internet community consisted primarily of computer scientists and engineers. This community developed and used services like electronic mail, file transfer, remote login, and electronic bulletin boards (newsgroups, notes files, etc.). Prior to the

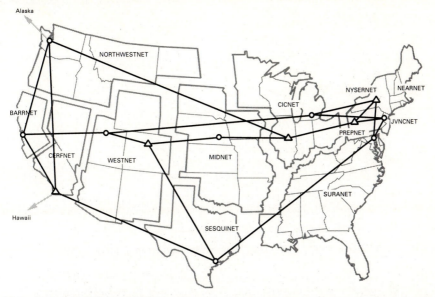

Figure 18.2   By July 1988 the NSFNET backbone had grown to interconnect a number of regional, or mid-level networks at 1.5 Mbits/sec. This map shows some of these mid-level networks. Though it oversimplifies the actual network, the regions served by the mid-level networks are separated for clarity. Triangles indicate supercomputer centers at the mid-level node

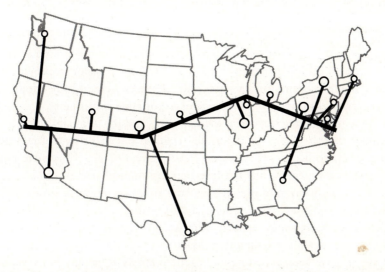

Figure 18.3   By the end of 1991, sixteen NSFNET backbone sites were interconnected with a 45 Mbits/sec infrastructure. This infrastructure is approximated for clarity in the figure above. Large circles indicate NSF-sponsored supercomputer centers. Each node provides connectivity to at least one—and in many cases, several—mid-level networks

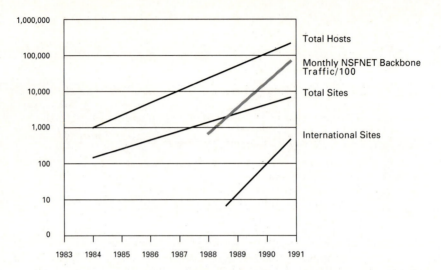

Figure 18.4   Growth of the Internet in terms of number of attached hosts, number of sites (networks), and the number of packets traversing the NSFNET backbone (monthly, in units of 100 packets). Host and site numbers provided by SRI; NSFNET statistics provided by Merit Computer Network, NSFNET Backbone project

NSFNET, immigration into the Internet culture was quite regulated in that a research project with DARPA was generally a prerequisite to having an ARPANET connection. The NSFNET, which transparently connected to the existing Internet, eliminated this regulated growth. A new mode of network use emerged as a result of allowing more sites and users to connect to the Internet: provision of services to the noncomputer scientist. As the NSFNET and other national networks, such as BITNET,[1] began to provide similar services to the academic community at large, these services were quickly adopted by physicists, chemists, biologists, and others outside of the original community.

Perhaps the main difference between the new users and the original Internet community was not so much that they were not computer scientists but that they had no interest in the network beyond its ability to provide access to supercomputers. They were not joining a community but rather were sharing the Internet community's infrastructure.

The Internet's transition from research network to service network continues today. The fact that the IETF, an organization created and operating within the Internet community, in 1991 formed working groups to deal with user services and network management and support issues illustrates this ongoing transition.

As foreign sites have been added rapidly to the Internet, it has grown to literally encircle the globe. As a result, another change has been seen: every hour[*] is rush hour! In the early days of the NSFNET backbone project, it was common to exchange new versions of the

---

[*]   Except, according to the Merit NSFNET Backbone Project, early Sunday mornings.

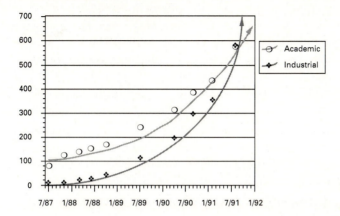

Figure 18.5   Growth of the NSFNET in terms of academic versus. industrial sites. These numbers come from the NSFNET Network Services Center Bulletin and are based on information from mid-level network managers

packet switch software by downloading it to floppy disks and rebooting the switches during the early morning hours (e.g., 2 am). This would affect few users because at 2 am Central Time it was midnight at the farthest western node in the network and 3 am at the farthest eastern node. With the Internet reaching to the Pacific Rim, Europe, and the Middle East, there is no longer a window of time that does not overlap business hours somewhere on the network.

The smoothing of the daily usage cycle has not yet become a real issue on the Internet because even though many users are connected in the Pacific Rim it is likely that only a handful would be actively using resources in the US at any given time. But as the capacity of international connections grows to support better interaction and more users, the difference in response time and throughput between resources in a user's region and those across the globe will be much smaller. When those far-away resources begin to appear as though they were local, usage will increase and any notion of a circadian cycle for network traffic will go away.

18.2.2   Growth in the Industrial Sector

By far, the most rapidly growing segment of the new Internet community consists of corporations. Figure 18.5 shows the growth trends of academic sites versus industrial sites. From this information, we can see that in late 1991 there was a crossover in the two growth curves, with industrial sites now outnumbering academic sites. More importantly, the growth in industrial sites is far more rapid than the growth in academic sites.

Initially, corporations connected to the Internet to support joint research with universities and to gain access to resources on the network, such as supercomputer centers. This early corporate access to the Internet through NSFNET was allowed only for these and other noncommercial purposes. Currently a number of organizations are providing Internet access to corporations as a commercial service. This new industry is resulting in two administratively separate "classes" of Internet infrastructure—a government research infrastructure and various commercial Internet infrastructures.

Services and modes of use that are acceptable on the commercial infrastructure may or may not be acceptable on the government research infrastructure. This will result in one of several things. Policy-based routing, where various services are blocked from using the government research infrastructure, is one possible solution. Another is a relaxation of the policies governing the use of the research infrastructure. Policy-based routing currently cannot be implemented on the basis of individual connections, but can be implemented on the basis of network sites. This presents a difficulty for those sites that wish to provide both commercial services and noncommercial services. Without policy-based routing, it will be difficult to enforce the differences in usage policies. As a result, the entire Internet infrastructure will essentially support the least restrictive of policies. The debate regarding commercial Internet usage will be active for some time.

Some organizations that provide access to data, for example Chemical Abstracts in Columbus, Ohio, are experimenting with the provision of data access services on the Internet. These types of organizations generally charge for their services, but current policies prevent them from charging for services provided over the research Internet infrastructure. Many of these services are targeted at academic researchers who use long distance telephone calls for access. Providing these commercial services on the Internet will result not only in better services for academic researchers but also in reduced access costs, eliminating the long distance telephone charges by using existing Internet infrastructure. Some usage policies make it difficult for service providers to improve their services, including lowering costs to researchers, by offering them through the Internet. Before commercial services can be developed and marketed on the Internet, policy makers need to take into account the possibility that many services would better serve the academic community if companies were allowed to provide them over the Internet.

Whereas the expansion of the Internet into more universities brought noncomputer scientists into the Internet community, the industrial sector represents the paying user. Unlike the academic user, the corporate user generally sees a line item in his or her budget for Internet services. If there are problems with the service, the corporate user can much more readily exert an economic influence on the network provider than can an academic user. For this reason, the addition of corporate users will put much more pressure on the Internet community to provide stable and predictable service.

In addition to the issue of service stability, corporate users demand more security from the Internet than do their academic counterparts. The November 1988 Internet Worm incident[2] brought home an important message to the Internet community. When the community was homogeneous, Internet security was treated much the same way that physical security is treated in small towns. If you leave your door unlocked, chances are that you know the person who might walk into your house uninvited and he will be either a friend or someone who has mistaken your house for another. No member of your community would exploit your open door. Today the Internet community is much larger and more heterogeneous, more like a large city. If you leave your door unlocked, someone might walk in and break or steal something. Evidence of change can be seen by the establishment of security organizations on the Internet, as well as through the warnings of recent reports such as the National Research Council's book *Computers at Risk: Safe Computing in the Information Age*. Cultural changes can be seen through the gradual disappearance of commonly used services, such as FINGER, and by the growing number of mail gateways that prevent direct access to their users' computers—not because of protocol incompatibilities (as was true in the past) but because of security.

Yet the issue of security is more than simply a necessary evil to protect corporate users on the Internet. The lack of adequate security and privacy stands squarely in the path of new and innovative services that the Internet can potentially offer. Consider the provision of access to databases on the Internet. These services require that accounts be set up and payment be arranged before access is granted. This involves either a telephone call or paper mail correspondence in which credit card numbers might be given in exchange for an account name and password. While none of these procedures are prohibitive, the ideal arrangement would be for the entire service, including account setup and billing, to be done over the network. Today this cannot be done because the Internet does not provide secure transit of information or authentication of messages. This means that an electronic message containing a credit card number or an account number and password could be intercepted and read by unauthorized persons, resulting in fraudulent use of the credit card or the service account. In addition, once an account is set up it would be possible for unauthorized persons to access the account by intercepting the password and masquerading as an authorized user.

Beyond security and authentication is the issue of copyright protection. Before information can be published on the network, the laws governing copyright must be adapted to provide for electronic as well as printed information. Because of the international scope of the Internet, electronic information available on the Internet in one country is accessible to Internet users in any other country. If copyright protection is not enforced in all countries on the Internet, publishers will be reluctant to use the Internet as a publishing medium.

18.2.3 Growth in Educational and Public Sectors

Penetration of the Internet beyond universities and corporate research laboratories has not yet been significant. Some factors for this include the lack of computer literacy among K-12 teachers, the lack of computer or network equipment in schools, and the expenses associated with establishing a local area network and a connection to the Internet.[3] Perhaps the latter factor—expense—is the largest. Computers in schools are increasing in numbers, however, and national programs like the NSF SuperQuest initiative are coupling individual schools with NSF supercomputer centers to transfer computer technology. At a number of the NSF supercomputer centers, for example, classrooms with personal computers at each desk are being used to teach several grade-school classes each day. Currently these programs are focused at using the personal computer alone. The next step will be collaborative software that will allow children to work together on a local area network, and eventually with colleagues at other schools on the Internet.

In the US, state and regional networks are beginning to work with K–12 school systems to provide access to the Internet. Even without a local area network, Internet access is now possible through dialup modems. Beyond physical access, then, there is a further enhancement of Internet technology that will cause a flood of new users: simple user interfaces to Internet services. For educational purposes, as well as for residential, simple user interfaces to electronic mail and to databases on the Internet will be required for widespread use. As user interfaces lower the threshold of computer expertise needed to take advantage of Internet resources, the growth in user population will be enormous.

Beyond this, the Internet community will be further expanded with the addition of noncomputer scientists, and noncomputer literates as well. The tolerance for interruptions or fluctuations in services decreases in proportion to the user's understanding of the system. This will require a heavy emphasis on user services.

18.3   CHANGES IN CAPABILITIES

As the NSFNET made supercomputer access more widespread, some of these Internet capabilities began to be stretched in terms of both capacity and functionality. When early remote login services, such as Telnet, were developed, the end user was assumed to be using a teletype (TTY) terminal. Telnet provided a mechanism for command lines to be typed in from a user's keyboard. When the user pressed "ENTER," the command was sent to a remote host and interpreted, and the output was sent back to the user's screen. By the mid 1980s, however, many users had personal computers or Unix workstations whose user interface capabilities included two-dimensional graphics. Today, these end systems are providing the user with capabilities like three- and four-dimensional graphics (three spatial dimensions plus time) as well.

Capabilities in terms of the capacity of the Internet itself and in terms of end systems on the Internet are discussed next, along with changes in the complexity of Internet technology and of Internet services.

18.3.1   Higher Capacity

Since 1985, local area networks have grown in capacity from 10 Mbits/sec, through 100 Mbits/sec, up to over 1 Gbits/sec. Whereas a high-end workstation in 1985 might have supported 3 Mbits/sec on Ethernet, in 1992 a high-end workstation might have supported 50 Mbits/sec on FDDI, an increase by a factor of about 17. Even greater throughput changes have been seen with departmental class computers and supercomputers. A user could send 10 Mbits/sec between two supercomputers over a local-area network (LAN) in 1985. In 1992 two supercomputers could exchange data at over 1 Gbits/sec over a high-performance LAN. This is an increase in capacity at the end system by a factor of 100 in terms of the amount of data that can potentially be sent over the network.

While the increase in the capacity of end systems ranged from factors of 17 to factors of 100 between 1985 and 1990, the capacity of the NSFNET backbone increased by a factor of nearly 800 during the same period. But this is only part of the story. Most Internet connections are provided by lines operating at 56 Kbits/sec or lower, which is quite insufficient for keeping up even with end systems (workstations, supercomputers, etc.).

In the next several years it will be possible to purchase access to the Internet at the traditional fixed capacity rates 1.5–45 Mbits/sec, as well as at intermediate and higher rates on a usage-sensitive basis. Telecommunications carriers are moving toward a standard optical channel format called the Synchronous Optical Network, or SONET, which is likely to be deployed at various rates between 52 Mbits/sec and 1.2 Gbits/sec in the near future. SONET is part of the Synchronous Digital Hierarchy (SDH) standards, and consists of multiples of the basic 55-Mbits/sec Optical Carrier called OC-1. Rates at OC-3 (155 Mbits/sec), OC-12 (622 Mbits/sec), OC-24 (1.2 Gbits/sec), and OC-48 (2.4 Gbits/sec) are the most likely to be implemented.

SONET technology will be coupled with a switching technology called the Asynchronous Transfer Mode (ATM), which uses fixed-size packets, or *cells*. Customer-oriented services that will be provided on top of this SONET/ATM infrastructure will be much more flexible and cost-effective than current leased line services. *Broadband Integrated Services Digital Network*, or B-ISDN, is a term used to describe the higher capacity, more flexible services—such as pay-per-use lines (at current 1.5-Mbits/sec and 45-Mbits/sec rates, as well as at intermediate and higher rates up to 600 Mbits/sec)—and specialized services such as high-resolution video.

Local area networks are also increasing in capacity. Currently, many sites are augmenting or replacing their 10-Mbits/sec Ethernet installations with the 100-Mbits/sec Fiber Distributed Data Interface (FDDI). At many supercomputer centers, 800-Mbits/sec High Performance Parallel Interface (HIPPI) channels, as well as the emerging Gbits/sec Fibre Channel technologies, are being used to construct local area networks. Recently, 1.6-Gbits/sec HIPPI channels have begun to emerge as well.

When the Internet begins to support capacities of 150 Mbits/sec and above, commensurate with local area and campus area networks, remote services and distributed services will operate at roughly the same level as local services. This will result in more widely used and offered distributed services, as will be discussed later. At the same time, researchers are developing capabilities that may require rates up to several hundred Mbits/sec, suggesting that regardless of the capacity of the Internet there will continue to be advanced services capable of

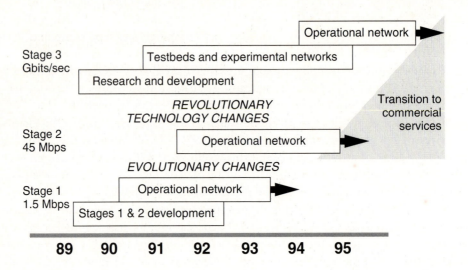

Figure 18.6   Program plan for the National Research and Education Network (NREN).
(Courtesy of Federal Research Internet Coordinating Council)

instantaneously using up all available capacity. Congestion-control algorithms that can adapt quickly to rapid changes in traffic levels and available capacity will be necessary.

The Corporation for National Research Initiatives (CNRI) is coordinating five gigabit network testbeds with funding from industry, the National Science Foundation (NSF), and the Defense Advanced Research Projects Agency (DARPA).[4] In addition to these five, gigabit research activities are proceeding at a number of universities, corporate and government research laboratories, and within regions of several Regional Bell Operating Companies. The emphasis of gigabit network research is on revolutionary, as opposed to evolutionary, developments, as illustrated in Figure 18.6.

Gigabit network research can be divided into several general areas: switching and transmission, protocols and architecture, and software and applications. What is interesting about the CNRI-coordinated program is that each testbed contains a mix of research in several areas and an interrelationship between the various activities. For this reason, it is instructive to look at these particular activities in that they are representative of a much broader research and development agenda being pursued by the research community as a whole.

The five gigabit testbeds shown in Figure 18.7 consist of research participants from more than 15 university and government research laboratories, and more than 10 communications and computing companies. The testbeds are investigating various ways to use ATM, SONET, and other technologies so that new Internet services can be supported. The main thrusts of the research in each of the five testbeds are discussed in the following sections.

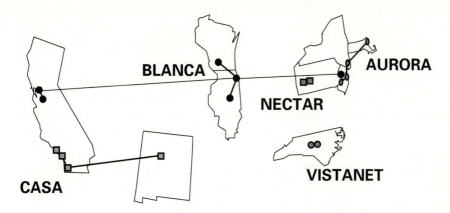

Figure 18.7 NSF- and DARPA-funded gigabit testbeds

AURORA

The AURORA testbed is a collaboration between researchers at the University of Pennsylvania, Bellcore, IBM Research, and the Massachusetts Institute of Technology. These researchers are focusing primarily on switching, protocols, and architectures for the provision of gigabit services to the end user. Several switching technologies are being investigated in the AURORA testbed, including IBM's PlaNET switch, Bellcore's Sunshine switch, and their interoperation. The Sunshine switch is a fixed-length ATM cell architecture. The PlaNET switch is a variable-length packet switch (otherwise similar to ATM, and called the Packet Transfer Mode, or PTM) that is architecturally compatible with a gigabit metropolitan area network technology called Orbit, which also was developed at IBM. ATM interfaces are being designed and built for several types of workstations in the AURORA testbed to investigate the use of ATM as a local and campus area network technology. Protocol research in AURORA includes transport protocols, as well as wide area network distributed virtual memory. Several applications are being investigated, including video conferencing and other real-time service capabilities. AURORA will use multiple SONET OC-12 622-Mbits/sec circuits provided by Bell Atlantic, MCI, and Nynex.

BLANCA

The BLANCA testbed consists of several groups of researchers who have been working together for several years on the XUNET wide area experimental network provided by AT&T Bell Laboratories. The research groups are located at the Universities of Illinois–Urbana-Champaign (computer science and the National Center for Supercomputing Applications), Wisconsin-Madison (computer science, physics, and the Space Science and Engineering Center), and California-Berkeley (electrical engineering, computer science, and astronomy). These researchers are attempting to address the entire range of issues relating to high-performance networks, from applications to distributed programming environments to network protocols and switching technology. AT&T's XUNET ATM switch technology will be used to interconnect HIPPI and Fibre Channel local area environments with the ATM wide-area network. Transport protocols supporting real-time channel services are being developed in BLANCA, and both traditional message-passing and distributed virtual memory schemes are being investigated for supporting distributed applications. Applications research includes distributed atmospheric simulation and visualization, radioastronomy imaging, biomedical imaging, and multimedia digital libraries. The network infrastructure, provided by the AT&T Bell Laboratories XUNET communications research program, will also include a connection to the Lawrence Livermore National Laboratory and Sandia-Livermore. The testbed will consist of 622-Mbits/sec segments in California and the Midwest interconnected with each other and with AT&T Bell Laboratories in Murray Hill, NJ, with 45-Mbits/sec circuits.

CASA

The CASA testbed includes researchers at the California Institute of Technology, NASA Jet Propulsion Laboratory, the University of California-Los Angeles, San Diego Supercomputer Center, and Los Alamos National Laboratory. CASA will focus primarily on distributed applications using large scale supercomputers. Software for distributing applications across multiple supercomputers will be used to solve large-scale simulation models. Scientists at UCLA are working to use multiple networked supercomputers to solve a coupled atmospheric and oceanic general circulation model at a level of detail not possible on a single supercomputer. Theoretical chemists at CalTech will use the CASA network to study chemical reaction dynamics using multiple networked supercomputers. At NASA's Jet Propulsion Laboratory, software developers are working to provide a real-time visualization interface to allow scientists to explore multiple databases through composite imaging. This project will include the integration of data from Landsat, and elevation and seismic databases into three-dimensional images. Using HIPPI crossbar switches and network equipment designed and developed at the Los Alamos National Laboratory, a network will be constructed from point-to-point 622-Mbits/sec SONET OC-12 circuits between sites in Los Angeles, San Diego, and Los Alamos.

NECTAR

The NECTAR testbed, which involves researchers at Carnegie-Mellon University and the Pittsburgh Supercomputer Center, is developing gigabit host interfaces and technology for interconnecting HIPPI local area networks with ATM/SONET-based wide area networks. This work includes investigation into the design of host communication software and off-board protocol processing. CMU is working with several companies to develop network hardware and intelligent host interfaces called *communication accelerator boards* (CABs). Several distributed applications are being used in the NECTAR testbed to develop distributed program execution and monitoring environments. These applications include a chemical process flowsheeting problem that models the control, design, and efficiency of large-scale chemical plants, and large-scale combinatorial optimization problems, such as the traveling salesman problem. The NECTAR testbed will interconnect the Pittsburgh Supercomputer Center computing facilities with Carnegie-Mellon University using a SONET OC-48 2.488-Gbits/sec circuit.

VISTANET

VISTANET is a research project involving scientists at the Microelectronics Center of North Carolina (MCNC) and the University of North Carolina. The research focuses on using SONET and ATM networks, interconnecting HIPPI local area networks, to implement a real-time volume-rendering system in a distributed computing environment. Applications work on the VISTANET testbed will concentrate on the design of a distributed radiation treatment planning system that will consist of a medical workstation, a remote Cray supercomputer, a MasPar SIMD processor, and a Pixel Planes-5 rendering engine. Its communications research thrust is focused on transport protocols, the ATM adaptation process, and gigabit-traffic characterization. The exploration of advanced graphics techniques for volume rendering as a technique for displaying complex data sets is an additional activity within the project. The VISTANET testbed will interconnect MCNC with the University of North Carolina Computer Science and Radiation Oncology Departments using a combination of OC-12C 622-Mbits/sec and OC-48 2.488-Gbits/sec circuits.

Other Gigabit Research Activities

The number of gigabit network symposiums, workshops, and conferences, and many papers on gigabit-related research being published, indicate the level of activity in this area. Virtually every supercomputer center is involved in high-performance applications research; many computer science departments and corporate laboratories, and certainly most of the Regional Bell Operating Companies and long distance carriers, are participating at some level in gigabit research.

Longer range research, not explicitly addressed in the testbeds described above, is being performed on optical transmission strategies and optical switching architectures.

18.3.2 Multiple Classes of Service, Protocols, and Added Complexity

What is likely to emerge to support new Internet capabilities and additional demands for capacity will be a scheme for supporting multiple classes of service, as well as multiple protocols. For example, some traffic might be earmarked for minimal delay, other traffic for reliable delivery, still other traffic for high throughput. This will bring an added dimension of complexity to network resource management and to network management as a whole. Classes of service associated with administrative policy (only certain traffic might be sent over a private segment of the Internet) and security will make the task of administering a connection to the Internet much more difficult. This added complexity will make mistakes on the part of administrators much more likely.

Added complexity was seen and addressed during the period of Internet expansion between 1985 and 1990. It resulted in further training of administrators and further centralization of control for wide area networks. The model of autonomous sites interconnected cooperatively with leased lines and routers will probably not be seen again. It is being replaced by models resembling the telephone service model, with centrally operated switches and clear demarcation between customer premises and operating entity responsibilities.

18.3.3 Transition from Text-Based to Multimedia Technologies

Clearly we are in a transition from text-based to image-based communication. The use of teleconferencing technology has proliferated in the corporate sector, and these capabilities are beginning to appear on networked workstations. In 1985, a supercomputer user would visually analyze results using contour plots on the early NSFNET. When the NSFNET was upgraded to provide some sites with 1.5-Mbits/sec throughput, two-dimensional color images took the place of contour plots. Today, with the availability of 45 Mbits/sec at some sites, three-dimensional images and animation are being used.

As was the case at every step in this evolution of visualization techniques, early developers produced custom systems that were subsequently produced for general use with simpler, more general user interfaces. The second-generation tools made it possible for the general user population to demand services that had been available only at high-end Internet nodes. The "trickle-down" effect of technology will result in high demand for interactive visualization tools and collaboration technologies (network teleconferencing, etc.), driving a demand for higher capacity Internet access.

High-definition television (HDTV) has caught the attention of the visualization community, as well as the end-users of scientific visualization technology. With appropriate compression technology, HDTV animation will be possible at under 20 Mbits/sec, and perhaps even lower. Though this is well within the capacity of a dedicated 45-Mbits/sec network, the widespread availability of equipment and software to use HDTV will mean that many users will be creating 20-Mbits/sec streams at any given time. In the aggregate, this will stress the capacity of the Internet.

18.3.4 Mobile Hosts and Users

Another technological change that will affect the Internet is the notion of mobile users and mobile hosts. The result will be increased complexity and an increased dependence on software for the operation of services. Not long after the rapid growth of the Internet began in the mid-1980s, centralized administration of a global host table was replaced by the distributed domain name system. As Internet hosts and users become mobile, new directory systems—most likely distributed and automated like the domain name system—will be needed to route information to those entities. Has this problem already been solved in the telephone world with the emergence of cellular telephones? No—if you were to call information and request my telephone number you would most likely get my home phone number and not my office number. You certainly would not be likely to get my cellular phone number.

18.4 CHANGES IN COMPUTATIONAL REQUIREMENTS: GRAND CHALLENGES[6]

In the mid-1980s, the National Science Foundation made supercomputers available to the academic research community through its supercomputer centers and the NSFNET. As a result, many scientists moved from departmental computers to supercomputers in fields like lattice gauge theory, chemistry, materials research, molecular mechanics, atmospheric sciences, and astronomy. The move from departmental class machines to supercomputers resulted in the expansion of computational research because the additional capacity in memory and CPU speed allowed researchers to scale their problems up in complexity and also to get answers faster. Being able to get answers in hours or days rather than weeks or months allowed the researchers to change the nature of the questions they were asking. The questions they could ask were more aggressive, and at the bottom line, they could ask more questions.

Today, researchers have reached a plateau in terms of memory size and processor power with conventional supercomputer designs. To move forward, several paths are being explored. The first, and perhaps the simplest route, is increased capacity in homogeneous environments, for example, multiple vector processor supercomputers or RISC workstations. A second route is also being explored that involves the use of heterogeneous resources and the mapping of various functions within applications to the most appropriate computer architecture. Both of these methods are discussed in more detail below.

18.4.1 High-Performance Computing and Communications Initiative

The High-Performance Computing and Communications (HPCC) initiative addresses these and other challenges through four interrelated programs:

- High-Performance Computing Systems (HPCS)
- Advanced Software Technology and Algorithms (ASTA)
- National Research and Education Network (NREN)
- Basic Research and Human Resources (BRHR).

Each of these programs aims at a particular aspect of high-performance information technology. HPCS will address future computing architectures, including computer-aided design tools and prototype systems, with the goal of seeing sustained teraflops performance

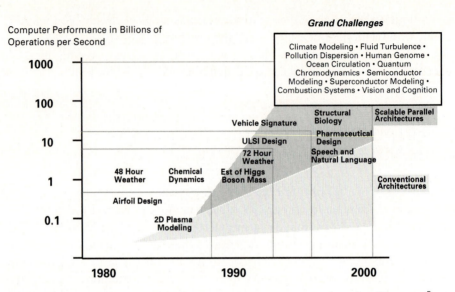

Figure 18.8   Grand Challenge applications versus processing needs and architectures[5]

by the mid-1990s through technologies that are scalable. (By *scalable* we mean that the same technology that runs on a desktop could be used to build a teraflops system.)

ASTA will address the software components and tools, including advanced computational algorithms, needed to solve the Grand Challenge problems that are described below. The program will also include the establishment of research centers and testbeds to provide researchers with access to advanced hardware and software technology.

The NREN program will concentrate on moving the US Internet forward in several ways. This will include consolidation of individual agency-run backbone networks and an upgrade path, including research in networking technology, to a Gbits/sec national network infrastructure.

The task of BRHR will be to support multidisciplinary research and to improve the computing and technology research infrastructure at individual research facilities; for example, at university and government centers. This program will also focus on technology transfer, education, and training in high-performance computing at all levels of the educational system.

Figure 18.8 illustrates the computational requirements of various current and emerging problems, showing the Grand Challenge problems. These are compared with trends in computing technology in terms of CPU performance. Note in particular that through conventional methods it is unlikely that we will reach the computational performance required for grand challenge problems.

Beyond computational hardware, to be addressed by HPCS, a significant improvement in effective performance will also be seen through advanced computational techniques. As

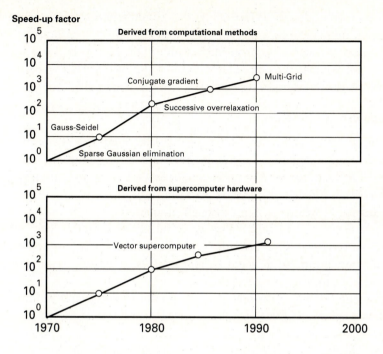

Speed-up factor

Derived from computational methods

Multi-Grid

Conjugate gradient

Successive overrelaxation

Gauss-Seidel

Sparse Gaussian elimination

Derived from supercomputer hardware

Vector supercomputer

1970   1980   1990   2000

Figure 18.9   Performance improvement for scientific computing problems

is shown in Figure 18.9, computational performance improvements have historically come not only from advanced hardware architectures but also from innovations in computational algorithms.

Participation in the HPCC initiative is planned on the part of eight federal agencies, with recommended total funding in Federal Fiscal Year 1992 at over $600 million. The agencies involved include DARPA, DOE, NASA, NSF, The National Institute for Standards and Technology (NIST), The National Oceanic and Atmospheric Administration, the Environmental Protection Agency, and the National Institutes for Health National Library of Medicine (NIH/NLM).

18.4.2   Survey of Applications

The Grand Challenge problems can be considered to be "drivers" of the HPCC initiative. Their requirements for CPU, memory, and I/O rates are stressing, or promising to stress, current technology. Before discussing distributed computing models and their impact on the network, it is important to understand, from a scientific standpoint, the goals of some of the Grand Challenges. One way of thinking about the Grand Challenges is in terms of two general categories: simulation modeling and computer-aided design and analysis. Simulation models involve the use of supercomputers to numerically simulate phenomena like air flow, chemical interactions, etc. Computer-aided design and examination includes the use of computers to augment human understanding by performing many simple operations (such as pattern matching on millions or billions of patterns) or by performing analysis operations on highly complex systems, such as VLSI circuits.

18.4.2.1 Simulation and Modeling

A number of Grand Challenge applications involve the modeling of complex natural systems, such as weather systems, climate, or the effects of air pollution. Other simulation activities include the design of custom materials, or the design and optimization of structures like aerospace vehicles, off-shore oil platforms, or ships.

The forecasting of weather systems through simulation has been done for some time in the US and in Europe. The forecasts that are possible with current supercomputers, however, are limited in several ways. First, the systems modeled are large-scale, with low spatial and temporal resolution. With these current models, it is possible to forecast general weather conditions for 4 to 5 days with approximately 75% accuracy. These forecasts are not of high enough resolution to predict severe weather activity, such as hurricanes or tornados, and they are not accurate enough to predict weather for areas much smaller than a several-state region. A goal of atmospheric scientists is to reach a point where forecasts can be made on local as well as regional conditions on a 6-hourly basis. To do this on conventional supercomputers with current computational methods would require performance in the 20-teraflops range.

Similar methods are being used to predict changes in the Earth's biosphere. Programs like NASA's Earth Observation System (EOS) promise to provide necessary data as input to numerical models. Researchers in the life, geophysical, computer, and computational sciences will need to work together to construct accurate models of the biosphere. These models will produce data on the order of tens of terabytes for a single model run, and this, combined with the large interdisciplinary teams, will stress data storage, analysis, and distribution technologies.

Computational methods are also used to study air pollution and to model engine combustion. In both cases, hundreds to thousands of chemical reactions combine with physical effects like air flow or temperature. But with current computational capabilities these models must oversimplify the phenomena. With combustion simulations, perhaps ten of four hundred chemical processes can be modeled. With pollution studies, where the scale of processes ranges from chemical reactions through the movement of large air masses, the interaction of multiple pollutants cannot be adequately studied.

Finally, models are used to simulate the interaction of drugs and to predict the characteristics of custom-designed materials. Drug interaction studies will lead to medicines that are specifically designed to attack diseases, while custom-material designs promise to lead to high-temperature superconductors.

18.4.2.2 *Computer-Aided Design and Analysis*

Computational biologists use computers to analyze complex molecules and cell structures. In the early 1980s, medical research databases contained several thousand molecular units that were used to compare and identify biomolecular structures. Today these databases contain over 30 million patterns. Programs within the NIH, NSF, and DOE will be adding data for billions of molecular units, ranging from structures found in simple organisms to those found in human beings, including the three billion base pairs of the human genome. As the pool of data continues to grow, the analysis and comparison of complex biological systems will require more advanced, possibly intelligent software, as well as more sophisticated interfaces to the databases.

The design of high-performance computing and communications technology is in itself a grand challenge. Over the past 30 years, the density of electronics has doubled roughly every other year. By the mid-1990s, we can expect the number of transistors per chip to reach 10 million. With devices of this scale, experimental testing is not feasible and thus designs must be verified and tested using computational methods. Without the computational methods, the exploration of alternative designs will not be practical on competitive time scales.

18.5 CHANGES IN MODALITIES OF NETWORK USE

Grand Challenge applications are most often associated with large-scale, CPU-intensive problems. As mentioned above, multiple supercomputers might be combined to provide the resources required to solve these problems. But distributed supercomputing, though an important part of solving Grand Challenges, is only part of the solution. In fact, distributed supercomputing will introduce additional problems in the computing and networking infrastructure by increasing the volume of data to be examined and the requirements for network communications. Figure 18.10 shows a number of types of applications, each with particular requirements in terms of the capacity of the network and in terms of the characteristics of the data exchange.

In the past, supercomputer applications were written as large software packages that performed every function from calculating, to data formatting and storage, to user input and visualization. As networks have increased in performance and as standard protocols and operating systems (primarily TCP/IP and Unix) have become available, the notion of distributing these application functions among several computers has become feasible. This has enabled a shift from centralized, multifunctional applications to specialized applications that could be linked together as building blocks.

In the early stages of this shift, post-processing applications were developed to help scientists analyze their data after the supercomputer application had finished running. Standard data file formats were developed that allowed many different data analysis applications to understand the formats in which supercomputer-generated data was stored. An example of a

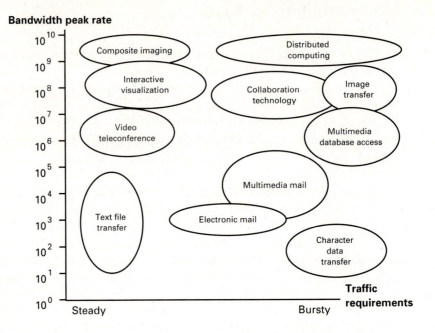

Figure 18.10   NREN applications by bandwidth and traffic characteristics[6]

post-processing data analysis application would be one that allows the user to convert raw data from the supercomputer application into a visual image or series of images.

At the same time, scientists were developing tools to allow them to utilize more elaborate visualization techniques interactively. As the supercomputer application was running, these tools allowed the scientist not only to visualize the output but to start, stop, or change the application based on the progress observed.

The disadvantages of developing interactive visualization capabilities within the supercomputer application itself were many. Each application required customized visualization functions, and for each new display device, user input device, or visualization technique, the entire application had to be modified. The complexity of these large, multifunctional applications dictated either large programming staffs or slow progress (see Figure 18.11).

Today computational scientists and experimental scientists are taking advantage of networks through the distribution of functions across network resources. Biomedical researchers connect laboratory instruments to the network through high-performance workstations, perform image reconstruction on a supercomputer, render images on a massively parallel computer, and display volumetric images at their workstations. Atmospheric scientists run portions of climate models on several supercomputers concurrently while creating images on one or more additional supercomputers and sending images to their own workstations and to colleagues' workstations.

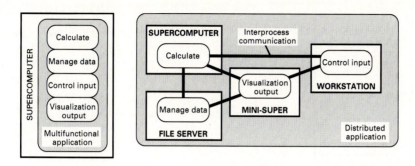

Figure 18.11 A single, multifunctional application is shown on the left, contrasted to a distributed multifunctional application on the right

Distributed computing capabilities are being investigated by computational scientists to reduce effective turn-around, to "navigate" through large amounts of experimental or computational data, and to increase the interactivity of their work. With each new prototype distributed system comes new insight into how to build general distributed computing tools. Once these tools become widely available and easier to use, distributed services will be commonplace on the Internet.

It is important to see which areas of the computational infrastructure are being distributed and what scientists hope to gain through distributed computing. Several examples of distributed application classes are discussed below, as well as the tools that are being developed to support the construction, execution, and analysis of distributed applications.

18.5.1 Taxonomies for Distributed Applications

It is true that the planned Gbits/sec Internet will provide upgraded versions of well-understood capabilities that are currently available, for example, the ability to transfer an entire encyclopedia in under 1 second. But the most intriguing capabilities are those that are not possible at all without very high performance computers and networks. Many of these are being driven by users attempting to solve scientific problems at the forefront of research: these are Grand Challenges as described earlier.

What are some ways that researchers are beginning to work on the Internet? The increased capacity and functionality provided by computing systems and local area networks over the past decade are beginning to be required on a wide-area scale as well. As shared file servers have become commonplace in LAN environments, researchers want the same functionality over wide area networks. Interactive visualization of processes was provided in the 1980s with local area network connections to supercomputers. In the 1990s this type of interaction will be commonplace, with two- and three-dimensional images or their geometric descriptions being transmitted in the same way that characters and files are transmitted today.

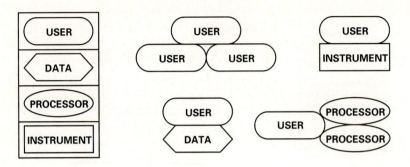

Figure 18.12   Four general types of distributed applications constructed from the four components at left: user–user, user–instrument or process, process–process, and user–digital library

Perhaps the most interesting applications that will be seen on the future Internet will not be those that we are developing today. When users have seen and used our new capabilities, their response will be "Now that I can do this, what would really be useful is if I could also _____." Those requests for new capabilities are likely to produce the Internet applications of the future.

This chapter proposes a taxonomy for distributed applications that encompasses new capabilities being developed today, and more importantly, can be used to postulate about capabilities that might be developed in the future. Computational scientists use the computing infrastructure (including networks) in the same way that experimental scientists use the laboratory. Even more, computational scientists use the network as a communication medium for collaborating with colleagues. Finally, computational and experimental science appear to be merging as state-of-the-art instruments rely more and more on computers to process data.

Consider four fundamental components of the computing infrastructure, each of which can be distributed (either through decomposition or multiple instances) and connected to components over a network. As discussed earlier, these components might also be mobile. These components, as shown in Figure 18.12, are:

- Users
- Processors
- Data
- Instruments or sensors.

In practical terms, each component either is a processor or is attached to the network by a processor. Figure 18.12 shows four types of network applications using these building blocks. The four classes of distributed applications will be discussed below, along with examples from ongoing distributed applications research. One might also consider a process as a component of distributed applications, and these could be in a fixed location, mobile, or distributed.

There are some important points that must be made to put this type of discussion into context. These capabilities are being developed with a view toward the technology that will be available in the mid-1990s. Supercomputers currently are measured in gigaflops and megaflops, and data sets are measured in gigabytes and megabytes. The capabilities we have been discussing assume teraflops supercomputers and terabytes of data. A problem that might take 100 hours of supercomputer time today would not require interactive visualization and steering, but it would if it ran in 10 minutes. The capabilities described here should not be mapped to current workstations and supercomputers but to those that we will be using several years from now.

18.5.1.1 *Process-to-Process Applications (Distributed Supercomputing)*

In a growing number of scientific and technological fields, the memory sizes and computing power of current supercomputers are insufficient to solve critical problems. Climate models, for example, are able to simulate phenomena only on a scale of tens of kilometers. To uniformly increase the resolution of these models by even a factor of 2 requires an increase in memory and CPU speeds by more than an order of magnitude.[*] To solve these problems, methods are being developed to harness the power and memory of multiple supercomputers.

Several models are being researched to divide large problems across multiple computers. These models are classified as task decompositions, time decompositions, and data decompositions. To illustrate these models, consider a general circulation model (GCM) used to model the Earth's atmosphere. This problem is being studied at UCLA in conjunction with the CASA gigabit testbed.[6] The GCM consists of an ocean systems model and an atmospheric model. These two models are run concurrently, and they exchange information, such as the temperature of the sea's surface and the movement of surface air masses.

Considering the GCM as a single application, running the atmospheric model on one supercomputer and the ocean systems model on another represents task decomposition. A finer granularity of task decomposition is employed on this model by running the physics calculations of the atmospheric model on one supercomputer and the dynamics calculations on another. A common example of task decomposition is to use a supercomputer to run a simulation model, a near-supercomputer for image processing, and a graphics workstation to render and display images.

A primary motivation for task decomposition is the fact that these applications involve many operations and many algorithms (e.g., one algorithm for solving air flow, a completely separate algorithm for state transition of water, and yet another algorithm for calculating surfaces for visualization), and each may run fastest on a specific computer architecture. The goal of task decomposition, then, is to achieve a nonlinear increase in

---

[*] Memory requirements increase by a factor of 8, and the length of a single time step must be reduced by half, thus doubling the number of time steps while at the same time having 8 times as many calculations to perform for each time step.

throughput, or to use N computers to reduce the computation time or to increase interactive response by a factor greater than N.

Data decomposition can also be applied to this application. To do this, the model data can be split among several processors. (The atmosphere and surface of the Earth are divided into a three-dimensional grid.) For example, the Northern Hemisphere might be simulated on one processor and the Southern Hemisphere on another, with the two components exchanging information for the boundary region at the Equator. This method of decomposition is also called spatial decomposition.

With time domain decomposition, several models would run concurrently, each computing for one time step. In this scenario, the process calculating for time step N will send data continuously to the process calculating for time step $N+1$. This process will begin computing time step $N+1$ as soon as enough data arrives from time step N. This allows overlapping processes to compute the model, with an improvement in throughput proportional to the amount of overlap that can be supported between time steps.

Though the distribution of supercomputing applications among multiple supercomputers is a relatively new technique, there are already examples of the use of several supercomputers to achieve significant performance increases. The understanding of which algorithms run best on scalar, vector, or massively parallel architectures is increasing rapidly.

The network requirements of these distributed applications will range from several million bits per second to several billion bits per second, depending on the particular application and algorithms used, the number of participating systems, and the user interfaces. Some systems may run for relatively long periods of time without using the network to exchange synchronization or boundary information; others may require a high degree of synchronization and data exchange and continuous access to the network (i.e., bursty transmission versus steady transmission).

A key requirement, in addition to the data transmission rate, is precise timing; data must arrive in perfect synchronization or the function running on one computer will be forced to wait, losing time. In these situations, one can compensate for the predictable delay associated with the speed of light, but it is likely that any performance gains that could be realized by distributed computing might be completely offset by unpredictable communications delays associated with the network.

Some distributed applications require relatively low network capacity (Mbits/sec or less), several relatively low memory requirements (16 Mbytes per component), and do not require interaction with the user. For example, physicists doing quantum Monte Carlo (QMC) work can utilize large numbers of workstations by starting up multiple QMC simulations with different input data, which generally involves different initial random number seeds. When these jobs are completed, the data files are collected at a central location for analysis.

Software systems like Express from Parasoft (developed at CalTech), Parallel Virtual Machine[7] from Oak Ridge National Laboratory, and the Distributed Queueing System[8] (DQS) from the Supercomputer Computations Research Institute at Florida State University provide support for this type of work. With DQS, for example, any networked work-station can make its idle resources available to a DQS resource pool. With this system, the QMC physicist can specify how many jobs to run and where to send the output data.

Imagine the effect these types of capabilities will have on the Internet. Various collabora-tive teams will make their computing resources available to each other, forming loosely coupled "metacomputers" at the national and international levels that exchange informa-tion continuously. The background traffic on the Internet produced by these collaborations will be significant. As supercomputer centers begin to offer distributed services as well, for example allowing distributed applications to run concurrently on supercomputers at sev-eral centers, not only will idle CPU cycles be utilized on the Internet, but idle network capacity will be utilized as well.

18.5.1.2 *User-to-Process (or Instrument) Applications (Remote Visualization and Control)*

Most sensor instruments manufactured today—medical instruments, for example—pro-duce data in digital form. They are coupled with computer systems for instrument control and data storage, and in many cases, these systems can be connected to a network. Exam-ples include nuclear magnetic resonance (NMR) spectrometers and radiotelescopes. For real-time interactive use of the instruments, a more powerful computer often is used for the image processing. In these cases, the computer system actually functions as the image-forming component of the instrument, essentially the "eyepiece." Thus the instruments must often be coupled with high-performance computers to allow the researcher to see the images interactively.

Over the past 15 years, supercomputers have been used to simulate phenomena, such as climatic changes, severe weather systems, economic systems, and chemical reactions, using numerical models. These models employ numerical equations representing the appropriate laws of physics, chemistry, economics, etc., to simulate the evolution of a phenomenon over a period of time.[*] Supercomputer simulations can now replace many physical experi-ments (e.g., wind tunnels), and are increasingly being used to perform numerical experi-ments for which physical ones are not possible (e.g., galaxy formation), not feasible (e.g., the Earth's climate), or more timely and expensive (e.g., drug interactions).

Researchers gain the most insight when they are able to work interactively with these models and instruments. To enable this, high-performance computing resources are required to transform raw data (either from an instrument or sensor, or from a supercom-puter simulation) into images. These images, many of which are three-dimensional sequences, must then be sent from the computing resource to the user. An example of the need for real-time interaction with an instrument is the use of a radiotelescope for observ-ing solar phenomena. In this case, the researcher will need to see images within seconds of the data collection to be able to see events, such as solar flares, that last only several min-

---

[*] These numerical simulations are the basis for what is called computational science.

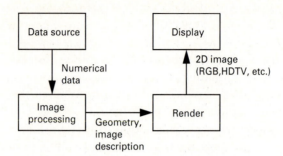

Figure 18.13   Scientific visualization components

utes. If the image processing takes several minutes, the researcher will see the event but will not be able to "zoom in" on it because it will have passed.

Several methods for remote interaction are being explored today. The visualization system is illustrated in Figure 18.13, with components including a data source (instrument or sensor, storage device, or process), a visualization process that transforms data into image representations, a rendering device that transforms image representations into displayable images, and a display device.

The network requirements of this system depend upon the location of the components. In one scenario, only the display device is located with the user, and the remaining components are located across the network. In this case, the data being sent over the network is a two-dimensional projection of the image, for example, a raster bitmap. Compression techniques can be employed to reduce the network requirements from Gbits/sec to Mbits/sec depending on the format and the resolution required by the user. With HDTV, full-motion, camera-quality, uncompressed image streams would be in the 3–4 Gbit/sec range. With compression that would not degrade visible image quality, this could be reduced to tens of Mbits/sec. Many images, however, require higher resolution than that offered by HDTV. Examples include medical and radioastronomy images. An image produced by a radiotelescope might be 24 bits of color and 4k×4K pixels. A single image of this size is roughly 50 Mbytes, but compression techniques could bring this down considerably, and as these are single images rather than animations, the time constraint of delivery is not a video frame rate but a human interaction issue.

The most common case for remote visualization is, and will continue to be, that in which the data source is in one location, the image processing in another, and the rendering and display in a third location. In this case the data being sent over the network is data from the source-to-image process, and geometric image representation from image process to the rendering or displaying device. Data compression in either of these paths must not involve information loss; i.e., the data must be decompressed at the other end without modification by the compression algorithms. Currently, the image process generally sends the entire image representation with each frame of an animation.

It is technically possible, however, to send the image description once and thereafter send display commands to move objects in the image, rather than sending the entire description of the next frame. This is done today with single images in collaborative software (e.g., rotation, pan, zoom, and light source commands are sent), allowing a user to manipulate an image, with the results being displayed on other workstations as well. This technique is also used in distributed games, for example, aerial dogfights between flight simulators on separate workstations. More work is required, however, to allow this technique to be used in scientific animation. The main area where work is needed is in the ability of visualization processing software to "recognize" objects within an image. In computer games, the scenes are constructed out of objects. With scientific images, however, the scenes are constructed out of numerical data and the objects are not defined a priori. Often the definition of objects or patterns in a scene is the whole point to the visualization in the first place, and the processor used to identify these objects is the user's brain.

Often the animation being visualized includes the element of time as an important variable. In these cases, images must be displayed with little or no deviation in frame delivery rate to preserve the temporal information. While isochronous network delivery is frequently cited as a requirement, this requirement might be relaxed somewhat if the display devices were to support the isochronism by buffering enough frames ahead of time to smooth out any fluctuation in frame delivery rates from the network.

18.5.1.3 User-to-Data Applications (Multimedia Digital Libraries)

One of the fundamental problems in computational science is the management and analysis of large amounts of data. A single supercomputer model might produce tens of gigabytes of data; with teraflops computers some Grand Challenge applications will produce terabytes of data. Satellite-based sensor systems, such as NASA's Earth Observation System, will produce 10 gigabytes every 4.5 minutes, or a steady stream of 300 Mbits/sec, continuously. Researchers must take this data and process it to gain insight. Often this involves visualization, as described earlier.

Researchers also require access to images, software, and other forms of data. Many institutions are researching methods for providing digital libraries that give scientists immediate access to many types of data, including images, text, software, and audio data. The utility of a digital library spans all areas of society, from grade-school students accessing text, image, video, and audio history data (e.g., seeing and hearing the broadcasts of Apollo 11's landing on the moon), to computational physicists verifying the conclusions of a research paper by examining the data firsthand.

Consider a scientist who is searching through software archives in the digital library. Rather than storing the resulting data set from a global climate model, a checkpoint of the process might be stored at various times during its execution in a form that would allow it to be restarted from that point in the model evolution. Later, a scientist could restart the simulation model at the point in time where a particular phenomenon begins, analyzing this phenomenon in detail without having to rerun the entire model from the beginning and without having to store all of the previously generated data. With many Grand Challenge applications, the amount of resources required for computation will be so large that many scientists will form teams to run and examine large-scale computational models. Each member of the team will then require access to the resulting data to perform their individual research.

It is likely that interaction with a digital library will involve a number of network services similar to those associated with other network uses. These services will include real-time interaction with images and sequences of images, instantaneous transfer of large data sets, and even interacting with supercomputers to analyze data or run software from the digital library.

In the preceding example, the scientists might want to use visualization systems, perhaps even a supercomputer, to examine raw data located within several different archives on the Internet. Unlike simply browsing images or image sequences, which might be done at several Mbits/sec with high-definition displays and compression–decompression techniques, this example might involve moving tens of megabytes or gigabytes between the separate archives and the visualization processing systems described earlier.

18.5.1.4   *User-to-User Applications (Collaboration)*

Research is being performed to investigate and develop mechanisms for multimedia collaboration support on networks, using workstations to exchange text, audio, images, and even video with one or more remote colleagues. A scenario where this type of application might be useful would be several atmospheric scientists studying a global climate model. One scientist might be producing an animation from model data stored in a digital library, while a second scientist might be running the same model with different initial conditions. These scientists could discuss the results of the two models to determine the effect of various initial conditions. Equally likely would be comparisons between existing and new model algorithms to determine the quality of the model algorithms themselves.

As with the digital library, these collaboration systems will have varying effects on the network. The video and audio teleconferencing portion will be possible using relatively low data rates, including compression and decompression techniques for high-definition display. For this portion, given robust compression algorithms, reliability and error rates are not as important, and thus network services like retransmission of lost or damaged portions of data will not be required. Given reasonable reliability, an occasional split second of lost video information is tolerable in video teleconferencing.

The most taxing network requirements will be in distributed data analysis, as described above in this section and also in the section on digital libraries. Consider not only the effect of a single application, but the aggregate of many users exchanging multimedia information at even modest rates. Suppose it is 1996, and an important discussion is scheduled to be multicast at 01:00 GMT regarding an experiment that day in the use of quantum physics for nanoprocessor design. Hundreds of computer engineers, physicists, and chemists would tune in to this multimedia address, which might include a panel discussion with experts participating from their workstations in Tokyo, Los Angeles, Washington, DC, and Caracas. At the conclusion of the discussion, a plan might be in place to perform several variations of the experiment to further investigate the conclusions. Participating researchers at a dozen institutes might volunteer, and a follow-up meeting might be scheduled for the next week.

What effects this type of capability would have on the Internet is clearly secondary to the benefits it would provide to the research community.

18.5.2 Emerging Distributed Computing Methods

Each of the applications and modalities of network use described above is essentially a distributed software application, with the differences between them having to do with what functions are performed by each component in the distributed system. Beyond these applications are two key technologies that will be instrumental in moving the capabilities described earlier into the mainstream of Internet use. The first step beyond custom distributed applications and prototypes will be tools that allow the user to construct a distributed application from existing software modules. These modules and the software required to build distributed systems will take into account differences in architectures and operating systems within the pool of available networked resources.

A major function required to distribute applications is a management scheme for keeping track of the various interprocess communication links between application components and for synchronizing the execution of those components. In some distributed applications packages today, the user can add, subtract, or change individual components, resulting in changes to the interprocess communication topology. An example of this is a multiuser audio and video teleconference. When a new user is added, additional interprocess communications links must be established to that user's computer.

Systems are being developed to monitor distributed applications and give the developer or the user information about the performance, failures, etc. These systems allow the developer to find problems in a distributed application, and allow the user to see quantitatively the costs and performance gains involved with distributing an application versus running it on a single computer.

Tools are also being developed to assist users in porting their applications between available architectures. In the case of supercomputers, a significant factor in the performance of an application is that it be designed in such a way as to take full advantage of the architecture of the supercomputer. When porting applications, or sections of applications, from one type of supercomputer to another, the required changes in the application structure will be proportional to the difference between the architectures of the two supercomputers.

The previous section described the use of several supercomputers to run distributed applications, subdividing functions so that each would run on the most suitable architecture. Today we find many applications that run on traditional supercomputers but contain portions that are much more suitably run on massively parallel supercomputers. In these cases, portions of the application are extracted and ported to the massively parallel super-computer.

More comprehensive systems are emerging that allow the user to specify which computers should be used to run the application; the application is automatically subdivided among selected machines. Algorithms are being researched to minimize the network interaction required among the computers running the application, and also to take into account and compensate for predictable network delays, such as signal propagation.

With distributed computing, it is not yet clear what details should be hidden from the application, what functions should be automated, etc. Distributed applications software described above performs many of the functions associated with an operating system. As these systems mature, it will become more clear what is needed to design an operating system that treats multiple, networked resources as routine details in the same way that current operating systems treat the components of an individual computer today. Rather than having each processor run its own operating system, one operating system would run on all of the computers, perhaps with each one performing specific, unique functions. This is often called a *metacomputer*, though the term also has been used to refer to a collection of computers that support distributed applications, as described in the previous section.

Beyond distributed application software is the distributed operating system. With distributed applications, a layer of software is added to the existing hierarchy to provide a uniform abstraction above multiple operating systems. The distributed application software is, in fact, a user-layer operating system on top of multiple existing operating systems. This layer currently introduces inefficiencies and overhead that will limit performance in the long run.

In the long run, a single operating system that can manage the resources of multiple networked processors, storage devices, etc., will allow the best performance and will complete the shift from distributed computing to distributed computers. The notion of distributed operating systems has been seen already within homogeneous environments, but the challenge will be in efficiently and seamlessly integrating the heterogeneous environment of scalar, vector, and massively parallel architectures.

REFERENCES

1 I.H. Fuchs, BITNET—Because It's Time, *Perspectives in Computing*, Vol. 3, No. 1, pp. 16–27, 1983.

2 Special Section on the Internet Worm, *Communications of the ACM*, Vol. 32, No. 6, 1989.

3 K. Klingenstein, A Coming of Age: Design Issues in the Low-End Internet, in *Building Information Infrastructure*, (B. Kahin, Ed.) McGraw-Hill, New York, 1992.

4 Information about the CNRI project is taken from *1991 Annual Testbed Reports*, Corporation for National Research Initiatives, and from the author's ongoing involvement in that effort. Reports were prepared by project participants in each of five testbeds.

5 Much of the material in the section can be found in greater detail in the President's FY92 and FY93 budgets in reports entitled *Grand Challenges: High Performance Computing and Communications*, both prepared by the Committee on Physical, Mathematical, and Engineering Sciences, Federal Coordinating Council for Science, Engineering, and Technology, and the Office of Science and Technology Policy.

Memory requirements increase by a factor of 8, and the length of a single time step must be reduced by half, doubling the number of time steps while at the same time having 8 times as many calculations to perform for each time step.

6 CASA Annual Report, from *1991 Annual Testbed Reports*, Corporation for National Research Initiatives. Reports were prepared by project participants in each of five testbeds.

7 A. Beguelin, J. Dongarra, G. Geist, R. Manchek, and V. Sunderam, Solving Computational Grand Challenges Using a Network of Supercomputers, in *Proceedings of the Fifth SIAM Conference on Parallel Processing*, Danny Sorenson, Ed., Philadelphia, 1991.

8 T. Green and J.Snyder, *DNQS, A Distributed Network Queueing System*, and DQS, *A Distributed Queueing System*, SCRI/FSU, 1991.

CHAPTER 19

Annotated Bibliography

JOHN S. QUARTERMAN

CONTENTS

19.1 INTRODUCTION

This bibliography covers introductory texts and basic references related to the Internet and the TCP/IP protocol suite. There are far more publications on networks and networking than can be listed here. But the reader should be able to use the references described here to get oriented, to learn the essential background, and to know where to go for more information.

General works on networks, including politics, come first. These are followed by protocol theory books. Most of the material is about specific topics related to the TCP/IP protocol suite, as it is actually used in real networks. The traditional TCP/IP core protocols (IP, ICMP, TCP, and UDP) are covered first, followed by basic distributed services, such as naming and time, and then traditional applications, such as Telnet, FTP, and SMTP. More general topics follow, including host system requirements, router requirements, and network management. The rest of the material is about more recent protocols and topics, such as remote procedure call and distributed file systems, distributed applications, and resource discovery.

This is a bibliography, so discussion is kept to a minimum. Any of the works described could have innumerable different short descriptions; those included here are meant to be illustrative and not definitive. The descriptions are also one person's opinions. (For some other opinions, see *RFC 1175*.) True relative worth of the items described, or of others not included, are left as an exercise for the reader.

19.2 ON-LINE INFORMATION

Because this is a bibliography, most of the information here is about paper publications. There is a wealth of on-line information about networks, protocols, and other subjects, but this is not the place to present it.

In this section we will describe only a few of the most commonly used on-line discovery or retrieval mechanisms. Anonymous FTP permits almost any Internet host to publish information over the network. Archie lets users find that information. Mail servers make similar information available to people who don't or can't retrieve it with FTP.

We must leave other information discovery, selection, or retrieval mechanisms, such as netfind, KIS, X.500, WAIS, Prospero, WWW, Gopher, etc., to other documents. Just as an indication of the wealth of material available, we list a couple of articles about libraries on line.

19.2.1 Anonymous FTP

To use anonymous FTP, use the FTP user client program on your host to connect to the anonymous FTP server host, and log in as user *anonymous*, with password *guest*, before retrieving files. The exact commands to use will depend on your local operating system.

Here is an example using the 4.3BSD FTP client to connect to nic.ddn.mil, change to the rfc subdirectory, and retrieve the *RFC* index.

```
% ftp nic.ddn.mil
Connected to nic.ddn.mil.
220-*****Welcome to the Network Information Center*****
            *****Login with username "anonymous" and password "guest"
            *****You may change directories to the following
            ddn-news              - DDN Management Bulletins
            domain                - Root Domain Zone Files
            iesg                  - IETF Steering Group
            ietf                  - Internet Engineering Task Force
            internet-drafts       - Internet Drafts
            netinfo               - NIC Information Files
            netprog               - Guest Software (ex. whois.c)
            protocols             - TCP-IP & OSI Documents
            rfc                   - RFC Repository
            scc                   - DDN Security Bulletins
            std                   - Internet Protocol Standards
220 And more!
Name (nic.ddn.mil:you): anonymous
331 Guest login ok, send "guest" as password.
Password:
230 Guest login ok, access restrictions apply.
ftp> cd rfc
250 CWD command successful.
ftp> get rfc-index.txt
200 PORT command successful.
150 Opening ASCII mode data connection for rfc-index.txt (166381 bytes).
^C
426 Transfer aborted. Data connection closed.
226 Abort successful
local: rfc-index.txt remote: rfc-index.txt
3584 bytes received in 2.8 seconds (1.3 Kbytes/s)
ftp> quit
221 Goodbye.
%
```

This example illustrates the use of control C (^C) to abort the transfer. This is useful when you start a transfer of a long file and realize you don't actually want it.

Some anonymous FTP servers are now requiring an electronic mail address as a password. This is intended to cut down on abuse by people transferring spurious files to the server.

19.2.2   Archie

Archie is an application that collects indexes of anonymous FTP servers (by polling them approximately monthly) and provides its clients with search access to those indexes.

- P. Deutsch, and A. Emtage, Archie: An Internet Electronic Directory Service, *ConneX-ions—The Interoperability Report*, Vol. 6, No. 2, pp. 2–9, Interop Company, Mountain View, TX, February 1992.

Archie is a good example of a widely used Internet service that was developed by essentially volunteer labor, and that has no organized means of support.

- P. Deutsch, On the Need to Develop Internet User Services, *Matrix News*, Vol. 1, No. 4, Matrix Information and Directory Services, Inc. (MIDS), Austin, TX, July 1991.

- B. Barron, The Left Hand Doesn't Know What the Right Hand Is Doing, *Matrix News*, Vol. 2, No. 4, Matrix Information and Directory Services, Inc. (MIDS), Austin, TX, April 1992.

Archie can be used either through Telnet, or better, through an archie client. For the former, Telnet to one of the archie server machines, such as archie.cs.mcgill.ca, and login as archie. Try to pick a server close to you; there are currently servers on at least three continents and in at least six countries. The archie command *servers* lists all archie servers. Archie has a help command that tells you how to actually use it.

The source for the archie client may be retrieved by anonymous FTP. Use anonymous FTP to connect to one of the archie servers, and to look in the directory /archie/clients or /pub/archie/clients.

Comments and bug reports for archie may be sent to archie-admin@archie.cs.mcgill.ca.

19.2.3   Mail Document Servers

Many hosts on the Internet, and some on other networks, such as BITNET, support mail document servers. Such a facility allows remote users to retrieve information by electronic mail. It is usable even by people who are not on the Internet, as long as they can send mail to the Internet. Here are three examples of mail servers, at the DDN NIC, at SRI, and at ISI.

The mail server at the DDN (Defense Data Network) NIC (Network Information Center) will return any *RFC* by electronic mail if you send it a message with headers like this:

```
To: service@nic.ddn.mil
Subject: RFC 791
```

That is, the Subject: header line contains the keyword *RFC*, a space, and the *RFC* number. The *RFC* will be returned by mail to the address in the From: header of your message, as it is received by the NIC. The rest of the message is ignored. To get an index of *RFC*s, use

```
To: service@nic.ddn.mil
Subject: RFC Index
```

SRI supports a mail server that will return any *RFC* in response to a request of the following form:

To: mail-server@nisc.sri.com
Subject: anything

RFC 1280

The SRI mail server expects the query in the *body* of the message, unlike the DDN NIC mail server, which expects the query in the *Subject:* of the message.

ISI supports a mail server that expects queries in the body of the message; the content of the *Subject:* is ignored. The ISI server permits searches by organization or date, and keyword searches with wildcards. To get details on other commands, send the server a request for help:

To: RFC-INFO@ISI.EDU
Subject: anything

Help: Help

19.2.4 Libraries

Not many libraries have their actual collections on-line yet, but more and more make their card catalogs accessible over the Internet. Most of these are accessible by Telnet.

• B. Barron, Another Use of the Internet: Libraries on-line Catalogs, *ConneXions—The Interoperability Report*, Vol. 5, No. 7, pp. 15–19, Interop, Company, Mountain View, CA, July 1991.

• B. Barron, Libraries on the Matrix, *Matrix News*, Vol. 1, No. 6, Matrix Information and Directory Services, Inc. (MIDS), Austin, TX, September 1991.

19.3 NETWORKS

Protocols are used to build networks. Some books and other works discuss the networks themselves. Here we list two kinds of network books:

1 Those about the Matrix, which includes all networks worldwide that exchange at least mail or news. These include the UUCP mail network, the USENET news network, BITNET, and FidoNet, as well as commercial systems like CompuServe, and conferencing systems like the WELL or the World, as well as the Internet. Systems like Prodigy, or standalone BBSs that do not exchange mail or news with any other system, are not part of the Matrix. The Matrix is sometimes called the Net.

2 Those about the Internet, which is the set of networks using TCP/IP and directly connected for interactive end-to-end transfer. There are many networks within the Internet, including wide area networks like NSFNET, PSINet, AlterNet, CERFNET,

NORDUnet, and WIDE; regional networks like NEARNET or BARRNet; and agency, company, university, building, or workgroup networks.

If you can FTP to nic.ddn.mil, ftp.uu.net, or ftp.psi.com, you are on the Internet. If you can't FTP, but you can send mail to service@nic.ddn.mil, you are in the Matrix.

- J.S. Quarterman, Which Network, and Why It Matters, *Matrix News*, Vol. 1, No. 5, Matrix Information and Directory Services, Inc. (MIDS), Austin, TX, August 1991.

19.3.1   The Matrix

Some of these references are sometimes cited as being about the Internet. All of them include material about the Internet, but none of them are limited to the Internet. The common theme is actually communication across networks, so they are really about the Matrix, not just the Internet. The Matrix has about ten million users.

- J.S. Quarterman, How Big Is the Matrix? *Matrix News*, Vol. 2, No. 2, Matrix Information and Directory Services, Inc. (MIDS), Austin, TX, February 1992.

19.3.1.1 General

The most comprehensive book about the Matrix is called *The Matrix*. It also includes overviews of network service types, of several protocol suites (TCP/IP, ISO-OSI, Coloured Book, XNS, DNA, NCA, SNA, and SAA) and of many specific protocols. The bulk of the book consists of descriptions of specific networks. Technical information is included for each, plus information about user communities, administration, funding, history, and plans. This book goes into more depth than any of the others. It has 25 pages about USENET. It includes the most extensive description of the Internet, including NSFNET and all the regionals, published in one place. It was published 29 September 1989 and is thus somewhat out of date. Details are thus not always dependable (there is no description of the NSFNET T-1 backbone, or of the CIX), but the general context is still usable.

- J.S. Quarterman, *The Matrix: Computer Networks and Conferencing Systems Worldwide*, Digital Press, Bedford, MA 1990. Prentice Hall ISBN 0-13-565607-9.

Matrix News is a monthly newsletter about contextual issues that cross network, political, and geographical boundaries. It is available both on paper and on-line.

Matrix Information and Directory Services, Inc. (MIDS)
Building 2 Suite 300
1120 South Capitol of Texas Highway
Austin, TX 78746
USA
tel: +1-512-329-1087
fax: +1-512-327-1274
mids@tic.com

19.3.1.2 Directories

UDCN is a detailed directory to the domain, host, and contact level of several major networks, including the Internet and BITNET. It also includes brief essays on major technical topics by technical experts. For example, DNS is described by Mockapetris. It was published in 1990, and is somewhat out of date, but is still a good contextual reference, and many of the details are still accurate.

- T.L. LaQuey, *Users' Directory of Computer Networks*, Digital Press, MA, Bedford, 1990. Digital Press ISBN 1-55558-047-5; Prentice Hall ISBN 0-13-950262-9.

The European R&D E-Mail Directory is a directory of EUnet and EARN. This is a directory of the two major European international networks as of 1990: EUnet (similar to UUCP and USENET in the States), and the European Academic and Research Network (the European relative of BITNET). It includes some useful introductory information on electronic mail, domain addressing, and other issues from a perspective different from the usual North American, native English-speaker perspective. Availability of this book is not clear.

- A. Goos, and D. Karrenberg, *The European R&D E-Mail Directory*, Second Edition, EurOpen, 1990. ISBN 0-9513181-9-5.

  EurOpen
  Secretariat
  Owles Hall
  Buntingford Herts. SG9 9PL
  United Kingdom
  tel: +44-763-73039
  fax: +44-763-73255
  europen@eu.net

19.3.1.3 Desk References

"!%@::" is a quick desk reference to several hundred networks. Each network has two pages, with a set of basic textual information on one page, and a map on the other. It is sometimes known as "that darn book," from the unpronounceable title. It is currently in its third edition, and is the most up to date of the general books about the Matrix.

- D. Frey, and R. Adams, *!%@:: A Guide to Electronic Mail Networks and Addressing*, O'Reilly & Associates, Newton, MA 1991. ISBN 0- 937175-39-0.

19.3.2 The Internet

All of the references already listed include material about the Internet, although they are not limited to the Internet. Here we list books and other publications that are specifically about the Internet. The Internet currently has about 5 million users, and is growing exponentially. It has been doubling in size each year since 1988.

- M. Lottor, *Internet Growth (1981–1991); RFC 1296*, Network Working Group Request for Comments, *RFC 1296*, Network Information Systems Center, SRI International, Menlo Park, CA January 1992.

19.3.2.1 Newsletters

ConneXions—The Interoperability Report is a technical journal of Interop Company, which is the company that organizes the INTEROP conferences and vendor exhibits. It contains technical articles about protocols, book reviews, descriptions of networks, and other interesting material.

Interop Company
480 San Antonio Road, Suite 100
Mountain View, CA 94040
USA
tel: +1-415-941-3399
connexions@interop.com

Internet Society News is a membership newsletter of the Internet Society (ISOC), which is an international membership organization, formed in January 1992, that promotes the use of the Internet for research, scholarly communication, and collaboration, and serves as a forum and a focus for debate, development, and evolution of network policies, procedures, and technology, as well as advancing open scholarship in all countries.

The Internet Society
1895 Preston White Drive, Suite 100
Reston, VA 22091
USA
isoc@nri.reston.va.us

In addition, many of the IP service providers, such as PSI, CERFNET, and Merit, publish newsletters. See *RFC 1175* for a sampling.

19.3.2.2 Guides

Perhaps the most condensed guide to the Internet is *The Hitchhiker's Guide to the Internet*, which began life as an *RFC*.

- E. Krol, *The Hitchhiker's Guide to the Internet; RFC 1118*, Network Information Systems Center, SRI International, Menlo Park, CA September 1989.

The book with the most detailed and current description of Internet services is the *Internet Resource Guide* (IRG). The IRG contains listings of the resources available through the Internet. Such resources range from supercomputers to specialized protocol servers.

- NNSC, *Internet Resource Guide*, BBN, Cambridge, MA 1992. $15.00

NSF Network Service Center (NNSC)
Bolt Beranek and Newman Inc.

10 Moulton Street
Cambridge, MA 02138
USA
tel: +1-617-873-3400
nnsc@nnsc.nsf.net

The IRG is also available by anonymous FTP from nnsc.nsf.net, in both PostScript and plain text. Whole chapters and recent changes are available separately. Get the file resource-guide/README first.

To get on a list to be notified by anonymous FTP when new material is available, or to get a set of sections by mail, mail a human-readable request to: resource-guide-request@nnsc.nsf.net.

The *NorthWestNet User Services Internet Resource Guide* (NUSIRG) is sort of a cross between UDCN and IRG, but is more oriented toward the new user than either. It is full of useful information, but is not extremely accessible to naive users, and has some technical flaws.

- *NorthWestNet User Services Internet Resource Guide*, NorthWestNet, Bellevue, 1991

NUSIRG may be gotten by anonymous FTP from ftphost.nwnet.net in the directory nic/nwnet/user-guide. Start with the file README.nusirg. There's a PostScript and a plaintext version of each version, and two compressed tar archives of the whole book, one of the PostScript chapters, the other of plaintext.

NorthWestNet
NUSIRG Orders
15400 SE 30th Place, Suite 202
Bellevue, WA 98007
USA
tel: +1-206-562-3000
fax: +1-206-562-4822
nusirg-orders@nwnet.net

19.3.2.3 Users

At the moment there are only a few introductions to the Internet for new, and perhaps nontechnical, users. Half a dozen more will be published soon.

The following is an introduction to the Internet for new users. SRI plans to update it frequently.

- A. Marine, S. Kirkpatrick, V. Neou, and C. Ward, *Internet: Getting Started*, SRI International, Network Information Systems Center, Menlo Park, CA May 1992.

Another introduction to the Internet for new users; so far is available only on-line. Contact guide-bugs@cs.widener.edu for access details, or use archie to locate it.

- B. Kehoe, *Zen and the Art of the Internet: A Beginner's Guide to the Internet*, Department of Computer Science, Widener University, Chester, PA, 1992.

The following book is about the users of the Internet.

- C. Malamud, *Exploring the Internet*, Prentice Hall, Englewood Cliffs, NJ 1992. ISBN 0-13-296898-3.

19.3.3   Politics

The Internet and TCP/IP have always attracted political activity. Here are some articles related to a few periods in Internet history.

19.3.3.1   NSFNET

The existence of national backbone networks like NSFNET is now often taken for granted, but the creation of NSFNET was not a foregone conclusion. Here are a few papers from the early calls for NSFNET.

- G.C. Bell, Gordon Bell calls for a US research network, *IEEE Spectrum*, Vol. 25, No. 2, pp. 54–7, February 1988.

- D.M. Jennings, L.H. Landweber, I.H. Fuchs, D.J. Farber, and W.R. Adrion, Computer Networking for Scientists, *Science*, Vol. 231, No. 4741, pp. 943–950, 28 February 1986.

- G.M. Vaudreuil, The Federal Research Internet Committee and the National Research Internet, *Computer Communication Review*, 1 July 1988.

- C. Catlett, The NSFnet: Beginnings of a National Research Internet, *Academic Computing*, December 1988.

19.3.3.2   NREN

The High Performance Computing Act of 1991 directs the President to implement a National High-Performance Computing Program, which includes a National Research and Education Network (NREN). Before and after its approval, NREN has attracted much political activity.

Brian Kahin has organized an early attempt to publish articles about a broad range of public policy, technical, and economic issues related to NREN.

- B. Kahin, *Building Information Infrastructure: Issues in the Development of the National Research and Education Network*, McGraw-Hill, New York, 1992.

The Library and Information Technology Association (LITA) is a division of the American Library Association (ARL). This short but very useful book is evidence of strong interest in networking on the part of librarians. It includes a chronology of significant events related to NREN, starting in 1986; a nice capsule summary by Vint Cerf of the political structure and services of the Internet; and much information in other articles about libraries, user services, and social and behavioral considerations topics which have often been neglected in discussions of NREN.

- C. A. Parkhurst, *Library Perspectives on NREN: The National Research and Education Network*, LITA, Chicago, 1990. ISBN 0-8389-7477-5.

  LITA Publications
  ALANET ALA0085
  50 East Huron Street
  Chicago, IL 60602
  USA
  tel: +1 800-545-2433
  tel: +1 312-280-4270
  fax: +1 312-440-9374

Research and Education Networking: The Newsletter for Education, Information, and Research Networks is published by Meckler Corporation, beginning in October 1990. It is organized around NREN issues.

  meckler@trigger.jvnc.net
  800-635-5537

The following is a report from the System Security Study Committee:

- D. Clark, *Computers at Risk: Safe Computing in the Information Age*, National Academy Press, 1991.

19.3.4 Standards

How do protocols become Internet Standards, and what does that mean? The official description of the process is in an *RFC*; see Chapter 2 in this book.

The following book includes interesting—and opinionated—material on OSI and Internet standards processes:

- M.T. Rose, *The Simple Book: An Introduction to Management of TCP/IP-Based internets*, Prentice Hall Series in Innovative Computing, Prentice Hall, Englewood Cliffs, NJ 1990. ISBN 0-13-812611-9.

The following book includes a detailed examination of the IAB standards process, including comparisons to other standards processes, and speculations on the effects of networks on standards and standards on networks. The book is about standards for open systems related to POSIX and the historical UNIX operating system, and provides a more general context for how TCP/IP and other network protocols are used in open system environments and distributed computing:

- J.S. Quarterman and S. Wilhelm, *UNIX, POSIX, and Open Systems: The Open Standards Puzzle*, Addison-Wesley, Reading, MA 1993. ISBN 0-201-52772-3.

The status of most current OSI standards or standards projects is chronicled periodically by Lyman Chapin in *Computer Communication Review*, the journal of ACM SIGCOMM.

• L. Chapin, Status of OSI (and related) Standards 1 Mar 92, *Computer Communication Review*, ACM SIGCOMM; ACM Press, New York, pp. 114-138, March 1992.

19.3.5 Operations

Literature on the practical application of network protocols, software, and hardware is sparse. Most of what is available is related to UNIX system administration.

The following volume gives a list of recommended books:

• C. Spurgeon, *List of Recommended Books, TCP/IP and Ethernet*, BIG-LAN@suvm.acs.syr.edu (Campus-Size LAN Discussion Group), Internet, 7 June 1988.

The following is an introduction to management of TCP/IP-based internets:

• M.T. Rose, *The Simple Book: An Introduction to Management of TCP/IP-Based Internets*, Prentice Hall Series in Innovative Computing, Prentice Hall, Englewood Cliffs, NJ 1990. ISBN 0-13-812611-9.

A more general book on practical aspects of how to make real networks work is:

• S. Carl-Mitchell, and J.S. Quarterman, *Practical Internetworking with TCP/IP and UNIX*, Addison-Wesley, Reading, MA 1993.

System Administration

The following is the basic textbook for UNIX system administration. It includes a lot of information about practical ad hoc network management in general, and about TCP/IP in particular.

• E. Nemeth, G. Synder, and S. Seebass, *UNIX System Administration Handbook*, Prentice Hall, Englewood Cliffs, NJ, 1989.

UniForum is "The International Association of Open Systems Professionals." Open systems need networking, and UniForum has published some technical guides describing network protocols (*Network Applications* and *Network Substrata*) and electronic mail (*Electronic Mail De-Mystified*):

• J.S. Quarterman, Network Applications, UniForum, Santa Clara, CA, January 1991.

• J.S. Quarterman Network Substrata, UniForum, Santa Clara, CA, January 1991.

• S. Carl-Mitchell, Electronic Mail De-Mystified, UniForum, Santa Clara, CA, January 1992.

19.4 PROTOCOL THEORY

Protocol theory is a popular subject for books.

19.4.1 Current

Here are some current books and other references on protocol theory.

19.4.1.1 *Introductory*

A very readable and current description of how aspects of protocol theory, particularly layering models, are actually used in real networks, is:

- C. Malamud, *Stacks*, Prentice Hall, Englewood Cliffs, NJ 1991. ISBN 0-13-484080-1.

A brief introduction to protocol layers is given in the article:

- P.J. Denning, The Science of Computing: Computer Networks, *American Scientist*, Vol. 73, No. 2, pp. 127–129, March/April 1985.

19.4.1.2 *Textbooks*

One of the oldest textbooks on protocol theory has recently been updated:

- A.S. Tanenbaum, *Computer Networks*, Second Edition, Prentice Hall, Englewood Cliffs, NJ 1988.

The following is somewhat more oriented toward IBM protocols:

- M. Schwartz, *Telecommunication Networks*, Addison-Wesley, Reading, MA 1987.

A set, covering a wide range of specific protocols, is:

- R. Stallings, *Data and Computer Communications*, Macmillan, New York, 1985.

An analytical book, with some specific protocol descriptions, is:

- D. Bertsekas, and R. Gallager, *Data Networks*, Prentice Hall, Englewood Cliffs, NJ 1987.

The standard reference for the data link and physical layers is:

- J.E. McNamara, *Technical Aspects of Data Communication*, Third Edition, Digital Press, Bedford, MA 1988.

19.4.2 Historical

Much current literature on protocols assumes knowledge of historical developments. Fortunately, many influential papers are still available. Some of them still serve as good introductions to their subjects.

19.4.2.1 *Introductions and Opinions*

A useful historical introduction is given by:

- A.S. Tanenbaum, Network Protocols *ACM Computing Surveys*, Vol. 13, No. 4, pp. 453–489, 1981.

A book that predicted much of the current networking situation is:

- M.A. Padlipsky, *The Elements of Networking Style*, Prentice Hall, Englewood Cliffs, NJ 1985.

19.4.2.2 *Collections of Papers*

The following is a very useful collection of historically-important papers on networking developments.

- C. Partridge, *Innovations in Internetworking*, ARTECH House, Norwood, MA 1988.

IEEE has published some useful historical papers:

- IEEE, *Proceedings of the IEEE Computer Society International Conference (25th COMP-CON, September 1982)*, Society Press, Los Angeles, 1982.

- V.G. Cerf, and P. Kirstein, Issues in Packet Network Interconnection, *Proceedings of the IEEE*, Vol. 66, No. 11, pp. 1386–1408, November 1978. Also in Partridge, *Innovations in Internetworking*, 1988.

19.5 PROTOCOL MODELS AND PROTOCOL SUITES

Here are some references on specific protocol models and protocol suites. This being a book about the Internet, we concentrate on TCP/IP, but we also include some references about OSI, and about other protocol suites.

19.5.1 TCP/IP

Although the Internet is now officially multiprotocol, from its inauguration (January, 1 1983) it has used TCP/IP.

19.5.1.1 *The Internet Model*

The following two papers provide the basic description of the Internet Model:

- V.G. Cerf and R. Kahn, A Protocol for Packet Network Interconnection, *IEEE Transactions on Communications*, Vol. COM-22, No. 5, pp. 637–648, May 1974. Also in Partridge, *Innovations in Internetworking*, 1988.

- V.G. Cerf, and E. Cain, The DOD Internet Architecture Model, *Computer Networks*, Vol. 7, No. 5, pp. 307–318, October 1983.

The next paper contains useful commentary on the Internet Model:

- D. Clark, The Design Philosophy of the DARPA Internet Protocols, *Proceedings of the ACM SIGCOMM '88 Workshop*, pp. 106–114, ACM SIGCOMM, New York, 1988.

19.5.1.2 The TCP/IP Protocols

These books are overviews of the TCP/IP protocols and the principles behind them:

- D. Comer, *Internetworking with TCP/IP Principles*, Protocols, and Architecture, Prentice Hall, Englewood Cliffs, NJ 1988.

- W. Stallings, P. Mockapetris, S. McLeod, and T. Michel, *Department of Defense (DOD) Protocol Standards*, Vol. 3 of *Handbook of Computer Communications Standards*, Macmillan, New York, 1988.

19.5.1.3 Implementations

This book is about how to implement TCP/IP:

- D. Comer, and D.L. Stevens, *Internetworking with TCP/IP Volume II: Design, Implementation, and Internals*, Prentice Hall, Englewood Cliffs, NJ 1991.

The next book describes the 4.3BSD UNIX operating system, which is an update of 4.2BSD. The latter was the source of the most popular implementation of TCP/IP. The book includes detailed examinations of the implementations of TCP/IP and XNS, the socket programming interface, and the protocol implementation framework of the operating system:

- S.J. Leffler, M.K. McKusick, M.J. Karels, and J.S. Quarterman, *The Design and Implementation of the 4.3BSD UNIX Operating System*, Addison-Wesley, Reading, MA 1989.

The following book is about internetworking using a teaching operating system:

- D. Comer, *Internetworking with Xinu*, Vol. 2 of *Operating System Design*, Prentice Hall, Englewood Cliffs, NJ 1987.

19.5.2 OSI

The Open Systems Interconnection Reference Model has been adopted by both ISO and CCITT. People often refer to it even when discussing protocol suites other than OSI.

19.5.2.1   The OSI Reference Model

This model was first codified in 1980:

- H. Zimmermann, OSI Reference Model—The ISO Model of Architecture for Open Systems Interconnection, *IEEE Transactions on Communications*, Vol. COM-28, No. 4, pp. 425–432, April 1980. Also in Partridge, *Innovations in Internetworking*, 1988.

- ISO, *ISO Open Systems Interconnection-Basic—Reference Model, Second Edition*, ISO/TC 97/SC 16, No. ISO CD 7498-1, 1992.

Less known than the reference model, but perhaps as important, is the *Framework and Taxonomy of International Standardized Profiles* that ISO has promulgated for fitting together OSI protocols for actual applications.

- SGFS, *Information Technology—Framework and Taxonomy of International Standardized Profiles*, ISO/IEC JTC1 SGFS, Geneva, 15 May 1990.

19.5.2.2   The Protocols

The most readable book about OSI is the following:

- M.T. Rose, *The Open Book: A Practical Perspective on OSI*, Prentice Hall Series in Innovative Computing, Prentice Hall, Englewood Cliffs, NJ 1989. ISBN 0-13-643016-3.

Other OSI references include:

- K.G. Knightson, T. Knowles, and J. Larmouth, *Standards for Open Systems Interconnection*, McGraw-Hill, New York, 1988.

- W. Stallings, *The Open System Interconnection (OSI) Model and OSI-Related Standards*, Vol. 1 of *Handbook of Computer Communications Standards*, Howard W. Sams, Indianapolis, 1987.

For the current status of specific protocols, see the latest version of this article:

- L. Chapin, Status of OSI (and related) Standards 1 March 1992, *Computer Communication Review*, pp. 114–138, March 1992.

19.5.2.3   ISODE

The ISO Development Environment (ISODE) is a software package that permits development of OSI protocols on top of TCP, by simulating TP0. See the following works:

- M.T. Rose, and D.E. Cass, OSI Transport Services on Top of the TCP, *Computer Networks and ISDN Systems*, Vol. 12, 1987.

- M.T. Rose, and D.E. Cass, *ISO Transport Service on top of the TCP: Version: 3; RFC 1006*, Network Information Systems Center, SRI International, Menlo Park, CA, May 1987.

- M.T. Rose, ISODE: Horizontal Integration in Networking, *ConneXions—The Interoperability Report*, Vol. 1, No. 1, pp. 8-12, Interop Company, Mountain View, CA, May 1987.

- M.T. Rose, Building Distributed Applications in an OSI Framework, *ConneXions— The Interoperability Report*, Vol. 2, No. 3, pp. 2–7, Interop Company, Mountain View, CA, March 1988.

The ISODE Consortium was founded in March 1992 to evolve and promote ISODE. ic-info@isode.com

ISODE Consortium
US Office, c/o MCC
P.O. Box 200195
Austin, TX 78720
USA
tel: +1-512-338-3340
fax: +1-512-338-3600

ISODE Consortium
European Office
P.O. Box 505
London SW11 1DX
UK
tel: +44-71-223-4062
fax: +44-71-223-3846

19.5.3 DECnet

Digital Equipment Corporation's Digital Network Architecture (DNA), commonly known as DECnet, has been influential, particularly in congestion control and performance. See the following works:

- A.G. Lauck, D.R. Oran, and R.J. Perlman, Digital Network Architecture Overview, *Digital Technical Journal*, No. 3, pp. 10–24, September 1986.

- R. Jain, A Timeout-Based Congestion Control Scheme for Window Flow-Controlled Networks, *IEEE Journal on Selected Areas of Communications*, Vol. SAC-4, No. 7, pp. 1162–1167, October 1986. Also in Partridge, *Innovations in Internetworking*, 1988.

- R. Jain, K.K. Ramkrishnan, and D.M. Chiu, *Congestion Avoidance in Computer Networks with a Connectionless Network Layer*, Digital Equipment Corporation, Bedford, MA, 1987.

DECnet is one of the more commonly used network architectures:

- C. Malamud, *DEC Networks and Architectures*, McGraw-Hill, New York, 1989.

Digital is migrating DNA to conform to OSI:

- C. Malamud, *Analyzing DECnet/OSI Phase V*, Van Nostrand Reinhold, NY, 1992.

19.5.4   XNS

The Xerox Network Services protocols are not widely used today, but have been influential, particularly in the areas of remote procedure calls, external data formats, and naming:

- A. Birrell, and B. Nelson, Implementing Remote Procedure Calls, *ACM Transactions on Computer Systems*, Vol. 2, No. 1, pp. 39–59, February 1984. Also in Partridge, *Innovations in Internetworking*, 1988.

- Courier: The Remote Procedure Call Protocol, in *Xerox System Integration Standard*, Xerox Corporation, Stamford, CT, December 1981.

- M.D. Schroeder, A.D. Birrell, and R.M. Needham, Experience with Grapevine: The Growth of a Distributed System, *ACM Transactions on Computer Systems*, Vol. 2, No. 1, pp. 3–23, February 1984. Also in Partridge, *Innovations in Internetworking*, 1988.

19.5.5   NetWare

Single process PC operating systems like MS-DOS are not well adapted for networking, and are often replaced by network operating systems like Novell NetWare:

- C. Malamud, *Analyzing Novell Networks*, Van Nostrand Reinhold, NY, 1991.

19.5.6   AppleTalk

The following is a frequently mentioned book about AppleTalk:

- G.S. Sidhu, R.F. Andrews, and A.B. Oppenheimer, *Inside AppleTalk*, Second Edition, Addison-Wesley, Reading, MA 1990.

19.5.7   PC Interoperability

FTP Software publishes a guide for making PCs that run MS-DOS or MS Windows interoperate with TCP/IP:

- *PC-TCP Interoperability Guide*, FTP Software, Inc., Wakefield, MA 01880, 1992.

19.6   TCP/IP CORE PROTOCOLS

There is no point in discussing every protocol specification here, because they will change and there are too many of them. Instead, we list the current major protocol *RFCs* in Table 19.1, and we discuss where you should look later for the current *RFC* numbers.

Table 19.1 Major Internet Protocol RFCs

Acronym	Name	RFC	STD
Model and Taxonomy			
	IAB Official Protocol Standards	1280	1
	Assigned Numbers	1060	2
	Requirements Documents		
	Host Requirements—Communications	1122	3
	Host Requirements—Applications	1123	3
	Gateway Requirements	1009	4
Internet Layer			
IP	Internet Protocol	791	5
	IP Subnet Extension	950	5
	IP Broadcast Datagrams	919	5
	IP Broadcast Datagrams with Subnets	922	5
ICMP	Internet Control Message Protocol	792	5
IGMP	Internet Group Multicast Protocol	1112	5
Transport Layer			
TCP	Transmission Control Protocol	793	6
UDP	User Datagram Protocol	768	7
Application Layer			
TELNET	Telnet Protocol and Options	854,855	8
FTP	File Transfer Protocol	959	9
SMTP	Simple Mail Transfer Protocol	821	10
MAIL	Format of Electronic Mail Messages	822	11
CONTENT	Content Type Header Field	1049	11
NETBIOS	NetBIOS Service Protocols	1001,1002	19
ECHO	Echo Protocol	862	20
DISCARD	Discard Protocol	863	21
CHARGEN	Character Generator Protocol	864	22
QUOTE	Quote of the Day Protocol	865	23
USERS	Active Users Protocol	866	24
DAYTIME	Daytime Protocol	867	25
TIME	Time Server Protocol	868	26
Distributed Services			
NTP	Network Time Protocol	1119	12
DNS	Domain Name System	1034,1035	13
DNS-MX	Mail Routing and the Domain System	974	14
Network Management			
SNMP	Simple Network Management Protocol	1157	15
SMI	Structure of Management Information	1155	16
MIB-II	Management Information Base-II	1213	17
Routing			
EGP	Exterior Gateway Protocol	904	18

It is important to realize that just having the basic specification for a protocol, such as *RFC 791* for IP, is not enough. Many protocols have been updated or amended by later *RFCs*, such as *RFCs 950, 919*, and *922* for IP. The current list of *RFCs* for each protocol is given in the document "IAB Official Protocol Standards," which we describe below. Other *RFCs*, such as the *Requirements Documents*, also described below, may incorporate by reference, amend, correct, and supplement the primary specifications for a protocol. There may also be other Applicability Statements (AS) that incorporate by reference, amend, correct, or supplement the basic Technical Specifications (TS). You need to look at these contextual documents in addition to the basic protocol specifications.

19.6.1   *RFC*s

RFC stands for *Request for Comments*, because in the early days of the ARPANET (1969–1990, R.I.P.), the predecessor of the Internet, *RFCs* were working documents circulated among a relatively small group of network researchers (the Network Working Group) for comments.

If you are really interested in current *RFCs*, you probably want to subscribe to the electronic mailing list ietf@isi.edu. To subscribe, do *not* send mail to the list itself, since that would distribute your request to thousands of people who could do nothing about it. Instead, send mail to ietf-request@isi.edu asking to be put on the list. Be aware that this list contains not only announcements of new *RFCs*, but also discussions of related topics.

RFCs are normally obtained by anonymous FTP from one of a set of hosts that have agreed to make them available. That is, connect to such a host with FTP, log-in as user *anonymous* with password *guest*. Then change to the rfc directory, and get rfcnnn.txt, e.g., rfc791.txt. To find out which *RFCs* are current, first retrieve the file rfc-index.txt.

Paper copies of *RFCs* may be ordered from:

> Network Information Systems Center
> SRI International
> Room EJ291
> 333 Ravenswood Avenue
> Menlo Park, CA 94025
> USA

SRI publishes a six-volume set of *RFCs* and related material called the *Internet Technology Handbook;* these volumes may be obtained together, with updates, or separately, without updates:

- V. Cerf, *Internet Technology Handbook*, SRI International, Network Information Systems Center, Menlo Park, CA, November 1991. $785.00. Individual volumes at $150.00 each.

SRI also publishes a CD/ROM with all the *RFCs* currently on-line, plus much other information, including source and object code, as well as documentation.

- *TCP/IP CD*, SRI International, Network Information Systems Center, Menlo Park, CA, February 1992. $195.00.

The Internet Society (ISOC) plans to become the publisher of record of *RFC*s.

Internet Society
1895 Preston White Drive
Suite 100
Reston, VA 22091
USA

19.6.2 Internet Drafts

There is a series of documents called Internet Drafts, many of which are later adapted as *RFC*s. Internet Drafts are not published on paper, and are not archived, but are available by anonymous FTP and electronic mail while current.

To get an Internet Draft by mail, send mail to mail-server@nisc.sri.com, and in the body put a line

SEND internet-drafts/draft-xyzzy-phlugh-nn.txt

where *xyzzy-phlugh* is a title corresponding to the author and topic, and *nn* is a version number for that Internet Draft. This mail server expects the request for an Internet Draft in the body of the message, unlike the mail server mentioned above, which expects requests for *RFC*s in the Subject: line. For further information about Internet Drafts, send mail to internet-drafts@nri.reston.va.us.

19.6.3 IAB Official Protocol Standards and STDs

The current list of *RFC*s that specify protocols is given in an *RFC* with the title *IAB Official Protocol Standards*. This is one of the most frequently updated *RFC*s, so it is not good to depend on knowing its *RFC* number. Fortunately, it is also STD 1, that is, it is number one in a series of STD (standard) documents that are published within the *RFC* series. All of the original protocols in the STD series are listed in Table 19.1, except for six STDs for Telnet options:

- J. Postel, *IAB Official Protocol Standards; STD-1/RFC-1280*, Network Information Systems Center, SRI International, Menlo Park, CA, March 1992.

At least one mail server, SRI's, that returns *RFC* will also return STDs by number. Send a message

To: mail-server@nisc.sri.com
Subject: anything
STD 1

and the server will return STD 1. This mail server, unlike the one run by nic.ddn.mil, expects the request in the *body* of the message, not in the Subject: line. The contents of the Subject: line can be anything. For an STD like STD 3, which corresponds to several *RFCs*, the server will return all of the corresponding *RFCs*, after first sending you a preliminary acknowledgment message telling you what to expect.

The procedures by which protocols become Internet Standards are described in another chapter of the present book, and also in *RFC 1310*:

- L. Chapin, *The Internet Standards Process; RFC 1310*, Network Information Systems Center, SRI International, Menlo Park, CA, March 1992.

The following book contains a more contextual description of those procedures:

- J.S. Quarterman and S. Wilhelm, *UNIX, POSIX, and Open Systems: The Open Standards Puzzle*, Addison-Wesley, Reading, MA 1993.

19.6.4   Assigned Numbers

Assignments of protocol number, port numbers, etc. are kept in the document *Assigned Numbers*, which is STD 2.

- J. Reynolds and J. Postel, *Assigned Numbers; RFC 1060*, Network Information Systems Center, SRI International, Menlo Park, CA, March 1990.

19.6.5   Requirements Documents

In addition to STD 1, *IAB Official Protocol Standards*, there are two Requirements Documents. Requirements Documents specify protocols that are required for certain platforms. Two have been published so far. *Host Requirements* is actually a set of two *RFCs*:

- R. Braden, *Requirements for Internet Hosts—Communication Layers; RFC 1122*, Network Information Systems Center, SRI International, Menlo Park, CA, October 1989.

- R. Braden, *Requirements for Internet Hosts—Application and Support; RFC 1123*, Network Information Systems Center, SRI International, Menlo Park, CA, October 1989.

Requirements for IP Routers is a single *RFC*:

- R.T. Braden and J.B. Postel, Requirements for Internet gateways; *RFC 1009*, Network *Network Working Group Requests for Comments RFC 1009*, Network Information Systems Center, SRI International, Menlo Park, CA, June 1987.

19.6.6   Statuses and *STD*s

STD 1 assigns a set of default statuses to all Internet Standard protocols; see Chapter 4 for descriptions of these statuses. STD 1 makes IP Required, but leaves TCP and UDP as Recommended. Other STDs, such as STD 3 or STD 4, may make TCP or UDP Required. See STDs 1, 3, and 4 for details.

19.6.7   *FYI RFCs*

Another subseries of *RFC* is called *FYI*s, where *FYI* stands for *For Your Information*. These are introduced in *RFC 1150*. They may be obtained by mailservers that return *RFC*s, by substituting *FYI nnn* for *RFC mmm*. SRI also sells a set of *FYI*s on paper. Of particular interest is *FYI 3, RFC 1175*, which is a bibliography of internetworking information:

- K.L. Bowers, T.L. LaQuey, J.K. Reynolds, K. Roubicek, M.K. Stahl, and A. Yuan, *FYI on where to start: A bibliography of internetworking information, FYI 3, RFC 1175*, Network Information Systems Center, SRI International, Menlo Park, CA, 1990 August.

19.7   BASIC DISTRIBUTED SERVICES

The *RFC*s listed in Table 19.1 are still the best reference for the Internet Domain Name Service (DNS), although there are descriptions of it in the LaQuey and Stallings books already cited, as well as in some others.

The OSI Directory Service is described in the book:

- M.T. Rose, *The Little Black Book: Mail–Bonding with OSI Directory Services*, Prentice Hall Series in Innovative Computing, Prentice Hall, Englewood Cliffs, NJ 1991. ISBN 0-13-683210-5.

19.8   TRADITIONAL APPLICATIONS

Most of the directories and introductions already cited cover file transfer (FTP and rcp) and remote login (Telnet and rlogin).

Electronic mail is covered in the guides, directories, and desk references already cited, as well as in most of the protocol implementation books.

This book is about Internet mail, technology:

- M.T. Rose, *The Internet Message: Closing the Book with Electronic Mail*, Prentice Hall Series in Innovative Computing, Prentice Hall, Englewood Cliffs, NJ 1992. ISBN 0-13-092941-7.

These two references have extensive coverage of electronic mail:

- S. Carl-Mitchell, *Electronic Mail De-Mystified*, UniForum, Santa Clara, CA January 1992.

- S. Carl-Mitchell, and J.S. Quarterman, *Practical Internetworking with TCP/IP and UNIX*, Addison-Wesley, Reading, MA 1993.

Few people take the time to read the most basic text on electronic mail formats: *RFC 822*, the central specification for the Internet mail format. More should read it:

- D.H. Crocker, *Standard for the Format of ARPA Internet Text Messages; RFC 822*, Network Information Systems Center, SRI International, Menlo Park, CA 13 August 1982.

RFC 822 has recently been extended to handle multimedia mail. These extensions are known as Multipurpose Internet Mail Extensions (MIME). These two specifications achieved Proposed Standard state in summer 1992, so they will not be full Internet Standards until at least summer 1993:

- N. Borenstein and N. Freed, *MIME (Multipurpose Internet Mail Extensions) Mechanisms for Specifying and Describing the Format of Internet Message Bodies; RFC 1341*, Network Information Systems Center, SRI International, Menlo Park, CA, June 1992.

- K. Moore, *Representation of Non-ASCII Text in Internet Message Headers; RFC 1342*, Network Information Systems Center, SRI International, Menlo Park, CA, June 1992.

This *RFC* is about an approach to implementation. It is not on the IAB Standards Track and will not become a standard:

- N. Borenstein, *A User Agent Configuration Mechanism for Multimedia Mail Format Information; RFC 1343*, Network Information Systems Center, SRI International, Menlo Park, CA, June 1992.

This *RFC* may encourage work on mail transport gateways. It is not intended to be a standard:

- N. Borenstein, *Implications of MIME for Internet Mail Gateways; RFC 1344*, Network Information Systems Center, SRI International, Menlo Park, CA, June 1992.

This *RFC* documents one of several efforts to provide a universal framework for all character sets; it will probably not become a standard:

- K. Simonsen, *Character Mnemonics and Character Sets; RFC 1345*, Network Information Systems Center, SRI International, Menlo Park, CA, June 1992.

ISO 10646 is a Draft International Standard that attempts to incorporate all character sets, including those from another effort called UniCode.

19.9 OTHER APPLICATIONS

Many common TCP/IP applications are not Internet Standards.
This is one book about the X Window System.

- R. Scheifler, J. Gettys, and R. Newman, *X Window System: C Library and Protocol Reference*, Digital Press, Bedford, MA, 1988.

Much USENET news is carried over the Internet (although much is still carried over UUCP and other networks and transport mechanisms). News format is specified in *RFC 1036*. The usual news application protocol for use over TCP is NNTP (Network News Transfer Protocol), and is specified in *RFC 977*.

Index

Numerics

4.2BSD   602, 613, 614, 625,
    642, 643, 644, 645, 646
  ARP implementation   617
  FTP implementation   659
  rcp protocol   660
  rlogin protocol   656
  UDP checksums   638
4.3BSD   628, 644, 649
4.3BSD-Reno   645
  one-behind cache of
    PCBs   640
576-byte rule   649

A

ABORT   118, 119
abort   128
Abort (ABOR)   234
Abstract Syntax Notation One
    (ASN.1)   503, 665
  Basic Encoding Rules
    (BER)   503, 665
Access   410

Access control   377, 379,
    382, 388, 397, 412
Account (ACCT)   230
Accredited standards bodies   47
Accuracy   110
Acknowledgment (ACK)
    125
  -compression   633
  -smashing, see ACK-com-
    pression
Active connection   441
AD   95
Address mask   299
  request   111
  Request and Reply   111
Address Resolution Protocol
    (ARP)   95, 160, 177,
    299, 616, 617
  caches   170
Addressing   90
Addressing domains   712
Administrative domain   95
Admission controls   603
Advertised window, see offered
    window

Advertisements   111, 112
Agent   199
Aggregation   711
Alarm   553
Alert   502
Allocate (ALLO)   233
All-routes broadcast   279
All-routes discovery   280
Almquist   86
Anonymous FTP   752
AP-CCIRN   33
API   62
Append (with create)
    (APPE)   233
Apple bridges   286
AppleTalk   170, 768
Applicability Statements   62
Application layer   392
Application programming
    interfaces   62
Applications Area   51
Archie   490
Area Directors   46, 50
Area Partition Problem   165,
    170

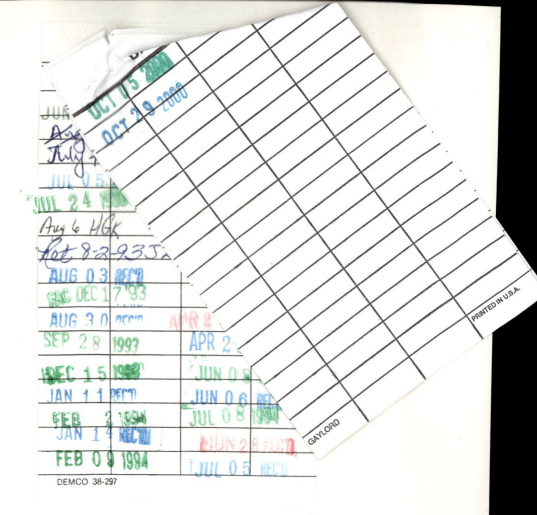